THE SOUTH PRECINCT OF DUTCHESS COUNTY NEW YORK 1740–1790

*divided into Philipse, Fredricksburgh, and South East Precincts in 1772
renamed Philipse, Fredericks, and South-East Towns in 1788
containing present-day Putnam County New York*

BY
PAMELA RICCIARDI PASCHKE

Copyright © 2018 Pamela Ricciardi Paschke

All rights reserved. No part of this book may be reproduced or transmitted in any form or by any means, electronic or mechanical, including photocopying, digitizing, or recording, without written permission from the author, except for the inclusion of brief quotations in a review.

Cover image taken from: Holland, Samuel, and Robert Sayer and John Bennett, *The provinces of New York, and New Jersey; with part of Pensilvania, and the province of Quebec* (London: Printed for Robt. Sayer & John Bennett, 1775), map, https://www.loc.gov/item/74694272/.

International Standard Book Numbers
Paperbound: 978-1-7327297-0-4
Hardbound: 978-1-7327297-1-1

LCCN: 2018275943

Published 2018 by:
PASCHKE PUBLISHING HOUSE
341 SW Second Street
Boca Raton, Florida 33432

Acknowledgements

To my husband, Paul, and my daughters Elesa, Emma, and Deanna
for their assistance with and support of this endeavor.
Their help with typing, proofreading, and editing
relived me of much angst. I am very grateful.

And thanks to the many others who helped and encouraged me
along the way, especially James Merrell and Ron Taylor
whose knowledge of the region and its history was invaluable.
And to the archivists at Columbia University
and to William Ruddock.

And thanks to all of the folks I never met who wrote the books
and articles included in the bibliography, and created, saved,
and donated the documents I was able to access in
manuscript collections at Columbia University
and the New York Historical Society.

TABLE OF CONTENTS

1 – AN INTRODUCTION TO SOUTH DUTCHESS AND ITS HISTORY 1
2 – TAX LISTS OF THE SOUTH PRECINCTS OF DUTCHESS COUNTY 13
   South(ern) Precinct:

February 1740/1 15		February 1758 68
February 1741/2 16		June 1758 72
February 1742/3 17		February 1759 77
February 1743/4 18		June 1759 82
February 1744/5 19		February 1760 87
February 1745/6 21		June 1760 92
February 1746/7 23		February 1761 98
June 1747 25		June 1761 103
June 1748 27		February 1762 108
February 1753 30		June 1762 114
June 1753 33		February 1763 119
February 1754 37		June 1763 124
June 1754 41		June 1765 129
February 1755 44		June 1766 135
June 1755 48		June 1767 140
February 1756 52		June 1768 146
June 1756 56		June 1769 151
February 1757 60		June 1770 157
June 1757 64		June 1771 163

   Philipse, Fredricksburgh, & South East Precincts:
      June 1772 170
              South East 170, Fredericksbourgh 171, Philipse's 175
      June 1773 177
              Philips's 177, Fredericks Burgh 179, South East 183
      June 1774 185
              South East 185, Fredricksburgh 186, Philipse's 191
      June 1775 193
              Philipse's 193, Fredricksburgh 195, South East 200
      June 1777 SouthEast, partial 202
      June 1778 203
              South East 203, Fredricksburgh 204, Philipse 209
      June 1779 211
              Philipse's 211, Fredricksburgh 213, South East 218
      1786 or 1787 Philipse's 220
   Summary of South Dutchess Tax Lists 1741–1779 222

3 – TENANT LISTS 223
    Beverly Robinson
        Lot Number 1 — 1777 and before 1768..225
        Lot Number 4 — 1777 and before 1768..226
        Lot Number 7 — 1777 and before 1768..230
    Philip Philipse (Mrs. Margret Philipse)
        Lot Number 8 — 1768 and prior 233

4 – MILITIA LISTS 235
    Provincial Troops 1758–1762
        Muster Roll 1758 235
        Muster Roll 1760 237
        Muster Roll 1762 239
    Militia Regiments in South Dutchess County 1776–1781 241
        Field's Third Militia Regiment 243
        Luddington's Seventh Militia Regiment...245

5 – FIRST CENSUS OF THE UNITED STATES 1790: 249
    Township of Frederickstown 250
    Township of Phillipstown..262
    Township of Southeast 267

APPENDIX A – Book of Taxes Dutchess County February 1739/40
    Fishkills Precinct (selected names)..269

APPENDIX B – Dutchess County Militia Beats
    1776: Fredricksburgh and South East...270
    1778: Luddington and Field Regiments...271

APPENDIX C – Tenant Farm Lot Maps 272
    Southern Portion of Robinson's Long Lot 4 273
    Robinson's Short Lot 7..274
    Philipse's Short Lot 8 275
    Philipse's Long Lot 6 — 1762 survey with tenant list...276
    May 1765 Agreement over Disputed Lands 278

BIBLIOGRAPHY 281

INDEX..285

LIST OF MAPS..317

Dutchess County

An Introduction to South Dutchess and its History

Many residents of colonial Dutchess County, New York[1] were tenant farmers, never owning land or having an estate to probate. In the southern part of the county the colonial proprietors rarely offered their farm lots for sale. In the 1770s and 1780s, some tenants purchased their farms, but others who may have lived there for decades had already died or moved away, leaving few records behind. With scant direct evidence of relationships in this era, lists of taxpayers, tenants, and militia provide a means to identify neighbors and trace migrations.

This book focuses on colonial records of residents of the South (or Southern) Precinct of Dutchess County, New York. The Dutchess property tax rolls span 1718–1779[2] but only provide separate lists for the South Precinct beginning in February 1740/1.[3] This volume presents the extant lists[4] from the precincts that served as the basis for Putnam County (cut from Dutchess in 1812). Included tenant lists, maps derived from surveys and deeds, and military records of the period, as well as the 1790 census enhance the utility of the taxpayer data. Collectively, these records facilitate further exploration of these colonial residents and their communities.

Effective use of these records requires an understanding of the history of the land, its early settlers, and other circumstances affecting settlement and recordkeeping. The following is a condensed version of those events and circumstances sufficient to provide a solid base of understanding. The bibliography provides numerous sources that address the history in greater depth.

History of the Land

When Europeans began settling in the area, the Wappinger, a family tribe of the Taconic natives, lived in the Highlands of southern Dutchess County. Several wealthy Dutchmen purchased parcels of land from the Wappinger on the east side of the Hudson River, and were granted patents for those parcels by the Colony of New York. Adolph Philipse received one such patent in 1697 after purchasing land from two Dutch land speculators.[5] His patent formed the basis for the South Precinct of Dutchess County and present-day Putnam County.

When granted, the Philipse patent (also called the Philipse Upper[6] or Highland patent) bordered the 1685 Col. Van Cortlandt and Co. patent (known as the Rombout patent) to the northwest, the 1697 Beekman patent to the northeast, the 1697 Manor of Cortlandt (in Westchester County) to the south, the Hudson River to the west, and the Colony of Connecticut to the east. In 1737, when Dutchess

---

1. The county is said to be named after the Duchess of York. Dutchess is an archaic spelling, used until Samuel Johnson's 1755 dictionary dropped the "t" to be consistent with the French "Duchesse." Those who postulate that the prevalence of Dutch settlers or ignorance created a misspelling appear to be misinformed.
2. Dutchess has the most complete set of colonial tax lists in the state. *New York Family History Research Guide and Gazetteer* (New York: New York Genealogical and Biographical Society, 2015), p.124.
3. For clarity, dual dates for January 1 through March 24 were used by the British colonists through 1751.
4. Lists for 1749-1752, 1764, and 1776 (and two and a half of the three precincts in 1777) are missing.
5. William S. Pelletreau, *History of Putnam County, New York: with Biographical Sketches of its Prominent Men* (Philadelphia: W.W. Preston, 1886), 14-16.
6. "Upper" distinguishes this parcel from Philipsburgh Manor, an earlier Philipse patent in Westchester County.

The South Precinct of Dutchess County New York 1740–1790

County was separated into seven precincts, the Philipse patent comprised the South Precinct,[7] bordered on the north by the Rombout and Beekman Precincts and to the south by the county line. In 1743 the government clarified that the precinct's eastern boundary extended beyond the Philipse patent lands to include the adjacent portion of The Oblong, a narrow strip that had been conveyed by the Colony of Connecticut to New York in 1732 in settlement of a border dispute.[8] This validated inclusion of the occupants of The Oblong (or Equivalent Lands) in the precinct tax rolls.

Adolph Philipse's land passed to his nephew Frederick in 1749, then to Frederick's heirs upon his death. A 1754 survey divided the patent lands into numbered lots: water lots 1–3 running south-north along the Hudson River, long lots 4–6 running west-east in the middle, and lots 7–9 running north-south along The Oblong line. The three heirs (Susanna née Philipse, wife of Beverly Robinson; Philip Philipse; and Mary Philipse, later wife of Roger Morris) took one of each of the three types of lots. (see Figure 1)

The 1754 division of the land among the Philipse heirs has generally been perceived as adhering to the boundaries of the original Philipse patent. However, subsequent events demonstrate that the 1754 map extended too far east and north. At various times between 1737 and 1771, the patent's east and north boundaries were challenged by Native Americans, tenants, and other patent holders. Conflicting claims to areas within the Philipse patent and adjacent sections (The Gore and the 20-Mile Lands) were resolved through additional deeds and patents, a "great rebellion," and contentious court cases.

Figure 1 shows the nine lot lines of the 1754 survey.[9] The Hudson River is to the west, The Oblong to the east, the Rombout and Beekman Precincts to the north, and The Manor of Courtlandt to the south. Because the South Precinct's borders were based on the original patents, its north and south lines were parallel. In the 1754 survey, the south border runs east-west,[10] but the north border is angled by three degrees. The dotted line labeled "north line of the South Precinct" shows the variance between the two borders.

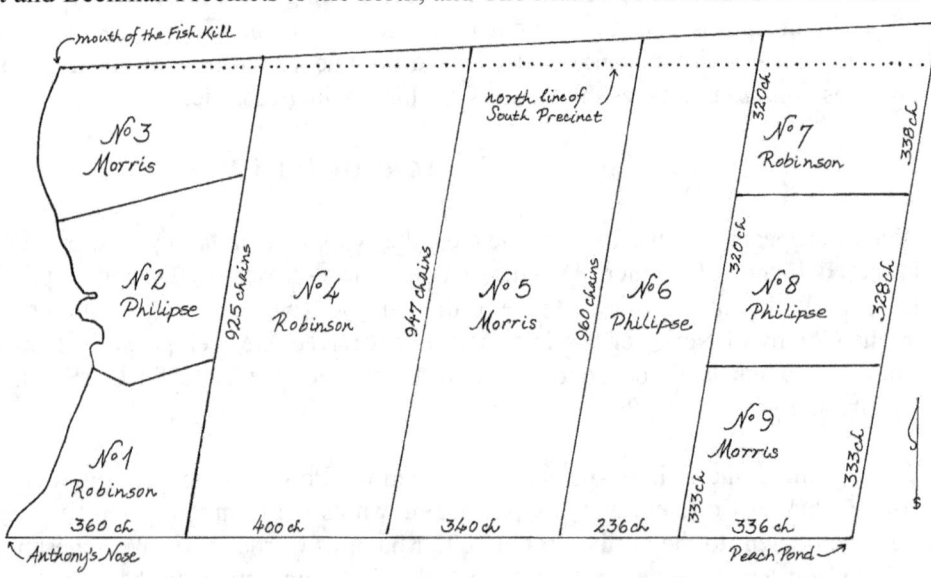

Figure 1 - The Philipse Patent Survey 1754[8]

---

7. *The Colonial Laws of New York from the Year 1664 to the Revolution*, v. II (Albany: JB Lyon State Printer, 1894), 957-957: Chapter 652, "An Act to divide Dutchess county into Precincts and to Repeal the Act therein Mentioned," passed 16 Dec 1737. "The South Precinct [is] to contain all that part of the High Lands granted by patent to Adolph Philipse."

8. *The Colonial Laws of New York* v. III, 337-8, passed 17 Dec 1743. Pelletreau, *History of Putnam County*, 108-112.

9. Map is based upon three deeds dated 7 February 1754 among the heirs, see Pelletreau, *History of Putnam County*, 54-64 (contrast this map to that in Pelletreau's book facing page 16). The conversion from chains to miles is 0.0125 mi/chain. This colonial survey did not adjust for the effect of magnetic declination on true north.

10. As the compass pointed in 1754. Surveying tools adjusting to "true north" were not used until the 1780s.

Introduction

The following sections summarize conflicting claims over the lands included in the 1754 survey. In creating a condensed history, judgement has been used to include or exclude events, details, and circumstances. Consult the footnoted sources and bibliography for more information.

THE NORTH BOUNDARY, THROUGH 1771 (THE GORE)

The Philipse heirs disputed the interpretation of the original descriptions of the north line of the Philipse patent and aggressively pursued claims to lands considered to be part of the Beekman and Rombout patents. They believed that ambiguous references to the Highlands and Fish Kill in the early patents entitled them to additional land. Their claim to the disputed areas termed The Gore was resolved with the Beekman patent owners by compromise in January 1758, and with the Rombout patent successor owners in January 1771.[11] The resulting northern border of the Philipse lands was no longer a straight line (see Figure 2). While the Philipse heirs asserted ownership to these lands based upon their interpretation of descriptions in the patents, the lands were conveyed to them by deeds.

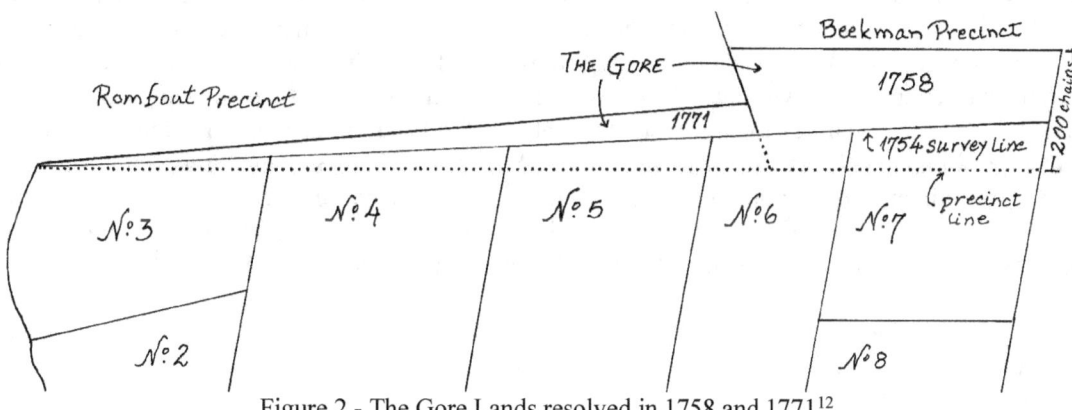

Figure 2 - The Gore Lands resolved in 1758 and 1771[12]

The Beekman concession began at a point on The Oblong line due east from the mouth of the Fish Kill (east end of the precinct line), then 200 chains northerly along The Oblong line, then due west to the Rombout dividing line. The Rombout concession was a line angled six degrees north of due east, from the mouth of the Fish Kill to the Beekman line. Because of magnetic declination, the due east-west lines used for these colonial surveys do not fall on a due east-west line on a current map.[13]

No subsequent divisions or precinct boundaries treated these conveyed parcels as part of the Philipse patent lands. When Putnam County was created, these Philipse Gore acquisitions remained in Dutchess County. Tenants of The Gore are not in the tax lists in this book, but may appear in tenant and other lists and related maps for those areas included in the 1754 survey.

THE EAST BOUNDARY (THE OBLONG AND THE 20-MILE LANDS)

Contrary to the 1754 division and survey, the east boundary of the Philipse patent did not extend to The Oblong boundary of 1754. The 1697 patents granted to Philipse and Beekman described the eastern terminus as the "petition line" with Connecticut. A November 1683 agreement between New York and Connecticut set that boundary line to be 20 miles east of and parallel to the Hudson River; large bends

---

11. Pelletreau, *History of Putnam County,* 102-105.
12. Map based upon 8 January 1758 agreement between Beverly and Susanna Robinson, Philip Philipse, and Mary Philipse, and Henry Beekman, Catharine Pawling, and Robert Livingston, Dutchess County Deeds 3:190-192, and Pelletreau, *History of Putnam County,* 103-104 for the Rumbout (Rombout) settlement.
13. For historical magnetic declination maps, see https://maps.ngdc.noaa.gov/viewers/historical_declination/

in the river made this a curved boundary. In 1719, acknowledging that the boundary was not properly marked, the New York government determined that new lines were to be run and marked in order to clarify which colony had jurisdiction over the residents.[14] However, the survey was not completed and the border was not marked, perpetuating the ambiguity of the boundary between the two colonies.

In 1730, residents who believed they were east of the said 20-mile line, and so living in Connecticut, petitioned the New York Council to complete the survey and set the boundary line. To settle the issue, the two colonies agreed that the boundary between New York and Connecticut, rather than curving with the river, would be a straight line between two points: the first set 20 miles east of the river at Verplanck's Point (in Westchester County), and the second north at the Massachusetts line. To effect a land swap compromise, a parallel line 145 chains (just over one and three-quarter miles) to the east was surveyed, enclosing a strip of land to be ceded by Connecticut to New York in exchange for lands farther south. The ceded tract ran along the eastern borders of Westchester and Dutchess Counties.

The survey of this strip of the "equivalent" lands known as The Oblong was completed in the spring of 1731.[15] Immediately, conflicting claims to the lands arose. Two Englishmen received a patent from the King for the entire 62,000 acres of The Oblong; however, the Equivalent Land Company challenged this patent based upon its own New York provincial patent for 50,000 acres. And people of New Fairfield, Connecticut, claimed to have a prior patent for 10,000 acres partly included in the Equivalent Land Company claim and partly in lands to the west. After some 1735–37 legal wranglings, the English claimants grew silent, and the Equivalent Land Company assumed ownership. As a consequence, many New Fairfield and English tenants left (or were driven out of) The Oblong, and settled on other lands farther west, where many were considered by the Philipse proprietors to be squatters.[16]

The survey and compromise of 1731 failed to resolve ownership of the lands between the straight western boundary of The Oblong (the Line of Division) and the curved line running 20 miles east of the Hudson River (the eastern edge of the Philipse and Beekman patents). These un-patented lands had no common name, so will be referred to hereafter as the 20-Mile Lands. Not included in patents granted in The Oblong nor in the Beekman or Philipse patents, and not claimed by Connecticut, the lands reasonably appeared to

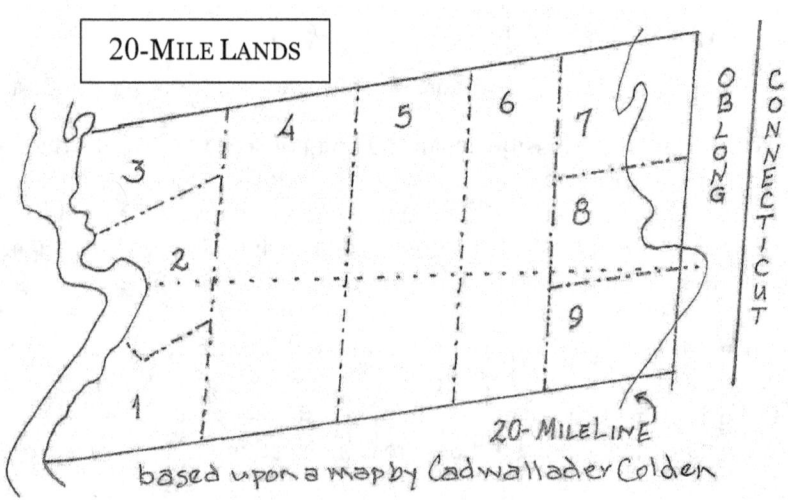

Figure 3 - Sketch of the 20-Mile Line ca 1733

belong to the Wappinger. Indeed, the Wappinger were living in the eastern end of the South Precinct. Nevertheless, Beekman and Philipse patent owners would later contend that the lands were theirs.

---

14. *The Colonial Laws of New York from the Year 1664 to the Revolution,* v. I (Albany: JB Lyon State Printer, 1894), 1039-1041: Chapter 384, "An Act for runing [sic] and Ascertaining the Lines of Partition & Division betwixt this Colony & the Colony of Connecticut," passed 25 Jun 1719.

15. Pelletreau, *History of Putnam County,* 111-112.

16. Kim, *Landlord and Tenant in Colonial New York,* 367-370.

Introduction

Figure 3 shows the general location of the 20-Mile Lands in relation to The Oblong and to the 1754 Philipse Lots. The placement of the 20-Mile line is taken from a map made by Cadwallader Colden around 1733[17]; while it may not be precise, it provides a general idea of the area east of the 20-Mile Line and west of The Oblong — home of the "squatters."

In 1752, the new attorney general William Kempe arrived with plans to reassert the 1730s English claims to The Oblong. Meeting resistance to concessions, Kempe saw an opportunity to go against the provincial proprietors another way. Recognizing that the 20-Mile Lands were not included in any of the existing patents, he aligned himself with "28 or more squatters" in a defense pact and began encouraging more settlement in the 20-Mile Lands. Kempe asserted that these lands belonged to the crown, and defended the squatters as English tenants. Indeed, more and more tenants began to defy the proprietors and request Kempe's help. But the resistance was met with a severe blow when Kempe died in July 1759.[18] It was also about this time that the Wappinger men were away fighting in the war with the French (see THE "INDIAN" LANDS section).

With Kempe and the Wappinger tribe gone, the Philipse heirs acknowledged that the 20-Mile Lands represented a flaw in the eastern line of the Philipse claim (and the 1754 division which included lands to The Oblong line), and commissioned a survey of two parcels of land in 1760: one of 4402 acres in The Gore and Lots 7 and 8, and another of 221 acres in Lot 9. Remarkable for its simplicity, the "survey," done by Cadwallader Colden makes no reference to the patent boundary 20 miles due east from the Hudson River, nor does it describe any landmarks save some marked stones near the northeast corner, and Peach Pond at the southeast corner. A rendition of the survey map[19] is as follows:

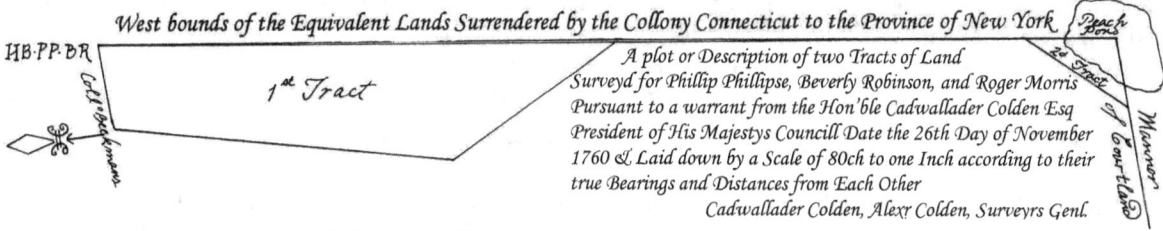

Figure 4 - Rendition of 1760 Patent Survey and Map (north arrow is to the left)

Despite the King's and New Fairfield's claims to the land and other obvious issues, the Philipse heirs received a provincial patent for these parcels in March 1761 and considered ownership of the 20-Mile Lands to be resolved. Almost immediately they began eviction proceedings against certain "squatters" on their newly patented land. Not surprisingly, all proceedings concluded in favor of the Philipse heirs.[20]

When placed onto a map of the Philipse lands, the new tracts line up as shown in Figure 5. Note that the largest portion of the lands acquired were in Beverly Robinson's Short Lot 7.

---

17. Cadwallader Colden, Map in "The Answer of the Proprietors of the Equivalent Lands to the Attorney Generals Bill in Chancery Before Governor Cosby," ca 1731-32, *[Oblong or Equivalent Land Papers]* (New York Historical Society Manuscript Collection).
18. Kim, *Landlord and Tenant in Colonial New York*, 370-373.
19. Report of survey dated 30 Dec 1760 for Phillipse, Robinson, and Morris; New York State Archives Record Series A0272, New York Department of State Applications for Land Grants 16:24. Figure 4 is based upon the image provided to the author by Reference Services.
20. Kim, *Landlord and Tenant in Colonial New York*, 373-374.

Frustrated that the Philipse heirs would eject tenants without "any manner of recompense for their labour, fatigue, and expense in cultivating manuring clearing fencing and improving said lands, nor for their buildings thereon erected, nor for their crops thereon then growing,"[21] the squatters refused to recognize the Philipse claim to the 20-Mile Lands. In continued defiance, they began collaborating with members of the Wappinger tribe who had returned to assert their own claim to a significant portion of the South Precinct.

Contrary to the expectations of the Philipse heirs, this issue was far from over.

THE EAST BOUNDARY, CONTINUED (THE ORIGINAL PATENT)

Adolph Philipse's original ownership claim was based upon his purchase from two Dutch men, Dorlandt and Seabrandt. These men obtained a license from the governor and purchased from the Wappinger a parcel stretching from Anthony's Nose to the Fishkill along the river, then "eastwards in the woods as farr [sic] along the said lands of Steph. Cortlandt and Co. [the Rombout Patent] aforesaid to a marked tree."[22] Dorlandt and Seabrandt sold their interest in the land to Adolph Philipse in June 1697 citing a similar land description, but substituting "backwards into the woods so farr [sic] as the land of Col. Cortlandt and Company extendeth" for the aforementioned "marked tree."[23] Neither deed indicated the acreage of the parcel, mentioned the Beekman Patent (located east of the Rombout patent), nor specifically described the eastern boundary.

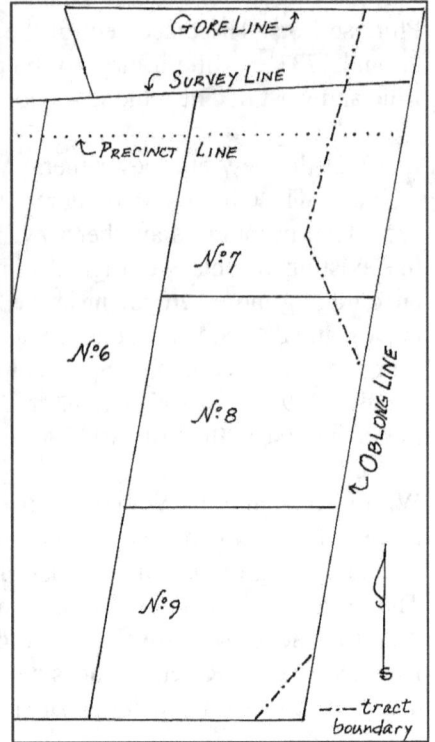

Figure 5 - The 1761 20-Mile Tracts

Using his 1697 deed, Adolph Philipse procured a provincial patent on 17 June 1697. The patent, however, inexplicably extended the north line easterly beyond the Rombout patent to include "the South bounds of Coll Henry Beeckman [sic] until it comes twenty Miles, or until the Division or Petition Line between our Colony of Connecticutt and our said Province, and Easterly by the said Division Line..."[24] Contrary to law, the patent description did not conform to the underlying license or deed – nevertheless, Philipse gained over 100,000 additional acres from these changes. The Philipse heirs later defended the patent against claims of fraud by asserting that Adolph Philipse indicated an eastern boundary 15 miles from the river in his patent application, and charging that it was the Colony of New York that extended the boundary five more miles east.[25] Not addressed was the fact that the original deed from the Wappinger referred to a marked tree, not a 15-mile distance.

---

21. Staughton Lynd, *Anti-Federalism in Dutchess County, New York: a Study of Democracy and Class Conflict in the Revolutionary Era* (Loyola Univ: Chicago, 1962), 47, citing Brief of Nimham (the Wappinger chieftain) before Chancery.
22. Pelletreau, *History of Putnam County*, 11-12, transcription of deed dated 15 July 1691 from seven members of the Wappinger tribe to the two purchasers.
23. Ibid 12-13, transcription of a deed dated 16 June 1697 from Dorlandt and Seabrandt to Adolph Philipse.
24. Ibid 14-16, transcription of the patent granted 17 June 1697 to Adolph Philipse from the governor of the Province of New Yorke. The petition and patent are indicated to be in the records of the Secretary of State of New York.
25. Ibid 83, transcription of the brief submitted by Philipse representatives.

Introduction

Figure 6 - Author's rendition of the Wappinger's plan showing lands sold compared to the entire tract[24]

The map in Figure 6, "laid down without actual survey," depicts the southernmost part of Dutchess County "The whole tract of land represented by this plan contains in quantity about two hundred and four thousand and eight hundred acres." The letter C in the plan represents the tree in the original deed and is "supposed to be about three miles distant" from the Hudson River, rather than the twenty miles represented by the letter E.[26] This clearly shows the disparity between the lands the natives contended they sold in 1697, and the land the Philipse heirs claimed Adolph Philipse purchased from Dorlandt and Seabrandt.

THE EAST BOUNDARY, CONTINUED (THE "INDIAN" LANDS)

The Wappinger tribe had remained on their lands in the southeast part of Dutchess County for all of these years. However, during the War with the French, the men left to fight and the women and children went to the tribe's Massachusetts settlement. Upon their return to Dutchess County in 1762, the Wappinger discovered that the Philipses had confiscated their lands. To reassert their ownership, the Wappinger sold titles or granted 999-year leases to many tenants in the disputed areas, who then refused to pay rent to the Philipses.[27] The Wappinger claimed to have originally sold only 5,000 acres of the patent lands to Dortlandt and Seabrandt,[28] and asserted that the rest of the land was still theirs. They argued that Adolph Philipse knew he had not purchased the land and that his "subsequent actions and statements demonstrated this fact."[29]

Indeed, Adolph Philipse did not divide his land, and as an absentee proprietor, did not collect rents from the residents, except some along the Hudson River. Some early residents obtained leases from the Wappinger, some from Connecticut, and others were squatters.[30] It wasn't until after the 1754 survey that the Philipse heirs divided the land into farms and began demanding leases and rents for the patent lands and northern Gore lands. The heirs believed that the 1754 division gave them a legal right to collect rents.

The Philipse heirs, led by Robinson, steadfastly claimed ownership to all of the lands in the 1754 division and, in 1764, initiated and won ejectment suits against fifteen of the "Indian" tenants.[31] In a 1764 petition, the tenants protested poor treatment by Robinson, stating that he refused to give

---

26. see New York State Archives, "Outline map of 204,800 acres of land in controversy," volume 18 page 128 [includes a map and description]. Figure 6 is based upon an image of that page provided by NYSA Reference Services, Albany, NY. See also Pelletreau, *History of Putnam County*, 79 for a similar map.

27. Irving Mark, *Agrarian Conflicts in Colonial New York 1711-1775* (New York: Columbia University Press, 1940), 132.

28. Other sources indicate the original lines encompassed 15,000 acres. In any case, it was far fewer than the patent.

29. Mark, *Agrarian Conflicts in Colonial New York,* 131 and 133. Particulars on Philipse's actions at pp 35-36.

30. Pelletreau, *History of Putnam County,* 283.

31. Sung Bok Kim, *Landlord and Tenant in Colonial New York: Manorial Society, 1664-1775* (Chapel Hill: Univ. of North Carolina Press, 1978), 379.

"obedient tenants a good or warrantable title by leases deed or any other title for leases for 3 lives or twenty years... he would not lease the land to the inhabitants who had lived on it for near 30 years past and had manured and cultivated the same but would oblige them to buy their farms paying money down or else to remove immediately."[32]

Rather than feeling defeated by the ejectments, the tenant resistance strengthened. No doubt they were encouraged by a 1762 proclamation by Cadwallader Colden, based upon the King's instructions, that persons who have "willfully or inadvertently" taken lands from the Indians "without any lawful authority" would be prosecuted.[33] The Wappinger, recognized as the original owners of the lands east of the Hudson River from New York City to the middle of the Beekman patent, possessed a reasonable claim to unsold land.

In March 1765 the Wappinger set out their claims against the Philipses by petition to then Lieutenant-Governor Colden and the council. To refute the Wappinger claim, Philipse heir Beverly Robinson proclaimed at the trial that he possessed a 1702 deed from the "native Indians" to Adolph Philipse containing a description of the land consistent with that of the patent (*i.e.*, extending 20 miles from the river).[34] He did not produce the required provincial license to support the deed's legitimacy. The lieutenant-governor and his council—all large landowners—neither examined the deed nor permitted the Wappinger to present evidence that it was a forgery. Notably, by declaring a need for the 1702 deed, Robinson tacitly acknowledged that the patent was in error when created – a fact which should technically render the patent invalid. Without citing legal justification, the council decided that the 1702 deed rectified the eastern boundary discrepancy between the 1697 deed and patent. The proceedings were quickly concluded, the native's claims were dismissed, and the Philipse heirs solidified their legal ownership of the extended patent (and 20-Mile) lands.[35]

THE GREAT REBELLION OF 1766

The Colony now recognized the Philipse heirs as owners of all of the lands included in the 1754 division and the 20-Mile lands of the Beekman Gore ceded to them in 1758. But the tenants and natives had not given up. With many tenants ejected, and others offered lease terms of only one year with bonds of £1,000, the settlers began organizing a firm resistance to the landlords, seeking justice for themselves and their neighbors.

After spreading beyond the South Precinct to other proprietary lands to the north and south, the conflict came to a head with perhaps two thousand tenants participating in the "great rebellion of 1766." Much happened in a short time: there were many confrontations, meetings, protests, and marches. The landlords first sought the help of the Dutchess militia to quell the uprising; having no success with the militia, they appealed to the King. British troops arrived, burning and plundering homes and skirmishing with tenants. After a British soldier was killed, the tenants surrendered. Some tenants fled, but fifty or sixty were brought to trial and received varying sentences, with one condemned to death.[36]

---

32. Lynd, *Anti-Federalism in Dutchess County, New York*, 48, citing a petition in the Samuel Munroe papers at the New York Historical Society.

33. Kim, *Landlord and Tenant in Colonial New York*, 355, citing Deposition of Gideon Prindle, 28 Feb 1765, Unsorted Legal MSS, Kempe Papers; king's "Additional Instructions," 9 Dec 1761, *Colden Papers*, VI 101-103.

34. Pelletreau, *History of Putnam County,* 16-18, transcription of a deed dated 13 August 1702 from eight "Indians." to Philipse, now in the manuscript papers of the Philipse-Gouverneur family at Columbia University, New York. Robinson took the deed from his pocket, but did not submit it to the council, nor let it be examined.

35. Mark, *Agrarian Conflicts in Colonial New York*, 133-135.

36. Lynd, *Anti-Federalism in Dutchess County, New York*, 50. The death sentence was subsequently commuted.

Introduction

With the uprising crushed, the rebels had a choice to make: either stay and pay rents under the landlord's terms or settle elsewhere. Some initially chose to return to Massachusetts or Connecticut,[37] but lured by available land, some migrated north to other New York counties, or to the unsettled region that would become Vermont. Former Dutchess County residents settled the towns of Manchester, Dorset, and Danby,[38] and likely other Vermont towns as well.[39]

It wasn't until after the Revolutionary War that the lands held by Tories Robinson and Morris were confiscated by the New York government and sold to individuals, many of whom were tenants, including recent arrivals.[40] The Morrises had previously sold some of their farms, but most were occupied by lease. Only Philip Philipse's Lots 2, 6, and 8 were not subject to the seizure, however many of those farms were also sold in the ensuing years. Despite having to pay for farms they had built and nurtured, some residents were finally able to satisfy their desire for ownership; others lacked funds to purchase their farms, and moved away.

DIVISIONS AFTER 1771

In April 1772, due to significant population growth, the South Precinct was split into three precincts: Philipse along the Hudson River encompassing lots 1–4, Fredricksburgh for the interior lots 5–9, and South East for The Oblong lands.[41] Official districts continued to be based upon the 1754 division of the property into nine lots, but excluding the Rombout and Beekman Gores.

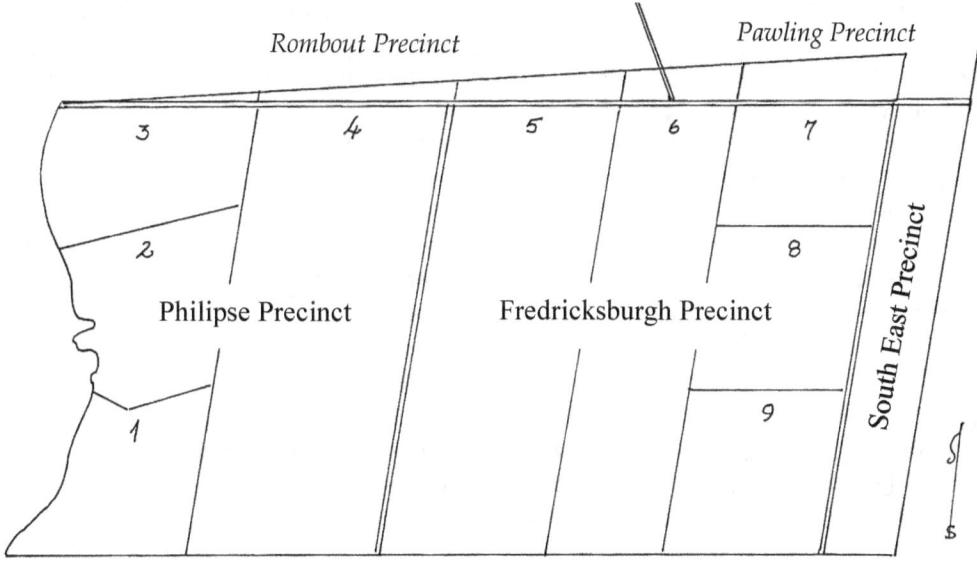

Figure 7 - Precincts in 1772 (precinct boundaries are shown with double lines)

---

37. John Broadhead, *Documents Relative to the Colonial History of the State of New York: procured in Holland, England, and France,* VII, 849, letter from Governor Moore to the Lords of Trade 12 Aug 1766.
38. R.C.Benton, *The Vermont Settlers and the New York Land Speculators* (Minn.: Housekeeper, 1894), 21.
39. Mark, *Agrarian Conflicts in Colonial New York*, 154.
40. For details of loyalist sales see William T Ruddock, *Confiscated Properties of Philipse Highland Patent Putnam County New York 1780-1785* (Westminster: Heritage, 2012).
41. *The Colonial Laws of New York from the Year 1664 to the Revolution,* V (Albany: JB Lyon State Printer, 1894), 395; Chapter 1555, "an Act for dividing the South Precinct in the County of Dutchess into three Precincts," passed 24 March 1772, and *Historical and Genealogical Record Dutchess and Putnam,* 101-102.

In March 1788 the State of New York divided its counties into towns. Philipse Precinct became Philips Town, Fredricksburgh Precinct became Fredericks Town, and South East Precinct became South-East Town. The legal description of the first two contained references to the bounds of the patent lands granted to Adolph Philipse and the lots assigned in 1754.[42] The area encompassing Fredericks Town and South-East Town was divided into four towns in 1795: Frederick, Franklin, Carmel, and South-East,[43] The west boundaries of lots 7–9 (the east boundary of lot 6) served as one dividing line. In later years, Frederick became Kent, Franklin became Patterson, and part of Philips Town (Philipstown) became Putnam Valley, with some boundary shifts along the way.

The last significant change to the boundaries of what would become Putnam County occurred in March 1806, when part of the northwest corner of the original Philipse Patent (a part then included in the Town of Philipstown) was annexed to the Town of Fishkill.[44] In 1812 Putnam was formed from the towns of Philipstown, Carmel, Frederick, Patterson, and Southeast.[45]

THE EARLY SETTLERS

Prior to 1740, few immigrants had settled in the South Precinct; but after 1740, the expansion began. In February 1740/1, the precinct tax list included 47 men; by February 1742/3 the list had 95 men; then, in 1753, just ten years later, it had increased to 352 men. Very few had ownership of their farms.

The first non-native settlers were drawn to land near the Hudson River. The Oblong and the eastern part of the Patent land drew settlement from New England. In 1756, New York historian Judge William Smith wrote of Dutchess County: "the inhabitants on the banks of the river are Dutch, but those more easterly, Englishmen, and, for the most part emigrants from Connecticut and Long Island."[46] Those early western settlers also included French Huguenots; and the eastern settlers included New England Quakers seeking religious tolerance.[47]

In addition to these general trends, as noted in the land history above, Connecticut had granted New Fairfield a patent for 10,000 acres in what later became part of New York; many of the residents of the southeastern area (The Oblong and Short Lot 9) were from New Fairfield.

OTHER INFLUENCES ON SETTLEMENT

The topography of much of the South Precinct was not conducive to settlement; but, as time went on, more roads and bridges were built, facilitating transportation and allowing access to markets. In 1756, Judge Smith noted "the south part of [Dutchess] county is mountainous and fit only for iron works..."[48]

---

42. *Laws of the State of New York*: passed at the Sessions of the Legislature held in the Years 1785, 1786, 1787 and 1788, inclusive, being the Eighth, Ninth, Tenth and Eleventh Sessions, Volume II (Albany: Weed Parsons, 1886), 752; Chap. 64: "An Act for dividing the counties of this state into towns," passed 7 March 1788.

43. *Laws of the State of New York*: passed at the Sessions of the Legislature held in the Years 1789, 1790, 1791, 1792, 1793, 1794, 1795 and 1796 inclusive, III (Albany: Weed Parsons, 1887), 563: Chap. 21. "An Act to divide Fredericks-Town and Southeast-Town in Dutchess county into four towns," passed 17 March 1795.

44. Pelletreau, *History of Putnam County*, 158.

45. *Laws of the State of New York Passed at the Thirty-Fifth Session of the Legislature:* Begun and held at the City of Albany, the Twenty-Eight Day of January 1812 (Albany: Southwick, 1812), 257; Chapter CXLIII passed 12 June 1812.

46. Frank Hasbrouck, *The History of Duchess* [sic] *County New York* (Poughkeepsie: S.A. Matthieu, 1909), 52. (intentionally spelled Duchess)

47. Ibid, 9.

48. Ibid, 52.

Introduction

However, in 1849, Blake clarified that the terrain of the eastern part of Putnam County was uneven and hilly, but highly cultivated. The central and western portions, which included the Highlands mountains, had steep, rocky ranges valuable for mines and quarries, separated by deep, narrow valleys with productive soil.[49]

Figure 8 depicts the rivers, ponds, streams, and mountains of The Oblong and the Philipse Patent, based upon a 1779 map by Claude Joseph Sauthier.[50] While the placement of the rivers and streams may not be precise, the extent of the mountainous regions in the west and northwest demonstrates why certain areas were settled sooner than others. Indeed, the mountain on the upper left is called "Breakneck Hill."

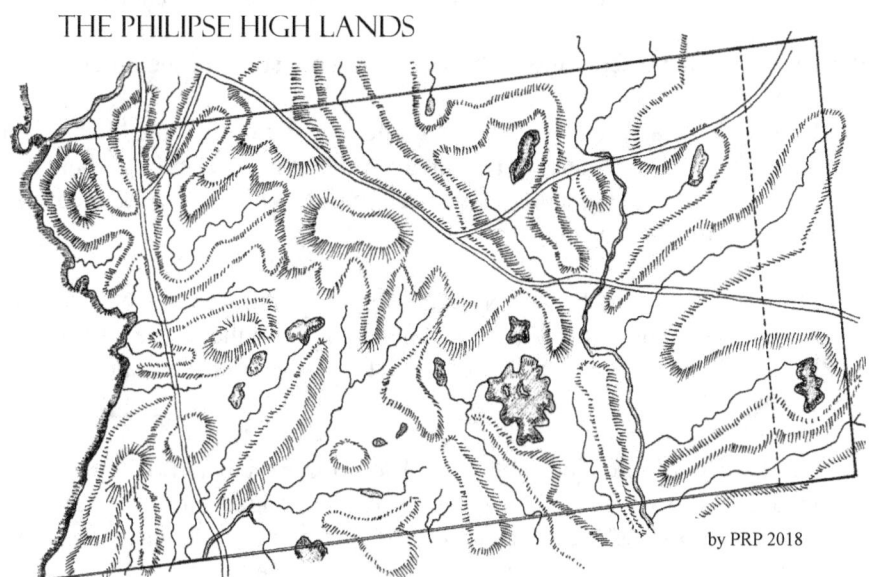

Figure 8 - Topography of Putnam County, NY; elevated areas are hatched, roads are depicted with double lines, and rivers and brooks are depicted with solid lines.

In 1819, regarding the three lots of Roger and Mary Morris, Henry Livingston noted that there were 4,600 acres under cultivation in Lot 3; 14,939 acres in Lot 5; and 7,348 acres in Lot 9. An additional 26,887 acres were uncultivated and unimproved. He also made the following observations:[51]

> "Lot No. 3 contains 9,200 acres, of these 2,000 are feasible and well improved. Hardly equal however to some parts of Lot 5 which lie in Carmel and various parcels on Lot No. 9. Three thousand more may be equal to the better parts of Lot No. 5 lying in Kent and the middling qualities of the same Lot in Carmel. The residue of this Lot is mountainous some altogether inaccessible, the buildings are erected upon a humble scale, all wood. Perhaps one-third of the field enclosures are stone. It is perfectly well watered by springs and rivulets. The farmers all reside at inconsiderable distances from either Fishkill or Cold Springs Landings. This adds value to their several estates.
>
> "Lot No. 5. The northern part of this Lot and that which lies in the town of Kent is mountainous and Rocky. Some of the valleys are excellent meadows and where the soil can be come at is good. But these estimable portions bear but a small proportion to the more rugged parts. The Southern division of this tract and which is the town of Carmel is hilly but cannot be deemed mountainous. Here extensive and excellent meadows every where meet the eye and tillage is well attended to....

---

49. William J. Blake, *History of Putnam County, N.Y.; with an Enumeration of its Towns, Villages, Rivers, Creeks, Lakes, Ponds, Mountains, Hills, and Geological Features; Local Traditions; and Short Biographical Sketches of Early Settlers, Etc.* (New York: Baker & Scribner, 1849), 15.

50. Claude Joseph Sauthier, *A Chorographical Map of the Province of New-York in North America, divided into counties, manors, patents and townships* (London: Fader, 1779), Library of Congress.

51. Pelletreau, *History of Putnam County*, 98-99. Emphasis retained.

The buildings on this Lot are generally below mediocrity. Many however are comfortable. *The day for elegance has not arrived.*

"Lot No. 9. Is so very like the south part of Lot 5 that a description of the one is a portrait of the other... Ponds also beautify this tract and small streams abound..."

Pelletreau in 1886 offered these observations about some of the other Putnam County lots:

Robinson's water lot 1. "Previous to the Revolution the inhabitants on this tract were very few in numbers... A few tenants were scattered on farms, but the rugged and mountainous nature of a large portion of the lot rendered it less desirable as a place of settlement than the fertile valleys in the eastern part of Philipse Patent."[52]

Philipse's water lot 2. "The proximity of this region to the Hudson River rendered it far more easy of access than the central portion of the patent, and the fertile portions were soon settled..." The old Post road, near the south part of the lot was the first road laid out in the Philipse patent, around 1730.[53]

Northern portion of long lots 4–6. The northern portion of these lots is mountainous and thinly inhabited. Lots 5 and 6 "were surveyed and divided into farms at an early day, but so far as the [northern portions] were concerned, did not readily find tenants." ... "As late as the Revolution the population did not number more than two or three hundred."[54]

Southern portion of long lot 4. The principal geographic features are two valleys, Peekskill and Canopus Hollows. They are bounded on either side by rugged mountains separated by "a wide extent of hilly, rocky, and broken ground."[55] The mountains were "unfavorable to the agriculturalist," but rich with iron ore. The first mineral exploration was in 1756, and mines were operated for many years.[56]

While Pelletreau's descriptions are not as colorful as Livingston's, both aid in understanding the difficulties in locating a productive farm lot, and why settlement was more rapid in some areas than others.

SUMMARY

The South Precinct of Dutchess County experienced rapid growth in the years leading up to the Revolution. Settlers included Dutch, French, German, and English stock, with much of the expansion coming from immigrants from Massachusetts, Connecticut, and Westchester and Long Island New York. Few early settlers purchased their farms and many did not have leases; but, by 1760, the landowners were demanding annual rents. It wasn't until after the Revolution that most residents had the opportunity, though perhaps not the wherewithal, to purchase their farms — by then, many of the earlier settlers had died or moved on. The accompanying new maps and new transcriptions of tax and tenant lists, combined with militia and census lists, provide the framework for identifying these early settlers and placing them in historical and genealogical context.

---

52. Pelletreau, *History of Putnam County*, 520.
53. Ibid, 545 and 547.
54. Ibid, 585 and 675-676.
55. Ibid, 714.
56. Ibid, 728-29.

TAX LISTS OF THE SOUTH PRECINCTS OF DUTCHESS COUNTY 1741–1779

Though the South Precinct was established in 1737, separate tax lists begin in February 1740/1. Previously, area residents were taxed in Fishkills Precinct (see Appendix A for names extracted from Fishkills in February 1739/40). Lists for 1749–1752 (Volume D) are missing; 1764 contains blank pages except for totals; there is no list for 1776; and 1777 stops abruptly, excluding nearly all of the southern precincts. The last labelled list in the tax books is for 1779; however, the last volume ends with an incomplete list from 1786 or 1787.[1]

The authority to assess and collect tax came from the provincial laws of New York, dating back to the late 1600s.[2] The New York General Assembly set the required taxes for support of the provincial government and for local government improvements like courthouses and gaols (jails).[3] The county assessors provided lists of freeholders, inhabitants, residents, and sojourners indicating the value of their real and personal property. The justices of the peace or supervisors then determined the tax rate to provide the requisite tax revenue. However, no one law defined who was to be taxed nor how the value of the property was to be determined.

Early laws provide insight into the assessment process. The Duke of York's Laws 1665–75 include a section called "Publicke Charges" calling for every inhabitant and owner of property to contribute to the costs of church and government in proportion to his ability to pay. The law required a true estimate of all personal and real estates for all males from age 16 upwards, excluding common land for free feed of cattle. Cattle, horses, sheep, and swine were assigned values, based upon age, from exempt to 12 pounds each. Assets of children and servants not taking wages were assessed to their parents and masters, and the sick, lame, and infirm were exempt.[4] These laws were replaced by the laws of the General Assembly.

The General Assembly laws, however, excluded specific guidance on assessing values. An act to "regulate the taxing of real and personal estates in the city & county of New York" passed in 1753 cited the "uncertain & unequal" method in use and clarified that 2/3 of rent or yearly income of real estate would determine its value.[5] In 1760, a law for Ulster County seeking "more equal taxation of estates," clarified that the value of whole estates, real and personal, would be set down based upon 10 pounds for each 100 pounds of full value.[6] A law in 1762 for Suffolk County for "better regulating the taxation of estates" specified that the assessor would record four pounds for every 100 pounds of real value.[7] While Dutchess County had no comparable law, it is clear that the assessed values served as *relative* values among the inhabitants, and not absolute values — and that methods of assessing values varied among counties.

---

1. While several precincts were not included, the presence of Clinton Pct. dates this list to no earlier than Clinton's 1786 formation. Precincts were replaced by Towns in 1788, so the list precedes that change.
2. Commissioners of Statutory Revision, *The Colonial Laws of New York from the Year 1664 to the Revolution* (Albany: Lyon, 1894) in four volumes, 1:59-60, 131, 308, 479, etc.
3. *The Colonial Laws of New York*, example 3:336. Dutchess County levy passed 17 Dec 1743.
4. Ibid, 1:59-60.
5. Ibid, 4:306.
6. Ibid, 4:503.
7. Ibid, 4:678.

Each year the assessors took an oath to rate and assess freeholders and inhabitants of the County. For Dutchess, it was: "I A:B: Do Swear that I will not pass any Account or any Article thereof Wherewith I do not think the County Justly Chargeable, nor will I Disallow Any Account or Any Article Thereof Wherewith I Think the County Justly Chargeable. So help me God."[8]

Caution

The tax books contain lists transcribed from the supervisors' original writings. As a result, transcription errors are inherent in the lists themselves, and may occur in subsequent transcriptions.

The order of the lists does not indicate neighbors. For the most part, new taxables were added to the end of the list each year, although sometimes a successor tenant retained the position in the list of his predecessor. As can be seen by comparing taxables to tenant lists and maps, or tracing taxables in the South Precinct of 1771 to the three successor precincts in 1772, few conclusions can be drawn about neighbors based upon placement on the lists.

Some handwriting contains ambiguously formed letters. A year by year comparison helped to decipher the names in many cases; however, the clarity of the script varied from list to list. When seeking an individual, consider alternate spellings by letter shape, not just sound.

Author Notes

The spellings in the original lists have been retained. Brackets enclose corrections for apparent or obvious enumeration or transcription errors. A question mark within brackets indicates a possible or probable error. Brackets also enclose spelling corrections when the mangling of a surname is so significant as to be misleading. These corrections were identified by comparing the lists year by year, looking for anomalies and inconsistencies. Some handwriting defied a precise transcription, necessitating reference to other entries and, in some cases, external sources. In searching the index, consider substituting c and k, e and i, e and a, i and y, e and o, etc. — creative spelling by the supervisors and scribes abounds.

The most prevalent abbreviation used in the tax books is for Junior, recorded as J^r, Junr or Jn^r (often scribbled and with a flair for the "r"). Rather than attempt to precisely determine which letters were included, a default of Jnr: denotes the presence of an abbreviation for Junior (similarly Sen: for Senior). For clarity, no superscripts are included herein, despite frequent use in the records. Most abbreviated names had the last letter raised, often with a flourish. These lists are a tool, the reader is encouraged to consult the original images.[9]

The lists herein include sequential numbering of the entries; these numbers do not appear in the originals, but serve to enhance usability. Most (not all) of the tax books also included the tax amount which is excluded from these lists. Note that in February 1761, the scribe skipped 37 names and inserted them at the end; however, the accompanying list includes them in the "correct" order (with notation to that effect). The original volume H includes 461 South Precinct names for June 1771, whereupon the scribe ran out of room. Volume I includes the complete list of 688 names, so only the complete list from Volume I appears herein.

---

8. "Supervizors Oath" inside cover of *Supervisor's Record 1753 to 1757 v. E, Dutchess County Clerks Office*.
9. See Bibliography on page 281 for sources.

BOOK OF TAXES 1729 to 1748, VOLUME C
DUTCHESS COUNTY CLERKS OFFICE

FEBRUARY 1740/1
SOUTHERN PRECINCT

... to be Paid at the Rate of two Pence / Pound

The Freeholders and Inhabitants are rated ... as follows

#	Name	Surname	Value £	#	Name	Surname	Value £
	Page 215				*Page 216*		
1	Francis	Nellson	16	26	Henry	Brewer	5
2	Thomas	Davinport	30	27	Jonathan	Sturdefunt	4
3	Joseph	Arkills	1	28	Jonathan	Sturdefunt Jnr:	2
4	Jacob	Sprinsteen	2	29	Jacob	Mandavill	6
5	Albert	Swim	3	30	Jacobus	Hennion	5
6	David	Hustis	9	31	David	Lancaster	1
7	John	Calkin Jnr:	10	32	Siber	Cranckheit	2
8	Jeremiah	Calkin	10	33	Nathan	Lane	15
9	John	Rodgers	4	34	Mossis	Husted	2
10	William	Baxter	1	35	Even	Brok	2
11	Abram	Otter	1	36	Ephraim	Forgason	2
12	Ebenezer	Jones	3	37	Anthony	Hill	2
13	Samuel	Jones	1	38	Thomas	Headen	3
14	John	Thompkins	1	39	Isaac	Forgason	1
15	Obediah	Thompkins	1	40	George	Hueston	1
16	Exd: of Francis	Drake Decd	2	41	Isaac	Names	2
				42	Daniell	Philip	1
17	Joseph	Thompkins	2	43	David	Tidd	1
18	James	Wellden	1	44	Benjamin	Earns	2
19	William	Lamb	2	45	William	Hunt	1
20	Issac	Fontyn	3	46	William	Brooster	2
21	John	Van Amburgh	9	47	Joseph	McGregory	4
22	Isaac	Van Amburgh	2				£ 201
23	Henry	Van Amburgh	7				
24	Peter	Du Bois	11				
25	Benjamin	Jaycocks	3				

February 1741/2
Southern Precinct

...to be paid at the rate of five pence one farthing / pound

The Freeholders & Inhabitants are ... Rated

#	Name	Surname	Value £	#	Name	Surname	Value £
	Page 236				*Page 237*		
1	Francis	Nellson	18	44	Benjamin	Earns	2
2	Thomas	Davinport	30	45	Iccabud	Viccary	2
3	Joseph	Arkills	1	46	William	Hunt	2
4	Jacob	Springsteen	3	47	William	Brewster	4
5	Abram	Hodges	1	48	Joseph	McGregory	1
6	David	Hustis	10	49	Joseph	Jaycocks	2
7	John	Calkin Jnr:	10	50	Joseph	Cowban	1
8	Jeremiah	Calkin	12	51	John	Eagleston	5
9	John	Rodgers	4	52	Josiah	Gregory	1
10	William	Baxter	1	53	John George	Garlinghousen	3
11	Abram	Otter	1	54	Hezekiah	Wright	3
12	Ebenezer	Jones	3	55	John	Drake	1
13	Samuell	Jones	1	56	Samuell	Bradly	1
14	John	Thompkins	1	57	Isaac	Rodes	1
15	Obediah	Thompkins	1	58	Giles	Robinson	1
16	Thomas	Kelek	1	59	Jacob	Craw	2
17	Joseph	Thompkins	10	60	Elijah	Thompkins	6
18	William	Lamb	2	61	Daniell	Townsen	6
19	Isaac	Fontyn	3	62	Joseph	Craine	1
20	John	Van Amburgh	10	63	David	Paddock	1
21	Isaac	Van Amburgh	2	64	James	Paddock	1
22	Henry	Van Amburgh	7	65	Daniel	Beckus	1
23	Peter	Du Bois	11	66	Philip	Minthorn	2
24	John	During	2	67	Peter	Benit Jnr:	1
25	Benjamin	Jaycocks	3	68	John	Langdon	1
26	Hendrick	Brewer	5	69	Silus	Wasebun	1
27	Jonathan	Sturdefunt	1	70	William	Sturdefunt	1
28	Jonathan	Sturdefunt Jnr:	1	71	Elisha	Luttington	1
29	Jacob	Mandavill	7	72	William	Yern	2
30	Jacobus	Hennion	5	73	Nathaniel	Porter	5
31	John	Campbell	1	74	Joseph	Barly	1
32	Sibit	Cranckhyt	2	75	William	Clarke	1
33	Nathan	Lane	15	76	Caleb	Claussen	1
34	Moses	Hustis	2				£ 267
35	Even	Brock	2				
36	Ephraim	Forgeson	2				
37	Anthony	Hill	3				
38	Thomas	Headon	3				
39	Isaac	Forgeson	1				
40	George	Hueston	1				
41	Joseph	Crane	1				
42	Daniell	Philips	1				
43	David	Tidd	1				

February 1742/3
Southern Precinct

The Freeholders & Inhabitants to pay at the rate of four pence / pound.

#	Name	Surname	Value £	#	Name	Surname	Value £
		Page 276				*Page 277*	
1	Francis	Nellson	18	50	Jonathan	Sturdefunt	1
2	Capt. Thomas	Davinport	35	51	Jacob	Craw	2
3	Jacob	Springsteen	3	52	Elijah	Thompkins	8
4	Abram	Hodges	1	53	Daniel	Townsen	6
5	David	Hustis	10	54	Joseph	Crane	3
6	John	Calkins Jnr: Eq^r	10	55	David	Paddock	3
7	Jeremiah	Calkin	12	56	James	Paddock	3
8	John	Rogers	4	57	Daniel	Beckus	1
9	Abram	Otter	1	58	Philip	Minthorn	2
10	Ebenezer	Jones	5	59	Peter	Bennet Jnr:	1
11	Samuel	Jones	1	60	John	Langdon	1
12	John	Thompkins	3	61	Silus	Washbun	3
13	Obediah	Thompkins	1	62	William	Sturdefunt	1
14	Thomas	Kelik	1	63	Elisha	Luttington	1
15	Joseph	Thompkins	10	64	William	Yurns	4
16	William	Lamb	1	65	Nathaniel	Porter	5
17	John	Van Amburgh	11	66	Joseph	Barley	2
18	Isaac	Van Amburgh	1	67	William	Clarke	1
19	Henry	Van Amburgh	7	68	Caleb	Clawsen	1
20	Peter	DuBois	13	69	Joseph	Lane	4
21	John	During	2	70	Joseph	Mead	2
22	Benjamin	Jaycock	2	71	Thomas	Kercome	2
23	Hendrick	Brewer Sen.	5	72	John	Jey	1
24	Jacob	Mandavill	7	73	William	Jey	1
25	Jacobus	Hennion	6	74	Jacobus	Crankhyt	3
26	John	Cambell	1	75	Jacobus	Crankhyt Jnr:	1
27	Siber	Cranckhyt	4	76	William	Forgeson	1
28	Nathan	Lane	8	77	Nathaniell	Robinson	2
29	Moses	Hustis	2	78	David	Astin	3
30	Ephraim	Fergeson	1	79	Caleb	Brundiges	1
31	Anthony	Hill	10	80	Thomas	Curry	1
32	Thomas	Headon	10	81	Daniell	Taylor	1
33	George	Hueston	2	82	John	Sprage	2
34	Joseph	Craw	1	83	John	Frost	2
35	Daniell	Philips	1	84	Joseph	Porter	2
36	David	Tidd	1	85	—	Perry	8
37	Benjamin	Earnell	1	86	Thomas	Stickny	2
38	Iccabud	Viccary	2	87	Cornelis	Fuller	1
39	William	Hunt	1	88	Samuel	Calkin	4
40	Joseph	McGregory	1	89	John	Hayns	2
41	Joseph	Jaycocks	2	90	Seth	Dean	2
42	Joseph	Corban	1	91	Thomas	Frost	1
43	John	Eggleston	3	92	William	Ballard	1
44	Josiah	Gregory	1	93	—	Cole	2
45	John George	Garlinghousen	4	94	—	Gray	2
46	Hezekiah	Wright	1	95	Jonathan	Sturdefunt	1
47	John	Drake	1				£ 340
48	Samuel	Bradly	1				
49	Isaac	Rhodes	6				

February 1743/4
Southern Precinct

The Freeholders & Inhabitants to pay at the rate of four pence one half penny / pound.

	Name	Surname	Value (£)		Name	Surname	Value
	Page 282			49	Elijah	Thompkins	9
1	Francis	Nellson	18	50	Daniell	Towsen	6
2	Thomas	Davinport	35	51	Joseph	Crane	4
3	Jacob	Springsteen	2	52	David	Paddock	4
4	Abram	Hodges	1	53	James	Paddock	4
5	David	Hustis	12	54	Daniell	Beckus	1
6	John	Calkins Jnr:	10	55	Philip	Minthorn	2
7	Jeremiah	Calkin	12	56	Peter	Bennet Jnr:	1
8	John	Rogers	4	57	Mathias	Du Bois	2
9	Abram	Otter	1	58	William	Sturdefunt	1
10	Ebenezer	Jones	6	59	Elisha	Luttington	1
11	Samuel	Jones	1	60	William	Yerns	5
12	John	Thompkins	4	61	Nathaniel	Porter	5
	Page 283			62	Joseph	Barley	2
13	Obediah	Thompkins	1		*Page 284*		
14	Thomas	Kelik	1	63	Caleb	Clawsen	1
15	John	Van Amburgh	12	64	Joseph	Lane	5
16	Isaac	Van Amburgh	1	65	Joseph	Meed	2
17	Henry	Van Amburgh	7	66	Thomas	Cercome	2
18	Peter	DuBois	15	67	John	Jey	1
19	John	During	2	68	William	Jey	1
20	Benjamin	Jaycock	2	69	Jacobus	Crankhyt	3
21	Hendrick	Brewer & Son	5	70	Jacobus	Crankhyt Jnr:	1
22	Jacob	Mondavill	9	71	William	Forgeson	1
23	Jacobus	Hennion	1	72	Nathaniell	Robinson	2
24	John	Campell	1	73	David	Astin	3
25	Sibet	Crankhyt	4	74	Caleb	Brundige	1
26	Nathan	Lane	8	75	Thomas	Curry	1
27	Moses	Hustis	2	76	John	Spragg	2
28	Ephraim	Fergeson	1	77	John	Frost	2
29	Anthony	Hill	10	78	Joseph	Porter	2
30	Thomas	Headon	10	79	—	Perry	8
31	George	Hueston	2	80	Thomas	Stickny	2
32	Joseph	Craw	1	81	Cornelis	Fuller	1
33	David	Tidd	1	82	Samuel	Calkin	5
34	Benjamin	Earnell	1	83	John	Haines	2
35	Iccabud	Viccary	2	84	Seth	Dean	3
36	William	Hunt	1	85	Thomas	Frost	1
37	Joseph	McGregory	1	86	William	Ballard	1
38	Joseph	Jaycocks	2	87	—	Cole	2
39	Joseph	Corbin	1	88	—	Gray	2
40	John	Egleston	3	89	Jonathan	Sturdefunt	1
41	Josiah	Gregory	1	90	William	Taylor [Teller]	3
42	John George	Garlinghousen	5	91	Thomas	Davinport Jnr:	10
43	Hezekiah	Wright	1	92	Teunis	Crankwright	1
44	John	Drake	1	93	Daniell	Fields	1
45	Samuel	Bradly	1	94	Abraham	Smith	2
46	Isaac	Rhodes	6	95	Luke	Covert	2
47	Jonathan	Sturdefunt Jnr:	1	96	Robert	Emmery	2
48	Jacob	Craw	2	97	Elie	Nellson	2

February 1743/4 continued

#	Name	Surname	Value	#	Name	Surname	Value
98	Joseph	Arcler	1	114	Nathan	Brewster	5
99	Abraham	Hodges	2	115	Robert	Jones	2
100	Hark S:	Crankhyt	1	116	Thomas	Richardson Sen:	3
101	Simon	Price	2	117	Richard	Hulse	3
102	John	Kelly	1	118	—	Perkins	2
103	Joshua	Arcly	1	119	—	Nicholls	3
104	Abraham	Buis	13	120	William	Sweet	4
105	John S	DuBois	6	121	Joseph	Sweet	2
106	Cornelis	Gerretsen	3	122	—	Case	1
107	Elijah	Gerretsen	1	123	Samuel	Field	15
108	Johannis	Buis	2	124	—	Nicholls at Joes Hills	1
109	William	Prickett	1				
110	—	Hatch	5	125	—	Stephens	4
111	Peter	Bennet	1	126	James	Dickenson	2
112	William	Daily	2	127	Benjamin	Franklin	1
	Page 285			128	—	Townsen	7
113	Edward	Daily	1				£ 457

February 1744/5
Southern Precinct

The Freeholders & Inhabitants to pay at the rate of eight pence three farthings / pound.

#	Name	Surname	Value	#	Name	Surname	Value
	Page 318		£	26	Moses	Hustis	2
1	Francis	Nellson	15	27	Ephraim	Forgeson	1
2	Thomas	Davinport	30	28	Anthony	Hill	15
3	Abram	Hoges	1	29	Thomas	Headon	15
4	David	Hustis	10	30	George	Hueston	4
	Page 319			31	Joseph	Craw	5
5	John	Calkin	10	32	David	Tidd	1
6	Jeremiah	Calkin	12	33	Benjamin	Earnoll	1
7	John	Rogers	4	34	Iccabud	Viccary	2
8	Abram	Otter	1	35	William	Hunt	2
9	Ebenezer	Jones	5	36	Joseph	McGregory	1
10	Samuell	Jones	1	37	Joseph	Jaycocks	2
11	John	Thompkins	4	38	Joseph	Corben	1
12	Obediah	Thompkins	1	39	John	Egleston	4
13	Elijah	Thompkins	10	40	Josiah	Gregory	1
14	Thomas	Kelek	1	41	John	Garlinghousen	5
15	John	Van Amburgh	12	42	Hezekiah	Wright	1
16	Henry	Van Amburgh	7	43	John	Drake	2
17	Peter	DuBois	15	44	Isaac	Rodes	6
18	John	During	1	45	Jonathan	Sturdefunt	1
19	Benjamin	Jaycocks	2	46	Jonathan	Sturdefunt Jnr:	1
20	Hendrick	Brewer & son	5	47	Jacob	Craw	1
21	Jacob	Mandavill	9	48	Daniel	Townsen	12
22	Jacobus	Hennion	1	49	Joseph	Crane	4
23	John	Campell	1	50	David	Paddock	4
24	Sibet	Crankhyt	3	51	James	Paddock	2
25	Nathan	Lane	9	52	Philip	Minthorn	4

February 1744/5 continued

	Name	Surname	Value		Name	Surname	Value
53	Peter	Bennet Jnr:	1	106	Thomas	Richardson	3
54	Mathew	Du Bois	2	107	Richard	Hultes	1
	Page 320			108	—	Perkins	1
55	Elisha	Luttington	1	109	—	Nicholls	3
56	William	Yerns	4	110	William	Sweet	3
57	Nathaniell	Porter	5	111	Joseph	Sweet	1
58	Joseph	Barly	3	112	—	Case	1
59	Caleb	Clawsen	1	113	Samuel	Fields	15
60	Joseph	Lane	6	114	—	Nicholls	1
61	Joseph	Mead	2			at Joes Hills	
62	Thomas	Cercome	4	115	—	Stevens	4
63	John	Jey	1	116	James	Dickenson	3
64	William	Jey	1	117	Benjamin	Franklin	1
65	Jacobus	Crankhyt	3	118	Robert	Townsen	1
66	Jacobus	Crankhyt Jnr:	1	119	Benjamin	Arnold	1
67	William	Forgeson	1	120	Mathew	Winter	1
68	Nathaniell	Robinson	2	121	Jesse	Smith	2
69	David	Astin	5	122	Marcus	Baxter	2
70	Caleb	Brundige	1	123	Lockart	Baxter	2
71	Thomas	Curry	1	124	Bartlet	Brundidge	2
72	John	Sprag	3	125	Samuell	Brewer	1
73	John	Frost	4	126	Richard	Curry	6
74	Joseph	Porter	2	127	Michaell	Shaw	1
75	Thomas	Stickny	2	128	Barnabas	Hamblin	1
76	Cornelis	Fuller	1	129	Samuell	Jenkins	1
77	Samuell	Calkin	5	130	Caleb	Hale	1
78	John	Hains	1	131	John	Wantsell	1
79	Seth	Dean	1	132	Joseph	Fields	14
80	Thomas	Frost	1	133	Samuell	Gates	2
81	William	Ballard	1	134	Amos	Dickenson	3
82	—	Cole	2	135	John	Dickenson	4
83	—	Gray	1	136	William	Bloomer	2
84	William	Teller	3	137	William	Underhill	3
85	Thomas	Davinport Jnr:	12	138	William	Rapalyea	4
86	Teunis	Krankright	1	139	Andrew	Rapalyea	1
87	Daniell	Fields	2	140	Timothy	Shaw	3
88	Abram	Smith	5	141	Joseph	Clinton	2
89	Luke	Covert	2	142	Joseph	Lockwood	3
90	Robert	Emmery	2	143	Nehemiah	Levet	1
91	Elie	Nellson	2	144	Jacob	Doty	1
92	Abram	Hadge	2	145	Titus	Wood	2
93	Joseph	Arcles	1	146	John	Barber	1
94	Hark S:	Crankhyt	1	147	Jonathan	Barber	1
95	John	Kelly	1	148	Moses	Nauthorp	15
96	Joshua	Arcles	1	149	Benjamin	Owins	1
97	Abraham	Buis	10	150	Peter	Hartwell	1
98	Hannis	Buis	1	151	Thomas	Townsen	3
99	William	Pricket	1	152	Benjamin	Andrews	1
100	Richard	Hatch	5	153	John	Lea	1
101	Peter	Bennet	1	154	William	Smith	1
102	William	Daiy	2		*Page 322*		
103	Edward	Daily	1	155	James	Sears	3
104	William	Brewster	5	156	Deacon	Hamlin	5
	Page 321						£ 540
105	Robert	Jones	2				

February 1745/6
Southern Precinct

The Freeholders & Inhabitants to pay at the rate of nine penies half penny / pound.

	Name	Surname	Value		Name	Surname	Value
			£	51	Philip	Minthorn	5
	Page 352			52	Peter	Bennet Jnr:	1
1	Francis	Nellson	15	53	Mathew	Du Bois	2
2	Thomas	Davinport	30	54	Elisha	Luttington	1
3	Thomas	Davinport Jnr:	12	55	William	Yerns	6
4	William	Davinport	2	56	Nathaniel	Porter	5
5	Jacob	Mandavill	10	57	Joseph	Barly	3
6	John	Nellson	2	58	Caleb	Clawsen	1
7	Abram	Hodges	1	59	Joseph	Lane	5
8	David	Hustis	8	60	Joseph	Meed	2
9	John	Calkin Jnr:	7	61	Thomas	Cercome	4
10	Jeremiah	Calkin	10	62	John	Jey	1
11	John	Rogers	5	63	William	Jey	1
12	Abram	Otter	1	64	Jacobus	Crākhyt	3
13	Ebenezer	Jones	5	65	Jacobus	Crankhyt Jnr:	1
14	Samuell	Jones	1	66	William	Forgeson	1
15	John	Tomkins	4	67	Nathaniel	Robinson	2
16	Elijah	Tomkins	8	68	David	Astin	5
17	Thomas	Kelk	2	69	Caleb	Brundidge	1
18	John	V: Amburgh	12	70	Thomas	Curry	1
19	Henry	V Amburgh	7		*Page 354*		
20	Peter	DuBois	15	71	John	Sprag	3
	Page 353			72	Joseph	Porter	2
21	John	During	1	73	Thomas	Stickny	2
22	Benjamin	Jaycocks	2	74	Cornelius	Fuller	2
23	Hend:k	Brewer & son	5	75	Samuel	Calkin	4
24	John	Campell	1	76	John	Hayns	1
25	Sibet	Crākhyt	1	77	Seth	Dean	3
26	Nathan	Lane	9	78	Thomas	Frost	2
27	Ephraim	Forgeson	1	79	—	Cole	3
28	Anthony	Hill	17	80	Edward	Gray	1
29	Thomas	Headon	16	81	William	Teller	3
30	George	Hueston	8	82	Teunis	Crankright	1
31	Joseph	Craw	1	83	Daniell	Field	1
32	David	Tidd	1	84	Abram	Smith	5
33	Benjamin	Earnoll	1	85	Luke	Covert	1
34	Iccabudd	Viccary	3	86	Robert	Emmery	2
35	William	Hunt	3	87	Elie	Nellson	3
36	Joseph	McGregory	1	88	Abram	Hadge	2
37	Joseph	Jaycocks	1	89	Joseph	Arcles	1
38	Joseph	Corben	2	90	Harh : S:	Crankhyt	6
39	John	Egleston	4	91	John	Kelly	1
40	Josiah	Gregory	1	92	Joshua	Arcles	1
41	Hezekiah	Wright	1	93	Abram	Buis	10
42	John	Drake	2	94	Hannis	Buis	3
43	Isaac	Rodes	6	95	Richard	Hatch	5
44	Jonathan	Sturdefunt	1	96	Peter	Bennet	1
45	Jonathan	Sturdefunt Jnr:	1	97	William	Daily	2
46	Jacob	Craw	1	98	Edward [William]	Brewster	12
47	Daniel	Townsen	12	99	Robert	Jones	2
48	Joseph	Crane	5	100	Thomas	Richardson	2
49	David	Paddock	3				
50	James	Paddock	2				

February 1745/6 continued

	Name	Surname	Value		Name	Surname	Value
101	Richard	Hulse	1	154	Elihu	Townsen	6
102	Valentine	Perkins	2	155	Caleb	Sweet	1
103	Ephraim	Nicholls	2	156	William	Masters	1
104	William	Sweet	2	157	James	Lovelace	2
105	William	Case	1	158	Allen	Ball	2
106	Joseph	Sweet	1	159	Elifelet	Ball	2
107	Samuel	Field	15	160	Benjamin	Allen	1
108	Nathaniel	Stevens	2	161	John	Potter	1
109	James	Dickenson	4	162	Simon	Wolf	2
110	Benjamin	Fräklin	2	163	Abiel	Hatch	2
111	Robert	Townsen	10	164	James	Hide	1
112	Benjamin	Arnold	1	165	Jabish	Hide	2
113	Mathew	Winter	1	166	John	Newberry	3
114	Jesse	Smith	2	167	Samuel	Utter	2
115	Marcus	Baxter	2	168	Benjamin	Merrick	1
116	Lockart	Baxter	2	169	Daniel	Gray	2
117	Bartlet	Brundige	3	170	James	Philips	1
118	Samuell	Brewer	1		*Page 356*		
119	Richard	Curry	7	171	William	Palmer	1
120	Michall	Shaw	1	172	Peter	Paddock	6
	Page 355			173	Thomas	Paddock	2
121	Barnabas	Hamlin	1	174	Silas	Sears	1
122	Samuel	Jenkins	2	175	Ebenezer	Jones	1
123	Caleb	Hale	1	176	Giles	Robinson	1
124	John	Wantsell	1	177	Ebenezer	Craw	1
125	Joseph	Field	14	178	Joseph	Crane Jnr:	1
126	Samuel	Gates	3	179	David	Patterson	1
127	Amos	Dickenson	4	180	Daniel	Bradly	1
128	John	Dickenson	5	181	William	Ballard	1
129	William	Bloomer	2	182	Nathaniel	Sheperdson	1
130	William	Underhill	4	183	Uriah	Townsen	4
131	William	Rapalyea	5	184	—	Latham	1
132	Andrew	Rapalyea	1	185	Jonathan	White	1
133	Timothy	Shaw	3	186	John	White	1
134	Joseph	Clinton	3	187	Russell	Gregory	1
135	Joseph	Lockwood	5	188	—	Collwell	1
136	Jacob	Doty	1	189	John	Calkin 3d	1
137	Titus	Wood	2	190	Thomas	Cotton	1
138	John	Barber	1	191	Benjamin	Utter	1
139	Jonathan	Barber	1	192	John	Utter	1
140	Moses	Nauthorp	17	193	Seth	Dean Jnr:	1
141	Benjamin	Owins	1	194	Nathan	Taylor Jnr:	1
142	Peter	Hartwell	1	195	Abell	Scribner	1
143	Thomas	Townsen	3	196	Peter	Randell	1
144	Benjamin	Andrews	2	197	Daniel	Parish	1
145	John	Lee	3	198	Jacob	Ellis	2
146	William	Smith	1	199	Edward	Ganung	2
147	James	Sears	5	200	—	Scribner	2
148	Deacon	Hamlin	5	201	John	Tid	1
149	Shubal	Rowly	4	202	George	Curry	2
150	Mathew	Rowly	1	203	Mathew	Roe	1
151	Anthony	Pattison	2	204	Uriah	Hill	1
152	Jacob	Philips	2	205	William	Drake	1
153	Philip	Philips	1				£ 657

February 1746/7
Southern Precinct

The Freeholders & Inhabitants to pay at 4 d /£ [pence/pound]

#	Name	Surname	Value (£)	#	Name	Surname	Value
	Page 401			51	Thomas	Cercomb	10
1	Francis	Nellson	20	52	John	Jey	3
2	Thomas	Davinport	30	53	William	Jey	2
3	Thomas	Davinport Jnr:	13	54	Jacobus	Crankhyt	3
4	William	Davinport	1	55	Jacobus	Crankhyt Jnr:	1
5	Jacob	Mandavill	13	56	William	Fergeson	1
6	John	Nellson	2	57	Nathaniell	Robinson	2
7	Abram	Hodges	2	58	David	Astin	4
8	David	Hustis	8	59	Caleb	Brundidge	2
9	John	Calkin Jnr:	7	60	Thomas	Curry	1
10	Jeremiah	Calkin	9	61	John	Spragg	3
11	John	Rogers	8	62	Joseph	Porter	1
12	Abram	Otter	3	63	Thomas	Stickney	3
13	Ebenezer	Jones	6	64	Cornelis	Fuller	2
14	Samuel	Jones	1	65	Samuell	Calkin	5
15	John	Tompkins	5	66	John	Haynes	1
16	Elijah	Tompkins	10	67	Seth	Dean	2
17	Thomas	Kelk	4	68	Thomas	Frost	2
18	John	Van Amburgh	14	69	Eleazer	Cole	3
19	Henry	Van Amburgh	12	70	Edward	Gray	1
20	Peter	Du Bois	18		*Page 403*		
	Page 402			71	William	Teller	4
21	John	During	2	72	Teunis	Crankhyt	1
22	Benjamin	Jaycocks	2	73	Daniell	Field	1
23	Hend:k	Brewer & son	5	74	Abram	Smith	6
24	Sibet	Crankhyt	1	75	Luke	Covert	2
25	Nathan	Lane	12	76	Robert	Emmery	2
26	Anthony	Hill	16	77	Elie	Nellson	4
27	Thomas	Headon	2	78	Joseph	Arclas	1
28	George	Hueston	7	79	Hark S:	Krankhyt	6
29	Joseph	Craw	1	80	John	Kelly	1
30	David	Tidd	6	81	Joshua	Arclas	1
31	Ben:	Earnoll	1	82	Abram	Buis	9
32	Iccabud	Viccary	5	83	Hannis	Buis	3
33	William	Hunt	2	84	Nath-ll	Hatch	12
34	Joseph	McGregory	1	85	Peter	Bennet	1
35	Joseph	Jaycocks	1	86	William	Daily	3
36	John	Egleston	2	87	William	Brewster	10
37	Josiah	Gregory	2	88	Thomas	Richardson	1
38	Hezekiah	Wright	1	89	Valentine	Perkins	3
39	John	Drake	5	90	William	Sweet	2
40	Isaac	Rodes	6	91	Samuell	Field	15
41	Jacob	Craw	1	92	Nathaniell	Stephens	1
42	Daniell	Townsen	12	93	James	Dickenson	5
43	Joseph	Crane	5	94	Benjamin	Franklin	1
44	David	Paddock	4	95	Robert	Townsen	10
45	James	Paddock	4	96	Benjamin	Arnold	1
46	Peter	Bennet Jnr:	1	97	Mathew	Winter	1
47	William	Yearns	8	98	Jesse	Smith	2
48	Nath-ll	Porter	2	99	Marcus	Baxter	2
49	Joseph	Lane	6	100	Benj-n	Brundidge	10
50	Joseph	Meed	4	101	Bartlet	Brundidge	5

February 1746/7 continued

	Name	Surname	Value		Name	Surname	Value
102	Sam-ll	Brewer	1	155	Dan-ll	Bradly	1
103	Richard	Curry	11	156	Nath-ll	Sheperson	1
104	Michael	Shaw	1	157	Uriah	Townsen	4
105	Barnabas	Hamblin	2	158	—	Latham	1
106	Samuell	Jenkins	2	159	Jonathan	White	1
107	Caleb	Hale	1	160	John	White	1
108	John	Wantsell	1	161	Russell	Gregory	1
109	Joseph	Field	8	162	Jno	Calkin 3d	6
110	Samuell	Gates	3	163	Seth	Dean Jnr:	1
111	Amos	Dickenson	3	164	Nathan	Taylor Jnr:	1
112	John	Dickenson	3	165	Abell	Scribner	1
113	William	Bloomer	2	166	Peter	Randall	1
114	William	Rapalyea	7	167	Jacob	Ellis	1
115	Timothy	Shaw	4	168	Edward	Gunning	1
116	Joseph	Lockwood	4	169	John	Tidd	1
117	Jacob	Doty	1	170	George	Curry	5
118	Titus	Wood	3		*Page 405*		
119	John	Barber	1	171	Mathew	Row	4
120	Jonathan	Barber	1	172	Uriah	Hill	3
	Page 404			173	William	Drake	1
121	William	Underhill	2	174	Joseph	Hunt	5
122	Moses	Nauthorp	8	175	Isaac	Terhill	1
123	Benjamin	Owins	1	176	John	V:Tessell	1
124	Peter	Hartwell	1	177	John	Harrick	3
125	Thomas	Townsen	1	178	Alex:	Dowell	2
126	Benjamin	Andrews	2	179	Robert	Farrinton	8
127	William	Smith	1	180	James	Maurade	2
128	James	Sears	6	181	Tim:	Farrinton	1
129	Deacon	Hamlin	8	182	W-m	Field	2
130	Shuball	Rowly	6	183	Nath-ll	Byington	2
131	Mathew	Rowly	1	184	Jacob	Finch	1
132	Anthony	Paterson	2	185	Francis	Purdy	1
133	Jacob	Philips	2	186	Thomas	Philips	2
134	Elihu	Townsend	5	187	Jeremiah	Jones	1
135	Caleb	Sweet	1	188	Ebenezer	King	1
136	Elifelet	Ball	1	189	John	Arcy	1
137	Ben:	Allen	1	190	Silas	Backer	4
138	John	Potter	1	191	Isaac	Chapman	2
139	Simon	Wolf	2	192	Leu:t	Taylor	4
140	James	Hide	1	193	Isaac	Crosby	2
141	Jabish	Hide	2	194	Ben:	Sears	3
142	John	Newberry	4	195	Samuell	Wright	1
143	Samuel	Utter	2	196	John	Wright	1
144	Ben:	Merrick	1	197	Hezekiah	Corkum	2
145	James	Philips	1	198	Edward	Richards	1
146	Wm	Palmer	1	199	Wellem	Teller	1
147	Peter	Paddock	6	200	—	Fowler	3
148	Thos	Paddock	2	201	David	Right	1
149	Silas	Sears	1	202	James	Nickerson	1
150	Ebenezer	Jones	1	203	Peter	Anjerijn	1
151	Giles	Robenson	1	204	Simon	Reyders	1
152	Ebenezer	Craw	1	205	John	Reyders	1
153	Joseph	Crane Jnr:	2	206	Philip	Cannon	1
154	David	Paterson	1	207	Peter	Wever	1

February 1746/7 continued

	Name	Surname	Value		Name	Surname	Value
208	Nicolas	Cartryt	3	212	Joseph	Odell	1
209	Tom	Forgeson	1	213	Benjamin	Bennit	1
210	John	Heady	7				£ 744
211	Old	Odell	1				

June 1747
Southern Precinct

Rate of 6 d [pence] /pound

	Name	Surname	Value		Name	Surname	Value
	Page 432		£	41	David	Paddock	3
1	Francis	Nellson	18	42	James	Paddock	3
2	Thomas	Davinport	30	43	Peter	Bennet Jnr:	1
3	Thomas	Davinport Jnr:	15	44	William	Yearns	6
4	William	Davinport	1	45	Nath-ll	Porter or Smith	2
5	Jacob	Mandavill	13	46	Joseph	Lane	6
6	John	Nellson	2	47	Joseph	Meed	4
7	Abram	Hodges	2	48	Thomas	Cercome	10
8	David	Hustis	10	49	John	Jey	3
9	John	Calkin Jnr:	6	50	William	Jey	3
10	Jeremiah	Calkin	7	51	Jacobus	Crankhyt	3
11	John	Roggers	10	52	Jacobus	Crankhyt Jnr:	1
12	Abram	Otter	1	53	Nath-ll	Robinson	2
13	Ebenezer	Jones	5	54	David	Astin	3
14	Samuell	Jones	1	55	Caleb	Brundidge	3
15	John	Tomkins	2	56	Thomas	Curry	1
16	Elijah	Tomkins	8	57	John	Spragg	3
17	Thomas	Kelk	4	58	Joseph	Porter	2
18	John	Van Amburgt	13	59	Thomas	Stickney	3
19	Henry	Van Amburgt	14	60	Cornelis	Fuller	2
20	Peter	DuBois	16	61	Samuell	Calkin	5
21	John	During	2	62	John	Hayns	1
22	Ben:	Jaycocks	2	63	Seth	Dean	1
23	Hend:k	Brower & Son	5	64	Thomas	Frost	2
24	Timothy	Concklin	1	65	Eleazer	Cole	3
25	Nathan	Lane	8	66	Edward	Gray	1
	Page 433			67	Wm	Teller	4
26	Anthony	Hill	16	68	Daniell	Field	2
27	Thomas	Headon	3	69	Abram	Smith	5
28	George	Hueston	7	70	Luke	Covert	1
29	Joseph	Craw	1	71	Elie	Nellson	4
30	David	Tidd	5	72	Joseph	Arcles	1
31	Iccabud	Viccary	5	73	Hark S	Krankhyt	6
32	William	Hunt	2	74	John	Kelly	1
33	Joseph	McGregory	2	75	Abram	Buis	9
34	Joseph	Jaycocks	1		*Page 434*		
35	Josiah	Gregory	3	76	Hannis	Buis	2
36	John	Drake	5	77	Nath-ll	Hatch	12
37	Isaac	Rodes	6	78	William	Brewster	10
38	Jacob	Craw	1	79	Valentine	Perkins	3
39	Daniell	Townsen	10	80	William	Sweet	2
40	Joseph	Crane	4	81	Samuell	Fields	1

June 1747 continued

	Name	Surname	Value		Name	Surname	Value
82	James	Dickeson	5	135	Giles	Robenson	1
83	Benjn	Franklin	1	136	Ebenezer	Craw	1
84	Robert	Townsen	9	137	Joseph	Crane Jnr:	2
85	Benjn	Arnold	1	138	David	Patterson	1
86	Mathew	Winter	2	139	Dan-ll	Bradly	1
87	Jesse	Smith	4	140	Nath-ll	Sheperdson	1
88	Marcus	Baxter	2	141	Uriah	Townsen	4
89	Benjn	Brundidge	8	142	Samuell	Latham	1
90	Bartlet	Brundidge	4	143	Jonathan	White	1
91	Samuell	Brewer	1	144	John	White	1
92	Richard	Curry	12	145	Russell	Gregory	1
93	Michael	Shaw	2	146	John	Calkin Justice	5
94	Barnabas	Hamlin	2	147	Seth	Dean Jnr:	1
95	Samuell	Jenkins	2	148	Abell	Scribner	1
96	Caleb	Hale	2	149	Peter	Randall	1
97	Joseph	Fields	8	150	Jacob	Ellis	3
98	Samuell	Gates	3	151	Edward	Gunning	2
99	Amos	Dickeson	3	152	George	Curry	5
100	John	Dickeson	3	153	Mathew	Row	5
101	William	Bloomer	2	154	Nathan	Taylor Jnr:	1
102	William	Rapalyea	6	155	Uriah	Hill	3
103	Timothy	Shaw	4	156	Wm	Drake	2
104	Joseph	Lockwood	4	157	Joseph	Hunt	5
105	Jacob	Doty	1	158	Isaac	Ter Hill	1
106	Titus	Wood	3	159	John	V Tessell	1
107	John	Barber	1	160	John	Harrick	3
108	Jonathan	Barber	1	161	Alex:	Dowell	2
109	Wm	Underhill	2	162	Robert	Farrinton	9
110	Moses	Nauthorp	8	163	James	Maurode	2
111	Peter	Hartwell	2	164	Tom	Farrinton	5
112	Thomas	Townsen	1	165	William	Fields	2
113	William	Smith	1	166	Nath-ll	Byington	2
114	James	Sears	6	167	Jacob	Finch	1
115	Deacon	Hamlin	6	168	Francis	Purdy	1
116	Shuball	Rowly	6	169	Thomas	Philips	2
117	Mathew	Rowly	1	170	Jeremiah	Jones	1
118	Anthony	Patterson	2	171	Ebenezer	King	1
119	Jacob	Philips	2	172	John	Arcy	1
120	Elihu	Townsend	5	173	Silas	Backer	4
121	Caleb	Sweet	1	174	Isaac	Chapman	2
122	Elifelet	Ball	1	175	Leu:t	Taylor	4
123	Ben:	Allen	1		*Page 436*		
124	John	Porter	1	176	Isaac	Crossby	2
125	Simon	Wolf	2	177	Ben:	Sears	4
	Page 435			178	Samuell	Wright	1
126	James	Hide	1	179	John	Wright	1
127	Jabish	Hide	1	180	Hezekiah	Corkum	2
128	John	Newberry	4	181	Edward	Richards	1
129	Samuel	Utter	2	182	Wellem	Teller	1
130	James	Philips	1	183	—	Fowler	3
131	Wm	Palmer	1	184	David	Right	1
132	Peter	Paddock	5	185	James	Nickerson	1
133	Ths	Paddock	2	186	Peter	Anjerijn	1
134	Silas	Sears	1	187	Simon	Reyders	2

June 1747 continued

	Name	Surname	Value		Name	Surname	Value
188	John	Reyders	2	204	Joseph	Merrit	2
189	Philip	Cannon	1	205	John	Lane	1
190	Peter	Wever	1	206	Joseph	Philips	1
191	Nicolas	Cartryt	3	207	Stephen	Carpenter	1
192	Tom	Forgeson	1	208	Coll	Willet	1
193	John	Heady	8	209	Samuell	Treadwell	1
194	Old	Odell	1	210	Ebenzer	Haviland	1
195	Joseph	Odell	1	211	Thomas	Haviland	1
196	Benjamin	Bennet	1	212	Peter	Dewil	1
197	Henry	Hedger	1	213	—	Haws	1
198	Nathan	Field	1	214	—	Covell	1
199	David	Halstead	1	215	John	Smith	2
200	Christopher	Isinghart	1	216	—	Williams	1
201	Danll	Cornwell	2	217	Thomas	Smith	1
202	Jonathan	Fowler	2				£ 742
203	John	Fowler	3				

JUNE 1748
SOUTHERN PRECINCT

Rate of 10 d [pence] ½ / pound

	Name	Surname	Value		Name	Surname	Value
	Page 525		£	29	Iccabud	Viccary	3
1	Francis	Nellson	13	30	William	Hunt	2
2	Thomas	Davinport	27	31	Joseph	McGregory	2
3	Thomas	Davinport Jnr:	16	32	William	Drake	3
4	William	Davinport	1	33	Joseph	Jaycocks	1
5	Jacob	Mandavill	13	34	Josiah	Gregory	4
6	Daniell	Sunderland	1	35	John	Drake	5
7	Abram	Hodges	2	36	Isaac	Rodes	6
8	David	Hustis	10	37	Jacob	Craw	1
9	John	Calkin Jnr:	5	38	Daniell	Townsen	6
	Page 526			39	Joseph	Crane	1
10	Jeremiah	Calkin	6	40	David	Paddock	2
11	John	Rogers	9	41	James	Paddock	2
12	Abram	Otter	1	42	William	Yerns	4
13	Ebenezer	Jones	3	43	—	Smith on Porters Place	2
14	Samuell	Jones	1	44	Joseph	Lane	6
15	Elijah	Tomkins	6	45	Joseph	Meed	4
16	Thomas	Kelek	4	46	Thomas	Kercome	9
17	John	Van Amburgh	14	47	John	Gay	2
18	Henry	Van Amburgh	15	48	William	Gay	5
19	Peter	Du Bois	16	49	Jacobus	Crankhyt	2
20	Benjamin	Jaycocks	2	50	Jacobus	Crankhyt Jnr:	1
21	Hendrick	Brewer	5	51	Nathaniell	Robinson	3
22	Timothy	Concklin	1	52	David	Astin	3
23	Nathan	Lane	8	53	Caleb	Brundidge	4
24	Anthony	Hill	17	54	Nathaniel	Tomkins	2
25	Thomas	Headon	3	55	John	Spragg	4
26	George	Hueston	7	56	Joseph	Porter	1
27	Joseph	Craw	1		*Page 527*		
28	Cap:	Underhill	5	57	Amos	Stickney	3

June 1748 continued

#	Name	Surname	Value	#	Name	Surname	Value
58	Cornelius	Fuller	1	111	Anthony	Patterson	2
59	Samuell	Calkin	4	112	Jacob	Philips	1
60	John	Hains	2	113	Elihu	Townsend	4
61	Seth	Dean	1	114	Caleb	Sweet	1
62	Thomas	Frost	2	115	Elifelet	Ball	1
63	Eleazer	Cole	3	116	John	Porter	1
64	Edward	Gray	1	117	Simon	Wolf [Dolf]	2
65	Wm	Teller	5	118	James	Hide	1
66	Abram	Smith	4	119	John	Newberry	4
67	Luke	Covert	1	120	Samuel	Utter	2
68	Elie	Nellson	4	121	Wm	Palmer	1
69	Hark :S	Kranck[hyt]	5	122	Peter	Paddock	5
70	David	Kelly	1	123	Thomas	Paddock	2
71	Hannis	Buis	2	124	Silas	Sears	1
72	Nathaniell	Hatch	10	125	Giles	Robinson	1
73	William	Brewster	9	126	Joseph	Crane Jnr:	2
74	Valentine	Perkins	2	127	David	Paterson	1
75	William	Sweet	1	128	Nathaniel	Paterson	1
76	Samuell	Field	20	129	Daniel	Bradly	1
77	James	Dickenson	6	130	Uriah	Townsend	4
78	Benjamin	Franklin	1	131	Samuell	Latham	1
79	Robert	Townsen	8	132	Jonathan	White	1
80	Benjamin	Arnold	1	133	Russell	Gregory	1
81	Mathew	Winter	2	134	John	Calkin Justice	5
82	Jesse	Smith	6	135	Seth	Dean Jnr:	1
83	Marcus	Baxter	3	136	Abell	Scribner	1
84	Benjamin	Brundidge	7	137	John	White	1
85	Bartlet	Brundidge	3	138	Jacob	Ellis	5
86	Samuell	Brewer	1	139	Edward	Gunning	3
87	Richard	Curry	12	140	George	Curry	5
88	Michal	Shaw	2	141	Mathew	Roe	5
89	Barnabas	Hamlin	2	142	Nathan	Taylor Jnr:	1
90	Samuell	Jenkins	2	143	Uriah	Hill	3
91	Caleb	Hale	2	144	Joseph	Hunt	6
92	Joseph	Field	9	145	Isaac	Terhill	1
93	Samuell	Gates	3	146	John	Kranck [Harrick?]	2
94	Amos	Dickenson	3	147	Alexander	Dewell	1
95	John	Dickenson	4	148	Robert	Farrington	9
96	William	Bloomer	2	149	James	Maurode	2
97	William	Rapalyea	6	150	Tom	Farrington	6
98	Timothy	Shaw	4	151	William	Field	4
99	Joseph	Lockwood	2	152	Nathiell	Byington	2
100	Titus	Wood	2	153	Jacob	Finch	1
101	John	Barber	1		*Page 529*		
102	Wm	Underhill	1	154	Francis	Purdy	1
103	Moses	Nauthorp	12	155	Thomas	Philips	2
104	Peter	Hartwell	2	156	Jeremiah	Jones	2
105	Thomas	Townsend	1	157	Ebenezer	King	1
	Page 528			158	John	Arcy	1
106	William	Smith	1	159	Josiah	Backer	3
107	Isaac	Chapman	3	160	Leu:t	Taylor	4
108	Deacon	Hamlin	8	161	Isaac	Crosby	2
109	Shuball	Rowly	6	162	Banjamin	Sears	4
110	Mathew	Rowly	1				

June 1748 continued

#	Name	Surname	Value	#	Name	Surname	Value
163	John	Wright	1	212	Nathan	Green	1
164	Hezekiah	Kercome	2	213	Seth	Nickerson	1
165	William	Taylor	1	214	William	Daily	2
166	Christopher	Fowler	5	215	Timothy	Clawsen	1
167	David	Wright	1	216	Benjamin	Roberts	1
168	Alexander	Nellson	1	217	James	Lovelace	1
169	Peter	Anjeryn	2	218	Richard	Hulse	1
170	Simon	Ryders	2	219	Jickin	Bottom	1
171	John	Ryders	2	220	Benjamin	Perry	4
172	Philip	Cannon	1	221	Elisha	Luttington	2
173	Peter	Weaver	1	222	David	Hunywell	1
174	Nicolas	Cartwright	3	223	Benjamin	Parish	1
175	Tom	Forguson	1	224	Daniel	Parish	1
176	John	Heady	8	225	Elisha	Baker	1
177	Benjamin	Bennet	1	226	Philip	Philips	1
178	Nathan	Field	2	227	Isaac	Aikins	1
179	David	Hallsted	2	228	Widow	Jones	1
180	Christopher	Isinghart	2	229	Abiel	Carpenter	1
181	David [Daniel]	Cornell	3	230	Jeremiah	Baily	1
182	Jonathan	Fowler	3	231	Jonathan	Sturdefunt	1
183	John	Fowler	4	232	Jonathan	Sturdefunt Jnr:	1
184	Joseph	Merrit	2	233	William	Sturdefunt	1
185	Joseph	Phillips	1	234	David	Sturdefunt	1
186	Thomas	Carpenter	1	235	John	Green	1
187	Coll:	Willet	5		*Page 531*		
188	Samuell	Treadwell	1	236	Ebenezer	Brewster	1
189	Ebenzer	Haviland	2	237	—	Bump	1
190	Thomas	Haviland	3	238	Samuel	More	1
191	Isaac	Haws	1	239	Isaac	Horner [Horton]	1
192	Seth	Covell	1	240	Jonathan	Lane	2
193	John	Smith	1	241	Caleb	Pells	3
	Page 530			242	Isaac	Willet	3
194	Thomas	Smith	1	243	Charles	Townsend	1
195	Oliver	Gray	2	244	Joseph	Chatterton	1
196	Edward	Gray	1	245	Iabah	Morris	3
197	Samuell	Banks	1	246	Joseph	Pell	2
198	Nathaniell	Foster	1	247	John	Williams	1
199	Samuell	Elwell	3	248	Israel	Honywell Jnr:	1
200	David	Cosby	1	249	Joseph	Concklin	1
201	Joshua	Crosby	1	250	Richard	Roads	1
202	Jabe	Berry	1	251	Michall	Slott	1
203	Joseph	Taylor	1	252	William	Tayler	1
204	Isaac	Smith	1	253	Peter	Ryals	1
205	Isaiah	Burchard	2	254	Philip	Barto	3
206	Hope	Covey	2	255	Isaac	Garrison	1
207	Hope	Covey Jnr:	1	256	John	Penny	1
208	Joseph	Covey	1	257	William	Penny	1
209	John	Covey	1	258	Thomas	Foster	1
210	Jonathan	Paddock	1	259	Thomas	Rickerson	1
211	John	Hill	2	260	John	Paddock	1

£ 791

The next book of taxes is missing: Volume D covered 1749-1752

Supervisor's Record 1753 to 1757, Volume E
Dutchess County Clerks Office

February 1753
Southern Precinct

at 3 d [pence] / pound

#	Name	Surname	Value £
	Page 46		
1	Francis	Nellson	10
2	Thomas	Davinport	15
3	Thomas	Davinport Jr	18
4	Jacob	Mandavill	10
5	Daniel	Southerland	2
6	David	Hustis	10
7	John	Calkin Justice	3
8	John	Calkin Jr	1
9	William	Gray	6
10	John	Rodgers	10
11	Abram	Otter	1
12	Elijah	Tompkins	6
13	Thomas	Kelk	1
14	John	Van Amburgh	12
15	Henry	Van Amburgh	12
16	Peter	Du Bois	12
17	Ebenezer	Jones	2
18	Benjamin	Jaycocks	1
19	Timothy	Concklin	1
20	Nathan	Lane	6
21	Tom	Haydons farm	4
22	George	Hueston	8
23	Joseph	Crane	1
24	Iccabud	Viccarys Widw	2
25	William	Hunt	3
26	Joseph	Gregory	1
27	William	Drake	3
28	Joseph	Jaycocks	1
29	Sias	Gregory	2
30	John	Drake	1
31	Isaac	Rodes	4
32	Daniel	Townsend	4
33	Joseph	Crane Jr	3
34	David	Paddock	1
35	William	Yerns	3
36	—	Smith on Porters Place	2
	Page 47		
37	Joseph	Lane	3
38	Joseph	Meed	3
39	John	Gee	1
40	William	Gee	3
41	Jacobus	Krankhite	1
42	Jacobus	Krankhite Jr	1
43	Nathaniel	Robinson	2
44	David	Astin	1
45	Caleb	Brundidge	1
46	Nathaniel	Tomkins	5
47	Cornelius	Fuller	1
48	John	Spragge	1
49	Samuell	Calkin	2
50	John	Hains	2
51	Seth	Dean	1
52	Thomas	Frost	1
53	Eleazer	Cole	2
54	Edward	Gray	1
55	William	Teller	8
56	Abram	Smith	3
57	Luke	Covert	1
58	Samuell	Jones	1
59	Elie	Nellson	2
60	Nathaniel	Hatch	4
61	Valentine	Perkins	1
62	William	Sweet	1
63	Samuel	Field	16
64	Joseph	Field	10
65	James	Dickenson	8
66	Amos	Dickenson	4
67	John	Dickenson	4
68	Robert	Townsend	1
69	Thomas	Townsend	1
70	Elihu	Townsend	4
71	Charles	Townsend	2
72	Zebulon	Townsend	1
73	Benjamin	Townsend	3
74	Robert	Townsend	3
75	Robert	Townsend Jr	2
76	Daniell	Townsend Jr	1
77	Daniell	Townsend Leuts Son	1
78	Benjamin	Arnold	1
79	Mathew	Winter	1
	Page 48		
80	Jesse	Smith	3
81	Marcus	Baxtert	1
82	Benjamin	Brundidge	5
83	Michael	Shaw	1
84	Barnabas	Hamblin	1
85	Caleb	Hazell	2
86	Samuell	Gates	1
87	William	Rapalyea	5

February 1753 continued

	Name	Surname	Value		Name	Surname	Value
88	Tim:	Shaws farm	2	141	John	Smith	1
89	John	Barber	1	142	Thomas	Smith	1
90	Peter	Hartwell	1	143	Oliver	Gray	2
91	William	Smith	1	144	Edward	Gray Jr	2
92	Isaac	Chapman	2	145	Samuel	Banks	2
93	Deacon	Hamblin	5	146	Nathaniel	Foster	2
94	Shuball	Rowly	3	147	Samuell	Ellwell	1
95	Jacob	Philips	1	148	Daniel	Cosby	2
96	Caleb	Sweet	1	149	Joshua	Cosby	2
97	Simon	Dolfs farm	1	150	Jabe	Berry	1
98	William	Palmer	1	151	Joseph	Taylor	1
99	John	Newberry	4	152	Isaac	Smith	1
100	Samuel	Otter	1	153	Hope	Covey Jr	3
101	Peter	Paddock	2	154	John	Covey	1
102	Thomas	Paddock	2	155	Jonathan	Paddock	1
103	Silas	Sears	1	156	John	Hill	1
104	Daniel	Bradly	1	157	Nathan	Green	2
105	Samuell	Latham	1	158	Seth	Nickerson	1
106	Russell	Gregory	1	159	Wm	Daily farm	1
107	John	White	1	160	Timothy	Clawson	1
108	Jacob	Ellis	3	161	Benjamin	Roberts	1
109	Philip	Cannon	1	162	James	Lovelace	1
110	George	Curry	1	163	Hickin	Bottom	1
111	Nathaniel	Taylor Jr	1	164	Elisha	Luttington	2
112	Joseph	Hunt	6	165	David	Honeywell	1
113	Isaac	Terhill	1	*Page 50*			
114	Alexander	Dewell	1	166	Elisha	Baker	1
115	Robert	Farrington Widw	1	167	Benjamin	Parish	1
116	Thomas	Farrington	2	168	Daniel	Parish	1
117	James	McReedy	2	169	Philip	Philips	1
118	Nathaniel	Byington	2	170	Jonathan	Sturdefunt	1
119	Jacob	Finch	1	171	Jonathan	Sturdefunt Jr	1
120	Francis	Purdy	1	172	William	Sturdefunt	1
121	Thomas	Philip	4	173	Mathew	Bump	1
122	Jeremiah	Jones	1	174	Samuel	More	2
Page 49				175	Isaac	Horton	1
123	Ebenezer	King	1	176	Jonathan	Lane	3
124	John	Ary	1	177	Caleb	Pells farm	2
125	Josiah	Baker	3	178	John	Williams	1
126	Leut:	Taylor	3	179	—	Pell & Dean	4
127	Isaac	Crosby	1	180	Israel	Honywell Jr: farm	1
128	Benjamin	Sears	2				
129	Hezekiah	Kercome	1	181	Joseph	Concklin	1
130	William	Taylor	1	182	Richard	Roads	1
131	Christopher	Fowler	3	183	Michael	Slott	1
132	Peter	Angerine	3	184	John	Penny	1
133	Simion	Ryders	4	185	William	Penny	2
134	John	Ryders	4	186	Thomas	Foster	1
135	Nicolas	Cartwright	2	187	Tom.	Richardson	1
136	Thomas	Ferguson	1	188	John	Paddock	1
137	Daniel	Cornell	8	189	Ezekiel	Meed	1
138	Joseph	Philips	1	190	Israel	Taylor	1
139	Isaac	Haws	1	191	William	Stevens	1
140	Seth	Covell	1	192	Edward	Griffen	2

February 1753 continued

#	Name	Surname	Value
193	William	Hill	5
194	Gershom	Mustoon	1
195	Peter	Robinson	1
196	Abram	Hodges Jr	1
197	—	Hamblin	1
198	Isaac	Otter	1
199	Elemuel	Kelk	1
200	John	Langdon	1
201	Seth	Paddock	2
202	Ebenezer	Jones Jr	1
203	Aaron	Calkin	1
204	Theophilus	Jones	1
205	Joshua	Hamblin	1
206	Elisha	Cole	1
207	Robert	Weekson	1
208	Ezekiel	Gee	1

Page 51

#	Name	Surname	Value
209	Gabriell	Nap	3
210	Jere.	Drakes farm	2
211	John	Tompkins [Hopkins?]	1
212	John	Van Tessell	1
213	Mr.	Kent	6
214	Jonathan	Astin	3
215	Abram	Slott	1
216	John	Kelly	1
217	Thomas	Kelly	1
218	Isaac	Peirce	2
219	Silas	Peirce	1
220	Joseph	Tompkins [Hopkins?]	3
221	William	Stone	1
222	Noah	Burbanks	1
223	David	Sturdefunt	1
224	Edmund	Baker	1
225	Benjamin	Winter	1
226	Caleb	Chase	1
227	Ebenezer	Chase	1
228	Caleb	Chase Jr	1
229	Elisha	Kelk	1
230	James	Sears	1
231	Peter	Hall	1
232	Nathaniel	House	1
233	Thomas	Gage	2
234	Job	Hogg	1
235	Elijah	Calkin	1
236	Samuel	Calkin Jr	1
237	Samuel	Goodspeed	1
238	Old	Bobbet	2
239	Shubal	Rowly Jr	1
240	John	Mahew	1
241	John	Mahew Jr	1
242	John	Merrick	1
243	Joseph	Hide	1
244	Joseph	Baker	1
245	Mody	Hows	2
246	James	Cowen	1
247	Edward	Hall	2
248	Ezekiel	Burgiss	1
249	Thomas	Kelly	1
250	Jonathan	Kelly	1
251	Francis	Baker	2

Page 52

#	Name	Surname	Value
252	Uriah	Lawrence	2
253	Isaac	Chase	1
254	Eleazer	Spragge	1
255	Nathaniel	Porter	1
256	Thomas	Crinnell	1
257	Joseph	Chittenton	1
258	William	Hedger	1
259	Thomas	Kirk	1
260	James	Philips	1
261	Moses	Gregory	1
262	—	Bazely on Powers Place	2
263	William	Rice	1
264	Joseph	Crow	2
265	Ebenezer	Crow	1
266	Elisha	Bangs	1
267	John	Scribner	1
268	Zadock	Scribner	1
269	Isaac	Hatch	2
270	Widw	Wilcocks	1
271	Jonathan	Hill	1
272	David	Kelly	1
273	Joseph	Barly	1
274	Christopher	Bobbet	1
275	Widw	Dickensons farm	2
276	Orlander	Mack	1
277	Malthia	Hatch	2
278	Elijah	Dean	1
279	Peleg	Ballard	1
280	Peleg	Ballard Jr	1
281	Nathaniel	Robinson Jr	1
282	Andrew	Rapalyea	1
283	Ruben	Kelly	1
284	Seth	Merrick	1
285	Martin	Smith	1
286	Gideon	Ellis	1
287	James	Colwill	1
288	Amos	Fuller	1
289	Thomas	Colwill	2
290	Jonathan	Runnells	1
291	William	Ballard	1
292	Nehemiah	Horton	1
293	Elijah	Kercome	1
294	Cornelius	Tompkins	2

Page 53

February 1753 continued

	Name	Surname	Value		Name	Surname	Value
295	Daniel	Gregory	1	329	—	Horsemore	1
296	Simon	Ellis	1	330	John	Slott	1
297	Samuel	Fuller	4	331	—	Dusenbury on Currys place	5
298	John	Van Vore	1				
299	Silas	Washbun	1	332	—	Crawford on Fowlers place	1
300	John	Meeks	2				
301	Josiah	Church	1	333	Caleb	Pells farm	1
302	Samuell	Carle	1	334	Edward	Ganung	1
303	Isaac	Barton	1	335	Daniel	Philips	1
304	Thomas	Curry	1	336	Samuell	Peters	4
305	Teunis	Krankhite	1	337	Henry	Brewer	1
306	Nathaniel	Baily	3		*Page 54*		
307	Jonathan	Palmer	1	338	Benjamin	Brundidge Jr	1
308	Silas	Paddock	2	339	Lazarus	Griffen	2
309	Robert	Ryder	4	340	—	Edderton	1
310	Jonathan	Ryder	1	341	Bethuel	Barnam	1
311	John	Field	2	342	John	Depie	1
312	Philip	Paddock	2	343	Solomon	Brundidge	1
313	Benjamin	Perry	2	344	Abram	Slott	1
314	James	Quinby	2	345	Joseph	Philips	1
315	Zachariah	Paddock Jr	2	346	Zachariah	Paddock	2
316	Stephen	Field	1	347	Abner	Bangs	2
317	John	Concklin	3	348	Jeremiah	Raly [Baily]	1
318	Joshua	Moss	2	349	Wm	Gray Eldest Son	1
319	John	Nellson	1	350	George	Curry	2
320	Moses	Nauthrop	5	351	—	Crawfoot on Fowlers place	1
321	Solomon	Farrington	1				
322	Nathan	Birdsell	10	352	David	Smith	1
323	Samuel	Casston	1	353	Robert	Weekson Eldest Son	1
324	Jeremiah	Linkhorn	1				
325	—	Sely on Astins place	1	354	Rowland	Perry	1
				355	Mathew	Rowly	1
326	Lewis	Winter	1				£ 730
327	John	Manly	1				
328	Uriah	Hill	5				

June 1753
Southern Precinct

at 10 pence / pound

	Name	Surname	Value		Name	Surname	Value
	Page 101		£	11	Abram	Otter	1
1	Francis	Nellson	10	12	Elijah	Tompkins	6
2	Thomas	Davinport	14	13	Thomas	Kellick	1
3	Thomas	Davinport Jnr:	18	14	John	Van Amburgh	12
4	Jacob	Mandavill	10	15	Henry	Van Amburgh	13
5	Daniel	Southerland	2	16	Peter	Du Bois	12
6	David	Hustis	11	17	Ebenezer	Jones	2
7	John	Calkin Justice	3	18	Benjamin	Jaycocks	2
8	John	Calkin Jnr:	1	19	Timothy	Concklin	2
9	William	Gray	5	20	Nathan	Lane	3
10	John	Rodgers	10	21	Tom	Haydons farm	1

June 1753 continued

	Name	Surname	Value		Name	Surname	Value
22	George	Hueston	8		*Page 103*		
23	Joseph	Crane	1	74	Daniel	Townsend Jr	1
24	Iccabud	Viccarys Widw	2	75	Daniel	Townsend Leuts Son	2
25	Joseph	Gregory	1				
26	William	Drake	4	76	Benjamin	Arnold	1
27	Joseph	Jaycocks	1	77	Jesse	Smith	4
28	Sias	Gregory	3	78	Marcus	Baxtert	1
29	John	Drake	1	79	Benjamin	Brundidge	5
30	Isaac	Rodes	5	80	Michael	Shad	1
31	Daniel	Townsend	4	81	Barnabas	Hamblin	2
	Page 102			82	Caleb	Hazell	2
32	Joseph	Crane Jr	2	83	Samuell	Gates	2
33	David	Paddock	1	84	William	Rapalyea	5
34	William	Yerns Widw.	2	85	John	Barber	2
35	—	Smith on Porters place	2	86	Peter	Hartwell	2
				87	William	Smith	1
36	Joseph	Lane	4	88	Isaac	Chapman	2
37	Joseph	Meed	4	89	Deacon	Hamblin	6
38	John	Gee	1	90	Shuball	Rowly	2
39	William	Gee	4	91	Jacob	Philip	1
40	Jacobus	Krankhite	1	92	Caleb	Sweet	1
41	Jacobus	Krankhite Jr	1	93	Simon	Dolfs farm	1
42	Nathaniel	Robinson	2	94	William	Palmer	1
43	David	Astin	2	95	John	Newberry	4
44	Caleb	Brundige	2	96	Samuel	Otter	2
45	Nathaniel	Tompkins	6	97	Peter	Paddock	3
46	Cornelius	Fuller	2	98	Thomas	Paddock	2
47	John	Spragge	1	99	Silas	Sears	2
48	Samuell	Calkin	2	100	Daniel	Bradly	1
49	John	Haines	2	101	Russell	Gregory	1
50	Thomas	Frost	2	102	John	White	1
51	Eleazer	Cole	3	103	Jacob	Ellis	3
52	Edward	Gray	2	104	Philip	Cannon	2
53	William	Teller	9	105	George	Curry	2
54	Abram	Smith	3	106	Nathaniel	Taylor Jr	1
55	Luke	Covert	1	107	Joseph	Hunt	5
56	Samuell	Jones	1	108	Isaac	Ter hill	1
57	Elie	Nellson	2	109	Alexander	Dewell	1
58	Nathaniel	Hatch	5	110	Robert	Farrington Widw	1
59	Valentine	Perkins	2	111	Thomas	Farrington	2
60	William	Sweet	1	112	James	McReedy	2
61	Samuel	Field	16	113	Nathaniel	Byington	3
62	Joseph	Field	9	114	Jacob	Finch	2
63	James	Dickenson	8	115	Thomas	Philips	4
64	Amos	Dickenson	4		*Page 104*		
65	John	Dickenson	4	116	Jeremiah	Jones	1
66	Robert	Townsend	1	117	Ebenezer	King	1
67	Thomas	Townsend	1	118	John	Ary	1
68	Elihu	Townsend	5	119	Josiah	Baker	3
69	Charles	Townsend	2	120	Leut:	Taylor	4
70	Zebulon	Townsend	1	121	Isaac	Crosby	2
71	Benjamin	Townsend	3	122	Benjamin	Sears	3
72	Robert	Townsend	3	123	Hezekiah	Kercome	1
73	Robert	Townsend Jr	2	124	William	Taylor	1

June 1753 continued

	Name	Surname	Value		Name	Surname	Value
125	Christopher	Fowler	3	179	Israel	Taylor	1
126	Peter	Anjerine	4	180	William	Stevens	1
127	Simion	Ryders	4	181	Edward	Griffen	3
128	Nicolas	Cartwright	3	182	William	Hill	6
129	Thomas	Ferguson	1	183	Gershom	Mustoon	1
130	Daniel	Cornell	7	184	Peter	Robinson	1
131	Joseph	Philips	1	185	Abram	Hodges	1
132	Isaac	Haws	1	186	Ebenezer	Hamblin	1
133	Seth	Covell	1	187	Isaac	Otter	2
134	John	Smith	1	188	Elemuel	Kelk	1
135	Thomas	Smith	1	189	John	Langdon	1
136	Oliver	Gray	2	190	Seth	Paddock	3
137	Edward	Gray Jr	2	191	Ebenezer	Jones Jr	2
138	Samuel	Banks	3	192	Aaron	Calkin	1
139	Nathaniel	Foster	2	193	Theophilus	Jones	1
140	Samuell	Ellwell	1	194	Joshua	Hamblin	2
141	David	Cosby	3	195	Elisha	Cole	1
142	Joshua	Cosby	3	196	Robert	Weekson	1
143	Jaby	Berry	1	197	Gabriell	Knap	4
144	Joseph	Taylor	1	198	John	Tompkins [Hopkins?]	1
145	Isaac	Smith	1				
146	Hope	Covey Jr	3	199	John	Van Tessell	3
147	John	Covey	1	*Page 106*			
148	Jonathan	Paddock	1	200	Mr.	Kent	6
149	John	Hill	1	201	Jonathan	Astin	3
150	Nathan	Green	2	202	Abraham	Slott	1
151	Seth	Nickerson	1	203	John	Kelly	1
152	Will.	Daily farm	2	204	Thomas	Kelly	1
153	Timothy	Clawson	1	205	Isaac	Peirce	2
154	Benjamin	Roberts	1	206	William	Stone	2
155	James	Loveless	1	207	Noah	Burbanks	1
156	Hickin	Bottom	1	208	David	Sturdefunt	1
157	Elisha	Luttington	2	209	Edmond	Baker	1
Page 105				210	Benjamin	Winter	1
158	David	Honeywell	1	211	Caleb	Chase	1
159	Elisha	Baker	1	212	Caleb	Chase Jr	1
160	Benjamin	Parish	2	213	Ebenezer	Chase	1
161	Daniel	Parish	1	214	Elisha	Kelk	1
162	Jonathan	Sturdefunt	1	215	James	Sears	2
163	Jonathan	Sturdefunt Jr	1	216	Peter	Hall	2
164	William	Sturdefunt	1	217	Nathaniel	House	2
165	Mathew	Bump	1	218	Thomas	Gage	3
166	Samuel	More	1	219	Job	Hogg	1
167	Isaac	Horton	1	220	Elijah	Calkin	1
168	Jonathan	Lane	3	221	Samuel	Calkin Jr	1
169	—	Pell & Dean	4	222	Samuel	Goodspeed	2
170	Joseph	Concklin	1	223	Old	Bobbet	3
171	Richard	Roads	2	224	Shubal	Rowly	1
172	Michael	Slott	1	225	John	Mahew	1
173	John	Penny	1	226	John	Mahew Jr	1
174	William	Penny	3	227	John	Merrick	1
175	Thomas	Foster	1	228	Joseph	Hide	1
176	Tom.	Richardson	1	229	Joseph	Baker	1
177	John	Paddock	1	230	Mody	House	2
178	Ezekiel	Meed	1	231	James	Cowen	2

June 1753 continued

#	Name	Surname	Value
232	Edward	Hall	2
233	Ezekiel	Burgiss	1
234	Thomas	Kelly	1
235	Jonathan	Kelly	1
236	Francis	Baker	2
237	Uriah	Lawrence	2
238	Isaac	Chase	1
239	Eleazer	Spragge	1
240	Thomas	Crinnell	1
241	Nathaniel	Porter	2

Page 107

#	Name	Surname	Value
242	Joseph	Chittendon	3
243	William	Hedger	1
244	Thomas	Kerk	1
245	Moses	Gregory	1
246	—	Bazely on Powers Place	3
247	William	Rice	1
248	Joseph	Crow	1
249	Ebenezer	Crow	1
250	Elisha	Bangs	1
251	John	Scribner	1
252	Isaac	Hatch	2
253	Widw	Wilcocks	1
254	Jonathan	Hill	1
255	Joseph	Barly	1
256	Christopher	Bobbet	1
257	Widw	Dickensons farm	5
258	Orlander	Mack	1
259	Malthias	Hatch	2
260	Peleg	Ballard	1
261	Peleg	Ballard Jr	1
262	Nathaniel	Robinson Jr	1
263	Andrew	Rapalyea	1
264	Ruben	Kelly	1
265	Seth	Merrick	1
266	Martin	Smith	1
267	Gideon	Ellis	1
268	James	Colwill	1
269	Amos	Fuller	1
270	Thomas	Colwill	2
271	Jonothan	Runnells	1
272	William	Ballard	1
273	Nehemiah	Hortin	1
274	Cornelius	Tompkins	2
275	Daniel	Gregory	1
276	Simon	Ellis	1
277	Samuell	Fuller	2
278	John	Meeks	2
279	Josiah	Church	1
280	Samuell	Carle	1
281	Isaac	Barton	1
282	Thomas	Curry	1
283	Teunis	Krankhite	1

Page 108

#	Name	Surname	Value
284	Nathaniel	Baily	3
285	Jonathan	Palmer	1
286	Silas	Paddock	2
287	Robert	Ryder	4
288	Jonathan	Ryder	1
289	John	Field	2
290	Philip	Paddock	2
291	Benjamin	Perry	2
292	James	Quinby	2
293	Zachary	Paddock Jr	3
294	Stephen	Field	1
295	John	Concklin	2
296	Joshua	Moss	2
297	John	Nellson	1
298	Moses	Nauthrop	4
299	Solomon	Farrington	1
300	Nathan	Birdsell	8
301	Jeremiah	Linkhorn	1
302	John	Manly	1
303	Uriah	Hill	5
304	John	Slott	1
305	—	Dusenbury on Curry place	4
306	—	Crawford on Fowler place	1
307	Caleb	Pells farm	6
308	Edward	Ganung	1
309	Daniel	Philips	1
310	Samuell	Peters	5
311	Henry	Brower	1
312	Benjamin	Brundidge Jr	1
313	Lazarus	Griffen	2
314		Edderton	1
315	Bethuell	Barnam	2
316	Solomon	Brundidge	1
317	Abram	Slott	1
318	Joseph	Philips	1
319	Zachary	Paddock Jr	2
320	Abner	Bangs	2
321	Jeremiah	Raly [Baily]	1
322	Wm	Grays Eldest Son	1
323	David	Smith	1
324	Robert	Weekson Eldest Son	1
325	Rowland	Perry	1

Page 109

#	Name	Surname	Value
326	Mathew	Rowly	2
327	Silas	Pearce	1
328	Benjamin	Lord	2
329	Bartlet	Brundidge	1
330	Thomas	Gray	1
331	Noah	Smith	1
332	—	Crosby On Smiths farm	2
333	—	Bangs on Sprags farm	2

June 1753 continued

	Name	Surname	Value		Name	Surname	Value
334	—	Hinkle	1	344	Sam.	Stringham	1
335	Isaac	Smiths Brother	1	345	John [?]	Single	1
336	John	How	1	346	Thomas	Townsend Jr	1
337	Jonathan	Bryant	1	347	Isaiah	Jaycocks	1
338	William	Lane	1	348	David	Hortin	1
339	Jonathan	Lockwood	1	349	Daniel	Runalds	1
340	Caleb	Hyat	1	350	John	Birdsell	2
341	Isaac	Perry	1	351	William	Nellson	1
342	—	Burgis On Totters farm	2	352	Moses	Hustis	1
343	—	Cole On Wil: Hunts farm	1				£ 778

FEBRUARY 1754
SOUTHERN PRECINCT

at 3 d [pence] ½ / pound

	Name	Surname	Value		Name	Surname	Value
	Page 115		£	34	Joseph	Lane	4
1	Francis	Nellson	10	35	Joseph	Meed	4
2	Thomas	Davinport	15	36	John	Gee	1
3	Thomas	Davinport Jnr:	18	37	William	Gee	5
4	Jacob	Mandavill	11	38	Kobus	Krankhite	1
5	Daniel	Southerland	1	39	Kobus	Krankhite Jnr:	1
6	David	Hustis	11	40	Nathaniel	Robinson	2
7	John	Calkin	3	41	David	Astin	3
8	John	Calkin Jnr:	1	42	Caleb	Brundidge	2
9	William	Gray	5	43	Nathaniel	Tomkins	6
10	John	Rogers	9	44	Cornelius	Fuller	2
11	Abram	Otter	1	45	John	Spragge	2
12	Elijah	Tompkins	5	46	Samuell	Calkin	2
13	Thomas	Kellick	1	47	John	Hains	2
14	John	Van Amburgh	12	48	Thomas	Frost	2
15	Henry	Van Amburgh	13	49	Eleazer	Cole	3
16	Peter	Du Bois	12	50	Edward	Gray	2
17	Ebenezer	Jones	3	51	William	Teller	9
18	Benjamin	Jaycocks	2	52	Abram	Smith	3
19	Timothy	Concklin	3	53	Luke	Covert	1
20	Nathan	Lane	3	54	Samuell	Jones	1
21	Tom	Haydons farm	1	55	Elie	Nellson	2
22	George	Hueston	7	56	Nathaniel	Hatch	5
23	Joseph	Crane	1	57	Valentine	Perkins	2
24	Iccabud	Viccarys Widw	2	58	William	Sweets farm	1
25	Joseph	Gregory	1	59	Samuel	Field	16
26	William	Drake	4	60	Joseph	Field	8
27	Sias	Gregory	3	61	James	Dickenson	6
28	John	Drake	1	62	Amos	Dickenson	4
29	Isaac	Rodes	5	63	John	Dickenson	4
30	Joseph	Crane Jnr:	2	64	Daniel	Townsend	4
31	David	Paddock	2	65	Robert	Townsend	1
32	William	Yerns Widw.	2	66	Thomas	Townsend	1
33	—	Smith on Porters Place	2	67	Elihu	Townsend	5
	Page 116			68	Charles	Townsend	2
				69	Zebulon	Townsend	1

February 1754 continued

	Name	Surname	Value		Name	Surname	Value
70	Benjamin	Townsend	3	122	Benjamin	Sears	3
71	Robert R	Townsend	3	123	Heskiah	Kercome	1
72	Robert U	Townsend	2	124	William	Taylor	1
73	Daniel	Townsend Jnr:	1	125	Christopher	Fowler	3
74	Daniel D:	Townsend	2	126	Peter	Angerine	4
75	Thomas	Townsend Jnr:	1	127	Simion	Ryders	4
	Page 117			128	Nicolas	Cartwright	3
76	Benjamin	Arnold	1	129	Daniel	Cornell	6
77	Jesse	Smith	4	130	Joseph	Philips	1
78	Marcus	Baxter	1	131	Isaac	Haws	1
79	Benjamin	Brundidge	5	132	Seth	Covell	1
80	Michael	Shad	1	133	John	Smith	1
81	Barnabas	Hamblin	2	134	Thomas	Smith	1
82	Caleb	Hayzer	2	135	Oliver	Gray	2
83	Samuel	Gates	2	136	Edward	Gray Jnr:	2
84	William	Rapalyea	5	137	Samuel	Banks	2
85	John	Barber	2	138	Nathaniel	Forster	2
86	Peter	Hartwell	2	139	Samuell	Ellwell	2
87	William	Smith	1	140	David	Cosby	3
88	Isaac	Chapman	2	141	Joshua	Cosby	3
89	Deacon	Hamblin	6	142	Jaby	Berry	1
90	Shubal	Rowly	2	143	Joseph	Taylor	1
91	Jacob	Philip	1	144	Isaac	Smith	1
92	Caleb	Sweet	1	145	Hope	Covey	3
93	Simon	Dolfs farm	2	146	John	Covey	1
94	William	Palmer	1	147	Jonathan	Paddock	1
95	John	Newberry	4	148	John	Hill	2
96	Samuel	Otter	2	149	Nathan	Green	2
97	Peter	Paddock	3	150	Seth	Nickerson	1
98	Thomas	Paddock	2	151	Will.	Dailys farm	2
99	Silas	Sears	2	152	Timothy	Clawson	1
100	Daniel	Bradly	1	153	Benjamin	Roberts	1
101	Russell	Gregory	1	154	James	Loveless	1
102	John	White	1	155	Hickin	Bottom	1
103	Jacob	Ellis	3	156	Elisha	Luttington	2
104	Philip	Cannon	1	157	David	Honywell	1
105	George	Curry	2	158	Elisha	Baker	1
106	Nathaniel	Taylor Jnr:	1	159	Benjamin	Parish	2
107	Joseph	Hunts Widw	2		*Page 119*		
108	Isaac	Terhill	1	160	Daniel	Parish	1
109	Alexander	Dewell	1	161	Jonathan	Sturdefunt	1
110	Robert	Farrington Widw	1	162	Jonathan	Sturdefunt Jnr:	1
111	Thomas	Farrington	3	163	William	Sturdefunt	1
112	James	McReedy	2	164	Mathew	Bump	1
113	Nathaniel	Byington	3	165	Samuel	Moore	1
114	Jacob	Finch	2	166	Isaac	Horton	1
115	Thomas	Philip	5	167	Jonathan	Lane	3
116	Jeremiah	Jones	1	168	—	Pell & Dean	4
117	Ebenezer	King	2	169	Joseph	Concklin	1
	Page 118			170	Richard	Roads	2
118	John	Ary	1	171	Michael	Slott	1
119	Josiah	Baker	3	172	John	Penny	1
120	Leut:	Taylor	4	173	William	Penny	3
121	Isaac	Crosby	2	174	Tom.	Foster	2

February 1754 continued

#	Name	Surname	Value
175	John	Paddock	1
176	Ezekiel	Meed	1
177	Israel	Taylor	1
178	William	Stevens	1
179	Edward	Griffen	3
180	William	Hill	6
181	Gershom	Mustoon	1
182	Peter	Robinson	1
183	Abram	Hodges	1
184	Ebenezer	Hamblin	1
185	Isaac	Otter	2
186	Elemuel	Kelk	1
187	John	Langdon	1
188	Seth	Paddock	3
189	Ebenezer	Jones Jnr:	2
190	Aaron	Calkin	1
191	Theophilus	Jones	1
192	Joshua	Hamlin	3
193	Elisha	Cole	1
194	Robert	Weekson	1
195	Gabriell	Knap	4
196	John	Tomkins [Hopkins?]	1
197	John	Van Tessell	2
198	Mr.	Kent	6
199	Jonathan	Astin	3
200	Abram	Slott	1
201	John	Kelly	1

Page 120

#	Name	Surname	Value
202	Thomas	Kelly	1
203	Isaac	Peirce	2
204	William	Stone	2
205	Noah	Burbanks	1
206	David	Sturdefunt	1
207	Edmond	Baker	1
208	Benjamin	Winter	1
209	Caleb	Chase	1
210	Ebenezer	Chase	1
211	James	Sears	2
212	Peter	Hall	2
213	Nathaniel	House	2
214	Thomas	Gage	3
215	Job	Hogg	1
216	Elijah	Calkin	1
217	Samuel	Calkin Jnr:	1
218	Samuel	Goodspeed	2
219	Old	Bobbet	3
220	Shubal	Rowly	1
221	John	Mahew	1
222	John	Mahew Jnr:	1
223	John	Merrick	1
224	Joseph	Hide	1
225	Joseph	Baker	1
226	Mody	House	2
227	James	Cowen	1
228	Edward	Hall	2
229	Ezekiel	Burgiss	1
230	Jonathan	Kelly	1
231	Francis	Baker	2
232	Uriah	Lawrence	2
233	Isaac	Chase	1
234	Eleazer	Spragge	1
235	Thomas	Crimell	1
236	Nathaniel	Porter	2
237	Jos	Chittendon	2
238	Thomas	Kerk	1
239	Moses	Gregory	1
240	—	Bazely on Powers place	2
241	William	Rice	1
242	Joseph	Crow	1
243	Ebenezer	Crow	1

Page 121

#	Name	Surname	Value
244	Elisha	Banks	1
245	John	Scribner	1
246	Isaac	Hatch	2
247	Widw	Willcocks	1
248	Jonathan	Hill	1
249	Joseph	Barly	1
250	Christopher	Bobbet	1
251	Widw	Dickensons farm	2
252	Orlander	Mack	1
253	Melletah	Hatch	1
254	Peleg	Ballard	1
255	Peleg	Ballard Jnr:	1
256	Andrew	Rapalyea	1
257	Ruben	Kelly	1
258	Seth	Merrick	1
259	Gideon	Ellis	1
260	James	Colwill	1
261	Thomas	Colwill	2
262	Amos	Fuller	1
263	Jonathan	Runnells	1
264	William	Ballard	1
265	Nehemiah	Horton	1
266	Cornelis	Tompkins	3
267	Simon	Ellis	1
268	Samuel	Fuller	3
269	John	Meeks	2
270	Josiah	Church	1
271	Samuell	Carle	1
272	Isaac	Barton	1
273	Thomas	Curry	1
274	Teunis	Krankhite	1
275	Nathaniel	Baily	1
276	Jonathan	Palmer	1
277	Silas	Paddock	2
278	Robert	Ryder	4

February 1754 continued

#	Name	Surname	Value	#	Name	Surname	Value
279	Jonathan	Ryder	1	321	Thomas	Gray	1
280	John	Field	2	322	Noah	Smith	1
281	Philip	Paddock	2	323	—	Crosby on Smiths farm	2
282	Benjamin	Perry	2	324	Joseph	Bangs	2
283	James	Quinby	2	325		Hinkle	1
284	Zachary	Paddock Jnr:	2	326	Isaac	Smiths Brother	1
285	Stephen	Field	1	327	John	How	1
Page 122				*Page 123*			
286	John	Concklin	2	328	Jonathan	Lockwood	1
287	Joshua	Moss	1	329	Caleb	Hyatt	1
288	John	Nellson	1	330	Isaac	Perry	1
289	Moses	Nauthrop	4	331	—	Burgiss on Totters farm	2
290	Solomon	Farrington	1	332	—	Cole on Hunts farm	2
291	Nathan	Birdsell	8				
292	Jeremiah	Linkhorn	1				
293	John	Manly	2				
294	Uriah	Hill	6	333	Sam	Stringham	1
295	John	Slott	1	334	Isaiah	Jaycocks	1
296	Moses	Dusenbury	3	335	David	Horton	1
297	Daniel	Crawford	1	336	Daniel	Runnels	1
298	Caleb	Pells farm	6	337	William	Nellson	1
299	Edward	Ganung	1	338	John	Birdsell	2
300	Daniel	Philips	1	339	Moses	Hustis	1
301	Samuell	Peters	3	340	Elisha	Kelk	1
302	Henry	Brower	1	341	Jonathan	Bryant	1
303	Benjamin	Brundidge Jnr:	1	342	William	Lane	1
304	Lazarus	Griffen	2	343	John	Ryder	4
305	—	Edderton	1	344	William	Dusenbury	1
306	Bethuell	Barnam	2	345	John	Lane	1
307	Solomon	Brundige	1	346	Jonathan	Fowler	4
308	Abram	Slott	1	347	Joseph	Hopkins	3
309	Joseph	Philips	1	348	John	Green	2
310	Zachary	Paddock	2	349	Elithan	Done	1
311	Abner	Bangs	2	350	Thomas	Higgins	1
312	Jeremiah	Baily	1	351	Thomas	Hinkly	1
313	Will.	Grays Son	1	352	Josiah	Hinkly	1
314	David	Smith	1	353	Israel	Cole	1
315	Robert	Weeksons Son	1	354	Abram	Underhill	1
316	Rowland	Perry	1	355	James	Russell	1
317	Mathew	Rowly	2	356	Edward	Haws	1
318	Silas	Peirce	1	357	John	Lawrence	2
319	Benjamin	Lord	1	358	John	McFarthing	1
320	Bartlet	Brundidge	2				£ 787

June 1754
Southern Precinct

at 10 d [pence] / pound

#	Name	Surname	Value
	Page 172		
1	Francis	Nellson	10
2	Thomas	Davinport	14
3	Thomas	Davinport Jnr	17
4	Jacob	Mandavill	11
5	David	Hustis	12
6	John	Calkin	2
7	John	Calkin Jnr	1
8	William	Gray	5
9	John	Rogers	9
10	Abram	Otter	1
11	Elijah	Tompkins	5
	Page 173		
12	Thomas	Kellik	1
13	John	Van Amburgh	13
14	Henry	Van Amburgh	13
15	Peter	Du Bois	11
16	Ebenezer	Jones	3
17	Benjamin	Jaycocks	3
18	Timothy	Concklin	3
19	Nathan	Lane	3
20	Tom	Haydons farm	1
21	George	Hueston	6
22	Joseph	Crane	1
23	Iccabud	Viccarys Estate	2
24	Joseph	Gregory	1
25	William	Drake	4
26	Sias	Gregory	3
27	John	Drake	1
28	Isaac	Rodes	5
29	Joseph	Crane Jnr	1
30	David	Paddock	1
31	William	Yerns Widw	1
32	—	Smith on Porters place	2
33	Joseph	Lane	4
34	Joseph	Meed	4
35	John	Gee	1
36	William	Gee	4
37	Cobus	Crankhite	1
38	Cobus	Crankhite Jnr	2
39	Nathaniel	Robinson	2
40	David	Austin	1
41	Caleb	Brundidge	2
42	Nathaniel	Tompkins	6
43	Cornelius	Fuller	1
44	John	Spragge	1
45	Samuel	Calkin	2
46	John	Haines	2
47	Thomas	Frost	2
48	Eleazer	Cole	3
49	Edward	Gray	2
50	William	Teller	9
51	Abram	Smith	3
52	Luke	Covert	1
53	Samuell	Jones	1
	Page 174		
54	Elia	Nellson	3
55	Nathaniel	Hatch	6
56	Valentine	Perkins	2
57	Samuel	Field	16
58	Joseph	Field	8
59	James	Dickenson	6
60	Amos	Dickenson	4
61	John	Dickenson	4
62	Daniel	Townsend	4
63	Robert	Townsend	1
64	Thomas	Townsend	1
65	Elihu	Townsend	5
66	Charles	Townsend	2
67	Zebulon	Townsend	1
68	Benjamin	Townsend	3
69	Robert R:	Townsend	3
70	Robert U:	Townsend	2
71	Daniel	Townsend Jnr	1
72	Daniel D.	Townsend	2
73	Thomas	Townsend Jnr	1
74	Benjamin	Arnold	1
75	Jesse	Smith	4
76	Benjamin	Brundidge	5
77	Michael	Shaw	1
78	Barnabas	Hamblin	2
79	Caleb	Hayzer	2
80	Samuell	Gates	2
81	William	Rapalyea	5
82	John	Barber	2
83	Peter	Hartwell	2
84	Isaac	Chapman	2
85	Deacon	Hamblin	6
86	Shubel	Rowly	2
87	Jacob	Philip	1
88	Caleb	Sweet	1
89	Simon	Dolfs farm	2
90	William	Palmer	1
91	John	Newberry	4
92	Samuel	Otter	2
93	Peter	Paddock	3
94	Thomas	Paddock	2
95	Silas	Sears	1
	Page 175		
96	Daniel	Bradly	1
97	Russell	Gregory	1
98	John	White	1
99	Jacob	Ellis	3

June 1754 continued

#	Name	Surname	Value		#	Name	Surname	Value
100	Philip	Cannon	1		154	Jonathan	Sturdefunt	1
101	George	Curry	2		155	William	Sturdefunt	1
102	Nathaniel	Taylor Jnr	2		156	David	Sturdefunt	1
103	Joseph	Hunts Widw	1		157	Mathew	Bump	1
104	Isaac	Tarhill	1		158	Samuel	More	1
105	Sander	Dewall	1		159	Isaac	Horton	1
106	Robert	Farrington Widw	1		160	Jonathan	Lane	3
107	James	McReedy	3		161	Jo:	Conklin	1
108	Nathaniel	Byington	3		162	Richard	Roads	2
109	Jacob	Finch	2		163	Michael	Slott	1
110	Thomas	Philip	5		164	John	Penny	1
111	Ebenezer	King	2		165	William	Penny	3
112	John	Ary	1		166	Tom.	Foster	2
113	Josiah	Baker	3		167	John	Paddock	1
114	Leut:	Taylor	4		168	Ezekiel	Meed	1
115	Isaac	Crosby	2		169	Israel	Taylor	1
116	Benjamin	Sears	3		170	William	Hill	6
117	Hezekiah	Kercomb	2		171	Gershom	Muston	1
118	William	Taylor	1		172	Peter	Robinson	1
119	Christopher	Fowler	3		173	Abram	Hodges	1
120	Peter	Angerine	4		174	Ebenezer	Hamblin	1
121	Simon	Ryders	4		175	Isaac	Otter	2
122	Nicolas	Cartwright	3		176	Elemuel	Kelk	1
123	Joseph	Philips	1		177	John	Songworth	1
124	Isaac	Haws	1		178	Seth	Paddock	3
125	Seth	Covell	1		179	Ebenezer	Jones Jnr	2
126	John	Smith	1		*Page 177*			
127	Thomas	Smith	1		180	Aaron	Calkin	1
128	Oliver	Gray	1		181	Theophilus	Jones	1
129	Edward	Gray Jnr	2		182	Joshua	Hamblin	3
130	Samuel	Banks	2		183	Elisha	Cole	1
131	Nathaniel	Forster	2		184	Robert	Weekson	1
132	Samuell	Ellwell	2		185	Gabriel	Knap	4
133	David	Cosby	3		186	John	Tompkins [Hopkins?]	1
134	Joshua	Cosby	3					
135	Jaby	Berry	1		187	John	Van Tessell	2
136	Joseph	Taylor	1		188	Mr.	Kent	6
137	Isaac	Smith	1		189	Jonathan	Astin	3
Page 176					190	John	Kelly	1
138	Hope	Covey	4		191	Thomas	Kelly	1
139	John	Covey	1		192	Isaac	Peirce	2
140	Jonathan	Paddock	1		193	William	Stone	2
141	John	Hill	2		194	Noah	Burbanks	1
142	Nathan	Green	2		195	David	Smith	1
143	Seth	Nickerson	1		196	Edmund	Baker	1
144	Will	Daily farm	1		197	Benjamin	Winter	1
145	Timothy	Clawson	1		198	Caleb	Chase	1
146	Benjamin	Roberts	1		199	Ebenezer	Chase	1
147	James	Loveless	1		200	James	Sears	3
148	Hickin	Bottom	1		201	Peter	Hall	2
149	Elisha	Luttington	2		202	Nathaniel	House	1
150	David	Honywell	1		203	Thomas	Gage	3
151	Elisha	Baker	1		204	Job	Hogg	1
152	Benjamin	Parish	2		205	Elijah	Calkin	1
153	Daniel	Parish	1		206	Samuel	Calkin Jnr	1

June 1754 continued

#	Name	Surname	Value	#	Name	Surname	Value
207	Samuel	Goodspeed	2	260	Thomas	Curry	1
208	Old	Bobbit	3	261	Teunis	Crankhite	1
209	Shubal	Rowly	1	262	Nathaniel	Bailiff	1
210	John	Mahew	1	263	Silas	Paddock	2
211	John	Mahew Jnr	1		*Page 179*		
212	John	Merrick	1	264	Robert	Ryder	4
213	Joseph	Baker	1	265	Jonathan	Ryders	1
214	Moody	House	1	266	John	Field	2
215	James	Cowen	1	267	Philip	Paddock	2
216	Edward	Hall	2	268	Benjamin	Perry	2
217	Ezekiel	Burgiss	1	269	James	Quinby	2
218	Jonathan	Kelly	1	270	Zachary	Paddock Jnr	2
219	Francis	Baker	2	271	Stephen	Field	1
220	Uriah	Lawrence	2	272	John	Concklin	2
221	Isaac	Chase	1	273	Joshua	Moss	1
	Page 178			274	John	Nellson	1
222	Eleazer	Spragge	1	275	Moses	Nauthrop	4
223	Thomas	Crinnell	1	276	Nathan	Birdsell	8
224	Nathaniel	Porter	2	277	Jeremiah	Linkhorn	1
225	Jos	Chittenton	1	278	John	Manly	2
226	Thomas	Kerk	1	279	Uriah	Hill	6
227	Moses	Gregory	1	280	John	Slott	1
228	—	Bazely on Powers place	2	281	Moses	Dusinbury	3
				282	Daniel	Crawford	2
229	William	Rice	1	283	Caleb	Pells farm	6
230	Joseph	Crow	1	284	Edward	Ganung	1
231	Ebenezer	Crow	1	285	Daniel	Philips	1
232	Elisha	Banks	1	286	Samuel	Peters	3
233	John	Scribner	1	287	Henry	Brewer	1
234	Isaac	Hatch	2	288	Ben:	Brundidge Jnr	1
235	Widw	Wilcocks	1	289	Lazarus	Griffen	2
236	Jonathan	Hill	1	290		Edderton	1
237	Jo.	Barly	1	291	Bethuel	Barnam	1
238	Christopher	Bobbit	1	292	Joseph	Philips	1
239	Widw	Dickersons farm	2	293	Zachary	Paddock	2
240	Orlander	Mack	1	294	Abner	Bang	2
241	Malthia	Hatch	1	295	Jeremiah	Baily	1
242	Peleg	Ballard	1	296	Will:	Grays Son	1
243	Peleg	Ballard Jnr	1	297	Robert	Weeksons Son	1
244	Andrew	Rapalyea	1	298	Rowland	Perry	1
245	Ruben	Kelly	1	299	Mathew	Rowly	2
246	Seth	Merrick	1	300	Silas	Peirce	1
247	Gideon	Ellis	1	301	Bartlet	Brundidge	2
248	James	Colwill	1	302	Noah	Smith	1
249	Thomas	Colwill	2	303	—	Crosby	2
250	Amos	Fuller	1	304	Joseph	Bangs	2
251	Jonathan	Runnells	1	305	—	Hinkle	1
252	William	Ballard	1		*Page 180*		
253	Nehemiah	Horton	1	306	John	How	1
254	Cornelis	Tompkins	3	307	Isaac	Smiths Brother	1
255	Simon	Ellis	1	308	Jonathan	Lockwood	1
256	Samuel	Fuller	1	309	Caleb	Hyat	1
257	John	Meeks	3	310	Isaac	Perry	1
258	Samuel	Carle	1	311		Burgiss	2
259	Isaac	Barton	1	312		Cole	2

June 1754 continued

#	Name	Surname	Value	#	Name	Surname	Value
313	Sam	Stringham	1	343	Abram	Krankhite	1
314	Isaiah	Jaycocks	1	344	Teunis	Brewer	1
315	David	Horton	1	345	John	Chugel	1
316	Daniel	Runnells	1	346	Daniel	Taylor	1
317	William	Nellson	1	347	William	Roads	1
318	John	Birdsell	1		*Page 181*		
319	Moses	Hustis	1	348	John	Simkins	1
320	Elisha	Kelk	1	349	Joseph	Underwood	1
321	Jonathan	Bryant	1	350	William	Shaw Jnr	1
322	William	Lane	1	351	Elisha	Meed	1
323	John	Ryder	4	352	Richard	Christian	1
324	William	Dusenbury	1	353	Andrew	Hill	2
325	John	Lane	1	354	William	Chatterdon	1
326	Jonathan	Fowler	6	355	Stephen	Farrington	1
327	Joseph	Hopkins	3	356	Joseph	Brundidge	1
328	John	Green	2	357	Gilbert	Concklin	1
329	Elnathan	Done	1	358	John	Pray	1
330	Thomas	Higgins	1	359	John	Heddy	1
331	Thomas	Hinkly	1	360	Henry	Haynes	1
332	Josiah	Hinkly	1	361	Andrew	Berger Jnr:	1
333	Israel	Cole	1	362	William	Dicks	1
334	Abram	Underhill	1	363	Peter	Ryall	1
335	James	Russell	1	364	Jonathan	Knap	1
336	Edmund	Haws	1	365	Jeremiah	Hueston	1
337	John	Lawrence	2	366	William	Mast	1
338	John	McFarthing	1	367	Israel	Honeywell	6
339	Peter	Terhill	1	368	Thomas	Haviland	6
340	Teunis	Krankhite Sen:	1	369	Thomas	Oakley	6
341	Thomas	Clemons	1				£793
342	Siber	Krankhite	1				

FEBRUARY 1755
SOUTHERN PRECINCT

at 4 d [pence] / pound

#	Name	Surname	Value	#	Name	Surname	Value
	Page 278			17	Benjamin	Jaycocks	3
1	Francis	Nellson	10	18	Timothy	Concklin	3
2	Thomas	Davinport	14	19	Nathan	Lane	4
3	Thomas	Davinport Jnr:	16	20	Tom	Haydons Farm	1
4	Jacob	Mandavill	11	21	George	Hueston	6
5	David	Hustis	12	22	Joseph	Crane	1
6	John	Calkin	2	23	Iccabud	Viccarys Estate	2
7	John	Calkin Jnr:	1	24	Joseph	Gregory	1
8	William	Gray	4	25	William	Drake	4
9	John	Rogers	10	26	Sias	Gregory	3
10	Abram	Otter	1	27	John	Drake	1
11	Elijah	Tompkins	5	28	Isaac	Rodes	5
12	Thomas	Kellick	1	29	Joseph	Crane Jnr:	1
13	John	Van Amburgh	14	30	David	Paddock	1
14	Henry	Van Amburgh	13	31	William	Yerns Widw	1
15	Peter	Du Bois	6	32	—	Smith on Porters Place	2
16	Ebenezer	Jones	3				

February 1755 continued

	Name	Surname	Value		Name	Surname	Value
33	Joseph	Lane	4	86	Jacob	Philip	1
34	Joseph	Meed	4	87	Caleb	Sweet	1
35	John	Gee	1	88	Simon	Dolfs farm	1
36	William	Gee	4	89	William	Palmer	1
37	Cobus	Crankhite	1	90	John	Newberry	4
38	Cobus	Crankhite Jnr:	1	91	Samuell	Otter	3
39	Nathaniel	Robinson	2	92	Peter	Paddock	3
	Page 279			93	Thomas	Paddock	2
40	David	Austin	1	94	Silas	Sears	1
41	Caleb	Brundidge	2	95	Daniel	Bradly	1
42	Nathaniel	Tompkins	6	96	Russell	Gregory	1
43	Cornelius	Fuller	1	97	John	White	1
44	John	Spragge	1	98	Jacob	Ellis	3
45	Samuell	Calkin	2	99	Philip	Cannon	1
46	John	Hains	2	100	George	Curry	2
47	Thomas	Frost	2	101	Joseph	Hunts Widw	1
48	Eleazer	Cole	3	102	Isaac	TerHill	1
49	Edward	Gray	2	103	Sander	Dewell	1
50	William	Teller	10	104	Robert	Ferringtons W:w	1
51	Abram	Smith	3	105	James	McReedy	3
52	Luke	Covert	1	106	Nathaniel	Byington	3
53	Samuell	Jones	1	107	Jacob	Finch	2
54	Elie	Nellson	3	108	Thomas	Philip	5
55	Nathaniel	Hatch	6	109	Ebenezer	King	2
56	Valentine	Perkins	1	110	John	Ary	1
57	Samuell	Field	16	111	Josiah	Baker	3
58	Joseph	Field	8	112	Leut:	Taylor	4
59	James	Dickenson	6	113	Isaac	Crosby	2
60	Amos	Dickenson	4	114	Benjamin	Sears	3
61	John	Dickenson	4	115	Hezekiah	Kercomb	2
62	Daniell	Townsend	4	116	William	Taylor	1
63	Robert	Townsend	1	117	Christopher	Fowler	4
64	Thomas	Townsend	1	118	Peter	Angerine	4
65	Elihu	Townsend	5	119	Simon	Ryders	4
66	Charles	Townsend	2	120	Nicolas	Cartwright	3
67	Zebulon	Townsend	1	121	Joseph	Philip	1
68	Benjamin	Townsend	3	122	Isaac	Haws	1
69	Robert R:	Townsend	3	123	Seth	Covell	1
70	Robert U:	Townsend	2		*Page 281*		
71	Daniel	Townsend Jnr:	1	124	John	Smith	1
72	Daniel D.	Townsend	1	125	Thomas	Smith	1
73	Benjamin	Arnold	1	126	Oliver	Gray	1
74	Jesse	Smith	4	127	Edward	Gray Jnr:	2
75	Benjamin	Brundidge	6	128	Samuell	Banks	2
76	Michael	Shaw	1	129	Nathaniel	Forster	2
77	Barnabas	Hamblin	2	130	Samuell	Ellwell	2
78	Caleb	Hayzer	2	131	David	Cosby	3
79	Samuell	Gates	2	132	Joshua	Cosby	3
80	William	Rapalyea	4	133	Jaby	Berry	1
81	John	Barber	2	134	Joseph	Taylor	1
	Page 280			135	Isaac	Smith	1
82	Peter	Hartwell	2	136	Hope	Covey	4
83	Isaac	Chapman	2	137	John	Covey	1
84	Deacon	Hamblin	6	138	Jonathan	Paddock	1
85	Shubal	Rowly	2	139	John	Hill	2

February 1755 continued

	Name	Surname	Value		Name	Surname	Value
140	Nathan	Green	2	194	Ebenezer	Chase	1
141	Seth	Nickerson	1	195	James	Sears	3
142	Will:	Dailys farm	1	196	Peter	Hall	2
143	Timothy	Clawson	1	197	Nathaniel	House	1
144	Benjamin	Roberts	1	198	Thomas	Gage	3
145	James	Loveless	1	199	Job	Hogg	1
146	Hickin	Bottom	1	200	Elijah	Calkin	1
147	Elisha	Luttington	2	201	Samuell	Calkin Jnr:	1
148	David	HonyWell	1	202	Samuell	Good Speed	2
149	Elisha	Baker	1	203	Old	Bobbit	3
150	Benjamin	Parish	2	204	Shubal	Rowly	1
151	Daniel	Parish	1	205	John	Mahew	1
152	Jonathan	Sturdefunt	1	206	John	Mahew Jnr:	1
153	William	Sturdefunt	1	207	John	Merrick	1
154	David	Sturdefunt	1		*Page 283*		
155	Mathew	Bump	1	208	Joseph	Baker	1
156	Samuell	More	1	209	Moody	House	2
157	Isaac	Horton	2	210	James	Cowen	1
158	Jonathan	Lane	4	211	Edward	Hall	2
159	Jo:	Conklin	1	212	Ezekiel	Burgiss	2
160	Richard	Roads	2	213	Jonathan	Kelly	1
161	Michael	Slott	1	214	Francis	Baker	2
162	John	Penny	1	215	Uriah	Lawrence	2
163	William	Penny	3	216	Isaac	Chase	1
164	Tom:	Foster	2	217	Eleazer	Spragge	1
165	John	Paddock	1	218	Nathaniel	Porter	2
	Page 282			219	Jo:	Chittenton	1
166	Ezekiel	Meed	1	220	Thomas	Kerk	1
167	Israel	Taylor	1	221	Moses	Gregory	1
168	William	Hill	6	222	William	Rice	1
169	Peter	Robinson	1	223	Joseph	Crow	1
170	Abram	Hodges	1	224	Ebenezer	Crow	1
171	Ebenezer	Hamblin	1	225	Elisha	Banks	1
172	Isaac	Otter	2	226	John	Scribner	1
173	Elemuel	Kelk	1	227	Isaac	Hatch	2
174	Seth	Paddock	3	228	—	Pembleton	1
175	Ebenezer	Jones Jnr:	2	229	Jonathan	Hill	1
176	Aaron	Calkin	1	230	Jo:	Barly	1
177	Theophilus	Jones	1	231	Christopher	Bobbit	1
178	Joshua	Hamblin	3	232	Widw	Dickensons farm	3
179	Elisha	Cole	1	233	Orlander	Mack	1
180	Robert	Weekson	1	234	Malthia	Hatch	1
181	Gabriel	Knap	4	235	Peleg	Ballard	1
182	John	Hopkins	1	236	Peleg	Ballard Jnr:	1
183	John	Van Tessell	2	237	Andrew	Rapelyea	1
184	Mr.	Kent	6	238	Ruben	Kelly	1
185	Jonathan	Austin	3	239	Seth	Merrick	1
186	John	Kelly	1	240	Gideon	Ellis	1
187	Thomas	Kelly	1	241	James	Colwill	1
188	Isaac	Peirce	2	242	Thomas	Colwill	2
189	William	Stone	2	243	Amos	Fuller	1
190	Noah	Burbanks	1	244	William	Ballard	1
191	David	Smith	1	245	Nehemiah	Horton	1
192	Edmund	Baker	1	246	Cornelis	Tompkins	3
193	Caleb	Chase	1	247	Simon	Ellis	1

February 1755 continued

	Name	Surname	Value		Name	Surname	Value
248	Samuel	Fuller	1	301	John	Birdsell	1
249	John	Meeks	2	302	Moses	Hustis	1
Page 284				303	Elisha	Kelk	1
250	Samuell	Carle	1	304	Jonathan	Bryant	2
251	Isaac	Barton	1	305	William	Lane	1
252	Teunis	Crankhite	1	306	John	Ryder	4
253	Nathaniel	Bailiff	2	307	William	Dusenbury	2
254	Silas	Paddock	2	308	John	Lane	1
255	Robert	Ryders	4	309	Joseph	Hopkins	3
256	Jonathan	Ryders	1	310	John	Green	2
257	John	Field	2	311	Elnathan	Done	1
258	Philip	Paddock	2	312	Thomas	Higgins	1
259	Benjamin	Perry	2	313	Thomas	Hinkly	1
260	James	Quinby	2	314	Josiah	Hinkly	1
261	Zachary	Paddock Jnr:	2	315	Israel	Cole	2
262	Stephen	Field	1	316	Abram	Underhill	1
263	Joshua	Moss	1	317	James	Russell	1
264	John	Nellson	1	318	Edmund	Haws	1
265	Moses	Nauthrop	4	319	John	Lawrence	2
266	Nathan	Birdsell	9	320	John	McFarthing	1
267	Jeremiah	Linkhorn	1	321	Teunis	Krankhite Sen:	1
268	John	Manly	2	322	Thomas	Clemens	2
269	Moses	Dusenbury	5	323	Sibet	Krankhite	1
270	Daniel	Crawford	2	324	Abram	Krankhite	1
271	Edward	Ganung	1	325	Teunis	Brewer	1
272	Daniel	Philip	1	326	John	Chugel	1
273	Samuell	Peters	4	327	Daniel	Taylor	1
274	Ben:	Brundidge Jnr:	1	328	William	Roads	1
275	Lazarus	Griffen	1	329	John	Simkins	1
276	—	Edderton	1	330	Joseph	Underwood	1
277	Bethuel	Barnam	1	331	William	Shaw	1
278	Joseph	Philip	1	332	Migell	Shaw Jnr:	1
279	Zachary	Paddock	2	*Page 286*			
280	Abner	Bang	2	333	Elisha	Meed	1
281	Jeremiah	Baily	1	334	Andrew	Hill	2
282	Will:	Grays Son	1	335	Will	Chatterdon	1
283	Robert	Weeksons Son	1	336	Stephen	Farrington	1
284	Rowland	Perry	1	337	Joseph	Brundidge	1
285	Mathew	Rowly	2	338	Gilbert	Concklin	1
286	Bartlet	Brundidge	2	339	John	Pray	1
287	Noah	Smith	1	340	John	Heddy	2
288	Joseph	Bangs	2	341	Henry	Haynes	1
289	—	Hinkle	1	342	Andrew	Burgis Jnr:	1
290	John	How	1	343	William	Dicks	1
291	Isaac	Smiths Bro:	1	344	Daniel	Akins	2
Page 285				345	Peter	Ryal	1
292	Jonathan	Lockwood	1	346	Jonathan	Knap	1
293	Caleb	Hyat	1	347	Jeremiah	Hueston	1
294	Isaac	Perry	1	348	William	Mast	1
295	Mathias	Burgiss	3	349	Israel	Honeywell	5
296	Rufus	Coles	1	350	Thomas	Haviland	6
297	Isaiah	Jaycocks	1	351	Thomas	Oakly	6
298	David	Horton	1	352	John	Clark	1
299	Daniel	Runnells	1	353	Johannis	Brewer	1
300	William	Nellson	2	354	Ruben	Hamblin	1

February 1755 continued

#	Name	Surname	Value
355	Robert	Fuller	2
356	Thomas	Dayton	1
357	William	Shaw	1
358	Jeremiah	Giffords	2
359	Heman	King	1
360	Jonathan	Hopkins	2
361	Jeremiah	Hueson	1
362	Benjamin	Howland	1
363	Joseph	Brooks	1
364	Peter	Purdy	1
365	Ezekiel	Meed	1
366	Christopher	Cartwright	1
367	Nehemiah	Wood	1
368	Christopher	Ellis	1
369	Humpfrey	Ruff	1
370	Philip	Ruff	1
371	William	Dean	1
372	Collo:	Willets farm	6
373	Josiah	Merrits farm	6
374	Mathew	Du Bois Jnr:	2
	Page 287		
375	Abraham	Du Bois	1
376	John	Backer	1
377	Nathan	Taylor Jnr:	1
378	John	Gray	2
379	Samuell	Yeomans	1
380	Anthony	Yeomans	1
			£809

JUNE 1755
SOUTHERN PRECINCT

at 1 shilling 6 pence / pound

#	Name	Surname	Value
	Page 291		
1	Francis	Nellson	10
2	Thomas	Davinport	14
3	Thomas	Davinport Jnr:	16
4	Jacob	Mandavill	11
5	David	Hustis	12
6	John	Calkin	2
7	John	Calkin Jnr:	1
8	William	Gray	4
9	John	Rogers	10
10	Abram	Otter	1
11	Elijah	Tompkins	5
12	Thomas	Kellick	1
13	John	Van Amburgh	14
14	Henry	Van Amburgh	13
15	Peter	Du Bois	6
16	Ebenezer	Jones	3
17	Benjamin	Jaycocks	3
18	Timothy	Concklin	3
19	Nathan	Lane	3
20	Tom	Haydons farm	1
21	George	Hueston	5
22	Joseph	Crane	1
23	Joseph	Gregory	1
24	William	Drake	4
25	Sias	Gregory	3
26	John	Drake	1
27	Isaac	Rodes	5
28	Joseph	Crane Jnr:	1
29	David	Paddock	1
30	William	Yerns Widw	1
31	John	Smith	2
32	Joseph	Lane	4
33	Joseph	Meed	4
34	John	Gee	1
35	William	Gee	4
36	Cobus	Krankhite	1
37	Cobus	Krankhite Jnr:	1
38	David	Austin	1
39	Caleb	Brundidge	2
	Page 292		
40	Nathaniel	Tompkins	6
41	Cornelis	Fuller	1
42	John	Spragge	1
43	Samuell	Calkin	3
44	John	Hains	2
45	Thomas	Frost	2
46	Eleazer	Cole	4
47	Edward	Gray	2
48	William	Teller	10
49	Abram	Smith	3
50	Luke	Covert	1
51	Samuell	Jones	1
52	Elie	Nellson	3
53	Nathaniel	Hatch	6
54	Valentine	Perkins	1
55	Samuell	Field	16
56	Joseph	Field	6
57	James	Dickenson	6
58	Amos	Dickenson	4
59	John	Dickenson	4
60	Daniel	Townsend	4
61	Robert	Townsend	1
62	Thomas	Townsend	1

June 1755 continued

	Name	Surname	Value		Name	Surname	Value
63	Elihu	Townsend	5	116	Simon	Ryders	4
64	Charles	Townsend	2	117	Nicolas	Cartwright	3
65	Zebulon	Townsend	1	118	Joseph	Philip	1
66	Benjamin	Townsend	3	119	Isaac	Haws	1
67	Robert R:	Townsend	3	120	Seth	Covell	1
68	Robert U	Townsend	2	121	John	Smith	1
69	Daniel	Townsend Jnr:	1	122	Thomas	Smith	1
70	Daniel D.	Townsend	1	*Page 294*			
71	Benjamin	Arnold	1	123	Oliver	Gray	1
72	Jesse	Smith	4	124	Edward	Gray Jnr:	2
73	Benjamin	Brundidge	5	125	Samuell	Banks	2
74	Michaell	Shaw	1	126	Nathaniel	Forster	2
75	Caleb	Hayzer	2	127	Samuell	Ellwell	2
76	Samuell	Gates	2	128	David	Cosby	3
77	William	Rapelyea	5	129	Joshua	Cosby	3
78	John	Barber	2	130	Jaby	Berry	1
79	Peter	Hartwell	2	131	Joseph	Taylor	1
80	Isaac	Chapman	2	132	Isaac	Smith	1
Page 293				133	Hope	Covey	4
81	Deacon	Hamblin	6	134	John	Covey	1
82	Shubal	Rowly	2	135	Jonathan	Paddock	1
83	Jacob	Philip	1	136	John	Hall	2
84	Caleb	Sweet	1	137	Nathan	Green	2
85	Simon	Dolfs farm	1	138	Seth	Nickerson	1
86	William	Palmer	1	139	Will:	Dailys farm	1
87	John	Newberry	4	140	Timothy	Clawson	1
88	Samuell	Other	3	141	Benjamin	Roberts	1
89	Peter	Paddock	3	142	James	Loveless	1
90	Thomas	Paddock	2	143	Hickin	Bottom	1
91	Silas	Sears	1	144	Elisha	Luttington	2
92	Daniel	Bradly	1	145	David	Honeywell	1
93	Russell	Gregory	1	146	Eisha	Baker	1
94	John	White	1	147	Banjamin	Parish	1
95	Jacob	Ellis	4	148	Daniel	Parish	1
96	Philip	Cannon	1	149	Johathan	Sturdefunt	1
97	Joseph	Hunts Widw	1	150	William	Sturdefunt	1
98	George	Curry	2	151	David	Sturdefunt	1
99	Isaac	TerHill	1	152	Mathew	Bump	1
100	Sander	Dewell	1	153	Samuell	Morce	1
101	Robert	Farringtons Widw	1	154	Isaac	Horton	2
				155	Jonathan	Lane	4
102	James	McReedy	3	156	Jo:	Concklin	1
103	Nathaniel	Byington	3	157	Richard	Roads	2
104	Jacob	Finch	2	158	Michael	Slott	1
105	Thomas	Philip	5	159	John	Penny	1
106	Ebenezer	King	2	160	William	Penny	3
107	John	Ary	1	161	Tom	Foster	2
108	Josiah	Baker	4	162	John	Paddock	1
109	Leut:	Taylor	5	163	Ezekiel	Meed	1
110	Isaac	Crosby	2	164	Israel	Taylor	1
111	Benjamin	Sears	3	*Page 295*			
112	Hesekiah	Kercomb	2	165	William	Hill	5
113	William	Taylor	1	166	Peter	Robinson	1
114	Christopher	Fowler	4	167	Abram	Hodges	1
115	Peter	Angerine	5	168	Ebenezer	Hamblin	1

June 1755 continued

#	Name	Surname	Value
169	Isaac	Otter	2
170	Elemuel	Kelk	1
171	Seth	Paddock	3
172	Ebenezer	Jones Jnr:	2
173	Aaron	Calkin	1
174	Theophilus	Jones	1
175	Joshua	Hamblin	3
176	Elisha	Cole	1
177	Robert	Weekson	1
178	Gabriel	Nap	5
179	John	Hopkins	1
180	John	Van Tessell	2
181	Mr.	Kent	6
182	Jonathan	Austin	3
183	John	Kelly	1
184	Thomas	Kelly	1
185	Isaac	Peirce	2
186	William	Stone	2
187	Noah	Burbancks	1
188	David	Smith	1
189	Edmund	Baker	1
190	Caleb	Chase	1
191	Ebenezer	Chase	1
192	James	Sears	4
193	Peter	Hall	2
194	Nathaniel	House	1
195	Thomas	Gage	3
196	Job	Hogg	1
197	Elijah	Calkin	1
198	Samuell	Calkin Jnr:	1
199	Samuell	Good Speed	2
200	Old	Bobbit	3
201	Shubal	Rowly	1
202	John	Mahew	1
203	John	Mahew Jnr:	1
204	John	Merrick	3
205	Joseph	Baker	1
206	Moody	House	1

Page 296

#	Name	Surname	Value
207	James	Cowen	1
208	Edward	Hall	2
209	Ezekiel	Burgiss	2
210	Jonathan	Kelly	1
211	Francis	Baker	2
212	Uriah	Lawrence	2
213	Isaac	Chase	1
214	Eleazer	Spragge	1
215	Nathaniel	Porter	3
216	Jo:	Chittenton	1
217	Thomas	Kerk	1
218	Moses	Gregory	1
219	William	Rice	1
220	Joseph	Craw	1
221	Ebenezer	Craw	1
222	Elisha	Banks	1
223	John	Scribner	1
224	Isaac	Hatch	2
225	—	Pembleton	1
226	Jonathan	Hill	1
227	Jo:	Barly	1
228	Christopher	Bobbit	1
229	Widw	Dickensons farm	3
230	Malthia	Hatch	2
231	Peleg	Ballard	1
232	Peleg	Ballard Jnr:	1
233	Andrew	Rapelyea	1
234	Seth	Merrick	2
235	Gideon	Ellis	1
236	James	Colwill	1
237	Thomas	Calwill	2
238	Amos	Fuller	1
239	William	Ballard	1
240	Nehemiah	Horton	1
241	Cornelis	Tompkins	4
242	Simon	Ellis	1
243	Samuel	Fuller	1
244	John	Meeks	2
245	Samuell	Carle	1
246	Isaac	Barton	2
247	Teunis	Crankhite	1
248	Nathaniel	Bailiff	2

Page 297

#	Name	Surname	Value
249	Silas	Paddock	2
250	Robert	Ryders	4
251	John	Field	2
252	Philip	Paddock	2
253	Benjamin	Perry	3
254	James	Quinby	2
255	Zachary	Paddock Jnr:	2
256	Stephen	Field	1
257	Joshua	Moss	1
258	John	Nellson	1
259	Moses	Nauthrop	5
260	Nathan	Birdsell	9
261	Jeremiah	Linkhorn	1
262	John	Manly	2
263	Moses	Dusenbury	5
264	Daniel	Crawford	2
265	Edward	Ganung	1
266	Daniel	Philip	1
267	Samuell	Peters	5
268	Ben:	Brundidge Jnr:	1
269	Lazarus	Griffen	1
270	—	Edderton	1
271	Bethuel	Barnam	1
272	Joseph	Philip	1
273	Zachary	Paddock	2
274	Abner	Bang	2
275	Jeremiah	Baily	1
276	Will:	Grays Son	1

June 1755 continued

	Name	Surname	Value		Name	Surname	Value
277	Robert	Weeksons Son	1	331	Joseph	Brundidge	1
278	Rowland	Perry	2	332	Gilbert	Concklin	2
279	Mathew	Rowly	2		*Page 299*		
280	Bartlet	Brundidge	2	333	John	Pray	1
281	Noah	Smith	1	334	John	Headdy	3
282	Joseph	Bangs	2	335	Henry	Haynes	1
283	—	Kinkle [Hinkle]	1	336	Andrew	Burgiss Jnr:	1
284	John	How	2	337	Daniel	Akins	2
285	Isaac	Smiths Bro:	1	338	Peter	Ryal	1
286	Jonathan	Lockwood	2	339	Jeremiah	Hueston	1
287	Caleb	Hyat	1	340	William	Most	1
288	Isaac	Perry	1	341	Israel	Honeywell	5
289	Mathias	Burgiss	3	342	Thomas	Haviland	6
290	Rufus	Coles	1	343	Thomas	Oakly	6
	Page 298			344	John	Clark	1
291	Josiah [Isaiah]	Jaycocks	1	345	Ruben	Hamblin	1
292	David	Horton	2	346	Robert	Fuller	2
293	Daniel	Runnells	1	347	Thomas	Dayton	1
294	William	Nellson	2	348	Jeremiah	Giffords	2
295	John	Birdsell	1	349	Heman	King	1
296	Moses	Hustis	1	350	Jonathan	Hopkins	2
297	Elisha	Kelk	1	351	Jeremiah	Hueson	1
298	Jonathan	Bryant	2	352	Benjamin	Howland	1
299	William	Lane	1	353	Joseph	Brooks	1
300	John	Ryder	4	354	Peter	Purdy	1
301	William	Dusenbury	3	355	Ezekiel	Meed	2
302	John	Lane	1	356	Christopher	Cartwright	1
303	Joseph	Hopkins	3	357	Nehemiah	Wood	1
304	John	Green	2	358	Christopher	Ellis	1
305	Elnathan	Done	1	359	Humfrey	Ruff	1
306	Thomas	Higgins	1	360	Philip	Ruff	1
307	Thomas	Hinkly	1	361	William	Dean	1
308	Josiah	Hinkly	1	362	Collo:	Willets farm	6
309	Israel	Cole	2	363	Joseph	Merrits farm	6
310	Abram	Underhill	1	364	Mathew	Du Bois Jnr:	2
311	James	Russell	1	365	Abraham	Du Bois	1
312	Edmund	Haws	1	366	John	Backer	1
313	John	Lawrence	2	367	Nathan	Taylor Jnr:	2
314	John	McFarthing	2	368	John	Gray	2
315	Teunis	Krankhite Sen:	1	369	Timothy	Vickorie	1
316	Thomas	Clemens	2	370	Joseph	Vickorie	1
317	Sibet	Krankhite	1	371	Benjamin	Vickorie	1
318	Abram	Krankhite	1	372	Ruben	Kelly	1
319	Teunis	Brewer	1	373	Jasper	Crankhirt	1
320	John	Chugal	1	374	Justice	Wealer	1
321	Daniel	Taylor	1		*Page 300*		
322	William	Roads	1	375	John	Jones	1
323	John	Simkins	1	376	David	Randolph	1
324	Joseph	Underwood	1	377	Fredrick	Gea	1
325	William	Shaw	1	378	Walter	Huson	1
326	Migell	Shaw Jnr:	1	379	Oliver	Odel	1
327	Elisha	Meed	1	380	James	Standly	1
328	Andrew	Hill	3	381	John	Ferris	1
329	Will	Chitterton	1	382	John	Slott	1
330	Stephen	Farrington	1	383	Uriah	Hill	2

June 1755 continued

	Name	Surname	Value		Name	Surname	Value
384	William	Dean	1	389	Solomon	Ferrington	1
385	Ebenezer	Merrit	1	390	Justice	Lane	1
386	Moses	Brundidge	1	391	Peter	Ter Hills Farm	1
387	Thomas	Underhill	1				£840
388	Samuell	Casten	1				

FEBRUARY 1756
SOUTHERN PRECINCT

at 4 d [pence] / pound

	Name	Surname	Value		Name	Surname	Value
	Page 351			40	Nathaniel	Tompkins	2
1	Francis	Nellson	9	41	Cornelis	Fuller	1
2	Thomas	Davinport	14	42	John	Spragge	1
3	Thomas	Davinport Jnr:	16	43	Samuell	Calkin	2
4	Jacob	Mandavill	11	44	John	Hains	2
5	David	Hustis	10	45	Thomas	Frost	2
6	John	Calkin	2	46	Eleazer	Cole	3
7	John	Calkin Jnr:	1	47	Edward	Gray	2
8	William	Gray	4	48	William	Teller	9
9	John	Rogers	11	49	Abram	Smith	3
10	Abram	Otter	1	50	Luke	Covert	1
11	Elijah	Tompkins	5	51	Samuell	Jones	1
12	Thomas	Kellick	1	52	Elie	Nellson	3
13	John	Van Amburgh	14	53	Nathaniel	Hath	6
14	Henry	Van Amburgh	10	54	Valentine	Perkins	1
15	Peter	Du Bois	16	55	Samuel	Field	17
16	Ebenezer	Jones Near the River	3	56	Joseph	Field	6
17	Benjamin	Jaycocks	3	57	James	Dickenson	6
18	Timothy	Concklin	3	58	Amos	Dickenson	4
19	Nathan	Lane	3	59	John	Dickenson	4
20	Tom	Haydons farm	1	60	Daniel	Townsend	4
	Page 352			61	Robert	Townsend	1
21	George	Hueston	5	62	Thomas	Townsend	1
22	Joseph	Crane	1		*Page 353*		
23	Joseph	Gregory	1	63	Elihu	Townsend	5
24	William	Drake	4	64	Charles	Townsend	2
25	Sias	Gregory	4	65	Zebulon	Townsend	1
26	John	Drake	1	66	Benjamin	Townsend	3
27	Isaac	Rodes	5	67	Robert R:	Townsend	3
28	Joseph	Crane Jnr:	1	68	Robert U:	Townsend	1
29	David	Paddock	1	69	Daniel	Townsend Jnr:	1
30	William	Yerns Widw:	1	70	Daniel D.	Townsend	1
31	John	Smith	2	71	Benjamin	Arnold	1
32	Joseph	Lane	4	72	Jesse	Smith	4
33	Joseph	Meed	4	73	Benjamin	Brundidge	4
34	John	Gee	1	74	Michael	Shaw	1
35	William	Gee	4	75	Caleb	Hayser	2
36	Cobus	Crankhite	1	76	Samuell	Gates	1
37	Cobus	Crankhite Jnr:	1	77	William	Rapelyea	5
38	David	Austin	1	78	John	Barber	2
39	Caleb	Brundidge	1	79	Peter	Hartwell	2
				80	Isaac	Chapman	2

February 1756 continued

	Name	Surname	Value		Name	Surname	Value
			81				
	Deacon	Hamblin	6	134	Will	Daily's farm	2
82	Shubal	Rowly	2	135	Timothy	Clawson	1
83	Jacob	Philip	1	136	Benjamin	Roberts	1
84	Caleb	Sweet	2	137	James	Loveless	1
85	William	Palmer	1	138	Hickin	Bottom	1
86	John	Newberry	4	139	Elisha	Luttington	3
87	Samuell	Other	3	140	David	Honeywell	1
88	Peter	Paddock	2	141	Elisha	Baker	1
89	Thomas	Paddock	2	142	Benjamin	Parish	1
90	Silas	Sears	1	143	Daniel	Parish	1
91	Daniel	Bradly	1	144	Jonathan	Sturdefunt	1
92	Russell	Gregory	1	145	William	Sturdefunt	1
93	John	White	1	146	David	Sturdefunt	1
94	Jacob	Ellis	4		*Page 355*		
95	Philip	Cannon	1	147	Mathew	Bump	1
96	Joseph	Hunts Widw:	1	148	Samuell	More	1
97	George	Curry	2	149	Isaac	Horton	2
98	Isaac	Terhill	1	150	Jonathan	Lane	4
99	Sander	Dewell	1	151	Jo-	Concklin	1
100	Robert	Farringtons Widw:	1	152	Richard	Roads	2
				153	Michael	Slott	1
101	James	McReedy	3	154	John	Penny	1
102	Nathanll:	Byington	2	155	William	Penny	3
103	Jacob	Finch	2	156	Tom	Foster	2
104	Thomas	Philip	5	157	John	Paddock	1
	Page 354			158	Ezekiel	Meed	1
105	Ebenezer	King	1	159	Israel	Taylor	1
106	Josiah	Baker	3	160	William	Hill	5
107	Leut:	Taylor	4	161	Peter	Robinson	1
108	Isaac	Crosby	1	162	Abram	Hodges	1
109	Benjamin	Sears	3	163	Ebenezer	Hamblin	1
110	Hesekiah	Kercomb	2	164	Isaac	Otter	1
111	Christopher	Fowler	4	165	Elemuel	Kelk	1
112	Peter	Angerine	5	166	Seth	Paddock	3
113	Simon	Ryders	3	167	Ebenezer	Jones Jnr:	2
114	Joseph	Philip	1	168	Aaron	Calkin	1
115	Isaac	Haws	1	169	Theophilus	Jones	1
116	Seth	Covell	1	170	Joshua	Hamblin	3
117	John Thomas	Smith	1	171	Elisha	Cole	1
118	Oliver	Gray	1	172	Robert	Weekson	1
119	Edward	Gray Jnr:	2	173	Gabriel	Nap	5
120	Samuell	Banks	2	174	John	Hopkins	1
121	Nathaniel	Forster	2	175	John	Van Tessell	1
122	Samuell	Ellwell	2	176	Mr.	Kent	6
123	David	Cosby	3	177	Jonathan	Austin	3
124	Joshua	Cosby	3	178	John	Kelly	1
125	Jaby	Berry	1	179	Thomas	Kelly	1
126	Joseph	Taylor	1	180	Isaac	Peirce	2
127	Isaac	Smith	2	181	William	Stone	1
128	Hope	Covey	5	182	Noah	Burbancks	1
129	John	Covey	1	183	David	Smith	1
130	Jonathan	Paddock	1	184	Edmund	Baker	1
131	John	Hall	2	185	Caleb	Chase	1
132	Nathan	Green	2	186	Ebenezer	Chase	1
133	Seth	Nickerson	1	187	James	Sears	4

February 1756 continued

#	Name	Surname	Value
188	Peter	Hall	2
Page 356			
189	Nathaniel	House's farm	1
190	Thomas	Gage	3
191	Job	Hogg	1
192	Elisha	Calkin	1
193	Samuell	Calkin Jnr:	1
194	Samuell	Good Speed	2
195	Old	Bobbit	2
196	Shubal	Rowly	1
197	John	Mahew	1
198	John	Merrick	3
199	Joseph	Baker	1
200	Moody	House	1
201	James	Cowen	1
202	Edward	Hall	2
203	Ezekiel	Burgis	2
204	Jonathan	Kelly	1
205	Francis	Baker	2
206	Uriah	Lawrence	2
207	Isaac	Chase	1
208	Eleazer	Spragge	1
209	Nathaniel	Porter	4
210	Jo:	Chittenton	1
211	Thomas	Kerk	1
212	Moses	Gregory	2
213	William	Rice	1
214	Joseph	Craw	1
215	Ebenezer	Craw	1
216	Elisha	Banks	1
217	John	Scribner	1
218	Shubal	Wixon	1
219	—	Pembleton	1
220	Jonathan	Hill	1
221	Jo:	Barly	1
222	Christopher	Bobbit	1
223	Widw:	Dickensons farm	4
224	Malthia	Hatch	3
225	Peleg	Ballard	1
226	Peleg	Ballard Jnr:	1
227	Seth	Merrick	2
228	Gideon	Ellis	1
229	Andrew	Rapelye	1
230	Thomas	Colwill	2
Page 357			
231	Amos	Fuller	1
232	William	Ballard	1
233	Cornelius	Tompkins	3
234	Simon	Ellis	1
235	Samuell	Fuller	1
236	John	Meeks	2
237	Isaac	Barton	2
238	Teunis	Crankhite	1
239	Nathaniel	Bailiff	2
240	Silas	Paddock	2
241	Robert	Ryders	4
242	John	Field	3
243	Philip	Paddock	3
244	Benjamin	Perry	3
245	James	Quinby	3
246	Zachary	Paddock Jnr:	2
247	Stephen	Field	1
248	Joshua	Moss	1
249	John	Nellson	1
250	Moses	Nauthrop	5
251	Nathan	Birdsell	10
252	Jeremiah	Linkhorn	1
253	John	Manly	1
254	Moses	Dusenbury	4
255	Daniel	Crawford	2
256	Edward	Ganung	1
257	Daniel	Philip	1
258	Samuell	Peters	5
259	Ben:	Brundidge Jnr:	1
260	Lazarus	Griffen	1
261		Edderton	1
262	Bethuel	Barnam	1
263	Joseph	Philip	1
264	Zachary	Paddock	2
265	Abner	Bang	2
266	Jeremiah	Baily	1
267	Will:	Grays Son William	1
268	Robert	Weeksons Son Peleg	1
269	Rowland	Perry	1
270	Mathew	Rowly	1
271	Bartlet	Brundidge	2
272	Noah	Smith	1
Page 358			
273	Elijah	Wixson	1
274	Joshua	Hinkle	1
275	John	How	2
276	Isaac	Smiths Bro: Charles	1
277	Jonathan	Lockwood	2
278	Isaac	Perry	1
279	Mathias	Burgis	3
280	Rufus	Coles	1
281	Isaiah	Jaycocks	1
282	David	Horton	2
283	Daniel	Runnells	1
284	William	Nellson	2
285	John	Birdsell	2
286	Moses	Hustis	1
287	Elisha	Kelk	1
288	Jonathan	Bryant	2
289	William	Lane	1
290	John	Ryder	3
291	William	Dusenbury	3

February 1756 continued

	Name	Surname	Value		Name	Surname	Value
292	John	Lane	1	341	Ezekiel	Meed	2
293	Joseph	Hopkins	4	342	Nehemiah	Wood	1
294	John	Green	2	343	Christopher	Ellis	1
295	Thomas	Higgins	1	344	Humfrey	Ruff	1
296	Thomas	Hinkly	1	345	Philip	Ruff	1
297	Josiah	Hinkly	1	346	William	Dean	1
298	Israel	Cole	2	347	Collo:	Willets farm	5
299	Abram	Underhill	1	348	Joseph	Merrits farm	5
300	James	Russell	1	349	Abraham	Du Bois	2
301	Edmund	Haws	1	350	John	Baker	1
302	John	Lawrence	2	351	Nathan	Taylor Jnr:	1
303	John	McFarthing	2	352	John	Gray	1
304	Teunis	Krankhite Jonse	1	353	Joseph	Viccorie	1
				354	Ruben	Kelly	1
305	Thomas	Clemens	3	355	Justice	Whealer	1
306	Sibet	Krankhite	1	356	John	Jones	1
307	Abram	Krankhite	1	357	David	Randolph	1
308	Teunis	Brewer	1	*Page 360*			
309	John	Chugal	1	358	Fredrick	Gea	1
310	Daniel	Taylor	1	359	Walter	Huson	1
311	John	Simkins	1	360	Oliver	Odel	1
312	Joseph	Underwood	1	361	James	Standly	1
313	William	Shaw	1	362	John	Ferris	1
314	Migell	Shaw Jnr:	1	363	John	Slott	1
315	Elisha	Meed	1	364	Uriah	Hill	2
Page 359				365	William	Dean Jnr:	1
316	Andrew	Hill	3	366	Ebenezer	Merrit	1
317	Will	Chatterton	1	367	Moses	Brundidge	1
318	Stephen	Farrington	1	368	Thomas	Underhill	1
319	Joseph	Brundidge	1	369	Samuell	Casten	1
320	Gilbert	Concklin	2	370	Solomon	Ferrington	1
321	John	Haddy	3	371	Jonathan	Kent	1
322	Henry	Hanes	1	372	Henry	Terbus Jnr:	1
323	Andrew	Burgis Jnr:	1	373	John	Curtis	1
324	David	Akins	2	374	John	Wright	1
325	Peter	Ryal	1	375	Jacob	Doty	1
326	Jeremiah	Hueston	1	376	Silas	Washburn	2
327	William	Mash	1	377	Samuel	Brewer	1
328	Israel	Honeywell	5	378	John	Price	1
329	Thomas	Haviland	5	379	Eber	Herriton	1
330	Thomas	Oakly	5	380	Richard	Hoppe	1
331	John	Clark	1	381	Richard	Arundel	1
332	Ruben	Hamblin	1	382	Hezekiah	Meed	1
333	Robert	Fuller	1	383	John	Brewer	1
334	Thomas	Dayton	1	384	William	Teller Son	1
335	Jeremiah	Giffords	2	385	Joshua	Barnum	2
336	Heman	King	1	386	Timothy	Stevens	2
337	Jonathan	Hopkins	1	387	Joshua	Porter	1
338	Benjamin	Howland	1	388	James	Colwill	2
339	Joseph	Brooks	1				£824
340	Peter	Purdy	1				

JUNE 1756
SOUTHERN PRECINCT

at 1 shilling 8 pence / pound

#	Name	Surname	Value
	Page 416		
1	Francis	Nellson	8
2	Thomas	Davinport	14
3	Thomas	Davinport Jnr:	16
4	Jacob	Mandavill	11
5	David	Hustis	10
6	John	Calkin	2
7	John	Calkin Jnr:	1
8	William	Gray	4
9	John	Rogers	12
10	Abram	Otter	1
11	Elijah	Tompkins	5
12	Thomas	Kellick	1
13	John	Van Amburgh	14
14	Henry	Van Amburgh	9
15	Peter	Du Bois	16
16	Ebenezer	Jones Near the River	3
17	Benjamin	Jaycocks	3
18	Timothy	Concklin	3
19	Nathan	Lane	3
20	Tom	Haydons farm	1
21	George	Hueston	5
22	Joseph	Crane	1
23	Joseph	Gregory	1
24	William	Drake	4
25	Sias	Gregory	4
26	John	Drake	1
27	Isaac	Rodes	5
28	Joseph	Crane Jnr:	1
29	David	Paddock	1
30	William	Yerns Widw:	1
31	John	Smith	2
32	Joseph	Lane	4
33	Joseph	Meed	4
34	John	Gee	1
35	William	Gee	3
36	Cobus	Crankhite	1
37	Cobus	Crankhite Jnr:	1
38	David	Austin	1
39	Caleb	Brundidge	1
	Page 417		
40	Nathaniel	Tompkins	2
41	Cornelis	Fuller	1
42	John	Spragge	1
43	Samuell	Calkin	2
44	John	Hains	2
45	Thomas	Frost	2
46	Eleazer	Cole	3
47	Edward	Gray	2
48	William	Teller	9
49	Abram	Smith	4
50	Luke	Covert	1
51	Samuell	Jones	1
52	Elie	Nellson	1
53	Nathaniel	Hatch	5
54	Valentine	Perkins	2
55	Samuell	Field	17
56	Joseph	Field	7
57	James	Dicketson	6
58	Amos	Dicketson	4
59	John	Dicketson	3
60	Daniel	Townsend	4
61	Robert	Townsend	1
62	Thomas	Townsend	1
63	Elihu	Townsend	5
64	Charles	Townsend	2
65	Zebulon	Townsend	2
66	Benjamin	Townsend	3
67	Robert U:	Townsend	1
68	Robert R:	Townsend	3
69	Daniel	Townsend Jnr:	1
70	Benjamin	Arnold	1
71	Daniel D.	Townsend	1
72	Jesse	Smith	4
73	Benjamin	Brundidge	4
74	Michael	Shaw	1
75	Caleb	Hayser	1
76	Samuell	Gates	1
77	William	Rapelyea	5
78	John	Barber	2
79	Peter	Hartwell	2
80	Isaac	Chapman	2
81	Deacon	Hamblin	6
	Page 418		
82	Shubal	Rowly	2
83	Jacob	Philip	1
84	Caleb	Sweet	2
85	William	Palmer	1
86	John	Newberry	5
87	Samuell	Other	3
88	Peter	Paddock	2
89	Thomas	Paddock	2
90	Daniel	Bradly	1
91	Russell	Gregory	1
92	John	White	1
93	Jacob	Ellis	4
94	Philip	Cannon	1
95	George	Curry	2
96	Isaac	Terhill	1
97	Sander	Dewell	1
98	Robert	Farringtons Widw:	1
99	James	McReedy farm	2

June 1756 continued

	Name	Surname	Value		Name	Surname	Value
100	Nathanll:	Byngton	2	154	John	Paddock	1
101	Jacob	Finch	2	155	Ezekiel	Meed	1
102	Thomas	Philip	5	156	Israel	Taylor	2
103	Ebenezer	King	1	157	William	Hill	5
104	Josiah	Baker	3	158	Peter	Robinson	1
105	Leut:	Taylor	3	159	Abram	Hodges	2
106	Isaac	Crosby	1	160	Ebenezer	Hamblin	1
107	Benjamin	Sears	3	161	Isaac	Otter	1
108	Hesekiah	Kercomb	2	162	Elemuel	Kelk	1
109	Christopher	Fowler	4	163	Seth	Paddock	4
110	Peter	Angerine	5	164	Ebenezer	Jones Jnr:	2
111	Simon	Ryders	3		*Page 420*		
112	Joseph	Philip	1	165	Aaron	Calkin	1
113	Isaac	Haws	2	166	Theophilus	Jones	1
114	Seth	Covell	1	167	Joshua	Hamblin	3
115	Thomas	Smith	1	168	Elisha	Cole	1
116	Oliver	Gray	2	169	Robert	Weekson	1
117	Edward	Gray Jnr:	2	170	Gabriel	Nap	5
118	Samuell	Banks	2	171	John	Hopkins	1
119	Nathaniel	Forster	2	172	John	Van Tessell	1
120	Samuell	Ellwell	2	173	Mr:	Kent	6
121	David	Cosby	3	174	Jonathan	Austin	3
122	Joshua	Cosby	3	175	John	Kelly	1
123	Jaby	Berry	1	176	Thomas	Kelly	1
	Page 419			177	Isaac	Peirce	2
124	Joseph	Taylor	1	178	William	Stone	2
125	Isaac	Smith	2	179	Noah	Burbancks	1
126	Hope	Covey	4	180	David	Smith	1
127	John	Covey	1	181	Edmund	Baker	1
128	Jonathan	Paddock	1	182	Caleb	Chase	1
129	Edward	Hall	2	183	Ebenezer	Chase	1
130	Nathan	Green	2	184	James	Sears	4
131	Seth	Nickerson	1	185	Peter	Hall	2
132	Will	Daily's farm	2	186	Nathaniel	Houses farm	1
133	Timothy	Clawson	1	187	Thomas	Gage	2
134	Benjamin	Roberts	1	188	Elisha	Calkin	1
135	James	Loveless	1	189	Samuell	Calkin Jnr:	1
136	Hickin	Bottom	1	190	Samuell	Goodspeed	2
137	Elisha	Luttington	3	191	Old	Bobbit	3
138	David	Honeywell	1	192	Shubal	Rowly	1
139	Benjamin	Parish	2	193	John	Mahew	1
140	Daniel	Parish	1	194	John	Merrick	3
141	Jonathan	Sturdefunt	2	195	Moody	House	2
142	William	Sturdefunt	1	196	James	Cowen	1
143	David	Sturdefunt	1	197	Edward	Hall	1
144	Mathew	Bump	1	198	Ezekiel	Burgis	1
145	Samuell	More	1	199	Jonathan	Kelly	1
146	Isaac	Horton	2	200	Francis	Baker	1
147	Jonathan	Lane	4	201	Uriah	Lawrence	3
148	Jo:	Concklin	1	202	Eleazer	Spragge	1
149	Richard	Roads	1	203	Nathaniel	Porter	5
150	Michael	Slott	1	204	Jo	Chittenton	1
151	John	Penny	1		*Page 421*		
152	William	Penny	3	205	Moses	Gregory	2
153	Tom	Foster	2	206	William	Rise	1

June 1756 continued

#	Name	Surname	Value
207	Joseph	Craw	1
208	Ebenezer	Craw	1
209	Elisha	Banks	1
210	John	Scribner	1
211	Shubal	Wixon	1
212	Jonathan	Hill	1
213	Jo	Barly	1
214	Christopher	Bobbit	1
215	Widw:	Dickensons farm	4
216	Malthia	Hatch	3
217	Peleg	Ballard	1
218	Peleg	Ballard Jnr:	1
219	Seth	Merrick	2
220	Gideon	Ellis	1
221	Thomas	Colwill	2
222	Amos	Fuller	1
223	William	Ballard	1
224	Cornelis	Tompkins	3
225	Simon	Ellis	1
226	Samuell	Fuller	1
227	John	Meeks	2
228	Isaac	Barton	2
229	Nathaniel	Bailiff	2
230	Robert	Ryders	4
231	John	Field	3
232	Philip	Paddock	2
233	Benjamin	Perry	2
234	James	Quinby	4
235	Zachary	Paddock Jnr:	2
236	Stephen	Field	1
237	Joshua	Moss	1
238	John	Nellson	1
239	Moses	Nauthrop	5
240	Nathan	Birdsell	10
241	Jeremiah	Linkhorn	1
242	John	Manly	1
243	Silas	Paddock	1
244	Moses	Dusenbury	4
245	Daniel	Crawford	2

Page 422

#	Name	Surname	Value
246	Edward	Ganung	1
247	Daniel	Philip	1
248	Samuell	Peter	5
249	Ben:	Brundidge Jnr:	1
250	Lazarus	Griffen	1
251		Edderton	1
252	Bethuel	Barnam	1
253	Joseph	Philip	1
254	Zachary	Paddock	2
255	Abner	Bang	2
256	Jeremiah	Baily	1
257	Will:	Grays Son William	1
258	Robert	Weeksons Son Peleg	1
259	Rowland	Perry	1
260	Mathew	Rowly	1
261	Noah	Smith	1
262	Elijah	Wixson	1
263	Joshua	Hinkle	1
264	John	How	2
265	Isc:	Smths: Brother Charles	1
266	Jonathan	Lockwood	2
267	Isaac	Perry	1
268	Mathias	Burgis	4
269	Rufus	Coles	1
270	Isaiah	Jaycocks	1
271	Daniel	Runnells	1
272	William	Nellson	2
273	John	Birdsell	1
274	Moses	Hustis	1
275	Elisha	Kelk	1
276	Jonathan	Bryant	2
277	William	Lane	1
278	John	Ryder	3
279	William	Dusenbury	2
280	John	Lane	1
281	Joseph	Hopkins	4
282	John	Green	2
283	Thomas	Higgins	1
284	Thomas	Hinkly	1
285	Josiah	Hinkly	1
286	Israel	Cole	2
287	Abram	Underhill	1

Page 423

#	Name	Surname	Value
288	James	Russell	1
289	John	Lawrence	2
290	John	McFarthing	2
291	Teunis	Krankhites Jonse	1
292	Thomas	Clemens	3
293	Sibet	Krankhite	1
294	Abram	Krankhite	1
295	Teunis	Brewer	1
296	Daniel	Taylor	1
297	John	Simkins	1
298	Joseph	Underwood	1
299	William	Shaw	1
300	Michael	Shaw Jnr:	1
301	Elisha	Meed	1
302	Adrew	Hill	3
303	Will	Chatterton	1
304	Stephen	Farrington	1
305	Gilbert	Concklin	2
306	John	Haddy	3
307	Henry	Hanes	1
308	Andrew	Burgis Jnr:	1
309	David	Akins	3
310	Peter	Ryal	1

June 1756 continued

	Name	Surname	Value		Name	Surname	Value
311	Jeremiah	Hueston	1	352	John	Curtiss	1
312	William	Marsh	1	353	John	Wright	1
313	Israel	Honeywell	5	354	Silas	Washburn	2
314	Thomas	Haviland	5	355	Samuell	Brewer	1
315	Thomas	Oakly	5	356	John	Price	1
316	John	Clark	1	357	Ebert	Herriton	1
317	Ruben	Hamblin	1	358	Richard	Hoppe	1
318	Robert	Fuller	1	359	Richard	Arundall	1
319	Jeremiah	Giffords	2	360	Hezekiah	Meed	1
320	Heman	King	1	361	William	Tellers Son	1
321	Jonathan	Hopkins	1	362	Joshua	Barnum	2
322	Joseph	Brooks	1	363	Timothy	Stephens	3
323	Peter	Purdy	1	364	Joshua	Porter	2
324	Ezekiel	Meed	2	365	James	Colwill	2
325	Nehemiah	Wood	1	366	Ezekiel	Gee	2
326	Christopher	Ellis	1	367	Samll:	Drake	1
327	Humfry	Ruff	1	368	Uriah	Drake	1
328	Philip	Ruff	1	369	Joshua	Tompkins	2
329	William	Dean	1	370	Josiah	Ingerson	2
Page 424				371	Richard	Griffen	1
330	Collo:	Willets farm	5	*Page 425*			
331	Joseph	Merrits farm	5	372	Joseph	Waters	2
332	Abraham	Du Bois	2	373	Benjamin	Underhill	1
333	John	Baker	1	374	Michael	Lownsbury	1
334	Nathan	Taylor Jnr:	1	375	William	McReedy	1
335	Joseph	Viccorie	1	376	Isaac	Garrison	1
336	Ruben	Kelly	1	377	Henry	Boice	1
337	Justice	Whealer	1	378	Joshua	Gea	1
338	John	Jones	1	379	David	Meruce	1
339	Fredrick	Gea	1	380	John	Langdon	2
340	Walter	Hueson	1	381	Isaac	Langdon	1
341	Oliver	Odell	1	382	John	Langdon Isaac's Broth:	1
342	James	Standly	1	383	—	Fowler & Dennis on Nathanll: Robin[son]s farm	2
343	John	Ferris	1	384	Nathaniel	Robinson Jnr:	1
344	John	Slott	1	385	Ebenezer	Robinson	1
345	Uriah	Hill	3	386	Simon	Deason	2
346	William	Dean	1	387	Benjamin	Perry Jnr:	1
347	Moses	Brundidge	1				£831
348	Thomas	Underhill	1				
349	Solomon	Ferrington	1				
350	Jonathan	Kent	1				
351	Henry	Terbos Jnr:	1				

February 1757
Southern Precinct

at 4 pence / pound

#	Name	Surname	Value	#	Name	Surname	Value
	Page 530			49	Luke	Covert	1
1	Francis	Nellson	7	50	Samuell	Jones	1
2	Thomas	Davinport	14	51	Elie	Nellson	1
3	Thomas	Davinport Jnr:	16	52	Nathaniel	Hatch	5
4	Jacob	Mandavil	11	53	Valentine	Perkins	2
5	David	Hustis	10	54	Samuell	Field	18
6	John	Calkin	2	55	Joseph	Field	7
7	John	Calkin Jnr:	1	56	James	Dickenson	6
8	William	Gray	5	57	Amos	Dickenson	4
9	John	Rogers	12	58	John	Dickenson	4
10	Abram	Otter	1	59	Daniel	Townsend	4
11	Elijah	Tompkins	5	60	Robert	Townsend	1
12	Thomas	Kellick	1	61	Thomas	Townsend	1
13	John	Van Amburgh	14	62	Elihu	Townsend	5
14	Henry	Van Amburghs Widw:	5	63	Charles	Townsend	2
				64	Zebulon	Townsend	2
15	Peter	Du Boys	17	65	Benjamin	Townsend	3
16	Ebenezer	Jones Near the River	3	66	Robert U:	Townsend	1
				67	Robert R:	Townsend	3
17	Benjamin	Jaycocks	3	68	Daniel	Townsend Jnr:	1
18	Timothy	Concklin	3	69	Benjamin	Arnold	1
19	Nathan	Lane	3	70	Daniel D.	Townsend	1
20	George	Hueston	5	71	Jesse	Smith	4
21	Joseph	Crane	1	72	Benjamin	Brundidge	5
22	Joseph	Gregory	1		*Page 532*		
23	William	Drake	4	73	Michael	Shaw	1
24	Sias	Gregory	4	74	Caleb	Hayser	1
25	John	Drake	1	75	Samuell	Gates	1
26	Isaac	Rodes	5	76	William	Rapelyea	5
27	Joseph	Crane Jnr:	1	77	John	Barber	2
28	David	Paddock	1	78	Peter	Hartwell	2
29	William	Yerns Widw:	1	79	Deacon	Hamblin	6
30	John	Smith	2	80	Shubal	Rowly	2
	Page 531			81	Jacob	Philip	1
31	Joseph	Lane	3	82	Caleb	Sweet	2
32	Joseph	Meed	4	83	William	Palmer	1
33	John	Gee	1	84	John	Newberry	5
34	William	Gee	3	85	Samuell	Other	2
35	Cobus	Crankhite	1	86	Peter	Paddock	2
36	Cobus	Crankhite Jnr:	2	87	Thomas	Paddock	1
37	David	Austin	1	88	Daniel	Bradly	1
38	Caleb	Brundidge	1	89	Russell	Gregory	1
39	Nathaniel	Tompkins	2	90	John	White	1
40	Cornelis	Fuller	1	91	Jacob	Ellis	4
41	John	Spragge	1	92	Philip	Cannon	1
42	Samuell	Calkin	2	93	George	Cary	2
43	John	Hains	2	94	Isaac	Terhills Widw:	1
44	Thomas	Frost	2	95	Sander	Dewell	1
45	Eleazer	Cole	2	96	Robert	Farringtons Widw:	1
46	Edward	Gray	2	97	James	McReedy farm	1
47	William	Teller	9	98	Nathaniel	Byngton	2
48	Abram	Smith	3	99	Jacob	Finch	2

February 1757 continued

	Name	Surname	Value		Name	Surname	Value
100	Ths:	Philip	5	154	Peter	Robinson	1
101	Ebenezer	King	1	155	Abram	Hodges	2
102	Josiah	Baker	4	156	Ebenezer	Hamblin	2
103	Leut:	Taylor	3	157	Isaac	Otter	1
104	Isaac	Crosby	1		*Page 534*		
105	Benjamin	Sears	3	158	Elemuel	Kelk	1
106	Hesekiah	Kercomb	1	159	Seth	Paddock	4
107	Christopher	Fowler	4	160	Ebenezer	Jones Jnr:	2
108	Peter	Angerine	5	161	Aaron	Calkin	1
109	Simon	Ryders	3	162	Theophilus	Jones	1
110	Isaac	Chapman	2	163	Joshua	Hamblin	3
111	Isaac	Hoss	2	164	Robert	Weekson	1
112	Thomas	Smith	1	165	Gabriel	Knap	5
113	Oliver	Gray	1	166	John	Van Tassell	1
114	Edward	Gray Jnr:	2	167	Mr:	Kent	6
115	Samuell	Banks	2	168	Jonathan	Austin	3
	Page 533			169	John	Kelly	1
116	Nathaniel	Forster	2	170	Thomas	Kelly	1
117	Samuell	Ellwell	2	171	Isaac	Peirce	2
118	David	Cosby	3	172	William	Stone	2
119	Joshua	Cosby	3	173	Noah	Burbancks	1
120	Jaby	Berry	1	174	David	Smith	1
121	Joseph	Taylor	1	175	Edmund	Baker	1
122	Isaac	Smith	2	176	Caleb	Chase	1
123	Hope	Covey	5	177	Ebenezer	Chase	1
124	John	Covey	1	178	James	Sears	4
125	Jonathan	Paddock	1	179	Peter	Hall	2
126	Edward	Hall	2	180	Nathaniel	House's farm	1
127	Nathan	Green	2	181	Thomas	Gage	2
128	Seth	Nickerson	1	182	Elisha	Calkin	1
129	Will	Dailys farm	2	183	Samuel	Calkin Jnr:	1
130	Timothy	Clawson	1	184	Samuell	Good speed	2
131	Benjamin	Roberts	1	185	Old	Bobbit	3
132	James	Loveless	1	186	Shubal	Rowly	1
133	Hickin	Bottom	1	187	John	Mahew	1
134	Elisha	Luttington	4	188	John	Merrick	3
135	David	Honeywell	1	189	Moody	House	2
136	Benjamin	Parish	2	190	James	Cowen	1
137	Daniel	Parish	1	191	Elisha	Cole	2
138	Jonathan	Sturdefunt	2	192	John	Hall	1
139	William	Sturdefunt	1	193	Ezekiel	Burgis	1
140	David	Sturdefunt	1	194	Jonathan	Kelly	1
141	Mathew	Bump	1	195	Francis	Baker	1
142	Samuell	More	1	196	Uriah	Lawrence	3
143	Isaac	Horton	2	197	Eleazer	Spragge	1
144	Jonathan	Lane	5	198	Nathaniel	Porter	5
145	Jo:	Concklin	1	199	Moses	Gregory	2
146	Richard	Roads	1		*Page 535*		
147	Michael	Slott	1	200	William	Rice	1
148	William	Penny	3	201	Joseph	Craw	1
149	Tom:	Foster	2	202	Ebenezer	Craw	1
150	John	Paddock	1	203	Elisha	Banks	1
151	Ezekiel	Meed	2	204	John	Scribner	1
152	Israel	Taylor	1	205	Jonathan	Hill	1
153	William	Hill	6	206	Jo	Barly	1

February 1757 continued

#	Name	Surname	Value
207	Christopher	Bobbit	1
208	Christopher	Dickenson's farm	4
209	Malthia	Hatch	3
210	Peleg	Ballard	1
211	Peleg	Ballard Jnr:	1
212	Seth	Merrick	2
213	Gideon	Ellis	1
214	Thomas	Colwill	2
215	Amos	Fuller	1
216	William	Ballard	1
217	Cornelius	Tompkins	3
218	Simon	Ellis	1
219	Samuell	Fuller	1
220	John	Meeks	2
221	Isaac	Barton	2
222	Nathaniel	Bailiff	2
223	Robert	Ryders	4
224	John	Field	3
225	Philip	Paddock	2
226	Benjamin	Perry	2
227	James	Quinby	4
228	Zachary	Paddock Jnr:	2
229	Stephen	Field	1
230	Joshua	Moss	1
231	John	Nellson	1
232	Moses	Nauthrop	5
233	Jonathan [Nathan]	Birdsell	10
234	Jeremiah	Linkhorn	1
235	John	Manly	1
236	Silas	Paddock	1
237	Moses	Dusenbury	3
238	Daniel	Crawford	1
239	Edward	Ganung	1
240	Daniel	Philip	1
241	Samuell	Peter	5

Page 536

#	Name	Surname	Value
242	Ben:	Brundidge Jnr:	1
243	Lazarus	Griffen	1
244	Bethual	Barnam	1
245	Joseph	Philip	1
246	Zachary	Paddock	2
247	Abner	Bang	2
248	Jeremiah	Baily	1
249	William	Grays Son Wm.	1
250	Robt:	Weeksons Son Peleg	1
251	Rowland	Perry	1
252	Mathew	Rowly	1
253	Noah	Smith	1
254	Elijah	Weekson	1
255	Joshua	Hinkle	1
256	John	How	2
257	Jonathan	Lockwood	1
258	Isaac	Perry	1
259	Mathias	Burgis	4
260	Rufus	Coles	1
261	Isaiah	Jaycocks	1
262	Daniel	Runnells	1
263	William	Nellson	2
264	John	Birdsell	1
265	Moses	Hustis	1
266	Elisha	Kelk	1
267	Jonathan	Bryant	1
268	William	Lane	1
269	John	Ryder	3
270	William	Dusenbury	4
271	John	Lane	1
272	Joseph	Hopkins	4
273	John	Green	2
274	Thomas	Higgins	1
275	Thomas	Hinkly	1
276	Josiah	Hinkly	1
277	Israel	Cole	2
278	Abram	Underhill	1
279	James	Russell	1
280	John	Lawrence	2
281	John	McFarthing	2
282	Teunis	Krankhites Jonse	1
283	Thomas	Clemens	3
284	Sibet	Krankhite	1

Page 537

#	Name	Surname	Value
285	Abram	Krankhite	1
286	Teunis	Brewer	1
287	Daniel	Taylor	2
288	John	Simkins	1
289	Joseph	Underwood	1
290	William	Shaw	1
291	Michael	Shaw Jnr:	1
292	Elisha	Meed	1
293	Andrew	Hill	3
294	Will	Chatterton	1
295	Stephen	Farrington	1
296	Gilbert	Concklin	2
297	John	Haddy	3
298	Henry	Hanes	1
299	Andrew	Burgis Jnr:	1
300	David	Akins	6
301	Peter	Ryal	1
302	Jeremiah	Hueston	1
303	William	Mash	1
304	Israel	Honeywel	5
305	John	Clarke	1
306	Ruben	Hamblin	1
307	Robert	Fuller	1
308	Jeremiah	Giffords	2
309	Heman	King	1
310	Jonathan	Hopkins	1
311	Joseph	Brooks	1
312	Ezekiel	Meed	2
313	Nehemiah	Wood	1

February 1757 continued

	Name	Surname	Value		Name	Surname	Value
314	Christopher	Ellis	1	356	Benjamin	Underhill	2
315	Humfry	Ruff	1	357	Michael	Lownsburg	1
316	Philip	Ruff	1	358	William	McCreedy	1
317	William	Dean	1	359	Henry	Boyce	1
318	Joseph	Merrits farm	5	360	Joshua	Gea	1
319	Abraham	Du Boys	2	361	David	Meruce	1
320	John	Baker	1	362	John	Langdon	2
321	Nathan	Taylor Jnr:	1	363	Isaac	Langdon	1
322	Joseph	Viccorie	1	364	John	Langdon Isaac's Brother	1
323	Ruben	Kelly	1				
324	Justice	Wheeler	1	365	—	Fowler & Dennis on Natll: Robs: farm	2
325	John	Jones	1				
326	Fredrick	Gea	1	366	Nathaniel	Robinson Jnr:	1
Page 538				367	Ebenezer	Robinson	1
327	Walter	Hueson	1	368	Simon	Deacon	2
328	Oliver	Odell	1	*Page 539*			
329	James	Standly	1	369	Benjamin	Perry Jnr:	1
330	John	Ferris	2	370	Josiah	Ingerson	2
331	John	Slott	1	371	Abram	Mabee	2
332	Uriah	Hill	2	372	Abram	Mabee Jnr:	1
333	Moses	Brundidge	1	373	Isaac	Fitch	2
334	Thomas	Underhill	1	374	John	Rodes	1
335	Solomon	Ferrington	1	375	Benjamin	Odel	1
336	Jonathan	Kent	1	376	Thomas	Crosbary	3
337	Henry	Ter Bos Jnr:	2	377	John	Cronckhite	1
338	John	Wright	1	378	John	Tarbell	1
339	Silas	Washburn	2	379	John	Williams	1
340	Samuell	Brewer	1	380	Samuel	Carll	1
341	Ebert	Herriton	1	381	Samuel	Yeomans	1
342	Richard	Hoppe	1	382	Cornelis	Gea	1
343	Richard	Arundal	1	383	George	Fields	1
344	Hezekiah	Meed	1	384	Jonathan	Jones	1
345	William	Tellers Son	1	385	Philip	Philips	1
346	Joshua	Barnum	3	386	Mathew	Benedicts farm on the: Oblong	1
347	Timothy	Stephens	2				
348	Joshua	Porter	2	387	Daniel	Sunderhill	1
349	James	Colwill	2	388	Samuell	Mora	1
350	Ezekiel	Gee	2	389	Jeremiah	Springsteen	1
351	Samuell	Drake	1	390	Jonathan	Lane Jnr:	1
352	Uriah	Drake	1	391	George	Cooper	1
353	Joshua	Tompkins	2	392	Abram	Moss	1
354	Richard	Griffen	1				£832
355	Joseph	Waters	2				

SUPERVISOR'S RECORD 1757 to 1761, VOLUME F
DUTCHESS COUNTY CLERKS OFFICE

JUNE 1757
SOUTHERN PRECINCT

at 2 shillings / pound

#	Name	Surname	Value
	Page 3		
1	Francis	Nellson	6
2	Thomas	Davinport	14
3	Thomas	Davinport Jnr:	16
4	Jacob	Mandavill	11
5	David	Hustis	10
6	John	Calkin	2
7	John	Calkin Jnr:	1
8	William	Gray	4
9	John	Rogers	12
10	Abram	Otter	1
11	Elijah	Tompkins	4
12	Thomas	Hellick	1
13	John	Van Amburgh	14
14	Peter	Du Boys	17
15	Ebenezer	Jones Near the River	3
16	Benjamin	Jaycocks	3
17	Timothy	Conklin	2
18	Nathan	Lane	3
19	George	Hueston	5
20	Joseph	Crane	1
21	Joseph	Gregory	1
22	William	Drake	4
23	Sias	Gregory	4
24	John	Drake	1
25	Isaac	Rodes	5
26	Joseph	Crane Jnr:	1
27	David	Paddock	1
28	William	Yerns Widw:	1
29	John	Smith	2
30	Joseph	Lane	3
31	Joseph	Meed	4
32	John	Gee	1
33	William	Gee	3
34	Cobus	Crankhite	1
35	Cobus	Crankhite Jnr:	2
36	David	Austin	1
37	Caleb	Brundidge	1
38	Nathaniel	Tompkins	1
39	Cornelis	Fuller	1
	Page 4		
40	John	Spragge	1
41	Samuell	Calkin	2
42	John	Hains	2
43	Thomas	Frost	2
44	Eleazer	Cole	2
45	Edward	Gray	2
46	William	Teller	9
47	Abram	Smith	3
48	Luke	Covert	1
49	Samuell	Jones	1
50	Elie	Nellson	1
51	Nathaniel	Hatch	5
52	Valentine	Perkins	2
53	Samuell	Field	18
54	Joseph	Field	7
55	James	Dickenson	6
56	Amos	Dickenson	3
57	John	Dickenson	4
58	Daniel	Townsend	4
59	Robert	Townsend	1
60	Thomas	Townsend	1
61	Elihu	Townsend	5
62	Charles	Townsend	2
63	Zebulon	Townsend	2
64	Benjamin	Townsend	3
65	Robert U:	Townsend	1
66	Robert R:	Townsend	3
67	Daniel	Townsend Jnr:	1
68	Benjamin	Arnold	1
69	Daniel D.	Townsend	1
70	Jesse	Smith	4
71	Benjamin	Brundidge	4
72	Michael	Shaw	1
73	Caleb	Hayser	1
74	Samuell	Gates	1
75	William	Rapelyea	5
76	John	Barber	2
77	Peter	Hartwell	2
78	Deacon	Hamblin	6
79	Jacob	Philip	1
80	Caleb	Sweet	2
81	William	Palmer	1
	Page 5		
82	John	Newberry	5
83	Samuell	Other	2
84	Peter	Paddock	2
85	Thomas	Paddock	1
86	Daniel	Bradly	1
87	Russell	Gregory	1
88	John	White	1
89	Jacob	Ellis	4
90	Philip	Cannon	1
91	George	Cary	2
92	Isaac	Ter Hills Widw:	1

June 1757 continued

	Name	Surname	Value		Name	Surname	Value
93	Sander	Dewell	1	147	Ezekiel	Meed	2
94	Robert	Farringtons Widw:	1	148	Israel	Taylor	1
95	James	McReeds farm	1	149	William	Hill	7
96	Nathaniel	Byngton	2	150	Peter	Robinson	1
97	Jacob	Finch	1	151	Abram	Hodges	2
98	Thomas	Philip	5	152	Ebenezer	Hamblin	2
99	Ebenezer	King	1	153	Isaac	Otter	1
100	Josiah	Baker	4	154	Elemuel	Kelk	1
101	Leut:	Taylor	3	155	Seth	Paddock	3
102	Isaac	Crosby	1	156	Ebenezer	Jones Jnr:	2
103	Benjamin	Sears	3	157	Abram [Aaron]	Calkin	1
104	Hesekiah	Kercomb	2	158	Theophilus	Jones	1
105	Christopher	Fowler	1	159	Joshua	Hamblin	3
106	Peter	Angevine	5	160	Robert	Weekson	1
107	Simon	Ryder	3	161	Gabriel	Knap	5
108	Isaac	Chapman	2	162	John	Van Tassell	1
109	Isaac	Hass	2	163	Mr:	Kent	6
110	Thomas	Smith	1	164	Jonathan	Austin	4
111	Oliver	Gray	1		*Page 7*		
112	Edward	Gray Jnr:	2	165	John	Kelly	1
113	Samuell	Banks	2	166	Thomas	Kelly	1
114	Nathaniel	Forster	2	167	Isaac	Peirce	2
115	Samuell	Ellwell	2	168	William	Stone	2
116	David	Cosby	3	169	Noah	Burbanks	1
117	Joshua	Cosby	3	170	David	Smith	1
118	Jaby	Berry	1	171	Edmund	Baker	1
119	Joseph	Taylor	1	172	Caleb	Chase	1
120	Isaac	Smith	2	173	Ebenezer	Chase	1
121	Hope	Covey	5	174	James	Sears	4
122	John	Covey	1	175	Peter	Hall	2
	Page 6			176	Nathaniel	Houses farm	1
123	Jonathan	Paddock	1	177	Thomas	Gage	2
124	Nathan	Green	2	178	Elisha	Calkin	1
125	Seth	Nickerson	1	179	Samuel	Calkin Jnr:	1
126	Timothy	Clawson	1	180	Samuel	Goodspeed	2
127	Benjamin	Roberts	1	181	Old	Bobbits farm	2
128	James	Loveless	1	182	John	Mahew	1
129	Hickin	Buttom	1	183	John	Merrick	3
130	Elisha	Luttington	3	184	Moody	House	2
131	David	Honeywell	1	185	James	Cowen	1
132	Benjamin	Parish	2	186	Elisha	Cole	2
133	Daniel	Parish	1	187	John	Hall	1
134	Jonathan	Sturdefunt	1	188	Ezekiel	Burgis	1
135	William	Sturdefunt	1	189	Jonathan	Kelly	1
136	David	Sturdefunt	1	190	Francis	Baker	1
137	Mathew	Bump	1	191	Uriah	Lawrence	3
138	Samuel	More	1	192	Eleazer	Spragge	1
139	Isaac	Horton	2	193	Nathaniel	Porter	5
140	Jonathan	Lane	4	194	Moses	Gregory	2
141	Jo:	Conklin	1	195	William	Rice	1
142	Richard	Roads	1	196	Joseph	Craw	1
143	Michael	Slott	1	197	Ebenezer	Craw	1
144	William	Penny	3	198	Elisha	Bangs	1
145	Tom:	Foster	2	199	Jonathan	Hill	1
146	John	Paddock	1	200	Jo	Barly	1

June 1757 continued

	Name	Surname	Value		Name	Surname	Value
201	Christopher	Bobbit	1	254	Daniel	Runnells	1
202	Malthia	Hatch	1	255	William	Nellson	1
203	Peleg	Ballard	1	256	John	Birdsell	1
204	Peleg	Ballard Jnr:	1	257	Moses	Huestis	1
	Page 8			258	Elisha	Kelk	1
205	Seth	Merrick	2	259	Jonathan	Bryant	1
206	Gideon	Ellis	1	260	William	Lane	1
207	Thomas	Colwill	2	261	John	Ryder	3
208	Amos	Fuller	1	262	William	Dusenbury	4
209	William	Ballard	1	263	John	Lane	2
210	Cornelis	Tompkins	3	264	Joseph	Hopkins	4
211	Simon	Ellis	1	265	John	Green	2
212	Samuell	Fuller	1	266	Thomas	Higgins	1
213	John	Meeks	2	267	Thomas	Hinkly	1
214	Isaac	Barton	1	268	Josiah	Hinkly	1
215	Nathaniel	Bailiff	2	269	Israel	Cole	1
216	Robert	Ryders	3	270	Abram	Underhill	1
217	John	Field	3	271	James	Russell	1
218	Philip	Paddock	2	272	John	Lawrence	2
219	Benjamin	Perry	2	273	John	McFarthing	1
220	James	Quinby	4	274	Teunis	Krankhites Johnse	1
221	Zachary	Paddock Jnr:	2	275	Thomas	Clemens	2
222	Stephen	Field	1	276	Sibet	Krankhite	1
223	Joshua	Moss	1	277	Abram	Krankhite	1
224	John	Nellson	1	278	Teunis	Brewer	1
225	Moses	Nauthrop	5	279	Daniel	Taylor	1
226	Jonathan [Nathan]	Birdsell	9	280	John	Simkins	1
227	Jeremiah	Linkhorn	1	281	Joseph	Underwood	1
228	John	Manly	3	282	William	Shaw	1
229	Silas	Paddock	1	283	Michael	Shaw Jnr:	1
230	Moses	Dusenbury	3	284	Amos	Dickenson Jnr:	1
231	Daniel	Crawford	1	285	Elisha	Meed	2
232	Edward	Ganung	1	286	Andrew	Hill	3
233	Daniel	Philip	1	287	William	Chatterton	1
234	Samuell	Peter	5		*Page 10*		
235	Ben:	Brundidge Jnr:	1	288	Stephen	Farrington	1
236	Lazarus	Griffen	1	289	Gilbert	Conklin	2
237	Bethual	Barnam	1	290	John	Haddy	3
238	Joseph	Philip	1	291	Henry	Hanes	1
239	Zachary	Paddock	2	292	Andrew	Burgis Jnr:	1
240	Abner	Bang	2	293	David	Akins	5
241	Jeremiah	Baily	1	294	Peter	Ryal	1
242	Wm:	Grays Son William	1	295	Jeremiah	Hueston	1
243	Robt:	Weeksons Son Peleg	1	296	William	Mash	1
244	Joseph	Cromwell	4	297	Israel	Honeywell	5
245	Rowland	Perry	1	298	John	Clarke	1
246	Noah	Smith	1	299	Ruben	Hamblin	1
	Page 9			300	Robert	Fuller	1
247	Elijah	Weekson	1	301	Jeremiah	Giffords	2
248	Joshua	Hinkle	1	302	Heman	King	1
249	John	How	1	303	Jonathan	Hopkins	1
250	Jonathan	Lockwood	1	304	Joseph	Brooks	1
251	Isaac	Perry	1	305	Ezekiel	Meed	2
252	Mathias	Burgis	4	306	Nehemiah	Wood	1
253	Isaiah	Jaycocks	1	307	Christopher	Ellis	1

June 1757 continued

	Name	Surname	Value
308	Humfry	Ruff	1
309	Philip	Ruff	1
310	William	Dean	1
311	Joseph	Merrits farm	5
312	Abraham	DuBoys	2
313	John	Baker	1
314	Nathan	Taylor Jnr:	1
315	Joseph	Viccorie	1
316	Ruben	Kelly	1
317	John	Jones	1
318	Fredrick	Gea	1
319	Walter	Hueson	1
320	Oliver	Odell	1
321	James	Standly	4
322	John	Ferris	2
323	John	Scott	1
324	Uriah	Hill	2
325	Moses	Brundidge	1
326	John	Lamesie	1
327	Thomas	Underhill	1
328	Solomon	Ferrington	1
329	John	Wright	1

Page 11

	Name	Surname	Value
330	Silas	Washburn	2
331	Samuell	Brewer	1
332	Ebert	Herriton	1
333	Richard	Hoppe	1
334	Richard	Arundel	1
335	Hezekiah	Meed	1
336	William	Tellers Son	1
337	Joshua	Barnum	3
338	Timothy	Stevens	2
339	Joshua	Porter	2
340	James	Colwill	2
341	Ezekiel	Gee	1
342	Samuell	Drake	1
343	Uriah	Drake	1
344	Joshua	Tompkins	3
345	Richard	Griffen	1
346	Joseph	Waters	3
347	Benjamin	Underhill	2
348	Michael	Lounsburg	1
349	William	McCreedy	1
350	Henry	Boyce	1

	Name	Surname	Value
351	Joshua	Gea	1
352	John	Langdon	4
353	Isaac	Langdon	1
354	Jno:	Langdon Is' Brother	1
355	—	Fowler & Dennis on Natll: Robinsons farm	2
356	Nathaniel	Robinson Jnr:	1
357	Ebenezer	Robinson	1
358	Simon	Deacon	3
359	Benjamin	Perry Jnr:	1
360	Josiah	Ingerson	1
361	Abram	Mabee	2
362	Abram	Mabee Jnr:	1
363	Isaac	Fitch	2
364	John	Rodes	1
365	Benjamin	Odel	1
366	Daniel	Bull	1
367	Thomas	Crosbary	3
368	John	Crankhite	1
369	John	Tarbell	1
370	John	Williams	1

Page 12

	Name	Surname	Value
371	Samuel	Carll	1
372	Samuel	Yeomans	1
373	George	Fields	1
374	Jonathan	Jones	1
375	Philip	Philips	1
376	Matw:	Benedicts farm on the Oblong	1
377	Daniel	Sunderhill	1
378	Jeremiah	Springsteen	1
379	Jonathan	Lane Jnr:	1
380	George	Cooper	1
381	Abram	Moss	1
382	Benjamin	Gifford	3
383	Christopher	Dickenson	1
384	John	Bogardus	2
385	Henry	Krankhite	1
386	Gilson	Clap	3
387	Jonathan	Lane Jnr:	1
388	Richard	Griffen	1
389	Iccabud	Rose	2
			£812

February 1758
Southern Precinct

at 7 pence / pound

#	Name	Surname	Value	#	Name	Surname	Value
		Page 124		50	Elie	Nellson	1
1	Francis	Nellson	6	51	Nathaniel	Hatch	6
2	Thomas	Davinport	12	52	Valentine	Perkins	2
3	Thomas	Davinport Jnr:	16	53	Samuel	Field	16
4	Jacob	Mandavill	11	54	Joseph	Field	8
5	David	Hustis	10	55	James	Dickinson	8
6	John	Calkin	2	56	Amos	Dickinson	3
7	John	Calkin Jnr:	1			*Page 126*	
8	William	Gray	4	57	John	Dickenson	4
9	John	Rogers	12	58	Daniel	Townsend	4
10	Abram	Otter	1	59	Robert	Townsend	1
11	Elijah	Tompkins	4	60	Thomas	Townsend	1
12	Thomas	Hellick	1	61	Elihu	Townsend	4
13	John	Van Amburghs Estate	14	62	Charles	Townsend	2
14	Peter	Du Bois	17	63	Benjamin	Townsend	3
15	Ebenezer	Jones near the river	3	64	Robert U.	Townsend	1
				65	Robert R.	Townsend	3
		Page 125		66	Daniel	Townsend Jnr:	1
16	Benjamin	Jaycocks	3	67	Daniel D.	Townsend	1
17	Timothy	Conklin	2	68	Jesse	Smith	4
18	Nathan	Lane	3	69	Benjamin	Brundidge	6
19	George	Hueston	5	70	Michael	Shaw	1
20	Joseph	Crane	1	71	Caleb	Hayser	2
21	Joseph	Gregory	1	72	Samuel	Gates	1
22	William	Drake	4	73	William	Rapelyea	5
23	Sias	Gregory	4	74	John	Barber	2
24	John	Drake	1	75	Peter	Hartwell	2
25	Isaac	Rhodes	5	76	Dacon	Hamblin	7
26	Joseph	Crane Jnr:	1	77	Jacob	Philip	1
27	David	Paddock	1	78	Caleb	Sweet	2
28	William	Yerns Widw:	1	79	William	Palmer	1
29	John	Smith	2	80	John	Newberry	5
30	Joseph	Lane	3	81	Samuel	Other	2
31	Joseph	Meed	4	82	Peter	Paddock	2
32	John	Gee	4	83	Thomas	Paddock	1
33	William	Gee	3	84	Daniel	Bradly	1
34	Cobus	Krankhite	1	85	Russell	Gregory	1
35	Cobus	Kranhite Jnr:	2	86	John	White	1
36	David	Austin	1	87	Jacob	Ellis	3
37	Caleb	Brundidge	1	88	Philip	Cannon	1
38	Nathaniel	Tompkins	1	89	George	Cary	2
39	Cornelis	Fuller	1	90	Isaac	Terhills Widw:	1
40	John	Spragge	1	91	Sander	Dewell	1
41	Samuel	Calkin	2	92	Robert	Farringtons Widw:	1
42	John	Hains	2	93	James	Mc Reeds farm	1
43	Thomas	Frost	2	94	Nathaniel	Byington	2
44	Eleazer	Cole	2	95	Jacob	Finch	1
45	Edward	Gray	2	96	Thomas	Philip	5
46	William	Teller	9	97	Ebenezer	King	1
47	Abram	Smith	3			*Page 127*	
48	Luke	Covert	1	98	Josiah	Baker	4
49	Samuel	Jones	1	99	Lieut	Taylor	2

February 1758 continued

#	Name	Surname	Value
100	Isaac	Crosby	1
101	Benjamin	Sears	3
102	Christopher	Fowler	1
103	Peter	Angewine	5
104	Simon	Ryders	3
105	Isaac	Chapman	2
106	Isaac	Hause	1
107	Thomas	Smith	1
108	Oliver	Gray	1
109	Edward	Gray Jnr:	2
110	Samuel	Banks	2
111	Nathaniel	Forster	2
112	Samuel	Elwell	2
113	David	Cosby	3
114	Joshua	Cosby	3
115	Jaby	Berry	1
116	Joseph	Taylor	1
117	Isaac	Smith	2
118	Hope	Covey	5
119	John	Covey	1
120	Jonathan	Paddock	1
121	Nathan	Green	2
122	Seth	Nickerson	1
123	Timothy	Clawson	1
124	Benjamin	Roberts	1
125	James	Loveless	1
126	Hickin	Bottom	1
127	Elisha	Luttington	3
128	David	Honeywell	1
129	Benjamin	Parish	2
130	Daniel	Parish	1
131	Jonathan	Sturdefunt	1
132	William	Sturdefunt	1
133	David	Sturdefunt	1
134	Mathew	Bump	1
135	Samuel	Moore	1
136	Isaac	Horton	2
137	Jonathan	Lane	4
138	Jo:	Conklin	1

Page 128

#	Name	Surname	Value
139	Richard	Rodes	1
140	Michael	Slott	1
141	William	Penny	3
142	Tom	Foster	2
143	John	Paddock	1
144	Ezekiel	Meed	1
145	Israel	Taylor	1
146	William	Hill	7
147	Peter	Robinson	1
148	Abram	Hodges	2
149	Ebenezer	Hamblin	2
150	Isaac	Otter	2
151	Elemuel	Kelk	1
152	Seth	Paddock	2
153	Ebenezer	Jones Jnr:	2
154	Abram [Aaron]	Calkin	1
155	Theophilius	Jones	1
156	Joshua	Hamblin	3
157	Robert	Weekson	1
158	Gabriel	Knap	6
159	John	Van Tessell	1
160	Mr:	Kent	6
161	Jonathan	Austin	3
162	John	Kelly	1
163	Thomas	Kelly	1
164	Isaac	Peirce	3
165	William	Stone	2
166	Noah	Burbanks	1
167	David	Smith	1
168	Edmund	Baker	1
169	Caleb	Chase	1
170	Ebenezer	Chase	1
171	James	Sears	4
172	Peter	Hall	2
173	Nathanel	Houses farm	1
174	Thomas	Gage	2
175	Samuel	Goodspeed	2
176	Old	Bobbits farm	3
177	Elisha	Calkin	1
178	John	Mahew	1
179	John	Merrick	3

Page 129

#	Name	Surname	Value
180	Moody	House	2
181	James	Cowen	1
182	Elisha	Cole	2
183	John	Hall	1
184	Ezekiel	Burgis	1
185	Jonathan	Kelly	1
186	Francis	Baker	1
187	Uriah	Lawrence	3
188	Eleazer	Spragge	1
189	Nathaniel	Porter	4
190	Moses	Gregory	3
191	William	Rice	1
192	Joseph	Craw	1
193	Ebenezer	Craw	1
194	Elisha	Bangs	1
195	Jonathan	Hill	1
196	Jo:	Barly	1
197	Christopher	Bobbit	1
198	Malthia	Hatch	1
199	Peleg	Ballard	1
200	Peleg	Ballard Jnr:	1
201	Seth	Merrick	2
202	Thomas	Colwill	2
203	Amos	Fuller	1
204	William	Ballard	1
205	Cornelis	Tompkins	3
206	Simon	Ellis	1
207	John	Meeks	2

February 1758 continued

	Name	Surname	Value		Name	Surname	Value
208	Isaac	Barton	1	262	Josiah	Hinkly	1
209	Nathaniel	Bailiff	2	*Page 131*			
210	Robert	Ryders	3	263	Israel	Cole	1
211	John	Field	2	264	Abram	Underhill	1
212	Philip	Paddock	2	265	James	Russell	1
213	Benjamin	Perry	3	266	John	Lawrence	2
214	James	Quimby	3	267	John	McFarthing	1
215	Zachary	Paddock Jnr:	2	268	Tunis	Krankhite Johnse	1
216	Stephen	Field	3	269	Thomas	Clemens	2
217	Joshua	Moss	1	270	Sibet	Krankhite	1
218	John	Nellson	1	271	Abram	Krankhite	1
219	Moses	Nauthrop	4	272	Teunis	Brewer	1
220	Nathan	Birdsell	9	273	Daniel	Taylor	2
Page 130				274	John	Simkins	1
221	Jeremiah	Linkhorn	1	275	Joseph	Underwood	1
222	John	Manly	3	276	William	Shaw	1
223	Silas	Paddock	1	277	Michael	Shaw Jnr:	1
224	Moses	Dusenbury	3	278	Amos	Dickenson Jnr:	1
225	Daniel	Crawford	1	279	Elisha	Meed	1
226	Edward	Ganung	1	280	Andrew	Hill	3
227	Daniel	Philip	1	281	William	Chitterton	1
228	Samuel	Peters	5	282	Stephen	Farrington	1
229	Ben	Brundidge Jnr:	1	283	Gilbert	Conklin	2
230	Lazarus	Griffen	1	284	John	Haddy	3
231	Bethuel	Barnam	1	285	Andrew	Burgis Jnr:	1
232	Joseph	Philip	1	286	David	Akins	5
233	Zachary	Paddock	2	287	Peter	Ryal	1
234	Abner	Bang	2	288	Jeremiah	Hueston	1
235	Jeremiah	Baily	1	289	William	Marsh	1
236	Wm:	Grays Son Wm:	1	290	Israel	Honeywell	5
237	Robt:	Weeksons Son Peleg	1	291	John	Clarke	1
238	Joseph	Cromwel	4	292	Ruben	Hamblin	1
239	Rowland	Perry	1	293	Robert	Fuller	1
240	Noah	Smith	1	294	Jeremiah	Gifford	2
241	Elijah	Weekson	1	295	Heman	King	1
242	Joshua	Hinkle	1	296	Jonathan	Hopkins	1
243	John	How	1	297	Joseph	Brooks	1
244	John	Lockwood	1	298	Ezekiel	Meed	1
245	Isaac	Perry	1	299	Nehemiah	Wood	1
246	Mathias	Burgis	4	300	Christopher	Ellis	1
247	Isaiah	Jaycocks	1	301	Humfry	Ruff	1
248	David	Runnells	1	302	Philip	Ruff	1
249	William	Nellson	1	303	William	Dean	1
250	John	Birdsel	1	*Page 132*			
251	Moses	Huestis	1	304	Joseph	Merrits farm	5
252	Elisha	Kelk	1	305	John	Baker	1
253	Jonathan	Bryant	1	306	Nathan	Taylor Jnr:	1
254	William	Lane	1	307	Joseph	Viccory	1
255	John	Ryder	3	308	Ruben	Kelly	1
256	William	Dusenbury	3	309	John	Jones	1
257	John	Lane	1	310	Fredrick	Gea	1
258	Joseph	Hopkins	4	311	Walter	Hueson	1
259	John	Green	2	312	Oliver	Odle	1
260	Thomas	Higgins	1	313	James	Standly	1
261	Thomas	Kinkly [Hinkly]	1	314	John	Ferris	2

February 1758 continued

	Name	Surname	Value		Name	Surname	Value
315	John	Scott	1	367	Jonathan	Lane Jnr:	1
316	Uriah	Hill	4	368	George	Cooper	1
317	Moses	Brundidge	1	369	Abram	Moss	1
318	John	Lamesie	1	370	Benjamin	Gifford	3
319	Solomon	Ferrington	1	371	Christopher	Dickenson	1
320	John	Wright	1	372	John	Bogardus	2
321	Silas	Washburn	2	373	Henry	Crankhite	1
322	Samuel	Brewer	1	374	Cornelis	Cooper	1
323	Ebbert	Herriton	1	375	Gilson	Clap	3
324	Richard	Hoppe	1	376	Jonathan	Lane Jnr:	1
325	Richard	Arundal	1	377	Iccabud	Rose	1
326	Joshua	Barnam	3	378	Joseph	Stocker	1
327	Timothy	Stephens	2	379	Obediah	Basely	1
328	Joshua	Porter	2	380	Samuel	Elwell Jnr:	1
329	James	Colwill	2	381	Isaac	Elwell	1
330	Ezekiel	Gee	1	382	Jonathan	Hunlock	1
331	Samuel	Drake	1	383	Jacobs	Philips Jnr:	1
332	Uriah	Drake	1	384	John	Calkin 3rd:	1
333	Joshua	Tompkins	1	385	John	Clawson	1
334	Richard	Griffen	1		*Page 134*		
335	Joseph	Waters	3	386	Edward	Dolph or Wolf	1
336	Benjamin	Underhill	2	387	Joseph	Duwey	1
337	William	McReedy	1	388	Benjamin	Roberts Jnr:	1
338	Henry	Boyce	1	389	Augustine	Baseley	1
339	Joshua	Gee	1	390	Jehiel	Basely	1
340	John	Langdon	2	391	Ebenezer	Bennet	1
341	Isaac	Langdon	1	392	Old	Bennet	1
342	John	Langdon Is: Brother	1	393	William	Rapelje Jnr:	1
343	—	Fowler & Dennis on Nathll: Robn: Place	2	394	Elihu	Gage	1
				395	Anthony	Gage	1
344	Nathaniel	Robinson Jnr:	1	396	Moses	Gage	1
	Page 133			397	Richard	Wearing	1
345	Ebenezer	Robinson	1	398	John	Bloomer	1
346	Simon	Deacon	2	399	Thomas	Townsend Jnr:	1
347	Benjamin	Perry Jnr:	1	400	Christopher	Townsend	1
348	Josiah	Ingerson	3	401	Hugh	Baily	1
349	Abram	Mabee	2	402	Timothy	Sweet	1
350	Abram	Mabee Jnr:	1	403	James	Anderson	1
351	Isaac	Fitch	2	404	David	Paddock Jnr:	1
352	John	Rodes	1	405	John	Tomkins	1
353	Benjamin	Odle	1	406	Samuel	Benedict	1
354	Daniel	Bull	1	407	Jebes	Elwell	1
355	Thomas	Crossbary	3	408	Nathan	Crosby	1
356	John	Crankhite	1	409	John	Garrison	1
357	John	Tarwell	1	410	Amos	Pine	1
358	John	Williams	1	411	David	Burchad	1
359	Samuel	Carll	1	412	Thomas	Hodges Farm	1
360	Samuel	Yeomans	1	413	Elisha	Morehouse	1
361	George	Fields	1	414	Stephen	Rockwell	1
362	Jonathan	Jones	1	415	Elkeny	Hinkly	1
363	Philip	Philips	1	416	Elisha [Elijah]	White	1
364	Mathew	Benedicts farm on the Oblong	1	417	Azariah	Meed	1
				418	Edward	Rice	1
365	Daniel	Sunderhill	1	419	Ebenezer	Kelly	1
366	Jeremiah	Springsteen	1	420	Ephraim	Smith	1

February 1758 continued

#	Name	Surname	Value	#	Name	Surname	Value
421	William	Merrit	1	438	Elijah	Calkin	1
422	Joseph	Baker	1	439	Josiah	Benjamins	1
423	Thomas	Fowler	1	440	Simon	Covill	1
424	John	Bloomer Near the N. River	1	441	Joseph	Robins	1
				442	Josiah	Swift	1
425	Thomas	Cromw[e]ll	1	443	Josiah	Swift Jnr:	1
426	Robert	Bloomer	1	444	Gedeon	Crowfoot	1
	Page 135			445	John	Garrison near Wekepe	1
427	Nathaniel	Plumsteed	1				
428	James	Paddock	1	446	Thomas	Pew	1
429	Thomas	Nickerson	1	447	Daniel	Brundige	1
430	Joseph	Nickerson	1	448	Solomon	Jenkins	1
431	Ebenezer	Weekson	1	449	Solomon	Brundidge	1
432	John	Stephens	1	450	Benjamin	Serringe	1
433	Nathaniel	Hatch Jnr:	1	451	Thomas	Baxter	1
434	Jeremiah	Calkin Jnr:	1	452	Anthony	Hill	1
435	David	French	1	453	Samuel	Carter	2
436	Eliezer	Miller	1	454	John	Gean	3
437	John	Hill Jnr:	1				£873

JUNE 1758
SOUTHERN PRECINCT

at 2 shillings / pound

#	Name	Surname	Value	#	Name	Surname	Value
	Page 140			25	David	Paddock	1
1	Francis	Nellson	6	26	William	Yerns's Widw:	1
2	Thomas	Davinport	12	27	John	Smith	2
3	Thomas	Davinport Jnr:	16	28	Joseph	Lane	3
4	Jacob	Mandavill	10	29	Joseph	Meed	4
5	John	Calkin	2	30	John	Gee	4
6	John	Calkin Jnr:	1	31	William	Gee	3
7	William	Gray	4	32	Cobus	Krankhite Jnr:	2
8	John	Rogers	12	33	David	Austin	1
9	Elijah	Tompkins	4	34	Abram	Otter	1
10	Thomas	Hellick	1		*Page 141*		
11	John	Van Amburghs Estate	10	35	Caleb	Brundidge	1
12	Peter	Du Bois	16	36	Nathaniel	Tompkins	1
13	Ebenezer	Jones Near the river	3	37	Cornelius	Fuller	1
				38	John	Spragge	1
14	Benjamin	Jaycocks	3	39	Samuel	Calkin	2
15	Timothy	Concklin	2	40	John	Hains	2
16	Nathan	Lane	3	41	Thomas	Frost	1
17	George	Hueston	5	42	Eleazer	Cole	2
18	Joseph	Crane	1	43	Edward	Gray	2
19	Joseph	Gregory	1	44	William	Teller	9
20	William	Drake	4	45	Abram	Smith	3
21	Sias	Gregory	4	46	Luke	Covert	1
22	John	Drake	2	47	Samuel	Jones	1
23	Isaac	Rhodes	5	48	Elie	Nellson	1
24	Joseph	Crane Jnr:	1	49	Nathaniel	Hatch	7

June 1758 continued

	Name	Surname	Value
50	Valentine	Perkins	2
51	Samuel	Field	16
52	Joseph	Field	8
53	James	Dickinson	8
54	Amos	Dickinson	3
55	John	Dickenson	4
56	Daniel	Townsend	4
57	Robert	Townsend	1
58	Thomas	Townsend	1
59	Elihu	Townsend	4
60	Charles	Townsend	2
61	Benjamin	Townsend	3
62	Robert U.	Townsend	1
63	Robert R.	Townsend	3
64	Daniel	Townsend Jnr:	1
65	Daniel D.	Townsend	1
66	Jesse	Smith	4
67	Benjamin	Brundidge	6
68	Michael	Shaw	4
69	Caleb	Hayser	2
70	Samuel	Gates	1
71	William	Rapelyea	5
72	John	Barber	2
73	Peter	Hartwell	2
74	Dacon	Hamblin	7
75	Jacob	Philip	1

Page 142

	Name	Surname	Value
76	Caleb	Sweet	2
77	William	Palmer	1
78	John	Newberry	5
79	Samuel	Other	2
80	Peter	Paddock	2
81	Thomas	Paddock	1
82	Daniel	Bradly	1
83	Russell	Gregory	1
84	John	White	1
85	Jacob	Ellis	3
86	Philip	Cannon	1
87	George	Cary	2
88	Isaac	Terhill Widw:	1
89	Sander	Dewell	1
90	Robert	Farringtons Widw:	1
91	James	Mc Reeds farm	1
92	Jacob	Finch	1
93	Thomas	Philip	5
94	Ebenezer	King	1
95	Josiah	Baker	4
96	Lieut	Taylor	2
97	Isaac	Crosby	1
98	Benjamin	Sears	3
99	Christopher	Fowler	1
100	Peter	Angwine	5
101	Simon	Ryders	3
102	Isaac	Chapman	2
103	Isaac	Hause	1
104	Thomas	Smith	1
105	Oliver	Gray	1
106	Edward	Gray Jnr:	2
107	Samuel	Banks	2
108	Nathaniel	Forster	2
109	Samuel	Elwell	2
110	David	Cosby	3
111	Joshua	Cosby	3
112	Jaby	Berry	1
113	Joseph	Taylor	1
114	Isaac	Smith	2
115	Hope	Covey	5
116	John	Covey	1

Page 143

	Name	Surname	Value
117	Jonathan	Paddock	1
118	Nathan	Green	2
119	Seth	Nickerson	1
120	Timothy	Clawson	1
121	Benjamin	Roberts	1
122	Elisha	Luttington	3
123	David	Honeywell	1
124	Benjamin	Parish	2
125	Jonathan	Sturdefunt	1
126	William	Sturdefunt	1
127	David	Sturdefunt	1
128	Mathew	Bump	1
129	Samuel	More	1
130	Isaac	Horton	1
131	Jonathan	Lane	2
132	Jo:	Conklin	4
133	Richard	Roades	1
134	Michael	Slot	1
135	William	Penny	3
136	Tom	Forster	2
137	John	Paddock	1
138	Ezekiel	Meed	1
139	Israel	Taylor	1
140	William	Hill	7
141	Peter	Robinson	1
142	Abram	Hodges	2
143	Ebenezer	Hamblin	2
144	Isaac	Otter	2
145	Elemuel	Kelk	1
146	Seth	Paddock	2
147	Ebenezer	Jones Jnr:	2
148	Abram [Aaron]	Calkin	1
149	Theophilius	Jones	1
150	Joshua	Hamblin	3
151	Robert	Weekson	1
152	Gabriel	Knap	5
153	John	Van Tessell	4
154	Mr:	Kent	6
155	Jonathan	Austin	3
156	John	Kelly	1
157	Thomas	Kelly	1

June 1758 continued

#	Name	Surname	Value	#	Name	Surname	Value
	Page 144			211	John	Nellson	1
158	Isaac	Peirce	3	212	Moses	Nauthop	4
159	William	Stone	2	213	Nathan	Birdsell	9
160	Noah	Burbanks	1	214	Jeremiah	Linkhorn	1
161	David	Smith	1	215	John	Manly	3
162	Edmund	Baker	1	216	Silas	Paddock	1
163	Caleb	Chase	1	217	Moses	Dusenbury	3
164	Ebenezer	Chase	1	218	Edward	Ganung	1
165	James	Sears	4	219	Daniel	Philip	1
166	Peter	Hall	2	220	Samuel	Peters	5
167	Nathaniel	Hoses farm	1	221	Lazarus	Griffen	1
168	Thomas	Gage	2	222	Bethual	Barnam	1
169	Samuel	Goodspeed	2	223	Joseph	Philip	1
170	Old	Bobbits farm	3	224	Zachary	Paddock	2
171	Elisha	Calkin	1	225	Abner	Bang	2
172	John	Mahew	1	226	Jeremiah	Baily	1
173	John	Merrick	3	227	Wm:	Grays Son William	1
174	Moody	House	2	228	Robt:	Weeksons Son Peleg	1
175	James	Cowen	1	229	Joseph	Cromwel	3
176	Elisha	Cole	2	230	Rowland	Perry	1
177	John	Hall	1	231	Noah	Smith	1
178	Ezekiel	Burgis	1	232	Elijah	Weekson	1
179	Jonathan	Kelly	1	233	Joshua	Hinkle	1
180	Francis	Baker	1	234	John	How	1
181	Uriah	Lawrence	3	235	John	Lockwood	1
182	Eleazer	Sprage	1	236	Isaac	Perry	1
183	Nathaniel	Porter	5	237	Mathias	Burgis	4
184	Moses	Gregory	3	238	Josiah	Jaycocks	1
185	William	Rice	1	239	Daniel	Runnells	1
186	Joseph	Craw	1		*Page 146*		
187	Elisha	Bangs	1	240	William	Nellson	1
188	Jonathan	Hill	1	241	John	Birdsell	1
189	Jo:	Barly	1	242	Moses	Huestis	1
190	Christopher	Bobbit	1	243	Elisha	Kelk	1
191	Malthia	Hatch	1	244	Jonathan	Bryant	1
192	Peleg	Ballard	1	245	William	Lane	1
193	Peleg	Ballard Jnr:	1	246	John	Ryder	3
194	Seth	Merrick	2	247	William	Dusenbury	3
195	Thomas	Colwill	2	248	John	Lane	1
196	Amos	Fuller	1	249	Joseph	Hopkins	4
197	William	Ballard	1	250	John	Green	2
198	Cornelis	Tompkins	3	251	Thomas	Higgins	1
	Page 145			252	Thomas	Hinkly	1
199	Simon	Ellis	1	253	Josiah	Hinkly	1
200	John	Meeks	2	254	Israel	Cole	1
201	Isaac	Barton	1	255	Abram	Underhill	1
202	Nathaniel	Bailiff	2	256	James	Russell	1
203	Robert	Ryders	3	257	John	Lawrence	2
204	John	Field	3	258	Tunis	Krankites Johnse	1
205	Philip	Paddock	2	259	Thomas	Clemens	2
206	Benjamin	Perry	3	260	Sibet	Krankhite	1
207	James	Quimby	3	261	Abram	Krankhite	1
208	Zachary	Paddock Jnr:	2	262	Teunis	Brewer	1
209	Stephen	Field	3	263	Daniel	Taylor	2
210	Joshua	Moss	1	264	Joseph	Underwood	1

June 1758 continued

	Name	Surname	Value		Name	Surname	Value
265	William	Shaw	1	319	Joshua	Tompkins	1
266	Michael	Shaw Jnr:	1	320	Richard	Griffen	1
267	Amos	Dickenson Jnr:	1	321	Joseph	Waters	3
268	Elisha	Meed	2	322	Benjamin	Underhill	2
269	Andrew	Hill	3	323	William	Dean	1
270	William	Chitterton	1		*Page 148*		
271	Stephen	Farrington	1	324	William	McReady	1
272	Gilbert	Concklin	2	325	Henry	Boyce	1
273	John	Haddy	3	326	Joshua	Gee	1
274	Andrew	Burgis Jnr:	1	327	John	Langdon	2
275	David	Akins	2	328	Isaac	Langdon	1
276	Peter	Ryal	1	329	Jno:	Langdon Isaacs Brother	1
277	Jeremiah	Hueston	1	330	—	Fowler & Dennis on Nathll: Robinsons Place	2
278	William	Mash	1				
279	Israel	Honeywell	5	331	Nathaniel	Robinson Jnr:	1
280	John	Clarke	1	332	Ebenezer	Robinson	1
281	Ruben	Hamblin	2	333	Simon	Deacon	4
	Page 147			334	Benjamin	Perry Jnr:	2
282	Robert	Fuller	1	335	Josiah	Ingerson	3
283	Jeremiah	Gifford	2	336	Abram	Mabee	2
284	Heman	King	1	337	Abram	Mabee Jnr:	1
285	Jonathan	Hopkins	1	338	Isaac	Fitch	2
286	Joseph	Brooks	1	339	John	Rhodes	2
287	Nehemiah	Wood	1	340	Benjamin	Odle	2
288	Christopher	Ellis	1	341	Daniel	Bull	3
289	Humfrey	Ruff	1	342	Thomas	Crosbary	3
290	Philip	Ruff	1	343	John	Crankhite	1
291	Joseph	Merrits farm	5	344	John	Tarwell	1
292	John	Baker	1	345	John	Williams	1
293	Nathan	Taylor Jnr:	2	346	Samuel	Carll	1
294	Joseph	Gregory	1	347	Samuel	Yeomans	1
295	Ruben	Kelly	1	348	George	Fields	1
296	John	Jones	3	349	Jonathan	Jones	2
297	Fredrick	Gea	2	350	Philip	Philips	1
298	Walter	Hueson	1	351	Matw:	Benedicts farm on the Oblong	1
299	Oliver	Odle	1				
300	James	Standley	3	352	Jeremiah	Springsteen	1
301	John	Ferris	2	353	Daniel	Sunderhill	1
302	John	Scott	1	354	Jonathan	Lane Jnr:	1
303	Caleb	Pells farm	4	355	George	Cooper	1
304	Uriah	Hill	4	356	Benjamin	Gifford	3
305	Moses	Brundidge	1	357	Christopher	Dickenson	4
306	John	Lamesie	1	358	John	Bogardus	3
307	Solomon	Ferrington	1	359	Henry	Krankhite	1
308	John	Wright	1	360	Cornelis	Cooper	1
309	Silas	Washburn	2	361	Gilson	Clap	3
310	Ebbert	Herriton	1	362	Jonathan	Lane Jnr:	1
311	Richard	Hoppe	1	363	Iccabud	Rose	5
312	Richard	Arundal	1		*Page 149*		
313	Joshua	Barnam	3	364	Joseph	Stocker	1
314	Timothy	Stephens	2	365	Obediah	Basely	1
315	Joshua	Porter	2	366	Samuel	Elwell Jnr:	1
316	James	Colwill	2	367	Isaac	Elwell	1
317	Samuel	Drake	1	368	Jonathan	Hunlock	1
318	Uriah	Drake	1	369	Jacob	Philips Jnr:	1

June 1758 continued

#	Name	Surname	Value	#	Name	Surname	Value
370	John	Calkin 3rd:	1	410	Robert	Bloomer	1
371	John	Clawson	1	411	Nathaniel	Plumsteed	1
372	Edward	Dolph or Wolf	1	412	James	Paddock	1
373	John	Duwey	1	413	Thomas	Nickerson	1
374	Benjamin	Roberts Jnr:	1	414	Joseph	Nickerson	1
375	Augustine	Basely	1	415	Ebenezer	Weekson	1
376	Ebenezer	Bennet	1	416	John	Stephens	1
377	Old	Bennet	1	417	Nathaniel	Hatch Jnr:	1
378	William	Rapelyea Junior	1	418	Jeremiah	Calkin Jnr:	1
379	Elihu	Gage	1	419	David	French	1
380	Anthony	Gage	1	420	Eliazer	Miller	1
381	Moses	Gage	1	421	John	Hill Jnr:	1
382	Richard	Wearing	1	422	Elijah	Calkin	1
383	John	Bloomer	1	423	Simon	Covill	1
384	Thomas	Townsend Jnr:	1	424	Joseph	Robins	1
385	Christopher	Townsend	1	425	Josiah	Swift	1
386	Hugh	Baily	1	426	Josiah	Swift Jnr:	1
387	Timothy	Sweet	1	427	Gideon	Crowfoot	1
388	James	Anderson	1	428	John	Garrison Near Wekepe	1
389	David	Paddock Jnr:	1	429	Thomas	Pew	1
390	John	Tompkins	1	430	Daniel	Brundidge	1
391	Samuel	Benedict	1	431	Solomon	Jenkins	1
392	Jebes	Elwell	1	432	Benjamin	Serring	1
393	Nathan	Crosby	1	433	Anthony	Hill	1
394	John	Garrison	1	434	Samuel	Carter	2
395	Amos	Pine	1	435	John	Gean	3
396	David	Burchad	1	436	Ephraim	Shead	1
397	Thomas	Hodges Farm	1	437	Rubin	Close	5
398	Elisha	Morehouse	1	438	Josiah	Akin	1
399	Stephen	Rockwell	1	439	David	Tuttle	1
400	Elkeny	Hinkly	1	440	Thomas	West	1
401	Elijah	White	1	441	Ephraim	Pearce	1
402	Azariah	Meed	1	442	Joseph	Huested	5
403	Edward	Rice	1	443	Caleb	Huested	5
404	Ebenezer	Kelly	1	444	John	Hunt	5
	Page 150			445	Jeremiah	Witnah	1
405	Ephraim	Smith	1		*Page 151*		
406	William	Merrit	1	446	Solomon	Brundige	1
407	Thomas	Fowler	1	447	John	Lumarey	1
408	John	Bloomer Near the River	1	448	Joseph	Chatterton	1
409	Thomas	Cromwell	1				£898

FEBRUARY 1759
SOUTHERN PRECINCT

at 16 d ½ [1 shilling 4 ½ pence] pr. pound

	Name	Surname	Value		Name	Surname	Value
	Page 266			49	Elie	Nellson	1
1	Francis	Nellson	6	50	Nathaniel	Hatch	8
2	Thomas	Davinport	11	51	Valentine	Perkins	2
3	Thomas	Davinport Jnr:	16	52	Samuel	Field	18
4	Jacob	Mandavill	10	53	Joseph	Field	8
5	John	Calkin	2	54	James	Dickinson	11
6	John	Calkin Jnr:	2	55	Amos	Dickinson	3
7	William	Gray	4	56	John	Dickenson	4
8	John	Rogers	13	57	Daniel	Townsend	4
	Page 267			58	Robert	Townsend	2
9	Elijah	Tompkins	4	59	Thomas	Townsend	1
10	Thomas	Hellick	1	60	Elihu	Townsend	4
11	John	Van Amburghs Estate	10	61	Charles	Townsend	2
12	Peter	Duboys	17	62	Benjamin	Townsend	3
13	Ebenezer	Jones Near the River	3	63	Robert U:	Townsend	1
14	Benjamin	Jaycocks	2	64	Robert R:	Townsend	3
15	Timothy	Conklin	2	65	Daniel	Towsend Jnr:	1
16	Nathan	Lane	3	66	Daniel D.	Townsend	[-]
17	George	Hueston	5	67	Jesse	Smith	4
18	Joseph	Crane	1	68	Benjamin	Brundage	5
19	Joseph	Gregory	1	69	Michael	Shaw	1
20	William	Drake	4	70	Caleb	Hayser	2
21	Sias	Gregory	4	71	Samuel	Gates	1
22	John	Drake	2	72	William	Rapelyea	5
23	Isaac	Rhodes	5	73	John	Barber	2
24	Joseph	Gregory Jnr:	[-]	74	Peter	Hartwell	2
25	David	Paddock	1	75	Lewis	Jones	1
26	William	Yerns's ~~Widow~~ farm	2	76	Dacon	Hamblin	7
27	John	Smith	[-]	77	Jacob	Philip	1
28	Joseph	Lane	3	78	Caleb	Sweet	2
29	Joseph	Meed	4	79	William	Palmer	1
30	John	Gee	1	80	John	Newberry	4
31	Joseph	Crane Jnr:	2	81	Samuel	Other	3
32	William	Gee	2	82	Peter	Paddock	2
33	Cobus	Krankhite Jnr:	[-]	83	Thomas	Paddock	1
34	David	Austin	1	84	Daniel	Bradley	1
35	Abram	Otter	1	85	Russell	Gregory	1
36	Caleb	Brundage	1	86	John	White	1
37	Nathaniel	Thompkins	1	87	Jacob	Ellis	4
38	Cornelius	Fuller	2	88	Philip	Cannon	1
39	John	Sprage	1	89	George	Cary	2
40	Samuel	Calkin	3	90	Isaac	Ter Hills Widw:	[-]
41	John	Hains	2		*Page 269*		
42	Thomas	Frost	1	91	Sander	Dewel	1
43	Eleazer	Cole	2	92	Robert	Farringtons Widw:	1
44	Edward	Gray	2	93	James	Mc Reeds farm	[-]
45	William	Teller	9	94	Jacob	Finch	2
46	Abram	Smith	3	95	Thomas	Philip	5
47	Luke	Covert	1	96	Ebenezer	King	1
	Page 268			97	Josiah	Baker	4
48	Samuel	Jones	1	98	Lieut:	Taylor	2
				99	Isaac	Crosby	1

February 1759 continued

#	Name	Surname	Value	#	Name	Surname	Value
100	Benjamin	Sears	3	154	Gabriel	Knap	5
101	Christopher	Fowler	1	155	John	Van Tessell	1
102	Peter	Augwine	4	156	Mr:	Kent	8
103	Semion	Ryders	3	157	Jonathan	Austin	3
104	Isaac	Chapman	2	158	John	Kelly	1
105	Isaac	Hause	2	159	Thomas	Kelly	1
106	Thomas	Smith	1	160	Isaac	Piere	3
107	Oliver	Gray	1	161	William	Stone	2
108	Edward	Gray Jnr:	2	162	Noah	Burbanks	1
109	Samuel	Banks	2	163	David	Smith	1
110	Nathaniel	Forster	3	164	Edmund	Baker	1
111	Samuel	Elwell	3	165	Caleb	Chase	1
112	David	Crosby	3	166	Ebenezer	Chase	1
113	Joshua	Cosby	3	167	James	Sears	4
114	Jaby	Berry	1	168	Peter	Hall	2
115	Joseph	Taylor	2	169	Nathaniel	Hoses farm	1
116	Isaac	Smith	2	170	Thomas	Gage	3
117	Hope	Covy	6	171	Samuel	Good Speed	3
118	John	Covy	1		*Page 271*		
119	Jonathan	Paddock	1	172	Elisha	Calkin	1
120	Nathan	Green	2	173	John	Mahew	1
121	Seth	Nickerson	2	174	John	Merrick	3
122	Timothy	Clawson	1	175	Moody	House	2
123	Benjamin	Roberts	1	176	James	Cowen	1
124	Elisha	Luttington	4	177	Elisha	Cole	3
125	David	Honeywell	1	178	John	Hall	1
126	Benjamin	Parish	2	179	Ezekiel	Burgis	1
127	Jonathan	Sturdefunt	1	180	Jonathan	Kelly	1
128	William	Sturdefunt	1	181	Francis	Baker	2
129	David	Sturdefunt	1	182	Uriah	Lawrance	4
130	Mathew	Bump	1	183	Ezekiel [Eleazer]	Sprage	1
	Page 270			184	Nathaniel	Porter	6
131	Samuel	More	1	185	Moses	Gregory	3
132	Isaac	Horton	1	186	William	Rice	1
133	Jonathan	Lane	2	187	Joseph	Craw	1
134	Jo:	Concklin	1	188	Elisha	Bangs	1
135	Richard	Roads	[-]	189	Jonathan	Hill	1
136	Michael	Slot	1	190	Jo:	Barly	[-]
137	William	Penny	3	191	Christopher	Bobbit	1
138	Tom	Forster	2	192	Mathia	Hatch	[-]
139	John	Paddock	2	193	Peleg	Ballard	1
140	Ezekiel	Meed	1	194	Peleg	Ballard Jnr:	1
141	Israel	Taylor	1	195	Seth	Merrick	2
142	William	Hill	7	196	Thomas	Colwill	2
143	Peter	Robinson	1	197	Amos	Fuller	1
144	Abram	Hodges	3	198	William	Ballard	1
145	Ebenezer	Hamblin	[-]	199	Cornelis	Tompkins	3
146	Isaac	Otter	2	200	Simon	Ellis	1
147	Elemuel	Kelk	1	201	John	Meeks	2
148	Seth	Paddock	2	202	Isaac	Barton	1
149	Ebenezer	Jones Jnr:	2	203	Nathan	Bailiff	2
150	Aron	Calkin	1	204	Robert	Ryders	3
151	Theophilius	Jones	1	205	John	Field	3
152	Joshua	Hamblin	3	206	Philip	Paddock	[-]
153	Robert	Weekson	1	207	Benjamin	Perry	3

February 1759 continued

	Name	Surname	Value		Name	Surname	Value
208	James	Quimby	3	261	Sibert	Krankhite	1
209	Zachary	Paddock Jnr:	2	262	Abram	Krankhite	1
210	Stephen	Field	5	263	Teunis	Brewer	1
211	Joshua	Moss	2	264	Daniel	Taylor	2
	Page 272			265	Joseph	Underwood	[-]
212	John	Nellson	1	266	William	Shaw	1
213	Moses	Nauthrop	4	267	Michael	Shaw Jnr:	1
214	Nathan	Birdsill	11	268	Amos	Dickinson Jnr:	1
215	Jeremiah	Linkhorn	1	269	Elisha	Meed	1
216	John	Manly	3	270	Andrew	Hill	3
217	Silas	Paddock	2	271	William	Chitterton	1
218	Moses	Dusenbury	3	272	Stephen	Farrington	1
219	Edward	Ganung	1	273	Gilbert	Concklin	2
220	Daniel	Philip	1	274	John	Haddy	3
221	Samuel	Peters	5	275	Andrew	Burgis Jnr:	1
222	Lazarus	Griffin	1	276	David	Akins	2
223	Bethual	Barnam	1	277	Peter	Ryal	1
224	Joseph	Philip	1	278	Jeremiah	Hueston	1
225	Zachary	Paddock	2	279	William	Mash	1
226	Abner	Bang	1	280	Israel	Honeywell	6
227	Jeremiah	Baily	1	281	John	Clarke	1
228	Wm:	Grays Son William	1	282	Rubin	Hamblin	2
229	Robt:	Weekson's's Son Peleg	1	283	Robert	Fuller	1
230	Joseph	Cromwell	4	284	Jeremiah	Gifford	2
231	Rowland	Perry	2	285	Heman	King	1
232	Noah	Smith	3	286	Jonathan	Hopkins	1
233	Elijah	Weekson	1	287	Joseph	Brooks	[-]
234	Joshua	Kinkle [Hinkle]	1	288	Nehemiah	Wood	1
235	John	How	1	289	Christopher	Ellis	1
236	John	Lockwood	1	290	Humfrey	Ruff	1
237	Isaac	Perry	1	291	Philip	Ruff	1
238	Mathias	Burgis	5	292	Joseph	Merret	6
239	Josiah	Jaycocks	1	293	John	Baker	1
240	Daniel David	Runnells	1	294	Nathan	Taylor Jnr:	2
241	William	Nellson	1	295	Joseph	Gregory	1
242	John	Birdsell	1	296	Rubin	Kelly	1
243	Moses	Huestis	1		*Page 274*		
244	Elisha	Kelk	1	297	John	Jones	3
245	Jonathan	Bryant	2	298	Fredrick	Gea	1
246	William	Lane	1	299	Walter	Hueson	1
247	John	Ryders	3	300	Oliver	Odle	[-]
248	William	Dusenbury	3	301	James	Standley	[-]
249	John	Lane	1	302	John	Ferris	2
250	Joseph	Hopkins	4	303	John	Scott	1
251	John	Green [Geen]	2	304	Caleb	Pells farm	4
252	Thomas	Higgins	2	305	Uriah	Hill	3
253	Thomas	Hinkly	1	306	Moses	Brundage	1
254	Josiah	Hinkly	[-]	307	John	Lamesie	1
	Page 273			308	Solomon	Ferrington	1
255	Israel	Cole	1	309	John	Wright	2
256	Abram	Underhill	1	310	Silas	Washburn	2
257	James	Russell	1	311	Ebbert	Herriton	1
258	John	Lawrence	2	312	Richard	Hoppe	1
259	Tunis	Krankhites Johnse	1	313	Richard	Arundal	1
260	Thomas	Clemens	2	314	Joshua	Barnam	4

February 1759 continued

#	Name	Surname	Value	#	Name	Surname	Value
315	Timothy	Stephans	3	367	Samuel	Elwell Jnr:	1
316	Joshua	Porter	2	368	Isaac	Elwell	1
317	James	Colwill	2	369	Jonathan	Hunlock	2
318	Samuel	Drake	1	370	Jacob	Philip Jnr:	1
319	Uriah	Drake	1	371	John	Calkin 3rd:	1
320	Joshua	Tompkins	1	372	John	Clawson	1
321	Richard	Griffin	1	373	Edward	Dolph or Wolf	1
322	Joseph	Waters	3	374	John	Dewey	2
323	Benjamin	Underhill	2	375	Benjamin	Roberts Jnr:	1
324	William	Dean	1	376	Augustine	Basely	2
325	William	McReedy	1	377	Eleazer	Bennet	1
326	Henry	Boyce	1	378	Thomas	Bennet	1
327	Joshua	Gee	1	379	William	Rapelyea Jnr:	1
328	John	Langdon	2	380	Elihu	Gage	1
329	Isaac	Langdon	1		*Page 276*		
330	Jno: Langdon	Isaac's Brother	1	381	Anthony	Gage	1
331	Fowler & Dennis on Nathaniel Robinsons place		2	382	Moses	Gage	1
				383	Richard	Wearing	1
332	Nathaniel	Robinson Jnr:	1	384	John	Bloomer	1
333	Ebenezer	Robinson	1	385	Thomas	Townsend Jnr:	1
334	Simon	Deacon	5	386	Christopher	Townsend	1
335	Benjamin	Perry Jnr:	2	387	Hugh	Baily	1
336	Josiah	Ingerson	3	388	Timothy	Sweet	[-]
337	Abram	Mabee	2	389	James	Anderson	2
	Page 275			390	David	Paddock Jnr:	1
338	Abram	Mabee Jnr:	1	391	John	Thompkins	1
339	Isaac	Fitch	2	392	Samuel	Bennedict	1
340	John	Rhodes	1	393	Jabes	Elwell	1
341	Benjamin	Odle	2	394	Nathan	Crosby	1
342	Daniel	Bull	3	395	John	Garrison	1
343	Thomas	Crosbary	3	396	Amos	Pine	[-]
344	John	Crankhite	1	397	David	Burchad	1
345	John	Tarwell	1	398	Thomas	Hodges Farm	2
346	John	Williams	1	399	Elisha	Morehouse	1
347	Samuel	Carll	[-]	400	Stephan	Rockwell	1
348	Samuel	Yeomans	1	401	Elkeny	Hinkly	1
349	George	Fields	1	402	Elijah	White	1
350	Jonathan	Jones	1	403	Azariah	Meed	1
351	Philip	Philips	1	404	Edward	Rice	2
352	Mathw:	Benedicts farm on the Oblong	2	405	Ebenezer	Kelly	1
				406	Ephraim	Smith	2
353	Jeremiah	Springsteen	1	407	William	Merrit	[-]
354	Daniel	Sunderhill	1	408	Thomas	Fowler	1
355	Jonathan	Lane Jnr:	1	409	John	Bloomer (Near the River)	1
356	George	Cooper	2				
357	Benjamin	Gifford	4	410	Thomas	Cromwell	1
358	Christopher	Dickinson	4	411	Robert	Bloomer	1
359	John	Bogardus	4	412	Robert	Bloomer	1
360	Henry	Krankhite	1	413	Nathan	Plumsteed	1
361	Cornelius	Cooper	[-]	414	James	Paddock	2
362	Gilson	Clap	3	415	Thomas	Nickerson	[-]
363	Jonathan	Lane Jnr:	1	416	Joseph	Nickerson	[-]
364	Ichabod	Rose	[-]	417	Ebenezer	Wickson	1
365	Joseph	Stocker	1	418	John	Stephans	1
366	Obediah	Basely	2	419	Nathaniel	Hatch Jnr:	2

February 1759 continued

	Name	Surname	Value
420	Jeremiah	Calkin Jnr:	1
421	Ebenezer	French	1
422	Eleazer	Miller	1
Page 277			
423	John	Hill Jnr:	1
424	Elijah	Calkin	2
425	Simon	Covill	1
426	Joseph	Robins	1
427	Josiah	Swift	1
428	Josiah	Swift Jnr:	1
429	Gideon	Crowfoot	1
430	John	Garrison Near Wekepe	1
431	Thomas	Pew	1
432	Daniel	Brundage	1
433	Solomon	Jenkins	1
434	Benjamin	Serring	1
435	Anthony	Hill	1
436	Samuel	Carter	5
437	John	Green	[-]
438	Ephraim	Shead	[-]
439	Rubin	Close	5
440	Josiah	Akin	2
441	David	Tuttle	1
442	Thomas	West	[-]
443	Ephraim	Pearce	1
444	Joseph	Huested	7
445	Caleb	Huested	5
446	John	Hunt	[-]
447	Jeremiah	Witnah	1
448	Solomon	Brundage	1
449	John	Lumerey	2
450	Joseph	Chatterton	1
451	Elisha	Oakley	1
452	Nathaniel	Brundage	1
453	John	Bates	4
454	Benjamin	Lord	1
455	Peter	Anderson	2
456	Charles	Mc Ready	1
457	Mathew	Mc Caby	1
458	Joseph	Gee	1
459	Eleazer	Youmans	1
460	Caus [Hans]	Crankhite	1
461	John	Foster	1
462	Stephan	Hopkins	1
463	Seth	Hoems	1
464	James	Pardy	1
Page 278			
465	Ebenezer	Pardy	1
466	Stephan	Pardy	1
467	Daniel	Ball	1
468	Josiah	Hall	1
469	John	June	1
470	Joseph	Shearwood	1
471	Benjamin	Haviland	3
472	Peter	Terry	2
473	William	Haviland	2
474	Nehemiah	Barlow	1
475	Peter	Esmon	2
476	John	Brown	1
477	Daniel	Butler	1
478	Jonathan	Hungerford	1
479	Isaac	Chace	1
480	Silvenus	Coole	1
481	Ebenezer	Perry	1
482	Thomas	Hearns	1
483	Phenias	Touner	2
484	George	Darby	1
485	David	Hill	1
486	Noah	Lee	1
487	Benjamin	Hatch	1
488	John	Porter	2
489	James	Keler	1
490	George	Haborn	3
491	Benjamin	Burch	1
492	Joseph	Dewey Jnr:	1
493	Joseph	Collins	1
494	Berzelel	Tyler	1
495	Thomas	Trobrig	1
496	Samuel	Calkins Jnr:	1
497	Nathaniel	Stone	1
498	Wheter	Robeson	1
499	Benjamin	Borlew	1
500	John	Brade	1
501	Jonathen	Hobey	1
502	John	Sprague Jnr:	1
503	Josiah	Robison	1
504	Michael	Evans	1
505	Peter	Terre	2
506	Gilbert	Trevers	1
507	Solomon	Field	2
508	Samuel	Price [Prince?]	1
Page 279			
509	Ebenezer	Brown	1
510	Joseph	Foster	1
511	—	Lawrence (on Shaws farm)	2
512	Nathaniel	Arnold	1
513	Solomon	Parre	1
514	Elisha	Perre	1
515	James	Perre	1
516	William	Daily Jnr:	1
517	Jonathan	Hoagg	4
518	David	Akins farm	2
519	Stephan	Crane	1
520	Jonathan	Vieree	1
521	Nathan	Green Jnr:	1
522	Nathaniel	Green	1
523	Ebenezer	Gage	1
524	Nehemiah	Jones	1
525	Reubin	Crosby	1

February 1759 continued

#	Name	Surname	Value		#	Name	Surname	Value
526	David	Crosby	1		534	Jeremiah	Calkin	1
527	Joshua	Barnum Jnr:	1		535	David	Seers	2
528	Uriah	Townsend	2		536	Benjamin	Vickry	1
529	Silas	Gray	1		537	John	Hagur	1
530	David	Calkin	1		538	Capt Beverlie	Robinson farm	2
531	Simon	Calkin	1		539	Hezeka	Carter	1
532	Ebenezer	Ward	4					£1,021
533	Levy	Marks	2					

JUNE 1759
SOUTHERN PRECINCT

at 3 shillings 6 pence pr. pound

#	Name	Surname	Value		#	Name	Surname	Value
	Page 340				36	John	Sprage	1
1	Francis	Nellsons Estate	6		37	Samuel	Calkin	3
2	Thomas	Devenport	10		38	John	Hains	2
3	Thomas	Devenport Jnr:	16		39	Thomas	Frost	1
4	Jacob	Mandavil	10		40	Eleazer	Cole	2
5	John	Calkin	2		41	Edward	Gray	2
6	John	Calkin Jnr:	2		42	William	Tellers Estate	8
7	William	Gray	4		43	Abram	Smith	3
8	John	Rogers	13		44	Luke	Covert	1
9	Elijah	Tomkins	4		45	Samuel	Jones	1
10	Thomas	Hallack	1		46	Elie	Nellson	1
11	John	Van Amburghs Estate	10		47	Valentine	Perkins	2
12	Peter	Du Boise	16		48	Samuel	Field	16
13	Ebenezer	Jones Near the river	3		49	Joseph	Field	9
					50	James	Dickinson	10
14	Benjamin	Jaycocks	2		51	Amos	Dickinson	2
15	Timothy	Concklin	2		52	John	Dickinson	4
16	Nathan	Lane	1		53	Daniel	Townsend	4
17	George	Hueston	5		54	Robert	Townsend	1
18	Joseph	Crane	1		55	Thomas	Townsend	1
19	Joseph	Gregory	1		56	Elihu	Townsend	1
20	William	Drake	4		57	Charles	Townsend	2
21	Sias	Gregory	4		58	Benjamin	Townsend	3
22	John	Drake	2		59	Robert U:	Townsend	1
23	Isaac	Rhodes	5		60	Robert R:	Townsend	3
24	David	Paddock	1		61	Daniel	Townsend Jnr:	1
25	William	Yerns's Widw: farm	2		62	Jesse	Smith	4
26	Joseph	Lane	3		63	Benjamin	Brundage	5
27	Joseph	Meed	3		64	Michael	Shaw	1
	Page 341				65	Caleb	Hayser	2
28	John	Gee	1		66	Samuel	Gates	1
29	Joseph	Crane Jnr:	2		67	William	Rapelyea	5
30	William	Gee	2		68	John	Barber	2
31	David	Austin	1		69	Peter	Hartwell	2
32	Abram	Otter	1		70	Lewis	Jones	1
33	Caleb	Brundage	1		71	Dacon	Hamblin	4
34	Nathaniel	Tompkins	1			*Page 342*		
35	Cornelius	Fuller	2		72	Jacob	Philip	1

June 1759 continued

	Name	Surname	Value		Name	Surname	Value
73	Caleb	Sweet	3	127	Jo:	Concklin	1
74	William	Palmer	1	128	Michael	Slot	1
75	John	Newberry	4	129	William	Penny	3
76	Samuel	Other	3	130	Tom	Forster	2
77	Peter	Paddock	1	131	John	Paddock	2
78	Thomas	Paddock	2	132	Ezekiel	Meed	1
79	Daniel	Bradley	1	133	Israel	Taylor	1
80	Russell	Gregory	1	134	William	Hill	6
81	John	White	1	135	Peter	Robinson	1
82	Jacob	Ellis	3	136	Abram	Hodges	3
83	Philip	Cannon	1	137	Isaac	Otter	2
84	George	Cary	2	138	Elemuel	Kelk	1
85	Sander	Dewel	1	139	Seth	Paddock	2
86	Robert	Farringtons Widw:	1	140	Ebenezer	Jones Jnr:	2
87	Jacob	Finch	2	141	Aaron	Calkin	1
88	Thomas	Philip	6	142	Theophilius	Jones	1
89	Ebenezer	King	1	143	Joshua	Hamblin	3
90	Josiah	Baker	4	144	Robert	Weekson	1
91	Lieut:	Taylor	2	145	Gabriel	Knap	5
92	Isaac	Crosby	1	146	John	Van Tessell	1
93	Benjamin	Sears	3	147	Mr:	Kent & Son Moss	8
94	Christopher	Fowler	1	148	Jonathan	Austin	3
95	Peter	Angwine	4	149	John	Kelly	1
96	Simon	Ryders	3	150	Thomas	Kelly	1
97	Isaac	Chapman	2	151	Isaac	Pierce	3
98	Isaac	Hause	2	152	William	Stone	3
99	Thomas	Smith	1	153	David	Smith	1
100	Oliver	Gray	1	154	Edmund	Baker	1
101	Edward	Gray Jnr:	2	155	Caleb	Chase	1
102	Samuel	Banks	2	156	Ebenezer	Chase	1
103	Nathaniel	Forster	3	157	James	Sears	4
104	Samuel	Elwell	3	158	Peter	Hall	2
105	David	Crosby	3		*Page 344*		
106	Joshua	Casby	3	159	Nathaniel	Houses farm	1
107	Jaby	Berry	1	160	Thomas	Gage	3
108	Joseph	Taylor	2	161	Samuel	Goodspeed	3
109	Isaac	Smith	2	162	Elisha	Calkin	1
110	Hope	Covey	6	163	John	Mahew	1
111	John	Covey	1	164	John	Merrick	3
112	Jonathan	Paddock	2	165	Moody	House	2
113	Nathan	Green	2	166	James	Cowen	1
114	Seth	Nickerson	2	167	Elisha	Cole	3
	Page 343			168	John	Hall	1
115	Timothy	Clawson	1	169	Ezekiel	Burgis	1
116	Benjamin	Roberts	1	170	Jonathan	Kelly	1
117	Elisha	Luttington	4	171	Francis	Baker	2
118	David	Honeywell	1	172	Uriah	Lawrance	4
119	Benjamin	Parish	2	173	Ezekiel [Eleazer]	Sprague	1
120	Jonathan	Sturdefunt	1	174	Nathaniel	Porter	6
121	William	Sturdefunt	1	175	Moses	Gregory	3
122	David	Sturdefunt	1	176	William	Rice	1
123	Mathew	Bump	1	177	Joseph	Craw	1
124	Samuel	More	1	178	Elisha	Banks	1
125	Isaac	Horton	1	179	Jonathan	Hill	1
126	Jonathan	Lane	2	180	Christopher	Bobbit	1

June 1759 continued

#	Name	Surname	Value	#	Name	Surname	Value
181	Malthia	Hatch	4	234	John	Ryders	3
182	Peleg	Ballard	1	235	William	Dusenbury	3
183	Peleg	Ballard Jnr:	1	236	John	Lane	1
184	Seth	Merrick	2	237	Joseph	Hopkins	4
185	Thomas	Colwill	2	238	John	Green [Geen]	2
186	Amos	Fuller	1	239	Thomas	Higgins	2
187	William	Ballard	1	240	Thomas	Hinkley	1
188	Cornelius	Tompkins	3	241	Israel	Cole	1
189	Simon	Ellis	1	242	Abram	Underhill	1
190	John	Meeks	2	243	James	Russell	1
191	Isaac	Barton	1		*Page 346*		
192	Nathan	Bailiff	2	244	John	Lawrance	2
193	Robert	Ryder	3	245	Tunis	Krankhites	1
194	John	Field	3	246	Thomas	Clemens	2
195	Benjamin	Perry	3	247	Sibert	Krankhite	1
196	James	Quimby	3	248	Abram	Krankhite	1
197	Zachary	Paddock Jnr:	2	249	Teunis	Brewer	1
198	Stephan	Field	5	250	Daniel	Taylor	2
199	Joshua	Moss	1	251	William	Shaw	1
200	John	Nellson	1	252	Michael	Shaw Jnr:	1
	Page 345			253	Amos	Dickinson Jnr:	1
201	Moses	Nauthrop	4	254	Elisha	Meed	1
202	Nathan	Birdsal	10	255	Andrew	Hill	3
203	Jeremiah	Linkhorn	1	256	William	Chitterton	1
204	John	Manley	3	257	Stephan	Ferrington	1
205	Silas	Paddock	2	258	John	Haddy	2
206	Moses	Dusenbury	3	259	Andrew	Burgis Jnr:	1
207	Edward	Ganung	1	260	David	Akins	2
208	David	Philip	1	261	Peter	Ryal	1
209	Samuel	Peters farm	2	262	Jeremiah	Hueston	1
210	Lazarus	Griffin	1	263	William	Mash	1
211	Bethual	Barnum	1	264	Israel	Honneywell	6
212	Joseph	Philip	1	265	John	Clarke	1
213	Zachary	Paddock	2	266	Rubin	Hamblin	2
214	Abner	Bangs	2	267	Robert	Fuller	2
215	Jeremiah	Baily	1	268	Jeremiah	Gifford	2
216	Wm:	Grays Son William	1	269	Heman	King	1
217	Robt:	Weekson's Son Peleg	1	270	Jonathan	Hopkins	1
218	Joseph	Cromwell	4	271	Nehemiah	Wood	1
219	Rowland	Perry	2	272	Christopher	Ellis	1
220	Noah	Smith	3	273	Humfry	Ruff	1
221	Elijah	Weekson	1	274	Philip	Ruff	1
222	Joshua	Finckle [Hinkle]	1	275	Joseph	Merrits	6
223	John	Haw	1	276	John	Baker	1
224	John	Lockwood	1	277	Nathan	Taylor Jnr:	2
225	Isaac	Perry	1	278	Joseph	Gregory	1
226	Mathias	Burgis	5	279	Rubin	Kelly	1
	~~Josiah~~	~~Jaycocks~~		280	John	Jones	3
227	Daniel	Runnells	1	281	Walter	Hughson	1
228	William	Nellson	1	282	John	Ferris	2
229	John	Birdsill	1	283	John	Scott	1
230	Moses	Huestis	1		*Page 347*		
231	Elisha	Kelk	1	284	Caleb	Pells farm	4
232	Jonathan	Bryant	1	285	Moses	Brundage	1
233	William	Lane	1	286	John	Lamesie	1

June 1759 continued

	Name	Surname	Value
287	Solomon	Ferrington	1
288	John	Wright	2
289	Silas	Washburn	2
290	Ebbert	Herriton	1
291	Richard	Hoppe	1
292	Richard	Arundal	1
293	Joshua	Barnum	4
294	Timothy	Stephans	3
295	Joshua	Porter	2
296	James	Colwell	2
297	Samuel	Drake	1
298	Uriah	Drake	1
299	Joshua	Tompkins	1
300	Richard	Griffin	1
301	Benjamin	Underhill	2
302	William	Dean	1
303	William	McReady	1
304	Henry	Boyce	1
305	Joshua	Gee	1
306	John	Langdon	2
307	Jno: Langdon	Isaac's Brother	2
308	— Fowler & Dennis on Nathl: Robin: place		2
	~~Nathaniel~~	~~Robinson Jnr:~~	
309	Ebenezer	Robinson	1
310	Simon	Deacon	5
311	Benjamin	Perry Jnr:	2
312	Josiah	Ingerson	4
313	Abram	Mabee	1
314	Abram	Mabee Jnr:	1
315	Isaac	Fitch	2
316	John	Rhodes	1
317	Benjamin	Odle	2
318	Daniel	Bull	3
319	Thomas	Crosbary	3
320	John	Tarwell	1
321	John	Williams	1
322	Samuel	Yeomans	1

Page 348

	Name	Surname	Value
323	Jonathan	Jones	1
324	Philip	Philipse	1
325	Mathew	Benedicts farm Oblong	2
326	Jeremiah	Springsteen	1
327	Daniel	Sunderhill	1
328	Jonathan	Lane Jnr:	1
329	Benjamin	Gifford	4
330	Christopher	Dickinson	4
331	John	Bogardus	4
332	Henry	Krankhite	1
333	Joseph	Stocker	1
334	Obediah	Basely	2
335	Samuel	Elwell Jnr:	1
336	Isaac	Elwell	1
337	Jonathan	Hunlock	2

	Name	Surname	Value
338	Jacob	Philipse Jnr:	1
339	John	Calkin 3rd: Estate	1
340	John	Clawson	1
341	Edward	Dolph or Wolf	1
342	John	Dewey	2
343	Benjamin	Roberts Jnr:	1
344	Augustin	Basely	2
345	Eleazer	Bennet	1
346	Thomas	Bennet	1
347	William	Rapelyea Jnr:	1
348	Elihu	Gage	1
349	Anthony	Gage	1
350	Moses	Gage	1
351	Richard	Wearing	1
352	John	Bloomer	1
353	Thomas	Townsend Jnr:	1
354	Christopher	Townsend	1
355	Hugh	Baily	1
356	James	Anderson	2
357	David	Paddock Jnr:	1
358	John	Tompkins Jnr:	1
359	Samuel	Bennedict	1
360	Jabez	Elwell	1
361	Nathan	Crosby	1
362	John	Garrison	1
363	David	Burchad	1
364	Thomas	Hodges Farm	2
365	Elisha	Morehouse	1

Page 349

	Name	Surname	Value
366	Stephan	Rockwell	1
367	Elijah	White	1
368	Azariah	Meed	1
369	Edward	Rice	2
370	Ebenezer	Kelly	1
371	Ephraim	Smith	2
372	Thomas	Fowler	1
373	John	Bloomer Near the River	1
374	Thomas	Cromwell	1
375	Robert	Bloomer	1
376	Robert	Bloomer	1
377	Nathan	Plumsted	1
378	James	Paddock	1
379	Ebenezer	Weekson	1
380	John	Stephans	1
381	Nathaniel	Hatch Jnr:	2
382	Jeremiah	Calkin Jnr:	1
383	Ebenezer	Franch	1
384	Eleazer	Miller	2
385	John	Hill Jnr:	1
386	Elijah	Calkin	2
387	Simon	Covil	1
388	Joseph	Robins	1
389	Josiah	Swift	1
390	Josiah	Swift Jnr:	1

June 1759 continued

#	Name	Surname	Value
391	Gideon	Crowfoot	1
392	John	Garrison Near Wekepe	1
393	Thomas	Pew	1
394	Daniel	Brundage	1
395	Solomon	Jenkins	1
396	Benjamin	Serring	1
397	Anthony	Hill	1
398	Samuel	Carter	4
399	Rubin	Close	5
400	Josiah	Akin	2
401	David	Tuttle	1
402	Ephraim	Pierce	1
403	Joseph	Huested	5
404	Caleb	Huested	3
405	Jeremiah	Witnah	1
406	Solomon	Brundage	1
407	John	Lumerey	2
408	Joseph	Chatterton	1
409	Elisha	Oakley	1
410	Nathaniel	Brundage	1
411	John	Bates	4

Page 350

#	Name	Surname	Value
412	Benjamin	Lord	1
413	Peter	Anderson	2
414	Charles	Mc Ready	1
415	Mathew	Mc Caby	1
416	Joseph	Gee	1
417	Eleazer	Youmans	1
418	Hans	Krankhite	1
419	John	Foster	1
420	Stephan	Hopkins	1
421	Seth	Hoems	1
422	James	Pardy	1
423	Stephan	Pardy	1
424	Ebenezer	Pardy	1
425	Dan	Ball	1
426	Josiah	Hall	1
427	John	June	1
428	Joseph	Shearwood	1
429	Benjamin	Haviland	3
430	Peter	Terry	2
431	William	Haviland	2
432	Nehemiah	Barlow	1
433	Peter	Ismon	2
434	John	Brown	1
435	Daniel	Butler	1
436	Jonathan	Hungerford	1
437	Silvenus	Cole	1
438	Ebenezer	Perry	1
439	Thomas	Hearns	1
440	Phineas	Towner	2
441	George	Darby	1
442	David	Hill	1
443	Noah	Lee	1
444	Benjamin	Hatch	2
445	John	Porter	2
446	James	Keeler	1
447	George	Haborn	3
448	Benjamin	Burch	1
449	Joseph	Duwey Jnr:	1
450	Joseph	Collins	1
451	Berzelel	Tyler	1
452	Thomas	Trobrig	1
453	Samuel	Calkin Jnr:	1
454	Nathaniel	Stone	1
455	Wheten	Robinson	1

Page 351

#	Name	Surname	Value
456	Benjamin	Borlew	1
457	John	Brade	1
458	Jonathan	Hobey	1
459	John	Sprague Jnr:	1
460	Josiah	Robinson	1
461	Michael	Evans	1
462	Gilbert	Trevers	1
463	Solomon	Field	2
464	Samuel	Prince	1
465	Ebenezer	Brown	1
466	Joseph	Foster	1
467	—	Lawrance on Shaws farm	2
468	Nathaniel	Arnold	1
469	Solomon	Parre	1
470	Elisha	Perre	1
471	James	Perre	1
472	William	Daly Jnr:	1
473	Jonathan	Hoeg	1
474	David	Akins farm	2
475	Stephan	Crane	1
476	Jonathan	Viere	1
477	Jonathan	Green Jnr:	1
478	Nathaniel	Green	1
479	Ebenezer	Gage	1
480	Nehemiah	Jones	1
481	Reubin	Crosby	1
482	David	Crosby	1
483	Joshua	Barnum Jnr:	1
484	Uriah	Townsend	2
485	Silas	Gray	1
486	David	Calkin	1
487	Ebenezer	Ward	4
488	Levi	Marks	2
489	Jeremiah	Calkin	1
490	David	Sears	2
491	Benjamin	Vickrey	1
492	John	Hagur	1
493	Capt Beverlie	Robinsons farm	2
494	Hezekiah	Carter	1
495	Jeremiah	Butler	1
496	Ezekiel	Gee	1

Page 352

June 1759 continued

	Name	Surname	Value		Name	Surname	Value
497	Abraham	Mors	1	506	Nathaniel	Sheperson	1
498	Henry	Vanheyning	1	507	Stephen	Concklin	1
499	Lewis	Jones	1	508	Samuel	Jones	1
500	Daniel	Crawford	1	509	Peter	Boncker	1
501	Hezekiah	Kircum	1	510	Reubin	Hamlen	1
502	Elijah	Smith	1	511	David	Hamlen	1
503	John	Eager	1	512	—	Bauldin on Paddocks farm	1
504	Stephan	Pine	1				£984
505	Jacobus	Brouer	1				

FEBRUARY 1760
SOUTH PRECINCT

at 2/5 [2 shillings 5 pence] pr. pound

	Name	Surname	Value		Name	Surname	Value
	Page 432			35	Samuel	Calkin	3
1	Francis	Nelsons Estate	6	36	John	Hains	3
2	Thomas	Devenport's Estate	10	37	Thomas	Frost	1
3	Thomas	Devenport Jnr:	16	38	Eleazer	Cole	2
4	Jacob	Mandavil	10	39	Edward	Gray	2
5	John	Calkin	3	40	William	Tellers Estate	8
	Page 433			41	Abraham	Smith	3
6	John	Calkin Jnr:	1		*Page 434*		
7	William	Gray	3	42	Luke	Covert	1
8	John	Rogers	13	43	Samuel	Jones	1
9	Elijah	Thompkins	3	44	Elie	Nelson	1
10	Thomas	Hallock	1	45	Valentine	Perkins	3
11	John	Van Amburghs Estate	10	46	Samuel	Field	14
12	Peter	Du Boys	16	47	Joseph	Field	9
13	Ebenezer	Jones | Near the River	3	48	James	Dickinson	9
				49	Amos	Dickinson	2
14	Benjamin	Jaycocks	2	50	John	Dickinson	4
15	Timothy	Concklin	2	51	Daniel	Townsend	4
16	Nathan	Lane	2	52	Robert	Townsend	1
17	George	Huestin	5	53	Thomas	Townsend	1
18	Joseph	Crane	1	54	Elihu	Townsend	1
19	William	Drake	4	55	Charles	Townsend	2
20	Sias	Gregory	1	56	Benjamin	Townsend	3
21	John	Drake	2	57	Robert U.	Townsend	1
22	Isaac	Rhodes	4	58	Robert R.	Townsend	3
23	David	Paddock	1	59	Daniel	Townsend Jnr:	1
24	William	Yerns's Widw: farm	2	60	Jesse	Smith	4
25	Joseph	Lane	3	61	Benjamin	Brundage	5
26	Joseph	Meed	3	62	Michal	Shaw	1
27	John	Gee	1	63	Caleb	Hayser	2
28	Joseph	Crane Jnr:	2	64	Samuel	Gates	1
29	William	Gee	2	65	William	Rapelyea	4
30	David	Austin	1	66	John	Barber	2
31	Caleb	Brundage	1	67	Peter	Hartwell	2
32	Nathaniel	Tomkins	1	68	Lewis	Jones	1
33	Cornelius	Fuller	2	69	Dacon	Hamblin	4
34	John	Sprage	1	70	Jacob	Philip	1

February 1760 continued

#	Name	Surname	Value
71	Caleb	Sweet	3
72	William	Palmer	1
73	John	Newbury	5
74	Samuel	Otters Estate	1
75	Peter	Paddock	2
76	Thomas	Paddock	2
77	Daniel	Bradley	1
78	Russell	Gregory	1

Page 435

#	Name	Surname	Value
79	John	White	1
80	Jacob	Ellis	3
81	Philip	Canon	1
82	George	Cary	2
83	Sander	Dewel	1
84	Robert	Farringtons Widw:	1
85	Jacob	Finch	2
86	Thomas	Philip	6
87	Ebenzer	King	1
88	Josiah	Baker	4
89	Lieut:	Taylor	3
90	Isaac	Crosby	1
91	Benjamin	Sears	3
92	Christopher	Fowler	1
93	Peter	Angwine	4
94	Simon	Ryders	3
95	Isaac	Chapman	2
96	Isaac	House	2
97	Thomas	Smith	1
98	Oliver	Gray	2
99	Edward	Gray's Son	2
100	Samuel	Banks	2
101	Nathaniel	Forster	3
102	Samuel	Elwell	3
103	David	Cosby	3
104	Joshua	Cosby	3
105	Jaby	Berry	1
106	Joseph	Taylor	2
107	Isaac	Smith	3
108	Hope	Covy	7
109	John	Covy	1
110	Jonathan	Paddock	2
111	Nathen	Green	2
112	Seth	Nickerson	2
113	Timothy	Clawson	1
114	Benjamin	Roberts	1

Page 436

#	Name	Surname	Value
115	Elisha	Luttington	4
116	David	Honeywell	1
117	Benjamin	Parish	2
118	Jonathan	Sturdefunt	1
119	William	Sturdefunt	1
120	David	Sturdefunt	1
121	Matthew	Bump	1
122	Samuel	More	1
123	Isaac	Horton	1
124	Jonathen	Lane	2
125	Jo	Concklin	1
126	Michal	Slot	1
127	William	Penny	3
128	Tom	Forster	2
129	John	Paddock	2
130	Ezekiel	Meed	1
131	Israel	Taylor	1
132	William	Hill	6
133	Peter	Robinson	1
134	Abram	Hodges	4
135	Isaac	Otter	2
136	Elemuel	Kelk	1
137	Seth	Paddock	2
138	Ebenezer	Jones Jnr:	2
139	Aron	Calkin	1
140	Theophilius	Jones	1
141	Joshua	Hamblin	4
142	Robert	Weekson	1
143	Gabriel	Knap	5
144	John	Van Tessel	1
145	Mr:	Kent	10
146	Jonathan	Austen	3
147	John	Kelly	1
148	Thomas	Kelly	1
149	Isaac	Pierce	3
150	William	Stone	3
151	David	Smith	2
152	Edmund	Baker	1

Page 437

#	Name	Surname	Value
153	Caleb	Chase	1
154	Ebenezer	Chase	1
155	James	Sears	4
156	Peter	Hall	2
157	Nathaniel	House's farm	1
158	Thomas	Gage	3
159	Samuel	Goodspeed	3
160	Elisha	Calkin	1
161	John	Mahew	1
162	John	Merrick	3
163	Moody	House	2
164	James	Cowen	2
165	Elisha	Coole	3
166	John	Hall	1
167	Ezekiel	Burgis	1
168	Jonathan	Kelly	2
169	Francis	Baker	2
170	Uriah	Lawrenc	4
171	Esekiel [Eleazer]	Sprague	1
172	Nathaniel	Porter	6
173	Moses	Gregory's Estate	1
174	William	Rice's Estate	1
175	Joseph	Craw	1
176	Elisha	Banks	1
177	Jonathan	Hill	1

February 1760 continued

	Name	Surname	Value		Name	Surname	Value
178	Christopher	Bobbet	2	231	William	Lane	2
179	Malthia	Hatch	4	232	John	Ryders	3
180	Peleg	Ballard	1	233	William	Dusenbury	3
181	Peleg	Ballard Jnr:	[-]	234	John	Lane	1
182	Seth	Merrick	2	235	Joseph	Hopkins	4
183	Thomas	Colvill	2	236	John	Green [Geen]	2
184	Amos	Fuller	1	237	Thomas	Higgins	2
185	William	Ballard	1	238	Thomas	Hinkley	1
186	Cornelius	Tompkins	3	239	Israel	Cole	1
187	Simon	Ellis	1	240	Abrahan	Underhill	1
	Page 438			241	James	Russell	1
188	John	Meeks	2	242	John	Lawrance	2
189	Isaac	Barton	1	243	Teunis	Krankheyt	[-]
190	Nathen	Bailif	2	244	Thomas	Clemens	2
191	Robert	Ryder	3	245	Sibert	Krankheyt	1
192	John	Field	3	246	Abraham	Krankheyt	1
193	Benjamin	Perry	3	247	Teunis	Brewer	1
194	James	Quimby	3	248	Daniel	Taylor	2
195	Zachary	Paddock Jnr:	3	249	William	Shaw	1
196	Stephen	Field	4	250	Michal	Shaw Jnr:	1
197	Joshua	Moss	1	251	Amos	Dickinson Jnr:	1
198	John	Nelson	1	252	Elisha	Meed	1
199	Moses	Nauthrop	4	253	Andrew	Hill	2
200	Nathan	Birdsill	10	254	William	Chitterton	1
201	Jeremiah	Linckhorn	1	255	Stephen	Ferrington	1
202	John	Manley	3	256	John	Haddy	2
203	Silas	Paddock	2	257	Andrew	Burgis Jnr:	1
204	Moses	Dusenbury	3	258	David	Akins	2
205	Edward	Ganung	1	259	Peter	Ryal	1
206	David	Philip	1	260	Jeremiah	Huiston	1
207	Samuel	Peters farm	1	261	Israel	Honeywell	6
208	Lazarus	Griffen	1		*Page 440*		
209	Bethual	Barnum	1	262	John	Clarke	1
210	Joseph	Philip	1	263	Rubin	Hamblin	2
211	Abner	Bangs	2	264	Robert	Fuller	2
212	Zachary	Paddock	2	265	Jeremiah	Gifford	2
213	Jeremiah	Baily	2	266	Heman	King	2
214	Wm:	Grays Son William	1	267	Jonathen	Hopkins	1
215	Robert	Weekson's son Peleg	1	268	Nehemiah	Wood	2
216	Joseph	Crommell	5	269	Christopher	Ellis	1
217	Rowland	Perry	3	270	Humfry	Ruff	1
218	Noah	Smith	2	271	Philip	Ruff	1
219	Elijah	Weekson	1	272	Joseph	Merrits	6
220	Joshua	Finckle [Hinkle]	1	273	Nathen	Taylor Jnr:	2
221	John	Haw	1	274	Rubin	Kelly	1
222	Jonathen	Lookwood	1	275	John	Jones	2
223	Isaac	Perry	2	276	Walter	Hughson	1
224	Mathias	Burgis	3	277	John	Ferris	2
225	Daniel	Runnells	1	278	Caleb	Pells farm	6
	Page 439			279	Moses	Brundage	1
226	William	Nelson	1	280	John	Lamorie	1
227	John	Birdsill	2	281	Solomon	Ferrington	1
228	Moses	Huestis	1	282	John	Wright	2
229	Elisha	Kelk	1	283	Silas	Washburn	3
230	Jonathen	Bryant	1	284	Ebbert	Herrington	1

February 1760 continued

	Name	Surname	Value
285	Richard	Hoppe	1
286	Richard	Arundal	1
287	Joshua	Barnum	4
288	Timothy	Stephens	3
289	Joshua	Porter	2
290	James	Colwell	2
291	Samuel	Drake	1
292	Uriah	Drake	1
293	Joshua	Tomkins	1
294	Richard	Griffin	1
295	Benjamin	Underhill	2
296	William	Dean	1
297	William	McReady	1

Page 441

	Name	Surname	Value
298	Henry	Boyce	1
299	Joshua	Gee	1
300	John	Langdon	2
301	John Langdon Isaac's Brother		1
302	—	Fowler & Dennis on Nath. Robins: place	2
303	Ebenezer	Robinson	1
304	Simon	Deacon	5
305	Benjamin	Perry Jnr:	2
306	Josiah	Ingerson	4
307	Abraham	Maybee	1
308	Abraham	Maybee Jnr:	1
309	Isaac	Fitch	2
310	John	Rodes	1
311	Benjamin	Odle	2
312	Daniel	Bull	2
313	Thomas	Crosbary	3
314	John	Tarwell	1
315	John	Williams	1
316	Jonathen	Jones	1
317	Philip	Philipse	1
318	Mathew	Benedicts farm Oblong	2
319	Jeremiah	Springsteen	1
320	Daniel	Sunderhill	1
321	Jonathen	Lane Jnr:	1
322	Benjamin	Gifford	5
323	Christopher	Dickinson	4
324	John	Bogardus	3
325	Henry	Krankheyt	1
326	Joseph	Stocker	1
327	Obediah	Basely	2
328	Samuel	Elwell Jnr:	1
329	Isaac	Elwell	1
330	Jonathan	Hunlock	2
331	Jacob	Philipse Jnr:	1
332	John	Clawson Estate	1

Page 442

	Name	Surname	Value
333	Edward	Dolph or Wolf	1
334	John	Dewey	2
335	Benjamin	Roberts Jnr:	1
336	Augustin	Basely	2
337	Eleazer	Bennet	1
338	Thomas	Bennet	1
339	William	Rapelyea Jnr:	1
340	Elihu	Gage	2
341	Anthony	Gage	1
342	Moses	Gage	1
343	Richard	Wearing	1
344	John	Bloomer	1
345	Thomas	Townsend Jnr:	2
346	Christopher	Townsend	1
347	Hugh	Baily	1
348	James	Anderson	2
349	David	Paddock Jnr:	1
350	John	Tompkins Jnr:	1
351	Samuel	Benedict	1
352	Jabez	Elwill	1
353	Nathan	Crosby	1
354	John	Garrison	1
355	David	Burchad	1
356	Thomas	Hodges Farm	2
357	Elisha	Morehouse	1
358	Stephen	Rockwell	1
359	Elijah	White	2
360	Azariah	Meed	1
361	Edward	Rice	2
362	Ebenezer	Kelly	1
363	Ephraim	Smith	2
364	Thomas	Fowler	1
365	John	Bloomer near the River	1
366	Thomas	Crommell	1
367	Nathan	Plumstead	1
368	James	Paddock	1
369	Ebenezer	Weekson	2

Page 443

	Name	Surname	Value
370	John	Stephens	1
371	Jeremiah	Calkin Jnr:	1
372	Ebenezer	Franch	1
373	Eleazer	Miller	2
374	John	Hill Jnr:	1
375	Elijah	Calkin	2
376	Simon	Covil	1
377	Joseph	Robins	1
378	Josiah	Swift	1
379	Josiah	Swift Jnr:	1
380	Gedion	Crowfoot	1
381	John	Garrison near Wickepe	[-]
382	Thomas	Pew	1
383	Daniel	Brundage	1
384	Sollomon	Jenkins	1
385	Benjamin	Serring	1
386	Anthony	Hill	1
387	Samuel	Carter	4

February 1760 continued

	Name	Surname	Value		Name	Surname	Value
388	Rubin	Close	5		*Page 445*		
389	Josiah	Akin	1	442	Benjamin	Barleu	1
390	David	Tuttle	1	443	John	Brade	1
391	Ephraim	Pierce	1	444	Jonathen	Hobey	1
392	Joseph	Huested	5	445	John	Sprague Jnr:	1
393	Caleb	Huested	3	446	Josiah	Robinson	1
394	Jeremiah	Witnah	1	447	Michael	Evans	1
395	Solomon	Brundage	1	448	Gilbert	Trevers	1
396	John	Lumery	1	449	Solomon	Field	2
397	Joseph	Chatterton	1	450	Samuel	Prince	1
398	Elisha	Oakly	1	451	Ebenezer	Brown	1
399	John	Bates	4	452	Joseph	Foster	1
400	Benjamin	Lord	1	453	—	Lawrence on Shaws farm	2
401	Peter	Anderson	1	454	Nathaniel	Arnold	1
402	Charles	Mc Ready	1	455	Solomon	Perry	1
403	Matthew	Mc Caby	1	456	Elisha	Perre	1
404	Joseph	Gee	1	457	James	Perre	1
405	Eleazer	Yoemans	2	458	William	Daily Jnr:	1
	Page 444			459	David	Akin's farm	2
406	Hans	Krankheyt	1	460	Stephen	Crane	1
407	John	Foster	1	461	Jonathen	Viere	1
408	Stephen	Hopkins	1	462	Jonathen	Green Jnr:	1
409	Seth	Hoems	1	463	Nathaniel	Green	1
410	James	Pardy	1	464	Ebenezer	Gage	1
411	Stephen	Pardy	1	465	Nehemiah	Jones	1
412	Ebenzer	Pardy	1	466	Reubin	Crosby	1
413	Daniel	Ball	1	467	David	Crosby	1
414	John	June	1	468	Joshua	Barnum Jnr:	1
415	Joseph	Shearwood	1	469	Uriah	Townsend	2
416	Benjamin	Haviland	2	470	Silas	Gray	1
417	Peter	Terry	2	471	David	Calkin	1
418	William	Haviland	2	472	Ebenezer	Ward	4
419	Nehemiah	Barlow	1	473	Levi	Marks	1
420	Peter	Ismond	2	474	Jeremiah	Calkin	1
421	John	Brown	1	475	David	Sears	2
422	Daniel	Butler	1	476	Benjamin	Vickrey	1
423	Jonathen	Hungerford	2	477	John	Hagur	1
424	Silvenus	Cole	1		*Page 446*		
425	Ebenezer	Perry	1	478	Capt Beverly	Robinson's farm	2
426	Thomas	Hearns	1	479	Hezekiah	Carter	1
427	Phineas	Towner	2	480	Jeremiah	Butler	1
428	George	Darby	1	481	Ezekiel	Gee	1
429	David	Hill	1	482	Abraham	Mors	1
430	Noah	Lee	1	483	Henry	Van Heyning	1
431	Benjamin	Hatch	2	484	Lewis	Jones	1
432	John	Porter	2	485	Daniel	Crawford	1
433	James	Keeler	1	486	Elijah	Smith	1
434	George	Haborn	3	487	John	Eagar	1
435	Benjamin	Burch	1	488	Jacobus	Brower	1
436	Joseph	Collins	1	489	Nathaniel	Sheperson	1
437	Berzelel	Tyler	1	490	Stephen	Concklin	1
438	Thomas	Trobrig	1	491	Samuel	Jones	1
439	Samuel	Calkin Jnr:	1	492	Peter	Boncker	1
440	Nathaniel	Stone	1	493	Reubin	Hamblin	1
441	Wheten	Robinson	1	494	David	Hamblin	1

February 1760 continued

#	Name	Surname	Value
495	—	Baulding on Paddocks farm	1
496	Moss	Kent	2
497	Mellitiah	Hatch	6
498	Peter	Habond	3
499	Benjamin	Nauthrop	2
500	Joseph	Nauthrop	2
501	William	Brownell	1
502	John	Haviland	1
503	Zadock	Scribner	1
504	William	Porter	1
505	Joseph	Forster	1
506	James	Forster	1
507	Prince	Hopkins	1
508	Ebenezer	Unisted	1
509	Silvenus	Hopkins	1
510	John	Kingsley	1
511	—	Palmer Living with Kingsley	1
512	Seth	Holms	1
513	John	Corby [Carly]	1
514	Thomas	Lovelis	1

Page 447

#	Name	Surname	Value
515	Stephen	Hopkins	1
516	Zebulon	Brigs	1
517	Joseph	Barber	3
518	Jacob	Briggs	1
519	Ebenezer	Craw	1
520	Joseph	Vickrey	1
521	Joseph	Bessee	1
522	Charles	Basely	1
523	William	Maxfield	1
524	Eleazer	Hamblin	1
525	Elemuel	Price	1
526	James	Coller	1
527	Joshua	Lewis	1
528	Isaac	Fox	1
529	Lemuel	Fox	1
530	William	Dailey	1
531	William	Dailey Jnr:	1
532	Edward	Daily	1
533	Henry	Hall	1
534	Reubin	Rublee	1
535	Hezekiah	Meed	1
536	Nathaniel	Shepardson	[-]
537	Jacob	Burgis	1
538	John	Barto	6
539	Elisha	Budd	1
540	Ephraim	Pierce	1
541	Joseph	Baker	2
542	Eben.	Lockwood	1
543	Basely	King	1
544	George	Cooper	2
545	—	Barret on Scots farm	1
546	Thomas	Sarls	1
547	Thomas	Woodward	1
548	Jacobus	Brewer	1
549	Joseph	Pearish	1

Page 448

#	Name	Surname	Value
550	Simon	Calkins	1
551	Daniel	Parish	1
552	Peter	Ryal	1
			£1,045

JUNE 1760
SOUTHERN PRECINCT

at 6/9 [6 shillings 9 pence] pr. pound

#	Name	Surname	Value
	Page 453		
1	Major Philips	Philipse	5
2	Francis	Nelson's Estate	6
3	Thomas	Devenport's Estate	6
4	Thomas	Devenport Jnr:	16
5	Jacob	Mandevil	10
6	John	Calkin	3
7	John	Calkin Jnr:	1
8	William	Gray	3
9	John	Rogers	13
10	Thomas	Hallock	1
11	John	Van Amburgh's Estate	10
12	Elijah	Tompkins	3
13	Peter	Duboys	16
14	Ebenezer	Jones	3
15	Benjamin	Jaycocks	2
16	Timothy	Concklin	2
17	Nathen	Lane	2
18	George	Hughstin	5
19	Joseph	Crane	1
20	William	Drake	4
21	Sias	Gregory's Estate	1
22	John	Drake	2
23	Isaac	Roades	4
24	David	Paddock	1
25	William	Yern's widw	2
26	Joseph	Lane	3
27	Joseph	Meed	3

June 1760 continued

	Name	Surname	Value		Name	Surname	Value
28	John	Gee	1	81	Philip	Cannon	1
29	Joseph	Crane Jnr:	2	82	George	Cary	2
30	William	Gee	2	83	Sanders	Duvel	1
31	David	Austin	1	84	Robert	Farrington's wid.	1
32	Caleb	Brundage	1	85	Jacob	Finch	1
33	Nathaniel	Tomkins	1	86	Thomas	Philip	6
Page 454				87	Ebenezer	King	1
34	Cornelius	Fuller	2	88	Josiah	Baker	4
35	John	Sprague	1	89	Lieut.	Taylor	2
36	Samuel	Calkin	2	90	Isaac	Crosby	1
37	John	Hains	3	91	Benjamin	Sears	3
38	Thomas	Frost	1	92	Christopher	Fowler	1
39	Eleazer	Cole	2	93	Peter	Angwine	5
40	Edward	Gray	2	94	Simon	Ryders	2
41	William	Teller's Estate	8	95	Isaac	Chapman	2
42	Abraham	Smith	3	96	Isaac	House	1
43	Luke	Covert	1	97	Thomas	Smith	1
44	Samuel	Jones	1	98	Oliver	Gray	2
45	Elie	Nelson	1	99	Edward	Gray Jnr:	3
46	Valentine	Perkins	2	100	Samuel	Banks	2
47	Samuel	Field	14	101	Nathaniel	Forster	3
48	Joseph	Field	9	102	Samuel	Elwell	2
49	James	Dickinson	9	103	David	Cosby	3
50	Amos	Dickinson's Estate	3	104	Joshua	Cosby	3
51	John	Dickinson	4	105	Jaby	Berry	1
52	Daniel	Townsend	4	106	Joseph	Taylor	2
53	Robert	Townsend	1	107	Isaac	Smith	3
54	Thomas	Townsend	1	108	Hope	Covy	6
55	Elihu	Townsend	2	109	John	Covy	1
56	Charles	Townsend	2	110	Jonathen	Paddock	2
57	Benjamin	Townsend	3	111	Nathan	Green	2
58	Robert U.	Townsend	1	112	Seth	Nickerson	2
59	Robert R.	Townsend	2	113	Timothy	Clawson	1
60	Daniel	Townsend Jnr:	2	114	Benjamin	Roberts	1
61	Jesse	Smith	4	*Page 456*			
62	Benjamin	Brundage	5	115	Elisha	Luttington	2
63	Micheal	Shaw	1	116	David	Honeywell	1
64	Caleb	Hayser	2	117	Benjamin	Parish	2
65	Samuel	Gates	1	118	Jonathen	Sturdefunt	1
66	William	Rappelyea	4	119	William	Sturdefunt	1
67	John	Barber	2	120	David	Sturdefunt	1
68	Peter	Hartwell	2	121	Mathew	Bump	1
69	Lewis	Jones	1	122	Samuel	More	1
70	Deacon	Hamblin	3	123	Isaac	Horton	2
71	Jacob	Philip	1	124	Jonathen	Lane	2
72	Caleb	Sweet	3	125	Jo	Concklin	1
73	William	Palmer	1	126	Micheal	Slott	1
74	John	Newbury	4	127	William	Penny	3
Page 455				128	Tom	Forster	2
75	Samuel	Otter's Estate	1	129	John	Paddock	2
76	Peter	Paddock's Estate	2	130	Ezekiel	Meed	1
77	Thomas	Paddock	1	131	Israel	Taylor	1
78	Daniel	Bradley	1	132	William	Hill	7
79	Russel	Gregory	1	133	Peter	Robinson	1
80	John	White	1	134	Abraham	Hodges	3

June 1760 continued

#	Name	Surname	Value	#	Name	Surname	Value
135	Isaac	Otter	2	189	John	Field	3
136	Edmund	Kelk	1	190	Benjamin	Perry's Estate	1
137	Seth	Paddock	3	191	James	Quimby's	3
138	Ebenezer	Jones Jnr:	2	192	Zachary	Paddock Jnr:	3
139	Aron	Calkin	1	193	Stephen	Field	4
140	Theophilus	Jones	1	194	Joshua	Moss	1
141	Joshua	Hamblin	4		*Page 458*		
142	Robert	Weekson	1	195	John	Nelson	1
143	Gabriel	Knap	5	196	Moses	Nauthrop	4
144	John	Van Tessel	1	197	Nathen	Birdsill	10
145	Mr	Kent	9	198	Jeremiah	Linckhorn	1
146	Jonathen	Austin	3	199	John	Manley	3
147	John	Kelly	1	200	Silas	Paddock	2
148	Thomas	Kelly	1	201	Moses	Dusenbury	3
149	Isaac	Pierce	2	202	Edward	Ganung	1
150	William	Stone	3	203	David	Philip	1
151	David	Smith	2	204	Samuel	Peters' farm	3
152	Edmund	Baker	1	205	Lazarus	Griffen	1
153	Caleb	Chase	1	206	Bethual	Barnum	1
154	Ebenezer	Chase	1	207	Joseph	Philips	1
155	James	Sears	3	208	Abner	Bangs	2
	Page 457			209	Zachary	Paddock	2
156	Peter	Hall	2	210	Jeremiah	Baily	2
157	Thomas	Gage	3	211	William	Gray's William	1
158	Samuel	Goodspeed	2	212	Robert	Weekson's son Peleg	1
159	Elisha	Calkin	1	213	Joseph	Crommell	5
160	John	Meyhew	1	214	Rowland	Perry	3
161	John	Merrick	3	215	Noah	Smith	2
162	Moody	House	2	216	Elijah	Weekson	1
163	James	Cowen	1	217	Joshua	Finckle [Hinkle]	1
164	Elisha	Coole	3	218	John	Haw	1
165	John	Hall	1	219	Jonathen	Lockwood	1
166	Ezekiel	Burgis	1	220	Isaac	Perry	2
167	Jonathen	Kelly	2	221	Mathias	Burgis	3
168	Francis	Baker	2	222	Daniel	Runnels	1
169	Uriah	Lawrence	4	223	William	Nelson	1
170	Eleazer	Sprage	1	224	John	Birdsill	1
171	Nathaniel	Porter	6	225	Moses	Huested	1
172	Moses	Gregory's Estate	1	226	Elisha	Kelk	1
173	William	Rice's Estate	1	227	Jonathen	Bryant	1
174	Joseph	Craw	1	228	William	Lane	2
175	Elisha	Banks	1	229	John	Ryders	3
176	Jonathen	Hill	1	230	William	Dusenbury	3
177	Christopher	Bobbet	2	231	John	Lane	1
178	Malthia	Hatch	3	232	Joseph	Hopkins	4
179	Seth	Merrick	2	233	John	Green [Geen]	2
180	Thomas	Colvil	2	234	Thomas	Higgins	2
181	Amos	Fuller	1	235	Thomas	Hinkley	1
182	William	Ballard	1		*Page 459*		
183	Cornelius	Tompkins	3	236	Israel	Coole	1
184	Simion	Ellis	2	237	Abram	Underhill	1
185	John	Weeks	2	238	James	Russel	1
186	Isaac	Barton	1	239	John	Lawrence	2
187	Nathaniel	Bailyff	2	240	Thomas	Clements	2
188	Robert	Ryder	3	241	Sibert	Krankheyt	1

June 1760 continued

	Name	Surname	Value		Name	Surname	Value
242	Abraham	Krankheyt	1	296	—	Fowler & Dennis on Nathal: Robertson's place	2
243	Teunis	Brewer	1	297	Ebenezer	Robinson	1
244	Daniel	Taylor	2	298	Simon	Deacon	4
245	William	Shaw	1	299	Benjamin	Perry Jnr:	1
246	Micheal	Shaw Jnr:	1	300	Josiah	Ingerson	4
247	Elisha	Meed	1	301	Abraham	Maybee	1
248	Andrew	Hill	2	302	Abraham	Maybee Jnr:	1
249	William	Chetterton	1	303	Isaac	Finch's widow	1
250	Stephen	Ferrington	1	304	John	Roades	1
251	John	Haddy	3	305	Benjamin	Odle	2
252	Andrew	Bergis Jnr:	1	306	Daniel	Bull	1
253	David	Akins Jnr:	2	307	Thomas	Crosbury	3
254	Peter	Ryal	1	308	John	Tarwell	1
255	Jeremiah	Huestin	1	309	John	Williams	1
256	Israel	Honeywell	6	310	Jonathen	Jones	1
257	John	Clarke	1	311	Philip	Philips	1
258	Reubin	Hamblin	2	312	Matthew	Benedict's farm Oblong	1
259	Robert	Fuller	2				
260	Jeremiah	Gifford	2	313	Jeremiah	Springsteen	1
261	Haman	King	2	314	Daniel	Sunderhill	1
262	Jonathen	Hopkins	1	315	Jonathen	Lane Jnr:	1
263	Nehemiah	Wood	2	316	Benjamin	Gifford	5
264	Christopher	Ellis	1	317	John	Bogardus	3
265	Humfry	Ruff	1	318	Henry	Krankheyt	1
266	Philip	Ruff	1		*Page 461*		
267	Joseph	Merrits	6	319	Joseph	Stacker	1
268	Nathen	Taylor Jnr:	1	320	Obediah	Basely	2
269	Reubin	Kelly	1	321	Samuel	Elwell Jnr:	1
270	John	Jones	2	322	Isaac	Elwell	1
271	Walter	Hughson	1	323	Jonathen	Hunlock	1
272	John	Ferris	2	324	Jacob	Philipse Jnr:	1
273	Caleb	Pell's farm	6	325	John	Clawson's Estate	1
274	Moses	Brundage	1	326	Edward	Dolf or Wolf	1
275	John	Lamorie	2	327	Joseph	Dewey	1
276	Solomon	Ferrington	1	328	Augustin	Baseley	2
	Page 460			329	Eleazer	Bennet	1
277	John	Wright	2	330	Thomas	Bennet	1
278	Silas	Washburn	3	331	William	Rappelyea Jnr:	1
279	Ebbert	Herrington	1	332	Elihu	Gage	1
280	Richard	Hoppe	2	333	Anthony	Gage	1
281	Joshua	Barnum	4	334	Moses	Gage	1
282	Timothy	Stephen's farm	1	335	Richard	Wearing	1
283	Joshua	Porter	2	336	John	Bloomer	1
284	James	Colvill	3	337	Thomas	Townsend Jnr:	2
285	Samuel	Drake	1	338	Christopher	Townsend	1
286	Uriah	Drake	1	339	Hugh	Baily	1
287	Joshua	Tompkins	1	340	James	Anderson	2
288	Richard	Griffen	1	341	David	Paddock Jnr:	1
289	Benjamin	Underhill	1	342	John	Tompkins Jnr:	1
290	William	Dean	1	343	Samuel	Benedict	1
291	William	McReady	1	344	Jabez	Elwell	1
292	Henry	Boyce	1	345	Nathan	Crosby	1
293	Joshua	Gee	1	346	John	Garrison	1
294	John	Langdon	1	347	Thomas	Hodges farm	1
295	John Langdon	Isaac's Brother	1				

June 1760 continued

#	Name	Surname	Value
348	Elisha	Morehouse	1
349	Stephen	Rockwell	1
350	Elijah	White	1
351	Azariah	Meed	1
352	Edward	Rice	2
353	Ebenezer	Kelly	1
354	Ephraim	Smith	2
355	Thomas	Fowler	1
356	John	Bloomer near the river	1
357	Thomas	Crommell	1
358	Nathen	Plumstead	1

Page 462

#	Name	Surname	Value
359	James	Paddock	1
360	Ebenezer	Weekson	1
361	John	Stephens	1
362	Jeremiah	Calkin Jnr:	1
363	Ebenezer	French	1
364	Eleazer	Miller	1
365	John	Hill Jnr:	1
366	Elijah	Calkin	1
367	Josiah	Swift	1
368	Josiah	Swift Jnr:	1
369	Gedion	Crowfoot	1
370	Thomas	Pew	1
371	Daniel	Brundage	1
372	Solomon	Jenkins	1
373	Benjamin	Serring	1
374	Anthony	Hill	1
375	Samuel	Carter	4
376	Reubin	Close	4
377	Josiah	Akin	1
378	David	Tuttle	1
379	Ephraim	Pierce	1
380	Joseph	Huested	5
381	Caleb	Huested	3
382	Jeremiah	Witnah	1
383	Solomon	Brundage's farm	1
384	Joseph	Chatterton	1
385	Elisha	Oakley	3
386	John	Bates	4
387	Benjamin	Lord	1
388	Peter	Anderson	1
389	Charles	Mc Ready	1
390	Matthew	Mc Caby	1
391	Joseph	Gee	1
392	Eleazer	Yoemans	2
393	Hans	Krankheyt	1
394	John	Forster	1
395	Stephens	Hopkins	1
396	Seth	Hoems	1
397	James	Pardy	1
398	Stephen	Pardy	1
399	Ebenezer	Pardy	1

Page 463

#	Name	Surname	Value
400	Daniel	Ball	1
401	John	June	1
402	Joseph	Shearwood	1
403	Benjamin	Haviland	3
404	William	Haviland's farm	1
405	Nehemiah	Barlow	1
406	Peter	Ismond	2
407	John	Brown	1
408	Daniel	Butler's farm	1
409	Jonathan	Hungerford	2
410	Silvenus	Coole	1
411	Ebenezer	Perry	1
412	Thomas	Hearns	1
413	Phinease	Towner	2
414	George	Darby	1
415	David	Hill	1
416	Noah	Lee	1
417	Benjamin	Hatch	2
418	John	Porter	2
419	James	Keeler	1
420	George	Haborn	2
421	Benjamin	Burch	1
422	Joseph	Collins Jnr:	1
423	Berzelel	Tyler	1
424	Thomas	Trobrig	1
425	Samuel	Calkin Jnr:	1
426	Nathaniel	Stone	1
427	Wheton	Robinson	1
428	Benjamin	Barleu	1
429	John	Brade	1
430	Jonathen	Hobey	1
431	John	Sprague Jnr:	1
432	Isaiah	Robinson	1
433	Gilbert	Travers	1
434	Solomon	Field	2
435	Samuel	Prince	1
436	Ebenezer	Brown	1
437	Joseph	Forster	1
438	Nathaniel	Arnold	1

Page 464

#	Name	Surname	Value
439	Solomon	Perre	1
440	Elisha	Perre	1
441	James	Perre	1
442	William	Daily Jnr:	[-]
443	David	Akins farm	2
444	Stephen	Crane	1
445	Jonathen	Viere	1
446	Ebenezer	Gage	1
447	Nehemiah	Jones	1
448	Reubin	Crosby	1
449	David	Crosby	1
450	Joshua	Barnum Jnr:	1
451	Uriah	Townsend	2
452	Silas	Gray	1
453	David	Calkin	1

June 1760 continued

	Name	Surname	Value		Name	Surname	Value
454	Jeremiah	Calkin	1	495	Jacob	Brigs	1
455	David	Sears	2	496	Ebenezer	Craw	1
456	Benjamin	Vickrey	1	497	Joseph	Vickrey	1
457	John	Hagur	1	498	Joseph	Bessee	1
458	Capt. Beaverly Robinson's farm		5	499	Charles	Basely	1
				500	William	Maxfield	1
459	Hezekiah	Carter	1	501	Eleazer	Hamblin	1
460	Jeremiah	Butler	1	502	Elemuel	Price	1
461	Ezekiel	Gee	1	503	James	Coller	1
462	Abraham	Mors	1	504	Joshua	Lewis	1
463	Lewis	Jones	1	505	Isaac	Fox	1
464	Daniel	Crawford	1	506	William	Dailey	2
465	Elijah	Smith	1	507	Edward	Dailey	1
466	John	Eagar	1	508	Henry	Hall	1
467	Jacobus	Brower	1	509	Reubin	Rublee	1
468	Nathaniel	Sheperson	1	510	Hezekiah	Meed	1
469	Stephen	Concklin	1	511	Jacob	Burgis	1
470	Samuel	Jones	1	512	John	Barto	6
471	Peter	Bonker	1	513	Elisha	Budd	1
472	Reubin	Hamblin	1	514	Ephraim	Pierce	1
473	David	Hamblin	1	515	Joseph	Baker	1
474	Thomas	Baulding	2	516	Eben	Lockwood	1
475	Moss	Kent	3	517	Baseley	King	1
476	Malleciah	Hatch	6	518	George	Cooper	1
477	Peter	Habond	2		*Page 466*		
	Page 465			519	—	Barret on Scots farm	1
478	Benjamin	Nauthrop	2	520	Thomas	Sarls	1
479	Joseph	Nauthrop	2	521	Thomas	Woodard	1
480	William	Brownell	1	522	Jacobus	Brewer	1
481	Zadock	Scribner	1	523	Joseph	Parish	1
482	William	Porter	1	524	Simon	Calkins	1
483	Joseph	Forster	1	525	Daniel	Parish	1
484	James	Forster	1	526	Peter	Ryal	1
485	Prince	Hopkins	1	527	—	Craft on Widw Lathen's place	1
486	Ebenezer	Unisted	1				
487	Silvenus	Hopkins	1	528	Simeon	Bundy	1
488	John	Kingsley	1	529	The French man on Robert Shaw's place		1
489	— Palmer living with Kingsley		1				
490	John	Carly	1	530	William	Fenton	1
491	Thomas	Lovelis	1	531	Joseph	Lee	1
492	Stephens	Hopkins	1	532	Benjamin	Moss	1
493	Zebulon	Brigs	1				£994
494	Joseph	Barber	3				

Supervisor's Record 1761 to 1764, Volume G
Dutchess County Clerks Office

February 1761
South Precinct

at 2/9 [2 shillings 9 pence] pr. pound

#	Name	Surname	Value
	Page 66		
1	Major Philip	Philipse	5
2	Francis	Nelsons farm	7
3	Thomas	Devenports farm	7
4	Thomas	Devenport Jnr:	14
5	Jacob	Mandevill	9
6	John	Calkin	3
7	John	Calkin Jnr:	1
8	William	Gray	3
9	John	Rogers	13
10	Thomas	Hallock	1
	Page 67		
11	John	Van Amburgh's Estate	10
12	Elijah	Tompkins	3
13	Capt. Peter	Duboys	16
14	Ebenezer	Jones	3
15	Benjamin	Jaycocks	1
16	Timothy	Concklin	2
17	Nathen	Lane	2
18	George	Hughstin	5
19	Joseph	Crane	1
20	William	Drake	4
21	John	Drake	2
22	Isaac	Roades	4
23	David	Paddock	2
24	Samuel	Towner	2
25	Joseph	Lane	3
26	Joseph	Meed	3
27	John	Gee	2
28	Joseph	Crane Jnr:	2
29	William	Gee	2
30	David	Austin	1
31	Caleb	Brundage	1
32	Nathaniel	Tomkins	2
33	Cornelius	Fuller	2
34	John	Sprague	1
35	Samuel	Calkin	2
36	John	Hains	3
37	Thomas	Frost	2
38	Eleazer	Coole	2
39	Edward	Gray	2
40	William	Tellers Estate	9
41	Abraham	Smith	3
42	Luke	Covert	1
43	Samuel	Jones	1
44	Elie	Nelson	1
45	Valentine	Perkins	2
46	Samuel	Fields	10
47	Joseph	Field	9
48	James	Dickenson	7
49	Amos	Dickenson's Estate	3
50	John	Dickenson	4
51	Daniel	Townsend	4
	Page 68		
52	Robert	Townsend	1
53	Thomas	Townsend	1
54	Elihu	Townsend	2
55	Charles	Townsend	2
56	Benjamin	Townsend	3
57	Robert U.	Townsend	1
58	Robert R.	Townsend	3
59	Daniel	Townsend Jnr:	2
60	Jesse	Smith	4
61	Benjamin	Brundage's farm	5
62	Michal	Shaw	1
63	Caleb	Hayser	2
64	Samuel	Gates	1
65	William	Rappelyea	4
66	John	Barber	3
67	Peter	Hartwell's farm	1
68	Deacon	Hamblin	3
69	Jacob	Philip	1
70	Caleb	Sweet	3
71	William	Palmer	1
72	John	Newbury	4
73	Samuel	Otters Estate	1
74	Peter	Paddock's Estate	2
75	Thomas	Paddock	1
76	Daniel	Bradley	1
77	Russel	Gregory	1
78	John	White	1
79	Philip	Cannon	1
80	George	Cary	2
81	Sander	DeVel	1
82	Robert	Farrington's wid.	1
83	Jacob	Finch	1
84	Thomas	Philip	6
85	Ebenezer	King	1
86	Josiah	Baker	3
87	Lieut.	Taylor	2
88	Isaac	Crosby	1
89	Benjamin	Sears	3
90	Christopher	Fowler	1
91	Peter	Angwine	5
92	Symon	Ryders	3
93	Isaac	Chapman	2

February 1761 continued

	Name	Surname	Value		Name	Surname	Value
94	Isaac	Hass	1	147	William	Stone	3
95	Thomas	Smith	1	148	David	Smith	2
96	Oliver	Gray	2	149	Edmund	Baker	1
Page 69				150	Caleb	Chase	1
97	Edward	Gray Jnr:	4	151	Ebenezer	Chase	1
98	Samuel	Banks	2	152	James	Sears	2
99	Nathaniel	Forster	3	153	Peter	Hall	3
100	Samuel	Elwell	2	154	Thomas	Gage	2
101	David	Cosby	3	155	Samuel	Goodspeed	2
102	Joshua	Cosby	3	156	Elisha	Calkin	1
103	Jaby	Berry	1	157	John	Mayhew	1
104	Joseph	Taylor	2	158	John	Mirrick	3
105	Isaac	Smith	3	159	Moody	House	2
106	Hope	Covy	6	160	James	Cowen	1
107	John	Covy	1	161	Elisha	Coole	4
108	Jonathen	Paddock	2	162	John	Hall	1
109	Nathan	Green	2	163	Ezekiel	Burgis	1
110	Seth	Nickerson	2	164	Jonathen	Kelly	1
111	Timothy	Clawson	1	165	Francis	Baker	2
112	Benjamin	Roberts	1	166	Uriah	Lawrence	4
113	Elisha	Luttington	2	167	Eleazer	Sprague	1
114	David	Honeywell	1	168	Nathaniel	Porter	6
115	Benjamin	Parish	2	169	Moses	Gregory's Estate	1
116	Jonathen	Sturdefunt	1	170	William	Rice's Estate	1
117	William	Sturdefunt	1	171	Joseph	Craw	1
118	David	Sturdefunt	1	172	Elisha	Banks	1
119	Matthew	Bump	1	173	Jonathen	Hill	1
120	Samuel	More	1	174	Christopher	Bobbit	3
121	Isaac	Horton	2	175	Seth	Mirrick	2
122	Jonathen	Lane	2	176	Thomas	Colvill	2
123	Jo	Concklin	1	177	Amos	Fuller	2
124	Michal	Slott	1	178	William	Ballard	1
125	William	Penny	3	179	Cornelius	Tompkins	3
126	Tom	Forster	2	180	Simon	Ellis	2
127	John	Paddock	1	181	John	Weeks	2
128	Esekiel	Meed	1	182	Isaac	Barton	1
129	Israel	Taylor	1	*Page 71*			
130	William	Hill	7	183	Nathaniel	Bailyff	2
131	Peter	Robertson	1	184	Robert	Ryder	4
132	Abraham	Hodges	3	185	John	Field	4
133	Isaac	Utter	2	186	John	Yoemans	2
134	Elemuel	Kelk	1	187	Zachary	Paddock Jnr:	3
135	Seth	Paddock	4	188	Stephen	Field	4
136	Ebenezer	Jones Jnr:	2	189	John	Nelson	1
137	Aron	Calkin	1	190	Moses	Nauthrop	1
138	Theophilis	Jones	1	191	Nathen	Birdsill	10
139	Joshua	Hamblin	4	192	Jeremiah	Linkhorn	1
Page 70				193	John	Manley	3
140	Robert	Weekson	1	194	Silas	Paddock	2
141	Gabriel	Knap	3	195	Moses	Dusenbury	3
142	John	Van Tessel	2	196	Edward	Ganung	1
143	Mr:	Kent	8	197	Daniel	Philip	1
144	Jonathen	Austin	5	198	Samuel	Peters	3
145	Thomas	Kelley	1	199	Lazarus	Griffen	1
146	Isaac	Pierce	2	200	Bethual	Barnum	1

February 1761 continued

#	Name	Surname	Value
201	Joseph	Philips	1
202	Abner	Bangs	2
203	Zachary	Paddock	2
204	Wid:	Bailey	2
205	William	Gray's William	1
206	Robert	Weekson's Son Peleg	1
207	Joseph	Crommel	5
208	Rowland	Perry	4
209	Noah	Smith	2
210	Elijah	Weekson	1
211	Joshua	Finkle [Hinkle]	1
212	John	How	2
213	Jonathen	Lockwood	1
214	Isaac	Perry	2
215	Mathias	Burgis	3
216	Daniel	Reynolds [Runnels]	1
217	William	Nelson	2
218	John	Birdsill	2
219	Elisha	Kellick	1
220	Jonathen	Bryant	2
221	William	Lane	2

Page 72

#	Name	Surname	Value
222	John	Ryders	3
223	William	Dusenbury	3
224	John	Lane	1
225	Joseph	Hopkins	4
226	John	Geen	3
227	Thomas	Higgens	2
228	Thomas	Hinkley	1
229	Israel	Coole	2
230	Abram	Underhill	1
231	James	Russel	1
232	John	Lawrence	2
233	Thomas	Clements	2
234	Sibert	Krankheyt	1
235	Abraham	Krankheyt	1
236	Teunis	Brewer	1
237	Daniel	Taylor	2
238	William	Shaw	1
239	Michal	Shaw Jnr:	1
240	Elisha	Meed	1
241	William	Chetterton	1
242	Stephen	Ferrington	1
243	John	Haddy	4
244	Andrew	Bergis Jnr:	1
245	David	Akin Jnr:	2
246	Jeremiah	Huesten	1
247	Israel	Honeywell	5
248	John	Clarke	1
249	Robert	Fuller	2
250	Widow	Hill	2
251	Hamon	King	2
252	Jonathen	Hopkins	2
253	Nehemiah	Wood	2
254	Christopher	Ellis	1
255	Humfry	Ruff	1
256	Philip	Ruff	1
257	Joseph	Merritt	6
258	Nathen	Taylor Jnr:	2
259	Reubin	Killy	1
260	John	Jones	2
261	Walter	Hughson	1
262	John	Ferris	2
263	Caleb	Pells farm	6
264	Moses	Brundage	1
265	John	Lamorie	2
266	Solomon	Ferrington	1

Page 73

#	Name	Surname	Value
267	John	Wright	2
268	Silas	Washburn	3
269	Richard	Hoppe	1
270	Joshua	Barnum	4
271	Timothy	Stephen's farm	1
272	James	Colvil	2
273	Samuel	Drake	1
274	Uriah	Drake	1
275	Joshua	Thompkins	1
276	Richard	Griffen	1
277	Benjamin	Underhill	1
278	William	Dean	1
279	William	McReady	1
280	Joshua	Gee	1
281	John	Langdon	1
282	John	Langdon Isaac's Brother	1
283	Caleb	Fowler & Dennis on N. Robertson p.	3
284	Ebenezer	Robertson [Robinson]	1
285	Simon	Deacon	4
286	Benjamin	Perry Jnr:	1
287	Josiah	Ingerson	4
288	Abraham	Maybee	1
289	Abraham	Maybee Jnr:	1
290	Isaac	Finch's widow	1
291	John	Roades	1
292	Benjamin	Odle	1
293	Daniel	Bull	2
294	Thomas	Crosbury	3
295	John	Tarwell	1
296	John	William	1
297	Jonathen	Jones	1
298	Philip	Philipse	1
299	Matthew	Benedict's farm on Oblong	1
300	Daniel	Southerhill	1
301	Jonathen	Lane Jnr:	1
302	Benjamin	Gifford	5
303	John	Bogardus	3
304	Henry	Krankheyt	1
305	Joseph	Stacker	1

February 1761 continued

	Name	Surname	Value		Name	Surname	Value
306	Obediah	Baseley	2	550	Benjamin	Serring's farm	2
307	Samuel	Elwell Jnr:	1	551	Samuel	Carter	2
308	Isaac	Elwell	1	552	Reubin	Close	4
	Page 74			553	Josiah	Akin	1
309	Jonathen	Hunlock	1	554	David	Tuttle	1
310	Jacob	Philipse Jnr:	1	555	Ephraim	Pierce	1
311	John	Clawson's Estate	1	556	Joseph	Huested	5
312	Edward	Dolf or Wolf	2		[*back to Page* 74]		
313	Joseph	Dewey	2	327	Caleb	Huested	3
314	Augustin	Baseley	1	328	Jeremiah	Witnah	1
315	Eleazer	Bennet	1	329	Joseph	Chatterton	1
316	Thomas	Bennet	1	330	Elisha	Oakley	3
317	William	Rappelyea Jnr:	1	331	John	Bates	4
318	Elihu	Gage	1	332	Charles	Mc Ready	2
319	Anthony	Gage	1	333	Matthew	Mc Caby	1
320	Moses	Gage	1	334	Joseph	Gee	1
321	Richard	Wearing	1	335	Eleazer	Yoemans	1
322	John	Bloomer	1	336	Hans	Krankheyt	1
323	Thomas	Townsend Jnr:	2	337	Stephen	Hopkins	1
324	Christopher	Townsend	1	338	Seth	Holmes	1
325	Hugh	Bailey	1	339	James	Pardy	1
326	James	Anderson	2	340	Stephen	Pardy	1
	[*ahead to Page 78*]			341	Ebenezer	Pardy	1
520	David	Paddock Jnr:	1	342	Daniel	Ball	1
521	John	Tomkins Jnr:	1	343	John	June	1
522	Samuel	Benedict	1	344	Joseph	Sheerwood	1
523	Jabez	Elwell	1	345	Benjamin	Havilands farm	3
524	Nathen	Crosbee	1	346	Nehemiah	Barlow	1
525	John	Garrison	1	347	Peter	Ismond	2
526	Thomas	Hodges farm	1	348	John	Brown	1
527	Elisha	Morehouse	1	349	Jonathan	Hungarford	2
528	Stephen	Rockwell	1	350	Silvenus	Coole	1
	Page 79			351	Ebenezer	Perry	1
529	Elijah	White	1	352	Thomas	Hearns	1
530	Azariah	Meed	1	353	Phinease	Towner	2
531	Edward	Rice	3	354	George	Darby	1
532	Ebenezer	Kelly	1		*Page 75*		
533	Ephraim	Smith	1	355	David	Hill	1
534	Thomas	Fowler	3	356	Noah	Lee	1
535	John	Bloomer near the River	1	357	Benjamin	Hatch	3
				358	John	Porter's farm	2
536	Thomas	Crommell	1	359	George	Hawborn	3
537	Nathen	Plumstead	1	360	Benjamin	Burch	1
538	James	Paddock	1	361	Joseph	Collins Jnr:	1
539	Ebenezer	Wixson	1	362	Berzelel	Tyler	1
540	John	Stephens	2	363	Thomas	Trobrig	1
541	Jeremiah	Calken Jnr:	1	364	Samuel	Calkin Jnr:	1
542	Ebenezer	French	1	365	Nathaniel	Stone	1
543	Eleazer	Miller	2	366	Wheton	Robertson [Robinson]	1
544	Elijah	Calkin	1				
545	Josiah	Swift Jnr:	1	367	Benjamin	Barlow	1
546	Gedion	Crowfoot	1	368	John	Bradey	1
547	Thomas	Pew	1	369	Jonathen	Hobey	1
548	Daniel	Brundage	1	370	John	Sprague Jnr:	1
549	Solomon	Jenkins	2	371	Isaiah	Robinson	1

February 1761 continued

#	Name	Surname	Value
372	Gilbert	Travers	1
373	Solomon	Field	2
374	Ebenezer	Brown	1
375	Joseph	Forster	1
376	Nathaniel	Arnold	1
377	Solomon	Perry	1
378	Elisha	Perry	1
379	James	Perry	1
380	David	Akins farm	2
381	Stephen	Crane	1
382	Jonathen	Vickry	1
383	Ebenezer	Gage	1
384	Nehemiah	Jones	1
385	Reubin	Crosby	1
386	David	Crosby	1
387	Joshua	Barnum Jnr:	1
388	Uriah	Townsend	2
389	Silas	Gray	1
390	David	Calkin	1
391	David	Sears	3
392	Benjamin	Vickry	1
393	John	Hagar	1
394	Capt. Beaverly	Robertsons [Robinson] farm	5
395	Hezekiah	Carter	2
396	Jeremiah	Butler	1

Page 76

#	Name	Surname	Value
397	Abraham	Mors	1
398	Lewis	Jones	2
399	Daniel	Crawford	1
400	Elijah	Smith	1
401	John	Eagar	1
402	Jacobus	Brower	1
403	Nathaniel	Shepardson	1
404	Stephen	Concklin	1
405	Samuel	Jones	1
406	Peter	Banker	1
407	Reubin	Hamblin	1
408	David	Hamblin	1
409	Thomas	Baulding	3
410	Moss	Kent	4
411	Mallethiah	Hatch	6
412	Nathen	Birdsill	2
413	Joseph	Nauthrop	4
414	William	Brownell	1
415	Zadock	Scribner	1
416	William	Porter	1
417	James	Forster	1
418	Prince	Hopkins	1
419	Ebenezer	Unisted	1
420	Silvenus	Hopkins	1
421	—	Palmer living with Kingsly	1
422	John	Carly	1
423	Thomas	Lovelis	1
424	Zabuday	Briggs	1
425	Joseph	Barber	2
426	Ebenezer	Craw	1
427	Joseph	Vickry	1
428	Joseph	Bessee	1
429	Charles	Baseley	1
430	William	Maxfield	1
431	Eleazer	Hamblin	2
432	Elemuel	Price	1
433	James	Coller	1
434	Isaac	Fox	1
435	William	Daily	2
436	Henry	Hall	1
437	Reubin	Rubley	1
438	Hezekiah	Meed Jnr:	1
439	Jacob	Burgis	2
440	John	Barto's farm	1

Page 77

#	Name	Surname	Value
441	Elisha	Budd	1
442	Ephraim	Pierce	[-]
443	Joseph	Baker	1
444	Eben	Lockwood	1
445	Baseley	King	1
446	Thomas	Sarls	1
447	Thomas	Woodard	1
448	Jacobus	Brewer	1
449	Joseph	Parish	1
450	Daniel	Parish	1
451	Peter	Ryal	1
452	—	Craft on Wid: Lathens Place	1
453	Simeon	Bundy	1
454	The French man on Robert Shaws p.		1
455	William	Fenton	1
456	Joseph	Lee	1
457	Benjamin	Moss	1
458	William	Calkins	1
459	Caleb	Lockwood	1
460	Abraham	Covert	1
461	Joseph	Tucker	1
462	Robert	Porter	1
463	James	Bell	1
464	Isaac	Lownsbury	1
465	Seth	Sears	1
466	Dan	Gregory	1
467	Samuel	Lucas	1
468	Noah	Burbanks	1
469	Solomon	Byington	1
470	Nathaniel	Byington	[-]
471	Jabish	Tuttle	1
472	Stephen	Fenton	1
473	John	Smith	1
474	Nathanll:	Robinson Jnr:	1
475	Danill:	Jones	1
476	Silvenis	Thompkins	1

February 1761 continued

	Name	Surname	Value
477	Richard	Inckinbottom	1
478	James	Covey	1
479	William	Merrit	1
480	John	Gould	1
481	Josiah	Bobbit	1
482	Samuel	Tanner	2
483	Timothy	Hatch	2
484	Jacob	Wanser	2
485	Nathaniel	Hays	1
	Page 78		
486	Jehiel	Stevens	1
487	Moses	Williams	1
488	Nathaniel	Finch	1
489	Jedediah	Frost	1
490	John	Blosum	1
491	Silas	Sears	1
492	Nathaniel	Green	1
493	Peter	Maybee	1
494	John	Lownsbury	1
495	Thomas	Lownsbury	1
496	John	Ganung	1
497	Jacob	Finch Jnr:	1
498	Joshua	Parker	1
499	Jabish	Utter	1
500	David	Haukins	1
501	Joseph	Ganung	1
502	Andrew	Rubbelyea	1
503	Ede	Backer	1
504	Shuerman	Travis	1
505	Jacob	Ellice	1
506	Wid:	Ballard	1
507	John	Mirrick Jnr:	1
508	Joseph	Nauthrop	1
509	Jehiel	Baseley	1
510	Lucas	Carter	1
511	Stephen	Osborn	1
512	Andrew	Barger Jnr:	1
513	Anthony	Yoemans	1
514	David	Bruister	1
515	James	King	1
516	Abraham	Yoemans	1
517	Thomas	Adams	1
518	Daniel	Secor	2
519	Samuel	Berned	2

[see 520-556 with *Page 74*]

£1,032

JUNE 1761
SOUTH PRECINCT

at 5/4 [5 shillings 4 pence] pr. pound

	Name	Surname	Value
	Page 88		
1	Major Philip	Philipse	5
2	Thomas	Devenports farm	7
3	Thomas	Devenport Jnr:	13
4	Jacob	Mandevill	9
5	John	Calkin	3
6	John	Calkin Jnr:	1
7	William	Gray	3
8	John	Rogers	13
9	Thomas	Hallock	1
10	John	Van Amburgh's Estate	10
11	Elijah	Tompkins	4
12	Peter	Duboys	16
13	Ebenezer	Jones	3
14	Benjamin	Jaycocks	1
15	Timothy	Concklin	3
16	Nathen	Lane	2
17	George	Hughson	4
18	Joseph	Crane	1
19	William	Drake	4
20	John	Drake	1
21	Isaac	Roades	4
22	David	Paddock	1
23	Samuel	Towner	2
24	Joseph	Lane	3
25	Joseph	Meed	3
26	John	Gee	2
27	Caleb	Brundage	1
28	Nathaniel	Tompkins	2
29	Cornelius	Fuller	2
30	John	Sprague	1
31	Samuel	Calkin	2
32	John	Hains	3
33	Thomas	Frost	2
34	Eleazer	Coole	2
35	Joseph	Crane Jnr:	2
36	William	Gee	2
37	Edward	Gray	2
38	Abraham	Smith	3
39	Luke	Covert	1
40	Samuel	Jones	1
	Page 89		
41	Elie	Nelson	1
42	Valentine	Perkins farm	2

June 1761 continued

	Name	Surname	Value		Name	Surname	Value
43	Samuel	Field	10	97	David	Cosby	3
44	Joseph	Field	9	98	Joshua	Cosby	3
45	James	Dickenson	7	99	Jaby	Berry	1
46	Amos	Dickenson	3	100	Joseph	Taylor	2
47	John	Dickenson	4	101	Isaac	Smith	3
48	Daniel	Townsend	4	102	Hope	Covy	6
49	Robert	Townsend	1	103	John	Covy	1
50	Thomas	Townsend	1	104	Jonathen	Paddock	2
51	Elihu	Townsend	2	105	Nathan	Green	2
52	Charles	Townsend	2	106	Seth	Nickerson	3
53	Benjamin	Townsend	3	107	Timothy	Clawson	1
54	Robert U.	Townsend	1	108	Benjamin	Roberts	1
55	Robert R.	Townsend	3	109	Elisha	Luttington	2
56	Daniel	Townsend Jnr:	2	110	David	Honeywell	1
57	Jesse	Smith	4	111	Benjamin	Parish	2
58	Robert	Shaw	1	112	Jonathen	Sturdefunt	1
59	Caleb	Hayser	2	113	William	Sturdefunt	1
60	Samuel	Gates	1	114	David	Sturdefunt	1
61	William	Rapelyea	3	115	Matthew	Bump	1
62	John	Barber	3	116	Samuel	More	1
63	Peter	Hartwell's farm	1	117	Isaac	Horton	2
64	Deacon	Hamblin	3	118	Jonathen	Lane	2
65	Jacob	Philip	1	119	Jo.	Concklin	1
66	Caleb	Sweet	1	120	Michal	Slott	1
67	William	Palmer	1	121	William	Penny	3
68	John	Newbury	4	122	Tom	Forster	2
69	Samuel	Otters Estate	1	123	John	Paddock	1
70	Peter	Paddock's Estate	2	124	Esekiel	Meed	1
71	Thomas	Paddock	1	125	Israel	Taylor	1
72	Daniel	Bradley	1		*Page 91*		
73	Russel	Gregory	1	126	William	Hill	7
74	John	White	1	127	Peter	Robertson	1
75	Philip	Cannon	1	128	Abraham	Hodges	3
76	George	Cary	2	129	Isaac	Otter	1
77	Sander	Dewil	1	130	Seth	Paddock	4
78	Robert	Farrington's wid.	1	131	Ebenezer	Jones Jnr:	2 [3]
79	Jacob	Finch	1	132	Aron	Calkin	1
80	Thomas	Philip	5	133	Theophilus	Jones	1
81	Ebenezer	King	1	134	Joshua	Hamblin	4
	Page 90			135	Robert	Weekson	1
82	Josiah	Baker	3	136	Gabriel	Knaps Estate	1
83	Lieut.	Taylor	2	137	John	Van Tessel	3
84	Isaac	Crosby	1	138	Mr:	Kent	8
85	Benjamin	Sears	3	139	Jonathen	Austin	4
86	Christopher	Fowler	1	140	Thomas	Kelly	1
87	Peter	Angwine	5	141	Isaac	Pierce	2
88	Simeon	Ryder	5	142	William	Stone	4
89	Isaac	Chapman	2	143	David	Smith	2
90	Isaac	Hause	1	144	Edmund	Baker	1
91	Thomas	Smith	1	145	Caleb	Chase	1
92	Oliver	Gray	1	146	Ebenezer	Chase	1
93	Edward	Gray Jnr:	4	147	James	Sears	2
94	Samuel	Bangs	2	148	Peter	Hall	3
95	Nathaniel	Forster	4	149	Thomas	Gage	2
96	Samuel	Elwell	2	150	Samuel	Goodspeed	2

June 1761 continued

	Name	Surname	Value		Name	Surname	Value
151	John	Mayhew	1	205	Isaac	Perry	2
152	John	Merrick	3	206	Mathias	Burgis	3
153	Moody	House	2	207	Daniel	Runnels	1
154	James	Cowen	1	208	William	Nelson	2
155	Elisha	Coole	4	209	John	Birdsill	2
156	John	Hall	1	210	Elisha	Kelk	1
157	Ezekiel	Burgis	1	211	Jonathen	Bryant	2
158	Jonathen	Kelly	1		*Page 93*		
159	Francis	Baker	2	212	William	Lane	2
160	Uriah	Lawrence	4	213	John	Ryder	5
161	Eleazer	Sprague	1	214	William	Dusenbury	3
162	Nathaniel	Porter	6	215	John	Lane	1
163	Joseph	Craw	1	216	Joseph	Hopkins	4
164	Elisha	Bangs	2	217	John	Geen	2
165	Christopher	Bobbet	3	218	Thomas	Higgens	2
166	Seth	Merrick	2	219	Thomas	Hinkley	1
167	Thomas	Colvill	2	220	Abraham	Underhill	1
168	Amos	Fuller	2	221	James	Russel	1
	Page 92			222	John	Lawrence	2
169	William	Ballard	1	223	Thomas	Clements	2
170	Cornelius	Tompkins	3	224	Sibert	Krankheyt	1
171	Simon	Ellis	2	225	Abraham	Krankheyt	1
172	John	Weeks	2	226	Teunis	Brewer	1
173	Isaac	Barton	1	227	Daniel	Taylor	2
174	Nathaniel	Bailiff	2	228	William	Shaw	1
175	—	Peck	3	229	Michal	Shaw Jnr:	1
176	John	Field	4	230	Elisha	Meed	1
177	John	Yoemans	2	231	William	Chatterton	1
178	Zachary	Paddock Jnr:	3	232	Stephen	Ferrington	1
179	Stephen	Field	4	233	John	Haddy	4
180	John	Nelson	1	234	Andrew	Bergis Jnr:	1
181	Moses	Nauthrop	1	235	David	Akin Jnr:	2
182	Nathen	Birdsill	10	236	Jeremiah	Huesten	1
183	Jeremiah	Linckhorn	1	237	John	Clarke	1
184	John	Manley	3	238	Robert	Fuller	2
185	Silas	Paddock	2	239	Widow	Hill	2
186	Moses	Dusenbury	3	240	Hamon	King	2
187	Edward	Ganung	1	241	Jonathen	Hopkins	2
188	Daniel	Philip	1	242	Nehemiah	Wood	2
189	Samuel	Peters	3	243	Christopher	Ellis	1
190	Lazarus	Griffen	1	244	Humfry	Ruff	1
191	Bethual	Barnum	1	245	Philip	Ruff	1
192	Joseph	Philips	1	246	Joseph	Merritts	6
193	Abner	Bangs	2	247	Nathen	Taylor Jnr:	2
194	Zachary	Paddock	2	248	Reubin	Kelly	1
195	Widow	Bailey	1	249	John	Jones	2
196	William	Grays Son William	1	250	Walter	Hughson	1
197	Peleg	Weekson	1	251	John	Ferris	2
198	Joseph	Crommell	5	252	Caleb	Pells farm	3
199	Rowland	Perry	4	253	Moses	Brundage	1
200	Noah	Smith	2	254	John	Lamorie	2
201	Elijah	Weekson	1		*Page 94*		
202	Joshua	Hinckley	1	255	Solomon	Farrington	1
203	John	How	2	256	John	Wright	1
204	Jonathen	Lockwood	1	257	Silas	Washburn	3

June 1761 continued

	Name	Surname	Value		Name	Surname	Value
258	Richard	Hoppe	1	310	Thomas	Townsend Jnr:	1
259	Joshua	Barnum	3	311	Christopher	Townsend	1
260	Timothy	Stephens farm	1	312	Hugh	Bailey	1
261	James	Colvills farm	1	313	David	Paddock Jnr:	1
262	Samuel	Drake	1	314	John	Tompkins Jnr:	1
263	Uriah	Drake	1	315	Samuel	Benedict	1
264	Joshua	Tompkins	1	316	Jabez	Elwell	1
265	Richard	Griffen	1	317	Nathen	Crosbee	1
266	Benjamin	Underhill	1	318	John	Garrison	1
267	William	Dean	1	319	Thomas	Hodges farm	1
268	William	McReady	1	320	Stephen	Rockwell	1
269	John	Langdon	1	321	Elijah	White	1
270	Joshua	Gee	1	322	Azariah	Meed	1
271	John	Langdon Isaac's Brothers	1	323	Edward	Rice	3
				324	Ebenezer	Kelly	1
272	Caleb	Fowler	4	325	Ephraim	Smith	1
273	Ebenezer	Robertson	1	326	Thomas	Fowler	3
274	Simon	Deacon	5	327	John	Bloomer near the River	1
275	Benjamin	Perry Jnr:	1				
276	Josiah	Ingerson	4	328	Thomas	Crommell	1
277	Abraham	Maybee	1	329	Nathen	Plumstead	1
278	Abraham	Maybee Jnr:	1	330	James	Paddock	1
279	Isaac	Finch's wid	1	331	Ebenezer	Wickson	1
280	John	Roades	1	332	John	Stephens	2
281	Benjamin	Odle	1	333	Ebenezer	French	1
282	Daniel	Bull	2	334	Eleazer	Miller	1 [2]
283	Thomas	Crosbury	3	335	Elijah	Calkin	1
284	John	Tarwell	1	336	Josiah	Swift Jnr:	1
285	John	Jones	1	337	Gedion	Crowfoot	1
286	Philip	Philips	1	338	Thomas	Pew	1
287	Matthew	Benedict's farm Oblong	1	339	Daniel	Brundage	1
				340	Solomon	Jenkins	2
288	Daniel	Sunderhill	1	341	Benjamin	Serring's farm	2
289	Jonathen	Lane Jnr:	1	*Page 96*			
290	Benjamin	Gifford	4	342	Samuel	Carter	2
291	John	Bogardus	3	343	Reubin	Close	3
292	Henry	Krankheyt	1	344	Josiah	Akin	1
293	Joseph	Stocker	1	345	Jabes	Tuttle	1
294	Obediah	Baseley	2	346	Ephraim	Pierce	1
295	Samuel	Elwell Jnr:	1	347	Joseph	Huested	4
296	Isaac	Elwell	1	348	Caleb	Huested	3
297	Jonathen	Hunlock	1	349	Jeremiah	Witnah	1
298	Jacob	Philipse Jnr:	1	350	Joseph	Chetterton	1
Page 95				351	Elisha	Oakley	3
299	John	Clawson's Estate	1	352	Charles	Mc Ready	2
300	Edward	Dolph	1	353	Matthew	Mc Caby	1
301	Joseph	Dewey	1	354	Joseph	Gee	1
302	Augustin	Baseley	1	355	Eleazer	Yoemans	1
303	Eleazer	Bennet	1	356	Hans	Krankheyt	1
304	William	Rappelyea Jnr:	1	357	Stephen	Hopkins	1
305	Elihu	Gage	1	358	Seth	Holmes	1
306	Anthony	Gage	1	359	James	Pardy	1
307	Moses	Gage	1	360	Stephen	Pardy	1
308	Richard	Wearing	1	361	Daniel	Ball	1
309	John	Bloomer	1	362	Ebenezer	Pardy	1

June 1761 continued

	Name	Surname	Value		Name	Surname	Value
363	John	June	1	416	Abraham	Mors	1
364	Joseph	Shearwood	1	417	Lewis	Jones	2
365	Benjamin	Haviland farm	3	418	Daniel	Crawford	1
366	Nehemiah	Barlow	1	419	Elijah	Smith	1
367	John	Brown	1	420	John	Eagar	1
368	Jonathan	Hungarford	1	421	Jacobus	Brower	1
369	Silvenus	Coole	1	422	Stephen	Concklin	1
370	Ebenezer	Perry	1	423	Samuel	Jones	2
371	Thomas	Hearns	1	424	Peter	Boncker	1
372	Phineas	Towner	1	425	Reubin	Hamblin	1
373	George	Darby	1	426	David	Hamblin	1
374	David	Hill	1	*Page 98*			
375	Noah	Lee	1	427	Thomas	Baulding	3
376	Benjamin	Hatch	3	428	Moss	Kent	3
377	John	Porter's farm	2	429	Mallethah	Hatch	4
378	George	Hawborn	3	430	Nathen	Birdsill	2
379	Benjamin	Burch	[-]	431	Joseph	Nauthrop	4
380	Joseph	Collins Jnr:	1	432	William	Brownell	1
381	Berzelel	Tyler	1	433	Zadoc	Scribner	1
382	Thomas	Trobrig	1	434	William	Porter	1
383	Samuel	Calkin Jnr:	1	435	James	Forster	1
384	Nathaniel	Stone	1	436	Prince	Hopkins	1
Page 97				437	Ebenezer	Humstead	1
385	Wheton	Robinson	1	438	Silvenus	Hopkins	1
386	Benjamin	Barleu	1	439	— Palmer Living with Kingsley		1
387	John	Braide	1	440	John	Carley	1
388	Jonathen	Hobey	2	441	Thomas	Loveless	1
389	John	Sprague Jnr:	1	442	Zabedee	Brigs	1
390	Isaiah	Robinson	1	443	Joseph	Barber	1
391	Gilbert	Travers	1	444	Ebenezer	Craw	1
392	Solomon	Field	2	445	Joseph	Vickrey	1
393	Ebenezer	Brown	1	446	Joseph	Bessie	1
394	Joseph	Forster	1	447	Charles	Baseley	1
395	Nathaniel	Arnold	1	448	William	Maxfield	1
396	Solomon	Perry	1	449	Eleazer	Hamblin	2
397	Elisha	Perry	1	450	Elemuel	Price	1
398	James	Perry	1	451	James	Coller	1
399	David	Akins farm	1	452	William	Dailey	2
400	Stephen	Crane	1	453	Henry	Hall	1
401	Jonathen	Vickry	1	454	Reubin	Rublee	1
402	Ebenezer	Gage	1	455	Hezekiah	Meed Jnr:	1
403	Nehemiah	Jones	1	456	Jacob	Burgis	2
404	Reubin	Crosby	1	457	John	Barto's farm	1
405	David	Crosby	1	458	Elisha	Budd	1
406	Joshua	Barnum Jnr:	1	459	Joseph	Baker	1
407	Uriah	Townsend	1	460	Eben	Lockwood	1
408	Silas	Gray	1	461	Baseley	King	1
409	David	Calkin	1	462	Thomas	Sarls	1
410	David	Sears	3	463	Thomas	Woodard	1
411	Benjamin	Vickry	1	464	Jacobus	Brewer	1
412	John	Hager	1	465	Caleb	Nelson	3
413	Capt. Beaverly Robinson's farm		5	466	Justice	Nelson	3
				467	Isaac	Teller	5
414	Hezekiah	Carter	2	*Page 99*			
415	Jeremiah	Butler	1	468	Jeremiah	Teller	2

June 1761 continued

#	Name	Surname	Value
469	Stephen	Pine	1
470	William	Devenport	1
471	Robert	Hughson	1
472	Sebel	Gregory	1
473	Peter	Drake	1
474	— Shearwood on Caleb Sweet's place		2
475	Joseph	Parish	1
476	Daniel	Parish	1
477	Peter	Ryal	1
478	— Craft on wid. Lathens place		1
479	Simeon	Bundy	1
480	The French man on Robert Shaw's place		1
481	William	Fenton	1
482	Benjamin	Moss	1
483	William	Calkins	1
484	Abraham	Covert	1
485	Joseph	Tucker	1
486	Robert	Porter	1
487	James	Bell	1
488	Isaac	Lownsbury	1
489	Seth	Sears	1
490	Daniel	Gregory	1
491	Samuel	Lucas	1
492	Noah	Burbanks	1
493	Solomon	Byington	1
494	Jabish	Tuttle	1
495	Stephen	Fenton	1
496	John	Smith	1
497	Nathanll:	Robinson Jnr:	1
498	Daniel	Jones	1
499	Silvenus	Tompkins	1
500	Richard	Inckinbottom	1
501	James	Covey	1
502	William	Merritt	1
503	John	Gould	[erased]
504	Josiah	Bobbet	1
505	Jacob	Wanser	2
506	Nathaniel	Hays	1
507	Jehiel	Stephens	1
508	Moses	Williams	1
509	Jedediah	Frost	1
	Page 100		
510	Silas	Sears	1
511	Nathaniel	Green	1
512	Peter	Maybee	1
513	John	Lownsbury	1
514	Thomas	Lownsbury	1
515	John	Ganung	1
516	Jacob	Finch Jnr:	1
517	Joshua	Parker	1
518	Jabish	Utter	1
519	David	Hawkins	1
520	Joseph	Ganung	1
521	Andrew	Rubbelyeer	1
522	Ede	Backer	1
523	Shurman	Travis	1
524	Jacob	Ellis	1
525	John	Merrick Jnr:	1
526	Jehiel	Baseley	2
527	Lucas	Carter	1
528	Stephen	Osborn	1
529	Andrew	Barger Jnr:	1
530	Anthony	Yoemans	1
531	David	Bruister	1
532	James	King	1
533	Thomas	Adams	1
534	Thomas	Nickerson	1
535	Eben	Robinson	1
536	Nathaniel	Nickerson	1
537	Isakor	Nickerson	1
538	Samuel	Yoeman's	1
539	Daniel	Secar	2
540	Samuel	Bernod	2
541	Benjamin	Hutchins	1
542	Ephraim	Bartley	1
543	Joshua	Nelson	1
			£978

February 1762
Southern Precinct

at 2/3 [2 shillings 3 pence] pr. pound

#	Name	Surname	Value
	Page 234		
1	Major Philip	Philipse	5
2	William	Devenport	7
3	Thomas	Devenport	13
4	Jacob	Mandeville	9
5	John	Calkin	3
6	William	Gray	3
7	John	Rogers	12
8	Thomas	Hallock	1
9	John Van Amburgh's Estate		10
10	Elijah	Tompkins	4
11	Peter	Duboys	16

February 1762 continued

	Name	Surname	Value		Name	Surname	Value
12	Ebenezer	Jones	3	66	Thomas	Paddock	3
13	Benjamin	Jaycocks	1	67	Russel	Gregory	1
14	Timothy	Concklin	4	68	John	White	1
15	Nathen	Lane	2	69	Philip	Cannon	1
16	George	Hughson	4	70	George	Cary	2
17	Joseph	Crane	1	71	Sander	Devil	1
18	William	Drake	4	72	Jacob	Finch	1
19	John	Drake	1	73	Thomas	Philip	5
20	Isaac	Roades	4	74	Ebenezer	King	1
21	David	Paddock	1	75	Josiah	Baker	3
22	Samuel	Towner	2	76	Lieut.	Taylor	2
23	Joseph	Lane	3	77	Isaac	Crosby	1
24	Joseph	Meed	3	78	Benjamin	Sears	3
25	John	Gee	2		*Page 236*		
26	Caleb	Brundage	1	79	Christopher	Fowler	1
27	Nathaniel	Tompkins	2	80	Peter	Angwine	5
28	Cornelius	Fuller	2	81	Simon	Ryder	5
29	Samuel	Calkin	2	82	Isaac	Chapman	2
30	John	Hains	3	83	Isaac	Hause	1
31	Thomas	Frost	2	84	Thomas	Smith	1
32	Eleazer	Coole	2	85	Oliver	Gray	1
33	Joseph	Crane Jnr:	2	86	Edward	Gray Jnr:	3
34	William	Gee	2	87	Samuel	Bangs	3
35	Edward	Gray	2	88	Nathaniel	Forster	4
36	Abraham	Smith	2	89	Samuel	Elwell	2
37	Luke	Covert	1	90	David	Cosby	3
38	Elie	Nelson	1	91	Jaby	Berry	2
39	Valentine	Perkins farm	2	92	Joseph	Taylor	2
	Page 235			93	Isaac	Smith	3
40	Samuel	Field	10	94	Hope	Covy	5
41	Joseph	Field	7	95	John	Covy	1
42	James	Dickenson	6	96	Jonathen	Paddock	2
43	Amos	Dickenson	3	97	Nathen	Green	2
44	John	Dickenson	4	98	Seth	Nickerson	3
45	Daniel	Townsend	4	99	Timothy	Clawson	1
46	Thomas	Townsend	1	100	Benjamin	Roberts	1
47	Elihu	Townsend	2	101	Elisha	Luttington	2
48	Charles	Townsend	2	102	David	Honeywell	1
49	Benjamin	Townsend	4	103	Benjamin	Parish	2
50	Robert U.	Townsend	1	104	William	Sturdefunt	1
51	Robert R.	Townsend	3	105	David	Sturdefunt	1
52	Daniel	Townsend Jnr:	2	106	Matthew	Bump	1
53	Jesse	Smith	3	107	Isaac	Horton	2
54	Robert	Shaw	1	108	Jonathen	Lane	2
55	Caleb	Hayser	2	109	Jo.	Concklin	1
56	Samuel	Gates	1	110	Michal	Slott	2
57	William	Rapelyea	3	111	William	Penny	3
58	John	Barber	2	112	Tom	Forster	2
59	Peter	Hartwell's farm	1	113	John	Paddock	1
60	Deacon	Hamblin	3	114	Esekiel	Meed	1
61	Jacob	Philip	1	115	Israel	Taylor	1
62	Caleb	Sweet	2	116	William	Hill	7
63	William	Palmer	1	117	Peter	Robinson	1
64	John	Newbury	4	118	Abraham	Hodges	5
65	Samuel	Otters Estate	1	119	Joshua	Cosby	3

February 1762 continued

#	Name	Surname	Value	#	Name	Surname	Value
	Page 237			172	John	Manley	3
120	Isaac	Utter	1	173	Silas	Paddock	2
121	Seth	Paddock	4	174	Moses	Dusenbury	3
122	Ebenezer	Jones Jnr:	2	175	Edward	Ganung	1
123	Theophilus	Jones	1	176	Daniel	Philip	1
124	Joshua	Hamblin	4	177	Samuel	Peters	3
125	Robert	Weekson	1	178	Lazarus	Griffen	1
126	Aaron	Calkin	1	179	Bethuel	Barnum	1
127	Gabriel	Knaps Estate	1	180	Joseph	Philips	1
128	John	Van Tessel	1	181	Abner	Bangs	3
129	Mr:	Kent	7	182	Zachary	Paddock	2
130	Jonathen	Austen	4	183	Wid.	Bailey	1
131	Thomas	Kelly	1	184	William	Grays Son William	1
132	Isaac	Pierce	2	185	Peleg	Weekson	1
133	William	Stone	4	186	Joseph	Crommell	5
134	David	Smith	2	187	Rowland	Perry	4
135	Edward [Edmund]	Baker	1	188	Noah	Smith	2
136	Caleb	Chase	1	189	Elijah	Weekson	1
137	James	Sears	2	190	Joshua	Hinckley	1
138	Peter	Hall	3	191	John	How	2
139	Thomas	Gage	2	192	Jonathen	Lockwood	1
140	Samuel	Goodspeed	3	193	Isaac	Perry	2
141	John	Mayhew	1	194	Mathias	Burgis	2
142	John	Merrick	3	195	William	Nelson	2
143	Moody	House	2	196	John	Birdsill	2
144	James	Cowen	1	197	Elisha	Kelk	1
145	Elisha	Coole	4	198	Jonathen	Bryant	2
146	Ezekiel	Burgis	1	199	William	Lane	2
147	Jonathen	Kelly	1	200	John	Ryder	5
148	Francis	Baker	2	201	William	Dusenbury	3
149	Uriah	Lawrence	4	202	John	Lane	1
150	Eleazer	Sprague	1	203	Joseph	Hopkins wid	1
151	Nathaniel	Porter	5		*Page 239*		
152	Joseph	Craw	1	204	John	Geen	2
153	Elisha	Bangs	2	205	Thomas	Higgens	2
154	Christopher	Bobbit's farm	3	206	Thomas	Hinkley	1
155	Seth	Merrick	2	207	Abraham	Underhill	1
156	Thomas	Colvill	2	208	James	Russel	1
157	Amos	Fuller	2	209	John	Lawrence	2
158	William	Ballard	1	210	Thomas	Clements	2
159	Cornelius	Tompkins	3	211	Sibert	Krankheyt	1
160	Simon	Ellis	2	212	Teunis	Brewer	1
161	Nathaniel	Bailiff	2	213	Daniel	Taylor	2
162	Eliphalet	Peck on Robert Ryders farm	3	214	William	Shaw	1
				215	Michal	Shaw Jnr:	1
	Page 238			216	William	Chetterton	1
163	Ebenezer	Chase	1	217	Stephen	Ferrington	1
164	John	Field	4	218	Andrew	Barger Jnr:	1
165	John	Yoemans	2	219	David	Akins Jnr:	2
166	Zachary	Paddock Jnr:	3	220	Jeremiah	Huestin	1
167	Stephen	Field	4	221	John	Clarke	1
168	John	Nelson	1	222	Robert	Fuller	2
169	Moses	Nauthrop	1	223	Widow	Hill	2
170	Nathen	Birdsill	9	224	Hamon	King	2
171	Jeremiah	Linckhorn	1	225	Jonathen	Hopkins	2

February 1762 continued

#	Name	Surname	Value
226	Nehemiah	Wood	2
227	Christopher	Ellis	1
228	Humfry	Ruff	1
229	Philip	Ruff	1
230	Joseph	Merrits	6
231	Nathen	Taylor Jnr:	3
232	Reubin	Kelly	1
233	John	Jones	3
234	Walter	Hughson	1
235	John	Ferris	2
236	Caleb	Pell's farm	3
237	John	Lamorie	3
238	Solomon	Farrington	1
239	John	Wright	1
240	Silas	Washburn	3
241	Richard	Hopper	1
242	Joshua	Barnum	3
243	James	Colvill's farm	1
244	Samuel	Drake	1
245	Uriah	Drake	2

Page 240

#	Name	Surname	Value
246	Joshua	Tompkins	1
247	Richard	Griffen	2
248	William	Dean	1
249	William	McReady	1
250	John	Langdon	1
251	Joshua	Gee	1
252	John	Langdon Isaac's Brother	1
253	Caleb	Fowler	4
254	Ebenezer	Robertson	1
255	Simon	Deacon	5
256	Benjamin	Perry Jnr:	1
257	Josiah	Ingerson	4
258	Abraham	Maybee	1
259	Abraham	Maybee Jnr:	1
260	Isaac	Finch's wid	1
261	John	Roades	1
262	Benjamin	Odle	2
263	Daniel	Bull	2
264	Thomas	Crosbury	3
265	Philip	Philips	1
266	Matthew	Benedick's farm Oblong	1
267	Daniel	Sunderhill	1
268	Jonathen	Lane Jnr:	1
269	Benjamin	Gifford	5
270	John	Bogardus	3
271	Henry	Krankheyt	1
272	Joseph	Stocker	1
273	Obediah	Baseley	2
274	Samuel	Elwell Jnr:	1
275	Isaac	Elwell	1
276	Jonathen	Hunlock	1
277	Jacob	Philips Jnr:	1
278	John	Clawson's Estate	1
279	Edward	Dolf	1
280	Joseph	Dewey	1
281	Augustin	Baseley	1
282	Eleazer	Bennet	1
283	William	Rappelyea Jnr:	1
284	Elihu	Gage	1
285	Anthony	Gage	1
286	Moses	Gage	1

Page 241

#	Name	Surname	Value
287	Richard	Wearing	2
288	John	Bloomer	1
289	Thomas	Townsend Jnr:	1
290	Christopher	Townsend	1
291	Hugh	Bailey	1
292	David	Paddock Jnr:	1
293	John	Tompkins Jnr:	1
294	Samuel	Benedict	1
295	Jabez	Elwell	1
296	Nathen	Crosby	1
297	John	Garrison	1
298	Thomas	Hodges farm	1
299	Stephen	Rockwell	1
300	Elijah	White	1
301	Azariah	Meed	1
302	Edward	Rice	3
303	Ebenezer	Kelly	1
304	Ephraim	Smith	1
305	Thomas	Fowler	3
306	John	Bloomer Near the River	1
307	Thomas	Crommell	1
308	Nathen	Plumstead	1
309	Ebenezer	Wickson	1
310	John	Stephens	2
311	Ebenezer	French	1
312	Eleazer	Miller	1
313	Elijah	Calkin	1
314	Josiah	Swift Jnr:	1
315	Gedion	Crofoot	1
316	Thomas	Pew	1
317	Daniel	Brundage	1
318	Solomon	Jenkins	2
319	Benjamin	Serrings farm	2
320	Samuel	Carter	2
321	Reubin	Close	3
322	Josiah	Akin	1
323	Jabes	Tuttle	1
324	Ephraim	Pierce	1
325	Joseph	Huestead	4
326	Caleb	Huestead	2
327	Jeremiah	Witnah	2
328	Joseph	Chatterton	1

Page 242

#	Name	Surname	Value
329	Elisha	Oakley	3

February 1762 continued

#	Name	Surname	Value
330	Charles	Mc Ready	1
331	Matthew	Mc Caby	1
332	Joseph	Gee	1
333	Eleazer	Yoemans	1
334	Seth	Holmes	1
335	James	Pardy	1
336	Stephen	Pardy	1
337	Daniel	Ball	1
338	Ebenezer	Pardy	1
339	John	June	1
340	Joseph	Sheerwood	1
341	Benjamin	Havilands farm	3
342	Nehemiah	Barlow	1
343	John	Brown	1
344	Silvenus	Coole	1
345	Thomas	Hearns	1
346	Phineas	Towner	1
347	George	Darbey	1
348	David	Hill	1
349	Noah	Lee	1
350	Benjamin	Hatch	3
351	George	Hawborn	3
352	Joseph	Collins Jnr:	1
353	Thomas	Trobrig	1
354	Samuel	Calkin Jnr:	1
355	Nathaniel	Stone	1
356	Wheten	Robinson	1
357	Benjamin	Barlo[w]	1
358	Jonathen	Hobey	2
359	John	Sprague Jnr:	1
360	Isaiah	Robinson	1
361	Gilbert	Travers	1
362	Solomon	Field	2
363	Ebenezer	Brown	1
364	Nathaniel	Ernold	1
365	Solomon	Perry	1
366	Elisha	Perry	1
367	James	Perry	1
368	David	Akins farm	1
369	Stephen	Crane	1
370	Jonathen	Vickery	1

Page 243

#	Name	Surname	Value
371	Ebenezer	Gage	1
372	Nehemiah	Jones	1
373	Reubin	Crosby	1
374	David	Crosby	1
375	Joshua	Barnum Jnr:	1
376	Silas	Gray	1
377	David	Calkin	1
378	David	Sears	3
379	Benjamin	Vickry	1
380	Capt. Beaverley	Robinson's farm	5
381	Hezekiah	Carter	2
382	Abraham	Mors	1
383	Luwis	Jones	2
384	Daniel	Crawford	1
385	John	Eagar	1
386	Peter	Boncker	1
387	Reubin	Hamblin	1
388	David	Hamblin	1
389	Thomas	Baulding	4
390	Moss	Kent	3
391	Melthiah	Hatch	4
392	Nathen	Birdsill	3
393	Joseph	Nauthrop	3
394	William	Brownell	1
395	Zadoc	Scribner	1
396	William	Porter	1
397	Prince	Hopkins	1
398	Ebenezer	Humsted	1
399	Silvenus	Hopkins	1
400	—	Palmer living with King[s]ley	1
401	John	Carley	1
402	Thomas	Loveless	1
403	Zabedee	Briggs	1
404	Ebenezer	Craw	1
405	Charles	Baseley	2
406	William	Maxfield	1
407	Eleazer	Hamblin	2
408	Elemuel	Price	1
409	William	Dailey	2
410	Henry	Hall	1
411	Reubin	Rublee	1
412	Joseph	Vickry	1

Page 244

#	Name	Surname	Value
413	Hezekiah	Meed Jnr:	1
414	Jacob	Burgis	2
415	John	Barto's farm	1
416	Elisha	Budd	2
417	Joseph	Baker	1
418	Eben	Lockwood	1
419	Baseley	King	1
420	Thomas	Sarls	1
421	Thomas	Woodard	1
422	Jacobus	Brewer	1
423	Caleb	Nelson	3
424	Isaac	Teller	6
425	Jeremiah	Teller	1
426	Stephen	Peyn	1
427	William	Devenport	-
428	Robert	Hughson	1
429	Sebel	Gregorys farm	1
430	Peter	Drake	1
431	David	Shearwood on Caleb Sweet's place	2
432	Joseph	Parish	1
433	Daniel	Parish	1
434	Peter	Ryal	1

February 1762 continued

	Name	Surname	Value		Name	Surname	Value
435	John Thauny	Craft on wid. Lathens place	1	480	Stephen	Osborn	1
436	Simeon	Bundy	1	481	Andrew	Berger Jnr: 2 in the dist	1
437	Samuel	Bernard Jnr:	1	482	Anthony	Yoemans	1
438	William	Fenton	1	483	David	Bruyster	1
439	Benjamin	Moss	1	484	James	King	1
440	William	Calkins	1	485	Thomas	Adams	1
441	Abraham	Covert	1	486	Thomas	Nickerson	1
442	James	Bell	1	487	Eben	Robinson	1
443	Isaac	Lownsbury	2	488	Nathaniel	Nickerson	1
444	Seth	Sears	1	489	Isaker	Nickerson	1
445	Daniel	Gregory	1	490	Samuel	Yoemans	1
446	Samuel	Lucas	1	491	Daniel	Secor	2
447	Noah	Burbanks	1	492	Samuel	Bernod	2
448	Solomon	Byington	1	493	Benjamin	Hutchens	1
449	Jabish	Tuttle	1	494	Joshua	Nelson	1
450	Stephen	Fenton	1	495	Timothy	Dillevan	1
451	John	Smith	1	496	—	Secor on Barton's place	1
452	Nathaniel	Robinson Jnr:	1	497	Ephraim	Jones	1
453	Daniel	Jones	1		*Page 246*		
454	Silvenus	Tompkins	1	498	Francis	Bryer	1
455	Justice	Nelson	3	499	James	Lumerey	1
	Page 245			500	Joseph	Rockwell	2
456	Richard	Inckenbottom	1	501	Eliphel	Nickerson	1
457	James	Covey	1	502	Benjamin	Lord	1
458	William	Merrit	1	503	Simeon	TerBoss	1
459	Josiah	Bobbit	1	504	Peter	Anderson	2
460	Nathaniel	Hays	1	505	Jonathen	Odle	1
461	Jehiel	Stephens	1	506	Isaac	Lumerey	1
462	Jedediah	Frost	1	507	Anthony	Field	1
463	Nathaniel	Green	1	508	John	Armstrong	1
464	Peter	Maybee	1	509	John	Armstrong Jnr:	1
465	John	Lownsbury	1	510	Henry	Jones	1
466	Thomas	Lownsbury	1	511	Abraham	Highet	1
467	John	Gannung	1	512	John	Adams	1
468	Jacob	Finch Jnr:	1	513	Nehemiah	Horton	1
469	Joshua	Parker	1	514	William	Van Tessel	1
470	Jabish	Utter	1	515	James	Roades	1
471	David	Hawkins	1	516	William	Gee	1
472	Joseph	Ganung	1	517	Peter	Moe	1
473	Andrew	Rubelyeer	1	518	Caleb	Lockwood	1
474	Ede	Backer	1	519	Rossell	Gee	1
475	Shurman	Travis	1	520	Benjamin	Teed	1
476	Jacob	Ellis	1	521	John	Meeks	2
477	John	Mirck Jnr:	1	522	Jesse	Smith Jnr:	1
478	Jehiel	Baseley	2				£958
479	Lucas	Carter	1				

June 1762
Southern Precinct

at 5 shillings pr. pound

#	Name	Surname	Value
	Page 250		
1	Major Philip	Philipse	5
2	William	Devenport	7
3	Thomas	Devenport	13
4	Jacob	Mandevil	10
5	John	Calkin	3
6	William	Gray	3
7	John	Rogers	12
8	Thomas	Hallock	1
9	John	Van Amburgh's Estate	8
10	Elijah	Tompkins	5
11	Peter	Duboys	16
12	Ebenezer	Jones	3
13	Benjamin	Jaycocks	2
14	Timothy	Concklin	4
15	Nathen	Lane	3
16	George	Hughson	4
17	Joseph	Crane	1
18	William	Drake	4
19	John	Drake	1
20	Isaac	Roades	4
21	David	Paddock	2
22	Samuel	Towner	4
23	Joseph	Lane	3
24	Joseph	Meed	4
25	John	Gee	3
26	Caleb	Brundage	1
27	Nathaniel	Tompkins	2
28	Cornelius	Fuller	2
29	Samuel	Calkin	3
30	John	Hains	4
31	Thomas	Frost	2
	Page 251		
32	Eleazer	Coole	2
33	William	Gee	2
34	Edward	Gray	2
35	Abraham	Smith	2
36	Luke	Covert	1
37	Elie	Nelson	1
38	Valentine	Perkins farm	2
39	Joseph	Crane Jnr:	3
40	Samuel	Field	10
41	Joseph	Field	7
42	James	Dickenson	6
43	Amos	Dickenson	4
44	John	Dickenson	5
45	Daniel	Townsend	4
46	Thomas	Townsend	1
47	Elihu	Townsend	1
48	Charles	Townsend	3
49	Benjamin	Townsend	5
50	Robert R.	Townsend	4
51	Daniel	Townsend Jnr:	3
52	Jesse	Smith	3
53	Robert	Shaw	1
54	Caleb	Hayser	2
55	Samuel	Gates	1
56	William	Rappeljea	3
57	John	Barber	3
58	Peter	Hartwell's farm	2
59	Deacon	Hamblin	3
60	Jacob	Philip	1
61	Caleb	Sweet	3
62	William	Palmer	2
63	John	Newbury	4
64	Samuel	Utters Estate	2
65	Thomas	Paddock	4
66	Russel	Gregory	1
67	John	White	1
68	Philip	Cannon	1
69	George	Cary	3
70	Sander	Devel	1
71	Thomas	Philip	5
72	Ebenezer	King	1
73	Josiah	Baker	3
74	Lieut.	Taylor	3
75	Isaac	Crosby	2
	Page 252		
76	Benjamin	Sears	4
77	Christopher	Fowler	2
78	Peter	Angwine	5
79	Simon	Ryder	5
80	Isaac	Hause	1
81	Thomas	Smith	1
82	Edward	Gray Jnr:	4
83	Samuel	Bangs	4
84	Nathaniel	Forster	5
85	Samuel	Elwell	2
86	David	Cosby	3
87	Jaby	Berry	2
88	Joseph	Taylor	2
89	Isaac	Smith	4
90	Hope	Covy	6
91	Jonathen	Paddock	4
92	Nathen	Green	3
93	Seth	Nickerson	3
94	Timothy	Clauson	1
95	Benjamin	Roberts	1
96	Elisha	Luttington	4
97	David	Honeywell	1
98	Benjamin	Parish	2
99	William	Sturdefunt	1
100	David	Sturdefunt	1
101	Matthew	Bump	1

June 1762 continued

	Name	Surname	Value		Name	Surname	Value
102	Isaac	Horton	2	156	Nathaniel	Bailiff	1
103	Jonathen	Lane	2	157	Eliphalet	Peck	3
104	Jo.	Concklin	1	158	Ebenezer	Chase	1
105	Michal	Slott	2		*Page 254*		
106	William	Penny	4	159	John	Field	5
107	Tom	Forster	2	160	John	Yoemans	3
108	John	Paddock	2	161	Zachary	Paddock Jnr:	4
109	Ezekiel	Meed	1	162	Stephen	Field	5
110	Israel	Taylor	1	163	John	Nelson	2
111	William	Hill	7	164	Moses	Nauthrop	1
112	Peter	Robinson	1	165	Nathen	Birdsill	10
113	Abraham	Hodges	4	166	Jeremiah	Linckhorn	1
114	Joshua	Cosby	3	167	John	Manley	4
115	Isaac	Chapman	2	168	Silas	Paddock	3
116	Isaac	Utter	1	169	Edward	Ganung	1
117	Seth	Paddock	5	170	Daniel	Philip	1
	Page 253			171	Samuel	Peters	4
118	Ebenezer	Jones Jnr:	2	172	Lazarus	Griffen	1
119	Theophilus	Jones	1	173	Joseph	Philips	2
120	Joshua	Hamblin	4	174	Abner	Bangs	4
121	Robert	Weekson	1	175	Zachary	Paddock	2
122	Aaron	Calkin	2	176	Wid.	Bailey	2
123	Gabriel	Knaps Estate	2	177	William	Grays Son William	1
124	John	Van Tessel	1	178	Peleg	Weekson	1
125	Mr:	Kent	7	179	Joseph	Crommell	5
126	Jonathen	Austen	4	180	Rowland	Perry	5
127	Thomas	Kelley	2	181	Noah	Smith	3
128	Isaac	Pierce	2	182	Elijah	Weekson	1
129	William	Stone	4	183	Joshua	Hinckley	1
130	David	Smith	2	184	John	How	2
131	Edward [Edmund]	Baker	1	185	Jonathen	Lockwood	1
132	Caleb	Chase	1	186	Isaac	Perry	3
133	James	Sears	2	187	Mathias	Burgis	3
134	Peter	Hall	3	188	William	Nelson	2
135	Thomas	Gage	2	189	John	Birdsill	3
136	Samuel	Goodspeed	4	190	Elisha	Kelk	1
137	John	Mayhew	1	191	Jonathen	Bryant	2
138	John	Merrick	3	192	William	Lane	2
139	Moody	House	3	193	John	Ryder	5
140	James	Cowen	2	194	William	Dusenbury	3
141	Elisha	Coole	4	195	John	Lane	1
142	Ezekiel	Burgis	1	196	Joseph	Hopkins wid	1
143	Jonathen	Kelley	2	197	Moses	Dusenbury	4
144	Francis	Baker	2	198	John	Geen	2
145	Uriah	Lawrence	5	199	Thomas	Higgens	2
146	Nathaniel	Porter	6		*Page 255*		
147	Joseph	Craw	1	200	Thomas	Hinkley	1
148	Elisha	Bangs	2	201	Abraham	Underhill	1
149	Christopher	Bobbits farm	1	202	James	Russel	1
150	Seth	Merrick	2	203	John	Lawrence	2
151	Thomas	Colvil	2	204	Thomas	Clements	2
152	Amos	Fuller	2	205	Sibert	Krankheyt	1
153	William	Ballard	1	206	Teunis	Brewer	1
154	Cornelius	Tompkins	3	207	Daniel	Taylor	2
155	Simeon	Ellis	3	208	William	Shaw	1

June 1762 continued

#	Name	Surname	Value
209	Michal	Shaw Jnr:	1
210	William	Chetterton	1
211	Stephen	Ferrington	1
212	Andrew	Berger Jnr:	1
213	David	Akins Jnr:	2
214	Jeremiah	Huestin	2
215	John	Clarke	2
216	Robert	Fuller	2
217	Wid:	Hill	2
218	Haman	King	2
219	Jonathen	Hopkins	2
220	Nehemiah	Wood	2
221	Christopher	Ellis	1
222	Philip	Ruff	2
223	Joseph	Merrits	6
224	Nathen	Taylor Jnr:	4
225	Reubin	Kelley	1
226	John	Jones	3
227	Walter	Hughson	1
228	John	Ferris	2
229	Caleb	Pells farm	3
230	John	Lamorie	2
231	Solomon	Farrington	1
232	John	Wright	1
233	Silas	Washburn	3
234	Richard	Hopper	1
235	Joshua	Barnum	4
236	James	Colvel's farm	1
237	Samuel	Drake	1
238	Uriah	Drake	2
239	Joshua	Tompkins	1
240	Richard	Griffen	3

Page 256

#	Name	Surname	Value
241	William	Dean	1
242	John Langdon ^	McReady	2
243	Joshua	Gee	1
244	Caleb	Fowler	4
245	Ebenezer	Robertson	1
246	Simon	Deacon	6
247	Benjamin	Perry Jnr:	1
248	Josiah	Ingerson	4
249	Abraham	Maybee	2
250	Abraham	Maybee Jnr:	2
251	Isaac	Finch's wid	2
252	John	Roades	2
253	Benjamin	Odle	2
254	Daniel	Bull	3
255	Thomas	Crosbury	4
256	Philip	Philips	2
257	Matthew	Benedicks farm	2
258	Daniel	Southerland	2
259	Jonathen	Lane Jnr:	1
260	Benjamin	Gifford	6
261	John	Bogardus	4
262	Henry	Krankheyt	1
263	Joseph	Stocker	1
264	Obediah	Baseley	3
265	Samuel	Elwell Jnr:	3
266	Isaac	Elwell	2
267	Jonathen	Hunlock	1
268	Jacob	Philips Jnr:	1
269	John	Clauson's Estate	1
270	Edward	Dolf	2
271	Joseph	Dewey	1
272	Augustin	Baseley	1
273	Eleazer	Bennet	1
274	William	Rappelyea Jnr:	1
275	Elihu	Gage	1
276	Anthony	Gage	1
277	Moses	Gage	1
278	Richard	Wearing	2
279	John	Bloomer	1
280	Thomas	Townsend Jnr:	1

Page 257

#	Name	Surname	Value
281	Christopher	Townsend	1
282	Hugh	Bailey	1
283	David	Paddock Jnr:	1
284	John	Tompkins Jnr:	1
285	Samuel	Benedict	1
286	Jabez	Elwell	1
287	Nathen	Crosby	1
288	John	Garrison	1
289	Thomas	Hodges farm	1
290	Stephen	Rockwell	1
291	Elijah	White	2
292	Azariah	Meed	1
293	Edward	Rice	4
294	Ebenezer	Kelley	1
295	Ephraim	Smith	2
296	Thomas	Fowler	3
297	John Bloomer	Near the River	1
298	Thomas	Crommell	1
299	Nathen	Plumstead	2
300	Ebenezer	Weekson	2
301	John	Stephens	2
302	Ebenezer	French	2
303	Elijah	Calkin	2
304	Josiah	Swift Jnr:	1
305	Gedion	Croofoot	2
306	Thomas	Pew	1
307	Daniel	Brundage	2
308	Solomon	Jenkins	2
309	Samuel	Carter	2
310	Reubin	Close	4
311	Josiah	Akin	2
312	Jabish	Tuttle	2
313	Ephraim	Pierce	1
314	Joseph	Huestead	4
315	Caleb	Huestead	1
316	Jeremiah	Witnah	2

June 1762 continued

	Name	Surname	Value
317	Joseph	Chetterton	1
318	Elisha	Oakley	3
319	Charles	Mc Ready	1
320	Matthew	Mc Caby	1
321	Joseph	Gee	1
322	Eleazer	Yoemans	1

Page 258

	Name	Surname	Value
323	Seth	Holmes	1
324	James	Pardy	1
325	Stephen	Pardy	1
326	Daniel	Ball	1
327	Ebenezer	Pardy	1
328	John	June	1
329	Joseph	Shearwood	1
330	Benjamin	Haviland	4
331	Nehemiah	Barlow	1
332	John	Brown	1
333	Silvenus	Coole	1
334	Thomas	Hearns	1
335	Phineas	Towner	1
336	George	Darbey	1
337	David	Hill	1
338	Benjamin	Hatch	4
339	George	Hawborn	3
340	Joseph	Collen's Jnr:	1
341	Thomas	Trobrigg	1
342	Samuel	Calkin Jnr:	1
343	Nathaniel	Stone	1
344	Wheten	Robinson	2
345	Benjamin	Barlow	1
346	Jonathen	Hobey	2
347	John	Sprague Jnr:	1
348	Isaiah	Robinson	1
349	Gilbert	Travis	2
350	Solomon	Field	3
351	Ebenezer	Brown	1
352	Nathaniel	Arnold	1
353	Solomon	Perry	1
354	Elisha	Perry	1
355	James	Perry	1
356	David	Akins farm	1
357	Stephen	Crane	1
358	Jonathen	Vickry	1
359	Ebenezer	Gage	1
360	Nehemiah	Jones	1
361	Reubin	Crosby	2
362	Joshua	Barnum Jnr:	1
363	David	Crosby	1

Page 259

	Name	Surname	Value
364	Silas	Gray	1
365	David	Calkin	1
366	David	Sears	4
367	Benjamin	Vickry	2
368	Capt. Beaverley Robinson's farm		7
369	Hezekiah	Carter	2
370	Abraham	Mors	2
371	Lewis	Jones	2
372	Daniel	Crawford	1
373	John	Eagar	1
374	Peter	Boncker	1
375	Reubin	Hamblin	2
376	David	Hamblin	1
377	Thomas	Baulding	4
378	Moss	Kent	4
379	Melthia	Hatch	5
380	Nathen	Birdsill Jnr:	3
381	Joseph	Nauthrop	3
382	William	Brownell	1
383	Zadoc	Scribner	1
384	William	Porter	1
385	Prince	Hopkins	1
386	Ebenezer	Humstead	1
387	— Palmer Living with Kingsley		1
388	John	Carley	1
389	Thomas	Lovelass	1
390	Zebedee	Briggs	1
391	Charles	Baseley	2
392	William	Maxfield	1
393	Eleazer	Hamblin	2
394	Elemuel	Price	1
395	William	Dailey	2
396	Henry	Hall	1
397	Reubin	Rublee	1
398	Joseph	Vickry	1
399	Silvenus	Hopkins	1
400	Hezekiah	Meed Jnr:	1
401	Jacob	Burgis	2
402	John	Barto's farm	1
403	Elisha	Budd	2
404	Joseph	Baker	1
405	Eben	Lockwood	1

Page 260

	Name	Surname	Value
406	Baseley	King	1
407	Thomas	Sarls	1
408	Thomas	Woodard	1
409	Jacobus	Brewer	1
410	Caleb	Nelson	3
411	Justice	Nelson	3
412	Isaac	Teller	4
413	Jeremiah	Teller	1
414	Stephen	Peyn	2
415	Robert	Hughson	1
416	Silas	Gregory's farm	2
417	Peter	Drake	1
418	David	Shearwood	2
419	Daniel	Parish	1
420	Peter	Ryal	1
421	John Thauny	Craft on wid. Lathens place	1

June 1762 continued

	Name	Surname	Value		Name	Surname	Value
422	Simeon	Bundy	1	470	Benjamin	Hutchens	1
423	Benjamin	Moss	1	471	Joshua	Nelson	1
424	William	Calkins	1	472	—	Secor on Bartons place	1
425	Isaac	Lownsbury	2	473	Ephraim	Jones	1
426	Seth	Sears	1	474	Francis	Bryer	1
427	Daniel	Gregory	1	475	James	Lumery	1
428	Samuel	Lucas	1	476	Joseph	Rockwell	2
429	Noah	Burbanks	1	477	Eliphel	Nickerson	1
430	Solomon	Byington	1	478	—	Jones on Benjamin Lord's place	1
431	Jabish	Tuttle	1				
432	Stephen	Fenton	1	479	Simeon	TerBoss	2
433	John	Smith	1	480	Peter	Anderson	2
434	Nathaniel	Robinson Jnr:	1	481	Isaac	Lumery	1
435	Daniel	Jones	1	482	Anthony	Field	1
436	Silvenus	Tompkins	1	483	John	Armstrong	1
437	James	Covey	1	484	John	Armstrong Jnr:	1
438	William	Merrit	2	485	Abraham	Height	1
439	Josiah	Bobbit	1	486	John	Adams	1
440	Nathaniel	Hays	1	487	Nehemiah	Horton	1
441	Jehiel	Stephens	1	488	William	Van Tessel	1
442	Jedediah	Frost	1	489	James	Roades	1
443	Nathaniel	Green	1	490	William	Gee	1
444	Peter	Maybee	1		*Page 262*		
445	John	Lownsbury	1	491	Peter	Moe	1
446	Thomas	Lownsbury	1	492	Caleb	Lockwood	1
447	John	Ganung	1	493	Rossell	Gee	1
	Page 261			494	Benjamin	Teed	1
448	Jacob	Finch Jnr:	1	495	John	Meeks	2
449	Joshua	Parker	1	496	Jesse	Smith Jnr:	1
450	Jabish	Utter	2	497	Benjamin	Weed	1
451	David	Hawkins	1	498	Moses	Fowler	2
452	Joseph	Ganung	1	499	Joseph	Bates	1
453	Andrew	Rubeljear	2	500	—	Maybee on the farm that was N. Robinson's	2
454	Ede	Backer	1				
455	Shurman	Travis	1	501	John	Yoemans Sen:	1
456	Jacob	Ellis	1	502	—	Oakley	2
457	John	Mirck Jnr:	1	503	—	Munsell	1
458	Jehiel	Baseley	3	504	Gilbert	Dickenson [Dickson]	1
459	Lucas	Carter	1	505	—	Ketterfield	2
460	Anthony	Yoemans	1	506	Thomas	Adams	1
461	David	Bruyster	1	507	Widow	Nickerson	1
462	James	King	1	508	Timothy	Delavan	1
463	Thomas	Nickerson	1	509	John	Cannon	1
464	Eben	Robinson Near Capt Browns	2	510	—	Barret on Chaises place	1
				511	Josiah	Wilcocks	2
465	Nathaniel	Nickerson	2	512	Capt	Brown	2
466	Izaker	Nickerson	1	513	Nathaniel	Hughson	1
467	Samuel	Yoemans	1	514	James	Wilson	2
468	Daniel	Secoor	2	515	Jared	Carter	1
469	Samuel	Bernod	2			£1,076	

February 1763
Southern Precinct

at 1/9 [1 shilling 9 pence] pr. pound

#	Name	Surname	Value	#	Name	Surname	Value
	Page 398			51	Jesse	Smith	3
1	Philip	Philipse	5	52	Robert	Shaw	1
2	William	Devenport	7	53	Caleb	Hayser	3
3	Thomas	Devenport	13		*Page 400*		
4	Jacob	Mandevil	10	54	Samuel	Gates	1
5	John	Calkin	3	55	William	Rapelyea	3
6	William	Gray	3	56	John	Barber	3
7	John	Rogers	12	57	Abraham	Hartwell	3
8	John	Van Amburgh's Estate	8	58	Deacon	Hamblin	3
9	Elijah	Tompkins	5	59	Jacob	Philip	1
10	Peter	Duboys	16	60	Caleb	Sweet	3
11	Ebenezer	Jones	3	61	William	Palmer	2
12	Benjamin	Jaycocks	2	62	John	Newbury	4
13	Timothy	Concklin	4	63	Samuel	Utters Estate	2
14	Nathen	Lane	3	64	Thomas	Paddock	4
	Page 399			65	Russel	Gregory	1
15	George	Hughson	5	66	John	White	1
16	Joseph	Crane	1	67	George	Cary	4
17	William	Drake	4	68	Thomas	Philip	5
18	John	Drake	1	69	Ebenezer	King	1
19	Isaac	Roades	4	70	Josiah	Baker	3
20	David	Paddock	2	71	Lieut.	Taylor	3
21	Samuel	Towner	4	72	Isaac	Crosby	2
22	Joseph	Lane	4	73	Benjamin	Sears	4
23	Joseph	Meade	4	74	Christopher	Fowler	2
24	John	Gee	2	75	Peter	Angwine	5
25	Caleb	Brundage	1	76	Simon	Ryder	5
26	Nathaniel	Tompkins	2	77	Isaac	Hause	2
27	Cornelius	Fuller	2	78	Thomas	Smith	1
28	Samuel	Calkin	2	79	Edward	Gray Jnr:	4
29	John	Hains	4	80	Samuel	Bangs	3
30	Thomas	Frost	2	81	Nathaniel	Forster	5
31	Eleazor	Coole	2	82	Samuel	Elwell	2
32	William	Gee	2	83	David	Cosby	3
33	Edward	Gray	2	84	Jaby	Berry	2
34	Abraham	Smith	3	85	Joseph	Taylor	2
35	Luke	Covert	1	86	Isaac	Smith	4
36	Elie	Nelson	2	87	Hope	Covey	6
37	Valentine	Perkins farm	2	88	Jonathen	Paddock	4
38	Joseph	Crane Jnr:	2	89	Nathen	Green	3
39	Samuel	Field	10	90	Seth	Nickerson	3
40	Joseph	Field	7	91	Timothy	Clauson	1
41	James	Dickenson	6		*Page 401*		
42	Amos	Dickenson	4	92	Benjamin	Roberts	1
43	John	Dickenson	4	93	Elisha	Luttington	2
44	Daniel	Townsend	4	94	David	Honeywell	1
45	Thomas	Townsend	1	95	Benjamin	Parish	2
46	Elihu	Townsend	2	96	William	Sturdefunt	1
47	Charles	Townsend	2	97	David	Sturdefunt	1
48	Benjamin	Townsend	5	98	Matthew	Bump	1
49	Robert R.	Townsend	4	99	Isaac	Horton	2
50	Daniel	Townsend Jnr:	3	100	Jonathen	Lane	2

February 1763 continued

#	Name	Surname	Value	#	Name	Surname	Value
101	Jo.	Concklin	1	155	John	Field	6
102	Michal	Slott	2	156	John	Yoemans	3
103	William	Penny	4	157	Zachary	Paddock Jnr:	4
104	Tom	Forster	2	158	Stephen	Field	5
105	John	Paddock	2	159	John	Nelson	2
106	Ezekiel	Meade	2	160	Moses	Nauthrop	1
107	Israel	Taylor	1	161	Nathen	Birdsill	10
108	William	Hill	7	162	Jeremiah	Linckhorne	1
109	Peter	Robinson	1	163	John	Manley	3
110	Abraham	Hodges	4	164	Silas	Paddock	3
111	Joshua	Cosby	3	165	Edward	Ganung	1
112	Isaac	Chapman	2	166	Samuel	Peters	4
113	Isaac	Utter	1	167	Lazarus	Griffen	1
114	Seth	Paddock	5	168	Abner	Bangs	4
115	Ebenezer	Jones Jnr:	2	169	Zachary	Paddock	2
116	Theophilus	Jones	1	170	Widow	Bailey	2
117	Joshua	Hamblin	5		*Page 403*		
118	Robert	Weekson	1	171	William	Gray's Son William	1
119	Aaron	Calkin	2	172	Peleg	Weekson	1
120	Gabriel	Knap's Estate	2	173	Joseph	Crommell	5
121	John	Van Tessel	1	174	Rowland	Perry	5
122	Mr:	Kent	7	175	Noah	Smith	3
123	Jonathen	Austin	4	176	Elijah	Weekson	1
124	Thomas	Kelley	2	177	Joshua	Hinckley	1
125	Isaac	Pierce	2	178	John	Howard	2
126	William	Stone	4	179	Jonathen	Lockwood	1
127	David	Smith	2	180	Isaac	Perry	3
128	Edward [Edmund]	Baker	2	181	Mathias	Burgis	3
129	Caleb	Chase	1	182	William	Nelson	2
130	James	Sears	2	183	John	Birdsill	2
131	Peter	Hall	4	184	Elisha	Kelk	1
	Page 402			185	Jonathen	Bryant	2
132	Thomas	Gage	2	186	William	Lane	2
133	Samuel	Goodspeed	4	187	John	Ryder	5
134	John	Mayhew's Estate	1	188	William	Dusenbury	3
135	John	Mirck	3	189	John	Lane	1
136	Moody	House	3	190	Joseph	Hopkins wid	1
137	James	Cowen	2	191	Moses	Dusenbury	3
138	Elisha	Coole	4	192	John	Geen	2
139	Ezekiel	Burgis	1	193	Thomas	Higgens	2
140	Jonathen	Kelley	2	194	Thomas	Hinkley	1
141	Francis	Baker	2	195	Abraham	Underhill	1
142	Uriah	Lawrence	6	196	James	Russel	1
143	Nathaniel	Porter	6	197	John	Lawrence	2
144	Joseph	Craw	1	198	Thomas	Clements	2
145	Elisha	Bangs	2	199	Sibert	Krankheyt	1
146	Seth	Mirrick	2	200	Teunis	Brewer	1
147	Thomas	Colvil	2	201	Daniel	Taylor	2
148	Amos	Fuller	2	202	William	Shaw	1
149	William	Ballard	1	203	Michal	Shaw Jnr:	1
150	Cornelius	Tompkins	3	204	William	Chetterton	1
151	Simeon	Ellis	3	205	Stephen	Ferrington	1
152	Nathaniel	Bailiff	1	206	Andrew	Berger Jnr:	1
153	Eliphalet	Peck	4	207	David	Akins Jnr:	2
154	Ebenezer	Chase	1	208	Jeremiah	Huestin	2

February 1763 continued

	Name	Surname	Value		Name	Surname	Value
209	John	Clarke	2	262	John	Clauson	2
210	Robert	Fuller	2	263	Edward	Dolf	2
	Page 404			264	Joseph	Dewey	1
211	Widow	Hill	2	265	Augustin	Baseley	1
212	Haman	King	2	266	Eleazer	Bennet	1
213	Jonathen	Hopkins	2	267	William	Rapelyea Jnr:	1
214	Nehemiah	Wood	2	268	Elihu	Gage	2
215	Christopher	Ellis	1	269	Anthony	Gage	1
216	Philip	Ruff	1	270	Moses	Gage	1
217	Joseph	Merrits	6	271	Richard	Wearing	2
218	Nathen	Taylor Jnr:	4	272	John	Bloomer	1
219	Reubin	Kelley	1	273	Thomas	Townsend Jnr:	2
220	John	Jones	2	274	Christopher	Townsend	1
221	Walter	Hughson	1	275	Hugh	Bailey	1
222	John	Ferris	2	276	David	Paddock Jnr:	1
223	Caleb	Pells farm	3	277	John	Tompkins Jnr:	1
224	John	Lamorie	3	278	Samuel	Benedict	1
225	Solomon	Ferrington	1	279	Jabez	Elwell	1
226	John	Wright	1	280	Nathen	Crosby	1
227	Silas	Washburn	3	281	John	Garrison	1
228	Richard	Hopper	1	282	Thomas	Hodges farm	1
229	Joshua	Barnum	4	283	Stephen	Rockwell	1
230	James	Colvils farm	1	284	Elijah	White	2
231	Samuel	Drake	1	285	Hezekiah	Meade	1
232	Uriah	Drake	2	286	Edward	Rice	4
233	Joshua	Tompkins	2	287	Ebenezer	Kelley	1
234	Richard	Griffen	2	288	Ephraim	Smith	2
235	William	Dean	1	289	Thomas	Fowler	3
236	John	Langdon	2		*Page 406*		
237	Joshua	Gee	1	290	John Bloomer near the River		1
238	Caleb	Fowler	4	291	Thomas	Crommell	1
239	Ebenezer	Robertson	1	292	Nathen	Plumsted	2
240	Simon	Deacon	6	293	Ebenezer	Weekson	2
241	Benjamin	Perry Jnr:	1	294	John	Stephens	2
242	Josiah	Ingerson	5	295	Ebenezer	French	2
243	Abraham	Maybee	2	296	Elijah	Calkin	2
244	Abraham	Maybee Jnr:	1	297	Josiah	Swift Jnr:	1
245	Isaac	Finch's wid	1	298	Gedion	Crofoot	1
246	John	Roades	2	299	Thomas	Pew	1
247	Benjamin	Odle	2	300	Daniel	Brundage	2
248	Daniel	Bull	2	301	Solomon	Jenkins	2
249	Thomas	Crosbury	4	302	Samuel	Carter	2
	Page 405			303	Reubin	Close	4
250	Philip	Philips	2	304	Josiah	Akin	2
251	Matthew	Benedick's farm	2	305	Jabish	Tuttle	2
252	Daniel	Southerland	2	306	Ephraim	Pierce	1
253	Jonathen	Lane Jnr:	1	307	Joseph	Huested	4
254	Benjamin	Gifford	5	308	Caleb	Huested	2
255	John	Bogardus	4	309	Jeremiah	Witnah	2
256	Henry	Krankheyt	1	310	Joseph	Chetterton	2
257	Joseph	Stocker	1	311	Elisha	Oakley	3
258	Obediah	Baseley	3	312	Charles	Mc Ready	2
259	Samuel	Elwell Jnr:	3	313	Matthew	Mc Caby	1
260	Isaac	Elwell	2	314	Joseph	Gee	1
261	Jacob	Philips Jnr:	1	315	Seth	Holmes	1

February 1763 continued

	Name	Surname	Value		Name	Surname	Value
316	James	Pardy	1	368	Moss	Kent	3
317	Stephen	Pardy	1	369	Melthia	Hatch	5
318	Daniel	Ball	1	370	Nathen	Birdsill Jnr:	3
319	Ebenezer	Pardy	1	371	Joseph	Nauthrop	3
320	John	June	1	372	William	Brownell	1
321	Joseph	Shearwood	1	373	William	Porter	2
322	Benjamin	Haviland	2	374	Prince	Hopkins	1
323	Nehemiah	Barlow	1	375	Ebenezer	Humsted	1
324	John	Brown	1	376	—	Palmer with Kingsley	1
325	Silvenus	Coole	1	377	John	Carley	1
326	Thomas	Hearns	1	378	Thomas	Lovelass	1
Page 407				379	Zabedee	Briggs	1
327	Phineas	Towner	1	380	Charles	Baseley	2
328	George	Darbey	1	381	Eleazer	Hamblin	2
329	David	Hill	1	382	Elemuel	Price	1
330	Benjamin	Hatch	3	383	William	Dailey	2
331	George	Hawborn	3	384	Reubin	Rublee	1
332	Joseph	Collons	1	385	Joseph	Vickry	1
333	Thomas	Trobrig	1	386	Silvenus	Hopkins	1
334	Samuel	Calkin Jnr:	1	387	Hezekiah	Meade Jnr:	1
335	Nathaniel	Stone	1	388	Jacob	Burgis	2
336	Wheton	Robinson	2	389	Thomas	Barto's farm	1
337	Benjamin	Barber	2	390	Elijah	Budd	2
338	Jonathen	Hobey	2	391	Joseph	Baker	1
339	Isaiah	Robinson	1	392	Eben	Lockwood	1
340	Gilbert	Travis	2	393	Baseley	King	1
341	Solomon	Field	3	394	Thomas	Sarls	1
342	Ebenezer	Brown	1	395	Thomas	Woodard	1
343	Nathaniel	Arnold	1	396	Jacobus	Brewer	1
344	Solomon	Perry	1	397	Caleb	Nelson	3
345	James	Perry	1	398	Justice	Nelson	3
346	David	Akins farm	1	399	Isaac	Teller	4
347	Stephen	Crane	1	400	Jeremiah	Teller	1
348	Jonathen	Vickry	1	401	Stephen	Pine	1
349	Ebenezer	Gage	1	*Page 409*			
350	Nehemiah	Jones	1	402	Robert	Hughson	1
351	Reubin	Crosby	2	403	Josiah	Gregory's farm	2
352	Joshua	Barnum Jnr:	1	404	Peter	Drake	1
353	David	Crosby	1	405	David	Shearwood	2
354	Silas	Gray	1	406	Daniel	Parish	1
355	David	Calkin	1	407	Peter	Ryal	1
356	David	Sears	4	408	John Thauny	Craft on widow Lathen	1
357	Benjamin	Vickry	2				
358	Capt. Beaverley	Robinson's farm	7	409	Benjamin	Bundy [Moss]	1
				410	William	Calkins	1
359	Hezekiah	Carter	2	411	Isaac	Lownsberry	2
360	Abraham	Mors	2	412	Seth	Sears	2
361	Luwis	Jones	3	413	Daniel	Gregory	1
362	Daniel	Crawford	1	414	Samuel	Lucas	1
363	John	Eagar	1	415	Noah	Burbanks	1
364	Peter	Boncker	1	416	Solomon	Byington	1
Page 408				417	Jabish	Tuttle	1
365	Reubin	Hamblin	2	418	Stephen	Fenton	1
366	David	Hamblin	1	419	Nathaniel	Robinson Jnr:	1
367	Thomas	Baulding	4	420	James	Covey	1

February 1763 continued

	Name	Surname	Value		Name	Surname	Value
421	William	Merrit	2	474	Rossell	Gee	1
422	Josiah	Bobbit	2	475	Benjamin	Teed	1
423	Jehiel	Stephens	1	476	John	Meeks	2
424	Jedediah	Frost	1	477	Jesse	Smith Jnr:	1
425	Nathaniel	Frost [Green]	1	478	Benjamin	Weed	1
426	Peter	Maybee	1		*Page 410[a]*		
427	John	Lownsberry	1	479	Moses	Fowler	2
428	Thomas	Lownsberry	1	480	John	Maybee	2
429	John	Ganung	1	481	John	Yoemans Sen:	1
430	Jacob	Finch Jnr:	1	482	Robert	Oakley	1
431	Joshua	Parker	1	483	Ebenezer	Munsell	2
432	Jabish	Utter	2	484	Gilbert	Dickenson [Dickson]	1
433	David	Hawkins	1	485	—	Kitterfield	2
434	Joseph	Ganung	1	486	Thomas	Adams	1
435	Andrew	Rubelyeer	2	487	Widow	Nickerson	1
436	Ede	Backer	1	488	Timothy	Delavan	1
437	Shuerman	Travis	1	489	John	Cannon	2
438	Jacob	Ellis	1	490	Isaac Barrit on Chaises place		1
439	John	Mirck Jnr:	1	491	Josiah	Wilcocks	3
440	Jehiel	Baseley	4	492	Capt	Brown	2
	Page 410			493	Nathaniel	Hughson	1
441	Lucas	Carter	1	494	James	Wilson	2
442	Anthony	Yoemans	1	495	Jared	Carter	1
443	James	King	1	496	Comfort	Luddington	1
444	Thomas	Nickerson	1	497	Joseiah	Benjamins	1
445	Eben	Robinson Near Capt Brown	2	498	Samuel	Perry	1
				499	Elisha	Calkin	1
446	Nathaniel	Nickerson	2	500	James	Townsend	1
447	Izaker	Nickerson	1	501	Roger	Haviland	2
448	Samuel	Yoemans	1	502	Thomas	Ferguson	1
449	John	Secar	2	503	Joseph	Colvil	1
450	Samuel	Bernod	2	504	Nathaniel	Byington	1
451	Benjamin	Hutchens	1	505	Reubin	Bloomer	1
452	Joshua	Nelson	1	506	Jacob	Doty	1
453	James	Secor	2	507	Samuel	Hall	2
454	Ephraim	Jones	1	508	David	Pearce	1
455	Francis	Bryer	1	509	John	Barber Jnr:	1
456	James	Lumery	1	510	Isaac	Mirrick	1
457	Joseph	Rockwell	2	511	Solomon	Hopkins	1
458	Eliphelet	Nickerson	1	512	Isaiah	Hopkins	1
459	Stephen	Concklin	1	513	Jonathen	Washburn	1
460	Simeon	TerBoss	2	514	Uriah	Whitney	2
461	Peter	Anderson	2	515	John	Clarke Jnr:	2
462	Isaac	Lumery	1	516	William	Judd	1
463	Anthony	Field	1	517	Reubin	Chase	1
464	John	Armstrong	1		*Page 411*		
465	John	Armstrong Jnr:	1	518	William	Underhill	1
466	Abraham	Height	1	519	Augustin	Underhill	1
467	John	Adams	1	520	Seth	Olmsted	1
468	Nehemiah	Horton	1	521	Joseph	Robins	1
469	William	Van Tessel	1	522	Joshua	Porter	1
470	James	Roades	1	523	John	Roberts	1
471	William	Gee	1	524	Benjamin	Roberts Jnr:	1
472	Peter	Moe	1	525	Theodorus	Crosby	1
473	Caleb	Lockwood	1	526	Samuel	Burchard	1

February 1763 continued

#	Name	Surname	Value	#	Name	Surname	Value
527	Nehemiah	Bailey	1	543	James	Forster	1
528	Caleb	Palmer	1	544	Stephen	Tompkins	1
529	John	Manley Jnr:	1	545	Eleazor	Baker	1
530	Ebenezer	Munson Jnr:	1	546	John	Haviland	1
531	Elisha	Kent Jnr:	1	547	David	Tuttle	1
532	Richard	Gray	1	548	Elisha	Beadle	1
533	Benoney	Gray	1	549	Jonathen	Pine	1
534	Augustin	Wright	1	550	Abraham	Craft	1
535	John	Rubelyear	1	551	Malcom	Morrison	3
536	Gedion	Ellis	1	552	Samuel	Pears	1
537	Nathen	Green Jnr:	1	553	Jedediah	Davis	1
538	Benjamin	Sears Jnr:	1	554	James	Knap	1
539	Stephen	Murch	1		*Page 412*		
540	Stephen	Meade	1	555	Jonathen	Knap	1
541	Joseph	Forster	1	556	Gilbert	Clap	1
542	Obadiah	Horton	1				£1,132

JUNE 1763
SOUTHERN PRECINCT

at 5/1 [5 shilling 1 pence] pr. pound

#	Name	Surname	Value	#	Name	Surname	Value
	Page 415			30	Thomas	Frost	2
1	Major Philip	Philipse	5	31	William	Gee	3
2	William	Devenport	6	32	Edward	Gray	2
3	Thomas	Devenport	13	33	Abraham	Smith	3
4	Jacob	Mandevell	10	34	Luke	Covert	1
5	John	Calkin	3	35	Elie	Nelson	1
6	William	Gray	3	36	Valentine	Perkins farm	2
7	John	Rogers	12		*Page 416*		
8	John	Van Amburghs Estate	7	37	Joseph	Crane Jnr:	2
9	Elijah	Tompkins	5	38	Samuel	Field	11
10	Peter	Duboys	16	39	Joseph	Field	8
11	Ebenezer	Jones	3	40	James	Dickenson	6
12	Benjamin	Jaycocks	2	41	Amos	Dickenson	4
13	Timothy	Concklin	4	42	John	Dickenson	5
14	Nathen	Lane	3	43	Daniel	Townsend	4
15	George	Hughson	5	44	Thomas	Townsend	1
16	Joseph	Crane	1	45	Elihu	Townsend	2
17	William	Drake	4	46	Charles	Townsend	2
18	John	Drake	1	47	Benjamin	Townsend	5
19	Isaac	Roades	5	48	Robert R.	Townsend	4
20	David	Paddock	2	49	Daniel	Townsend Jnr:	3
21	Samuel	Towner	4	50	Jesse	Smith	3
22	Joseph	Lane	3	51	Robert	Shaw	1
23	Joseph	Meade	4	52	Caleb	Hayser	3
24	John	Gee	2	53	Samuel	Gates	1
25	Caleb	Brundage	1	54	William	Rappelyea	3
26	Nathaniel	Tomkins	2	55	John	Barber	3
27	Cornelius	Fuller	2	56	Abraham	Hartwell	3
28	Samuel	Calkin	2	57	Deacon	Hamblin	3
29	John	Hains	4	58	Jacob	Philip	1

June 1763 continued

#	Name	Surname	Value	#	Name	Surname	Value
59	Caleb	Sweet	3	113	Theophilus	Jones	1
60	William	Palmer	2	114	Joshua	Hamblin	5
61	John	Newbury	4	115	Robert	Weekson	1
62	Samuel	Utters Estate	2	116	Aaron	Calkin	2
63	Thomas	Paddock	4	117	Gabriel	Knaps Estate	2
64	Russel	Gregory	1	118	John	Van Tessel	1
65	John	White	1	119	Mr:	Kent	6
66	George	Curry	4	120	Jonathen	Austin	4
67	Thomas	Philip	5	121	Thomas	Kelley	1
68	Ebenezer	King	1	122	Isaac	Pierce	2
69	Josiah	Baker	4	123	William	Stone	4
70	Lieut.	Taylor	3	124	David	Smith	2
71	Isaac	Crosby	2	125	Edward [Edmund]	Baker	2
72	Benjamin	Sears	4	126	Caleb	Chase	1
73	Christopher	Fowler	1	127	James	Sears	2
74	Peter	Angwine	5		*Page 418*		
75	Simon	Ryder	5	128	Peter	Hall	4
76	Isaac	Hause	1	129	Thomas	Gage	2
77	Thomas	Smith	1	130	Samuel	Goodspeed	4
78	Edward	Gray Jnr:	4	131	John	Mayhew's Estate	1
79	Samuel	Bangs	3	132	John	Mirck	3
80	Nathaniel	Forster	5	133	Moody	House	3
81	Samuel	Elwell	2	134	James	Cowen	2
	Page 417			135	Elisha	Coole	4
82	David	Cosby	3	136	Ezekiel	Burgis	1
83	Jaby	Berry	2	137	Jonathen	Kelley	2
84	Joseph	Taylor	2	138	Francis	Baker	2
85	Isaac	Smith	3	139	Uriah	Lawrence	6
86	Hope	Covy	6	140	Nathaniel	Porter	6
87	Jonathan	Paddock	4	141	Joseph	Craw	1
88	Nathen	Green	3	142	Elisha	Bangs	2
89	Seth	Nickerson	3	143	Seth	Mirrick	2
90	Timothy	Clauson	1	144	Thomas	Colvill	2
91	Benjamin	Roberts	1	145	Amos	Fuller	2
92	Benjamin	Parish	2	146	William	Ballard	1
93	William	Sturdefunt	1	147	Cornelius	Tompkins	4
94	David	Sturdefunt	1	148	Simon	Ellis	3
95	Matthew	Bump	1	149	Nathaniel	Bailiff	1
96	Isaac	Horton	2	150	Eliphalet	Pick	4
97	Jonathan	Lane	2	151	Ebenezer	Chase	1
98	Joseph	Concklin	1	152	John	Field	6
99	Michal	Slott	2	153	John	Yoemans Jnr:	3
100	William	Penney	4	154	Zachary	Paddock Jnr:	4
101	Tom	Forster	2	155	Stephen	Field	5
102	John	Paddock	2	156	John	Nelson	2
103	Ezekiel	Meade	2	157	James	Birdsill	10
104	Israel	Taylor	1	158	Jeremiah	Linckhorne	1
105	William	Hill	7	159	John	Manley	3
106	Peter	Robinson	1	160	Silas	Paddock	3
107	Abraham	Hodges	4	161	Edward	Ganung	1
108	Joshua	Cosby	3	162	Samuel	Peters	4
109	Isaac	Chapman	2	163	Lazarus	Griffen	1
110	Isaac	Utter	1	164	Abner	Bangs	4
111	Seth	Paddock	5	165	Zachary	Paddock	2
112	Ebenezer	Jones Jnr:	2	166	Widow	Bailey	2

June 1763 continued

	Name	Surname	Value		Name	Surname	Value
167	William	Grays Son William	1	220	Solomon	Ferrington	1
168	Peleg	Weekson	1	221	John	Wright	1
169	Joseph	Crommell	5	222	Silas	Washburn	3
170	Rowland	Perry	5	223	Richard	Hopper	1
171	Noah	Smith	3	224	Joshua	Barnum	4
	Page 419			225	James	Colvils farm	1
172	Elijah	Weekson	1	226	Samuel	Drake	1
173	Joshua	Hinckley	1	227	Uriah	Drake	2
174	John	How	2	228	Joshua	Tompkins	2
175	Jonathen	Lockwood	1	229	Richard	Griffen	2
176	Isaac	Perry	3	230	William	Dean	1
177	Mathias	Burgis	3	231	John	Langdon	1
178	William	Nelson	1	232	Joshua	Gee	1
179	John	Birdsill	2	233	Caleb	Fowler	4
180	Elisha	Kelk	1	234	Ebenezer	Robinson	1
181	Jonathen	Bryant	2	235	Simon	Deacon	6
182	William	Lane	2	236	Benjamin	Perry	1
183	John	Ryder	5	237	Josiah	Ingerson	5
184	William	Dusenbury	3	238	Abraham	Maybee	2
185	John	Lane	1	239	Abraham	Maybee Jnr:	1
186	Joseph	Hopkins widow	1	240	Isaac	Finch's widow	1
187	Moses	Dusenbury	3	241	John	Roades	2
188	John	Geen	2	242	Benjamin	Odle	2
189	Thomas	Higgens	2	243	Daniel	Bull	2
190	Thomas	Hinkley	1	244	Thomas	Crosbury	4
191	Abraham	Underhill	1	245	Philip	Philips	2
192	James	Russel	1	246	Matthew	Benedick's farm	2
193	Thomas	Clements	2	247	Daniel	Southerland	2
194	Sibert	Krankheyt	1	248	Jonathen	Lane Jnr:	1
195	Teunis	Brewer	1	249	Benjamin	Gifford	5
196	Daniel	Taylor	2	250	John	Bogardus	4
197	William	Shaw	1	251	Henry	Krankheyt	1
198	Michal	Shaw Jnr:	1	252	Joseph	Stocker	2
199	William	Chetterton	1	253	Obediah	Baseley	3
200	Stephen	Farrington	1	254	Samuel	Elwell Jnr:	3
201	Andrew	Berger Jnr:	1	255	Isaac	Elwell	2
202	David	Akins Jnr:	3	256	Jacob	Philipse	1
203	Jeremiah	Huestin	2	257	John	Clauson	2
204	John	Clarke	2	258	Edward	Dolff	2
205	Robert	Fuller	2		*Page 421*		
206	Widow	Hill	2	259	Joseph	Dewey	1
207	Haman	King	2	260	Augustin	Baseley	1
208	Jonathen	Hopkins	2	261	Eleazer	Bennet	1
209	Nehemiah	Wood	2	262	William	Rappelyea Jnr:	1
210	Christopher	Ellis	1	263	Elihu	Gage	2
211	Philip	Ruff	1	264	Anthony	Gage	1
212	Joseph	Merrits	6	265	Moses	Gage	1
213	Nathen	Taylor Jnr:	4	266	Richard	Wearing	2
214	Reubin	Kelley	1	267	John	Bloomer	1
215	John	Jones	2	268	Thomas	Townsend Jnr:	2
	Page 420			269	Christopher	Townsend	1
216	Walter	Hughson	1	270	Hugh	Bailey	1
217	John	Ferris	2	271	David	Paddock Jnr:	1
218	Caleb	Pells farm	3	272	John	Tomkins Jnr:	1
219	John	Lamory	3	273	Samuel	Benedict	1

June 1763 continued

	Name	Surname	Value		Name	Surname	Value
274	Jabez	Elwell	1	328	Benjamin	Barber	2
275	Nathen	Crosby	1	329	Jonathen	Hobey	2
276	John	Garrison	2	330	Isaiah	Robinson	1
277	Thomas	Hodges farm	1	331	Solomon	Field	3
278	Stephen	Rockwell	1	332	Ebenezer	Brown	1
279	Elijah	White	2	333	Nathaniel	Arnold	1
280	Hezekiah	Meade	1	334	Solomon	Perry	1
281	Edward	Rice	4	335	James	Perry	1
282	Ebenezer	Kelly	1	336	David	Akins farm	2
283	Ephraim	Smith	2	337	Stephen	Crane	1
284	Thomas	Fowler	3	338	Jonathen	Vickry	1
285	John Bloomer near the River		1	339	Ebenezer	Gage	1
286	Thomas	Crommell	1	340	Nehemiah	Jones	1
287	Nathaniel	Plumstead	2	341	Reubin	Crosby	2
288	Ebenezer	Weeksons Estate	1	342	Joshua	Barnum Jnr:	1
289	Ebenezer	French	2	343	David	Crosby	1
290	Elijah	Calkin	2	344	Silas	Gray	1
291	Josiah	Swift Jnr:	1	345	David	Calkin	1
292	Gedion	Crofoot	2	346	David	Sears	4
293	Thomas	Pew	1	347	Benjamin	Vickry	2
294	Daniel	Brundage	3	348	Capt. Beverley Robinson's farm		7
295	Solomon	Jenkins	2		*Page 423*		
296	Samuel	Carter	2	349	Hezekiah	Carter	2
297	Reubin	Close	4	350	Abraham	Moss	2
298	Josiah	Akin	2	351	Lewis	Jones	3
299	Jabish	Tuttle	2	352	Daniel	Crawford	1
300	Ephraim	Pierce	1	353	John	Eagar	1
301	Joseph	Huested	4	354	Peter	Boncker	1
302	Caleb	Huested	2	355	Reubin	Hamblin	2
303	Jeremiah	Witnah	2	356	David	Hamblin	1
	Page 422			357	Thomas	Baulding	4
304	Joseph	Chetterton	2	358	Moss	Kent	4
305	Elisha	Oakley	3	359	Melthia	Hatch	5
306	Charles	Mc Ready	2	360	Nathen	Birdsill Jnr:	3
307	Matthew	Mc Caby	1	361	Joseph	Nauthrop	3
308	Joseph	Gee	1	362	William	Brownell	1
309	Seth	Holmes	1	363	William	Porter	2
310	James	Pardy	1	364	Prince	Hopkins	1
311	Stephen	Pardy	1	365	Ebenezer	Humsted	1
312	Daniel	Ball	1	366	— Palmer Living with Kingsley		1
313	Ebenezer	Pardy	1	367	John	Carley	1
314	John	June	1	368	Thomas	Lovelass	1
315	Joseph	Shearwood	1	369	Zabedee	Briggs	2
316	Benjamin	Haviland	2	370	Charles	Baseley	3
317	John	Brown	1	371	Eleazer	Hamblin	2
318	Silvenus	Coole	1	372	Reubin	Rubleey	1
319	Thomas	Hearns	1	373	Joseph	Vickry	2
320	George	Darbey	1	374	Silvenus	Hopkins	1
321	David	Hill	1	375	Hezekiah	Meade Jnr:	1
322	Benjamin	Hatch	3	376	Jacob	Burgis	2
323	George	Hawborn	3	377	Thomas	Barto's farm	1
324	Thomas	Trobridge	1	378	Elijah	Budd	2
325	Samuel	Calkin Jnr:	1	379	Joseph	Baker	1
326	Nathaniel	Stone	1	380	Eben	Lockwood	1
327	Wheaton	Robinson	2				

June 1763 continued

#	Name	Surname	Value
381	Baseley	King	1
382	Thomas	Sarls	1
383	Thomas	Woodard	1
384	Jacobus	Brewer	1
385	Caleb	Nelson	3
386	Justice	Nelson	3
387	Isaac	Teller	5
388	Jeremiah	Teller	1
389	Stephen	Pine	1
390	Robert	Hughson	1
391	Josiah	Gregory's farm	2
392	Peter	Drake	1
393	David	Shearwood	2
394	Daniel	Parish	1
395	Peter	Ryal	1

Page 424

#	Name	Surname	Value
396	John thauny	Craft	1
397	Benjamin	Moss	1
398	William	Calkin	1
399	Isaac	Lownsberry	2
400	Seth	Sears	2
401	Daniel	Gregory	1
402	Samuel	Lucas	1
403	Noah	Burbanks	1
404	Solomon	Byington	1
405	Jonathen	Tuttle	1
406	Stephen	Fenton	1
407	Nathaniel	Robinson Jnr:	1
408	James	Covey	1
409	William	Merritt	2
410	Josiah	Bobbet	2
411	Jehiel	Stephens	1
412	Nathaniel	Green	1
413	Peter	Maybee	1
414	John	Lownsberry	1
415	Thomas	Lownsberry	1
416	John	Ganung	1
417	Jacob	Finch Jnr:	1
418	Joshua	Parker	1
419	Jabish	Otter	1
420	David	Hawkins	1
421	Joseph	Ganung	1
422	Andrew	Rubelyeer	2
423	Ede	Backer	1
424	Shurman	Travis	1
425	Jacob	Ellis	1
426	John	Mirrick Jnr:	1
427	Jehiel	Baseley	5
428	Lucas	Carter	1
429	James	King	1
430	Thomas	Nickerson	1
431	Eben	Robinson near Capt Browns	2
432	Nathaniel	Nickerson	2
433	Izaker	Nickerson	1
434	Samuel	Yoemans	1
435	John	Secar	2
436	Samuel	Bernod	2
437	Joshua	Nelson	1
438	James	Secor	2

Page 425

#	Name	Surname	Value
439	Ephraim	Jones	1
440	Francis	Bryer	1
441	James	Lumery	1
442	Joseph	Rockwell	2
443	Elipet A.	Nickerson	1
444	Stephen	Concklin	1
445	Peter	Anderson	3
446	Isaac	Lumery	1
447	Anthony	Field	1
448	John	Armstrong	1
449	John	Armstrong Jnr:	1
450	Abraham	Height	1
451	John	Adams	1
452	Nehemiah	Horton	1
453	William	Van Tessel	1
454	James	Roades	1
455	William	Gee	1
456	Peter	Mowe	1
457	Caleb	Lockwood	1
458	Roswell	Gee	1
459	Benjamin	Teed	1
460	John	Meeks	2
461	Jesse	Smith Jnr:	1
462	Benjamin	Weed	2
463	Moses	Fowler	2
464	John	Maybee	2
465	John	Yoemans Sen:	1
466	Robert	Oakley	1
467	Ebenezer	Munsell	2
468	Gilbert	Dickenson [Dickson]	1
469	—	Ketterfield	3
470	Thomas	Adams	1
471	Widow	Nickerson	1
472	Timothy	Delavan	1
473	John	Cannon	2
474	Isaac Barret on Chaises place		1
475	Josiah	Wilcocks	3
476	Capt	Brown	2
477	James	Wilson	2
478	Jared	Carter	1
479	Comfort	Luddington	1
480	Josiah	Benjamins	1
481	Samuel	Perry	1
482	Elisha	Calkin	1
483	James	Townsend	1
484	Roger	Haviland	2

Page 426

#	Name	Surname	Value
485	Thomas	Ferguson	1
486	Joseph	Colvil	1

June 1763 continued

	Name	Surname	Value		Name	Surname	Value
487	Nathaniel	Byington	1	518	John	Rubelyeer	1
488	Reubin	Bloomer	1	519	Gedion	Ellis	1
489	Jacob	Doty	1	520	Nathen	Green Jnr:	1
490	Samuel	Hall	2	521	Benjamin	Sears Jnr:	1
491	David	Pierce	1	522	Stephen	Murch	1
492	John	Barber Jnr:	1	523	Stephen	Meade	1
493	Isaac	Mirrick	1	524	Joseph	Forster	1
494	Solomon	Hopkins	1	525	Obediah	Horton	1
495	Isaiah	Hopkins	1	526	James	Forster	1
496	Jonathen	Washburn	1	527	Stephen	Tomkins	1
497	Uriah	Whitney	2	528	Eleazor	Baker	1
498	John	Clarke Jnr:	2		*Page 427*		
499	William	Judd	1	529	John	Haviland	1
500	Reubin	Chase	1	530	David	Tuttle	1
501	William	Underhill	1	531	Elisha	Beadle	2
502	Augustin	Underhill	1	532	Jonathen	Pine	1
503	Seth	Olmsted	1	533	Abraham	Craft	1
504	Joseph	Robins	1	534	Malcom	Morrison	5
505	Joshua	Porter	1	535	Samuel	Pears	1
506	John	Roberts	1	536	Jedediah	Davis	1
507	Benjamin	Roberts Jnr:	1	537	James	Knap	1
508	Theodorus	Crosby	1	538	Jonathen	Knap	1
509	Samuel	Burchard	1	539	Gilbert	Clap	2
510	Nehemiah	Bailey	1	540	Henry	Wooden	2
511	Caleb	Palmer	1	541	Tartulus	Dickenson	2
512	John	Manley Jnr:	1	542	Joseph	Bates	1
513	Ebenezer	Munson Jnr:	1	543	William	Yoemans	1
514	Elisha	Kent Jnr:	1	544	—	Lane on Dowel farme	1
515	Richard	Gray	1	545	Mr.	Gregory	1
516	Benoney	Gray	1				£1,129
517	Augustin	Wright	1				

SUPERVISOR'S RECORD 1765 to 1770, VOLUME H
DUTCHESS COUNTY CLERKS OFFICE

JUNE 1765
SOUTHERN PRECINCT

at 4/7 [4 shillings 7 pence] pr. pound

	Name	Surname	Value		Name	Surname	Value
	Page 90			11	Timothy	Concklin	4
1	William	Devenport	5	12	George	Lane	2
2	Thomas	Devenport	13	13	George	Hughson	4
3	Jacob	Mandevil	10	14	William	Drake	4
4	John	Calkin	3	15	John	Drake	1
5	William	Gray	3	16	John [Isaac]	Roades	4
6	John	Rogers	11	17	David	Paddock	2
7	John	Van Amburghs Estate	7	18	Samuel	Towner	5
8	Elijah	Tompkins	5	19	Joseph	Lane	3
9	Capt. Peter	Duboys	11	20	Joseph	Meade	3
10	Ebenezer	Jones	3	21	John	Gee	2

June 1765 continued

#	Name	Surname	Value	#	Name	Surname	Value
22	Caleb	Brundage	1	75	Samuel	Elwell	3
23	Nathaniel	Tompkins	2	76	David	Cosby	3
24	Cornelius	Fuller	2	77	Jaby	Berry	2
25	Samuel	Calkin	1	78	Joseph	Taylor	2
26	John	Hains	1	79	Isaac	Smith	3
27	Thomas	Frost	1	80	Hope	Covy	6
28	William	Gee	3	81	Jonathen	Paddock	4
29	Edward	Gray	2	82	Nathen	Green	3
30	Abraham	Smith Estate	2	83	Seth	Nickerson	3
31	Luke	Covert	1	84	Timothy	Clauson	1
32	Elie	Nelson	1	85	Benjamin	Roberts	1
	Page 91			86	Benjamin	Parish's farm	2
33	Joseph	Crane Jnr:	2	87	William	Sturdefunt	1
34	Samuel	Field	11	88	David	Sturdefunt	1
35	Joseph	Field	6	89	Matthew	Bump	1
36	James	Dickenson	6	90	Isaac	Horton	2
37	Amos	Dickenson	4	91	Joseph	Concklin	1
38	John	Dickenson	5	92	Michal	Slott	2
39	Daniel	Townsend	4	93	William	Penny	4
40	Uriah	Townsend	2	94	Thomas	Forster	2
41	Charles	Townsend	2	95	John	Paddock	2
42	Benjamin	Townsend	5	96	Ezekiel	Meade	2
43	Robert R.	Townsend	4	97	Israel	Taylor	1
44	Daniel	Townsend Jnr:	2	98	William	Hill	7
45	Jesse	Smith	3	99	Abraham	Hodges	2
46	Robert	Shaw	1	100	Joshua	Cosby	3
47	Caleb	Hayson	3	101	Isaac	Chapman	2
48	Samuel	Gates farm	1	102	Seth	Paddock	5
49	William	Rappelyeas farm	2	103	Ebenezer	Jones Jnr:	2
50	Abraham	Hartwell	3	104	Theophilus	Jones	1
51	Deacon	Hamblin	3	105	Joshua	Hamblin	5
52	Jacob	Philip	1	106	Robert	Weekson	1
53	Caleb	Sweet	3	107	Aron	Calkin	2
54	William	Palmer	2	108	Gabriel	Knaps Estate	2
55	John	Newbury	4	109	John	Van Tessel	2
56	Robert	Mooney	3	110	Mr:	Kent	4
57	Thomas	Paddock	4	111	Jonathen	Austin	5
58	Russel	Gregory	1	112	Thomas	Kelley	1
59	John	White	1	113	Isaac	Pierce	2
60	George	Curry	3	114	John	Martine	4
61	Thomas	Philip	3	115	David	Smith	2
62	Ebenezer	King	1	116	Edmund	Baker	2
63	Josiah	Baker	3	117	James	Sears	2
64	Lieut.	Taylor	2	118	Peter	Hall	4
65	Isaac	Crosby	2	119	Thomas	Gage	2
66	Benjamin	Sears	4		*Page 93*		
67	Christopher	Fowler	1	120	Samuel	Goodspeed	4
68	Peter	Angwine	4	121	John	Mayhews Estate	1
69	Simeon	Ryder	5	122	John	Mirck	2
70	Isaac	Hause	2	123	Moody	House	3
71	Thomas	Smith	1	124	James	Cowen	2
72	Edward	Gray Jnr:	4	125	Elisha	Coole	4
73	Samuel	Bangs	2	126	Ezekiel	Burgis	1
74	Nathaniel	Forster	5	127	Jonathen	Kelley	1
	Page 92			128	Uriah	Lawrence	4

June 1765 continued

	Name	Surname	Value		Name	Surname	Value
129	Nathaniel	Porter	6	183	Stephen	Farrington	1
130	Joseph	Craw's farm	1	184	Mr.	Peck the Minister	1
131	Elisha	Bangs	2	185	Andrew	Berger Jnr:	1
132	Seth	Mirrick	2	186	Jeremiah	Hustin	2
133	Thomas	Colvil	2	187	David	Akins Jnr:	3
134	Amos	Fuller	2	188	John	Clarke	2
135	Cornelius	Tompkins	4	189	Robert	Fullers farm	2
136	Simeon	Ellis	3	190	Widow	Hill	2
137	Nathaniel	Bailiff	1	191	Haman	King	2
138	James	Dickens Jnr:	2	192	Jonathen	Hopkins	2
139	Ebenezer	Chase's farm	1	193	Nehemiah	Wood	2
140	John	Field	5	194	Christopher	Ellis	1
141	John	Yoemans Jnr:	3	195	Philip	Ruff	2
142	Zachary	Paddock Jnr:	4	196	Joseph	Merritts	6
143	Stephen	Field	5	197	Nathen	Taylor Jnr:	4
144	John	Nelson	2	198	Reubin	Kelley	1
145	James	Birdsill	10	199	John	Jones	1
146	Jeremiah	Linckhorne	1	200	John	Ferris's farm	1
147	John	Manley	3	201	Caleb	Pells farm	3
148	Silas	Paddock	3	202	John	Lamory	3
149	Edward	Ganung	1	203	Solomon	Farrington	1
150	Samuel	Peters	4	204	John	Wright	1
151	Lazarus	Griffen	1	205	Silas	Washburn	2
152	Abner	Bangs Estate	3	206	Richard	Hopper	1
153	Zachary	Paddock	2	207	Joshua	Barnum	3
154	Widow	Bailey	1	208	Abraham	Maybee	2
155	William	Grays Son William	1	209	Samuel	Drake	1
156	Peleg	Weekson	1	*Page 95*			
157	Joseph	Crommell	4	210	Uriah	Drake	2
158	Rowland	Perry	6	211	Joshua	Tompkins	2
159	Noah	Smith	3	212	William	Dean	1
160	Elijah	Weekson	1	213	John	Langdon	1
161	Joshua	Hinckley	1	214	Joshua	Gee	1
162	John	How	2	215	Caleb	Fowler	5
163	Jonathen	Lockwood	1	216	Ebenezer	Robinson	1
164	Mathias	Burgis	3	217	Simon	Deacon	7
Page 94				218	Benjamin	Perry	1
165	William	Nelson	1	219	Josiah	Ingersons farm that was	3
166	John	Birdsill	2				
167	Elisha	Kelk	1	220	Abraham	Maybee	2
168	Jonathen	Bryant	2	221	Abraham	Maybee Jnr:	1
169	William	Lane	2	222	Isaac	Finch's widow	1
170	John	Ryder	4	223	John	Roades	2
171	William	Dusenbury	3	224	Benjamin	Odle	2
172	Joseph	Hopkins widow	1	225	Daniel	Bull	2
173	Moses	Dusenbury	4	226	Thomas	Crosbury	3
174	John	Geen	2	227	Thomas	Maggot	2
175	Thomas	Higgins	2	228	Matthew	Benedict's farm	2
176	Abraham	Underhill	1	229	Jonathen	Lane Jnr:	1
177	Thomas	Clements	2	230	Benjamin	Gifford	4
178	Sibert	Krankheyt	1	231	John	Bogardus	3
179	Teunis	Brewer	1	232	Henry	Krankheyt	1
180	Daniel	Taylor	1	233	Obediah	Baseley	3
181	Michal	Shaw Jnr:	1	234	Samuel	Elwell Jnr:	2
182	William	Chitterton	1	235	Isaac	Elwell	1

June 1765 continued

#	Name	Surname	Value	#	Name	Surname	Value
236	Jacob	Philips	1	290	John	June	1
237	John	Clauson	2	291	Joseph	Sheerwood	1
238	Edward	Dolff	2	292	Benjamin	Haviland	2
239	Augustin	Baseley	1	293	Silvenus	Coole	1
240	Ebenezer	Bennet	1	294	Thomas	Hearns	1
241	William	Rappleyea	1	295	George	Darby	1
242	Elihu	Gage	1	296	David	Hill	1
243	Anthony	Gage	1	297	Benjamin	Hatch	3
244	Moses	Gage	1		*Page 97*		
245	Richard	Wearing	2	298	George	Hawborn	3
246	John	Bloomer	1	299	Thomas	Trobridge	1
247	Thomas	Townsend Jnr:	2	300	Samuel	Calkin Jnr:	2
248	Christopher	Townsend	2	301	Nathaniel	Stone	1
249	David	Paddock	2	302	Wheaton	Robinson	2
250	John	Tomkins	1	303	Benjamin	Barbers farm	1
251	Samuel	Benedict	1	304	Jonathen	Hobey	2
252	Jabez	Elwell	1	305	Solomon	Field	3
	Page 96			306	Ebenezer	Brown	1
253	Nathen	Crosby	1	307	Nathaniel	Arnold	1
254	John	Garrison	2	308	Solomon	Perry	1
255	Thomas	Hodges farm	1	309	James	Perry	1
256	Stephen	Rockwell	1	310	David	Akins farm	2
257	Elijah	White	2	311	Stephen	Crane	1
258	Hezekiah	Meade	1	312	Jonathen	Vickry	1
259	Edward	Rice	4	313	Ebenezer	Gage	1
260	Ebenezer	Kelley	1	314	Nehemiah	Jones	2
261	Ephraim	Smith	2	315	Reubin	Crosby	2
262	Thomas	Fowler	3	316	Joshua	Barnum Jnr:	1
263	John	Bloomer	1	317	David	Crosby	1
264	Thomas	Crommell	1	318	Silas	Gray	1
265	Nathaniel	Plumsted	1	319	David	Calkin	1
266	Ebenezer	Benidict	2	320	David	Sears	3
267	Ebenezer	French	2	321	Capt. Beaverley	Robinson	12
268	Elijah	Calkin	2	322	Hezekiah	Carter	2
269	Josiah	Swift Jnr:	1	323	Luwis	Jones	2
270	Gedion	Crofoot	2	324	Daniel	Crawford	1
271	Thomas	Pew	1	325	John	Eagar	1
272	Daniel	Brundage	3	326	Peter	Bonker	1
273	Solomon	Jenkins	2	327	Reubin	Hamblin	1
274	Reubin	Close	4	328	David	Hamblin	1
275	Josiah	Akin	2	329	Thomas	Baulding	4
276	Jabish	Tuttle	1	330	Moss	Kent	4
277	Ephraim	Pierce	1	331	Malthia	Hatch	5
278	Joseph	Huested	4	332	Nathen	Birdsill Jnr:	3
279	Caleb	Huested	2	333	Joseph	Nauthrop	2
280	Jeremiah	Witnah	2	334	William	Porter	2
281	Joseph	Chetterton	1	335	Prince	Hopkins	1
282	Elisha	Oakley	1	336	Ebenezer	Humsted	1
283	Charles	Mc Ready	2	337	John	Carley	1
284	Matthew	Mc Caby	1	338	Thomas	Lovelass	1
285	Joseph	Gee	1	339	Zabedee	Briggs	2
286	Seth	Holmes	1	340	Charles	Baseley	4
287	James	Pardy	1	341	Eleazer	Hamblin	2
288	Stephen	Pardy	1		*Page 98*		
289	Daniel	Ball	1	342	Reubin	Rubly	1

June 1765 continued

	Name	Surname	Value		Name	Surname	Value
343	Joseph	Vickry	1	395	Samuel	Yoemans	1
344	Silvenus	Hopkins	1	396	Samuel	Bernod	2
345	Hezekiah	Meade Jnr:	1	397	Joshua	Nelson	1
346	Jacob	Burgis	2	398	James	Secar	2
347	Thomas	Barto's farm	1	399	Ephraim	Jones	2
348	Elijah	Bud	2	400	Francis	Bryer	1
349	Joseph	Baker	1	401	James	Lumery	1
350	Eben	Lockwood	1	402	Joseph	Rockwell	1
351	Baseley	King	1	403	—	Jones on Eliphet A. Nickersons	1
352	Thomas	Sarls	1				
353	Thomas	Woodard	1	404	Stephen	Concklin	1
354	Caleb	Nelson	3	405	Peter	Anderson	2
355	Justice	Nelson	3	406	Isaac	Lumery	1
356	Jeremiah	Nelson	1	407	Anthony	Field	1
357	Stephen	Pine	1	408	John	Armstrong	1
358	Robert	Hughson	2	409	Abraham	Height	1
359	Josiah	Gregory's farm	3	410	John	Adams	1
360	Peter	Drake	1	411	William	Van Tessel	1
361	David	Sheerwood	2	412	James	Roades	1
362	Daniel	Parish	1	413	William	Gee	1
363	John thauny	Craft	1	414	Peter	Mock [Moe]	1
364	William	Calkin	1	415	Caleb	Lockwood	1
365	Isaac	Lownsbury	3	416	John	Meeks	2
366	Seth	Sears	2	417	Jesse	Smith	1
367	Daniel	Gregory	1	418	Benjamin	Weed	2
368	Samuel	Lucas	1	419	Moses	Fowler	3
369	Noah	Burbanks	1	420	John	Maybee	2
370	Solomon	Byington	1	421	John	Yoemans Jnr:	1
371	Jonathen	Tuttle	1	422	Robert	Oakley	1
372	Stephen	Fenton	1	423	Ebenezer	Mansell	2
373	Nathaniel	Robinson Jnr: farm	1	424	Gilbert	Dickson	1
				425	Samuel	Dickenson	2
374	James	Covey	1	426	Thomas	Adams	1
375	William	Merritt	2	427	Widow	Nickerson	1
376	Josiah	Bobbet	2	428	Timothy	DeLavan	1
377	Jehiel	Stephens	1	*Page 100*			
378	Nathaniel	Green	1	429	Isaac Barret on Chases place		1
379	Peter	Maybee	1	430	Josiah	Wilcocks	2
380	John	Lownsbury	2	431	Capt	Brown	2
381	Thomas	Lownsbury	2	432	James	Wilson	3
382	John	Ganung	1	433	Jared	Carter	1
383	David	Hawkins	1	434	Comfort	Luddington	1
384	Joseph	Ganung	1	435	Samuel	Perry	1
385	Andrew	Rubelyeer	1	436	Elisha	Calkin	2
386	Ede	Baker	1	437	James	Townsend	1
Page 99				438	Roger	Haviland	2
387	Shuerman	Travis	1	439	Thomas	Ferguson	1
388	Jacob	Ellis	1	440	Joseph	Colvil	1
389	David	Mirrick Jnr:	1	441	Nathaniel	Byington	1
390	Jehiel	Baseley	5	442	Samuel	Hall	2
391	James	King	1	443	David	Pierce	1
392	Thomas	Nickerson's farm	1	444	Isaac	Mirrick	1
393	Eben	Robinson (near Capt Browns)	2	445	Solomon	Hopkins	1
				446	Isaiah	Hopkins	1
394	Nathaniel	Nickerson	2	447	Jonathen	Washburn	2

June 1765 continued

	Name	Surname	Value		Name	Surname	Value
448	Uriah	Whitney	1	501	Joshua	Lumery	1
449	William	Judd	1	502	Henry	Jones	1
450	Reubin	Chase	1	503	James	Barrit	1
451	William	Underhill	1	504	Gilbert	Lane	1
452	Augustin	Underhill	1	505	Joseph	Hoyt	3
453	Joseph	Robins	1	506	Widow Hall on Meades place		2
454	Joshua	Porter	1	507	John	Win	1
455	John	Roberts	1	508	Moses	Meed	1
456	Benjamin	Roberts Jnr:	1	509	Jonathen	Stockem	1
457	Theodorus	Crosby	1	510	Charles	How	1
458	Samuel	Burchard	1	511	Luwis	Jones Jnr:	1
459	Nehemiah	Bailey	2	512	Byal	Bashford	2
460	Caleb	Palmer	1	513	Isaac	Garrison	1
461	John	Manley Jnr:	1	514	James	Bawlding	1
462	Ebenezer	Munson Jnr:	1	515	Henry	Garleck	1
	Page 101			516	Thomas	More	1
463	Elisha	Kent Jnr:	2	517	Richard	Carpenter	1
464	Richard	Gray	1	518	Jonathen	Stedwell	2
465	Benoney	Gray	1	519	Richard	Peters	2
466	Augustin	Wright	1	520	—	Cocke on Wheaton	2
467	Gedion	Ellis	1			Robinson's place	
468	Nathen	Green Jnr:	1	521	Joseph	Southerland	1
469	Benjamin	Sears Jnr:	1	522	Daniel	Southerland Jnr:	1
470	Stephen	Meade	1	523	John	Moss Jnr:	2
471	Joseph	Forster	1	524	Isaac	Sloot	1
472	Obediah	Horton	1	525	Simeon	Schouten	1
473	James	Forster	1	526	Reubin	Bond	1
474	Stephen	Tompkins	1	527	John	Avery	1
475	Eleazor	Baker	1	528	Joseph	Darby	1
476	John	Haviland	1	529	Elisha	Baker	1
477	David	Tuttle	1	530	Cornelius	Fuller	1
478	Elisha	Beadle	2		*Page 103*		
479	Jonathen	Pine	1	531	Jeremiah	Burgis	1
480	Abraham	Craft	1	532	Richard	Heirs	1
481	Meliom	Morrison	9	533	John	Humstead	1
482	Samuel	Pierce	1	534	Isaac	Ruscky	1
483	Jedediah	Davis	1	535	Gedion	Prindle	4
484	James	Knap	1	536	Rowlin	Russel	1
485	Jonathen	Knap	1	537	Stephen	Hopkins	1
486	Gilbert	Clap	2	538	Obediah	Wood	1
487	Henry	Wooden	2	539	James	Carle	1
488	Tartulus	Dickenson	8	540	Samuel	Carle	1
489	William	Yoemans	1	541	James	Forster	1
490	—	Lane, on Dowels farm	2	542	Timothy	Hatch	2
491	Mr.	Gregory	1	543	Jurdin	Cock	1
492	Benjamin	Lord	1	544	James	Hughson	1
493	Elisha	Coole Jnr:	1	545	Robert	Townsend	1
494	Andrew	Attwood	1	546	Matuel	Baker	1
495	Samuel	Washburn	1	547	Thomas	Baseter	1
	Page 102			548	Nathaniel	Austin	1
496	Charles	Arrewah	2	549	Simeon	Calkin	1
497	Solomon	Lane	1	550	Nathaniel	Finch	1
498	Elisha	Horton	1	551	Philip	Minthorn	1
499	John	Dike	1	552	Philip	Minthorne Jnr:	1
500	Daniel	Warren	3	553	James	Brown	1

June 1765 continued

	Name	Surname	Value		Name	Surname	Value
554	Eliza	Caby	1	556	Seth	Perry	1
555	Joshua	Deacon	1				£1,103

JUNE 1766
SOUTHERN PRECINCT

at 5/6 [5 shillings 6 pence] pr. pound

	Name	Surname	Value		Name	Surname	Value
	Page 178			43	Robert R.	Townsend	3
1	William	Devenport	5	44	Daniel	Townsend Snr	2
2	Thomas	Devenport	14		*Page 179*		
3	Jacob	Mandevil	10	45	Jesse	Smith	2
4	John	Calkin	3	46	Robert	Shaw	1
5	William	Gray	3	47	Caleb	Hazell	3
6	John	Rogers	10	48	Samuel	Gates farm	1
7	John	Van Amburgh's Estate	7	49	William	Rappelyea	4
8	Elijah	Tompkins	5	50	—	Leggit, on Abraham Hartwell's place	3
9	Capt. Peter	Duboys	11				
10	Ebenezer	Jones	3	51	Deacon	Hamblin	3
11	Timothy	Concklin	4	52	Jacob	Philip	1
12	George	Lane	2	53	Caleb	Sweet	1
13	George	Hughson	5	54	William	Palmer	2
14	William	Drake	4	55	John	Newbury	4
15	John	Drake	1	56	Robert	Mooney	3
16	Isaac	Roades	4	57	Thomas	Paddock	4
17	David	Paddock	1	58	Russel	Gregory	1
18	Samuel	Towner	5	59	John	White	1
19	Joseph	Lane	3	60	George	Curry	2
20	Joseph	Meade	2	61	Thomas	Philip's Estate	3
21	John	Gee	1	62	Ebenezer	King	1
22	Caleb	Brundage	1	63	Josiah	Baker	3
23	Nathaniel	Tompkins	2	64	Lieut.	Taylor	1
24	Cornelius	Fuller	3	65	Isaac	Crosby	3
25	Samuel	Calkin	2	66	Benjamin	Sears	4
26	John	Hains	2	67	Christophr	Fowler	1
27	Thomas	Frost	1	68	Peter	Anguwine	4
28	William	Gee	3	69	Simeon	Ryder	5
29	Edward	Gray	1	70	Isaac	House	2
30	Abraham	Smith's Estate	1	71	Thomas	Smith	1
31	Luke	Covert	1	72	Edward	Gray Jnr:	4
32	Elie	Nelson	1	73	Samuel	Bangs	3
33	Joseph	Crane Jnr:	3	74	Nathaniel	Forster	4
34	Samuel	Field	11	75	Samuel	Elwell	3
35	Joseph	Field	6	76	David	Cosby	3
36	James	Dickenson	6	77	Jaby	Berry	2
37	Amos	Dickenson	4	78	Joseph	Taylor	2
38	John	Dickenson	5	79	Isaac	Smith	4
39	Daniel	Townsend	4	80	Hope	Covy	6
40	Uriah	Townsend	2	81	Jonathen	Paddock	4
41	Charles	Townsend	2	82	Nathen	Green	2
42	Benjamin	Townsend	5	83	Seth	Nickerson	3

June 1766 continued

#	Name	Surname	Value	#	Name	Surname	Value
84	Timothy	Clauson	1	136	Nathaniel	Bailiff	1
85	Benjamin	Parish's farm	2	137	James	Dickens Jnr:	2
86	William	Sturdefunt	1	138	Ebenezer	Chase's farm	1
87	David	Sturdefunt	1	139	John	Field	4
Page 180				140	John	Yoemans Jnr:	3
88	Mathew	Bump	1	141	Zachary	Paddock Jnr:	3
89	Isaac	Horton	2	142	Stephen	Field	6
90	Joseph	Concklin	1	143	John	Nelson	1
91	Michal	Slott	2	144	James	Birdsill	9
92	William	Penny	4	145	Jeremiah	Linkhorn	1
93	Thomas	Forster	2	146	John	Manley	3
94	John	Paddock	2	147	Silas	Paddock	2
95	Ezekiel	Meade	1	148	Edward	Ganung	1
96	Israel	Taylor	1	149	Samuel	Peters	4
97	William	Hill	7	150	Lazarus	Griffen	1
98	Abraham	Hodges	1	151	Abner	Bangs Estate	3
99	Joshua	Cosby	3	152	Zachary	Paddock	2
100	Isaac	Chapman	2	153	Widow	Bailey	2
101	Seth	Paddock	4	154	William	Gray's son Wm.	1
102	Ebenezer	Jones Jnr:	2	155	Peleg	Weekson	1
103	Theophilus	Jones	2	156	Joseph	Crommell	4
104	Joshua	Hamblin	4	157	Rowland	Perry	6
105	Robert	Weekson	1	158	Noah	Smith	4
106	Aron	Calkin	2	159	Elijah	Weekson	1
107	Hannah	Knap	2	160	Joshua	Hinkley	1
108	John	Van Tessel	1	161	John	How	2
109	Mr	Kent	2	162	Jonathen	Lockwood	1
110	Jonathen	Austin	4	163	Mathias	Burgis	3
111	Thomas	Kelley	1	164	William	Nelson	1
112	Isaac	Pierce	3	165	John	Birdsill	2
113	John	Martine	4	166	Elisha	Kelk	1
114	David	Smith	2	167	Jonathen	Bryant	2
115	Edmund	Baker	1	168	William	Lane	2
116	James	Sears	2	169	John	Ryder	4
117	Peter	Hall	4	170	William	Dusenbury	3
118	Thomas	Gage	2	171	John	Geen	2
119	Samuel	Goodspeed	3	172	Thomas	Higgins	2
120	John	Mayhew's Estate	1	173	Abraham	Underhill	2
121	John	Mirrick	2	174	Thomas	Clements	2
122	Moody	House	3	*Page 182*			
123	James	Cowen	3	175	Silbert	Krankheyt	1
124	Elisha	Coole	4	176	Daniel	Taylor's Estate	1
125	Ezekiel	Burgis	1	177	Michal	Shaw Jnr:	1
126	Jonathen	Kelley	2	178	Stephen	Ferrington	1
127	—	Taylor on Uriah Lawrence's farm	4	179	Mr	Peck the Minister	1
				180	Andrew	Berger Jnr:	1
128	Nathaniel	Porter	5	181	Jeremiah	Huestin	2
129	Joseph	Craw s farm	1	182	David	Akins farm	3
Page 181				183	John	Clarke	2
130	Elisha	Bangs	2	184	Robert	Fuller's farm	3
131	Seth	Mirrick	2	185	Widow	Hill	2
132	Thomas	Colvil	2	186	Haman	King	3
133	Amos	Fuller	2	187	Jonathen	Hopkins	2
134	Cornelius	Tompkins	2	188	Nehemiah	Wood	2
135	Simeon	Ellis	3	189	Christopher	Ellis	1

June 1766 continued

	Name	Surname	Value		Name	Surname	Value
190	Philip	Ruff	2	244	Samuel	Benedict	1
191	Joseph	Merrits	6	245	Jabish	Elwell	2
192	Nathen	Taylor Jnr:	2	246	Nathen	Crosby	2
193	Reubin	Kelley	2	247	John	Garrison	2
194	John	Jones	1	248	Thomas	Hodges farm	1
195	John	Ferris Farm	1	249	Stephen	Rockwell	1
196	Caleb	Pell's farm	3	250	Elijah	White	2
197	John	Lamory	3	251	Hezekiah	Meade	1
198	Solomon	Farrington	1	252	Edward	Rice	3
199	John	Wright	1	253	Ebenezer	Kelley	1
200	Silas	Washburn	2	254	Ephraim	Smith	2
201	Richard	Hopper	1	255	Thomas	Fowler	3
202	Joshua	Barnum	3	256	John Bloomer (near the river		1
203	Abraham	Maybee, Taylor	3	257	Thomas	Crommell	1
204	Samuel	Drake	1	258	Nathaniel	Plumsted	1
205	Uriah	Drake	2	259	Ebenezer	Benedict	2
206	Joshua	Tompkins	1	260	Ebenezer	French	1
207	William	Dean	1	261	Elijah	Calkin	1
208	John	Langdon	2	262	Josiah	Swift Jnr:	1
209	Caleb	Fowler	6	263	Gedion	Crowfoot	2
210	Ebenezer	Robinson	1	264	Thomas	Pew	1
211	Simon	Deacon	7		*Page 184*		
212	Benjamin	Perry	1	265	Daniel	Brundage	3
213	Solomon	Smith	2	266	John [Solomon] Jenkins		2
214	Abraham	Maybee	2	267	Reubin	Close	4
215	Abraham	Maybee Jnr:	1	268	Josiah	Akin	2
216	Isaac	Finch's widow	1	269	Jabish	Tuttle	1
217	John	Roades	1	270	Ephraim	Pierce	1
218	Benjamin	Odle	2	271	Joseph	Huested	3
219	Daniel	Bull	3	272	Caleb	Huested	2
	Page 183			273	Jeremiah	Witnah	1
220	Thomas	Crosbury	3	274	Elisha	Oakley	1
221	Thomas	Maggot	2	275	Charles	Mc Ready	1
222	Matthew	Ben[e]dick's farm	2	276	Matthew	Mc Caby	1
223	Benjamin	Gifford	4	277	Joseph	Gee	1
224	James	Henry	2	278	Seth	Holmes	1
225	Henry	Krankheyt	1	279	James	Pardy	1
226	Obidiah	Baseley	3	280	Stephen	Pardy	1
227	Samuel	Elwell Jnr:	3	281	Daniel	Ball	1
228	Isaac	Elwell	1	282	John	June	1
229	Jacob	Philips	1	283	Joseph	Shurwood	1
230	John	Clauson	2	284	Benjamin	Haviland	2
231	Edward	Dolf	2	285	Silvenus	Coole	2
232	Augustin	Baseley	2	286	Thomas	Hearns	1
233	Ebenezer	Bennet	1	287	George	Darbey	1
234	William	Rappelyea	1	288	David	Hill	1
235	Elihu	Gage	1	289	Benjamin	Hatch	3
236	Anthony	Gage	1	290	George	Hawborn	3
237	Moses	Gage	1	291	Thomas	Trobridge	1
238	Richard	Wearing	7	292	Samuel	Calkin Jnr:	2
239	John	Bloomer	2	293	Nathaniel	Stone	1
240	Thomas	Townsend Jnr:	2	294	Wheton	Robinson	2
241	Christopher	Townsend	2	295	Benjamin	Barber's farm	2
242	David	Paddock	2	296	Jonathan	Hobey	2
243	John	Tompkins	1	297	Solomon	Field	3

June 1766 continued

#	Name	Surname	Value
298	Ebenezer	Brown	1
299	Nathaniel	Arnold	1
300	Solomon	Perry	1
301	James	Perry	1
302	David	Akins farm	2
303	Stephen	Crane	1
304	Jonathen	Vickry	1
305	Ebenezer	Gage	1
306	Nehemiah	Jones	2
307	Reubin	Crosby	2
308	Joshua	Barnum Jnr:	1
309	David	Crosby Jnr:	1

Page 185

#	Name	Surname	Value
310	Silas	Gray	1
311	David	Calkin	1
312	David	Sears	4
313	Capt. Beaverley	Robinson	16
314	Hezekiah	Carter	2
315	Lewis	Jones	2
316	Daniel	Crawford	1
317	John	Eager	1
318	Peter	Bonker	1
319	Reubin	Hamblin	2
320	David	Hamblin	1
321	Thomas	Baldwin	4
322	Moss	Kent	5
323	Malthia	Hatch	4
324	Nathan	Birdsill	3
325	Joseph	Nauthrop	2
326	William	Porter	1
327	Prince	Hopkins	1
328	Ebenezer	Humstead	1
329	John	Carley	1
330	Thomas	Lovelass	1
331	Zebedee	Briggs	2
332	Charles	Baseley	4
333	Eleazer	Hamblin	2
334	Reubin	Rubley	1
335	Joseph	Vickry	1
336	Silvenus	Hopkins	2
337	Hezekiah	Meade Jnr:	1
338	Jacob	Burgis	2
339	John	Barto's farm	1
340	Elijah	Budd	2
341	Joseph	Baker	1
342	Eben	Lockwood	1
343	Baseley	King	1
344	Thomas	Sarls	1
345	Thomas	Woodard	1
346	Caleb	Nelson	3
347	Justice	Nelson	3
348	Jeremiah	Nelson	1
349	Stephen	Pine	1
350	Robert	Hughson	1
351	Josiah	Gregory's farm	3
352	Peter	Drake	2
353	David	Sheerwood	2
354	Daniel	Parish	1
355	John thauny	Craft	1

Page 186

#	Name	Surname	Value
356	William	Calkin	1
357	Isaac	Lownsbury	3
358	Seth	Sears	2
359	Daniel	Gregory	1
360	Samuel	Lucas	1
361	Noah	Burbanks	1
362	Solomon	Byington	1
363	Jonathen	Tuttle	1
364	Stephen	Fenton	1
365	Nathaniel	Robinson Jnr: farm	2
366	James	Covy	1
367	William	Merrit	2
368	Isaiah	Bobbet	2
369	Jehiel	Stephens	1
370	Nathaniel	Green	2
371	Peter	Maybee	1
372	John	Lownsbury	2
373	Thomas	Lownsbury	2
374	John	Ganung	1
375	David	Hawkins	1
376	Joseph	Ganung	1
377	Andrew	Rubelyeer	1
378	Ede	Baker	1
379	Sheurman	Travis	1
380	Jacob	Ellis	1
381	David	Mirrick Jnr:	1
382	Jehiel	Baseley	5
383	James	King	1
384	Eben	Brown (Capt Browns	2
385	Nathaniel	Nickerson	2
386	Samuel	Yoemans	1
387	Samuel	Bernod	2
388	Joshua	Nelson	1
389	James	Secord	2
390	Ephraim	Jones	2
391	Francis	Bryer	1
392	James	Lumery	1
393	—	Jones on Eliphel A. Nickerson's farm	2
394	Stephen	Concklin	1
395	Peter	Anderson	2
396	Isaac	Lumery	2
397	John	Armstrong	1
398	Abraham	Height	1
399	John	Adams	1

Page 187

#	Name	Surname	Value
400	William	Van Tessel	1
401	James	Roades	1

June 1766 continued

	Name	Surname	Value		Name	Surname	Value
402	William	Gee	1	456	Benjamin	Sears Jnr:	1
403	Peter	Mock [Moe]	1	457	Stephen	Meade	1
404	Caleb	Lockwood	1	458	Joseph	Forster	1
405	John	Meeks	2	459	Obbidiah	Horton	1
406	Jesse	Smith Jnr:	1	460	James	Forster	1
407	Benjamin	Weed	2	461	Stephen	Tompkins	1
408	Moses	Fowler	4	462	Eleazer	Baker	1
409	John	Maybee	2	463	John	Haviland	1
410	John	Yoemans Jnr:	1	464	David	Tuttle	1
411	Robert	Oakley	1	465	Elisha	Beadle	2
412	Ebenezer	Mansell	2	466	Jonathen	Pine	1
413	Gilbert	Dickson	1	467	Abraham	Craft	1
414	Samuel	Dickenson	2	468	Malcom	Morrison	8
415	Thomas	Adams	1	469	Samuel	Pierce	1
416	Widow	Nickerson	1	470	Jedediah	Davis	1
417	Timothy	DeLavan	2	471	Jonathen	Knap	1
418	Isaac	Barrit	1	472	Gilbert	Clap's farm	1
419	Josiah	Wilcocks	1	473	Henry	Wooden	2
420	Capt.	Brown	2	474	Tertullus	Dickenson	6
421	James	Wilson	3	475	William	Yoemans	1
422	Jared	Carter	1	476	George Lane, on Dowels farm		2
423	Comfort	Luddington	1	477	Mr	Gregory	1
424	Samuel	Perry	1	478	Elisha	Coole Jnr:	1
425	Elisha	Calkin	2	479	Andrew	Attwood	1
426	James	Townsend	1	480	Samuel	Washboun	1
427	Roger	Haviland	2	481	Charles	Arrawah	2
428	Thomas	Ferguson	1	482	Solomon	Lane	1
429	Joseph	Colvil	1	483	Elisha	Horton	1
430	Samuel	Hall	2	484	John	Dyck	1
431	David	Pierce	1	485	Daniel	Warren	3
432	Isaac	Merrick	1	486	Joshua	Lumery	1
433	Solomon	Hopkins	1		*Page 189*		
434	Isaiah	Hopkins	1	487	Henry	Jones	1
435	Jonathen	Washburn	2	488	James	Barritt	1
436	Uriah	Whitney	1	489	Gilbert	Lane	1
437	William	Judd	1	490	Joseph	Height	4
438	Reubin	Chase	1	491	Widow Hall on Meades Place		2
439	William	Underhill	1	492	John	Win	1
440	Joseph	Robins	1	493	Moses	Meade	1
441	Joshua	Porter	1	494	Jonathen	Stockham	1
442	John	Roberts	1	495	Charles	How	1
443	Benjamin	Roberts Jnr:	1	496	Ryal	Bashford	3
	Page 188			497	Isaac	Garrison	1
444	Theodorus	Crosby	1	498	James	Baldwin	1
445	Samuel	Burchard	2	499	Henry	Garlick	1
446	Nehemiah	Bailey	2	500	Thomas	More	1
447	Caleb	Palmer	1	501	Richard	Carpenter	1
448	John	Manley	1	502	Jonathen	Stedwell	2
449	Ebenezer	Munson Jnr:	1	503	Richard	Peters	2
450	Elisha	Kent Jnr:	2	504	—	Cooke on Wheaton Robinson's pla[ce]	2
451	Richard	Gray	1				
452	Benony	Gray	1	505	Joseph	Southerland	1
453	Augustin	Wright	1	506	Daniel	Southerland Jnr:	1
454	Gedion	Ellis	1	507	John	Moss Jnr:	2
455	Nathen	Green Jnr:	2	508	Isaac	Slott	1

June 1766 continued

#	Name	Surname	Value	#	Name	Surname	Value
509	Reubin	Bond	1	550	Philip	Steebonck	1
510	John	Avery	1	551	James	Hughson	1
511	Joseph	Darbey	1	552	Richard	Arnold	2
512	Elisha	Baker	1	553	John	Baker	1
513	Cornelius	Fuller	1	554	Nathaniel	Jager	1
514	Jeremiah	Burgis	1	555	Stephen	Higbee	1
515	Richard	Hains [Hairs]	1	556	Charles	Hager	1
516	John	Humsted	1	557	Francis	Berger	1
517	Isaac	Ruscky	1	558	Peter	Berger	1
518	Gedion	Prindle	5	559	John	Langdon	1
519	Rowlin	Russel	1	560	Sibert	Krankheyt	1
520	Stephen	Hopkins	1	561	Thomas	Tompkins	1
521	Obidiah	Wood	1	562	Abner	Crosby	1
522	James	Carle	1	563	William	Stone	1
523	Samuel	Carle	1	564	Elnathen	Dunn	1
524	James	Forster	1	565	Daniel	Dunn	1
525	Timothy	Hatch	2	566	Zebulon	Bass	1
526	Jorden	Cooke	1	567	Francis	Baker's farm	1
527	James	Hughson	1	568	Thomas	Higgins Jnr:	1
528	Robert	Townsend	1	569	Samuel	Wright	1
529	Matuel	Baker	1	570	David	Porter	1
530	Thomas	Baseter	1	571	Isaiah	Bennet	1
Page 190				572	Thomas	Bridges [Burgis]	1
531	Nathaniel	Austin	1	573	Elijah	Hungerford	1
532	Simon	Calkin	1	574	Doctr: John	Calkin	2
533	Nathaniel	Finch	1	*Page 191*			
534	Philip	Minthorne	1	575	Anthony	Yoemans	1
535	Philip	Minthorne Jnr:	1	576	Richard	Arison [Garrison]	2
536	James	Brown	1	577	Joshua	Barns	2
537	Joshua	Deacon	1	578	Benjamin	Bloomer	1
538	Seth	Perry	1	579	Daniel	Southerland	1
539	Isaac	Perry	1	580	Nathaniel	Calkin	1
540	William	Clinton	1	581	Jonathen	Bennet	1
541	Shaw	Young	1	582	Stephen	Wilcocks	1
542	John	Wood	1	583	Samuel	Dailey	1
543	John	Wright Jnr:	1	584	Joshua	Crosby Jnr:	1
544	John	Brown	1	585	Simeon	Bundy Jnr:	1
545	Reubin	Drake	1	586	Daniel	Secord	1
546	John	Berger	1	587	Isaac	Secord	1
547	Isaac	Horten	1	588	John	Seacord	1
548	Thomas	Bryant	1				£1,142
549	Abraham	Coevert	1				

JUNE 1767
SOUTHERN PRECINCT

at 5/6 [5 shillings 6 pence] pr. pound

#	Name	Surname	Value	#	Name	Surname	Value
	Page 330			5	John	Rogers	10
1	William	Devenport	5	6	John	Van Amburgh's Estate	7
2	Thomas	Devenport	14	7	Elijah	Tompkins	5
3	Jacob	Mandevill	10	8	Capt. Peter	Duboys	11
4	John	Calkins farm	3	9	Ebenezer	Jones	2

June 1767 continued

#	Name	Surname	Value	#	Name	Surname	Value
10	Timothy	Concklin	4	63	Samuel	Bangs	4
11	George	Lane	2	64	Nathaniel	Forster	4
12	George	Hughson	5	65	Samuel	Elwell	3
13	William	Drake	3	66	David	Cosby	3
14	John	Drake	1	67	Jaby	Berry	1
15	Isaac	Roades	4	68	Joseph	Taylor	2
16	David	Paddock	1	69	Isaac	Smith	4
17	Samuel	Towner	5		*Page 332*		
18	Joseph	Lane	3	70	Jonathen	Paddock	4
19	Joseph	Meades farm	1	71	Nathen	Green	2
20	Caleb	Brundage	1	72	Seth	Nickerson	4
21	Nathaniel	Tompkins	2	73	Timothy	Clauson	1
22	Cornelius	Fuller	3	74	William	Sturdefunt	1
23	John	Hains	2	75	Joseph	Concklin	1
24	William	Gee	3	76	Michal	Slott	2
25	Edward	Gray	1	77	William	Penny	4
26	Abraham	Smith's Estate	1	78	Thomas	Forster	2
27	Luke	Coevert	1	79	John	Paddock	2
	Page 331			80	Ezekiel	Meade	1
28	Elie	Nelson	1	81	Israel	Taylor	1
29	Joseph	Crane Jnr:	3	82	William	Hill	7
30	Samuel	Field	10	83	Joshua	Cosby	3
31	Joseph	Field	6	84	Isaac	Chapman	2
32	James	Dickenson	6	85	Seth	Paddock	4
33	Amos	Dickenson	3	86	Ebenezer	Jones Jnr:	2
34	John	Dickenson	5	87	Theophilus	Jones	2
35	Daniel	Townsend	3	88	Joshua	Hamblin	4
36	Uriah	Townsend	2	89	Robert	Weekson	1
37	Charles	Townsend	2	90	Hannah	Knap	2
38	Benjamin	Townsend	5	91	John	Van Tessel	1
39	Robert	Townsend	3	92	Revd: Mr	Kent	3
40	Daniel D.	Townsend	1	93	Jonathen	Austins farm	3
41	Robert	Shaw	1	94	Thomas	Kelley	1
42	Caleb	Hazel	2	95	Isaac	Pierce	3
43	Gabriel	Legget on Hartwell's farm	2	96	John	Martine	4
				97	David	Smith	2
44	Deacon	Hamblin	1	98	Edmund	Baker	1
45	Jacob	Philip	1	99	James	Sears	1
46	Caleb	Sweet	1	100	Peter	Hall	5
47	William	Palmer	2	101	Thomas	Gage	2
48	John	Newbury	5	102	John	Mirrick	2
49	Robert	Mooney	5	103	Moody	House	3
50	Thomas	Paddock	4	104	James	Cowen	3
51	George	Curry	2	105	Elisha	Coole	2
52	Thomas	Philips Estate	2	106	Ezekiel	Burgis	1
53	Ebenezer	King	1	107	Jonathen	Kelley	2
54	Josiah	Baker	3	108	John	Taylor	4
55	Isaac	Crosby	3	109	Nathaniel	Porters Estate	2
56	Benjamin	Sears	4		*Page 333*		
57	Christopher	Fowler	1	110	Elisha	Bangs	2
58	Peter	Anguwine	4	111	Seth	Mirricks Estate	1
59	Simeon	Ryder	5	112	Thomas	Covil	2
60	Isaac	House	2	113	Amos	Fuller	2
61	Thomas	Smith	2	114	Cornelius	Fuller [Tompkins?]	2
62	Edward	Gray Jnr:	4	115	Simeon	Ellis	3

June 1767 continued

#	Name	Surname	Value	#	Name	Surname	Value
116	Nathaniel	Bailiff	1	170	John	Wright	1
117	James	Dickens Jnr:	2	171	Richard	Hopper	1
118	Jeremiah	Chase	1	172	Joshua	Barnum	3
119	John	Field	6	173	Samuel	Drake	1
120	John	Yoemans Jnr:	2	174	Uriah	Drake	2
121	Zachary	Paddock Jnr:	3	175	Joshua	Tompkins	1
122	Stephen	Field	6	176	William	Dean	1
123	John	Nelson	1	177	John	Langdon	1
124	James	Birdsill	9	178	Caleb	Fowler	6
125	Jeremiah	Linckhorne	1	179	Ebenezer	Robinson	1
126	John	Manley	3	180	Simon	Deacon	7
127	Silas	Paddock	2	181	Benjamin	Perry	1
128	Edward	Ganung	1	182	Solomon	Smith	2
129	Samuel	Peters	8	183	Abraham	Maybee	2
130	Lazarus	Griffen	1	184	Abraham	Maybee Jnr:	1
131	Widow	Bailey	2	185	Isaac	Finch's widow	1
132	Peleg	Weekson	1	186	John	Roades	1
133	Joseph	Crommell	4	187	Benjamin	Odle	2
134	Rowland	Perry	5	188	Daniel	Bull	3
135	Noah	Smith	1	189	Thomas	Maggot	3
136	Elijah	Weekson	1	190	Matthew	Benedick's farm	2
137	Joshua	Hinckley	1	191	Benjamin	Gifford	4
138	John	How	1		*Page 335*		
139	Mathias	Burgis	6	192	Henry	Krankheyt	1
140	William	Nelson	1	193	Obidiah	Baseley	3
141	John	Birdsills farm	1	194	Samuel	Elwell Jnr:	3
142	Elisha	Kelk	1	195	Isaac	Elwell	2
143	Jonathen	Bryant	2	196	Jacob	Philips	1
144	William	Lane	2	197	John	Clauson	3
145	John	Ryder	4	198	Edward	Dolf	2
146	William	Dusenbury	4	199	Augustin	Baseley	1
147	John	Geen	2	200	Ebenezer	Bennet	1
148	Thomas	Higgins	2	201	William	Rappelyea	2
149	Abraham	Underhill	1	202	Elihu	Gage	1
150	Thomas	Clements	2	203	Anthony	Gage	1
	Page 334			204	Richard	Wearing	1
151	Silbert	Krankheyt	1	205	John	Bloomer	2
152	Daniel	Taylor's Estate	1	206	Thomas	Townsend Jnr:	2
153	Michal	Shaw Jnr:	1	207	Christopher	Townsend	1
154	Stephen	Ferrington	1	208	David	Paddock	2
155	Andrew	Berger Jnr:	1	209	John	Tompkins	1
156	Jeremiah	Huesten	2	210	Samuel	Benedick	1
157	David	Akins	5	211	Jabish	Elwell	2
158	John	Clarke	2	212	Nathen	Crosby	2
159	Widow	Hill	2	213	John	Garrison	2
160	Haman	King	3	214	Thomas	Hodges's farm	1
161	Jonathen	Hopkins	2	215	Stephen	Rockwell	1
162	Nehemiah	Wood	2	216	Elijah	White	2
163	Christopher	Ellis	1	217	Hezekiah	Meade	1
164	Philip	Ruff	2	218	Edward	Rice	4
165	Joseph	Merrits	6	219	Ebenezer	Kelley	1
166	Reubin	Kelley	2	220	Ephraim	Smith	2
167	John	Jones	1	221	Thomas	Fowler	3
168	Caleb	Pell's farm	3	222	John	Bloomer near the River	1
169	John	Lamory	3				

June 1767 continued

	Name	Surname	Value		Name	Surname	Value
223	Thomas	Crommell	1	276	David	Hamblin	1
224	Nathaniel	Plumsted	1	277	Thomas	Baldwin	4
225	Ebenezer	Benedick	2	278	Moss	Kent	5
226	Ebenezer	French	1	279	Melthia	Hatch's farm	4
227	Elijah	Calkin	2	280	Nathan	Birdsill	4
228	Josiah	Swift Jnr:	2	281	Joseph	Nauthrop	2
229	Gedion	Crowfoot	2	282	William	Porter	1
230	Thomas	Pew	1	283	Prince	Hopkins	1
231	Daniel	Brundage	3	284	Ebenezer	Humsted	1
232	John [Solomon]	Jenkins	2	285	John	Carley	1
Page 336				286	Thomas	Lovelass	1
233	Reubin	Close	4	287	Zebedee	Briggs	2
234	Ephraim	Pierce	1	288	Eleazer	Hamblin	2
235	Joseph	Huested	3	289	Joseph	Vickry	1
236	Caleb	Huested	2	290	Silvenus	Hopkins's farm	1
237	Jeremiah	Witnah	1	291	Hezekiah	Meade Jnr:	1
238	Elisha	Oakley	1	292	John	Barto's farm	1
239	Charles	Mc Reedy	1	293	Elijah	Budd	2
240	Mathew	Mc Caby	1	294	Joseph	Baker	1
241	Joseph	Gee	1	295	Eben	Lockwood	1
242	Seth	Holmes	1	296	Baseley	King	1
243	James	Pardy	1	297	Thomas	Sarls	1
244	Stephen	Pardy	1	298	Thomas	Woodard	1
245	Daniel	Ball	1	299	Caleb	Nelson	2
246	John	June	1	300	Justice	Nelson	2
247	Joseph	Sheerwood	1	301	Stephen	Pine	1
248	Benjamin	Haviland	3	302	Robert	Hughson	1
249	Silvenus	Coole	2	303	Josiah	Gregory	3
250	George	Darbey	1	304	Peter	Drake	2
251	Benjamin	Hatch	4	305	David	Sherwood	2
252	George	Hawborn	4	306	John thauny	Craft	1
253	Thomas	Trobridge	1	307	Isaac	Lownsbury	3
254	Samuel	Calkin Jnr:	2	308	Seth	Sears	2
255	Nathaniel	Stone	1	309	Samuel	Lucas	1
256	Wheton	Robinson	2	310	Noah	Burbanks	1
257	Jonathan	Hobey	2	311	Stephen	Fenton	1
258	Solomon	Field	3	*Page 338*			
259	Ebenezer	Brown	1	312	Nathaniel	Robinson Jnr: farm	1
260	Nathaniel	Arnold	1				
261	Solomon	Perry	1	313	James	Covy	1
262	James	Perry	1	314	William	Merrit	2
263	Ebenezer	Gage	1	315	Isaiah	Bobbitt	2
264	Nehemiah	Jones	2	316	Nathaniel	Green	2
265	Reubin	Crosby	2	317	Peter	Maybee	1
266	Joshua	Barnum Jnr:	1	318	John	Lownsbury	3
267	David	Crosby Jnr:	3	319	Thomas	Lownsbury	3
268	David	Calkin Jnr:	1	320	David	Hawkins	1
269	David	Sears	4	321	Joseph	Ganung	1
270	Capt. Beaverley	Robinson	25	322	Andrew	Rubelyear	1
271	Lewis	Jones	2	323	Ede	Baker	1
Page 337				324	Sheurman	Travis	1
272	Daniel	Crawford	1	325	Jacob	Ellis	1
273	John	Eager	1	326	David	Mirrick	1
274	Peter	Bonker	1	327	Jehiel	Baseley	6
275	Reubin	Hamblin	1	328	James	King	1

June 1767 continued

#	Name	Surname	Value
329	Eben	Brown near Capt. Browns	2
330	Nathaniel	Nickerson's Estate	2
331	Samuel	Yoemans	1
332	Samuel	Bernod	2
333	Joshua	Nelson	1
334	James	Secord's farme	1
335	Ephraim	Jones	2
336	Francis	Bryer	1
337	James	Lumery	1
338	Benjamin	Jones	2
339	Stephen	Concklin	1
340	Peter	Anderson	2
341	Isaac	Lumery	1
342	John	Armstrong	1
343	Abraham	Height	1
344	John	Adams	1
345	William	Van Tessel	1
346	James	Roades	1
347	William	Gee	1
348	Peter	Moe	1
349	Caleb	Lockwood	1
350	John	Meeks	2
351	Moses	Fowler	5
352	John	Maybee's Estate	2
353	John	Yoemans	1

Page 339

#	Name	Surname	Value
354	Robert	Oakley	1
355	Gilbert	Dickson	1
356	Samuel	Dickenson	2
357	Thomas	Adams	1
358	Widow	Nickerson	1
359	Timothy	DeLavan	2
360	Isaac	Barrit	1
361	Capt.	Brown	2
362	James	Wilson	3
363	Elisha	Calkin	2
364	James	Townsend	1
365	Roger	Haviland	3
366	Thomas	Ferguson	1
367	Joseph	Colvil	2
368	Samuel	Hall	3
369	Isaac	Mirrick	1
370	Solomon	Hopkins	2
371	Widow	Washburn	1
372	William	Judd	1
373	Reubin	Chase	1
374	William	Underhill	1
375	Augustin	Underhill	1
376	Joseph	Robins	1
377	Joshua	Porter	1
378	John	Roberts	1
379	Benjamin	Roberts Jnr:	1
380	Theodorus	Crosby	2
381	Samuel	Burchard	2
382	Nehemiah	Bailey	1
383	Caleb	Palmer	1
384	John	Manley	1
385	Ebenezer	Munson Jnr:	2
386	Elisha	Kent Jnr:	2
387	Richard	Gray	1
388	Benoney	Gray	1
389	Augustin	Wright	1
390	Gedion	Ellis	1
391	Nathen	Green Jnr:	2
392	Benjamin	Sears Jnr:	1
393	Joseph	Forster	1
394	James	Forster	2

Page 340

#	Name	Surname	Value
395	Stephen	Tompkins	1
396	Eleazer	Baker	1
397	John	Haviland	2
398	Abraham	Craft	1
399	Malcom	Morrison	6
400	Samuel	Pierce	1
401	Gilbert	Clap	2
402	Henry	Wooden	2
403	Tertullus	Dickenson	8
404	William	Yoemans	1
405	George	Lane on Dowels farm	2
406	Mr	Gregory	1
407	Elisha	Coole Jnr:	1
408	Andrew	Attwood	1
409	Samuel	Washburn	1
410	Charles	Arrawah	2
411	Solomon	Lane	1
412	Elisha	Horton	1
413	John	Dyck's farm	1
414	Daniel	Warren	3
415	Joshua	Lumery	1
416	Henry	Jones	1
417	James	Barrett	1
418	Joseph	Height	3
419	Widow	Hall on Meades place	3
420	John	Win	1
421	Moses	Meade	1
422	Jonathen	Stockham	1
423	Byal	Bashford	3
424	Isaac	Garrison	1
425	James	Baldwin	1
426	Henry	Garlick	1
427	Jonathen	Stedwell	3
428	Richard	Peters	2
429	Joseph	Cocke	1
430	Daniel	Southerland Jnr:	1
431	John	Moss Jnr:	2
432	Isaac	Slott	1
433	Reubin	Bond	1
434	John	Averys farm	1
435	Joseph	Darbey	1

June 1767 continued

	Name	Surname	Value		Name	Surname	Value
	Page 341			489	Joshua	Crosby Jnr:	1
436	Jeremiah	Burgis	1	490	Simeon	Bundy	2
437	Richard	Hairs	1	491	Daniel	Secord	1
438	Isaac	Ruscky	1	492	Isaac	Secord	1
439	Gedion	Prindle's Estate	3	493	John	Seacord	1
440	Rowlin	Russel	1	494	Locklan	McDonald	3
441	Stephen	Hopkins's farm	1	495	Elexander	Grant	3
442	James	Carle	1	496	John	Birdsall	2
443	Samuel	Carle	1	497	John	Bates	1
444	Timothy	Hatch	2	498	Ethiel	Towner	3
445	James	Hughson	3	499	Elexander	Menzus	3
446	Robert	Townsend	1	500	Joshua	Hatfield	4
447	Matuel	Baker	1	501	Capt	Clarke's Farm	4
448	Thomas	Baxter	1	502	Andrew	Beardsley	2
449	Nathaniel	Finch	1	503	Josiah	Benjamin	1
450	Philip	Minthorne	1	504	Benjamin	Green	1
451	Philip	Minthorne Jnr:	1	505	Robert	Wats	1
452	Elias	Brown	1	506	Simeon	Mash	1
453	William	Clinton	1	507	Thomas	Menzus	4
454	Shaw	Young	1	508	Henry	Ludington	3
455	John	Wood	1	509	Roswell	Wilcocks	2
456	John	Wright Jnr:	1	510	David	Heacock	1
457	Reubin	Drake	2	511	Michael	Nowland	1
458	John	Berger	1	512	Samuel	Hunt	2
459	Thomas	Bryant	1	513	Joshua	Concklin	2
460	Philip	Steenbock	1	514	James	Calkins	1
461	Richard	Arnold	2	515	Doctr:	Beardsley	1
462	John	Baker	1		*Page 343*		
463	Nathaniel	Jager	1	516	Samuel	Towner	1
464	Stephen	Higbee's farm	1	517	Nathen	Lane	1
465	Charles	Hager	1	518	Samuel	Williams	1
466	Francis	Berger	1	519	Doctor	Daniels	1
467	Peter	Berger	1	520	Amos	Travis	1
468	John	Langdon	1	521	Titus	Travis	2
469	Sibert	Krankheyt	1	522	Benjamin	Birdsall	2
470	Thomas	Tompkins	1	523	James	Height	2
471	Abner	Crosby	1	524	Gabriel	Carpenter	2
472	William	Stone	2	525	Richard	Cornwell	1
473	Elnathen	Dann	1	526	Joseph	Philips	1
474	Daniel	Dunn	1	527	Anthony	Stock	2
475	Zebulon	Bass	1	528	John	Smith	2
	Page 342			529	Isaac	Hodges	1
476	Thomas	Higgins Jnr:	1	530	Thomas	Hughson	2
477	Samuel	Wright	1	531	Joseph	Horskins	1
478	David	Porter	1	532	David Hamblin	Joshua's Son	1
479	Isaiah	Bennet	2	533	Isaac	Austin	1
480	Thomas	Burgis	1	534	Johnson	Dakins	1
481	Elijah	Hungerford	1	535	Robert	Lang	1
482	Anthony	Yoemans	1	536	Samuel	Horton	1
483	Richard	Garrison	1	537	— Smith on	Langdon's farm	2
484	Joshua	Barns	4	538	Joseph	Prindle	1
485	Benjamin	Bloomer	1	539	Benjamin	Lord	1
486	Daniel	Southerland	1	540	Elijah	Fuller	1
487	Nathaniel	Calkin	2	541	Zachary	Paddock	2
488	Jonathen	Bennet	1	542	Daniel	Beagle	1

June 1767 continued

	Name	Surname	Value		Name	Surname	Value
543	Cornelius	Tompkins	2	546	Jacob	Maybee	1
544	Moses	Dusenbury	4				£1,110
545	Elijah	Oakley	1				

JUNE 1768
SOUTHERN PRECINCT

at 3/4 [3 shillings 4 pence] pr. pound

	Name	Surname	Value		Name	Surname	Value
	Page 350			42	William	Palmer	2
1	William	Devenport	5	43	John	Newbury	5
2	Thomas	Devenport	14	44	Robert	Money	4
3	Jacob	Mandevill	7	45	Thomas	Paddock	4
4	John	Rogers	7	46	George	Curry	2
5	John	Van Amburgh's Estate	7	47	Ebenezer	King	1
6	Elijah	Tompkins	4	48	Josiah	Baker	3
7	Capt. Peter	Duboys	11	49	Isaac	Crosby	3
8	Ebenezer	Jones	2	50	Benjamin	Sears	4
9	Timothy	Concklin	4	51	Christopher	Fowler	1
10	George	Lane	2	52	Peter	Anguwine	4
11	George	Hughson	5	53	Simeon	Ryder	5
12	William	Drake	3	54	Isaac	House	2
13	John	Drake	1	55	Thomas	Smith	3
14	Isaac	Roades	4		*Page 352*		
15	David	Paddock	1	56	Edward	Gray Jnr:	4
	Page 351			57	Samuel	Bangs	4
16	Samuel	Towner	4	58	Nathaniel	Forster	4
17	Joseph	Lane	3	59	Samuel	Elwell	2
18	Caleb	Brundage	1	60	David	Cosby	3
19	Nathaniel	Tompkins	2	61	Jaby	Berry	1
20	Cornelius	Fuller	3	62	Joseph	Taylor	2
21	John	Hains	2	63	Jonathen	Paddock	3
22	Edward	Gray	1	64	Nathen	Green	2
23	Luke	Covert	1	65	Seth	Nickerson	3
24	Elie	Nelson	1	66	Timothy	Clauson	1
25	Joseph	Crane Jnr:	3	67	William	Sturdefunt	1
26	Samuel	Field	10	68	Joseph	Concklin	1
27	Joseph	Field	6	69	Michal	Slott	2
28	James	Dickenson	3	70	William	Penny	4
29	Amos	Dickenson	3	71	Thomas	Forster	2
30	John	Dickenson	5	72	John	Paddock	2
31	Daniel	Townsend	3	73	Ezekiel	Meade	1
32	Uriah	Townsend	2	74	Israel	Taylor	1
33	Charles	Townsend	2	75	William	Hill	7
34	Benjamin	Townsend	5	76	Joshua	Cosby	3
35	Robert	Townsend	3	77	Isaac	Chapman	2
36	Daniel D.	Townsend	1	78	Seth	Paddock	4
37	Robert	Shaw	1	79	Ebenezer	Jones Jnr:	2
38	Caleb	Hazel	3	80	Theophilus	Jones	1
39	Gabriel	Legget on Hartwell's farm	2	81	Joshua	Hamblin	4
				82	Robert	Weekson	1
40	Jacob	Philip	1	83	Hannah	Knap	2
41	Caleb	Sweet	1	84	John	Van Tessel	1

June 1768 continued

	Name	Surname	Value		Name	Surname	Value
85	Revd: Mr	Kent	3	138	Daniel	Taylor	1
86	Thomas	Kelley	1	*Page 354*			
87	Isaac	Pierce	2	139	Michal	Shaw Jnr:	1
88	John	Martine	4	140	Andrew	Berger Jnr:	1
89	Edmund	Baker	1	141	Jeremiah	Huestin	2
90	James	Sears	1	142	David	Akins Jnr:	5
91	Peter	Hall	5	143	John	Clarke	2
92	Thomas	Gage	2	144	Widow	Hill	1
93	John	Mirrick	2	145	Haman	King	4
94	Moody	House	2	146	Jonathen	Hopkins	2
95	James	Cowen	2	147	Nehemiah	Wood	2
96	Elisha	Coole	4	148	Christopher	Wood [Ellis?]	1
97	Ezekiel	Burgis	1	149	Joseph	Merritts	4
Page 353				150	Reubin	Kelley	1
98	Jonathen	Kelley	1	151	John	Jones	2
99	John	Taylor on Lawrence's farm	4	152	Caleb	Pell's farm	3
				153	John	Lamory	3
100	Elisha	Bangs	2	154	John	Wright	2
101	Thomas	Colwill	2	155	Richard	Hopper	1
102	Amos	Fuller	2	156	Joshua	Barnum	4
103	Simeon	Ellis	2	157	Samuel	Drake	1
104	Nathaniel	Bailiff	1	158	Uriah	Drake	2
105	James	Dickenson Jnr:	2	159	Joshua	Tompkins	1
106	Jeremiah	Chase	1	160	William	Dean's farm	1
107	John	Field	6	161	John	Langdon	1
108	John	Yoemans Jnr:	2	162	Caleb	Fowler	6
109	Zachary	Paddock Jnr:	3	163	Ebenezer	Robinson	1
110	Stephen	Field	5	164	Simon	Deacons	7
111	John	Nelson	1	165	Benjamin	Perry	1
112	James	Birdsill	9	166	Solomon	Smith	2
113	Jeremiah	Linkhorne	1	167	Abraham	Maybee	2
114	John	Manley	3	168	Abraham	Maybee Jnr:	1
115	Silas	Paddock	2	169	John	Roades	1
116	Edward	Ganung	1	170	Benjamin	Odle	2
117	Samuel	Peters	6	171	Daniel	Bull	3
118	Lazarus	Griffen	2	172	Thomas	Maggot	3
119	Widow	Bailey	1	173	Matthew	Benedick's farm	2
120	Peleg	Weekson	1	174	Benjamin	Gifford	3
121	Joseph	Crommell	4	175	Henry	Krankheyt	1
122	Rowland	Perry	4	176	Obediah	Baseley	3
123	Noah	Smith	2	177	Samuel	Elwell Jnr:	2
124	Elijah	Weekson	1	*Page 355*			
125	Joshua	Hinckley	1	178	Isaac	Elwell	2
126	John	How	1	179	Jacob	Philips Jnr:	1
127	Mathias	Burgis	6	180	John	Clauson	3
128	William	Nelson	1	181	Edward	Dolf	3
129	Elisha	Kelk	1	182	Ebenezer	Bennet	1
130	Jonathen	Bryant	2	183	Elihu	Gage	1
131	William	Lane	2	184	Anthony	Gage	1
132	John	Ryder	5	185	Richard	Wearing	1
133	William	Dusenbury	4	186	John	Bloomer	1
134	John	Geen	2	187	Thomas	Townsend Jnr:	2
135	Thomas	Higgins	2	188	Christopher	Townsend	1
136	Thomas	Clements	1	189	David	Paddock Jnr:	1
137	Silbert	Krankheyt	1	190	John	Tompkins	1

June 1768 continued

	Name	Surname	Value		Name	Surname	Value
191	Samuel	Benedict	1	245	Capt. Beverley	Robinson	35
192	Jabish	Elwell	2	246	Lewis	Jones	2
193	Nathen	Crosby	2	247	Daniel	Crawford	1
194	John	Garrison	2	248	Peter	Bonker	1
195	Thomas	Hodges farm	1	249	Thomas	Baldwin	4
196	Stephen	Rockwell	1	250	Moss	Kent	5
197	Elijah	White	2	251	Nathan	Birdsill	4
198	Hezekiah	Meade	1	252	Joseph	Nauthrop	2
199	Edward	Rice	4	253	William	Porter's farm	1
200	Ebenezer	Kelly	1	254	Prince	Hopkins	1
201	Ephraim	Smith	2	255	Ebenezer	Humsted	1
202	Thomas	Fowler	3	256	John	Carly	1
203	John Bloomer	near the River	1	257	Thomas	Lovelass	1
204	Thomas	Crommell	1	258	Zebedee	Briggs	2
205	Nathaniel	Plumsted	1	259	Eleazer	Hamblin	3
206	Ebenezer	Benedick	2	260	Joseph	Vickry	1
207	Ebenezer	French	1		*Page 357*		
208	Elijah	Calkin	2	261	Silvenus	Hopkins's farm	1
209	Josiah	Swift Jnr:	1	262	Hezekiah	Meade Jnr:	1
210	Gedion	Crowfoot	2	263	John	Barto's farm	1
211	Thomas	Pew	1	264	Elijah	Budd	1
212	Daniel	Brundage	3	265	Eben	Lockwood	1
213	Solomon	Jenkins	2	266	Baseley	King	1
214	Reubin	Close	4	267	Thomas	Sarls	1
215	Joseph	Huested	3	268	Thomas	Woodard	1
216	Caleb	Huested	2	269	Caleb	Nelson	2
217	Jeremiah	Witnah	1	270	Justice	Nelson	3
218	Elisha	Oakley	1	271	Robert	Hughson	1
	Page 356			272	Peter	Drake	2
219	Charles	Mc Ready	1	273	John thauny	Craft	1
220	Mathew	Mc Caby	1	274	Isaac	Lownsberry	4
221	Seth	Holmes	1	275	Seth	Sears	2
222	James	Pardy	1	276	Samuel	Lucas	1
223	Stephen	Pardy	1	277	Noah	Burbanks	1
224	Daniel	Ball	1	278	Stephen	Fenton	1
225	John	June	1	279	James	Covey Jnr:	1
226	Benjamin	Haviland	3	280	William	Merrit	2
227	Silvenus	Coole	2	281	Nathaniel	Green	2
228	George	Darbey	1	282	Peter	Maybee	1
229	Benjamin	Hatch	3	283	John	Lownsberry	3
230	Thomas	Trobridge	1	284	Thomas	Lownsberry	3
231	Samuel	Calkin Jnr:	1	285	David	Hawkins	1
232	Nathaniel	Stone	1	286	Joseph	Ganung	1
233	Wheeton	Robinson	2	287	Andrew	Rubelyeer	1
234	Solomon	Field	3	288	Ede	Baker	1
235	Ebenezer	Brown	1	289	Shuerman	Travis	1
236	Nathaniel	Arnold	1	290	Jacob	Ellis	1
237	Solomon	Perry	1	291	David	Mirrick	1
238	Ebenezer	Gage	1	292	Jehiel	Baseley	6
239	Nehemiah	Jones	2	293	James	King	1
240	Reubin	Crosby	2	294	Samuel	Yoemans	1
241	Joshua	Barnum Jnr:	1	295	Samuel	Barnod	2
242	David	Crosby Jnr:	3	296	Joshua	Nelson	5
243	David	Calkin Jnr:	1	297	Ephraim	Jones	2
244	David	Sears	4	298	Francis	Bryer	1

June 1768 continued

#	Name	Surname	Value	#	Name	Surname	Value
299	James	Lumery	1	352	James	Forster	2
300	Benjamin	Jones	2	353	Stephens	Tompkins	2
301	Stephen	Concklin	2	354	Eleazer	Baker	1
302	Peter	Anderson	2	355	John	Haviland	2
303	Isaac	Lumery	2	356	Abraham	Craft	1
	Page 358			357	Malcom	Morrison	6
304	John	Armstrong	1	358	Samuel	Pierce	1
305	Abraham	Hyatt	1	359	Gilbert	Clap	2
306	John	Adams	1	360	Henry	Wooden	2
307	William	Van Tessel	1	361	Tertullis	Dickenson	8
308	James	Roades	2	362	William	Yoemans	1
309	William	Gee	1	363	Mr	Gregory	1
310	Peter	Moe	1	364	Elisha	Coole Jnr:	1
311	Caleb	Lockwood	1	365	Andrew	Attwood	1
312	John	Meeks	2	366	Samuel	Washburn	2
313	Moses	Fowler	5	367	Charles	Arrawah	2
314	John	Yoemans	1	368	Solomon	Lane	1
315	Robert	Oakley	1	369	Elisha	Horton	1
316	Gilbert	Dickson	1	370	Daniel	Warren	3
317	Samuel	Dickenson	2	371	Joshua	Lumery	1
318	Thomas	Adams	1	372	Henry	Jones	1
319	Widow	Nickerson	1	373	James	Barrett	1
320	Timothy	DeLavan	2	374	Joseph	Height	3
321	Isaac	Barrit	1	375	Widow	Hall	3
322	Capt.	Brown	2	376	John Wynn	on Meades place	1
323	James	Wilson	3	377	Moses	Meade	1
324	Elisha	Calkin	2	378	Jonathen	Stockham	1
325	James	Townsend	1	379	Byal	Bashford	2
326	Roger	Haviland	3	380	Isaac	Garrison	1
327	Thomas	Ferguson	1	381	James	Baldwin	1
328	Joseph	Colvill	2	382	Henry	Garlick	1
329	Samuel	Hall	2	383	John	Stedwell	3
330	Isaac	Merrick	1	384	Richard	Peters	2
331	Solomon	Hopkins	2	385	Daniel	Southerland Jnr:	1
332	Widow	Washburn	1	386	John	Moss Jnr:	2
333	Reubin	Chase	1	387	Reubin	Bunn	1
334	William	Underhill	1		*Page 360*		
335	Augustin	Underhill	2	388	Joseph	Darbey	1
336	Joseph	Robins	1	389	Jeremiah	Burgis	1
337	Joshua	Porter	1	390	Richard	Hairs	1
338	John	Roberts	1	391	Isaac	Ruscky	1
339	Benjamin	Roberts Jnr:	1	392	Stephen	Hopkins's farm	1
340	Theodorus	Crosby	2	393	James	Carle	1
341	Samuel	Burchard	2	394	Samuel	Carle	1
342	Nehemiah	Bailey	1	395	Timothy	Hatch	2
343	Caleb	Palmer	1	396	James	Hughson	2
344	Ebenezer	Munson Jnr:	1	397	Robert	Townsend	1
345	Elisha	Kent Jnr:	2	398	Mathuel	Baker	1
	Page 359			399	Thomas	Baxter	1
346	Richard	Gray	1	400	Philip	Minthorne	1
347	Benoney	Gray	1	401	Philip	Minthorne Jnr:	1
348	Augustin	Wright	1	402	William	Clinton	1
349	Nathen	Green Jnr:	2	403	Shaw	Young	2
350	Benjamin	Sears Jnr:	1	404	John	Wright Jnr:	1
351	Joseph	Forster	1	405	Reubin	Drake	1

June 1768 continued

	Name	Surname	Value		Name	Surname	Value
406	John	Berger	1	460	Nathen	Lane	1
407	Thomas	Bryant	1	461	Samuel	Williams	1
408	Philip	Steenbuck	1	462	Doctor	Daniels	1
409	Richard	Arnold	1	463	Amos	Travis	1
410	Nathaniel	Jager	1	464	Titus	Travis	2
411	Stephen	Higgbee's farm	1	465	Benjamin	Birdsill	2
412	Francis	Berger	1	466	James	Height	1
413	Peter	Berger	1	467	Gabriel	Carpenter	3
414	John	Langdon	1	468	Richard	Cornwell	1
415	Sibert	Krankheyt Jnr:	1	*Page 362*			
416	Thomas	Tompkins	1	469	Joseph	Philips	1
417	Abner	Crosby	1	470	Anthony	Stock	2
418	William	Stone	2	471	John	Smith	2
419	Elnathen	Dunn	1	472	Thomas	Hughson	2
420	Daniel	Dunn	1	473	Joseph	Horskins	1
421	Zebulon	Bass	1	474	David Hamblin	Joshua's Son	1
422	Thomas	Higgins Jnr:	1	475	Isaac	Austin	1
423	David	Porter	1	476	Johnson	Dakins	1
424	Isaiah	Bennet	1	477	Robert	Long	1
425	Thomas	Burgis	1	478	Samuel	Horton	1
426	Elijah	Hungerford	1	479	— Smith on	Langdon's farm	2
427	Anthony	Yoemans	1	480	Benjamin	Lord	1
Page 361				481	Elijah	Fuller	1
428	Benjamin	Bloomer	1	482	Zachary	Paddock	2
429	Daniel	Southerland	1	483	Cornelius	Tompkins	2
430	Nathaniel	Calkin	2	484	Moses	Dusenbury	4
431	Jonathen	Bennet	1	485	Jacob	Maybee	1
432	Joshua	Crosby Jnr:	1	486	Timothy	Shaw	2
433	Simeon	Bundy	2	487	John	Kelly	1
434	Daniel	Secord	2	488	Nathaniel	Nickerson's widow	1
435	Isaac	Secord	1	489	— Ketchum on Widow Maybee farm		1
436	John	Secord	1				
437	Locklan	McDonald	2	490	Nathan	Coole	1
438	Elexander	Grant	2	491	Joseph	Coole	1
439	John	Birdsill	2	492	Hezekiah	Avery	1
440	John	Bates	1	493	— Heddy on Joshua Barns farm		1
441	Ethiel	Towner	2				
442	Elexander	Menzus	3	494	— Willson on Elijah Oakley farm		1
443	Joshua	Hatfield	4				
444	Capt	Clarke's farm	4	495	Henry	Eldrige	1
445	Andrew	Beardsley	1	496	Cornelius	Swim	1
446	Josiah	Benjamin	1	497	Margaret	Smith	2
447	Benjamin	Green	1	498	Widow	Philipse	1
448	Robert	Watts	2	499	Charity	Austin	2
449	Simeon	Mash	1	500	Widow	Porter	2
450	Thomas	Menzus	5	501	Widow	Merrick	1
451	Henry	Luddington	3	502	Samuel	Bates	1
452	Roswell	Wilcocks	2	503	Thomas	Palmer	2
453	David	Heacock	1	504	Isaac	Gannung	1
454	Michal	Nowland	1	505	— Sniffen on widow Finch's farm		1
455	Samuel	Hunt	2				
456	Joshua	Concklin	2	506	Thomas	Williamson	1
457	James	Calkins	1	507	Widow	Hawborn	3
458	Doctor	Beardsley	1	*Page 363*			
459	Samuel	Towner	1	508	Benjamin	Titus	1

June 1768 continued

	Name	Surname	Value		Name	Surname	Value
509	Gilbert	Budd	1	540	Caleb	Veal	1
510	John	Terrill	3	541	Daniel	Seless	1
511	William	Henderson	3	542	John	Lawrence	1
512	Lazarus	Griffen	1	543	David	Corum [Cowen]	1
513	Isaac	Reade	1	544	Theophilus	Spencer	1
514	Ephraim	Jones	1	545	Seth	Nickerson Jnr:	1
515	Daniel	Pearce	1	546	Daniel	Haviland	1
516	Silvenus	Coole Jnr:	1	547	Benjamin	Higgins Jnr:	1
517	Uriah	Raymond	2	548	Eliphalet	Saunders	1
518	Joshua	Crosby Jnr:	1		*Page 364*		
519	Joshua	Burdock	1	549	Samuel	Height	1
520	Daniel	Osborn	1	550	James	Gardner	2
521	Stephen	Osborn	1	551	John	Townsend	1
522	John	Raymond	1	552	Jehiel	Stephens	1
523	Mial	Penny	1	553	Ebenezer	Robinson	2
524	George	Penny	1	554	Edward	Hunt	2
525	Ebenezer	Ryder	1	555	Stephen	Boothe	1
526	William	Stow	1	556	Robert	Wright	1
527	John	Carley Jnr:	1	557	Richard	Chapman	1
528	Edmund	Rathburn	1	558	John	Krankheyt	1
529	James	Bundy	1	559	Richard	Trusdell	1
530	Mathew	Stephen	2	560	Joseph	Height in Highland	5
531	Reubin	Close Jnr:	1	561	William	Wright	1
532	Theophilus	Hunt	1	562	William	Chatterton	1
533	Jedediah	Wyllis	1	563	James	Cock	1
534	Christopher	Dickenson	1	564	Joseph	Brundage	1
535	Ebenezer	Stone	1	565	Daniel	Knap	2
536	Nathaniel	Hall	1	566	Isaac	Horton	1
537	Ebenezer	Arnold	1	567	Joseph	Sherwood for Eagers farm	1
538	Edmund	Green	2				
539	Israel	Ward	2				£1,108

JUNE 1769
SOUTHERN PRECINCT

at 3/9 [3 shillings 9 pence] pr. pound

	Name	Surname	Value		Name	Surname	Value
	Page 447			15	David	Paddock	1
1	William	Devinport	5	16	Samuel	Towner	3
2	Thomas	Devinport	14	17	Joseph	Lane	3
3	Jacob	Mandeville	7	18	Caleb	Brundage	1
4	John	Rogers	7	19	Nathaniel	Tompkins	2
5	John	Van Amburgh's estate	7		*Page 448*		
6	Elijah	Tompkins	4	20	Cornelius	Fuller	3
7	Capt. Peter	Dubois	11	21	John	Hains	2
8	Ebenezer	Jones	2	22	Edward	Gray	1
9	Timothy	Concklin	4	23	Luke	Covert	1
10	George	Lane	2	24	Elie	Nelson	1
11	George	Hughson	4	25	Joseph	Crane Jnr:	3
12	William	Drake	3	26	Samuel	Field	10
13	John	Drake	1	27	Joseph	Field	6
14	Isaac	Roades	4	28	James	Dickenson	3

June 1769 continued

	Name	Surname	Value		Name	Surname	Value
29	Amos	Dickenson	3	82	Robert	Weekson	1
30	John	Dickenson	5	83	Hannah	Knap	2
31	Daniel	Townsend	3	84	John	Van Tessel	1
32	Uriah	Townsend	2	85	Revd: Mr	Kent	2
33	Charles	Townsend	1	86	Thomas	Kelley	1
34	Benjamin	Townsend	5	87	Isaac	Pierce	2
35	Robert	Townsend	3	88	John	Martine	4
36	Daniel D.	Townsend	1	89	Edmund	Baker	1
37	Robert	Shaw	1	90	James	Sears	1
38	Caleb	Hazell	3	91	Peter	Hall	5
39	Gabriel	Legget on Hartwells farm	2	92	Thomas	Gage	1
					Page 450		
40	Jacob	Philip	1	93	John	Merrick	3
41	Caleb	Sweet	1	94	Moody	House	2
42	William	Palmer	2	95	James	Cowen	3
43	John	Newbury	4	96	Elisha	Coole	4
44	Robert	Mooney	3	97	Ezekiel	Burgis	1
45	Thomas	Paddock	4	98	Jonathen	Kelley	1
46	George	Curry	2	99	Elisha	Bangs	2
47	Ebenezer	King	1	100	Thomas	Colville	2
48	Josiah	Baker	3	101	Amos	Fuller	2
49	Isaac	Crosby	3	102	Simeon	Ellis	2
50	Benjamin	Sears	4	103	Nathaniel	Bailiff	1
51	Christopher	Fowler	1	104	James	Dickenson Jnr:	2
52	Peter	Anguwine	4	105	Jeremiah	Chase	1
53	Simeon	Ryder	4	106	John	Field	6
54	Isaac	House's farm	3	107	John	Yoemans Jnr:	2
55	Thomas	Smith	3	108	Zachary	Paddock Jnr:	2
	Page 449			109	Stephen	Field	5
56	Edward	Gray Jnr:	1	110	John	Nelson	1
57	Samuel	Bangs	5	111	James	Birdsill	9
58	Nathaniel	Forster	4	112	Jeremiah	Linkhorn	1
59	Samuel	Elwell	2	113	John	Manley	3
60	David	Crosby	3	114	Silas	Paddock	1
61	Jaby	Berry	1	115	Edward	Ganung	1
62	Joseph	Taylors farm	3	116	Samuel	Peters	6
63	Jonathan	Paddock	3	117	Lazarus	Griffen	2
64	Nathen	Green	2	118	Widow	Bailey	1
65	Seth	Nickerson	3	119	Peleg	Weekson	1
66	Timothy	Clauson	1	120	Joseph	Crommell	4
67	William	Sturdefunt	1	121	Rowland	Perry	4
68	Joseph	Concklin	1	122	Noah	Smith	2
69	Michal	Slott	3	123	Elijah	Weekson	1
70	William	Penny	5	124	Joshua	Hinckley	1
71	Thomas	Forster	1	125	John	How	1
72	John	Paddock	2	126	Mathias	Burgis	4
73	Ezekiel	Meade	1	127	William	Nelson	1
74	Israel	Taylor	1	128	Jonathen	Bryant	2
75	William	Hill	7	129	William	Lane	2
76	Joshua	Crosby	3	130	John	Ryder	5
77	Isaac	Chapman	2		*Page 451*		
78	Seth	Paddock	4	131	William	Dusenbury	4
79	Ebenezer	Jones Jnr:	2	132	John	Geen	2
80	Theophilus	Jones	2	133	Thomas	Higgins	2
81	Joshua	Hamblin	4	134	Thomas	Clements farm	1

June 1769 continued

	Name	Surname	Value		Name	Surname	Value
135	Sibert	Krankheyt	1	189	Jabish	Ellwell	2
136	Daniel	Taylor	1	190	Nathen	Crosby	2
137	Michal	Shaw Jnr:	1	191	John	Garrison	2
138	Andrew	Berger Jnr:	1	192	Thomas	Hodges's farm	1
139	Jeremiah	Huestin	2	193	Stephen	Rockwell	1
140	David	Akins Jnr:	4	194	Elijah	White	2
141	John	Clarke	2	195	Hezekiah	Meade	1
142	Widow	Hill	1	196	Edward	Rice	4
143	Haman	King	4	197	Ebenezer	Kelly	1
144	Jonathen	Hopkins	2	198	Ephraim	Smith	2
145	Nehemiah	Wood	2	199	Thomas	Fowler	3
146	Christopher	Wood ? [Ellis?]	1	200	John Bloomer, near the river		1
147	Joseph	Merrits	4	201	Nathaniel	Plumsted	1
148	Reubin	Kelley	1	202	Ebenezer	Benedick	2
149	John	Jones	2	203	Elijah	Calkin	2
150	Caleb	Pells farm	3	204	Josiah	Swift Jnr:	1
151	John	Lamory	3	205	Gedion	Crowfoot	1
152	John	Wright	2	206	Thomas	Pew	1
153	Richard	Hopper	1	207	Daniel	Brundage	3
154	Joshua	Barnum	4	208	Thomas	Crummel	1
155	Samuel	Drake	1		*Page 453*		
156	Uriah	Drake	2	209	Solomon	Jenkins	2
157	Joshua	Tompkins	1	210	Reubin	Close	4
158	John	Langdon	1	211	Joseph	Huested	3
159	Caleb	Fowler	6	212	Caleb	Huested	2
160	Ebenezer	Robinson	1	213	Jeremiah	Witnah	1
161	Simon	Dacon	5	214	Elisha	Oakley	1
162	Benjamin	Perry	1	215	Charles	Mc Ready	1
163	Solomon	Smith	2	216	Mathew	Mc Caby	1
164	Abraham	Maybee	2	217	Seth	Holmes	1
165	Abraham	Maybee Jnr:	1	218	James	Pardy	1
166	John	Roades	1	219	Stephen	Pardy	1
167	Benjamin	Odle	2	220	Daniel	Ball	1
168	Daniel	Bull	3	221	John	June	1
169	Thomas	Maggot	3	222	Benjamin	Haviland	3
	Page 452			223	Silvenus	Coole	1
170	Matthew	Benedick's farm	2	224	George	Darby	1
171	Benjamin	Gifford	2	225	Benjamin	Hatch	3
172	Henry	Krankheyt	1	226	Thomas	Trobridge	1
173	Obediah	Baseley	2	227	Samuel	Calkin Jnr:	1
174	Samuel	Elwell Jnr:	2	228	Nathaniel	Stone	1
175	Isaac	Elwell	2	229	Wheeton	Robinson	1
176	Jacob	Philips Jnr:	1	230	Solomon	Field	3
177	John	Clauson	2	231	Ebenezer	Brown	1
178	Edward	Dolf	2	232	Solomon	Perry	1
179	Ebenezer	Bennet	1	233	Ebenezer	Gage	1
180	Elihu	Gage	1	234	Nehemiah	Jones	2
181	Anthony	Gage	1	235	Reubin	Crosby	2
182	Richard	Wearing	1	236	Joshua	Barnum Jnr:	1
183	John	Bloomer	1	237	David	Crosby Jnr:	3
184	Thomas	Townsend Jnr:	2	238	David	Calkin Jnr:	1
185	Christopher	Townsend	1	239	David	Sears	4
186	David	Paddock Jnr:	1	240	Capt. Beaverley Robinson		40
187	John	Tompkins	1	241	Lewis	Jones	2
188	Samuel	Benedick	1	242	Daniel	Crawford	1

June 1769 continued

	Name	Surname	Value		Name	Surname	Value
243	Peter	Bonker	1	296	Stephen	Concklin	2
244	Thomas	Baldwin	4	297	Peter	Anderson	2
245	Moss	Kent	5	298	Isaac	Lumery	2
246	Nathan	Birdsill	4	299	John	Armstrong	1
Page 454				300	Abraham	Hyat	1
247	Joseph	Nauthrop	2	301	John	Adams	1
248	William	Porter's farm	1	302	William	Van Tessel	1
249	Prince	Hopkins	1	303	James	Roades	2
250	Ebenezer	Humsted	1	304	William	Gee	1
251	John	Carley	1	305	Peter	Moe	1
252	Thomas	Lovelass	1	306	Caleb	Lockwood	1
253	Zebedee	Briggs	2	307	John	Meeks	2
254	Eleazer	Hamblin	3	308	Moses	Fowler	5
255	Joseph	Vickry	1	309	John	Yoemans	1
256	Silvenus	Hopkins's farm	1	310	Robert	Oakley	1
257	Hezekiah	Meade Jnr:	1	311	Gilbert	Dickson	2
258	John	Barto's farm	1	312	Samuel	Dickenson	2
259	Elijah	Budd	1	313	Thomas	Adams	1
260	Eben	Lockwood	1	314	Widow	Nickerson	1
261	Baseley	King	1	315	Timothy	DeLavan	2
262	Thomas	Sarls	1	316	Isaac	Barret	1
263	Thomas	Woodard	1	317	Capt.	Brown	2
264	Caleb	Nelson	2	318	James	Wilson	3
265	Justice	Nelson	2	319	Elisha	Calkin	2
266	Robert	Hughson	1	320	James	Townsend	1
267	Peter	Drakes farm	2	321	Roger	Haviland	3
268	John thauny	Craft	1	322	Thomas	Ferguson	1
269	Isaac	Lownsberry	4	323	Joseph	Colville	2
270	Seth	Sears	2	324	Samuel	Hall	2
271	Samuel	Lucas	1	*Page 456*			
272	Noah	Burbanks	1	325	Isaac	Merrick	1
273	Stephen	Fenton	1	326	Solomon	Hopkins	2
274	James	Covey Jnr:	1	327	Widow	Washburn	1
275	William	Merrit	2	328	Reubin	Chase	1
276	Nathaniel	Green	2	329	William	Underhill	1
277	Peter	Maybee	1	330	Augustin	Underhill	2
278	John	Lownsbury	3	331	Joseph	Robins	1
279	Thomas	Lownsbury	3	332	Joshua	Porter	1
280	David	Hawkins	1	333	John	Roberts	1
281	Joseph	Ganung	1	334	Benjamin	Roberts Jnr:	1
282	Andrew	Rubelyeer	1	335	Theodorus	Crosby	2
283	Edey	Backer	1	336	Samuel	Burchard's farm	1
284	Shuerman	Travis	1	337	Nehemiah	~~Nathaniel~~ Bailey	1
285	Jacob	Ellis	1	338	Caleb	Palmer	1
Page 455				339	Ebenezer	Munson Jnr:	1
286	David	Merrick	1	340	Elisha	Kent Jnr:	1
287	Jehiel	Baseley	5	341	Richard	Gray	1
288	James	King	1	342	Benoney	Gray	1
289	Samuel	Yoemans	1	343	Augustin	Wright	2
290	Samuel	Barnod	2	344	Nathen	Green Jnr:	2
291	Joshua	Nelson	5	345	Benjamin	Sears Jnr:	1
292	Ephraim	Jones	2	346	Joseph	Forster	1
293	Francis	Bryer	1	347	James	Forster	1
294	James	Lumery	1	348	Stephen	Tompkins	2
295	Benjamin	Jones	2	349	Eleazer	Baker	2

June 1769 continued

	Name	Surname	Value		Name	Surname	Value
350	John	Haviland	2	403	Richard	Arnold	1
351	Abraham	Craft	1	404	Nathaniel	Jager	1
352	Malcom	Morrison	6	405	Stephen	Higgby's farm	1
353	Samuel	Pierce	1	406	Francis	Berger	1
354	Gilbert	Clap	2	407	Peter	Berger	1
355	Henry	Wooden	3	408	John	Langdon	1
356	Tertullis	Dickenson's mill	8	409	Sibert	Krankheyt Jnr:	1
357	William	Yoemans	1	410	Thomas	Tompkins	1
358	Mr	Gregory	1	411	Abner	Crosby	1
359	Elisha	Coole Jnr:	1	412	William	Stone	2
360	Andrew	Attwood	1	413	Elnathen	Dunn	1
361	Samuel	Washburn	2	414	Daniel	Dunn	1
Page 457				415	Zebulon	Bass	1
362	Charles	Arrawah	2	416	Thomas	Higgins Jnr:	1
363	Solomon	Lane	1	417	David	Potter [Porter]	1
364	Elijah	Horton	1	418	Isaiah	Bennet	1
365	Daniel	Warren	3	419	Thomas	Burgis	1
366	Joshua	Lumery	1	420	Elijah	Hungerford	2
367	Henry	Jones	1	421	Anthony	Yoemans	1
368	James	Barrett	1	422	Benjamin	Bloomer	1
369	Joseph	Haight	3	423	Daniel	Southerland	1
370	Widow Hall, on Meades place		3	424	Nathaniel	Calkin	1
371	John	Wynn	1	425	Jonathen	Bennet	1
372	Moses	Meade	1	426	Joshua	Crosby	2
373	Jonathen	Stockham	1	427	Simeon	Bundy's farm	1
374	Byal	Bashford	2	428	Daniel	Secord	2
375	Isaac	Garrison	1	429	Isaac	Secord	1
376	James	Baldwin	1	430	John	Secord	1
377	Henry	Garlick	1	431	Lockland	McDonald	3
378	John	Stidwell	3	432	Alexander	Grant	2
379	Richard	Peters	2	433	John	Birdsill	2
380	Daniel	Southerland Jnr:	1	434	John	Bates	1
381	John	Moss Jnr:	2	435	Alexander	Mensus	4
382	Reubin	Bunn	1	436	Joshua	Hatfields farm	4
383	Joseph	Darbey	1	437	Andrew	Beardsley	1
384	Jeremiah	Burgis	2	438	Josiah	Benjamin's	1
385	Richard	Hares	1	439	Benjamin	Green	1
386	Isaac	Ruscky	1	440	Robert	Watts	2
387	Stephen	Hopkins farm	1	*Page 459*			
388	James	Carle	1	441	Simeon	Marsh	1
389	Samuel	Carle	1	442	Thomas	Menzus	6
390	Timothy	Hatch	2	443	Henry	Luddington	3
391	James	Hughson	2	444	Roswell	Wilcocks	2
392	Robert	Townsend	1	445	David	Heacock	1
393	Thomas	Baxter	1	446	Michael	Nowland	1
394	Philip	Minthorn	1	447	Samuel	Hunt	2
395	Philip	Minthorn Jnr:	1	448	Joshua	Concklin	2
396	Philip	Clinton	1	449	James	Calkins	1
397	Shaw	Young	2	450	Samuel	Towner	1
398	John	Wright Jnr:	1	451	Nathen	Lane	1
399	Reubin	Drake	1	452	Doctor	Daniels	1
400	John	Berger	1	453	Amos	Travis	1
Page 458				454	Titus	Travis	2
401	Thomas	Bryant	1	455	Benjamin	Birdsill South	2
402	Philip	Steenbuck	1	456	Gabriel	Carpenter	3

June 1769 continued

#	Name	Surname	Value
457	Richard	Cornwell	1
458	Joseph	Philip	1
459	Anthony	Stock	2
460	John	Smith	2
461	Thomas	Hughson	2
462	Joseph	Horskins	1
463	David Hamblin	Joshua's Son	1
464	Isaac	Austin	1
465	Johnson	Dakins	1
466	Robert	Long	1
467	Samuel	Horton	1
468	— Smith on	Langdons farm	2
469	Benjamin	Lord	1
470	Elijah	Fuller	1
471	Zachary	Paddock	2
472	Cornelius	Tompkins	3
473	Moses	Dusenbury	4
474	Jacob	Maybee	1
475	Timothy	Shaw	1
476	John	Kelley	1
477	Nathaniel	Nickerson's widow	1
478	— Ketchum, on widow Maybey pla		1

Page 460

#	Name	Surname	Value
479	Nathen	Cool	1
480	Joseph	Cool	1
481	Hezekiah	Avery	1
482	— Heddy on Joshua Barnums far		2
483	— Wilson on Elijah Oakleys farm		1
484	Henry	Aldridge	1
485	Cornelius	Swim	1
486	Margit	Smith	2
487	Widow	Philips	1
488	Charity	Austin	2
489	Widow	Merrick	1
490	Samuel	Bates	1
491	Thomas	Palmer	2
492	Isaac	Ganung	1
493	— Sniffen on widow Finchs farm		1
494	Thomas	Williamson	1
495	Widow	Hawborn	1
496	Benjamin	Titus	1
497	Gilbert	Budd	1
498	John	Terril	4
499	Lazarus	Griffen Jnr:	1
500	Isaac	Reade	1
501	Ephraim	Jones Upper	1
502	Daniel	Pierce	1
503	Silvenus	Cool Jnr:	1
504	Uriah	Raymond	2
505	Joshua	Crosby Jnr:	1
506	Joshua	Burdock	1
507	Daniel	Osborn	1
508	Stephen	Osborn	1
509	John	Raymond	1
510	Mial	Penny	2
511	George	Penny	1
512	Ebenezer	Ryder	1
513	William	Stow	1
514	John	Carley Jnr:	1
515	Edmund	Rathburn	1

Page 461

#	Name	Surname	Value
516	Matthew	Stephens	2
517	Reubin	Close Jnr:	1
518	Jedediah	Wyllis	1
519	Christopher	Dickenson	1
520	Nathaniel	Hall	1
521	Ebenezer	Arnold	1
522	Edmund	Green	2
523	Israel	Ward	2
524	Caleb	Veal	1
525	Daniel	Seless	1
526	John	Lawrence	1
527	David	Cowan	1
528	Theophilus	Spencer	1
529	Seth	Nickerson Jnr:	1
530	Daniel	Haviland	2
531	Benjamin	Higgins	1
532	Eliphalet	Saunders	1
533	Samuel	Haight	1
534	James	Gardner	2
535	John	Townsend	1
536	Ebenezer	Robinson	2
537	Edward	Hunt	2
538	Stephen	Boothe	1
539	Robert	Wright	1
540	Richard	Chapman	1
541	John	Krankheyt	1
542	Richard	Trusdell	1
543	Joseph	Haight in Highlands	4
544	William	Wright	1
545	William	Chetterton	1
546	James	Cock	1
547	Joseph	Brundage	1
548	Daniel	Knap	2
549	Isaac	Horton	1
550	Joseph	Sherwood for Eagers farm	1
551	Benjamin	Birdsell	2
552	Dennis	Wright	3
553	Lemuel	Wilmot	1
554	John	Hayns's farm	1
555	Silvenus	Brundage	2
556	Samuel	Utter	1
557	William	Maxvell	1
558	—	McNill & Collins	3
559	Asa	Hayns	1

June 1769 continued

	Name	Surname	Value
	Page 462		
560	John	Dean	1
561	Caleb	Dean	1
562	Jeremiah	Shafer	1
563	John	Dawn	1
564	James	Sears Jnr:	1
565	Moses	Knap	1
566	Moses	Knap Jnr:	1
567	James	Akelson	1
568	Jonathen	Pine	1
569	Thomas	Carle	2
570	Morton	Hall	1
571	Abraham	Haight	3
572	John	Taylor	2
573	Abner	Ston	2
574	Phenias	Baker	2
575	Jessil	Brown [Baker?]	1
576	William	Belden	1
577	—	Hull, near Zachariah Paddocks	4
578	Berry	Hopkins	1
579	Joseph	Hopkins	1
580	Samuel	Perry	1
581	Comfort	Luddington	1
582	Jesse	Smith	1
583	Samuel	Stringum	1
584	Banaga	Slaigh	1
			£1,121

JUNE 1770
SOUTHERN PRECINCT

at 4 shillings pr. pound

	Name	Surname	Value
	Page 624		
1	William	Devinport	5
2	Thomas	Devinport	14
3	Jacob	Mandeville	7
4	John	Rogers	7
5	John	Van Amburgh's Estate	7
	Page 625		
6	Elijah	Tompkins	4
7	Capt. Peter	Dubois	12
8	Ebenezer	Jones	2
9	Timothy	Concklin	4
10	George	Lane	2
11	William	Drake	3
12	John	Drake	1
13	Isaac	Roades	4
14	David	Paddock	1
15	Joseph	Lane	3
16	Caleb	Brundage	1
17	Nathaniel	Tompkins	2
18	Cornelius	Fuller	3
19	John	Hains	2
20	Luke	Covert	1
21	Elie	Nelson	1
22	Joseph	Crane Jnr:	3
23	Samuel	Field	8
24	Joseph	Field	6
25	James	Dickenson	4
26	Amos	Dickenson	2
27	John	Dickenson	5
28	Daniel	Townsend	3
29	Uriah	Townsend	2
30	Charles	Townsend	1
31	Benjamin	Townsend	5
32	Robert	Townsend	3
33	Daniel D.	Townsend	1
34	Robert	Shaw	1
35	Caleb	Hazell	3
36	Gabriel	Legget, on Hartwells farm	3
37	Jacob	Philip	1
38	Caleb	Sweet	1
39	William	Palmer	2
40	John	Newbury	4
41	Robert	Money	3
42	Thomas	Paddock	4
43	George	Curry's farm	2
44	Ebenezer	King	1
45	Josiah	Baker	4
	Page 626		
46	Isaac	Crosby	3
47	Benjamin	Sears	4
48	Christopher	Fowler	1
49	Peter	Anguwine	4
50	Simeon	Ryder	4
51	Thomas	Smith	4
52	Edward	Gray Jnr:	1
53	Samuel	Bangs	5
54	Nathaniel	Forster	5
55	Samuel	Elwell	2
56	David	Crosby	3
57	Jaby	Berry	2
58	Jonathen	Paddock	3
59	Nathen	Green	2
60	Seth	Nickerson	3

June 1770 continued

	Name	Surname	Value		Name	Surname	Value
61	Timothy	Clauson	1	115	Elijah	Weekson	1
62	William	Sturdefunt	1	116	Joshua	Hinckley	1
63	Joseph	Concklin	1	117	John	How	1
64	Michael	Slot	3	118	Mathias	Burgis	4
65	William	Penny	5	119	William	Nelson	1
66	Thomas	Forster	1	120	Jonathen	Bryant	2
67	John	Paddock	2	121	William	Lane	2
68	Israel	Taylor	1	122	John	Ryder	5
69	William	Hill	8	*Page 628*			
70	Joshua	Crosby	3	123	William	Dusenbury	5
71	Isaac	Chapman	1	124	John	Geen	2
72	Seth	Paddock	5	125	Thomas	Higgins	2
73	Ebenezer	Jones	2	126	Sibert	Krankheyt	1
74	Theophilus	Jones	2	127	Daniel	Taylor	1
75	Joshua	Hamblin	6	128	Michal	Shaw Jnr:	1
76	Robert	Weekson	1	129	Andrew	Berger Jnr:	1
77	Hannah	Knap	2	130	Jeremiah	Huestin	2
78	John	Van Tessel	1	131	David	Akin Jnr:	4
79	Revd: Mr	Kent	4	132	Widow	Hill	1
80	Thomas	Kelley	1	133	Haman	King	4
81	Isaac	Pearce	2	134	Jonathen	Hopkins	2
82	Edmund	Baker	1	135	Nehemiah	Wood	2
83	James	Sears	1	136	Christopher	Wood [Ellis?]	1
Page 627				137	Reubin	Kelley	1
84	Peter	Hall	6	138	John	Jones	2
85	Thomas	Gage	1	139	Caleb	Pells farm	3
86	John	Merrick	2	140	John	Lamorey	3
87	Moody	House	3	141	John	Wright	2
88	James	Cowen	2	142	Richard	Hopper	2
89	Elisha	Cole	5	143	Joshua	Barnum	4
90	Ezekiel	Burgis	1	144	Samuel	Drake	1
91	Jonathen	Kelley	1	145	Uriah	Drake	3
92	Elisha	Bangs	2	146	Joshua	Tompkins	2
93	Amos	Fuller	2	147	Caleb	Fowler	8
94	Simeon	Ellis	2	148	Ebenezer	Robinson	1
95	Nathaniel	Bailiff	1	149	Simon	Dacon	5
96	James	Dickinson Jnr:	3	150	Benjamin	Perry	1
97	Jeremiah	Chase	1	151	Solomon	Smith	3
98	John	Field	6	152	Abraham	Maybee	2
99	John	Yoemans Jnr:	2	153	Abraham	Maybee Jnr:	1
100	Zachary	Paddock	2	154	John	Roades	1
101	Stephen	Field	7	155	Benjamin	Odle	2
102	John	Nelson	1	156	Daniel	Bull	4
103	James	Birdsill	9	157	Thomas	Maggot	3
104	Jeremiah	Linkhorn	1	158	Matthew	Benedick's farm	2
105	John	Manly	2	159	Benjamin	Gifford	2
106	Silas	Paddock	1	160	Henry	Krankheyt	1
107	Edward	Ganung	1	*Page 629*			
108	Samuel	Peters	6	161	Obediah	Baseley	1
109	Lazarus	Griffen	2	162	Samuel	Elwell Jnr:	2
110	Widow	Bailey	1	163	Isaac	Elwell	2
111	Peleg	Weekson	1	164	Jacob	Philip Jnr:	1
112	Joseph	Crommell	4	165	John	Clauson	1
113	Rowland	Perry	3	166	Ebenezer	Bennet	1
114	Noah	Smith	2	167	Elihu	Gage	1

June 1770 continued

	Name	Surname	Value		Name	Surname	Value
168	Anthony	Gage	1	222	David	Sears	4
169	Richard	Wearing	1	223	Capt. Beverley	Robinson	80
170	Thomas	Townsend Jnr:	2	224	Lewis	Jones	2
171	Christopher	Townsend	1	225	Daniel	Crawford	1
172	David	Paddock Jnr:	1	226	Peter	Bonker	1
173	John	Tompkins	1	227	Thomas	Baldwin	5
174	Samuel	Benedick	1	228	Moss	Kent	6
175	Jabish	Ellwell	2	229	Nathan	Birdsill	3
176	Nathen	Crosby	2	230	Joseph	Nauthrop	3
177	John	Garrison	2	231	William	Porter's farm	1
178	Thomas	Hodge's farm	1	232	Prince	Hopkins	1
179	Stephen	Rockwell	1	233	Ebenezer	Humsted	1
180	Elijah	White	1	234	John	Carley	1
181	Hezekiah	Meade	1	235	Thomas	Lovelass	1
182	Edward	Rice	5		*Page 631*		
183	Ebenezer	Kelley	1	236	Zebedee	Briggs	1
184	Ephraim	Smith	3	237	Eleazer	Hamblin	4
185	Thomas	Fowler	4	238	Joseph	Vickry	1
186	John Bloomer	near the river	1	239	Silvenus	Hopkins farm	1
187	Nathaniel	Plumsted	1	240	Hezekiah	Meade Jnr:	1
188	Ebenezer	Benedick	2	241	John	Barto's farm	1
189	Elijah	Calkin	2	242	Elijah	Budd	2
190	Josiah	Swift Jnr:	1	243	Eben	Lockwood	1
191	Daniel	Brundage	4	244	Baseley	King	1
192	Thomas	Crommel	1	245	Thomas	Sarls	1
193	Solomon	Jenkins	3	246	Thomas	Woodard	1
194	Reubin	Close	4	247	Caleb	Nelson	3
195	Joseph	Huested	3	248	Justice	Nelson	3
196	Caleb	Huested	2	249	Robert	Hughson	2
197	Jeremiah	Witnah	1	250	Peter	Drakes farm	2
198	Elisha	Oakley	1	251	John thauny	Craft	1
199	Charles	Mc Ready	1	252	Isaac	Lownsbury	4
	Page 630			253	Seth	Sears	2
200	Mathew	Mc Caby	1	254	Samuel	Lucas	1
201	Seth	Holmes	1	255	Noah	Burbanks	1
202	James	Pardy	1	256	James	Covey Jnr:	2
203	Stephen	Pardy	1	257	William	Merrit	2
204	Daniel	Ball	1	258	Nathaniel	Green	1
205	John	June	1	259	Peter	Maybee	2
206	Benjamin	Haviland	4	260	John	Lownsbury	3
207	Silvenus	Cole	1	261	Thomas	Lownsbury	3
208	George	Darbey	1	262	David	Hawkins	1
209	Benjamin	Hatch	2	263	Joseph	Ganung	1
210	Thomas	Trobridge	1	264	Andrew	Rubelye	1
211	Nathaniel	Stone	1	265	Edey	Baker	2
212	Wheeton	Robinson	1	266	Jacob	Ellis	1
213	Solomon	Field	4	267	David	Merrick	1
214	Ebenezer	Brown	1	268	Jehiel	Beardsley	5
215	Solomon	Perry	1	269	James	King	1
216	Ebenezer	Gage	1	270	Samuel	Yoemans	1
217	Nehemiah	Jones	2	271	Samuel	Bernod	1
218	Reubin	Crosby	3	272	Joshua	Nelson	5
219	Joshua	Barnum Jnr:	1	273	Ephraim	Jones	2
220	David	Crosby Jnr:	3	274	Francis	Bryer	1
221	David	Calkin	1		*Page 632*		

June 1770 continued

#	Name	Surname	Value
275	James	Lumery	2
276	John	Armstrong	1
277	John	Adams	1
278	William	Van Tessel	1
279	James	Roades	2
280	William	Gee	1
281	Peter	Moe	1
282	John	Meeks	2
283	Moses	Fowler	6
284	John	Yoemans	1
285	Robert	Oakley	1
286	Gilbert	Dickson	2
287	Samuel	Dickinson	2
288	Thomas	Adams	1
289	William	Nickerson	1
290	Timothy	DeLavan	2
291	Isaac	Barret	1
292	Capt.	Brown	2
293	James	Wilson	4
294	Elisha	Calkin	1
295	James	Townsend	1
296	Roger	Haviland	3
297	Thomas	Ferguson	1
298	Joseph	Colvill	2
299	Samuel	Hall	2
300	Isaac	Merrick	1
301	Solomon	Hopkins	2
302	Widow	Washburn	1
303	Reubin	Chase	1
304	William	Underhill	1
305	Augustin	Underhill	2
306	Joseph	Robins	1
307	Joshua	Porter	1
308	John	Roberts	1
309	Benjamin	Roberts	1
310	Theodorus	Crosby	2
311	Samuel	Burchards farm	1
312	Nehemiah	Bailey	1

Page 633

#	Name	Surname	Value
313	Caleb	Palmer	1
314	Elisha	Kent Jnr:	1
315	Richard	Gray	1
316	Benoney	Gray	1
317	Augustin	Wright	2
318	Nathin	Green Jnr:	2
319	Benjamin	Sears Jnr:	1
320	Joseph	Forster	1
321	James	Forster	1
322	Stephen	Tompkins	2
323	Eleazer	Baker	2
324	John	Haviland	2
325	Abraham	Craft	1
326	Malcom	Morrison	7
327	Samuel	Pearce	2
328	Gilbert	Clap	2
329	Henry	Wooden	3
330	William	Yoemans	1
331	Mr	Gregory	2
332	Elisha	Coole Jnr:	1
333	Andrew	Attwood	1
334	Samuel	Washburn	2
335	Charles	Arrawah	2
336	Solomon	Lane	-
337	Elijah	Horton	1
338	Daniel	Warren	1
339	Joshua	Lumery	3
340	Henry	Jones	1
341	James	Barret	1
342	Joseph	Haight	3
343	Widow	Hall, on Meades place	1
344	John	Wynn	1
345	Moses	Meade	1
346	Jonathen	Stockham	1
347	Byal	Bashford	2
348	Isaac	Garrison	1
349	James	Baldwin	1
350	John	Stedwell	3
351	Richard	Peters	3

Page 634

#	Name	Surname	Value
352	Daniel	Southerland Jnr:	1
353	John	Moss Jnr:	1
354	Reubin	Bunn	1
355	Joseph	Darbey	1
356	Jeremiah	Burgis	2
357	Richard	Hares	1
358	Isaac	Ruscky	1
359	Stephen	Hopkins farm	1
360	James	Carl	2
361	Samuel	Carl	1
362	Timothy	Hatch	2
363	James	Hughson	2
364	Robert	Townsend	1
365	Thomas	Baxter	1
366	Philip	Minthorn	1
367	Philip	Minthorn Jnr:	1
368	Philip	Clinton	1
369	Shaw	Young	1
370	John	Wright Jnr:	1
371	Reubin	Drake	1
372	John	Berger	1
373	Thomas	Bryant	1
374	Philip	Steenbuck	1
375	Richard	Arnold	1
376	Nathaniel	Jager	1
377	Francis	Berger	1
378	Peter	Berger	1
379	John	Langdon Jnr:	1
380	Sibert	Krankheyt Jnr:	1
381	Thomas	Tompkins	1

June 1770 continued

#	Name	Surname	Value
382	Abner	Crosby	1
383	William	Stone	2
384	Elnathen	Dunn	1
385	Daniel	Dunn	1
386	Zebulon	Bass	1
387	Thomas	Higgins Jnr:	1
388	David	Potter [Porter]	1
389	Thomas	Burgis	1
390	Elijah	Hungerford	2

Page 635

#	Name	Surname	Value
391	Anthony	Yoemans	1
392	Benjamin	Bloomer	1
393	Daniel	Southerland	1
394	Nathaniel	Calkin	1
395	Jonathen	Bennet	1
396	Joshua	Crosby	2
397	Daniel	Secar	2
398	Isaac	Secar	1
399	John	Secar	2
400	Lockland	McDonald	4
401	Alexander	Grant	4
402	John	Birdsill	3
403	John	Bates	1
404	Alexander	Mensus	5
405	Joshua	Hatfields farm	4
406	Andrew	Beardsley	1
407	Josiah	Benjamin	2
408	Benjamin	Green	1
409	Robert	Watts	2
410	Simeon	Marsh	-
411	Thomas	Menzus	7
412	Henry	Luddington	3
413	Roswell	Wilcocks	2
414	David	Heacock	1
415	Michal	Nowland	1
416	Samuel	Hunt	2
417	Joshua	Concklin	2
418	James	Calkins	1
419	Samuel	Towner	1
420	Nathen	Lane	1
421	Doctor	Daniels	2
422	Amos	Travis	1
423	Titus	Travis	3
424	Benjamin	Birdsill south	2
425	Gabriel	Carpenter	1
426	Richard	Cornwell	1
427	Joseph	Philips	1
428	Anthony	Stock	2
429	John	Smith	2

Page 636

#	Name	Surname	Value
430	Thomas	Hughson	2
431	Joseph	Horskins	2
432	David Hamblin Joshua's son		2
433	Isaac	Austin	1
434	Johnson	Dakons	1
435	Robert	Long	1
436	Samuel	Horton	1
437	Elijah	Fuller	1
438	Zachary	Paddock	2
439	Cornelius	Tompkins	4
440	Moses	Dusenbury	5
441	Jacob	Maybee	1
442	Timothy	Shaw	2
443	John	Kelley	1
444	Nathaniel Nickerson's widow		1
445	—	Ketchum, on Widow Maybee pl	1
446	Nathen	Cole	1
447	Joseph	Cole	1
448	Hezekiah	Avery	1
449	—	Heddy, on Joshua Barnums far[m]	2
450	Robert	Wilson, on Oakleys farm	1
451	Henry	Aldridge	1
452	Cornelius	Swim	1
453	Charity	Austin	2
454	Widow	Merrick	1
455	Isaac	Gannung	1
456	—	Sniffen, on Widow Finchs farm	1
457	Thomas	Williamson	1
458	Widow	Hawborn	1
459	Gilbert	Budd	1
460	John	Terril	4
461	Lazarus	Griffen	1
462	Isaac	Reade	1
463	Ephraim	Jones, upper	1
464	Daniel	Pearce	1
465	Silvenus	Cole Jnr:	1
466	Uriah	Raymond	2

Page 637

#	Name	Surname	Value
467	Joshua	Crosby Jnr:	1
468	Joshua	Burdock	1
469	Daniel	Osborn	1
470	Stephen	Osborn	1
471	John	Raymond	1
472	Mial	Penny	2
473	George	Penny	1
474	Ebenezer	Ryder	1
475	William	Stow	1
476	John	Carley Jnr:	1
477	Edmund	Rathbun	1
478	Mathew	Stephens	2
479	Reubin	Close Jnr:	1
480	Jedediah	Willis	1
481	Nathaniel	Hall	1
482	Ebenezer	Arnold	1
483	Edmund	Green	1
484	Israel	Ward	3

June 1770 continued

#	Name	Surname	Value
485	Caleb	Veal	2
486	Daniel	Seless	2
487	John	Lawrence	2
488	David	Cowen	1
489	Theophilus	Spencer	1
490	Seth	Nickerson Jnr:	1
491	Daniel	Haviland	2
492	Benjamin	Higgins	1
493	Eliphalet	Saunders	1
494	Samuel	Haight	1
495	James	Gardner	2
496	John	Townsend	1
497	Ebenezer	Robinson	2
498	Edward	Hunt	2
499	Robert	Wright	1
500	Richard	Chapman	1
501	John	Krankheyt	1
502	Richard	Trusdell	1
503	Joseph	Haight	5
504	William	Wright	1

Page 638

#	Name	Surname	Value
505	William	Chatterton	1
506	James	Cock	1
507	Joseph	Brundage	1
508	Daniel	Knap	3
509	Isaac	Horton	1
510	Joseph	Sherwood for Eagers farm	1
511	Benjamin	Birdsill	2
512	Dennis	Wright	5
513	Lemuel	Wilmot	2
514	Silvenus	Brundage	2
515	Samuel	Utter	1
516	Asa	Hains	1
517	John	Dean	1
518	Caleb	Dean	1
519	Jeremiah	Shafer	1
520	John	Dawn	1
521	James	Sears Jnr:	1
522	Moses	Knap	1
523	Moses	Knap Jnr:	1
524	James	Akelson	1
525	Jonathen	Pine	1
526	Thomas	Karl	2
527	Morton	Hall	1
528	Abraham	Haight	3
529	John	Taylor	3
530	Abraham	Stone	2
531	Phenias	Baker	2
532	Jessel	Baker [Brown?]	1
533	William	Belden	1
534	—	Hull, near Zachary Paddock	6
535	Berry	Hopkins	1
536	Joseph	Hopkins	1
537	Samuel	Perry	1
538	Comfort	Luddington	1
539	Jesse	Smith	1
540	Samuel	Stringham	1
541	Banaga	Slaigh	1
542	Charles	Cullen	2
543	Niel	McNiel	3

Page 639

#	Name	Surname	Value
544	Susannah	Hughson	1
545	Matthew	Patterson	3
546	Joseph	Smith	1
547	Daniel	Martine	3
548	John	McLean	2
549	William	Colwill	2
550	Oliver	Hull	3
551	Ephraim	Lockwood	1
552	Joseph	Mead	1
553	John	Brewer	1
554	Josiah	Ingersol	2
555	Hachaliah	Merrit	2
556	—	Platt on John Bloomers farm	1
557	Jerod	Carter	1
558	William	Brady	3
559	Abner	Meade	1
560	Nathen	Disbrow	1
561	William	Stoakum	1
562	—	Linch on Solomon Lanes farm	2
563	John	Carpenter	3
564	John	Crane	1
565	Richard	Williams	1
566	John	Wright, near Capt. Peters	1
567	John	Wilson	1
568	James	Grant	2
569	—	Jones on Langdons farm	2
570	John	Avery	1
571	Joseph	Bates	1
572	John	Hunt	2
573	Simeon	Purdy	1
574	John	Gardner	1
575	Benjamin	Townsend	1
576	Eburn	Haight	1
577	Amos	Serrings	1
578	Daniel	Bobbet	1
579	Thomas	Peters	1
580	William	Wooden	1
581	Isaac	Wright	1

Page 640

#	Name	Surname	Value
582	Daniel	Ketchem	1
583	Joseph	Hitchcock	1
584	John	Leclear	1
585	John	Maybee	1

June 1770 continued

	Name	Surname	Value		Name	Surname	Value
586	William	Higbee	1	594	William	Underhill Jnr:	1
587	Thomas	Kirkhum	2	595	James	Wilson Jnr:	1
588	Zebulon	Kirkhum	2	596	William	Calkin	1
589	Peter	Clemmons	2	597	Daniel	Willson	1
590	Peter	Warring	2	598	William	Marsh	1
591	Doctor	Light	1	599	Nathaniel	Sacket	1
592	David	Waterbury	1	600	John	Oar	1
593	Waterbury	Hoyt	1				£1,223

SUPERVISOR'S RECORD 1771 to 1779, VOLUME I
DUTCHESS COUNTY CLERKS OFFICE

JUNE 1771
SOUTHERN PRECINCT

at 3s..5d [3 shillings 5 pence] pr. pound

	Name	Surname	Value		Name	Surname	Value
	Page 1			33	Robert	Shaw	1
1	William	Devenport	5	34	Caleb	Hazel	4
2	Thomas	Devenport	14	35	Gabriel	Legget	3
3	Jacob	MandeVille	7	36	Jacob	Philip	1
4	John	Rogers	7	37	Caleb	Sweet	1
5	John	Van Amburgh's estate	7	38	William	Palmer	3
6	Elijah	Tompkins	4	39	John	Newbury	4
7	Capt. Peter	Dubois	12	40	Robert	Money	1
8	Ebenezer	Jones	3	41	Thomas	Paddock	4
9	Timothy	Concklin	4	42	George	Curry's farm	2
10	George	Lane	2	43	Josiah	Baker	4
11	John	Drake Jnr:	3	44	Isaac	Crosby	2
12	Isaac	Roads	4	45	Benjamin	Sears	5
13	David	Paddock	1	46	Christopher	Fowler	1
14	Joseph	Lane	3	47	Peter	Anguwine	4
15	Caleb	Brundage	1	48	Simeon	Ryder	4
16	Nathaniel	Tompkins	2	49	Thomas	Smith	4
	Page 2			50	Edward	Gray Jnr: farm	2
17	Cornelius	Fuller	2	51	Samuel	Bangs	5
18	John	Hains	2	52	Nathaniel	Forster	5
19	Luke	Covert	1	53	Samuel	Elwell	2
20	Eli	Nelson	1	54	David	Crosby	3
21	Joseph	Crane Jnr:	2	55	Jaby	Berry	2
22	Samuel	Field	7	56	Jonathen	Paddock	4
23	Joseph	Field	5	57	Nathen	Green	2
24	James	Dickinson	4	58	Seth	Nickerson	5
25	Amos	Dickinson	1	59	Timothy	Clauson	1
26	John	Dickinson	6	60	William	Sturdefunt	1
27	Daniel	Townsend	2	61	Joseph	Concklin	1
28	Uriah	Townsend	2	62	Michael	Slott	3
29	Charles	Townsend	2	63	William	Penny	5
30	Benjamin	Townsend	5	64	Thomas	Forster	1
31	Robert	Townsend	4	65	John	Paddock	1
32	Daniel D.	Townsend	1	66	Israel	Taylor	1

June 1771 continued

#	Name	Surname	Value	#	Name	Surname	Value
	Page 3			119	John	Geen	2
67	William	Hill	8	120	Thomas	Higgins	1
68	Joshua	Crosby	3	121	Sibert	Krankheyt	1
69	Isaac	Chapman	1	122	Daniel	Taylor	1
70	Seth	Paddock	5	123	Michael	Shaw Jnr:	1
71	Ebenezer	Jones in Peeks Mill hollow	2	124	Andrew	Berger Jnr:	1
				125	Jeremiah	Huestin	2
72	Theophilus	Jones	1	126	David	Akin Jnr:	4
73	Joshua	Hamblin	6	127	Widow	Hill	1
74	Robert	Weekson	1	128	Haman	King	5
75	Hannah	Knap	3	129	Jonathen	Hopkins	2
76	John	Van Tessel	1	130	Nehemiah	Wood	2
77	Revd: Mr	Kent	4	131	Reubin	Kelley	1
78	Thomas	Kelley	1	132	John	Jones	2
79	Isaac	Pearce	2	133	Caleb	Pells farm	2
80	Edmund	Baker	2	134	John	Wright	2
81	James	Sears	2	135	Richard	Hopper	1
82	Peter	Hall	6	136	Joshua	Barnum	4
83	Thomas	Gage	1	137	Samuel	Drake Jnr:	1
84	John	Mirrick	2	138	Uriah	Drake	2
85	Moody	House	4	139	Joshua	Tompkins	2
86	James	Cowen	2	140	Caleb	Fowler	7
87	Elisha	Cool	5	141	Ebenezer	Robinson	2
88	Ezekiel	Burgis	1	142	Simon	Dacon	6
89	Jonathen	Kelley	1	143	Benjamin	Perry	1
90	Amos	Fuller	2	144	Solomon	Smith	3
91	Simeon	Ellis	3	145	Abraham	Maybee	2
92	Nathaniel	Bailiff	1	146	Abraham	Maybee Jnr:	2
93	James	Dickinson Jnr:	5	147	John	Roads	1
94	Jeremiah	Chase	1	148	Benjamin	Odle	2
95	John	Field	6	149	Daniel	Bull	4
96	John	Yoemans Jnr:	3	150	Matthew	Benedict's farm	2
97	Stephen	Field	7	151	Benjamin	Gifford	2
98	John	Nelson	1	152	Henry	Krankheyt	1
99	James	Birdsill	9	153	Obediah	Baseley	1
100	Jeremiah	Linkhorn	1	154	Samuel	Elwell Jnr:	2
101	Silas	Paddock	2	155	Isaac	Elwell	2
102	Edward	Ganung	1	156	Jacob	Philip Jnr:	1
103	Samuel	Peters	6	157	John	Clauson	1
104	Lazarus	Griffen	1	158	Ebenezer	Bennet	1
105	Widow	Bailey	1	159	Elihu	Gage	2
106	Peleg	Weekson	1	160	Anthony	Gage	1
107	Joseph	Crommel	4	161	Richard	Wearing	1
108	Rowland	Perry	3	162	Thomas	Townsend Jnr:	2
109	Noah	Smith	1	163	Christopher	Townsend	1
110	Elijah	Weekson	1	164	David	Paddock Jnr:	1
111	Joshua	Hinckly	1	165	John	Tompkins	1
112	John	How	1	166	Samuel	Benedict	1
113	Mathias	Burgis	4	167	Jabish	Ellwell	2
114	William	Nelson	1		*Page 5*		
115	Jonathen	Bryant	2	168	Nathen	Crosby	2
116	William	Lane	2	169	John	Garrison	1
117	John	Ryder	5	170	Thomas	Hodges farm	1
118	William	Dusenbury	5	171	Stephen	Rockwell	1
	Page 4			172	Elijah	White	1

June 1771 continued

	Name	Surname	Value		Name	Surname	Value
173	Hezekiah	Meade	1	227	Zebedee	Briggs	1
174	Edward	Rice	5	228	Eleazer	Hamblin	4
175	Ebenezer	Kelly	1	229	Joseph	Vickry	1
176	Thomas	Fowler	4	230	Hezekiah	Mead Jnr:	1
177	John Bloomer	near the river	1	231	John	Barto's farm	1
178	Nathaniel	Plumstead	1	232	Elijah	Budd	2
179	Ebenezer	Benedict	2	233	Eben	Lockwood	1
180	Elijah	Calkin	2	234	Baseley	King	2
181	Josiah	Swift Jnr:	1	235	Thomas	Sarls	1
182	Daniel	Brundage	5	236	Thomas	Woodard	1
183	Thomas	Crommel	1	237	Caleb	Nelson	3
184	Solomon	Jenkins	3	238	Justis	Nelson	3
185	Reubin	Cloos	4	239	Robert	Hughson	2
186	Joseph	Huested	3	240	Peter	Drake's farm	2
187	Caleb	Huested	2	241	John thauny	Craft	2
188	Jeremiah	Witnah	2	242	Isaac	Lownsbury	5
189	Elisha	Oakley	1	243	Seth	Sears	2
190	Charles	Mc Ready	1	244	Samuel	Lucas	1
191	Matthew	Mc Caby	1	245	Noah	Burbanks	1
192	Seth	Holms	1	246	James	Covey Jnr:	2
193	James	Pardy	1	247	William	Merrit	2
194	Stephen	Pardy	1	248	Nathaniel	Green	1
195	Daniel	Ball	1	249	Peter	Maybee	2
196	John	June	1	250	John	Lownsbury	3
197	Benjamin	Haviland	5	251	Thomas	Lownsbury	4
198	Silvenus	Cool	1	252	David	Hawkins	1
199	George	Darby	1	253	Joseph	Ganung	1
200	Benjamin	Hatch	2	254	Andrew	Rubelye	1
201	Thomas	Trobridge	1	255	Edy	Baker	2
202	Nathaniel	Stone	1	256	Jacob	Ellis	1
203	Wheeton	Robinson	1	257	David	Mirrick	2
204	Solomon	Field	3	258	Jehiel	Beardsley	6
205	Ebenezer	Brown	1	259	James	King	1
206	Solomon	Perry	1	260	Samuel	Yoemans	1
207	Ebenezer	Gage	1	261	Joshua	Nelson	5
208	Nehemiah	Jones	3	262	Ephraim	Jones	2
209	Reubin	Crosby	2	263	Francis	Bryor	1
210	Joshua	Barnum Jnr:	2	264	James	Lumery	2
211	David	Crosby Jnr:	4	265	John	Armstrong	1
212	David	Calkin	1	266	John	Adams	1
213	David	Sears	3	267	William	Van Tessel	1
214	Capt. Beverly	Robinson	80	268	James	Roads	2
215	Lewis	Jones	2	269	William	Gee	1
216	Daniel	Crawford	1	270	Peter	Moe	1
217	Peter	Bonker	1	271	John	Meeks	2
218	Thomas	Baldwin	5		*Page 7*		
219	Moss	Kent	6	272	Moses	Fowler	7
220	Nathen	Birdsill	2	273	John	Yoemans	2
	Page 6			274	Robert	Oakley	1
221	Joseph	Nauthrop	3	275	Gilbert	Dickinson [Dickson]	2
222	William	Porters farm	1	276	Samuel	Dickinson	4
223	Prince	Hopkins	1	277	Thomas	Adams	1
224	Ebenezer	Humstead	1	278	William	Nickerson	1
225	John	Carly	1	279	Timothy	DeLavan	2
226	Thomas	Lovelass	1	280	Isaac	Barret	1

June 1771 continued

	Name	Surname	Value		Name	Surname	Value
281	Capt.	Brown	2	335	Richard	Peters	3
282	James	Wilson	4	336	Daniel	Southerland Jnr:	1
283	Elisha	Calkin	1	337	John	Moss Jnr:	1
284	James	Townsend	1	338	Reubin	Bun[n]	1
285	Roger	Haviland	4	339	Joseph	Darby	1
286	Thomas	Ferguson	1	340	Jeremiah	Burgis	2
287	Joseph	Colvill	2	341	Richard	Hares	1
288	Samuel	Hall	2	342	Isaac	Ruscky	1
289	Isaac	Merrick	2	343	Stephen	Hopkins farm	1
290	Solomon	Hopkins	3	344	James	Carl	1
291	Reubin	Chase	1	345	Samuel	Carl	2
292	William	Underhill	2	346	Timothy	Hatch	2
293	Augustin	Underhill	3	347	James	Hughson	2
294	Joseph	Robins	1	348	Robert	Townsend	1
295	Joshua	Porter	1	349	Thomas	Baxter	1
296	John	Roberts	1	350	Philip	Minthorne	1
297	Benjamin	Roberts	1	351	Shaw	Young	2
298	Theodorus	Crosby	2	352	John	Wright Jnr:	1
299	Samuel	Burchards farm	1	353	Reubin	Drake	2
300	Nehemiah	Bailey	1	354	John	Berger	1
301	Caleb	Palmer	1	355	Thomas	Bryant	1
302	Elisha	Kent Jnr:	1	356	Philip	Steenbuck	1
303	Richard	Gray Jnr:	1	357	Richard	Arnold	1
304	Benoney	Gray	1	358	Nathaniel	Yager	1
305	Nathen	Green Jnr:	2	359	Francis	Berger	1
306	Benjamin	Sears Jnr:	2	360	Peter	Berger	1
307	Joseph	Forster	1	361	John	Langdon Jnr:	1
308	James	Forster	2	362	Sibert	Krankheyt Jnr:	1
309	Stephen	Tompkins	2	363	Thomas	Tompkins	1
310	Eleazer	Baker	1	364	Abner	Crosby	2
311	John	Haviland	1	365	Elnathen	Dun	1
312	Abraham	Craft	1	366	Daniel	Dun	1
313	Malcom	Morrison	9	367	Zebulon	Bass	1
314	Samuel	Perece [Pierce]	2	368	Thomas	Higgins Jnr:	1
315	Gilbert	Clap	2	369	David	Porter	1
316	Henry	Wooden	4	370	Thomas	Burgis	1
317	William	Yoemans	1	*Page 9*			
318	Mr	Gregory	2	371	Elijah	Hungerford	1
319	Elisha	Cool Jnr:	1	372	Anthony	Yoemans	1
320	Samuel	Washburn	4	373	Benjamin	Bloomer	1
321	Charles	Arwah	2	374	Daniel	Southerland	1
Page 8				375	Nathaniel	Calkin	1
322	Elijah	Horton	1	376	Jonathen	Bennet	1
323	Daniel	Warren	1	377	Joshua	Crosby Jnr:	1
324	Joshua	Lumery	1	378	Daniel	Secor	1
325	Henry	Jones	1	379	Isaac	Secor	2
326	James	Barret	1	380	Lockland	McDonald	4
327	Widow Hall, on Meads place		2	381	Alexander	Grant	4
328	John	Win	1	382	John	Birdsill	3
329	Moses	Meade	1	383	John	Bates	1
330	Jonathen	Stockham	1	384	Alexander	Mensus	4
331	Byal	Bashford	2	385	Joshua	Hatsfield farm	4
332	Isaac	Garrison	1	386	Andrew	Beardsley	1
333	James	Baldwin	1	387	Josiah	Benjamin	2
334	John	Stedwell	4	388	Benjamin	Green	1

June 1771 continued

	Name	Surname	Value		Name	Surname	Value
389	Robert	Watts	3	441	Joshua	Crosby Jnr:	[-]
390	Thomas	Mensus	7	442	Joshua	Burdock	1
391	Henry	Ludington	3	443	Daniel	Osborn	1
392	Roswell	Wilcocks	3	444	Stephen	Osborn	1
393	David	Heacock	1	445	John	Raymond	2
394	Michael	Nowland	1	446	Mial	Penny	1
395	Samuel	Hunt	2	447	George	Penny	1
396	Joshua	Concklin	2	448	Ebenezer	Ryder	1
397	James	Calkins	1	449	William	Stow	2
398	Samuel	Towner	1	450	John	Carly Jnr:	1
399	Nathen	Lane	1	451	Edmund	Rathborn	1
400	Doctor	Daniels	2	452	Mathew	Stephens	2
401	Amos	Travis	2	453	Reubin	Cloos Jnr:	1
402	Titus	Travis	3	454	Jedediah	Willis	1
403	Benjamin	Birdsill South	2	455	Nathaniel	Hall	2
404	Gabriel	Carpenter	1	456	Ebenezer	Arnold	1
405	Richard	Cornwell	2	457	Edmund	Green	1
406	Joseph	Philips	1	458	Israel	Ward	4
407	Thomas	Hughson	2	459	Caleb	Veal	2
408	Joseph	Horskins	2	460	Daniel	Seelass	2
409	David Hamblin Joshua's son		2	461	John	Lawrence	2
410	Isaac	Austin	1	462	David	Cowen	1
411	Johnson	Dacons	1	463	Theophilus	Spencer	1
412	Samuel	Horton	1	464	Seth	Nickerson Jnr:	2
413	Elijah	Fuller	1	465	Daniel	Haviland	3
414	Zachary	Paddock	2	466	Benjamin	Higgins	1
415	Cornelius	Tompkins	4	467	Eliphalet	Saunders	1
416	Moses	Dusenbury	5	468	Samuel	Haight	1
417	Jacob	Maybee	1	469	James	Gardner	2
418	Timothy	Shaw	2	470	John	Townsend	1
419	John	Kelly	2	471	Ebenezer	Robinson Jnr:	1
420	Nathaniel Nickerson's widow		1	*Page 11*			
421	Nathen	Cool	1	472	Edward	Hunt	2
422	Joseph	Cool	1	473	Robert	Wright	1
Page 10				474	Richard	Chapman	1
423	Hezekiah	Avery	1	475	John	Krankheyt	1
424	—	Heddy, on Joshua Barnum farm	2	476	Richard	Trusdell	1
425	Henry	Aldridge	1	477	Joseph	Haight	5
426	Cornelius	Swim	2	478	William	Wright	2
427	Charity	Austin	2	479	William	Chatterton	1
428	Widow	Merrick	1	480	James	Cook	1
429	Isaac	Ganung	1	481	Joseph	Brundage	1
430	—	Sniffen on widow Finch's farm	2	482	Daniel	Knap	3
				483	Isaac	Horton	1
431	Thomas	Williamson	1	484	Joseph	Sherwood for eagars farm	1
432	Widow	Hawborn	1				
433	Gilbert	Budd	1	485	Benjamin	Birdsill	1
434	John	Terril	4	486	Dennis	Wright	6
435	Lazarus	Griffen Jnr:	1	487	Lemuel	Wilmot	2
436	Isaac	Reade	1	488	Silvenus	Brundage	2
437	Ephraim	Jones upper	1	489	Samuel	Utter	1
438	Daniel	Pearce	1	490	Asa	Hains	1
439	Silvenus	Cool Jnr:	1	491	John	Dean	1
440	Uriah	Raymond	2	492	Caleb	Dean	1
				493	Jeremiah	Shafer	1

June 1771 continued

#	Name	Surname	Value
494	John	Dawn	1
495	James	Sears Jnr:	1
496	Moses	Knap	1
497	Moses	Knap Jnr:	1
498	Jonathen	Pine	1
499	Thomas	Karl	2
500	Mooton	Hall	1
501	Abraham	Haight	3
502	John	Taylor	1
503	Phinehas	Baker	2
504	Jessel	Baker [Brown?]	1
505	William	Belden	1
506	Joseph	Hull, near Zachary Padd[ock]	4
507	Berry	Hopkins	1
508	Joseph	Hopkins	1
509	Samuel	Perry	1
510	Comfort	Luddenton	1
511	Jesse	Smith	1
512	Samuel	Stringham	1
513	Benajah	Slaigh	1
514	Charles	Cullen	2
515	Neal	McNeal	[-]
516	Susannah	Hughson	1
517	Mathew	Patterson	4
518	Joseph	Smith	1
519	Daniel	Martine	3
520	John	McLane	3
521	William	Colwell	2

Page 12

#	Name	Surname	Value
522	Oliver	Hull	4
523	Joseph	Mead	2
524	John	Brewer	1
525	Josiah	Ingersol	2
526	Hachaliah	Merrit	2
527	—	Platt, on John Bloomers farm	2
528	Jared	Carter	1
529	William	Braidy	3
530	Abner	Mead	1
531	Nathen	Disbrow	1
532	William	Sloakum	1
533	—	Lynch, on Solomon Lanes farm	2
534	John	Carpenter	4
535	John	Crane	1
536	Richard	Williams	1
537	John	Wright near Capt. Peters	1
538	John	Wilson	1
539	James	Grant	2
540	—	Jones, on Langdons farm	2
541	John	Avery	1
542	Joseph	Bates	1
543	John	Hunt	2
544	Simion	Purdy	1
545	Benjamin	Townsend Jnr:	1
546	Eburn	Haight	1
547	Amos	Serrings	1
548	Daniel	Bobbet	1
549	Thomas	Peters	1
550	William	Wooden	1
551	Isaac	Wright	1
552	Daniel	Ketchem	2
553	Joseph	Hitchcock	1
554	John	LeClear	1
555	John	Maybee	1
556	William	Higby	2
557	Thomas	Kirkem	2
558	Zebulon	Kirkem	2
559	Peter	Clements	2
560	Peter	Warren	1
561	Doctor	Light	1
562	David	Waterbury	1
563	Waterbury	Hoyt	1
564	William	Underhill Jnr:	1
565	James	Wilson Jnr:	1
566	William	Calkin	1
567	Daniel	Willson	1
568	William	Marsh	1
569	John	Oar	1
570	Josiah	Folkenier	1

Page 13

#	Name	Surname	Value
571	John	Stephens	1
572	Widow	Terry	2
573	Samuel	Terry	1
574	Josiah	Baker Jnr:	1
575	John	Terry	1
576	John	Fuller	1
577	David	Fuller	1
578	Isaiah	Hopkins	1
579	Thomas	Hall	3
580	John	Smith	2
581	Dennis	Wortman	2
582	David	Frost	2
583	Charles	Arwah Jnr:	1
584	William	Mead	1
585	Charles	Surrine	1
586	William	Surrine	1
587	Jacob	Nnipfin [Kniffen]	3
588	David	Storms	2
589	Robert	Right	1
590	James	Searls	1
591	Lewis	Anguvine	1
592	Ephraham	Carpenter	1
593	John	Clarke	2
594	Shugel	Wickham	1
595	Nathen	Jones	1
596	Levy	Townsend	1

June 1771 continued

	Name	Surname	Value		Name	Surname	Value
597	John	Berritt	1	645	Jacob	Armstrong	1
598	John	Berrit Jnr:	1	646	Richard	Christian	1
599	Henry	Light	1	647	William	Col[e]grove	1
600	Jonathan	Parrish	2	648	Oliver	Odell	1
601	William	Penny Jnr:	1	649	Isaac	Taylor	1
602	William	Carpenter	1	650	Cornelius	Tanner	1
603	Edward	Dolff	1	651	Jonathen	Austin	1
604	Silvanus	Kelley	1	652	John	McDonnel	1
605	Zebedee	Kelley	1	653	Abraham	Post	1
606	David	Kelley	1	654	Thomas	Haywood	1
607	Jonathen	Krain	1	655	Absalom	Yeomans	1
608	Jonathen	Smith	1	656	Charles	Agar	1
609	John	Hinckley	1	657	Samuel	Warren	2
610	John	White	1	658	John	Smith, in the Highlands	1
611	Job	Burlingson	2				
612	Elbert	Solomons	1	659	Samuel	Jones	1
613	Samuel	Crosbey	1	660	Josiah	Jones	1
614	Thomas	Sears	2	661	Jonathan	Brundage	1
615	John	Tweedy	2	662	John	McKee	1
616	Joshua	Phillips	1	663	Thomas	Nickerson	1
617	Peleg	Baley	1	664	Joel	Runnells	1
618	James	Egleston	1	665	Peter	Brewer	1
619	Obediah	Chase	1	666	Oliver	Bailey	1
620	Jacob	Sunderland	1	667	Jonathan	Webb	1
621	Joseph	Dikeman	2	668	Benjamin	Jones Jnr:	1
Page 14				669	William	Snow	1
622	Thomas	Hinckley	1	670	Nathan	Paddock	1
623	David	Vickrey	1	*Page 15*			
624	John	Warren	2	671	James	Green	1
625	Asa	Barnum	1	672	Mathew	Bump	1
626	Peter	Chapman	1	673	John	Dan Jnr:	1
627	John	Stephens Jnr:	2	674	Solomon	Lockwood	1
628	Jehiel	Stephens	1	675	Francis	Good	1
629	Roger	Morris Esq:	10	676	Gilbert	Ganung	1
630	Tertullus	Dickinson	12	677	Jesse	Morcy	1
631	Iranen	Nickerson	1	678	Richard	Concklin	1
632	Edward	Nickerson	1	679	Silas	Parish	1
633	Isaac	Horton Jnr:	1	680	John	Ballid	1
634	Jedediah	Owens	1	681	John	Drake	1
635	Richard	Dean Jnr:	1	682	David	Lain	1
636	Gilbert	Bloomer	1	683	Capt.	Kid, on the farm was Maggots	4
637	Israel	Knap	1				
638	Stephen	Devenport	1	684	John	Secor	2
639	Richard	Hopper	1	685	Zebulon	Townsend	1
640	John	Gray	1	686	John	Button	1
641	Jonathen	Odle	1	687	John	Wallace	1
642	Gilbert	Drew	1	688	Charles	Theale	1
643	Isaac	Roads Jnr:	1				£1,377
644	John	Brown	1				

June 1772
South East Precinct

at 6/8 [6 shillings 8 pence] pr. pound

#	Name	Surname	Value	#	Name	Surname	Value
	Page 128			51	Nathan	Birdsell	2
1	Joseph	Crane	4	52	Prince	Hopkins	1
2	Samuel	Field	4	53	John	Carly	1
3	Joseph	Field	4	54	Zebedee	Briggs	2
4	Uriah	Townsend	2	55	Seth	Sears	2
5	Benjamin	Townsend	5	56	Nathaniel	Green	1
6	Robert	Townsend	4	57	Roger	Havylands Farm	4
7	Caleb	Sweet	1	58	Samuel	Hall	2
8	Isaac	Crosby	2	59	John	Roberts	1
9	Benjamin	Sears	5	60	Jesse	Lane	2
10	Simon	Ryder	4	61	Richard	Gray	1
11	Edward	Grays farm	4	62	Nathan	Green Jnr:	3
12	Samuel	Bangs	5	63	Benjamin	Sears Jnr:	2
13	Nathaniel	Forster	6	64	Joseph	Forster	1
14	Samuel	Elwell	2	65	John	Havyland	1
15	Nathen	Green	2	66	Shaw	Young	2
16	Seth	Nickerson	5	67	Thomas	Higgins Jnr:	2
17	Thomas	Forster	1	68	Thomas	Burgis	2
18	Mr	Kent	3	69	Joshua	Hatsfields farm	5
19	Peter	Hall	6	70	Widow	Hebburn	2
20	Thomas	Gage	2	71	Stephen	Osburn	1
21	John	Field	5	72	Ameniel	Penny	2
22	James	Birdsell	7	73	Ebenezer	Ryder	1
23	Noah	Smith	2	74	William	Stow	2
24	Mathias	Burgis	4	75	John	Carly Jnr:	1
25	John	Ryder	5	76	Mathew	Stephens	2
26	Thomas	Higgins	[-]	77	Seth	Nickerson Jnr:	2
27	Joshua	Barnum	4	78	Daniel	Haviland	3
28	Mathew	Benedicks Farm	2	79	Benjamin	Higgins	2
	Page 129			80	James	Sears	1
29	Samuel	Elwell Jnr:	2	81	Morten	Horten [Hall]	2
30	Isaac	Elwell	3	82	Joseph	Hull	6
31	Elihu	Gage	3	83	Berry	Hopkins	1
32	Anthony	Gage	1	84	Charles	Cullen	2
33	Richard	Warring	1	85	Oliver	Hull	4
34	Samuel	Benedict	1	86	William	Penny	2
35	Jabish	Ellwell	3	87	Jonathan	Crane	1
36	Able	Hodges Farm	2		*Page 130*		
37	Stephen	Rockwell	1	88	Thomas	Sears	2
38	Ebenezer	Benedict	2	89	John	Twedy	2
39	Seth	Holmes	2	90	Asa	Barnum	1
40	James	Purdys Farm	1	91	Peter	Chapman	1
41	Stephen	Purdys Farm	1	92	Nathan	Paddock	1
42	Daniel	Balls Farm	1	93	James	Green	1
43	John	Junes	1	94	Stephen	Field	4
44	Benjamin	Havyland	5	95	Thomas	Crumstock	5
45	Thomas	Trowbridge	1	96	Solomon	Maker	1
46	Solomon	Perrys Farm	1	97	John	McNichols	1
47	Ebenezer	Gage	1	98	John	Perry	1
48	Joshua	Barnum Jnr:	2	99	Roderick	McKinsey	1
49	Thomas	Baldwin	5	100	Nathaniel	Hampstead	1
50	Moss	Kent	4	101	Isaac	Crosby Jnr:	1

June 1772 South East continued

#	Name	Surname	Value	#	Name	Surname	Value
102	Marck	Gage	1	118	Thomas	Birdsell	2
103	William	Clinton	1	119	Samuel	Toweur	2
104	Elijah	Whitney	1	120	David	Wakeman	1
105	David	Perry	1	121	Joseph	Arnold	2
106	Eliah	Sweet	1	122	Aaron	Lancastor	2
107	Thomas	Killogg	1	123	Joseph	Stedwell	6
108	Jonathan	Paddocks farm	1	124	Joseph	Jennings	1
109	Ebenezer	Humstead	1	125	Nathaniel	Arnold	1
110	James	Joice	1	126	Timothy	Stephens	1
111	Elisha	Morehause	1	127	Eliakim	Barcrum	1
112	Stephen	Morehause	1	128	John	Ellwell	1
113	John	Forster	1	129	John	Bruyster	1
114	Elamuel	Birdsell	1	130	John	Hopkins	1
115	John	Twedy Jnr:	1	131	William	Pennys Farm	2
116	Samuel	Twedy Jnr:	1	132	Nathaniel	Stephenson	1
117	Samuel	Twedy	1				£282

JUNE 1772
FREDERICKSBOURGH PRECINCT

at 6/11 [6 shillings 11 pence] pr. pound

#	Name	Surname	Value	#	Name	Surname	Value
	Page 130			29	Simon	Ellis	3
1	Elijah	Hopkins [Tompkins]	4	30	—Dickenson & Wallis & Comp		6
2	Ebenezer	Jones	3	31	Jeremiah	Chase	1
3	David	Paddock	1	32	Jeremiah	Linkhorn	1
4	Caleb	Brundage	1	33	Silas	Baddock [Paddock]	2
5	Cornelius	Fuller	2	34	Samuel	Peters	7
6	John	Hains	2	35	Charles	Townsend	2
7	James	Dickenson	4	36	Benjamin	Townsend	2
8	John	Dickenson	6	37	Robert	Townsend	1
	Page 131			38	Daniel	Townsend Jnr:	1
9	Daniel	Townsend	2	39	Robert	Shaw	1
10	William	Palmer	3	40	Caleb	Hazell	4
11	John	Newbury	4	41	Gabriel	Legget	1
12	Robert	Mooney	2	42	Thomas	Paddock	3
13	Josiah	Baker	3	43	George	Currys farm	3
14	Thomas	Smith	4	44	Peter	Angevine	4
15	David	Crosby	3	45	Jabes	Berry	2
16	— Willis on	Clossens Farm	1	46	Jonathan	Baddock [Paddock]	3
17	William	Penny	3	47	Michael	Slut	3
18	Joshua	Crosby	3	48	John	Paddock	1
19	Isaac	Chapman	1	49	William	Hill	9
20	Theophilus	Jones	2	50	Joshua	Hamblin	6
21	Thomas	Kelley	1	51	Robert	Weekson	1
22	Edmund	Baker	2	52	Isaac	Pierce	2
23	Moody	House	4	53	John	Mirrick	2
24	James	Coven	2	54	Nathaniel	Bayly [Baliff]	1
25	Elisha	Cool	4	55	John	Yeoman Jnr:	3
26	Ezekiel	Burgis	1	56	Edward	Ganung	1
27	Jonathen	Kelley	2	57	Susana	Bayly	1
28	Amos	Fuller	2	58	Lazarus	Griffen	1

June 1772 Fredericksbourgh continued

	Name	Surname	Value		Name	Surname	Value
59	Peleg	Wickson	1	113	Isaac	Lownsberry	5
60	Rowland	Perry	4	114	James	Covey	2
61	William	Nelson	1	115	William	Murrit	2
62	Jonathan	Bryant	2	116	Peter	Maybee	2
63	John	Jean	2	117	John	Lounsburry	2
64	Joshua	Hinckley	1	118	Thomas	Lownsbury	4
65	Michael	Shaw Jnr:	1	119	Joseph	Gannung	1
66	Jeremiah	Hughson	2	120	Andrew	Rubley	1
67	David	Akens	3	121	Edy	Backer	2
68	Widow	Hills Farm	1	122	Jacob	Ellis	1
69	Haman	King	6	123	David	Merrit [Mirrick]	2

Page 132

	Name	Surname	Value		Name	Surname	Value
				124	Jehiel	Beardsly	5
70	Jonathan	Hopkins	2	125	Moses	Fowler	7
71	Ruben	Kelley	1	126	John	Yeomans	2
72	Caleb	Fowler	7	127	Ebenezer	Lockwood	1
73	Ebenezer	Robinson	2	128	John Thauny	Craft	1

Page 133

	Name	Surname	Value		Name	Surname	Value
74	Simon	Dakin	6				
75	Abraham	Maybee Jnr:	2	129	Samuel	Lucas	1
76	John	Roads	1	130	David	Hawkins	1
77	Daniel	Bull	4	131	James	King	1
78	Benjamin	Giffords	2	132	John	Adams	1
79	Obadiah	Beardsly	1	133	James	Roads	2
80	Jacob	Phillips Jnr:	2	134	Peter	Moe	1
81	Ebenezer	Bennet	1	135	Gilbert	Dickenson [Dickson]	3
82	Nathan	Crosby	3	136	Samuel	Dickenson	4
83	John	Garrison	1	137	Thomas	Adams	1
84	Elijah	White	1	138	Timothy	DeLavan	2
85	Hezekiah	Mead	1	139	Capt.	Brown	2
86	Edward	Rice	5	140	James	Willson	4
87	Thomas	Fowler	3	141	Thomas	Forguson	1
88	Elijah	Calkins	2	142	Joseph	Collwell	2
89	Josiah	Swift Jnr:	2	143	Isaac	Merrick	1
90	Daniel	Brundage	5	144	Salomon	Hopkins	3
91	Solomon	Jinkins	3	145	Ruben	Chase	1
92	Reuben	Cloos	3	146	William	Underhill	2
93	Jeremiah	Witerah	2	147	Augustin	Underhill	3
94	Charles	McCrady	1	148	Theodorus	Crosby	3
95	George	Darbey	1	149	Nehemiah	Bayly	1
96	Benjamin	Hatch	3	150	Caleb	Palmer	1
97	Salomon	Field	2	151	Eleazer	Backer	1
98	Ebenezer	Brown	2	152	Abraham	Craft	1
99	Nehemiah	Jones	3	153	Malcom	Morrison	9
100	Reuben	Crosby	2	154	Samuel	Pierce	1
101	David	Crosby Jnr:	4	155	Gilbert	Clap	2
102	David	Sears	2	156	Henry	Wooden	3
103	Daniel	Crawford	1	157	William	Yeomans	1
104	Peter	Bunker	1	158	Mr	Gregory	1
105	Moss	Kent	6	159	Elisha	Cole Jnr:	1
106	Joseph	Northrop	2	160	Samuel	Washburn	4
107	Thomas	Lovelass	1	161	Charles	Arwa	2
108	Eleazer	Hamblin	3	162	James	Barret	1
109	Joseph	Vickry	1	163	Moses	Mead	1
110	Hezekiah	Mead Jnr:	1	164	Jonathan	Stosckum	1
111	Barzillai	King	2	165	James	Baldwin	1
112	Robert	Hughson	1	166	Richard	Peters	3

June 1772 Fredericksbourgh continued

#	Name	Surname	Value	#	Name	Surname	Value
167	Daniel	Sunderland	1	221	Nathan	Lane	1
168	Jeremiah	Burgis	2	222	Doctor	Daniels	1
169	Richard	Airs	1	223	Benjamin	Birdsell	2
170	Isaac	Ruskey	1	224	Gabriel	Carpenter	1
171	James	Carl	1	225	Richard	Cornell	1
172	Samuel	Carl	2	226	Joseph	Philips	2
173	Timothy	Hatch	2	227	Thomas	Hughson	1
174	Phillip	Minthorn	1	228	Joseph	Horskins	2
175	John	Langdon Jnr:	1	229	David	Hamblin	2
176	Abner	Crosby	2	230	Isaac	Austin	1
177	Elnathan	Doone	1	231	Johnson	Dakin	1
178	Daniel	Doone	1	232	Samuel	Horton	1
179	Zebulon	Bass	1	233	Elijah	Fuller	1
180	Daniel	Sunderland Jnr:	1	234	Zachariah	Paddock	2
181	Nathaniel	Colkin	1	235	Jacob	Maybee	1
182	Daniel	Secor	1	236	Timothy	Shaw	2
183	Jonathen	Bennent	1	237	John	Kelly	2
184	Joshua	Crosby Jnr:	2	238	Widow	Nickerson	1
185	Isaac	Secor	2	239	Nathan	Cole	1
186	Lauchlan	McDonald	2	240	Joseph	Cole	1
187	Alexander	Grant	4	241	Charity	Austin	2
	Page 134			242	Widow	Mirrick	1
188	John	Birdsill	1	243	Isaac	Ganung	1
189	John	Bates	1	244	Samuel	Kniffen	2
190	Alexander	Mentzies	3	245	John	Terrill	4
191	Nathan	Green	2	246	Lazarus	Griffen Jnr:	1
192	William	Sturdewand	1	247	Ephraim	Jones the upper	2
193	Seth	Paddock	4	248	Daniel	Pierce	1
194	Stephen	Fields	5		*Page 135*		
195	Elijah	Wickson	1	249	Silvanus	Cole Jnr:	1
196	Nehemiah	Wood	2	250	Uriah	Raymond	2
197	Thomas	Townsend	1	251	Tobias [Joshua]	Burdock	1
198	Christopher	Townsend	1	252	George	Penny	1
199	John	Tompkins	1	253	Jerediah	Willis	1
200	Nathaniel	Stone	1	254	Israel	Ward	4
201	Francis	Bryer	1	255	Caleb	Veall	1
202	Isaac	Barret	1	256	Daniel	Seelass	2
203	James	Townsend	1	257	John	Lawrance	2
204	Benoney	Gray	1	258	David	Cowen	1
205	James	Forster	2	259	James	Gardner	2
206	John	Stedwell	3	260	John	Townsend	1
207	Thomas	Bexster	1	261	Ebenezer	Robinson Jnr:	1
208	Thomas	Tompkins	2	262	Edward	Hurts Estate	2
209	David	Porter	1	263	Robert	Wright	1
210	Andrew	Beardsly	1	264	Richard	Chapman	1
211	Josiah	Benjamen	2	265	John	Krackheit	1
212	Benjamen	Green	1	266	Richard	Trusdell	1
213	Robert	Watts	3	267	William	Chatterton	1
214	Thomas	Menzies	7	268	Joseph	Brundage	1
215	Henry	Ludenton	3	269	Daniel	Knap	3
216	Roswell	Willcocks	3	270	Dennis	Wright	5
217	David	Heacocks	2	271	Lemuel	Willmott	2
218	Michael	Newland	1	272	Samuel	Utter	1
219	Joshua	Concklin	2	273	Assa	Hains	2
220	James	Colkin	1	274	John	Dean	1

June 1772 Fredericksbourgh continued

#	Name	Surname	Value	#	Name	Surname	Value
275	Caleb	Dean	1	329	David	Fuller	1
276	Jeremiah	Sheifer	1	330	Josiah [Isaiah]	Hopkins	1
277	John	Dann	1	331	Thomas	Hall	3
278	Thomas	Carl	2	332	John	Smith	2
279	Abraham	Hyatt	2	333	Dennis	Worten	2
280	John	Taylor	1	334	David	Frost	1
281	Phinehas	Baker	1	335	Charles	Arwa Jnr:	1
282	Comfort	Ludenton	1	336	William	Mead	1
283	Jesse	Smith	2	337	Charles	Surine	1
284	Mathew	Patterson	3	338	William	Surine	1
285	Daniel	Matine	3	339	Jacob	Knilsen [Kniffen]	4
286	John	McLean	2	340	David	Storm	2
287	William	Collwell	2	341	James	Seails [Searls]	1
288	Joseph	Mead	3	342	Ephraim	Carpenter	1
289	John	Brewer	1	343	John	Clark	2
290	Hachaliah	Merrit	2	344	Shuble	Weikson	1
291	John	Platt	2	345	Levy	Townsend	1
292	William	Braidy	4	346	John	Barrick	1
293	Abner	Mead	1	347	Henry	Laight	1
294	Nathan	Disbrow	1	348	Jonathan	Parrish	2
295	William	Stokum	1	349	William	Carpenter	1
296	Thomas	Lynch	2	350	Silvanus	Killey	1
297	John	Carpenter	4	351	David	Killey	1
298	John	Crane	2	352	Zebedee	Killey	1
299	Richard	Williams	1	353	John	Hinckley	1
300	John Wright by J.Kniffen		1	354	John	White	1
301	John	Willson	1	355	Job	Burlison	1
302	James	Grant	2	356	Albert	Salomons	1
303	Eburir	Haight	1	357	Samuel	Crosby	1
304	Amos	Serrings	1	358	Joshua	Phillips	1
305	Daniel	Bobbet	2	359	Peleg	Bailey	1
306	Thomas	Peters	2	360	James	Egleston	1
307	William	Wooden	1	361	Obadiah	Chase	1
308	Isaac	Wright	1	362	Jacob	Sunderland	1
309	Daniel	Ketchem	3	363	Joseph	Dyckman	2
310	Joseph	Hitchcock	1	364	Thomas	Hinckly	1
	Page 136			365	David	Vickry	1
311	John	Lecler	1	366	John	Waring	2
312	John	Maybee	1	367	John	Stephens Jnr:	2
313	Thomas	Kirckem	2	368	Jehiel	Stephens	1
314	Zebulon	Kirckem	2	369	Roger	Morris	12
315	David	Waterbury	1	370	Tertules	Dickenson	12
316	Waterbury	Hoyt	1	371	Irane	Nickerson	1
317	William	Underhill Jnr:	1	372	Isaac	Roads Jnr:	1
318	James	Willson Jnr:	1		*Page 137*		
319	William	Calkins	1	373	Isaac	Taylor	1
320	Daniel	Willson	1	374	Jonathen	Austin	1
321	William	Marsh	1	375	Absalom	Yoemans	1
322	Josiah	Folkinar	1	376	Charles	Agar	1
323	John	Stephens	1	377	John	Smith Jnr:	1
324	Ezekiel	Dean	2	378	Samuel	Jones	1
325	Samuel	Terry	2	379	Josiah	Jones	1
326	Josiah	Baker Jnr:	1	380	John	McKee	1
327	John	Terry	1	381	Thomas	Nickerson	1
328	John	Fuller	1	382	Peter	Brewer	1

June 1772 Fredericksbourgh continued

	Name	Surname	Value		Name	Surname	Value
383	Oliver	Bailey	1	421	Josiah	Gregory	1
384	Jonathan	Webb	1	422	Benjamin	Minthorne	1
385	Benjamin	Jones Jnr:	1	423	John	Hains Jnr:	1
386	William	Snow	1	424	Samuel	Jenkins	1
387	Matthew	Bump	1	425	John	Ganung	1
388	John	Dann Jnr:	1	426	Josiah	Akins farm	1
389	Francis	Good	1	427	Oliver	Bates	1
390	Gilbert	Ganung	1		*Page 138*		
391	Jesse	Morcy	1	428	Duncan	McGregory	1
392	Silas	Parish	1	429	Stephen	Griffin	1
393	Alexander	Kidd	4	430	Caleb	Hazon Jnr:	1
394	John	Secor	2	431	Ebenezer	Washburn	1
395	John	Button	1	432	Elijah	Townsend	1
396	Charles	Theale	2	433	Robert	Fuller	1
397	Simeon	Tryon	3	434	William	Green	1
398	Abraham	Moe	1	435	George	Darbey Jnr:	1
399	John	Frost	1	436	Elijah	Hokam	1
400	Elemuel	Fuller	1	437	Joseph	Chandler	1
401	Nathaniel & Enoch	Scribner	4	438	Charles	Brown	1
402	William	Jones	1	439	Thomas	Griffis	1
403	Nathaniel	Finch	1	440	Solomon	Byington	1
404	Joseph	Dean	1	441	Ephraham	Nickerson	1
405	Edward	Arnold	1	442	Stephen	Baker	1
406	Fredrick	Pinckney	1	443	Simeon	Ellis Jnr:	1
407	Jonathan	Vickry	1	444	Isaac	Everitt	1
408	Jeremiah	Bailey	1	445	Isaac	Everitt Jnr:	1
409	Jeremiah	Mead	2	446	Abraham	Everitt	1
410	Jeremiah	Linchlon	1	447	Silvanus	Hamblin	1
411	Ebenezer	Burlisson	1	448	Benajah	Yarus	1
412	Jacob	Ganung	1	449	Samuel	Bangs farm	1
413	Thomas	Vickry	1	450	John	Fields farm	2
414	Samuel	Hains	1	451	James	Birdsill	2
415	John	Robinson	1	452	John	Tweedys farm	2
416	William	Henderson	10	453	David	Webb	1
417	Samuel	Bruyster	1	454	Gilbert	Hayt	1
418	John	Porter	1	455	Isaac	Philipse	1
419	William	Young	1	456	Joshua	Philipse	1
420	Samuel	Linchlon	1				£836

June 1772
Philipse's Precinct

at 5/9 [5 shillings 9 pence] pr. pound

	Name	Surname	Value		Name	Surname	Value
	Page 138			9	Isaac	Roads	4
1	William	Devenport	1	10	Joseph	Lane	2
2	Thomas	Devenport	15	11	Nathaniel	Tompkins	1
3	Jacob	Mandeville	7	12	Eli	Nelson	1
4	John	Rogers	6	13	Christopher	Fowler	1
5	John	Van Amburgh's Estate	7	14	Israel	Taylor	1
6	Capt. Peter	Dubois	12	15	Hannah	Knap	4
7	Timothy	Concklin	5	16	John	Nelson	1
8	George	Lane	2	17	Joseph	Crommells Estate	2

June 1772 Philipse's continued

#	Name	Surname	Value	#	Name	Surname	Value
18	John	How	1	72	Cornelius	Swim	2
19	William	Lane	3	73	Thomas	Williamson	1
20	William	Dusenbury	5	74	Gilbert	Budd	1
21	Sibert	Kranckheyt	1	75	Joseph	Haight	5
Page 139				*Page 140*			
22	Andrew	Barger Jnr:	1	76	William	Wright	1
23	John	Jones	4	77	Isaac	Horton	1
24	Caleb	Pells farm	2	78	Joseph	Sherwood	1
25	Richard	Hopper	1	79	Jonathen	Pine	1
26	Uriah	Drake	2	80	Joseph	Smith	1
27	Samuel	Drake Jnr:	1	81	John	Avery	2
28	Joshua	Tompkins	2	82	Peter	Warren	1
29	Solomon	Smith	2	83	Lazarus	Laight	1
30	Benjamin	Odle	1	84	Isaac	Horton Jnr:	1
31	Thomas	Crommell	1	85	Jerediah	Owens	1
32	Joseph	Huested	7	86	Richard	Denny Jnr:	2
33	Caleb	Huested	2	87	Gilbert	Bloomer	1
34	Elisha	Oakley	1	88	Israel	Knap	1
35	Matthew	McCabey	1	89	Stephen	Devenport	1
36	Beverley	Robinson	70	90	John	Gray	1
37	Lewis	Jones	1	91	Jonathen	Odle	1
38	Thomas	Searls	1	92	Gilbert	Drew	1
39	Thomas	Woodard	1	93	Jacob	Armstrong	1
40	Caleb	Nelson	2	94	Richard	Christian	1
41	Justus	Nelson	3	95	William	Colegrove	1
42	Peter	Drakes farm	2	96	Oliver	Odle	1
43	Joshua	Nelson	5	97	John	McDonald	1
44	John	Armstrong	1	98	Abraham	Post	2
45	William	Van Tassel	1	99	Thomas	Haywood	2
46	William	Gee	2	100	Samuel	Warren	3
47	John	Meeks	7	101	Jonathan	Brundage	1
48	Robert	Oakley	1	102	John	Drake	1
49	Stephen	Tompkins	2	103	David	Lane	1
50	Elijah	Horton	1	104	John	Wright	1
51	Joshua	Lamonaux	1	105	Joseph	Bard	2
52	John	Winn	1	106	Isaac	Lamoreaux	2
53	Byally	Bashford	2	107	Stephen	Concklin	1
54	Isaac	Garrison	1	108	John	Crumpton	2
55	Reuben	Bunn	1	109	Anthony	Fields	2
56	Reuben	Drake	3	110	Jerediah	Frost	1
57	John	Berger	1	111	Widow	Arkills	1
58	Thomas	Bryant	1	112	Jeremiah	McCudney	1
59	Philip	Steenbaugh	1	113	Arnold	Skolfield	1
60	Richard	Arnold	1	114	Gilbert	Oakley	1
61	Nathaniel	Jagger	1	115	Coll	Brinckerhoffs farm	1
62	Francis	Berger	1	116	Samuel	Jenkins	1
63	Sibert	Krankheyt Jnr:	2	117	Elijah	Smith	1
64	Benjamin	Bloomer	1	118	Joseph	Knap	1
65	Anthony	Yoemans	1	119	Silvanus	Haight	2
66	Samuel	Yoemans	1	120	Ezekiel	Gee	3
67	James	Lamonaux	2	121	William	Shaw	1
68	Cornelius	Tompkins	3	122	Samuel	Cornel	1
69	Moses	Dusenbury	5	123	Thomas	Sutton	1
70	Micajah	Avery	1	124	John	Haight	1
71	Henry	Aldridge	1	125	John	Barton	1

June 1772 Philipse's continued

	Name	Surname	Value		Name	Surname	Value
126	John	Lickely	1	133	Isaac	Springer	1
127	Abraham	Hall	1	134	John	Rogers Jnr:	1
128	Albert	Swims	1	135	Jeremiah	Johnson	1
129	Gilbert	Travis	1	136	Thomas	Hills	1
130	James	Perry	1	137	Samuel	Brewer	1
	Page 141			138	Benjamin	Slatt	1
131	Silvanus	Tompkins	1				£327
132	John Still	Purdy	1				

JUNE 1773
PHILLIPS'S PRECINCT

at 3/3 [3 shillings 3 pence] pr. pound

	Name	Surname	Value		Name	Surname	Value
	Page 143			37	Thomas	Searls	1
1	William	Davenport	1	38	Thomas	Woodard	1
2	Thomas	Davenport	15	39	Caleb	Nelson	3
3	Jacob	Mandevill	7	40	Justice	Nelson	3
4	Capt Peter	Duboys	12	41	Peter	Drakes farm	2
5	John	Rogers	6	42	Joshua	Nelson	5
6	John	Van Amburghs Estate	7	43	John	Armstrong	1
	Page 144			44	William	Van Tussel	1
7	Timothy	Conkling	4	45	William	Gee	2
8	George	Lane	2	46	John	Meeks	6
9	Isac	Roads	4	47	Robert	Oakley	1
10	Joseph	Lane	2	48	Joshua	Lamonaux	1
11	Nathaniel	Tomkins	2	49	John	Winn	1
12	Eli	Nelson	1	50	Byally	Bashford	[-]
13	Christopher	Fowler	1		*Page 145*		
14	Israel	Taylor	1	51	Isaac	Garrason	1
15	Hannah	Knapp	4	52	Ruben	Bunn	1
16	John	Nelson	1	53	Ruben	Drake	3
17	Joseph	Crommels Estate	2	54	John	Burger	1
18	John	How	[-]	55	Thomas	Bryant	1
19	William	Lane	[-]	56	Philip	Steenbaugh	1
20	William	Dusenbury	5	57	Richard	Arnold	2
21	Sibert	Krankheyt	[-]	58	Nathaniel	Jagger	1
22	Andrew	Berger Jnr:	1	59	Frans	Berger	1
23	John	Jones	[-]	60	Sibert	Krankheyt Jnr:	1
24	Caleb	Pells farm	2	61	Benjamin	Bloomer	1
25	Richard	Hopper	1	62	Anthony	Yeomans	1
26	Uriah	Drake	2	63	Samuel	Yeomans	1
27	Samuel	Drake Jnr:	1	64	Cournelius	Thomkins	3
28	Joshua	Tompkins	2	65	Moses	Dusenbury	5
29	Solomon	Smith	2	66	Micajah	Avery	1
30	Benjamin	Odle	1	67	Henry	Aldridge	2
31	Thomas	Crommell	1	68	Thomas	Williamson	1
32	Joseph	Huested	7	69	Gilbert	Budd	1
33	Caleb	Huested	2	70	Joseph	Haight	5
34	Matthew	Mc Caby	1	71	William	Wright	2
35	Beverley	Robinson	70	72	Isaac	Horton	2
36	Lewis	Jones	1	73	Joseph	Sherwood	1

June 1773 Phillips's continued

#	Name	Surname	Value	#	Name	Surname	Value
74	Jonathan	Pine Jnr:	1	118	John	Barton	1
75	Joseph	Smith	1	119	John	Likeley	1
76	John	Avery	2	120	Albert	Swim	1
77	Peter	Warren	1	121	James	Perrey	1
78	Lazerus	Laight	1	122	Silvanus	Tomkins	1
79	Isaac	Horten Jnr:	1	123	John Still	Purdy	1
80	Richard	Dennis Jnr:	1	124	Isaac	Springer	1
81	Gilbert	Bloomer	1	125	Thomas	Hills	1
82	Israel	Knop	1	126	Benjamin	Slatt	1
83	Stephen	Devenport	1	127	Samuel	Crummill	1
84	John	Gray	1	128	John	Agors	1
85	Jonathen	Odle	1	129	John	Hall	1
86	Gilbert	Drees	1	130	Isaac	Hall	1
87	Jacob	Armstrong	1	131	Elijah	Dinge	1
88	Richard	Christia	1	132	Thomas	Bashford	1
89	William	Colegrove	1	133	Isaac	Tallor	1
90	Oliver	Odle	1	134	Stephen	Lawrence	1
91	John	McDonald	1	135	Gabriel	Travis	1
92	Abraham	Post	2	136	Murte	Hagelston	1
93	Thomas	Haywood	1	137	Daniel	Odle	1
94	Samuel	Warren	3	138	William	Horton	2
95	Jonathan	Brundage	1	139	James	Sirrine	1

Page 146

#	Name	Surname	Value	#	Name	Surname	Value
96	John	Drake	2	140	William	White	1
97	David	Lane	1	141	Abraham	Croft	1
98	John	Wright	1	142	James	Jacocks	1
99	Joseph	Bard	[-]	143	Peter	Bell	1
100	Stephen	Conckling	1	144	Isaac	Odle	1
101	John	Crumpton	2	145	Henry	Post	1
102	Anthony	Field	2	146	Daniel	Wiltse	1
103	Jerediah	~~Field~~ Frost	1	147	Henry	Wiltse	1
104	Widow	Arkills	1	148	Caleb	Hamson	1
105	Jeremiah	McCudney	1	149	Nathaniel	Anderson	1
106	Arnold	Skolfield	1	150	John	Boyce	1
107	Gilbert	Oakley	1	151	Peter	Barger	1
108	Coll	Brinckerkoffs farm	1	152	William	Lankeston	1
109	Samuel	Jenkins	1	153	Elijah	Budd	1
110	Elijah	Smith	1	154	Uriah	Mackel [McKeel]	1
111	Joseph	Knapp	1	155	Isaac	Van Amber	1
112	Silvanus	Haight	2	156	John	Hallowday	1
113	Ezekiel	Gee	2	157	Clark	Ulsbron	1
114	William	Shaw	1	158	Peter	Recke	1
115	Samuel	Cornell	[-]	159	Peter	Morres	1
116	Thomas	Sutton	1				£332
117	John	Haight	1				

June 1773
Fredericks Burgh Precinct

at 3/8 [3 shillings 8 pence] pr. pound

	Name	Surname	Value		Name	Surname	Value
	Page 147			51	Edward	Young [Ganung]	1
1	Elijah	Tompkins	3	52	Peleg	Weekson	1
2	Ebenezer	Jones	3	53	Rowland	Perry	4
3	David	Paddock Jnr:	1	54	William	Nelson	1
4	Caleb	Brundage	2	55	Jonathan	Bryant	2
5	Cornelious	Fuller	2	56	John	Jean	2
6	James	Dickenson	5	57	Michael	Shaw Jnr:	2
7	John	Dickenson	7	58	Jeremiah	Hughson	2
8	Daniel	Townsend	2	59	David	Akins	3
9	William	Palmer	3	60	Widow	Hills	1
10	John	Newbury	5	61	Haman	King	7
11	Robert	Mooney	2	62	Jonathan	Hopkins	2
12	Josiah	Baker	3	63	Reuben	Kelly	1
13	Thomas	Smith	4	64	Caleb	Fowler	7
14	David	Crosby	3	65	Ebenezer	Robinson	2
15	—	Willis on Clossons farm	1	66	~~Simon~~	~~Dakin~~	[-]
16	William	Penny	3		*Page 149*		
17	Joshua	Crosby	3	67	Abraham	Maybee Jnr:	2
18	Isaac	Chapman	1	68	John	Roads	1
19	Theophilus	Jones	2	69	Daniel	Bull	4
20	Thomas	Killey	1	70	Benjamin	Gifford	2
21	Edmond	Barker [Baker]	2	71	Obediah	Bardsley	1
22	Moody	House	4	72	Jacob	Phillips Jnr:	1
	Page 148			73	Ebenezer	Bennet	1
23	James	Coven	2	74	Nathan	Crosby	3
24	Elijah [Elisha]	Cool	4	75	John	Garrison	1
25	Ezekiel	~~Burgis~~	~~2~~	76	Elijah	White	1
26	Jonathan	Kelly	2	77	Hezekiah	Mead	1
27	Simeon	Ellis	3	78	Edward	Rice	5
28	—	Dickenson & Wallis in Co	6	79	Thomas	Fowler	3
29	Jeremiah	Chase	[-]	80	Josiah	Swift Jnr:	1
30	Silas	Paddock	2	81	Daniel	Brundage	5
31	Samuel	Peters	7	82	Solomon	Jenkins	3
32	Charles	Townsend	2	83	Jeremiah	Whebney	2
33	Benjamin	Townsend	2	84	Charles	McCrady	1
34	Robert	Townsend	1	85	George	Darbey	1
35	Daniel	Townsend Jnr:	1	86	Benjamin	Hatch	3
36	Robert	Shaw	2	87	Solomon	Field	3
37	Caleb	Hazel	2	88	Ebenezer	Brown	2
38	Gabriel	Legget	1	89	Nehemiah	Jones	3
39	Thomas	Paddock	2	90	Reuben	Crosby	2
40	George	Curry's farm	3	91	David	Crosby Jnr:	4
41	Peter	Angewine	5	92	Peter	Banker	1
42	Jabez	Berry	2	93	Moss	Kent	7
43	Jonathan	Paddock	3	94	Joseph	Northroop	2
44	Michael	Slatt	3	95	Thomas	Lovlass	1
45	John	Paddock	1	96	Eleazer	Hamblin	3
46	William	Hill	9	97	Joseph	Vickrey	1
47	Robert	Weekson	1	98	Hezekiah	Mead Jnr:	1
48	Isaac	Pine [Pierce]	2	99	Barzilla	King	2
49	John	Mirreck	2	100	Robert	Huson	2
50	John	Yeomans Jnr:	4	101	Isaac	Lownsbury	6

June 1773 Fredericks Burgh continued

#	Name	Surname	Value	#	Name	Surname	Value
102	James	Covey	1	155	Isaac	Ruskey	1
103	William	Merritt	3	156	James	Carl	1
104	Peter	Maybee	2	157	Samuel	Carl	3
105	John	Lownsbury	3	158	Timothy	Hatch	2
106	Thomas	Lownsbury	5	159	John	Langdon Jnr:	1
107	Joseph	Gannung	1	160	Abner	Crosby	2
108	Andrew	Rubley	1	161	Elnathen	Done	1
109	Edy	Backer	2	162	Daniel	Done	1
110	Jacob	Ellis	2	163	Zebulon	Bass	2
	Page 150			164	Daniel	Sunderland Jnr:	1
111	David	Myrck	2	165	Daniel	Secord	1
112	Jehiel	Bardsley	5	166	Jonathan	Bennett	1
113	Moses	Fowler	8	167	Joshua	Crosby Jnr:	2
114	John	Yeomans	2	168	Isaac	Secor	2
115	Ebenezer	Larkwood	2	169	Loughlin	McDonald	2
116	John thuny	Craft	1	170	Alexander	Grant	6
117	Samuel	Lucas	2	171	John	Birdsell	2
118	David	Hawkins	1	172	John	Bates	1
119	James	King	1	173	Alexander	Minzies	3
120	John	Adams	1	174	Seth	Paddock	4
121	James	Roads	3	175	Stephen	Fields	5
122	Peter	Moe	1	176	Elijah	Weekson	1
123	Gilbert	Dickenson [Dickson]	3	177	Nehemiah	Wood	2
124	Samuel	Dickenson	4	178	Thomas	Townsend	1
125	Thomas	Adams	1	179	Christopher	Townsend	1
126	Timothy	DeLavan	2	180	John	Tompkins	1
127	Capt.	Brown	2	181	Nehemiah [Nathaniel]	Stone	1
128	James	Wilson	4	182	Francis	Brier	1
129	Thomas	Firguson	1	183	Isaac	Barret	1
130	Joseph	Colwell	3	184	James	Townsend	1
131	Isaac	Merick	1	185	Benoni	Gray	1
132	Solomon	Hopkins	4	186	James	Foster	2
133	Reuben	Chase	2	187	John	Stedwell	4
134	William	Underhill	2	188	Thomas	Baxter	1
135	Theodorus	Crosby	3	189	Thomas	Thompkins	2
136	Nehemiah	Bailey	1	190	David	Porter	1
137	Caleb	Palmer	1	191	Andrew	Bardsley	1
138	Eleazer	Baker	2	192	Josiah	Benjamin	3
139	Malcom	Morrison	10	193	Benjamin	Green	1
140	Samuel	Pine	1	194	Robert	Watts	3
141	Henry	Wooden	3		*Page 152*		
142	William	Yeomans	1	195	Thomas	Menzies	12
143	Mr.	Grigory	1	196	Henry	Ludenton	4
144	Elisha	Coole Jnr:	1	197	Roswell	Wilcocks	4
145	Samuel	Washburn	4	198	David	Heacock	2
146	Charles	Arway	3	199	Michael	Nowland	1
147	James	Barret	1	200	Joshua	Concklin	2
148	Moses	Mead	1	201	James	Colkins	1
149	Jonathan	Stoukum	1	202	Nathen	Lane	1
150	James	Baldwin	1	203	Doctor	Daniels	1
151	Richard	Peters	4	204	Benjamin	Birdsell	2
152	Daniel	Sunderland	1	205	Gabriel	Carpenter	1
153	Jeremiah	Burgis	3	206	Richard	Cornell	1
	Page 151			207	Joseph	Phillips	2
154	Richard	Airs	1	208	Thomas	Hughson	1

June 1773 Fredericks Burgh continued

	Name	Surname	Value		Name	Surname	Value
209	Joseph	Horskins	2	263	Matthew	Patterson	3
210	David	Hamblin	3	264	Daniel	Martine	3
211	Isaac	Austin	1	265	John	McLean	2
212	Johnson	Dacon	1	266	William	Collwell	3
213	Samuel	Horton	1	267	Joseph	Mead	2
214	Elijah	Fuller	1	268	John	Brewer	1
215	Zachariah	Paddock	2	269	Hachaliah	Merritt	2
216	Jacob	Maybee	1	270	John	Platt	2
217	Timothy	Shaw	2	271	William	Braidy	4
218	John	Kelly	2	272	Abner	Mead	1
219	Nathaniel	Nickersons wdo	1	273	Nathan	Disbrow	1
220	Nathan	Cole	1	274	William	Stokum	1
221	Joseph	Cole	2	275	Thomas	Lynch	2
222	Charity	Austin	2	276	John	Carpenter	4
223	Widow	Merrick	1	277	John	Crane	2
224	Isaac	Ganung	1	278	Richard	Williams	1
225	Samuel	Kuatson [Kniffen]	2		*Page 154*		
226	John	Terril	4	279	John	Wright near Jacob Knilsons	2
227	Lazarus	Griffen Jnr:	1				
228	Ephraham	Jones the Uper	2	280	John	Willson	1
229	Daniel	Pierce	1	281	James	Grant	3
230	Silvanus	Coole Jnr:	[-]	282	Eburn	Haight	1
231	Uriah	Ramond	2	283	Amos	Serrings	2
232	Joshua	Burdock	1	284	Daniel	Bobbett	2
233	George	Penny	1	285	Thomas	Peters	2
234	Jerediah	Willis	1	286	William	Wooden	1
235	Israel	Ward	4	287	Isaac	Wright	1
236	Caleb	Nail [Vail]	1	288	Daniel	Ketchem	3
	Page 153			289	Joseph	Hitchcocks	1
237	Daniel	Seelass	2	290	John	Le Clair	2
238	John	Lawrence	1	291	John	Maybee	1
239	David	Cowen	1	292	Thomas	Kurkham	2
240	James	Gardner	2	293	Zebulon	Kirkhum	2
241	John	Townsend	1	294	David	Waterbury	1
242	Ebenezer	Robinson Jnr:	1	295	Waterbury	Hoyt	1
243	Robert	Wright	1	296	William	Underhill Jnr:	1
244	Richard	Chapman	1	297	James	Willson Jnr:	1
245	John	Krankhight	1	298	William	Colkin	1
246	Richard	Truesdell	1	299	Daniel	Willson	1
247	William	Chatterton	1	300	Josiah	Falkennar	1
248	Joseph	Brundage	1	301	John	Stephens	1
249	Daniel	Knap	2	302	Ezekiel	Dean	2
250	Dennis	Wright	5	303	Samuel	Terry	2
251	Lemuel	Willmott	2	304	Josiah	Baker Jnr:	1
252	Samuel	Utter	1	305	John	Terry	1
253	Asa	Hains	2	306	John	Fuller	1
254	John	Dean	1	307	David	Fuller	1
255	Caleb	Dean	1	308	Isaiah	Hopkins	1
256	Jeremiah	Shaifer	1	309	Thomas	Hall	3
257	John	Dann	1	310	John	Smith	2
258	Thomas	Carl	2	311	Dennis	Horton	1
259	~~Abraham~~ John	Taylor	1	312	David	Frost	2
260	Phineas	~~Taylor~~ Baker	1	313	Charles	Arwa Jnr:	1
261	Cumfort	Ludenton	1	314	William	Mead	1
262	Jesse	Smith	1	315	Charles	Surine	2

June 1773 Fredericks Burgh continued

#	Name	Surname	Value	#	Name	Surname	Value
316	Jacob	Knilsen [Kniffen]	4	369	John	Frost	1
317	David	Storm	2	370	Elemuel	Fuller	1
318	Ephraham	Carpenter	1	371	Nathaniel & Enogh	Scribner	4
319	John	Clarke	2	372	William	Jones	1
320	Shuble	Weekson	1	373	Nathaniel	Finch	1
	Page 155			374	Edward	Arnold	1
321	Levy	Townsend	1	375	Fredrick	Pinkney	1
322	John	Barritt	1	376	Jonathan	Nickrey [Vickrey]	1
323	Henry	Laight	1	377	Jeremiah	Bailey	1
324	Jonathan	Parish	1	378	Jeremiah	Mead	2
325	William	Carpenter	1	379	Ebenezer	Burlesson	1
326	Silvanus	Kelley	1	380	Jacob	Ganung	1
327	David	Kelley	1	381	Samuel	Hains	1
328	Zebedee	Kelley	1	382	John	Robinson	1
329	John	Hinckley	1	383	William	Hinderson	10
330	John	White	1	384	Samuel	Bruyster	1
331	Albert	Solomons	1	385	Samuel	Linchlon	1
332	Samuel	Crosby	1	386	Isaiah [Josiah]	Grigory	1
333	Joshua	Phillips	1	387	Benjamin	Minthorn	1
334	Peleg	Bailey	1	388	John	Hains Jnr:	1
335	James	Egeleston	1	389	Samuel	Jenkins	1
336	Obediah	Chase	1	390	John	Ganung	1
337	Jacob	Sunderland	1	391	Josiah	Akins farm	1
338	Joseph	Dyckman	2	392	Oliver	Bales	1
339	Thomas	Hinckley	1	393	Duncan	McGregory	1
340	David	Nickry [Vickry]	1	394	Caleb	Hazor Jnr:	1
341	John	Wearing	4	395	Ebenezer	Washburn	1
342	Jehial	Stephens	1	396	Elijah	Townsend	1
343	Roger	Morris	40	397	Robert	Fuller	1
344	Tertullis	Dickenson	15	398	William	Green	1
345	Jonathan	Austen	1	399	George	Darby Jnr:	1
346	Absalom	Yeomans	1	400	Elijah	Hokum	1
347	Charles	Agar	1	401	Charles	Brown	1
348	John	Smith Jnr:	1	402	Joseph	Chandler	1
349	Samuel	Jones	2	403	Thomas	Griffen	1
350	Josiah	Jones	2	404	Solomon	Byington	1
351	John	McKee	1	405	Ephraham	Nickerson	1
352	Thomas	Nickerson	1	406	Stephen	Baker	1
353	Peter	Brewer	1		*Page 157*		
354	Oliver	Bailey	1	407	Simeon	Ellis Jnr:	1
355	Jonathan	Webb	1	408	Isaac	Everett	1
356	Benjamin	Jones Jnr:	1	409	Isaac	Everett Jnr:	1
357	William	Snow	1	410	George	Everett	1
358	Matthew	Bump	1	411	Silvanus	Hamblin	1
359	John	Dan Jnr:	1	412	Benajah	Yaeres	1
360	Francis	Good	1	413	Samuel	Bangs farm	1
361	Gilbert	Ganung	1	414	John	Fields farm	2
362	Jesse	Mercy	1	415	James	Birdsall	2
363	Alexander	Kidd	5	416	John	Tweedy's farm	1
	Page 156			417	David	Webb	1
364	John	Secor	2	418	Gilbert	Hyat	1
365	John	Button	1	419	Mahar	Nellson	1
366	Charles	Theal	3	420	John	Williams	1
367	Simeon	Tryon	2	421	Comfort	Chadwick	1
368	Abraham	Moe	1	422	Elijah	Oakley	1

June 1773 Fredericks Burgh continued

	Name	Surname	Value		Name	Surname	Value
423	Paul	Secord	1	458	Samuel	Towner	4
424	David	Hill	1	459	Gilbert	Merritt	1
425	Increase	Bennitt	1	460	Hezekiah	Willis	1
426	Samuel	Greggory	1	461	John	Welch	1
427	William	Hedger	1	462	William	Mertain	1
428	Silas	Austen	1	463	Josiah	Crosby	1
429	David	Smith	2	464	John	Crosby	1
430	Nathaniel	Rublee	1	465	John	Garner	1
431	Isaac	Birdsel	1	466	Edward	Penny	1
432	Seth	Paddock Jnr:	1	467	Moses	Richards	1
433	William	Palmer Jnr:	1	468	Nehemiah	Smith	1
434	Nathan	Palmer	1	469	—	Richards on Jones's farm	1
435	Eli	Crosby	1				
436	David	Fowler	3	470	John	Phillips	1
437	David	Patterson	1	471	James	Sears	1
438	William	Lovelace	1	472	—	Huested on Hunts farm	2
439	Joseph	Sunderlin	1				
440	Zebulon	Washburn	1	473	John	Slutt	2
441	Peter	Win	1	474	—	Weed on Wdo Baileys farm	2
442	Abraham	Birdsell	1				
443	Isaac	Bates	1	475	Reuben	Hinckley	1
444	Peter	Anderson	3	476	Isaac	Rhodes	1
445	Moses	Knap	2	477	Thomas	Vickrey	1
446	Jeremiah	Smith	1	478	Benjamin	Gifford Jnr:	1
447	Joseph	Grigery	1	479	Uriah	Wright	1
448	Jesse	Brown	1	480	—	Mertains on Closs's farm	4
Page 158							
449	Lewis	Forgerson	1	481	David	Garson	1
450	Nathaniel	Green	2	482	John	Lomree	1
451	Joshua	Merrick	1	483	Elisha	Lomree	1
452	Joel	Burlinson	1	484	Daniel	Cole	2
453	Nathan	Bailey	1	485	Joseph	Carpenter	1
454	William	Griffen	1	486	John	Berry	1
455	Eleany	Young	1	487	—	West Gate by the Store	1
456	Nathan	Yearns	1				£933
457	John	Hains Reed maker	1				

June 1773
South East Precinct

at 5/4 [5 shillings 4 pence] pr. pound

	Name	Surname	Value		Name	Surname	Value
Page 159				10	Simeon	Rider	4
1	Joseph	Crane	4	11	Edward	Gray's farm	4
2	Samuel	Field	4	12	Samuel	Bangs	5
3	Joseph	Field	4	13	Nathaniel	Foster	5
4	Uriah	Townsend	2	14	Samuel	Elwell	2
5	Benjamin	Townsend	5	15	Nathan	Green	2
6	Robert	Townsend	4	16	Seth	Nickerson	5
7	Caleb	Sweet	1	17	Thomas	Forster	1
8	Isaac	Crosby	2	18	Mr	Kent	2
9	Benjamin	Sears	5	19	Peter	Hall	5

June 1773 South East continued

	Name	Surname	Value		Name	Surname	Value
20	Thomas	Gage	2	74	Morton	Hall	2
21	John	Field	5	75	Joseph	Hull	6
22	James	Birdsell	9	76	Berry	Hopkins	2
23	Noah	Smith	2	77	Charles	Cullen	3
24	Matthias	Burges	5	78	Oliver	Hull	5
25	John	Ryder	5	79	William	Penny	2
26	Joshua	Barnum	3	80	Jonathan	Crane	1
27	Mathew	Benedicts farm	2	81	Thomas	Sears	3
28	Samuel	Ellwell Jnr:	3	82	John	Tweedy	2
29	Isaac	Ellwell	3	83	Azor	Barnum	1
30	Elisha [Elihu]	Gage	3	84	Peter	Chapman	1
31	Anthony	Gage	1		*Page 161*		
32	Richard	Warring	1	85	Nathan	Paddock	1
33	Samuel	Benedict	1	86	James	Green	1
34	Jabish	Ellwell	3	87	Stephen	Field	4
35	Abel	Hodges farm	2	88	Thomas	Cumstock	5
36	Stephen	Rockwell	1	89	Solomon	Maker	1
37	Ebenezer	Benedict	1	90	John	McNichols	1
38	James	Purdys farm	1	91	Rodrick	McKinsey	1
39	Dan	Balls farm	1	92	Nathaniel	Hemsted	1
40	John	June	1	93	Isaac	Crosby Jnr:	1
41	Benjamin	Haviland	6	94	Marck	Gage	1
	Page 160			95	William	Clinton	1
42	Thomas	Trobridge	1	96	David	Perry	2
43	Solomon	Perry's farm	1	97	Thomas	Killog	1
44	Ebenezer	Gage	2	98	Jonathan	Paddock Land	1
45	Joshua	Barnum Jnr:	2	99	Ebenezer	Humstead	1
46	Thomas	Baldwyn	5	100	Stephen	Monhouse	1
47	Moss	Kent	5	101	John	Foster	1
48	Nathan	Birdsell	3	102	Elemuel	Birdsill	-
49	Prince	Hopkins	1	103	John	Tweedy Jnr:	1
50	John	Carly	1	104	Samuel	Tweedy	1
51	Zebedee	Briggs	2	105	Thomas	Birdsell	2
52	Seth	Sears	3	106	David	Wakeman	1
53	Roger	Havelands farm	4	107	Joseph	Arnold	2
54	Samuel	Hall	3	108	Joseph	Stedwill	6
55	John	Roberts	1	109	Eliakim	Barcrum	1
56	Jesse	Lane	4	110	John	Ellwell	1
57	Richard	Gray	1	111	John	Hopkins	1
58	Nathan	Green Jnr:	3	112	William	Penny's farm	2
59	Benjamin	Sears Jnr:	3	113	Nathaniel	Stephensons	1
60	John	Haviland	1	114	David	Hoag Jnr:	1
61	Shaw	Young	2	115	William	Murch	1
62	Thomas	Higgins Jnr:	2	116	—	Cocker on Jno Ramonds farm	3
63	Thomas	Burgis	2				
64	Joshua	Hatfields farm	5	117	Seth	Sear Jnr:	1
65	Widow	Hibburn	2	118	Joseph	Field Jnr:	1
66	Ebenezer	Ryder	2	119	Abner	Doty	1
67	William	Stone	2	120	Isaac	Paddock	1
68	John	Carly Jnr:	1	121	James	Havaland	1
69	Matthew	Stephens	2	122	Ephraham	Smith's farm	1
70	Seth	Nickerson Jnr:	2	123	—	Cornwall	1
71	Daniel	Havaland	4	124	John	Ramond	1
72	Benjamin	Higgins	2	125	Benjamin	Roberts	1
73	James	Sears	[-]	126	Caleb	Roberts	1

June 1773 South East continued

	Name	Surname	Value		Name	Surname	Value
	Page 162			129	Jonathan	Carly	1
127	William	Young	2				£292
128	Samuel	Howland	1				

JUNE 1774
SOUTH EAST PRECINCT

at 3/9 [3 shillings 9 pence] pr. pound

	Name	Surname	Value		Name	Surname	Value
	Page 296			41	Ebenezer	Gage	2
1	Joseph	Crane	4	42	Joshua	Barnum Jnr:	2
2	Samuel	Field	4	43	Thomas	Baldwin	5
3	Joseph	Field	4	44	Moss	Kents farm	5
4	Uriah	Townsend	2	45	Nathen	Birdsall	4
5	Benjamin	Townsend	4	46	John	Carly	1
6	Robert	Townsend	4	47	Zebedee	Briggs	2
7	Caleb	Sweet	1	48	Seth	Sears	3
8	Isaac	Crosby	2	49	Roger	Havilands farm	4
9	Benjamin	Sears	5	50	Samuel	Hall	3
10	Simeon	Ryder	5	51	John	Roberts	1
	Page 297			52	Jesse	Lane	4
11	Samuel	Bangs	5	53	Nathen	Green	3
12	Nathaniel	Forster	5	54	Benjamin	Sears Jnr:	3
13	Samuel	Elwell	2	55	John	Haviland	1
14	Nathan	Green	1	56	Shaw	Young	2
15	Seth	Nickerson	6	57	Thomas	Higgins Jnr:	2
16	Thomas	Forster	1	58	Thomas	Burgis	2
17	Mr	Kent	2	59	Joshua	Hatfields farm	5
18	Peter	Hall	5	60	Ebenezer	Ryder	2
19	Thomas	Gage	2		*Page 298*		
20	John	Field	6	61	William	Stone	2
21	James	Birdsall	8	62	John	Corby [Carly] Jnr:	1
22	Noah	Smith	2	63	Seth	Nickerson Jnr:	2
23	Mathias	Burgis	5	64	Daniel	Haviland	5
24	John	Ryders farm	5	65	Benjamin	Higgins	2
25	Joshua	Barnum	3	66	Morton	Hall	2
26	Mathias	Benedicts farm	2	67	Joseph	Hull	6
27	—	Wieder for Elwells farm	3	68	Berry	Hopkins	2
				69	Charles	Cullen	3
28	Isaac	Elwell	3	70	William	Penny Jnr:	2
29	Elisha [Elihu]	Gage	3	71	Jonathen	Crane	1
30	Anthony	Gage	1	72	Thomas	Sears	3
31	Richard	Wearing	1	73	John	Tweedy	2
32	Samuel	Benedict	1	74	Azor	Burnum	1
33	Jabish	Elwell	3	75	James	Green	1
34	Able	Hodges farm	2	76	Stephen	Field	4
35	Stephen	Rockwell	1	77	Thomas	Cumstock	5
36	Ebenezer	Benedict	1	78	Rodrick	McKinsey	2
37	Dan	Balls farm	1	79	Nathaniel	Humstead	1
38	John	June	1	80	Mark	Gage	1
39	Benjamin	Haviland	6	81	William	Clinton	1
40	Solomon	Perry's farm	1	82	David	Perry's farm	2

June 1774 South East continued

#	Name	Surname	Value		#	Name	Surname	Value
83	Ebenezer	Humstead	2		102	John	Raymond	1
84	Stephen	Monhouse	1		103	Caleb	Roberts	1
85	John	Forster	1		104	William	Young	2
86	John	Tweedy Jnr:	1		105	Jonathen	Carley	1
87	Thomas	Birdsall	2		106	Nathaniel	Verney	1
88	Joseph	Arnold	2		107	Joseph	Townsend	1
89	Joseph	Stedwell's farm	6		108	Edward	Rice	1
90	John	Ellwell	1		109	Jeremiah	Burgis's farm	1
91	John	Hopkins	1		110	Elkney	Youngs	1
92	William	Penny's farm	3		111	Moses	Gage	1
93	Nathaniel	Stephenson	1			*Page 299*		
94	David	Hoag Jnr:	1		112	William	Mott	5
95	William	Marsh	1		113	George	Burtch	1
96	—	Cocker on Jno Raymond farm	3		114	Richard	Honeywell	1
					115	Ichabud	Gorum	1
97	Seth	Sears Jnr:	1		116	John	Stare	1
98	Joseph	Field Jnr:	1		117	Jeremiah	Wilcocks	1
99	Abner	Doty	1		118	Thomas	Fosters farm that Haviland now owns	2
100	James	Haviland	1					
101	Ephraim	Smith's farm	1					£284

JUNE 1774
FREDRICKSBURGH PRECINCT

at 6/. *[6 shillings] pr. pound*

#	Name	Surname	Value		#	Name	Surname	Value
	Page 299				26	Silas	Paddock	2
1	Elijah	Tompkins	2		27	Samuel	Peters	7
2	Ebenezer	Jones	3		28	Charles	Townsend	4
3	David	Paddock Jnr:	1		29	Benjamin	Townsend	2
4	Cornelius	Fuller	2		30	Robert	Townsend	1
5	James	Dickenson	5		31	Daniel	Townsend	1
6	John	Dickinson	7		32	Robert	Shaw	2
7	Daniel	Townsend	2		33	Caleb	Hazel	2
8	William	Palmer	3		34	Thomas	Paddock	2
9	John	Newbury	5		35	Peter	Badeau	3
10	Robert	Mooney	3		36	Peter	Anguvine	4
11	Josiah	Baker	3		37	Jabez	Berry	2
12	Thomas	Smith	4		38	Jonathan	Paddock	3
13	David	Crosby	3			*Page 300*		
14	—	Willis on Clossons Place	1		39	Michael	Slott	3
					40	John	Paddock	1
15	William	Penny	3		41	William	Hill	9
16	Joshua	Crosby	3		42	Isaac	Pine [Pierce]	2
17	Isaac	Chapman	1		43	John	Merrick	2
18	Theophilus	Jones	3		44	John	Yoemans Jnr:	4
19	Thomas	Kelley	1		45	Edward	Young [Ganung]	1
20	Edmund	Barker [Baker]	2		46	Peleg	Weekson	1
21	Moody	House	4		47	Rowland	Perry's farm	4
22	James	Coven	2		48	William	Nelson	1
23	Elisha	Cool	4		49	Jonathen	Bryant	2
24	Jonathen	Kelley	2		50	John	Jean	1
25	Simeon	Ellis	3		51	Michael	Shaw Jnr:	2

June 1774 Fredricksburgh continued

	Name	Surname	Value		Name	Surname	Value
52	Jeremiah	Hughson	2	106	John	Adams	1
53	David	Akins	4	107	James	Roads	3
54	Widow	Hill	1	108	Peter	Moe	1
55	Haman	King	8	109	Gilbert	Dickenson [Dickson]	3
56	Jonathen	Hopkins	2	110	Samuel	Dickenson	4
57	Reuben	Kelley	2	111	Thomas	Adams	1
58	Caleb	Fowler	8	112	Timothy	DeLavan	2
59	Ebenezer	Robinson	2	113	Capt.	Brown	2
60	Abraham	Maybee Jnr:	2	114	James	Brown [Wilson]	3
61	John	Roads	1	115	Thomas	Ferguson	1
62	Daniel	Bull	4	116	Joseph	Colwell	3
63	Benjamin	Gifford	2	117	Isaac	Mirrick	1
64	Obadiah	Beardsley	1	118	Solomon	Hopkins	5
65	Jacob	Philips Jnr:	2	119	Reuben	Chase	1
66	Ebenezer	Bennet	1	120	William	Underhill	2
67	Nathan	Crosby	4	121	Theodorus	Crosby	3
68	John	Garrison	1	122	Nehemiah	Bailey	1
69	Hezekiah	Mead	1	123	Caleb	Palmer	1
70	Edward	Rice	4	124	Ebenezer	Baker	4
71	Thomas	Fowler	3	125	Malcom	Morrison	10
72	Josiah	Swift Jnr:	2	126	Samuel	Pine	1
73	Daniel	Brundage	5	127	Henry	Wooden	3
74	Solomon	Jenkins	3	128	William	Yeomans	1
75	Jeremiah	Whibley	2	129	Mr.	Gregory	1
76	George	Darbey	1	130	Elisha	Coole Jnr:	2
77	Benjamin	Hatch	3	131	Samuel	Washburn	5
78	Solomon	Field	3	132	Charles	Arway	3
79	Ebenezer	Brown	2	133	James	Barrit	1
80	Nehemiah	Jones	4	134	Moses	Mead	1
81	Reuben	Crosby	2	135	Jonathen	Stockham	1
82	David	Crosby Jnr:	4	136	James	Baldwin	1
83	Peter	Bancker	1	137	Richard	Peters	4
84	Moss	Kent's farm	5	138	Daniel	Southerland	1
85	Joseph	Northrop	2	139	Jeremiah	Burgis	3
86	Ebenezer	Hamblin	3	140	Richard	Airs	1
87	Joseph	Vickry	1	141	Isaac	Rusky	1
88	Hezekiah	Mead Jnr:	1	142	James	Carl	2
89	Barzilla	King	2	143	Samuel	Carl	2
90	Robert	Hughson	3	144	Timothy	Hatch	2
91	Isaac	Lownsbury	7	145	Abner	Crosby	2
92	James	Covey	1		*Page 302*		
	Page 301			146	Elnathen	Dunn	1
93	William	Merrit	3	147	Daniel	Dunn	1
94	Peter	Maybee	2	148	Zebulon	Boss	2
95	John	Lownsbury	4	149	Joshua	Crosby Jnr:	2
96	Joseph	Ganung	1	150	Isaac	Secor	2
97	Andrew	Rubly	1	151	Laughlin	Mc Donald	1
98	Jacob	Ellis	2	152	Alexander	Grant	9
99	Dirck	Mirck	2	153	John	Birdsall	2
100	Moses	Fowler	8	154	John	Bates	1
101	John	Yoemans	2	155	Alexander	Menzies	4
102	Ebenezer	Lockwood	2	156	Seth	Paddock	4
103	John thauny	Craft	1	157	Stephen	Field	5
104	Samuel	Lucas	2	158	Elijah	Weekson	1
105	David	Hawkins	1	159	Nehemiah	Wood	2

June 1774 Fredricksburgh continued

	Name	Surname	Value		Name	Surname	Value
160	Christopher	Townsend	1	214	Ebenezer	Robinson Jnr:	1
161	John	Tompkins	1	215	Robert	Wright	1
162	Nehemiah [Nathaniel] Stone		1	216	John	Kranckheyt	1
163	Francis	Bryers farm	1	217	Richard	Truesdell	2
164	Isaac	Barret	1	218	Daniel	Knap	2
165	James	Townsend	1	219	Dennis	Wright	5
166	Benonai	Gray	1	220	Lemuel	Willmot	3
167	James	Forster	2	221	Asa	Hains	2
168	John	Stedwell	4	222	John	Dean	1
169	Thomas	Baxter	1	223	Caleb	Dean	1
170	David	Porter	1	224	John	Dan	1
171	Andrew	Beardsley	1	225	Thomas	Karl	3
172	Benjamin	Green	1	226	John	Taylor	1
173	Robert	Watts	3	227	Phinehas	Baker	1
174	Thomas	Menzies	12	228	Comfort	Ludenton	2
175	Henry	Ludenton	4	229	Matthew	Paterson	3
176	Roswell	Wilcocks	4	230	Daniel	Martin	3
177	David	Heacock	2	231	John	McLean	2
178	Michael	Nowland	1	232	William	Colwell	3
179	Joshua	Concklin	2	233	Joseph	Mead	2
180	James	Calkin	1	234	John	Brewer	1
181	Nathen	Lane	1	235	Hachaliah	Merritt	2
182	Benjamin	Birdsall	2	236	John	Platt	2
183	Joseph	Philips	3	237	William	Braidy	5
184	Thomas	Hughson	1	238	Abner	Mead	1
185	Joseph	Horskins	1	239	Nathan	Disbrow	1
186	Isaac	Austin	1	240	William	Stokum	1
187	Johnson	Deacon	1	241	Thomas	Lynch	2
188	Samuel	Horton	1	242	John	Carpenter	4
189	Elijah	Fuller	1	243	John	Crane	2
190	Zachariah	Paddock	2	244	Richard	Williams	1
191	Jacob	Maybee	1	245	John	Wright near Jacob Kniffens	2
192	Timothy	Shaw	2				
193	John	Kelley	2	246	John	Wilson	1
194	Nathaniel Nickerson's widow		1	247	James Grant's farm, that was		3
195	Nathen	Cool	1	248	Eburn	Haight	1
196	Joseph	Cool	2	249	Amos	Serrings	2
197	Charity	Austin, [and]		250	Daniel	Bobbet	3
198	Moses	Knap	2	251	Thomas	Peters	2
199	Samuel	Kniffen	2	252	William	Wooden	1
200	John	Terril	5	253	Isaac	Wright	1
	Page 303			254	Daniel	Ketchems	3
201	Lazarus	Griffen Jnr:	1		*Page 304*		
202	Daniel	Pine	1	255	Joseph	Hitchcocks	1
203	Uriah	Raymond	2	256	John	Le Clair	2
204	Joshua	Burdock	1	257	John	Maybee	1
205	George	Penny	1	258	Thomas	Kirkham	2
206	Jerediah	Willis	2	259	Zebulon	Kirkham	2
207	Israel	Ward	4	260	David	Waterbury	1
208	Caleb	Nail [Vail]	1	261	William	Underhill Jnr:	1
209	Daniel	Selass	2	262	James	Wilson Jnr:	1
210	John	Lawrence's farm	2	263	William	Calkin	1
211	David	Cowen	2	264	Daniel	Wilson	1
212	James	Gardner	2	265	Josiah	Falkanier	1
213	John	Townsend	2	266	John	Stephens	1

June 1774 Fredricksburgh continued

	Name	Surname	Value		Name	Surname	Value
267	Ezekiel	Dean	2	321	Matthew	Bump	1
268	Samuel	Terry	2	322	John	Dan Jnr:	1
269	Josiah	Baker Jnr:	2	323	Francis	Good	1
270	John	Terey	1	324	Gilbert	Ganung	1
271	John	Fuller	1	325	Jesse	Mercy	1
272	David	Fuller	1	326	Alexander	Kidd	3
273	Isaiah	Hopkins	1	327	John	Sacor	2
274	Thomas	Hall	3	328	Charles	Theale	3
275	John	Smith	2	329	Simion	Tryon	2
276	Dennis	Horton	1	330	Abraham	Moe	1
277	David	Frost	2	331	John	Frost	2
278	Charles	Arwah Jnr:	1	332	Elemuel	Fuller	1
279	William	Mead	1	333	Nathaniel & Enogh	Scribner	3
280	Charles	Surine	2	334	William	Jones	1
281	Jacob	Kniffen	4	335	Nathaniel	Finch	1
282	David	Storm	1	336	Edward	Arnold	1
283	Ephram	Carpenter	1	337	Fredrick	Pinckney	1
284	John	Clarke	2	338	Jeremiah	Bailey	1
285	Shubel	Weekson	1	339	Jeremiah	Mead	2
286	Levy	Townsend	1	340	Jacob	Ganung	1
287	John	Barret	1	341	Samuel	Hains	1
288	Henry	Laight	1	342	John	Robinson	1
289	Jonathan	Parish	2	343	William	Henderson	10
290	William	Carpenter	1	344	Samuel	Bruyster	1
291	Silvanus	Kelley	1	345	Isaiah [Josiah]	Gregory	1
292	David	Kelley	1	346	Benjamin	Minthorn	1
293	Zebedee	Kelley	1	347	John	Hains Jnr:	1
294	John	Hinckley	1	348	Samuel	Jenkins	1
295	John	White	1	349	John	Ganung	1
296	Samuel	Crosby	2	350	Josiah	Akins farm	1
297	Joshua	Philips	2	351	Oliver	Bates	1
298	Peleg	Bailey	1	352	Duncan	McGregory	1
299	James	Egelston	1	353	Caleb	Hazor Jnr:	1
300	Obadiah	Chase	2	354	Ebenezer	Washburn	1
301	Jacob	Sunderland	1	355	Elijah	Townsend	1
302	Joseph	Dyckman	2	356	Robert	Fuller	1
303	Thomas	Hinckley	1	357	William	Green	1
304	David	Vickry	1	358	George	Darby Jnr:	1
305	John	Wearing	4		*Page 306*		
306	Jehiel	Stephens	1	359	Elijah	Hokum	1
307	Roger	Morris	40	360	Charles	Brown	1
308	Tertullus	Dickenson	15	361	Joseph	Chandler	1
	Page 305			362	Thomas	Griffen	1
309	Jonathen	Austin	1	363	Solomon	Byington	1
310	Absolom	Yeomans	1	364	Ephraim	Nickerson	1
311	Charles	Agar	1	365	Stephen	Baker	1
312	John	Smith Jnr:	1	366	Simeon	Ellis Jnr:	1
313	Samuel	Jones	2	367	Isaac	Everitt	1
314	Josiah	Jones	2	368	Isaac	Everitt Jnr:	1
315	Thomas	Nickerson	1	369	George	Everitt	1
316	Peter	Brewer	1	370	Silvanus	Hamblin	1
317	Oliver	Bailey	1	371	Benajah	Yearns	1
318	Jonathen	Webb	2	372	Samuel	Bangs's farm	1
319	Benjamin	Jones Jnr:	1	373	John	Fields farm	2
320	William	Snow	1	374	James	Birdsall	2

June 1774 Fredricksburgh continued

	Name	Surname	Value
375	John	Tweedy's farm	1
376	David	Webb	1
377	Gilbert	Hyat	1
378	Mahar	Nelson	1
379	John	Williams	1
380	Comfort	Shadwick	1
381	Elijah	Oakley	2
382	Paul	Secord	1
383	Daniel	Hill	1
384	Increase	Bennet	1
385	Samuel	Gregory	1
386	Silas	Austin	1
387	David	Smith	2
388	Nathaniel	Rubly	1
389	Isaac	Birdsall	1
390	Seth	Paddock Jnr:	1
391	William	Palmer Jnr:	1
392	Nathan	Palmer	1
393	Eli	Crosby	1
394	David	Fowler	3
395	David	Patterson	1
396	William	Lovelace	1
397	Joseph	Sunderlin	1
398	Zebulon	Washburn	1
399	Peter	Winn	1
400	Abraham	Birdsall	1
401	Isaac	Bates	1
402	Peter	Anderson	3
403	Moses	Knap	2
404	Jeremiah	Smith	1
405	Joseph	Gregory	1
406	Jesse	Brown	1
407	Lewis	Ferguson	1
408	Nathaniel	Green	2
409	Joshua	Merrick	2

Page 307

410	Joel	Burlison	1
411	William	Griffen	1
412	John	Hains, Reed maker	1
413	Samuel	Towner	4
414	Gilbert	Merritt	1
415	Hezekiah	Willes	1
416	John	Welch	1
417	William	Martin	1
418	Josiah	Crosby	1
419	John	Crosby	1
420	John	Gardner	1
421	Edward	Penny	1
422	Moses	Richards	1
423	Nehemiah	Smith	1
424	—	Richards, on Jones's farm	1
425	John	Philips	2
426	—	Huested on Hunts farm	3
427	John	Slott	2

	Name	Surname	Value
428	—	Weed on Widow Bailey's farm	1
429	Reuben	Hinckley	1
430	Thomas	Vickry	1
431	Uriah	Wright	2
432	David	Garrison	1
433	John	Lumery	1
434	Elisha	Lumery	1
435	Daniel	Coole	2
436	Joseph	Carpenter	2
437	John	Berry	1
438	Samuel	Jones Jnr:	1
439	Job	Purlsend [Burlison]	1
440	Amos	Purtesend [Burlison]	1
441	Elias	Jones	1
442	Solomon	Lockwood	2
443	Solomon	Hains	1
444	Modak [Moody]	Hows Jnr:	1
445	Nathen	Paddock	1
446	Stephen	Paddock	1
447	Nathaniel	Paddock	1
448	Nathen	Sturdefunt	1
449	Peleg	Maker	1
450	Solomon	Maker	1
451	John	Holaday	1
452	Jacob	Dusenbury	1
453	Mr	McLean, on Capt. McDonalds farm	1
454	Allen	Cameron	1
455	Doctor Samuel, [Bryant and]		
456	Richd:	Bryant	2
457	Mr David	Cloos	2
458	John	Stuart	1
459	John	Henderson	1
460	Alpheaw	Hater	1

Page 308

461	Joseph	White	1
462	Nathan	Hinckley	1
463	John	Chase	1
464	John	Lester	1
465	Thadius	Wearing	2
466	Isaac	Crosby Jnr:	1
467	Solomon	Crosby	1
468	Peter	Hatfield	4
469	John	Kent	5
470	Jacob	Reed	1
471	Moses	Buckley	2
472	Henry	Lockwood	1
473	James	Dickinsons farm	3
474	John	Wallis's farm	3
475	Silvanus	Coole Jnr:	1
476	Andrew	Attwood	1
477	Benjamin	Chesman	1
478	Freeman	Hopkins	1
479	William	Craft	1

June 1774 Fredricksburgh continued

	Name	Surname	Value		Name	Surname	Value
480	Henry	Craft	1	515	William	Bashford	1
481	Elisha	Smith	1	516	Richard	Barker	1
482	Elisha	Baldwin	1	517	Daniel	Gregory	1
483	Henry	Baldwin	1	518	Jedediah	Davis	1
484	Marcus	Brundage	1	519	Solomon	Wood	1
485	Joel	Mead	1	520	Nathen	Teed	1
486	Joseph	Hopkins	1	521	Richard	Ketchem	1
487	Gilbert	Drew	2	522	Zephas	Ketchem	1
488	Joseph	Sarls	1	523	Michael	Louwnsbury	3
489	Thomas	Russel	1	524	Israel	Lucas	1
490	Richard	Price	3	525	Benjamin	Dean	1
491	Samuel	Hamerday	1	526	Alexander	Pears	1
492	John	Verkilyer	2	527	Moses	Winter	2
493	Samuel	Concklin	1	528	James	Haight	1
494	Solomon	Kirkum	1	529	Henry	Charlock	1
495	Silvanus	Merrit	1	530	Israel	Knap	1
496	Caleb	Peers	1	531	Thomas	Horton	1
497	Elisha	Hannis	1	532	Benjamin	Knap	1
498	Nathaniel	Bailey	1	533	Joseph	Moss	1
499	Henry	Lewis	1	534	Joseph	Randel	1
500	Peter	Moe	1	535	Lemuel	Menger	1
501	Elijah	Hunt	1	536	Benjamin	Menger	1
502	Joseph	Hitchcock at the stores	1	537	William	Carl	1
				538	Thomas	Carle Jnr:	1
503	William	Hitchcocks	1	539	John	Price	1
504	Anthony	Hill	1	540	William	Dutton	1
505	William	Hedden	1	541	Daniel	Sawyer	1
506	Joseph	Matthews	1	542	Peter	Sawyer	1
507	Samuel	Giffords	1	543	Zebulon	Townsend	1
508	Jacob	Birdsall	1	544	John	Shaw	2
509	James	Crawford	1	545	Ammiel	Penny	2
510	James	Surine	1	546	Jacob	Manuel	1
511	Major	Simkins	1	547	William	Folcomer	1
512	Justus	Barret	1	548	Jabish	Chase	1
	Page 309			549	Thomas	Ellis	1
513	John	Barret Jnr:	1	550	Oliver	Fox	1
514	George	Curry Jnr:	1				£1,031

June 1774
Philipse's Precinct

at 2/2. [2 shillings 2 pence] pr. pound

	Name	Surname	Value		Name	Surname	Value
	Page 309			10	Joseph	Lane	2
1	William	Davenport	1	11	Nathaniel	Tompkins	2
2	Thomas	Davenport	15		*Page 310*		
3	Jacob	Mandeville	7	12	Eli	Nelson	1
4	Capt Peter	Dubois	12	13	Christopher	Fowler	1
5	John	Rogers	6	14	Israel	Taylor	1
6	John [Van]	Amburgh's estate	6	15	Hannah	Knap	5
7	Timothy	Concklin	5	16	John	Nelson	1
8	George	Lane	3	17	Joseph	Crommel's estate	2
9	Isaac	Roads	5	18	William	Dusenbury	5

June 1774 Philipse's continued

#	Name	Surname	Value	#	Name	Surname	Value
19	Andrew	Berger Jur	1	73	Gilbert	Bloomer	1
20	Caleb	Pells farm	2	74	Israel	Knap	1
21	Richard	Hopper	1	75	Stephen	Davenport	2
22	Uriah	Drake	2	76	John	Gray	1
23	Samuel	Drake Jnr:	1	77	Jonathen	Odle	1
24	Joshua	Tompkins	2	78	Jacob	Armstrong	1
25	Solomon	Smith	2	79	William	Colegrove	1
26	Benjamin	Odle	1	80	Oliver	Odle	1
27	Joseph	Huested	7	81	John	McDonald	1
28	Caleb	Huested	2	82	Abraham	Post	2
29	Matthew	Mc Caby	1	83	Samuel	Warren	2
30	Beverly	Robinson	70	84	John	Drake	3
31	Lewis	Jones	1	85	David	Lane	1
32	Thomas	Sarls	1	86	Stephen	Concklin	2
33	Thomas	Woodard	1	87	Anthony	Field	2
34	Caleb	Nelson	3	88	Jedediah	Frost	1
35	Justice	Nelson	3	89	Widow	Arkills	1
36	Peter	Drakes farm	2	90	Jeremiah	McKudney	1
37	Joshua	Nelson	5	91	Arnold	Skolfield	1
38	John	Armstrong	1	92	Gilbert	Oakley	1
39	William	Van Tassel	1	93	Coll.	Brinckerkoffs farm	1
40	William	Gee	2	94	Samuel	Jenkins	1
41	John	Meeks	6	95	Elijah	Smith	1
42	Robert	Oakley	1	96	Joseph	Knap	1
43	Joshua	Lamoriaux	1	97	Silvanus	Haight	2
44	John	Winn	1	98	Ezekiel	Gee	2
45	John	Garrison	1	99	William	Shaw	1
46	Reuben	Bunn	1	100	Thomas	Sutton	1
47	Reuben	Drake	4	101	John	Haight	2
48	John	Burger	1	102	John	Barton	1
49	Thomas	Bryant	1	103	John	Likely	2
50	Philip	Steenbaugh	1	104	Albert	Swim	1
51	Richard	Arnold	2	105	Silvanus	Tompkins	1
52	Nathaniel	Jagger	1	106	John Still	Purdy	1
53	Francis	Berger's widow	1	107	Isaac	Springer	1
54	Sibert	Krankheyt	2	108	Thomas	Hills	1
55	Benjamin	Bloomer	1	109	Samuel	Crommell	2
56	Anthony	Yeomans	1	110	John	Agar	1
57	Samuel	Yeomans	1	111	John	Hall	1
58	Cornelius	Tompkins	4	112	Isaac	Hall	1
59	Moses	Dusenbury	5	113	Elijah	Dinger	1
60	Micajah	Avery	1	114	Thomas	Bashford	1
61	Henry	Eldridge widow	1		*Page 312*		
62	Thomas	Williamson	1	115	Stephen	Lawrence	1
	Page 311			116	Martin	Hazelton	1
63	Gilbert	Budd	2	117	James	Surene	1
64	Joseph	Haight	5	118	William	White	1
65	William	Wright	3	119	Abraham	Craft	1
66	Isaac	Horton	2	120	James	Jaycocks	1
67	Joseph	Sherwood	2	121	Peter	Bell	2
68	Jonathen	Pine Jnr:	1	122	Isaac	Odle	2
69	Joseph	Smith	1	123	Henry	Post	1
70	John	Avery	2	124	Daniel	Wilsie	2
71	Peter	Warren	1	125	Caleb	Hamson	2
72	Richard	Dennis Jnr:	2	126	Nathaniel	Anderson	1

June 1774 Philipse's continued

	Name	Surname	Value		Name	Surname	Value
127	John	Boice	1	138	John	Sherwood	1
128	Peter	Berger	2	139	Timothy	Oakley	1
129	William	Lankeston	1	140	Gabriel	Archer	1
130	Elijah	Budd	1	141	William	Chatterton	1
131	Uriah	Mitchel [McKeel]	1	142	Jonathen	Wright	1
132	Isaac	Van Amburgh	1	143	Isaac	Washburn	1
133	John	Hallowday	1	144	Henry	Wilsie	2
134	Peter	Ricks	1	145	Daniel	Bugbee	1
135	Peter	Montros	1	146	John	Comwell	1
136	Jeremiah	Sherwood	1				£344
137	Laurence	Powers	1				

JUNE 1775
PHILIPSE'S PRECINCT

at . pr. pound

	Name	Surname	Value		Name	Surname	Value
	Page 314			35	John	Armstrong	2
1	William	Davinport	1	36	William	Van Tassel	1
2	Thomas	Davinport	15	37	William	Gee	3
3	Jacob	Mandeville	8	38	John	Meeks	6
4	Capt Peter	Dubois	12	39	Robert	Oakley	1
5	John	Rogers	4	40	Joshua	Lamoriaux	1
6	John	Van Amburghs Estate	5	41	John	Win	1
7	Timothy	Concklin	5	42	John	Garrison	1
8	George	Lane	3	43	Reubin	Bunn	1
9	Isaac	Roads	5	44	Reuben	Drake	4
10	Joseph	Lane	2	45	John	Burger	1
11	Nathaniel	Tompkins	2	46	Thomas	Bryant	1
12	Cristopher	Fowler	1	47	Philip	Steenbaugh	1
13	Hannah	Knap	5	48	Richard	Arnold	2
14	John	Nelson	1	49	Nathaniel	Jagger	1
15	Joseph	Crommels estate	2	50	Francis	Berger s widow	1
16	William	Dusenbury	5	51	Sibert	Kranheyt	2
17	Caleb	Pells farm	2	52	Benjamin	Bloomer	2
18	Richard	Hopper	1	53	Anthony	Yeomans	1
19	Uriah	Drakes farm	1	54	Samuel	Yeomans	1
20	Samuel	Drake Jnr:	1	55	Cornelius	Tomkins	4
21	Joshua	Tompkins	2	56	Moses	Dusenbury	5
22	Solomon	Smith	2	57	Micajah	Avery	1
23	Benjamin	Odle	1	58	Henry	Eldridge's widow	2
	Page 315			59	Thomas	Williamson	1
24	Joseph	Huested	7	60	Gilbert	Budd	2
25	Caleb	Huested	2	61	Joseph	Haight	5
26	Matthew	Mc Caby	1	62	William	Wright	3
27	Beverly	Robinson	70	63	Isaac	Hoton	2
28	Lewis	Jones	1	64	Joseph	Shurwoods farm	2
29	Thomas	Sarls	1	65	Jonathen	Pine Jnr:	1
30	Thomas	Woodards farm	1	66	Joseph	Smith	1
31	Caleb	Nelson	3	67	John	Avery	2
32	Justis	Nelson	4	68	Peter	Warren	2
33	Peter	Drakes farm	2	69	Richard	Dennis Jnr:	2
34	Joshua	Nelson	5	70	Gilbert	Bloomer	2

June 1775 Philipse's continued

	Name	Surname	Value		Name	Surname	Value
71	Israel	Knap	2	116	Isaac	Odle	2
72	Stephen	Davinport	3	117	Henry	Post	1
73	John	Gray	1	118	Daniel	Wilsie	2
74	Jonathan	Odle	1	119	Caleb	Hampson	2
75	Jacob	Armstrong	1	120	Nathaniel	Anderson	1
76	William	Colegrove	2	121	John	Boice	1
77	Oliver	Odle	1	122	Peter	Berger	2
78	John	McDonald	1	123	William	Lancaster	1
79	Abraham	Post	2	124	Elijah	Budd	2
80	Samuel	Warrens farm	2	125	Uriah	Mitchel [McKeel]	1
81	John	Drake	3	126	John	Hollowday	1
82	David	Lanes farm	2	127	Peter	Ricks	1

Page 316

	Name	Surname	Value		Name	Surname	Value
				128	Peter	Montross	1
83	Stephen	Concklin	2	129	Jeremiah	Sherwood	1
84	Anthony	Field	2	130	Laurence	Powers	1
85	Jedediah	Frost	1	131	John	Shurwood	1
86	Widow	Arkills	1	132	Timothy	Oakley	1
87	Jeremiah	McKudney	1	133	Gabriel	Arsher	2
88	Gilbert	Oakley	1	134	William	Chatterton	1
89	Coll	Brinckerkoffs farm	1	135	Jonathen	Wright	2
90	Samuel	Jenkins	1	136	Isaac	Washburn	2
91	Elijah	Smith	1	137	Henry	Wilsie	2
92	Joseph	Knap	1	138	Daniel	Bugbee	2
93	Silvanus	Haight	2	139	John	Cornell	1
94	Ezekiel	Gee	2	140	Thomas	Davinport	1

Page 317

	Name	Surname	Value		Name	Surname	Value
95	William	Shaw	1	141	David	Hanen	1
96	Thomas	Sutton	1	142	Benjamin	Rogers	1
97	John	Haight	2	143	Daniel	Haight	1
98	John	Barton	1	144	John	Hopper	1
99	John	Likely	2	145	Thomas	Hanan	1
100	Albert	Swim	1	146	Jonathen	Owins	1
101	Silvanus	Tompkins	1	147	Reuben	Tompkins	1
102	John Still	Purdy	1	148	Joseph	Bard	1
103	Isaac	Springer	1	149	James	Bashford	1
104	Thomas	Hills	1	150	Peter	Terril	1
105	Samuel	Crommell	2	151	Joshua	Meed	1
106	John	Agar	1	152	James	Matthews	1
107	Isaac	Hall	2	153	Andrew	Doone	1
108	Elijah	Dinge	1	154	Nathen	Lane	1
109	Thomas	Bashford	1	155	Moses	Dusenbury Jnr:	1
110	Stephen	Lawrence	1	156	Elisha	Lamoriaux	1
111	Martin	Hazelton	1	157	Thomas	Sarls Jnr:	1
112	William	White	1	158	Jeremiah	White	1
113	Abraham	Craft	1				£370
114	James	Jaycocks	1				
115	Peter	Bill	2				

June 1775
Fredricksburgh Precinct

at 3/4 [3 shillings 4 pence] pr. pound

	Name	Surname	Value		Name	Surname	Value
	Page 317			51	David	Akins	4
1	Elijah	Tompkins	2	52	Widow	Hill	1
2	Ebenezer	Jones widow	2	53	Haman	King	8
3	David	Paddock	2	54	Jonathen	Hopkins	2
4	Cornelius	Fuller	2	55	Reuben	Kelley	2
5	James	Dickinson	4	56	Caleb	Fowler	8
6	John	Dickinson	7	57	Ebenezer	Robinson	2
7	Daniel	Townsend	1	58	Abraham	Maybee Jnr:	2
8	William	Palmer	2	59	John	Roads	1
9	John	Newbury	5	60	Daniel	Bull	5
10	Robert	Mooney	2	61	Jacob	Philips Jnr:	1
11	Josiah	Baker	4	62	Ebenezer	Bennet	1
12	Thomas	Smith	4	63	Nathan	Crosby	4
13	David	Crosby	3	64	John	Garrison	1
14	Hezekiah	Willis	1	65	Hezekiah	Mead	1
15	William	Penny	3	66	Edward	Rice	4
16	Joshua	Crosby	3	67	Thomas	Fowler	3
17	Isaac	Chapman	1	68	Josiah	Swift	2
18	Theophilis	Jones	2	69	Daniel	Brundage	5
19	Edmund	Baker	2	70	Solomon	Jenkins	3
20	Thomas	Kelley	1	71	Jeremiah	Whitney	2
21	Moody	House	4	72	Benjamin	Hatch	2
22	James	Coven	1	73	Solomon	Field	4
23	Elisha	Cool	5	74	Ebenezer	Brown	2
24	Jonathen	Kelley	2	75	Nehemiah	Jones	3
25	Simeon	Ellis	2	76	Reuben	Crosby	2
26	Silas	Paddock	2	77	David	Crosby Jnr:	4
27	Samuel	Peters	7	78	Peter	Bancker	1
28	Charles	Townsend	3	79	Moss	Kent's farm	5
29	Benjamin	Townsend	2	80	Joseph	Northrop	2
30	Robert	Townsend	1	81	Joseph	Vickry	1
31	Daniel	Townsend Jun	1	82	Hezekiah	Mead Jnr:	2
32	Robert	Shaw	2	83	Barzilla	King	2
33	Caleb	Hazell	3	84	Robert	Hughson	3
34	Thomas	Paddock	3	85	Isaac	Lownsbury	7
	Page 318			86	James	Covey	1
35	Peter	Badeau	3	87	William	Merritt	3
36	Peter	Anguvine	4	88	Peter	Maybee	2
37	Jabez	Berry	2	89	John	Lownsbury	4
38	Jonathan	Paddock	3	90	Joseph	Ganung	1
39	Michael	Slott	3	91	Andrew	Rubly	1
40	John	Paddock	1	92	Jacob	Ellis	2
41	William	Hill	10	93	David	Mirrick	2
42	Isaac	Pearce	2		*Page 319*		
43	John	Minck [Mirrck?]	2	94	Moses	Fowler	9
44	John	Yeomans Jnr:	3	95	John	Yeomans	1
45	Edward	Ganung	1	96	Ebenezer	Lockwood	2
46	Peleg	Weekson	1	97	John thauny	Craft	1
47	Jonathen	Bryant	2	98	David	Hawkins	1
48	John	Jean	1	99	John	Adams	1
49	Michael	Shaw Jnr:	1	100	James	Roads	3
50	Jeremiah	Hughsen	2	101	Gilbert	Dickinson [Dickson]	3

June 1775 Fredricksburg continued

	Name	Surname	Value		Name	Surname	Value
102	Samuel	Dickinson	4	156	Roswell	Wilcocks	4
103	Thomas	Adams	1	157	David	Heacock	2
104	Timothy	DeLavan	2	158	Michael	Nowland	1
105	Capt	Brown	2	159	Joshua	Conklin	2
106	Thomas	Ferguson	1	160	James	Calkin	1
107	Joseph	Colwell	3	161	Nathan	Lane	1
108	Isaac	Merrick	2	162	Benjamin	Birdsall	2
109	Solomon	Hopkins	5	163	Joseph	Philips	3
110	Reuben	Chase	1	164	Thomas	Hughson	1
111	William	Underhill	2	165	Joseph	Horskins	1
112	Theodorus	Crosby	3	166	Isaac	Austin	1
113	Caleb	Palmer	1	167	Johnson	Deacon	1
114	Malcom	Morrison	12	168	Samuel	Horton	1
115	Henry	Wooden	3	169	Elijah	Fuller	1
116	William	Yeomans	2	170	Zachariah	Paddock	2
117	Elisha	Coole Jnr:	2	171	Jacob	Maybee	1
118	Samuel	Washburn	5	172	Timothy	Shaw	2
119	Charles	Arwah	3	173	John	Kelley	2
120	James	Berrit	1	174	Nathaniel	Nickerson widow	1
121	Moses	Mead	1	175	Nathen	Cool	1
122	Jonathen	Stockum	1	176	Joseph	Cool	2
123	James	Baldwin	1	177	Charity	Austin, [and]	
124	Jeremiah	Burgis	3	178	Moses	Knap	2
125	Richard	Airs	1	179	Samuel	Kniffen	2
126	Isaac	Rusky	1	180	John	Terril	5
127	James	Carl	2	181	Lazurus	Griffen Jnr:	1
128	Samuel	Carl	2	182	Daniel	Pearce	2
129	Timothy	Hatch	2	183	Uriah	Raymond	2
130	Abner	Crosby	2	184	Joshua	Burdock	1
131	Zebulon	Boss	2	185	George	Penny	1
132	Joshua	Crosby Jnr:	2	186	Jerediah	Willis	2
133	Isaac	Sacor	3	187	Israel	Ward	4
134	Laughlin	Mc Donald	1	188	Caleb	Vail	1
135	Alexander	Grant	10	189	Daniel	Seless	2
136	John	Birdsall	2	190	David	Cowen	2
137	John	Bates	1	191	John	Townsend	2
138	Alexander	Menzies	4	192	Ebenezer	Townsend Jnr: [Robinson]	1
139	Seth	Paddock	4				
140	Stephen	Field	7	193	Robert	Wright	1
141	Elijah	Weekson	1	194	Richard	Truesdell	2
142	Nehemiah	Wood	2	195	Daniel	Knap	2
143	Christopher	Townsend	1	196	Dennis	Wright	4
144	John	Tompkins	1	197	Lemuel	Wilmot	2
145	Nathaniel	Stone	1	198	Asa	Hains	2
146	Isaac	Barret	1	199	John	Dean	1
147	James	Townsend	1		*Page 321*		
	Page 320			200	Caleb	Dean	1
148	Benonai	Gray	1	201	John	Dan	1
149	James	Forster	2	202	Thomas	Karl	3
150	Thomas	Baxter	1	203	Phinihas	Baker	1
151	John	Stidwill	4	204	Comfort	Ludenton	2
152	Andrew	Beardsley	1	205	Matthew	Paterson	3
153	Robert	Watts	3	206	Daniel	Martyne	3
154	Thomas	Menzies	14	207	John	McLean	2
155	Henry	Ludenton	4	208	William	Colwell	3

June 1775 Fredricksburg continued

#	Name	Surname	Value	#	Name	Surname	Value
209	John	Brewer	1	263	John	White	1
210	Hachaliah	Merritt	2	264	Samuel	Crosby	2
211	John	Platt	2	265	Joshua	Philips	2
212	William	Braidy	5	266	Peleg	Bailey	1
213	Abner	Mead	1	267	James	Egelston	1
214	Nathan	Disbrow	1	268	Obadiah	Chase	2
215	William	Stokum	1	269	Jacob	Sunderland	1
216	Thomas	Lynch	2	270	Joseph	Dyckman	2
217	John	Carpenter	4	271	Thomas	Hinckley	1
218	John	Crane	2	272	David	Vickry	1
219	Richard	Williams	1	273	John	Wearing	4
220	John	Wright	2	274	Jehiel	Stephens	1
221	John	Wilson	1	275	Roger	Morris	12
222	Daniel	Bobbit	3	276	Tertullus	Dickinson	13
223	Thomas	Peters	2	277	Jonathan	Austin	1
224	William	Wooden	1	278	Absolom	Yeomans	1
225	Isaac	Wright	1	279	Charles	Agar	1
226	Daniel	Ketchem	3	280	John	Smith Jnr:	1
227	Joseph	Hitchcock	1	281	Samuel	Jones	2
228	John	Le Clair	2	282	Josiah	Jones	2
229	John	Maybee	1	283	Thomas	Nickerson	1
230	Thomas	Kirkham	2	284	Peter	Brewer	1
231	Zebulon	Kirkham	2	285	Oliver	Bailey	1
232	David	Waterbury	1	286	Jonathen	Webb	1
233	William	Calkin	1	287	Benjamin	Jones Jnr:	1
234	Josiah	Falkenier	1	288	Matthew	Bump	1
235	Ezekiel	Dean	2	289	John	Dan Jnr:	1
236	Samuel	Terry	2	290	Francis	Good	1
237	Josiah	Baker Jnr:	2	291	Gilbert	Ganung	1
238	John	Terry	1	292	Jesse	Mercy	1
239	John	Fuller	1	293	Alexander	Kidd	3
240	David	Fuller	1	294	John	Secor	1
241	Isaiah	Hopkins	1	295	Charles	Theale	3
242	Thomas	Hall	3	296	Simeon	Tryon	2
243	John	Smith	1	297	Abraham	Moe	1
244	Dennis	Horton	1	298	John	Frost	2
245	David	Frost	2	299	Elemuel	Fuller	2
246	Charles	Arwah Jnr:	1	300	Nathaniel & Enoch	Scribner	3
247	William	Mead	1	301	William	Jones	1
248	Charles	Surine	2	302	Nathaniel	Finch	1
249	Jacob	Kniffen	4		*Page 323*		
250	David	Storm	1	303	Edward	Arnold	1
	Page 322			304	Fredrick	Pinckney	1
251	Ephram	Carpenter	1	305	Jeremiah	Bailey	1
252	John	Clarke	2	306	Jeremiah	Mead	1
253	Shubell	Weekson	1	307	Jacob	Ganung	1
254	Levy	Townsend	1	308	Samuel	Hains	1
255	John	Barret	1	309	John	Robinson	1
256	Henry	Laight	1	310	William	Henderson	9
257	Jonathan	Parish	2	311	Samuel	Bruyster	1
258	William	Carpenter	1	312	Josiah	Gregory	1
259	Silvanus	Kelley	1	313	John	Hains Jnr:	1
260	David	Kelley	1	314	Samuel	Jenkins	1
261	Zebedee	Kelley	1	315	John	Ganung	1
262	John	Hinckley	1	316	Josiah	Akins farm	1

June 1775 Fredricksburg continued

	Name	Surname	Value		Name	Surname	Value
317	Oliver	Bates	1	371	Samuel	Towner	4
318	Duncan	McGregory	1	372	Gilbert	Merritt	1
319	Caleb	Hazen Jnr:	1	373	Josiah	Crosby	1
320	Ebenezer	Washburn	1	374	Edward	Penny	1
321	Elijah	Townsend	1	375	Moses	Richards	3
322	Robert	Fuller	2	376	Nehemiah	Smith	2
323	Elijah	Hokum	1	377	— Richards on Soames's farm		2
324	Charles	Brown	1	378	John	Philips	2
325	Joseph	Chandler	1	379	— Huested on Hunt's farm		3
326	Thomas	Griffen	1	380	John	Slott	2
327	Solomon	Byington	1	381	Reuben	Hinckley	1
328	Ephraim	Nickerson	1	382	Uriah	Wright	2
329	Stephen	Baker	2	383	David	Garrison	1
330	Simeon	Ellis Jnr:	1	384	John	Lumery	2
331	Isaac	Everitt	1	385	Daniel	Coole	2
332	Isaac	Everitt Jnr:	1	386	John	Berry	1
333	George	Everitt	1	387	Samuel	Jones Jnr:	1
334	Benajah	Yearns	1	388	Job	Burlison	1
335	Samuel	Bangs's farm	1	389	Amos	Burlison	1
336	John	Fields's farm	2	390	Solomon	Lockwood	2
337	James	Birdsall	2	391	Solomon	Hains	1
338	John	Tweedy's farm	2	392	Eleazer	Hamblin	3
339	David	Webb	1	393	Eleazer	Baker	2
340	Gilbert	Hyat	1	394	Elnathan	Doane	1
341	Mahar	Nelson	1	395	Daniel	Doane	1
342	John	Williams	1	396	Jane	Bryer	1
343	Comfort	Shadwick	1	397	John	Bea	2
344	Elijah	Oakley	2	398	Abraham	Hill	1
345	David	Hill	1	399	Amos	Fuller	2
346	Increase	Bennet	1	400	William	Springer	1
347	Samuel	Gregory	1	401	Isaac	Ganung	2
348	Silas	Austin	1	402	Samuel	Hitchcock	1
349	David	Smith	2	403	Joshua	Main	2
350	Nathaniel	Rubly	1		*Page 325*		
351	Isaac	Birdsall	1	404	Thomas	Dakins	1
352	Seth	Paddock Jnr:	1	405	Doane	Griffen	1
	Page 324			406	Jonathen	Griffen [Burtch]	2
353	William	Palmer Jnr:	1	407	Jeremiah	Burtch	1
354	Nathen	Palmer	1	408	Joshua	Calkins	1
355	Eli	Crosby	1	409	Isaac	Townsend	1
356	David	Fowler	3	410	John	Raymond	1
357	David	Patterson	1	411	Elias	Benjamins	1
358	William	Lovelace	1	412	Jacob	Meed	3
359	Joseph	Southerlyn	1	413	Peter	Roberts	1
360	Zebulon	Washburn	2	414	Comfort	Nickerson	1
361	Peter	Win	1	415	Reubin	Ferris	5
362	Abraham	Birdsall	1	416	Jacob	Birdsall Jnr:	1
363	Isaac	Bates	1	417	John	Robinson, near Morrisons Store	1
364	Peter	Anderson	4				
365	Moses	Knap Jnr:	2	418	Cornbury	Merrit	1
366	Joseph	Gregory	2	419	Stephen	Umstead	1
367	Lewis	Ferguson	1	420	James	Darby	1
368	Joshua	Mirrick	2	421	Joseph	Tidd [Kidd]	4
369	William	Griffen	1	422	Moses	Sage	2
370	John	Hains, Reed-maker	1	423	William	Peters	1

June 1775 Fredricksburg continued

	Name	Surname	Value		Name	Surname	Value
424	Elisha	Gifford	1	477	Joseph	Hitchcock at the stores	1
425	William	Birdsall	1				
426	John	Green	1	478	William	Hitchcock	1
427	Moody	Hous Jnr:	1	479	Anthony	Hill	2
428	Isaac	Smith	2	480	William	Haddon	1
429	James	Green	2	481	Joseph	Matthews	1
430	Stephen	Paddock	1	482	Samuel	Giffords	1
431	Nathaniel	Paddock	1	483	Jacob	Birdsall	1
432	Nathen	Sturdefunt	1	484	James	Crawford	1
433	John	Hallowday	1	485	James	Surine	1
434	Jacob	Disbury	1	486	Major	Simkins	1
435	—	Macklean, on Capt McDonalds farm	1	487	Justus	Barret	1
				488	John	Barret Jnr:	1
436	Allen	Camaron	1	489	George	Curry Jnr:	1
437	Doctor Samuel	[Bryant and]		490	Richard	Barker	1
438	Richard	Bryant	2	491	Daniel	Gregory	2
439	Mr. David	Cloos	2	492	Jedediah	Davis	1
440	John	Stuart	1	493	Solomon	Wood	1
441	John	Henderson	1	494	Nathen	Teed	1
442	Joseph	White	1	495	Zophas	Ketchem	1
443	John	Chase	1	496	Benjamin	Dean	1
444	John	Lester	1	497	Alexander	Peers	1
445	Thaddeus	Wearing	1	498	Moses	Winter	2
446	Isaac	Crosby Jnr:	1	499	James	Haight	1
447	Solomon	Crosby	2	500	Henry	Sharlock	1
448	Peter	Hatfield	4	501	Israel	Knap	1
449	John	Kent	6	502	Thomas	Horton	1
450	Jacob	Reed	2	503	Benjamin	Knap	1
451	Moses	Buckley	2	504	Joseph	Moss	1
452	Henry	Lockwood	1	505	Joseph	Randell	1
453	James	Dickinson Jnr:	5	506	Lemuel	Munger	1
454	Benjamin	Cheeseman	[-]	507	James	Munger	1
Page 326				508	William	Carl	2
455	Freeman	Hopkins	1	*Page 327*			
456	William	Craft	1	509	Thomas	Carle Jnr:	1
457	Henry	Craft	1	510	John	Price	1
458	Elisha	Smith	1	511	William	Dutton	1
459	Elisha	Baldwin	1	512	Daniel	Sawyer	1
460	Henry	Baldwin	1	513	Peter	Sawyer	1
461	Marcus	Brundage	1	514	Zebulon	Townsend	1
462	Joel	Mead	1	515	John	Shaw	1
463	Joseph	Hopkins	1	516	Ammiel	Penny	2
464	Gilbert	Drew	2	517	William	Folcorner	1
465	Joseph	Sarls	1	518	Jabish	Chase	1
466	Thomas	Russel	1	519	Thomas	Ellis	1
467	Richard	Price	3	520	Oliver	Fox	1
468	John	Verkilyer	2	521	Johnson	Youmans	1
469	Samuel	Concklin	1	522	John	Crab	1
470	Solomon	Kirkum	1	523	Richard	Sturdefunt	1
471	Caleb	Peers	1	524	Samuel	Peers	2
472	Elisha	Hannis	1	525	Adonijah	Carl	1
473	Nathaniel	Bailey	1	526	Ezekiel	Kirkum	1
474	Henry	Lewis	2	527	Abraham	Cobert	1
475	Peter	Moe	1	528	John	Ferguson	1
476	Elijah	Hunt	1	529	Robert	Russel	1

June 1775 Fredricksburg continued

	Name	Surname	Value		Name	Surname	Value
530	Richard	Chapman	1	551	Samuel	Haight	1
531	Jacob	Sayca [?]	1	552	William	Verkilyer	1
532	Conrad	Harps	1	553	James	McFarthing	1
533	Thomas	Donaldson	1	554	John	Ganung Jnr:	1
534	William	Hughson	1	555	Stephen	Hyatt	1
535	William	Pinkerton	1	556	Gabriel	Carpenter	1
536	Stephen	Booth	1	557	John	Langdon	1
537	James	Barret Jnr:	1	558	John	Munrowe	1
538	Zopher	Kirkham	1	559	Rachael	Simmons	2
539	Ezekiel	Bugbee	1	560	Samuel	Dyck	1
540	Enoch	Shaw	1	561	Isaac	Chase	1
541	William	Barret	1		*Page 328*		
542	Daniel	Crawford	1	562	Josiah	Brundage	1
543	Doctor	Hambleton	1	563	Shuble	Dimmock	1
544	Philip	Smith	1	564	Uriah	Townsend	1
545	John	Merret	2	565	John	Utter	1
546	Joseph	Hitchcock Jnr:	1	566	Richard	Sturdefunt	1
547	Zebulon	Wright	1	567	Nathan	Disbury Jnr:	1
548	Hendrick	Slott	1	568	James	Wilson	5
549	Peter	Arwah Jnr:	1	569	Moses	Crosby	1
550	Ebenezer	Bedunah, Hatter	1				£1,037

JUNE 1775
SOUTH EAST PRECINCT

at 4/10 [4 shillings 10 pence] pr. pound

	Name	Surname	Value		Name	Surname	Value
	Page 328			25	Isaac	Elwell	3
1	Joseph	Crane	4	26	Elihu	Gage	3
2	Samuel	Field	4	27	Anthony	Gage	1
3	Joseph	Field	4	28	Samuel	Benedict	1
4	Uriah	Townsend	2	29	Jabish	Elwell	3
5	Benjamin	Townsend	4	30	Stephen	Rockwell	1
6	Robert	Townsend	4	31	Ebenezer	Benedict	1
7	Isaac	Crosby	3	32	John	June	1
8	Benjamin	Sears	5	33	Benjamin	Haviland	6
9	Simeon	Ryder	6	34	Solomon	Perry's farm	1
10	Samuel	Bangs	6	35	Ebenezer	Gage	2
11	Nathaniel	Forster	3	36	Joshua	Barnum Jnr:	2
12	Samuel	Elwell	2	37	Thomas	Baldwin	5
13	Nathan	Green	1	38	Moss	Kents farm	3
14	Seth	Nickerson	6	39	Nathan	Birdsall	4
15	Thomas	Forster	1	40	John	Carly	1
16	Mr	Kent	2	41	Zebidie	Briggs	2
17	Peter	Hall	5		*Page 329*		
18	Thomas	Gage	2	42	Seth	Sears	3
19	John	Field	7	43	Roger	Havilands farm	3
20	James	Birdsall	8	44	Samuel	Hall	3
21	Noah	Smith	2	45	John	Roberts	1
22	Mathias	Burgis	4	46	Jesse	Lane	3
23	Joshua	Barnum	3	47	Nathen	Green Jnr:	3
24	Mathias	Benedicts farm	2	48	Benjamin	Sears Jnr:	3

June 1775 South East continued

#	Name	Surname	Value	#	Name	Surname	Value
49	John	Haviland	1	96	Ichabud	Gorum's farm	1
50	Shaw	Young	2	97	John	Starr	1
51	Thomas	Higgins Jnr:	2	98	Jeremiah	Wilcocks	[-]
52	Thomas	Burgis	2	99	Thomas	Forsters farm	2
53	Ebenezer	Ryder	3	100	Weight	Ball	1
54	William	Stone	2	101	Daniel	Burtch	1
55	Seth	Nickerson Jnr:	2	102	Silas	Burtch	1
56	Daniel	Haviland	5	103	Joseph	Burtch	1
57	Benjamin	Higgins	2	104	—	Hinman	2
58	Morton	Hall	2	105	Ichabud	Humstead	1
59	Joseph	Hull	7	106	James	Steadwell	1
60	Berry	Hopkins	2	107	Jacob	Millard	1
61	Charles	Cullen	4	108	Jane	Haviland	1
62	William	Penny Jnr:	2	109	Samuel	Spencer	1
63	Jonathan	Crane	1	110	Caleb	Spencer	1
64	Thomas	Sears	3	111	Solomon	Haviland's farm	1
65	John	Tweedy	2	112	John	Brewster	1
66	Azor	Barnum	2	113	Barus	Hatfield	5
67	Thomas	Cumstock	5	114	Gilbut	Stedwell	5
68	Rodrich	Mc Kinsey	2	115	William	Fields	4
69	Nathaniel	Humstead	1	116	Reuben	Ryder	1
70	Mark	Gage	1	117	Zador	Ryder	1
71	William	Clinton	1	118	Thomas	Clements	1
72	David	Perry	1	119	John Wheeler	Forster	1
73	Stephen	Monhouse	1	120	Daniel	O'Hara	1
74	Ebenezer	Humstead	2	121	Elias	Jones	1
75	John	Forster	1	122	Silvanus	Gage	1
76	John	Tweedy Jnr:	1	123	Solomon	Crane	1
77	Thomas	Birdsall	2	124	John	Perry	1
78	Joseph	Arnold	2	125	John	Townsend	1
79	John	Elwell	1	126	David	Ryder	1
80	John	Hopkins	1	127	Widow Mary	Ryder	1
81	William	Penny's farm	3	128	John	Wilcocks	1
82	William	Mursh	1	129	Nathaniel	Forster Jnr:	2
83	Seth	Sears Jnr:	1	130	John	Crosby	2
84	Joseph	Field Jnr:	1	131	Elijah	Doty	2
85	James	Haviland	1	132	Eliakim	Barnum	1
86	William	Young	2	133	Elnathen	Marsh	2
87	Jonathen	Carly	1	134	Benajah	Tubbs	1
88	Nathaniel	Varney	1	135	Rowland	Russel	1
89	Edward	Rice's farm	1	136	William	Snow	1
90	Jeremiah	Burgis s farm	1	137	Jonathen	Paddock's farm	1
91	Elkney	Youngs	1	138	Nathin	Paddock	2
92	Moses	Gage	1	139	Daniel	Gay	1
93	William	Mott	6	140	Peter	Fields	1
	Page 330			141	Ebenezer	Burlosson	1
94	George	Burtch	2	142	Thomas	Senition	1
95	Richard	Honeywell	1				£305

June 1777
South East Precinct (partial)

#	Name	Surname	Value	#	Name	Surname	Value
	Page 445			52	Seth	Nickerson Jnr:	2
1	Joseph	Crane	4	53	Daniel	Haviland	6
2	Samuel	Field	4	54	Benjamin	Higgins	2
3	Joseph	Field	4	55	Morton	Hall	3
4	Uriah	Townsends farm	1	56	Joseph	Hull	7
5	Benjamin	Townsend	4	57	Berry	Hopkins	2
6	Robert	Townsend	4	58	Charles	Cullon	4
7	Isaac	Crosby	3	59	William	Penny Jnr:	3
8	Benjamin	Sears	4	60	Jonathen	Crane	1
9	Simeon	Ryder	4	61	Thomas	Sears	3
10	Samuel	Bangs	6	62	John	Twedy	1
11	Nathaniel	Forster	3	63	Azer	Burnum	3
12	Samuel	Elwell	2	64	Thomas	Cumstock	4
13	Nathan	Green	1	65	Rodrich	Mc Kinsey's estate	1
14	Seth	Nickerson	6	66	Nathaniel	Humstead	1
15	Thomas	Forster	6	67	Mark	Gage	1
16	Peter	Hall	4	68	William	Clinton	1
17	Thomas	Gage's farm	2	69	David	Perry	1
18	John	Field	7	70	Stephen	Morehous	1
19	James	Birdsall	8	71	Ebenezer	Humsted	2
20	Noah	Smith	2	72	John	Forster	1
21	Mathias	Burgis	4	73	John	Twedy Jnr:	1
22	Joshua	Barnum	3	74	Thomas	Birdsall	3
23	Matthew	Benedicts farm	2	75	Joseph	Arnold	1
24	Isaac	Elwell	3	76	John	Elwell	1
25	Elihu	Gage	3	77	John	Hopkins	1
26	Anthony	Gage	1	78	William	Penny's farm	4
27	Samuel	Benedict	1	79	William	Murch	1
28	Jabish	Elwell	2	80	Seth	Sears Jnr:	2
29	Stephen	Rockwell	2	81	Joseph	Field Jnr:	2
30	Ebenezer	Benedict	1	82	James	Haviland	1
31	John	June	1	83	William	Young	1
32	Benjamin	Haviland	6	84	Jonathen	Carly	1
33	Ebenezer	Gage	2	85	Edward	Rice s farm	1
34	Joshua	Barnum Jnr:	1	86	Jeremiah	Burgis farm	1
35	Thomas	Baldwin	5	87	Elkney	Youngs	1
36	Moss	Kents farm	2	88	Moses	Gage	1
37	Nathan	Birdsall	4	89	William	Mott	5
38	John	Carly	1	90	George	Burtch	2
39	Zebudie	Briggs	2	91	Richard	Honeywell	1
40	Seth	Sears	2	92	Ichabud	Goarmans farm	1
41	Roger	Havilands farm	3	93	John	Star	1
42	Samuel	Hall	3	94	James	Steadwell	1
43	Jesse	Lane	3	95	Jacob	Millard	1
44	Nathen	Green Jnr:	3	96	Isaac	Haviland	2
45	Benjamin	Sears Jnr:	4	97	Samuel	Spencer	1
	Page 446			98	Caleb	Spencer	1
46	John	Haviland	1	99	Solomon	Havilands farm	1
47	Shaw	Young	2	100	Barus	Hatfield	4
48	Thomas	Higgins Jnr:	2	101	Gilbert	Stedwell	4
49	Thomas	Burgis	1	102	William	Field	4
50	Ebenezer	Ryder, estate	2		[then blank, no lists for Fredricksburg or Philipse]		
51	William	Stone	2				

June 1778
South East Precinct

at	Name	Surname	pr. pound Value		Name	Surname	Value
	Page 506			51	Joseph	Hull	8
1	Joseph	Crane	5	52	Berry	Hopkins	3
2	Samuel	Field	4	53	Charles	Cullen	4
3	Joseph	Field	3	54	William	Penny Jnr:	4
4	Uriah	Townsend's farm	1	55	Jonathan	Crane	1
5	Benjamin	Townsend	4	56	Thomas	Sears	3
6	Robert	Townsend	4	57	John	Tweedy	1
7	Isaac	Crosby	3	58	Azor	Barnum	4
8	Benjamin	Sears	4	59	Thomas	Crumstock	4
9	Simeon	Ryder	4	60	Rodrich	Mc Kinsey's estate	1
10	Samuel	Bangs	6	61	Nathaniel	Humstead	1
11	Nathaniel	Forster	3	62	Mark	Gage	2
	Page 507			63	William	Clinton	1
12	Seth	Nickerson	6	64	Ebenezer	Olmstead	2
13	Thomas	Forster	1	65	Thomas	Birdsall	2
14	Peter	Hall	4	66	Joseph	Arnold	2
15	John	Field	9	67	John	Elwell	1
16	James	Birdsall	7		*Page 508*		
17	Noah	Smith	2	68	John	Hopkins	1
18	Mathias	Burgis's wife	1	69	William	Murch	1
19	Matthew	Benedicts farm	2	70	Seth	Sears Jnr:	1
20	Isaac	Elwell	5	71	Joseph	Field Jnr:	1
21	Elihu	Gage	3	72	William	Young	1
22	Anthony	Gage	1	73	Jonathen	Carley	1
23	Samuel	Benedict	1	74	Edward	Rice's farm	1
24	Jabish	Elwell	3	75	Jeremiah	Burgis's farm	1
25	Stephen	Rockwell	2	76	Elkney	Youngs	1
26	Ebenezer	Benedict	1	77	Moses	Gage	1
27	John	June	1	78	William	Mott	6
28	Benjamin	Haviland	7	79	George	Burtch	2
29	Ebenezer	Gage	2	80	Ichabud	Goarmans farm	1
30	Joshua	Barnum Jnr:	1	81	John	Starr	1
31	Thomas	Baldwin	5	82	James	Steadwell's farm	4
32	Moss	Kents farm	2	83	Jacob	Millard	5
33	Nathen	Birdsall	3	84	Isaac	Haviland	1
34	John	Carly	1	85	Caleb	Spencer	1
35	Zebedee	Briggs	2	86	Gilbert	Stedwell	1
36	Seth	Sears	3	87	William	Field	1
37	Roger	Havilands farm	4	88	Reuben	Ryder	1
38	Samuel	Hall	4	89	Zadoc	Ryder	1
39	Jesse	Lane	2	90	John Wheeler	Forster	1
40	Nathen	Green Jur	5	91	Elias	Jones	1
41	Benjamin	Sears Jur	4	92	Silvanus	Gage	1
42	John	Haviland	1	93	Solomon	Crane	1
43	Shaw	You[n]g	2	94	Widow Mary	Ryder	1
44	Thomas	Higgins Jnr:	2	95	Nathaniel	Forster	2
45	Thomas	Burgis	3	96	John	Crosby Jnr:	2
46	William	Stone	1	97	Elijah	Doty	2
47	Seth	Nickerson Jnr:	3	98	Eliakum	Barnum	1
48	Daniel	Haviland	7	99	Elnathan	Marsh	2
49	Benjamin	Higgins	2	100	Benajah	Tubbs	1
50	Morton	Hall	3	101	Rowland	Russel	1

June 1778 South East continued

#	Name	Surname	Value
102	Jonathen	Paddock's farm	1
103	Daniel	Gay	1
104	Peter	Field	2
105	Ebenezer	Burlisons widow	1
106	Thomas	Sention	1
107	Daniel	Burtch	1
108	Joseph	Burtch	1
109	Joshua	Nickerson	1
110	Thomas	Haviland	2
111	Zachariah	Hinman	2
112	Silas	Burtch	1
113	Ichabud	Olmstead	1
114	Elias	Benjamin	2
115	Abraham	Cannon	1
116	Nathaniel	Knott	1
117	Benjamin	Shearman's farm	1
118	Thomas	Nickerson	2
119	Thomas	Cheeseman	2
120	Edward	Penny	4
121	Thatcher	Hopkins	1
122	Joshua	Hatfield	1
	Page 509		
123	Dan & Wait	Ball	1
124	James	Green	1
125	Joseph	Drake	12
126	Allen	Ball	1
127	Thomas	Haviland Jnr:	1
128	Ezekiel	Osborn	1
			£301

JUNE 1778
FREDRICKSBURGH PRECINCT

at 10/. [10 shillings] pr. pound

#	Name	Surname	Value
	Page 509		
1	Elijah	Tompkins widow	2
2	Ebenezer	Jones widow	2
3	David	Paddock	2
4	Cornelius	Fuller	2
5	John	Dickenson	7
6	Daniel	Townsend	1
7	William	Palmer	2
8	John	Newbury	4
9	Robert	Mooney	2
10	Josiah	Baker	4
11	Thomas	Smith	4
12	David	Crosby	3
13	William	Penny	4
14	Joshua	Crosby	3
15	Isaac	Chapman	1
16	Theophilus	Jones	2
17	Edmund	Baker	2
18	Thomas	Baker [Kelly]	1
19	Moody	House	4
20	James	Covan	1
21	Elisha	Coole	5
22	Jonathen	Kelly	2
23	Simeon	Ellis	3
24	Silas	Paddock	2
25	Samuel	Peters	6
26	Charles	Townsend	2
27	Benjamin	Townsend	4
28	Robert	Townsend	1
29	Robert	Shaw	2
30	Thomas	Paddock	3
31	Peter	Badeau	4
32	Peter	Anguvine's estate	4
33	Jabez	Berry	2
34	Jonathen	Paddock	4
35	Michael	Slott	4
36	John	Paddock's widow	1
37	William	Hill	10
38	Isaac	Pearce	2
39	John	Minck [Mirrck?]	2
40	John	Yeomans estate	3
41	Peleg	Weekson	1
42	Jonathen	Bryant	2
43	John	Jean	2
44	Michael	Shaw Jnr:	2
	Page 510		
45	Jeremiah	Hughson	3
46	David	Akins	4
47	Widow	Hill	1
48	Haman	King	6
49	Jonathen	Hopkins	2
50	Reubin	Kelley	2
51	Caleb	Fowler	9
52	Ebenezer	Robinson	4
53	Abraham	Maybee Jnr:	2
54	John	Roads	1
55	Daniel	Bull	5
56	Jacob	Philips Jnr:	1
57	Ebenezer	Bennet	1
58	Nathen	Crosby	4
59	John	Garrison	1
60	Hezekiah	Mead Jnr:	2

June 1778 Fredricksburgh continued

	Name	Surname	Value		Name	Surname	Value
61	Edward	Rice	4	115	James	Baldwin	2
62	Thomas	Fowlers widow	2	116	Jeremiah	Burgis	3
63	Josiah	Swift	2	117	Richard	Airs	1
64	Daniel	Brundige	5	118	Isaac	Rusky	1
65	Solomon	Jenkins	4	119	James	Karl	2
66	Jeremiah	Whitney	2	120	Samuel	Karl	2
67	Solomon	Field	4	121	Timothy	Hatch	2
68	Ebenezer	Brown	1	122	Abner	Crosby	3
69	Nehemiah	Jones	4	123	Elijah	Whitney, or	
70	Reuben	Crosby	2	124	Zebulon	Bass widow	2
71	David	Crosby Jnr:	5	125	Joshua	Crosby Jnr:	2
72	Peter	Bunker	2	126	Isaac	Secord	3
73	Moss	Kent	8	127	John	Birdsall's estate	1
74	Joseph	Northrop	2	128	John	Bates, Estate	1
75	Joseph	Vickry	1	129	Alexander	Menzies estate	4
76	Barzilla	King	2	130	Seth	Paddock	4
77	Robert	Hughson	4	131	Stephen	Field	8
78	Isaac	Lownsbury	7	132	Elijah	Weekson	1
79	James	Covey	2	133	Nehemiah	Wood	3
80	William	Merritt	3	134	Christopher	Townsend	2
81	Peter	Maybee	3	135	John	Tompkins	1
82	John	Lownsbury	4	136	Isaac	Barret	1
83	Joseph	Ganung	3	137	James	Townsend	1
84	Andrew	Rubley	1	138	James	Forster	2
85	Jacob	Ellis	2	139	Thomas	Baxters estate	1
86	David	Merrick	3	140	John	Stedwell	5
87	Moses	Fowler	9	141	Robert	Watts	4
88	John	Yeomans	1	142	Thomas	Menzies	13
89	Ebenezer	Lockwood	2	143	Henry	Ludenton	5
90	John thauny	Craft	2	144	Roswell	Wilcocks	5
91	David	Hawkins Jnr:	1	145	David	Heacock	3
92	James	Roads	4	146	Michael	Nowland	1
93	Gilbert	Dickson	4	147	Joshua	Concklin	2
94	Samuel	Dickinson	6	148	James	Calkins	1
95	Thomas	Adams	1	149	Nathen	Lane's farm	1
96	Timothy	DeLavan	2	150	Benjamin	Birdsall	3
97	Capt	Brown	2	151	Joseph	Philips	3
	Page 511			152	Joseph	Horskins	3
98	Thomas	Ferguson	1		*Page 512*		
99	Joseph	Collvill	3	153	Isaac	Austin	1
100	Isaac	Merrick	1	154	Johnson	Dakin	1
101	Solomon	Hopkins	4	155	Samuel	Hortons estate	1
102	Reubin	Chase's estate	1	156	Elijah	Fuller	2
103	Abraham	DeLavan	2	157	Zachariah	Paddock	2
104	Theodorus	Crosby	3	158	Jacob	Maybee s estate	1
105	Caleb	Palmer	1	159	John	Kelley	2
106	Malcom	Morrison	12	160	Nathaniel	Nickerson	1
107	Henry	Wooden	3	161	Nathen	Cool	1
108	William	Yeomans	2	162	Joseph	Cool	2
109	Elisha	Cool Jnr:	2	163	Charity	Austin, [and]	
110	Samuel	Washburn	6	164	Moses	Knap	3
111	Charles	Arwah	3	165	Samuel	Kniffen	2
112	James	Barret	1	166	John	Tirrill	4
113	Moses	Mead	1	167	Lazurus	Griffen Jnr:	1
114	Jonathen	Stockum	1	168	Daniel	Pearce	2

June 1778 Fredricksburgh continued

#	Name	Surname	Value	#	Name	Surname	Value
169	Uriah	Raymond	2	223	David	Frost	3
170	Joshua	Burdock	1	224	Charles	Arwah Jnr:	2
171	George	Penny	1	225	William	Mead	1
172	Jedediah	Willis	2	226	Zebulon	Kirkum	2
173	Israel	Wards estate [with]		227	Charles	Surine	3
174	John	Matine	4	228	Jacob	Kniffen	4
175	Caleb	Vail	2	229	John	Clarke	2
176	Daniel	Seelass	2	230	Shubell	Weekson	1
177	David	Cowen	2	231	Levy	Townsend	1
178	John	Townsend	2	232	John	Barrit	1
179	Robert	Wright	2	233	Henry	Laight	1
180	Richard	Truesdell	1	234	Jonathan	Parish	2
181	Daniel	Knap	3	235	Silvanus	Kelley	1
182	Dennis	Wright	5	236	David	Kelley	1
183	Asa	Hains	3	237	Zebedee	Kelley	1
184	John	Dean	1	238	John	White	1
185	Caleb	Dean	2	239	Joshua	Philips	2
186	John	Dan	1	240	Peleg	Bailey	2
187	Thomas	Carles estate	3	241	James	Egelston	1
188	Phinehas	Baker	2	242	Obadiah	Chase	2
189	Comfort	Ludenton	2	243	Joseph	Dyckman	2
190	Matthew	Patterson	3	244	Thomas	Hinckley	1
191	Daniel	Wilson	3	245	John	Wearing	4
192	John	McLane	3	246	Jehiel	Stephens	1
193	William	Colwell	4	247	Tertullus	Dickinsons estate	2
194	Hachaliah	Merrits widow	2	248	Charles	Agar	1
195	John	Platt	2	249	Samuel	Jones	2
196	William	Braidy	4	250	Josiah	Jones	2
197	Abner	Mead	1	251	Thomas	Nickerson	1
198	Nathan	Disbrow	1	252	Peter	Brewer	1
199	Thomas	Lynch's estate	2	253	Matthew	Bump	1
200	John	Carpenter	4	254	John	Dan Jnr:	1
201	John	Crane	3	255	Gilbert	Ganungs estate	1
202	Richard	Williams	1	256	David	King	1
203	John	Wright	3	257	Alexander	Kidd	3
204	John	Wilson	1	258	John	Secor	2
205	Daniel	Bobbet	4		*Page 514*		
206	Thomas	Peters's estate	2	259	Charles	Theale	3
	Page 513			260	Abraham	Moe	1
207	William	Wooden	2	261	John	Frost	2
208	Daniel	Ketchem	3	262	Elemuel	Fuller	2
209	Nathen	Paddock	1	263	Nathaniel	Scribner	4
210	John	Le Clair	2	264	William	Jones	1
211	John	Maybee	2	265	Nathaniel	Finch	2
212	Thomas	Kirkham	2	266	Edward	Arnold	1
213	David	Waterbury	2	267	Fredrick	Pinckney	1
214	William	Calkin	2	268	Jeremiah	Bailey	1
215	Ezekiel	Dean	2	269	Jeremiah	Mead	1
216	Samuel	Terry	3	270	Jacob	Ganung	2
217	Josiah	Baker Jnr:	2	271	Samuel	Hains	2
218	John	Terry	1	272	James	Cox	2
219	David	Fuller	1	273	Samuel	Bruyster	1
220	Isaiah	Hopkins	1	274	Josiah	Gregory	1
221	Thomas	Hall	3	275	John	Hains	2
222	John	Smith	1	276	Samuel	Jenkins	1

June 1778 Fredricksburgh continued

	Name	Surname	Value		Name	Surname	Value
277	John	Ganung	1	331	Reuben	Hinckley	1
278	Josiah	Akins farm	1	332	David	Garrison	1
279	Oliver	Bates	1	333	John	Lamoreaux	2
280	Duncan	McGregory	1	334	Daniel	Kool	2
281	Caleb	Hazon	2	335	John	Berry	1
282	Elijah	Townsend	1	336	Samuel	Jones	1
283	Robert	Fuller	2	337	Job	Burlison	1
284	Joseph	Chandler	1	338	Solomon	Lockwood	2
285	Solomon	Byington	1	339	Eleazer	Baker	1
286	Ephraim	Nickerson	1	340	Eleazer	Hamblin	2
287	Stephen	Baker	2	341	Elnathan	Done	2
288	Isaac	Everitt	2	342	Daniel	Done	2
289	George	Everitt	1	343	John	Bea	2
290	Samuel	Bangs farm	1	344	Abraham	Hill	2
291	John	Fields	2	345	Isaac	Ganung	2
292	James	Birdsall	2	346	Joshua	Main	2
293	John	Tweedy's farm	2	347	Jonathen	Burtch	1
294	David	Webb	1	348	Jeremiah	Burtch	2
295	Gilbert	Hyat	1	349	Joshua	Calkins	1
296	Mahar	Nelson	2	350	Isaac	Townsend	2
297	John	Williams's estate	2	351	John	Raymond	1
298	Comfort	Shadwick	1	352	Jacob	Mead	3
299	Elijah	Oakley	2	353	Peter	Roberts	1
300	David	Hill	1	354	Reuben	Ferris	5
301	Increase	Bennet	1	355	John	Robinson near Robinson Store	1
302	David	Smith	2				
303	Nathaniel	Rubly	1	356	Stephen	Umpstead	1
304	Isaac	Birdsall	1	357	James	Darby	1
305	Seth	Paddock	2	358	Joseph	Kid	4
306	William	Palmer Jnr:	1	359	Elisha	Gifford	1
307	Nathen	Palmer	1	360	William	Birdsall	1
308	Eli	Crosby	2	361	John	Green	2
Page 515				362	Moody	House Jnr:	1
309	David	Fowler	3	*Page 516*			
310	William	Lovelace	1	363	Philip	Pelton	2
311	Joseph	Sunderland	1	364	James	Green's farm	2
312	Zebulon	Washburn	1	365	Stephen	Paddock	1
313	Peter	Win	1	366	Nathaniel	Paddock	1
314	Abraham	Birdsall	1	367	Nathun	Sturdefunt	1
315	Isaac	Bates	1	368	John	Halloway	1
316	Peter	Anderson	4	369	John	McLane on Capt McDonals farm	4
317	Moses	Knap Jnr: estate	2				
318	Joseph	Gregory	3	370	Doctor Samuel [Bryant and]		
319	Lewis	Ferguson	1	371	Ric'd	Bryant	1
320	Joshua	Merrick	2	372	Mr. David	Cloos	1
321	William	Griffith	1	373	John	Stuart	1
322	Samuel	Towner	6	374	John	Henderson	1
323	Gilbert	Merrit	1	375	Joseph	White	1
324	Josiah	Crosby	1	376	John	Chase	1
325	Moses	Richards	3	377	John	Lester	1
326	Nehemiah	Smith	2	378	Thaddeus	Wearing	2
327	Ezra	Richards	2	379	Solomon	Crosby	2
328	John	Philips farm	2	380	Peter	Hatfield	4
329	—	Huested on Hunts farm	3	381	John	Kent	6
330	John	Slotts estate	2	382	Jacob	Reade	2

June 1778 Fredricksburgh continued

#	Name	Surname	Value
383	Moses	Buckley	2
384	Henry	Lockwood	1
385	James	Dickenson Jnr:	2
386	Benjamin	Cheeseman	2
387	Freeman	Hopkins	2
388	Elisha	Smith	1
389	Elisha	Baldwin	2
390	Henry	Baldwin	1
391	Joel	Mead	2
392	Joseph	Hopkins	1
393	Gilbert	Drew	3
394	Thomas	Russel	1
395	Richard	Price	2
396	Samuel	Concklin	1
397	Solomon	Kirkham	1
398	Elisha	Hannis	1
399	Nathaniel	Bailey	1
400	Henry	Lewis	2
401	Elijah	Hunt	1
402	Joseph	Hitchcock	1
403	William	Hitchcock	1
404	William	Hadden	1
405	Samuel	Gifford	1
406	Jacob	Birdsall	2
407	James	Crawford	1
408	James	Surine	1
409	Major	Simpkins	1
410	Justus	Barret	1
411	John	Barrit Jnr:	1
412	Richard	Barker	1
413	Daniel	Gregory	3
414	Nathen	Teed	1
415	Alexander	Piers estate	1

Page 517

#	Name	Surname	Value
416	Moses	Winter	3
417	James	Haight	1
418	Henry	Charlock	2
419	Israel	Knap	2
420	Thomas	Horton	1
421	Benjamin	Knap	1
422	Joseph	Moss	1
423	Joseph	Randell	1
424	William	Carl	2
425	Thomas	Karls Jnr: estate	1
426	William	Dutton	1
427	Zebulon	Townsend	1
428	Ammiel	Penny	2
429	Jabish	Chase	1
430	Thomas	Ellis	1
431	Oliver	Fox	1
432	Johnson	Yeoman	2
433	John	Crab	2
434	Richard	Sturdefunt	1
435	Samuel	Peers estate	2
436	Abraham	Covert	2
437	John	Firguson	1
438	Richard	Chapman	1
439	Robert	Russel	2
440	William	Hughson	1
441	Ezekiel	Bugbee	2
442	Enoch	Shaw	1
443	William	Barret	1
444	Daniel	Crawford estate	1
445	Doctor	Hambleton	1
446	Philip	Smith	1
447	John	Merrit	1
448	Zebulon	Wright	1
449	Hendrick	Slott	1
450	Peter	Arwah	1
451	Samuel	Haight	1
452	William	Verkylyer	2
453	James	McFarlin	1
454	Stephen	Hyat	1
455	John	Langdon	1
456	Rachel	Simmons	2
457	Isaac	Chase	1
458	Josiah	Brundige	1
459	Shubell	Dimmock	1
460	Uriah	Townsend	1
461	John	Utter	1
462	Nathan	Disbury Jnr:	1
463	James	Wilson	5
464	Moses	Crosby	1
465	David	Nath	2
466	Ephraim	Jones	2
467	John	Verkylyer, on Dickenson farm	3
468	Benjamin	Golden's estate	3

Page 518

#	Name	Surname	Value
469	William	Snow	1
470	Absolom	Simmons	2
471	Silvanus	Travis	1
472	David	Akins farm	1
473	Mr. James	Sayers estate	2
474	Joel	Borland	1
475	Peter	Chapman's estate	1
476	Northrup	Fuller	1
477	Stephen	Griffith	1
478	Beverly Robinsons Jnr: farm		10
479	Lemuel	Mungers farm	2
480	Isaiah	Bennet	1
481	William	Higbee	1
482	Jabish	Smith	1
483	John	Brown	1
484	Isaa[c]	Baddeau	1
485	Caleb	Brundige	2
486	Ebenezer	Kool	1
487	Eleazer	Hason	2
488	Nathaniel	Jenkins	1
489	Russel	Gregory	1

June 1778 Fredricksburgh continued

#	Name	Surname	Value	#	Name	Surname	Value
490	Thomas	Gregory	1	527	Thadious	Raymond	1
491	Seth	Kirkum	1	528	Joseph	Teed Jnr:	1
492	Samuel	Wilson	1	529	Alpheus	Haddon	1
493	Samuel	Kniffen Jnr:	1	530	Berry	Chase	1
494	Isaac	Fuller	1	531	Edward	Smith	2
495	Joshua	Gregory	1	532	Joseph	Barber	1
496	William	Lawrence	2	533	Daniel	Parish	1
497	Isaac	Slott	1	534	Isaiah	Swift	1
498	Mary	Hanes widow	1	535	Walter	Covey	1
499	Gilbert	Shaw	1	536	William	Morse	1
500	Noah	Hill	1	537	James	Mead	1
501	Robert	Craggs estate	1	538	John	Hinckley	1
502	Amos	Townsend	1	539	Israel	Brown	1
503	Elnathen	Gregory	1	540	Israel	Pinckney	1
504	Asahel	Berry	1	541	Isaac	Townsend Jnr:	1
505	Noah	Burbanks	1	542	Jonas	Karl	1
506	Joseph	Anthony	1	543	Timothy	Carver	1
507	Ezra	Gregory	2	544	William	Wright	1
508	John	Russel	1	545	Night	Randell	1
509	Consider	Cushman	1	546	Jacob	Jewel	1
510	Amos	Utter	1	547	John	Davis	1
511	John	Hecock	1	548	Daniel	Hazelton	1
512	Caleb	Townsend	2	549	Joseph	Morse Jnr:	1
513	Oliver	Bailey	1	550	Nathaniel	Post	1
514	Moses	Reynolds	1	551	Cornelius	Brown	1
515	Isaac	Crank	1	552	William	Utter	1
516	Annanias	Akesley	1	553	Noah	Webb	1
517	Isaac	Drew	1	554	Abel	Vanscoy	1
518	William	Drew	1	555	Abner	Dotty	1
519	Elihu	Secord	2	556	Moses	Winter Jnr:	1
520	Lewis	Winter Jnr:	1	557	Isaac	Ganung	1
	Page 519			558	Israel	Mullinaus	1
521	Thomas	Mitchel	3	559	Timothy	Ludinton	1
522	Anthony	Post	2	560	Marmaduke	Forster	2
523	Martin	Post	2	561	Ebenezer	Ward	3
524	Philip	Pelton	2	562	Isaac	Ganung Jnr:	1
525	Daniel	Pelton	1	563	Justus	Murowe	1
526	Capt.	Pelton	1				£1,094

June 1778
Philipse Precinct

at . pr pound

#	Name	Surname	Value	#	Name	Surname	Value
	Page 519				*Page 520*		
1	William	Davinport	3	8	George	Lane	3
2	Thomas	Davinport	15	9	Isaac	Roads	5
3	Jacob	MandeVille	6	10	Nathaniel	Tompkins	3
4	Capt Peter	Dubois	12	11	Cristopher	Fowler	1
5	Benjamin	Rogers	4	12	Hannah	Knap	5
6	John	Van Amburghs estate	4	13	John	Nelson	2
7	Timothy	Concklin estate	5	14	Joseph	Crommel's estate	2

June 1778 Philipse continued

#	Name	Surname	Value	#	Name	Surname	Value
15	William	Dusenbury	5	69	Oliver	Odle	2
16	Caleb	Pells farm	2	70	John	McDonald	2
17	Richard	Hopper	2	71	Abraham	Post	5
18	Uriah	Drakes farm	2	72	John	Drake	3
19	Samuel	Drake Jnr:	1	73	Stephen	Concklin	2
20	Joshua	Tompkins	3	74	Anthony	Field	2
21	Solomon	Smith	2	75	Jedediah	Frost	1
22	Benjamin	Odle	1	76	Widow	Arkills	1
23	Joseph	Huestead	7	77	Jeremiah	McKudney	2
24	Matthew	McCaby	2	78	Gilbert	Oakley	2
25	Beverly	Robinsons farm	15	79	Coll:	Brinckerkoffs farm	2
26	Thomas	Sarls	1	80	Samuel	Jenkins	1
27	Thomas	Woodwards farm	3	81	Elijah	Smith	1
28	Caleb	Nelson	4	82	Joseph	Knap	1
29	Justus	Nelson	4	83	Ezekiel	Gee	3
30	Peter	Drakes farm	2	84	William	Shaw	1
31	Joshua	Nelson	4	85	Thomas	Sutton	1
32	John	Armstrong	2	86	John	Haight	6
33	William	Van Tassel	2	87	John	Barton	1
34	William	Gee	3	88	John	Likely	3
35	John	Meeks	3	89	Albert	Swim	1
36	Robert	Oakley	2	90	Silvanus	Tompkins	1
37	Joshua	Lamoreaux	1	91	John Still	Purdy	1
38	John	Winn	1	92	Thomas	Hills	1
39	Isaac	Garrison	1	93	Samuel	Crommell	3
40	Reuben	Bunn	1	94	John	Agard	1
41	Reuben	Drake	5	95	Thomas	Bashford	1
42	John	Berger	2	96	Stephen	Lawrence	1
43	Thomas	Bryant	2	97	William	White	1
44	Philip	Steenbaugh	2	98	Abraham	Craft	1
45	Richard	Arnold	2	99	James	Jaycocks	1
46	Nathaniel	Jagger	2	100	Peter	Bill	2
47	Sibert	Krankheyt	2	101	Isaac	Odle	3
48	Benjamin	Bloomer	2	102	Henry	Post	2
49	Anthony	Yeomans	1	103	Daniel	Wilsie	2
50	Samuel	Yeomans	1	104	Caleb	Hampson	2
51	Cornelius	Tompkins	4	105	Nathaniel	Anderson	2
52	Moses	Dusenbury	5	106	John	Boice	1
53	Micajah	Avery	1	107	Peter	Berger	3
54	Henry	Eldridge	2	108	William	Lancaster	1
55	Thomas	Williams	1	109	Elijah	Budd	3
56	Gilbert	Budd	2	110	Uriah	McKeel	1
57	William	Wright	3	111	John	Holliday	1
58	Joseph	Shurwoods farm	2	112	Peter	Rycks	3
59	Joseph	Smith	2	113	Jeremiah	Shearwood	2
60	John	Avery	2	114	John	Sherwood	2
61	Peter	Warren	2	115	Timothy	Oakley	1
	Page 521			116	Gabriel	Arsher	3
62	Richard	Dinnis	2		*Page 522*		
63	Gilbert	Bloomer	2	117	William	Chatterton	1
64	Israel	Knap	3	118	Jonathen	Wright	3
65	John	Gray	1	119	Isaac	Washburn	2
66	Jonathan	Odle	1	120	Henry	Wilsie	2
67	Jacob	Armstrong	1	121	Daniel	Buggbee	3
68	William	Colegrove	2	122	John	Cornells farm	1

June 1778 Philipse continued

	Name	Surname	Value		Name	Surname	Value
123	David	Hannon	1	148	Absolom	Nelson	3
124	Daniel	Haight	1	149	Archer	Reed	2
125	John	Hopper	1	150	Jacob	Reed	2
126	Thomas	Hamen	1	151	John	Halls farm	2
127	Jonathen	Owens	2	152	John	Smith	2
128	Reubin	Tompkins	1	153	Thomas	Smith	1
129	Joseph	Bard	1	154	James	Tompkins	1
130	James	Bashford	1	155	Charles	Post	1
131	Peter	Tirrill	1	156	Jacob	Tompkins	1
132	Joshua	Meade	1	157	Solomon	Smith Jnr:	1
133	Isaac	Mead	1	158	Adolphus	Bonker	1
134	Andrew	Done	1	159	Timothy	Schot	1
135	Nathen	Lane Jnr:	1	160	John	Knap	1
136	Moses	Dusenbury Jnr:	1	161	Barent	Dutcher	1
137	Elisha	Lamoreaux	2	162	Joseph	Garrison	1
138	Jeremiah	White	1	163	John	Heley	2
139	Jonathen	Austin	1	164	John	Van Tassel	1
140	Nathen	Lane	3	165	Jarvis	Dusenbury	1
141	Jonathan	Miller	1	166	Mordicai	Brown	1
142	Matthew	Snouk	1		*Page 523*		
143	Peter	Snouk	1	167	Joseph	Langdon	1
144	John	Rush	1	168	Lazarus	Light	1
145	James	Nelson	1	169	Caleb	Huested	3
146	Robert	Porter	2				£367
147	Widow	Arkills	1				

JUNE 1779
PHILIPSE'S PRECINCT

at 16s. pr pound

	Name	Surname	Value		Name	Surname	Value
	Page 534			21	Solomon	Smith	2
1	William	Davinport	3	22	Benjamin	Odle	1
2	Thomas	Davinport	13	23	Joseph	Huestead	7
3	Jacob	MandeVille	6	24	Matthew	Mc Caby	2
4	Capt Peter	Dubois	12	25	Beverly	Robinsons farm	15
5	Benjamin	Rogers	4	26	Thomas	Sarls	1
6	John Van Amburghs Estate		4	27	Thomas	Woodards farm	3
7	Timothy	Concklins Estate	5	28	Caleb	Nelson	3
8	George	Lane	4	29	Justus	Nelson	4
9	Isaac	Roads	5	30	Peter	Drakes farm	2
10	Nathaniel	Tompkins	4	31	Joshua	Nelson	4
11	Cristopher	Fowler	1	32	John	Armstrong	2
12	Hannah	Knap	5	33	William	Van Tassel	2
13	John	Nelson	2	34	William	Gee	2
14	Joseph	Crommells Estate	2	35	John	Meeks	2
15	William	Dus[e]nbury	5	36	Robert	Oakley	2
16	Caleb	Pells farm	2	37	Joshua	Lamoreaux	1
17	Richard	Hopper	2	38	John	Win	1
18	Uriah	Drakes Farm	3	39	Isaac	Garrison	1
19	Samuel	Drake Jnr:	1	40	Reuben	Bunn	1
20	Joshua	Tompkins	3	41	Reuben	Drakes farm	5

June 1779 Philipse's continued

	Name	Surname	Value		Name	Surname	Value
42	John	Berger	2	96	Abraham	Craft	1
43	Thomas	Bryant	2	97	James	Jacocks	1
44	Philip	Steenba[u]gh	2	98	Peter	Bill	2
45	Richard	Arnold	2	99	Isaac	Odle	3
46	Nathaniel	Jagger	2	100	Robert	Porter	2
47	Sybert	Krankheyt	2	101	Absolom	Nelson	3
48	Benjamin	Bloomer	2	102	Archer	Reed's farm	2
49	Anthony	Yeomans	2	103	Jacob	Reed	2
50	Samuel	Yeomans	2	104	John	Halls farm	2
51	Cornelius	Tompkins	5	105	John	Smith	2
52	Moses	Dusenbury	5	106	Thomas	Smith	1
53	Micajah	Avery	1	107	James	Tompkins	1
54	Henry	Eldridge	2	108	Charles	Post	1
55	Thomas	Williams	1	109	Jacob	Tompkins	1
56	Gilbert	Budd	2	110	Solomon	Smith	1
57	William	Wright	2	111	Timothy	Schott	1
58	Joseph	Sherwood	2	112	John	Knap	1
59	Joseph	Smith	2	113	Joseph	Garrison	1
60	John	Avery	2	114	John	Heley	2
61	Peter	Warren	2	115	John	Van Tassel	1
62	Richard	Denny	2	116	Jarvis	Dusenbury	2
63	Gilbert	Bloomer	2	117	Mordicai	Brown	1
64	Israel	Knap	3	118	Joseph	Langdon	1
65	John	Gray	2	119	Suzanne	Wright [Light?]	1
66	Jonathan	Odle	1	120	Caleb	Huestead	3
67	William	ColeGrove	2	121	Henry	Post	2
68	Oliver	Odle	2	122	Daniel	Wilsie	2
69	John	McDonald	2	123	Caleb	Hampson	2
70	Abraham	Post	6	124	Nathaniel	Anderson	2
71	John	Drake	3	125	John	Boice	1
72	Stephen	Concklin	2	126	Peter	Burger	3
73	Anthony	Field	2	127	William	Lancaster	1
74	Jedidiah	Frost	1	128	Elijah	Budd	1
75	Widow	Arkills	1	129	Uriah	McKeel	1
	Page 535			130	John	Holliday farm	1
76	Jeremiah	McKudney	2	131	Peter	Rycks	4
77	Gilbert	Oakley	2	132	Jeremiah	Sherwood	2
78	Coll	Brinckerkoffs farm	2	133	John	Sherwood	2
79	Samuel	Jenkins	1	134	Timothy	Oakley	1
80	Elijah	Smith	1	135	Gabriel	Archer	3
81	Joseph	Knap	1	136	William	Chatterdon	1
82	Ezekiel	Gee	3	137	Jonathan	Wright	3
83	William	Shaw	1	138	Isaac	Washburn	2
84	Thomas	Sutton	1	139	Henry	Wilsie	2
85	John	Haight	5	140	Daniel	Buggbee	3
86	John	Barton	1	141	John	Cornells farm	1
87	John	Likely	3	142	David	Hannon	1
88	Albert	Swim	1	143	Daniel	Haight	1
89	Silvanus	Tompkins	1	144	John	Hopper	1
90	John Still	Purdy	1	145	Thomas	Hammond	1
91	Thomas	Hills	1	146	Jonathan	Owens	2
92	Samuel	Cromwell	3	147	Reuben	Tompkins	2
93	Thomas	Bashford	2	148	Joseph	Bard	1
94	Stephen	Lawrence	1	149	James	Bashford	1
95	William	White	2	150	Peter	Terrills	1

June 1779 Philipse's continued

	Name	Surname	Value		Name	Surname	Value
	Page 536			158	Jonathan	Austin	1
151	Joshua	Meade	1	159	Nathan	Lane	3
152	Isaac	Mead	1	160	Jonathan	Miller	1
153	Andrew	Done	1	161	Matthew	Snouk	1
154	Nathan	Lane Jnr:	1	162	Peter	Snouk	1
155	Moses	Dusenbury Jnr:	2	163	John	Rush	1
156	Elisha	Lamoreaux	2	164	James	Nelson	1
157	Jeremiah	White	1				£367

June 1779
Fredricksburgh Precinct

at 60/. [3 pounds] pr. pound

	Name	Surname	Value		Name	Surname	Value
	Page 536			38	Isaac	Pearce	2
1	Elijah	Tompkins's widow	2	39	John	Minck [Mirrck?]	2
2	Ebenezer	Jones's widow	2	40	John	Yeomans Estate	3
3	David	Paddock	2	41	Peleg	Weekson	1
4	Cornelius	Fuller	2	42	Jonathan	Bryant	2
5	John	Dickenson	8	43	John	Jean	2
6	Daniel	Townsend	1	44	Michael	Shaw Jnr:	2
7	William	Palmer	2	45	Jeremiah	Hughson	3
8	John	Newbury	6	46	David	Akins	6
9	Robert	Mooney	3	47	Widow	Hill	1
10	Josiah	Baker	4	48	Haman	King	4
11	Thomas	Smith	4	49	Jonathen	Hopkins	2
12	David	Crosby	4	50	Reuben	Hopkins [Kelley]	2
13	William	Penny	6	51	Caleb	Fowler	9
14	Joshua	Crosby	3	52	Ebenezer	Robinson	4
15	Isaac	Chapman	1	53	Abraham	Maybee Jnr:	2
16	Theophilus	Jones	2	54	John	Roads	1
17	Edmund	Baker	2	55	Daniel	Bull	10
18	Thomas	Baker [Kelly]	1	56	Jacob	Philips Jnr:	3
19	Moody	House	4	57	Ebenezer	Bennet	1
20	James	Covan	1	58	Nathan	Crosby	4
21	Elisha	Cool	6		*Page 537*		
22	Jonathan	Kelley	2	59	John	Garrison	1
23	Simion	Ellis	3	60	Hezekiah	Mead Jnr:	2
24	Silas	Paddock	2	61	Edward	Rice	4
25	Samuel	Peters	6	62	Thomas	Fowlers widow	2
26	Charles	Townsend	2	63	Josiah	Swift	2
27	Benjamin	Townsend	4	64	Daniel	Brundage	5
28	Robert	Townsend	1	65	Solomon	Jenkins	4
29	Robert	Shaw	2	66	Jeremiah	Whitney	2
30	Thomas	Paddock	3	67	Solomon	Field	5
31	Peter	Badeau	4	68	Ebenezer	Brown	1
32	Peter	Angevine's estate	4	69	Nehemiah	Jones	5
33	Jabez	Berry	3	70	Reuben	Crosby	3
34	Jonathan	Paddock	4	71	David	Crosby Jnr:	8
35	Michael	Slott	4	72	Peter	Bancker	2
36	John	Paddocks widow	1	73	Moss	Kent	8
37	William	Hill	10	74	Joseph	Northrop	2

June 1779 Fredricksburgh continued

#	Name	Surname	Value	#	Name	Surname	Value
75	Joseph	Vickery	1	129	Seth	Paddock	4
76	Barzilla	King	2	130	Stephen	Field	8
77	Robert	Hughson	2	131	Elijah	Weekson	1
78	Isaac	Lownsbury	7	132	Nehemiah	Wood	3
79	James	Covey	2	133	Christopher	Townsend	2
80	William	Merrit	3	134	John	Tompkins	1
81	Peter	Maybee	3	135	Isaac	Barrit	1
82	John	Lownsbury	4	136	James	Townsend	1
83	Joseph	Ganung	3		*Page 538*		
84	Andrew	Rubly	1	137	James	Forster	2
85	Jacob	Ellis	2	138	Thomas	Baxters Estate	1
86	David	Merrick	3	139	John	Stedwell	5
87	Moses	Fowler	9	140	Robert	Watts	5
88	John	Yeomans	1	141	Thomas	Menzies	16
89	Ebenezer	Lockwood	2	142	Henry	Ludenton	6
90	John thauny	Craft	2	143	Roswell	Wilcocks	6
91	David	Hawkins Jnr:	1	144	David	Heacock	6
92	James	Roads	4	145	Michael	Nowland	1
93	Gilbert	Dicksons Estate	4	146	Joshua	Concklin	2
94	Samuel	Dickinsons farm	6	147	James	Calkin	1
95	Thomas	Adams	1	148	Nathan	Lane's farm	1
96	Timothy	DeLavan	2	149	Benjamin	Birdsall	3
97	Capt	Brown	2	150	Joseph	Philips	4
98	Thomas	Ferguson	1	151	Joseph	Horskins	3
99	Joseph	Colville	3	152	Isaac	Austin	1
100	Isaac	Merrick	2	153	Johnson	Dakin	1
101	Solomon	Hopkins	4	154	Samuel	Hortins Estate	1
102	Reuben	Chase's Estate	1	155	Elijah	Fuller	2
103	Abraham	DeLavan	2	156	Zachary	Paddock	4
104	Theodorus	Crosby	10	157	Jacob	Maybee's Estate	1
105	Caleb	Palmer	1	158	John	Kelly	2
106	Malcom	Morrisons farm	10	159	Nathaniel	Nickerson	1
107	Henry	Wooden	5	160	Nathan	Cool	1
108	William	Yeomans	2	161	Joseph	Cool	2
109	Elisha	Cool Jnr:	2	162	Charity	Austin, [and]	3
110	Samuel	Washburn	4	163	Moses	Knap	
111	Charles	Arwah	3	164	Samuel	Kniffen	2
112	James	Barret	1	165	John	Terrill	4
113	Moses	Mead	1	166	Lazurus	Griffen	1
114	Jonathan	Stockham	1	167	Daniel	Pearce	2
115	James	Baldwin	2	168	Uriah	Raymond	2
116	Jeremiah	Burgis	3	169	Joshua	Burdock	1
117	Richard	Airs	1	170	George	Penny	1
118	Isaac	Rusky	1	171	Jedediah	Willis	2
119	James	Carl	2	172	Israel	Wards Estate [with]	4
120	Samuel	Carl	2	173	John	Martine	
121	Timothy	Hatch	4	174	Caleb	Vail	2
122	Abner	Crosby	4	175	Daniel	Seelis	2
123	Elijah / Zebulon	Whitney or Bass's widow	2	176	David	Cowen	2
				177	John	Townsend	2
124	Joshua	Crosby Jnr:	3	178	Robert	Wright	2
125	Isaac	Secord	3	179	Richard	Truesdell	1
126	John Birdsall's Estate		1	180	Daniel	Knap	3
127	John	Bates's Estate	1	181	Dinnis	Wright	5
128	Alexander	Menzies Estate	8	182	Asa	Hains	3

June 1779 Fredricksburgh continued

	Name	Surname	Value		Name	Surname	Value
183	John	Dean	1	237	John	White	1
184	Caleb	Dean	2	238	Joshua	Philips	3
185	John	Dan	1	239	Peleg	Bailey	2
186	Thomas	Carls widow	3	240	James	Egilston	1
187	Phenihas	Baker	2	241	Obadiah	Chase	2
188	Comfort	Ludenton	2	242	Joseph	Dyckman	2
189	Matthew	Patterson	5	243	Thomas	Hinckley	1
190	Daniel	Wilson	3	244	John	Wearing	4
191	John	McLane	3	245	Jehiel	Stephens	1
192	William	Colville	4	246	Tertullus	Dickensons Estate	4
193	Hachaliah	Merrits Widow	2	247	Charles	Agar	1
194	John	Platt	2	248	Samuel	Jones	2
195	William	Braidy	6	249	Josiah	Jones	2
196	Abner	Mead	1	250	Thomas	Nickerson	1
197	Nathan	Disbrow	1	251	Peter	Brewer	1
198	Thomas	Lynch's Estate	2	252	Matthew	Bump	1
199	John	Carpenter	4	253	John	Dan Jnr:	1
200	John	Crane	3	254	Gilbert	Ganung's Estate	1
201	Richard	Williams	1	255	David	King	1
202	John	Wright	3	256	Alexander	Kid	4
203	John	Wilson	1	257	John	Secor	2
204	Daniel	Bobbet	5	258	Charles	Theal	4
205	Thomas	Peters's Estate	2	259	Abraham	Moe	1
206	William	Wooden	2	260	John	Frost	2
207	Daniel	Ketchem	3	261	Elemuel	Fuller	2
208	Nathan	Paddock	1	262	Nathaniel	Scribner	4
209	John	Leclair	2	263	William	Jones	1
210	John	Maybee	2	264	Nathaniel	Finch	2
211	Thomas	Kirkcum	2	265	Edward	Arnold	1
212	David	Waterbury	2	266	Fredrick	Pinckney	1
213	William	Calkin	2	267	Jeremiah	Bailey	1
214	Ezekiel	Dean	2	268	Jeremiah	Mead	1

Page 539

	Name	Surname	Value		Name	Surname	Value
				269	Jacob	Ganung	2
215	Samuel	Terry	3	270	Samuel	Hanes	2
216	Josiah	Baker Jnr:	2	271	James	Cox	6
217	John	Terry	1	272	Samuel	Bruyster	1
218	David	Fuller	1	273	Josiah	Gregory	1
219	Isaiah	Hopkins	1	274	John	Hains	2
220	Thomas	Hall	3	275	Samuel	Jenkins	1
221	John	Smith	1	276	John	Ganung	1
222	David	Frost	3	277	Josiah	Akins farm	4
223	Charles	Arwah	2	278	Oliver	Bates	1
224	William	Mead	1	279	Duncan	McGregory	1
225	Zebulon	Kirkum	2	280	Caleb	Hazon	2
226	Charles	Surine	3	281	Elijah	Townsend	1
227	Jacob	Kniffen	4	282	Robert	Fuller	2
228	John	Clarke	2	283	Joseph	Chandler	1
229	Shubael	Weekson	1	284	Solomon	Byington	1
230	Levy	Townsend	1	285	Ephraim	Nickerson	1
231	John	Barret	1	286	Stephen	Baker	2
232	Henry	Laight	1	287	Isaac	Everitt	2
233	Jonathan	Parish	2	288	George	Everitt	1
234	Silvanus	Kelley	1	289	Samuel	Bangs farm	1
235	David	Kelley	1	290	John	Fields	2
236	Zebedee	Kelley	1	291	James	Birdsall	2

June 1779 Fredricksburgh continued

	Name	Surname	Value		Name	Surname	Value
292	John	Tweedy's farm	2	346	Jonathen	Burtch	1
				347	Jeremiah	Burtch	2
293	David	Webb	1	348	Joshua	Calkin	1
294	Gilbert	Hyat	1	349	Isaac	Townsend	2
295	Machor	Nelson	2	350	John	Raymond	1
296	John	Williams Estate	2	351	Jacob	Mead	3
297	Comfort	Shadwick	1	352	Peter	Roberts	1
298	Elijah	Oakley	2	353	Reuben	Ferris	5
299	David	Hill	2	354	John	Robinson near Robinson Store	1
300	Increase	Bennet	1				
301	David	Smith	2	355	Stephen	Umpstead	1
302	Nathaniel	Rubly	1	356	James	Darby	1
303	Isaac	Birdsall	1	357	Joseph	Kidd	4
304	Seth	Paddock	2	358	Elisha	Gifford	1
305	William	Palmer Jnr:	1	359	William	Birdsall	1
306	Nathan	Palmer	1	360	John	Green	2
307	Eli	Crosby	2	361	Moody	House Jnr:	1
308	David	Fowler	3	362	Philip	Pelton	2
309	William	Lovelace	1	363	James	Greens farm	2
310	Joseph	Sunderland	1	364	Stephen	Paddock	1
311	Zebulon	Washburn	1	365	Nathaniel	Paddock	1
312	Peter	Winn	1	366	Nathan	Sturdefunt	1
313	Abraham	Birdsall	1	367	John	Halloway	1
314	Isaac	Bates	1	368	John	McLane, on Capt McDougalls farm	4
315	Peter	Anderson	4				
316	Moses	Knap's Jnr: Estate	2		*Page 541*		
317	Joseph	Gregory	3	369	Doctor Samuel [Bryant] and		1
318	Lewis	Ferguson	1	370	Richard	Bryant	
319	Joshua	Merrick	3	371	John	Stuart	1
320	William	Griffith	1	372	John	Henderson	1
321	Samuel	Towner	8	373	Joseph	White	1
322	Gilbert	Merritt	1	374	John	Chase	1
323	Josiah	Crosby	1	375	John	Lester	1
324	Moses	Richards	3	376	Thadeus	Wearing	2
325	Nehemiah	Smith	2	377	Solomon	Crosby	2
326	Ezra	Richards	2	378	Peter	Hatfield	4
327	John	Philips farm	2	379	Jacob	Reade	2
328	—	Huestead on Hunts farm	3	380	Moses	Buckley	3
329	John	Slotts Estate	2	381	Henry	Lockwood	1
330	Reuben	Hinckley	1	382	Benjamin	Cheeseman	2
331	David	Garrison	1	383	Freeman	Hopkins	2
332	John	Lamoreaux	2	384	Elisha	Smith	1
333	David	Cool	2	385	Elisha	Baldwin	2
334	John	Berry	1	386	Henry	Baldwin	1
335	Samuel	Jones	1	387	Joel	Mead	2
336	Job	Burlison	1	388	Joseph	Hopkins	1
337	Solomon	Lockwood	2	389	Gilbert	Drew	3
338	Eleazer	Baker	1	390	Thomas	Russel	1
339	Eleazer	Hamblin	2	391	Richard	Price	2
340	Elnathan	Done	2	392	Samuel	Concklin	1
341	Daniel	Done	2	393	Solomon	Kirkum	1
342	John	Bee	2	394	Elisha	Hannis	1
343	Abraham	Hill	2	395	Nathaniel	Bailey	1
344	Isaac	Ganung	2	396	Henry	Lewis	2
345	Joshua	Main	2	397	Elijah	Hunt	1

June 1779 Fredricksburgh continued

	Name	Surname	Value		Name	Surname	Value
398	Joseph	Hitchcock	1	452	Rachel	Seamons	2
399	William	Hitchcock	1	453	Isaac	Chase	1
400	William	Hadden	1	454	Josiah	Brundige	1
401	Samuel	Gifford	1	455	Shubael	Dimmock	1
402	Jacob	Birdsall	2	456	Uriah	Townsend	1
403	James	Crawford	1	457	John	Utter	1
404	James	Surine	1	458	Nathen	Disbury Jnr:	1
405	Major	Simpkins	1	459	James	Wilson	5
406	Justus	Barret	1	460	Moses	Crosby	1
407	John	Barret Jnr:	1	461	David	Nath	2
408	Richard	Barker	1	462	Ephraim	Jones	2
409	Daniel	Gregory	3	463	John	Verkilyer, on Dickenson farm	3
410	Nathen	Teed	1				
411	Alexander	Peers Estate	1	464	Benjamin	Goldens Estate	3
412	Moses	Winter	3	465	William	Snow	1
413	James	Haight	1	466	Absolom	Seamons	2
414	Henry	Charlock	2	467	Silvanus	Travis	1
415	Israel	Knap	2	468	David	Akins farm	1
416	Thomas	Horton	1	469	Mr. James	Sayers Estate	2
417	Benjamin	Knap	1	470	Joel	Borland	1
418	Joseph	Moss	1	471	Peter	Chapmans Estate	1
419	Joseph	Randell	1	472	Northrup	Fuller	1
420	William	Clarke	1	473	Stephen	Griffith	1
421	Thomas	Carl Jnr: Estate	1	474	Beverly Robinson's Jnr: farm		10
422	William	Dutton	1	475	Elemuel	Mungers farm	2
423	Zebulon	Townsend	1	476	Isaiah	Bennet	1
424	Ammiel	Penny	2	477	William	Higby	1
425	Jabish	Chase	1	478	Jabish	Smith	1
426	Thomas	Ellis	1	479	John	Brown	1
427	Oliver	Fox	1	480	Isaac	Badeau	1
428	Johnson	Yeomans	2	481	Caleb	Brundige	2
429	John	Crabb	2	482	Ebenezer	Cool	1
430	Richard	Sturdefunt	1	483	Eleazer	Hazon	2
431	Samuel	Peers Estate	2	484	Nathaniel	Jenkins	1
432	Abraham	Covert	2	485	Russel	Gregory	1
433	John	Ferguson	1	486	Thomas	Gregory	1
434	Richard	Chapman	1	487	Seth	Kirkum	1
435	Robert	Russel	2	488	Samuel	Wilson	1
436	William	Hughson	1	489	Samuel	Kniffen	1
437	Ezekiel	Bugbee	2	490	Isaac	Fuller	1
438	Enoch	Shaw	1	491	Joshua	Gregory	1
439	William	Barrit	1	492	William	Lawrence	2
440	Daniel	Crawford's Estate	1	493	Isaac	Slott	1
441	Doctor	Hambleton	1	494	Mary	Hains widow	1
Page 542				495	Gilbert	Shaw	1
442	Philip	Smith	1	496	Noah	Hill	1
443	John	Merrit	1	497	Robert	Craig's Estate	1
444	Zebulon	Wright	1	498	Amos	Townsend	1
445	Hendrick	Slott	1	499	Elnathan	Gregory	1
446	Peter	Arwah	1	500	Asahel	Berry	1
447	Samuel	Haight	1	501	Noah	Burbanks	1
448	William	Verkylyer	2	502	Joseph	Anthony	1
449	James	McFarlin	1	503	Ezra	Gregory	2
450	Stephen	Hyat	1	504	John	Russel	1
451	John	Langdon	1	505	Consider	Cushman	1

June 1779 Fredricksburgh continued

#	Name	Surname	Value	#	Name	Surname	Value
506	Amos	Utter	1	533	James	Mead	1
507	John	Heycock	1	534	John	Hinkley	1
508	Caleb	Townsend	2	535	Israel	Brown	1
509	Oliver	Bailey	1	536	Israel	Pinckney	1
510	Moses	Reynolds	1	537	Isaac	Townsend Jnr:	1
511	Isaac	Crank	1	538	Jonas	Karl	1
512	Annanias	Akesley	1	539	Timothy	Carver	1
	Page 543			540	William	Wright	1
513	Isaac	Drew	1	541	Night	Randell	1
514	William	Drew	1	542	Jacob	Jewel	1
515	Elihu	Secor	2	543	John	Davis	1
516	Lewis	Winter	1	544	Daniel	Hazelton	1
517	Thomas	Mitchel	3	545	Joseph	Mors Jnr:	1
518	Anthony	Post	2	546	Nathaniel	Post	1
519	Martin	Post	2	547	Cornelius	Brown	1
520	Philip	Pelton	2	548	William	Utter	1
521	Daniel	Pelton	1	549	Noah	Webb	1
522	Capt.	Pelton	1	550	Abel	Van Scey	1
523	Thadeus	Raymond	1	551	Abner	Doty	1
524	Joseph	Teed Jnr:	1	552	Moses	Winter Jnr:	3
525	Alpheus	Haddon	1	553	Isaac	Ganung	1
526	Berry	Chase	1	554	Israel	Mullineaux	1
527	Edward	Smith	4	555	Timothy	Ludenton	1
528	Joseph	Barber	1	556	Marmaduke	Forster	2
529	Daniel	Parish	1	557	Ebenezer	Ward	3
530	Isaiah	Swift	1	558	Isaac	Ganung	1
531	Walter	Covey	1	559	Justus	Munrowe	1
532	William	Mors	1				£1,156

JUNE 1779
SOUTH EAST PRECINCT

at 47/. [2 pounds 7 shillings] pr. pound

#	Name	Surname	Value	#	Name	Surname	Value
	Page 543			17	Noah	Smith	2
1	Joseph	Crane	5	18	Mathias	Burgis's wife	1
2	Samuel	Field	4	19	Matthew	Benedict's farm	2
3	Joseph	Field	3	20	Isaac	Elwell	5
4	Uriah	Townsends farm	1		*Page 544*		
5	Benjamin	Townsend	4	21	Elihu	Gage	3
6	Robert	Townsend	4	22	Anthony	Gage	1
7	Isaac	Crosby	3	23	Samuel	Benedict	1
8	Benjamin	Sears	4	24	Jabish	Elwell	3
9	Simeon	Ryder	4	25	Stephen	Rockwell	2
10	Samuel	Bangs	6	26	Ebenezer	Benedict	1
11	Nathaniel	Forster	4	27	John	June	1
12	Seth	Nickerson	6	28	Benjamin	Haviland	7
13	Thomas	Forster	1	29	Ebenezer	Gage	2
14	Peter	Hall	4	30	Joshua	Barnum Jnr:	1
15	John	Field	9	31	Thomas	Baldwin	5
16	James	Birdsall	7	32	Nathan	Birdsall	6

June 1779 South East continued

#	Name	Surname	Value	#	Name	Surname	Value
33	John	Carly	1	81	Jacob	Millard	1
34	Zebedee	Brigs	2	82	Isaac	Haviland	1
35	Seth	Sears	3	83	Caleb	Spencer	1
36	Roger	Havilands farm	4	84	Gilbert	Stedwell	4
37	Samuel	Hall	4	85	William	Field	5
38	Jesse	Lane	2	86	Reuben	Ryder	1
39	Nathan	Green Jnr:	5	87	Zadoc	Ryder	1
40	Benjamin	Sears Jnr:	4	88	John Wheeler	Forster	1
41	John	Haviland	1	89	Elias	Jones	1
42	Shaw	Young	2	90	Silvanus	Gage	1
43	Thomas	Higgins Jnr:	2	91	Solomon	Crane	1
44	William	Stone	1	92	Mary	Rider	1
45	Seth	Nickerson	3		*Page 545*		
46	Daniel	Haviland	7	93	Nathaniel	Forster	2
47	Benjamin	Higgins	2	94	John	Crosby	2
48	Morton	Hall	3	95	Elijah	Doty	2
49	Joseph	Hull	8	96	Eliakum	Barnum	1
50	Berry	Hopkins	3	97	Elnathan	Marsh	2
51	Charles	Cullen	4	98	Benajah	Tubbs	1
52	William	Penny Jnr:	4	99	Rowland	Russel	1
53	Jonathan	Crane	1	100	Jonathan	Paddocks farm	1
54	Thomas	Sears	3	101	Daniel	Gay	1
55	John	Twedy	1	102	Peter	Field	2
56	Azur	Barnum	4	103	Ebenezer	Burlisons widow	1
57	Thomas	Crumstock	4	104	Thomas	Sention	1
58	Rodrick	Mc Kinney's Estate	1	105	Daniel	Burtch	1
59	Nathaniel	Humsted	1	106	Joseph	Burtch	1
60	Mark	Gage	2	107	Joshua	Nickerson	1
61	William	Clinton	1	108	Thomas	Haviland	2
62	Ebenezer	Olmstead	2	109	Zachariah	Hinman	2
63	Thomas	Birdsall	2	110	Silas	Burtch	1
64	Joseph	Arnold	2	111	Ichabud	Olmstead	1
65	John	Elwell	1	112	Elias	Benjamin	2
66	John	Hopkins	1	113	Abraham	Cannon	1
67	William	Murik	1	114	Nathaniel	Knott	1
68	Seth	Sears Jnr:	1	115	Benjamin	Shearmans farm	1
69	Joseph	Field Jnr:	1	116	Thomas	Nickerson	2
70	William	Young	1	117	Thomas	Cheeseman	2
71	Jonathan	Carley	1	118	Edward	Penny	4
72	Edward	Rice's farm	1	119	Thatcher	Hopkins	1
73	Jeremiah	Burgis farm	1	120	Joshua	Hatfield	1
74	Alkanah	Youngs	1	121	Dan and Wait	Ball	1
75	Moses	Gage	1	122	James	Green	1
76	William	Mott	6	123	Joseph	Drake	12
77	George	Burtch	2	124	Allen	Ball	1
78	Ichabud	Goarmans farm	1	125	Thomas	Haviland Jnr:	1
79	John	Starr	1	126	Ezekiel	Osborn	1
80	James	Stedwells farm	1				£300

1786 OR 1787
PHILIPSE'S PRECINCT

at 2/9. pr pound

#	Name	Surname	Value	#	Name	Surname	Value
		Page 566		51	John	Nelson	2
1	William	Davenport	3	52	Richard	Arnold	2
2	Solomon	Cornwell	2	53	Widow	Dennick	1
3	Thomas	Sutton	1	54	William	Dennen	18
4	Mary	Davenport Jnr:	2	55	William	Lancaster	1
5	William	Davenport	1	56	Ezekiel	Avery	1
6	Matthew	Snook	2	57	Mary	Concklin	2
7	Uriah	McKeel	1	58	George	Lane	4
8	Thomas	Davenport	5	59	Isaac	Roads	3
9	Isaac	Davenport	1	60	Nathaniel	Tompkins	2
10	Reuben	Ferris	1	61	Hannah	Knap	6
11	Jonathan	Odell	1	62	William	Dusenbury	5
12	Justus	Nelson	4	63	Jesse	Owen	5
13	Caleb	Nelson	3	64	Andrew	Barton on Drakes farm	2
14	Joshua	Nelson	4				
15	Jacob	Nelson	1	65	—	Drew and Gals on Drakes farm	1
16	Sylvaninus	Haight	3				
17	Peter	Dubois	6	66	Joshua	Tompkins	2
18	Peter	Dubois Jnr:	2	67	Solomon	Smith	1
19	Judah	Crommell	3	68	Matthew	McCabe	2
20	John	Van Ambur	5	69	John	Armstrong	2
21	Gilbert	Bloomer	2	70	Hendrick	Dutcher	2
		Page 567		71	Jonathan	Owen	1
22	Sylvanus	Wood	1	72	Jane	Owen	3
23	Miles	Schoolfield	1	73	John	Berger	1
24	Ephraim	Sc[h]oolfield	1	74	Thomas	Obrian	2
25	John	Haight	7	75	Philip	Steenb[a]ugh	2
26	Stephen	Haight	1	76	Nathaniel	Gager	1
27	William	Wright	3	77	Sibert	Krankheyt	1
28	Gilbert	Weeks	3	78	John	Horton	2
29	Charity	Huested	3	79	Cornelius	Tompkins	3
30	Joseph	Huested	6	80	Moses	Dusenbury	3
31	Paul	Sparling	1	81	Isaac	Mead	2
32	Benjamin	Bloomer	3	82	James	Sherwood	2
33	Maurice	Smith	2	83	Isaac	Penoyer	1
34	Joshua	Meed	3	84	John	Avery	1
35	Gilbert	Budd	3	85	Richard	Denny	3
36	James	Yeomans	1	86	Israel	Kangs	4
37	Elijah	Budd	3	87	William	Colegrove	2
38	Thomas	Sarls	1	88	Oliver	Odle	2
39	John	Warren	1	89	John	McDaniel	1
40	William	Sarls	3	90	Abraham	Post	3
41	Banjamin	Rogers	4			*Page 568*	
42	Richard	Hopper	1	91	John	Drake	3
43	Christopher	Fowler	2	92	Francis	Strong on Nortons Place	2
44	Daniel	Haight	1				
45	Abraham	Baker	1	93	Charles	Post	1
46	Tanier	Warren	1	94	William	Mariner	1
47	Edward	Meeks	1	95	Daniel	DeLavans farm	1
48	John	Meeks	6	96	Gilbert	Oakley	2
49	Thomas	Oakley	2	97	Judge	Platts farm	1
50	James	Craft	1	98	Ezekiel	Gee	3

1786 or 1787 Philipse's continued

	Name	Surname	Value
99	John Barton	on Drakes farm	1
100	John	Likely	3
101	James Askel	on Swartwouts farm	1
102	Thomas	Hills	1
103	Jeremiah	Concklin	2
104	William	White	2
105	Abraham	Craft	1
106	James	Jacocks	1
107	Peter	Bell	2
108	John	Smith	2
109	John	Heley	1
110	John	Goldsilluk	2
111	Peter	Berger	2
112	Joshua	Horton	5
113	Thomas	Bashford	2
114	Timothy	Oakley	1
115	Henry	Post	2
116	Samuel	Smith	2
117	—	Chapman	1
118	Phinemon	Smith	1
119	Daniel	Bugbee	3
120	David	Hinyon	1
121	Rueben	Tompkins	2
122	Joseph	Bard	1
123	Richard	Saterly	1
124	John	Christian	1
125	Nathan	Lane Jnr:	1
126	Nathan	Lane Sen:	3
127	Jacob	Armstrong	1
128	John	Snock	1
129	James	Nelson	2
130	Amos	Odle	1
131	Squire	Baker	1
132	Henry	Dergey	1
133	Richard	Christian	1
134	Charles	Christian	1
135	Peter	Royal	2
136	Joseph	Horton	2
137	John	Russel	1
138	John	Barrit	1

	Name	Surname	Value
139	James	Perry	1
140	Abraham	Lockwood	1
141	Gabriel	Knapp	2
142	Isaiah	Jacocks	1
143	Sylvanus	Lockwood	1
144	Isaac	Roads	3
145	Titus	Travis	2
146	Israel	Lockwood	2
147	Cornelius	Tompkins Jnr:	2
148	Cornelius	Hills	3
149	Edward	Eldridge, on Drake's farm	1
150	John	Budd Sen:	2
151	Elisha	Barton on Drakes farm	1
152	Sylvanus	Covert	1
153	John	Denny	1
154	Moses	Dusenbury Jnr:	2
155	William	Dusenbury Jnr: son of Moses	1
156	Jacob	Reed	3
157	Gilbert	Lockwood	2
158	William	Lane	1

Page 569

	Name	Surname	Value
159	William	Dotton	1
160	Eliazer	Heeley	1
161	Squire	Wakeman	2
162	Abraham	Smith	1
163	William	Dusenbury Jnr:	1
164	James	Smith	1
165	William	Christian	1
166	Sylvanus	Tompkins	1
167	Isaac	Odle	2
168	John	Ager	1
169	Jacob	Armstrong	1
170	Joseph	Broadwick	2
171	Rueben	Shaw on Brinkerhoff farm	1
172	Richard	Christian	1
173	Philip	Pelton's farm	1
			£352

Summary of South Dutchess Tax Lists 1741-1779

Date	Households	Assessed Value £	Tax £.s.d.
Feb 1740/1	47	201	1.13.6
Feb 1741/2	76	267	5.16.9.3
Feb 1742/3	95	340	5.13.4
Feb 1743/4	128	457	8.11.4.2
Feb 1744/5	156	540	19.13.9.0
Feb 1745/6	205	658*	26.0.11.0
Feb 1746/7	213	744	12.8.0.0
June 1747	217	742	18.11.0.0
June 1748	260	791	4.12.1.2
Feb 1753	355	730	9.2.6
June 1753	352	778	32.8.4
Feb 1754	358	787	11.9.6.2
June 1754	369	793	33.0.10
Feb 1755	380	809	13.9.8
June 1755	391	840	63.0.0.
Feb 1756	388	824	13.14.8
June 1756	387	831	69.5.0
Feb 1757	392	832	10.8.0
June 1757	389	812	81.4.8
Feb 1758	454	873	25.9.3
June 1758	448	898	89.16.0
Feb 1759	539	1021	70.3.10½
June 1759	512	984	172.4.0
Feb 1760	552	1045	126.5.4
June 1760	532	994	335.9.6
Feb 1761	556	1031*	141.15.2
June 1761	543	981*	261.12.0
Feb 1762	522	958	107.15.5
June 1762	515	1072*	268.0.0
Feb 1763	556	1134*	99.4.0
June 1763	545	1128*	286.14.0
June 1764		1155	308.0.0
June 1765	556	1099*	251.17.1
June 1766	588	1142	314.1.0
June 1767	546	1112*	305.16.0
June 1768	567	1110*	185.0.0
June 1769	584	1119*	209.16.3
June 1770	600	1205*	241.0.0
June 1771	688	1377	235.4.9

Date	Households	Assessed Value £	Tax £.s.d.
Philipse			
June 1772	138	328*	94.6.0
June 1773	159	310*	50.7.6
June 1774	146	344	37.5.4
June 1775	158	370	
June 1777		377	
June 1778	168	367	
June 1779	164	367	293.12.0
Fredricksburgh			
June 1772	456	835*	288.15.5
June 1773	487	934*	171.4.8
June 1774	550	1029*	308.14.0
June 1775	569	1039*	173.3.4
June 1777		1050	
June 1778	562	1096	
June 1779	559	1155*	3465.0.0
SouthEast			
June 1772	132	283*	94.6.8
June 1773	129	294*	78.8.0
June 1774	118	284	53.5.0
June 1775	142	305	
June 1777		294	
June 1778	128	301	
June 1779	126	300	705.0.0

This list summarizes the number of households on each list, the total assessed value, and the tax assessed in £ (pounds), s (shillings), and d (pence).

The asterisk (*) identifies those aggregate assessed values that differ from the mathmatical totals of the detail values entered in the tax book. These discrepancies of £2 to £5 may result from transcription errors by the scribe or from changes made after the list was totaled by the assessor.

Tax lists for June 1764 and June 1777 were not entered into the Supervisor's Record; however, the total assessed values were included in annual summaries, and so appear above.

TENANT LISTS

The following tenant lists contain information extracted from two sources: the memorial of Beverly Robinson in the American Loyalist Claims originally filed with the Public Records Office in England, and Philipse family records in the manuscript collections of Columbia University in New York. The information included herein comes only from lists that provide the farm lot numbers.

The National Archives of the United Kingdom houses the original volumes of American Loyalist Claims, Series I and II (AO 12 and AO 13).[1] Beverly Robinson provided tenant lists for his Lots 1, 4, and 7 as evidence of his American losses.[2] Roger Morris (proprietor of Lots 3, 5, and 9), also a loyalist, did not provide tenant lists in his claim, reporting that his records were with his agent in New York.[3] Philip Philipse's heirs (proprietors of Lots 2, 6, and 8) were not loyalists and so, filed no claim. The Loyalist files and lists contain additional information, including some lease terms, lists of debts, and Loyalist tenant testimonies. The following lists contain the original spelling of all names.[4]

The tenant list for Lot 8 comes from the Philipse-Gouverneur family papers in the manuscript collection at Columbia University.[5]

See Appendix C for tenants of Lot 6 in 1762 and maps of farm lot locations for Lots 4, 6, 7, and 8. Early tenants of the Oblong can be found in Pelletreau's history of Putnam County.[6] Land purchasers after the Revolution for Lots 3, 4, 5, 7, and 9, and some Oblong parcels can be found in Ruddock's book on the loyalist properties confiscated and sold by the State of New York.[7]

---

1. Images available at Ancestry.com: go to Search>Card Catalog>UK, American Loyalist Claims, 1776-1835. These images were taken from microfilm which is available at the New York Public Library.
2. American Loyalist Claims Series 1, AO 12 piece 021: Evidence, New York, 1785-1786, Memorial of Beverly Robinson, pp. 77-79 (*Ancestry.com*, UK, American Loyalist Claims, 1776-1835, imageID=40939_307348-00328 to 00330); and American Loyalist Claims Series 2, AO 13 piece 116: Temporary Assistance N-R, New York, Memorial of Beverly Robinson pp. 571-574 (*Ancestry.com* UK, American Loyalist Claims, 1776-1835 imageID=40939_307033-00832 to 00834)
3. American Loyalist Claims Series 1, AO 12 piece 021, Memorial of Roger Morris p. 97 (*Ancestry.com*, UK, American Loyalist Claims, 1776-1835, imageID=40939_307348-00348).
4. See also Frederick C Haacker, *Early Settlers of Putnam County and Cortlandt Manor, New York*. (Typescript: author, 1954) pp. 5-10. His interpretations of the handwriting differ somewhat from mine, and he used only one set of lists; two are provided herein.
5. *Philipse – Gouverneur family papers, [ca. 1653]-1874*, Rare Book and Manuscript Library, Columbia University Library (New York City), MS#0994.
6. William S. Pelletreau, *History of Putnam County, New York: with Biographical Sketches of its Prominent Men* (Philadelphia: W.W. Preston, 1886), facing p. 17.
7. William T. Ruddock, *Confiscated Properties of Philipse Highland Patent, Putnam County, New York 1780-1785* (Westminster, Md: Heritage, 2012). For more loyalist lands see Dutchess County Deeds v. 8.

Other Information on the Robinson and Morris Lots

In the 17–18 December 1785 Memorial of Beverly Robinson, he testified to the following (all quotes, extracted from the record).[8]

> on Lot No. 1 there were 17 Tenants who rented 3230 Acres of Land for which they paid 135.15 currency Rent, besides which he [Robinson] had a Farm of 1500 Acres in his own Hands .... The remaining 5254 acres were untenanted. Every man had his Farm House & many of them Orchards.
>
> in Lot No. 4 settd. by 75 Tenants most of them under short Leases, in general very good Farms, great part of them lying in Peeks Kill Hollow & from 4 to 12 miles from Peeks Kill Landing on Hudson's River to which there is good Roads. ... There were 20 Tenants over & above those he has mentioned but not having granted them Regular Leases or entered them in his Rent Book he did not think it right to include them in his List of Tenants.
>
> Lot No. 7. On this Lot there were 54 Tenants who rented 9521 Acres, 599 Acres further part were wood Lots & on that account he considers them as being more Valuable than if settled 494 Acres which had been let to Alexr. Grant, he gave Grant £1100 to buy out his Lease ... He says this Lot separately considered is the most valuable of all.

In the 19 December 1785 Memorial of Roger Morris, he testified to the following (all quotes, extracted from the record).[9]

> As to Lot No. 3 – On this Lot Col Morris had 12 Tenants none of whom excepting one had Leases – Their Farms were not within any specific Boundaries. He is ignorant of the number of Acres there were in culture. The great advantage of it in point of Value was the Timber on it. ... He says he never was upon this Lot to examine it. He is utterly incapable of saying how much was in cultivation. He never sold any of this Lot nor made any advantage from the Timber. ... The Farms had Houses and Barns upon them.
>
> As to Lot No. 5 – On this Lot he believes there were 91 Tenants who were chiefly under Lease. ... The whole of this Lot was surveyed, but only between 16 and 17,000 acres laid out in particular Farms. ... The Tenants held Farms of from 100 to 4 and 500 Acres in Extent. He can't speak to the state of the Buildings. some very good, some indifferent. Says the same as to the payment of Rents, some were very regular, some otherwise.
>
> As to Lot No. 9. The number of Ten[an]ts on this Lot were 53 The Rent [£]305.17. ... This was all surveyed and mostly parted out into Farms. The Rents were not universally regulated by the Number of acres in each Farm. The Buildings were much in the same state as the former Lots. With respect to the value he says that some parts of the Estate were probably worth nothing others worth much more than he has charged it at.

---

8. American Loyalist Claims Series 1, AO 12 piece 021, Memorial of Beverly Robinson, pp. 76-77, 80-81.
9. American Loyalist Claims Series 1, AO 12 piece 021, Memorial of Roger Morris p. 97.

Tenant List Lot Number 1 - 1768 and 1777

American Loyalist Claims - Public Record Office, London

Rent Roll of Colonel Beverley Robinsons Estate in the County of Dutchess in New York in North America

A.O.13 Series II, piece 116 Temporary Assistance, page 574

Number of farm on Lot (No 1)	Tenants Names on Lot (No 1) in Philips's Precinct	no. of Acres in Each farm by Estimate	Rent pr Annum	Amt of Rent due from Each Tenant to the 1st May 1777
1	Thomas Williamson	250	3.0.0	2.17.6
2	Ely Nelson	250	2.10.0	12.17.0
3	Richd: Arnold	200	2.0.0	2.0.0
4	Hezekiah Avery	175	1.10.0	5.17.9
5	Jacob Mandivill	500	5.0.0	5.0.0
6	Richd Hopper	250	2.10.0	21.17.9
7	Chrisr: Fowler	300	2.15.0	51.18.6
8	David Lancaster	150	5.0.0	
9	Peter Warren	200	5.0.0	5.0.0
10	Peter Snoke	50	6.0.0	16.0.0
11	Abigal Arkles	175	1.10.0	
12	John Meeks	300	3.0.0	3.0.0
13	Jona: Owen	200	25.0.0	50.0.0
14	Isaac Garrison	50	6.0.0	68.0.0
15	John Cornwell	30	5.0.0	5.0.0
16	Sylvanus Haight	150	50.0.0	
17	Albert Swin	(a)	8.0.0	8.0.0
	My own Farm	1500		
		4730	£ 135.15.	£ 257.9.6

unsettled in this Lot 5254

(a) House & Garden

A.O.12 Series I, piece 021, page 77 (stamped), page 153 (pen)

Lot No 1	Tenants Names	Rents per Annum			Old Tenants before 1768
		in 1755 (from memory) £ s	1 May 1768 (from rent book)	1 May 1777	
1	Tho. Williamson	1.10	3.00	3.00	Saml. Moore
2	Ely Nelson	1.10	2.10	2.10	Jacobus Krankhite
3	Ricd. Arnold	1.10	2.00	2.00	Obediah Tomkins
4	Hezekiah Avery	1.10	1.10	1.10	John Avery settld. in 62
5	Jacob Mandiville	5.00	5.	5.00	1762 Jacob Mandiville
6	Richd. Hopper	1.10	1.10	2.10	
7	Christr. Fowler	2.15	2.15	2.15	Widow Trahill
8	Peter Snook	0.0	0.00	8.00	Settld. in 1771
9	Peter Warren	1.10	3.00	5.00	Henry Stanley
10	Widow Arkles	1.10	1.10	1.10	John Arkles
11	John Meckes	2.00	3.00	3.00	
12	Jona. Owen	5.00	5.00	25.0	Ebenzr. Jones
13	Isaac Garrisson	1.10	1.10	6.00	John Gee
14	David Lancaster			5.00	Lately Settled
15	John Cornwall			5.00	Settled in 1774
16	Sylv. Haight		50.0	50.0	My Mills
17	Albert Swim			8.00	Settled in 1769
18	My own Farm	2.00			Christ. Fowler
£		26.15	82.5	135.15	

TENANT LISTS 1768-1777

TENANT LIST LOT NUMBER 4 - 1768 and 1777

American Loyalist Claims - Public Record Office, London

Rent Roll of Colonel Beverley Robinsons Estate in the County of Dutchess in New York in North America

Number of farms on Lot (No 4)	Tenants Names on Lot (No 4) in Philips's Precinct	no. of Acres in Each farm by Estimation	Rent pr Annum	Amt of Rent due from Each Tenant to the 1st May 1777	Tenants Names	Lot No 4	Rents per Annum			Old Tenants before 1768
							in 1755 (from memory) £ s	1 May 1768 (from rent book)	1 May 1777	
1	Joseph Smith	55	5.0.0	31.12.9	Jos: Smith	1	2.0.0	3.0.0	5.0.0	Ezeke. Meade
2	John Hall	158	4.15.0		John Hall	2	3.0.0	4.15.0	4.15.0	Joseph Meade
3	Nathan Lane	162	5.0.0	4.15.6	Nathan Lane	3	3.10.0	4.17.0	5.0.0	Jos: Lane
4	Isaac Rhodes	398	9.0.0	50.17.3	Isaac Rhodes	4	5.0.0	9.0.0	9.0.0	Isaac Rhodes
5	John Avery	168	5.0.0	15.0.6	John Avery	5	3.0.0	5.0.0	5.0.0	Abm. Smith
6	Solomon Smith	167	5.0.0	4.6.0	Solomon Smith	6	2.10.0	5.0.0	5.0.0	
7	Elijah Dingee	96	4.0.0	10.0.0	Elij: Dingee	7	2.0.0	3.0.0	4.0.0	John How
8	Hannah Knap	255	7.13.0	16.0.4	Hannah Knap	8	4.0.0	7.13.0	7.13.0	Gabriel Knap
9	George Lane	228	6.17.0	6.17.0	Geo: Lane	9	3.10.0	6.17.0	6.17.0	Nathan Lane
10	Saml: Cromwell	239	5.0.0	10.0.0	Samuel Cromwell	10	2.0.0	5.0.0	5.0.0	Thos. Cromwell
11	Timy: Conklin	370	6.5.0	10.16.2	Timothy Conklin	11	2.10.0	6.5.0	6.5.0	Timy. Conklin
12	Wm: Dusenberry	404	9.0.0	79.0.6	Wm: Dusenberry	12	4.0.0	9.0.0	9.0.0	Richd. Curry
	Nathl: Jager		3.0.0	8.19.2	Nathll. Jager			3.0.0	3.0.0	*part farm No. 12*
13	Nathl: Tomkins	287	7.10.0	15.0.0	Nathl. Tomkins	13	3.10.0	7.10.0	7.10.0	Richd. Curry
14	Cors: Tomkins	245	7.10.0	22.10.0	Cors. Tomkins	14	3.10.0	7.10.0	7.10.0	do.
15	Moses Dusenberry	273	8.4.0	50.7.6	Moses Dusenberry	15	4.0.0	8.4.0	8.4.0	Gilbert Drew
16	Daniel Willsie	130	4.0.0	8.0.0	Danl. Wilsie	16		4.0.0	4.0.0	Stepn. Conklin
17	William Oakly	212	4.0.0	4.0.0	Willm. Oakley	17		4.0.0	4.0.0	Benj. Odell
18	Stephen Conklin	198	4.10.0	19.5.7	Stepn. Conklin	18	2.10.0	4.10.0	4.10.0	Saml. Drake Senr.
19	Benj: Odell	117	3.10.0	11.7.6	Benj. Odell	19	2.0.0	3.10.0	0.3.10	
20	Uriah Drake	188	5.6.0	20.12.0	Uriah Drake	20	2.0.0	5.0.0	5.6.0	

A.O.13 Series II, piece 116 Temp. Assistance, page 572-3

A.O.12 Series I, piece 021, New York, page 77-78 (stamped) page 153-5 (pen)

Tenant List Lot Number 4 - 1768 and 1777 continued

#	Name	Acres	£.s.d	Name	£.s.d	£.s.d	Name
21	Henry Wilsie	85	4.0.0	8.0.0	Henry Willsie	2.0.0	4.0.0	Stepn Tomkins
22	Peter Drake	85	3.6.0	17.4.9	Peter Drake	1.10.0	3.6.0	John Drake
22	Peter Drake	85	3.6.0	17.4.9	Peter Drake	1.10.0	3.6.0	John Drake
23	Saml Drake	47	7.4.0	7.4.0	Sam. Drake Junr.	2.0.0	7.4.0	Saml. Drake Senr.
24	Wm: Drake	435	6.0.0	20.2.5	Wm. Drake &	10.0.0	10.0.0	Willm. Drake
	Jos: Sherwood		4.0.0	20.0.0	Jor. Sherwood			
25	Danl: Bugbee	223	6.14.0	20.2.0	Danl. Bugbee	3.0.0	6.14.0	Bryaly Bassford
26	John Barger	263	1.2.0	2.4.0	John Barger		1.2.0	Lately Settd.
27	Thos: Bryant	145	1.0.0	1.19.0	Thos. Bryant		1.0.0	do.
28	Titus Travis	115	3.10.0	16.16.0	Titus Travis	2.0.0	3.10.0	Henry Jones
29	Abm: Post	256	7.14.0	7.14.0	Abm. Post	3.0.0	7.14.0	Lewis Jones
30	Joshua Tomkins	154	4.12.0	13.16.0	Josa. Tomkins	2.10.0	4.12.0	Josa Tomkins
31	John Sherwood	161	4.17.0	4.17.0	John Sherwood	2.0.0	4.17.0	Elijh. Horton
32	Sherwood & Smith	253	7.10.0	7.11.8	Sherwood & Powers	2.10.0	7.10.0	Obida. Horton
33	Reuben Drake	184	5.12.0	5.12.0	Reuben Drake	2.0.0	5.12.0	John Sherwood
34	Elisha Lamoreaux	133	4.0.0	8.0.0	Elisha Lamoreaux	1.10.0	4.0.0	Andw. Barger Junr.
35	Andrew Barger	197	6.0.0	42.0.0	Andw. Barger Senr.	3.0.0	6.0.0	Andw. Berger Senr. Jer. Cromton formerly
36	Gabriel Archer	175	6.0.0	6.0.0	Gabl. Archer	3.0.0	5.5.0	G Lane
37	Peter Bell	215	6.0.0	10.7.3	Peter Bell	3.10.0	6.10.0	Wm. Lane
38	Sibert Crankhite Junr:	296	2.10.0	2.10.0	Sibert A Crankhite	2.10.0	2.10.0	Sib. A Crankhite
39	Anty: Youmans	194	3.15.0	25.0.0	Anth. Youmans		3.15.0	Lately Settd.
40	Post & Odell	252	7.0.0	20.12.6	Post & Oddell	2.10.0	7.0.0	John Jones
41	Wm: Van Tassell	123	6.10.0	32.10.0	Will Van Tassells	2.0.0	6.10.0	John Van Tassells
42	John Lickley	129	6.9.0	6.9.0	John Lickley	1.10.0	6.9.0	Isaac Horton Jnr.
43	Jonan: Owen	168	5.0.0	6.14.8	Jonn. Owen	2.0.0	5.0.0	Jedidiah Owen
44	Peter Ricky	94	3.0.0	49.0.0	Peter Ricky	2.0.0	3.0.0	Jacobus Crankhite
45	ditto	189	5.10.0		ditto	2.10.0	5.10.0	Isaac Horton
46	Jeremiah McCurdy	175	7.0.	28.0.0	Jerm: McCudny		7.0.0	Joseph Darby
47	Hamson & Pottter	290	10.0.0	20.0.0	Caleb Hanson	5.0.0	5.0.0	Willm. Gee Senr.
					Rob: Potter		5.0.0	Do.
48	Wm: Gee Junr:	221	6.10.0	6.10.0	Will. Gee Jnr.	2.0.0	6.10.0	Will Gee Jnr.

TENANT LISTS 1768-1777

Tenant List Lot Number 4 - 1768 and 1777 continued

Number of farms on Lot (No 4)	Tenants Names on Lot (No 4) in Philips's Precinct	no. of Acres in Each farm by Estimation	Rent pr Annum	Amt of Rent due from Each Tenant to the 1st May 1777	Tenants Names	Lot No 4	Rents per Annum			Old Tenants before 1768
							in 1755 (from memory) £ s	1 May 1768 (from rent book)	1 May 1777	
49	Mathew McCabe	241	4.5.0	15.2.7	Math. McCabe	49	2.0.0	4.5.0	4.5.0	Mathw. McCabe
50	Anty: Field	508	9.0.0	36.0.0	Anthy. Field	50	4.0.0	9.0.0	9.0.0	Anthy. Field
51	Josa: Lamoreaux	273	2.10.0	12.6.3	Josha. Lamoriaux	51	1.10.0	2.10.0	2.10.0	Jas. Lamoriaux
52	John Armstrong	280	3.15.0	21.7.9	John Armstrong	52	2.0.0	3.15.0	3.15.0	Jos. Armstrong
	laid out by Survey	10909	£ 291.15	901.0.7						
farms not Surveyed, no. of acres by Estimation:										
53	Thomas Hills	100	2.0.0	10.0.0	Thos. Hills	53		2.0.0	2.0.0	Edw. Turner lately settd.
54	Joseph Bard	200	3.0.0	6.0.0	Joseph Bard	54		2.0.0	3.0.0	Cors. Gee lately settd.
55	Oliver Odell	200	3.0.0	58.10.0	Oliver Odell	55	2.0.0	3.0.0	3.0.0	Oliver Odell
56	Reuben Tomkins	150	3.0.0	4.0.0	Reuben Tomkins	56		2.0.0	3.0.0	Israel Taylor
57	Robt: & Gilbert Oakly	250	3.0.0	6.0.0	Robt. & Gilbt Oakly	57	2.0.0	3.0.0	3.0.0	Elisha Oakly
58	Saml: Youmans	200	3.0.0	45.0.0	Saml Youmans	58	2.0.0	3.0.0	3.0.0	Steph. Sheperdson
59	Richd: Saterly	150	3.0.0	48.0.0	Richd. Saterly	59	2.0.0	3.0.0	3.0.0	Rd. Slaterley
60	Jonn: Brundage	100	3.0.0	6.0.0	Jona. Brundage	60		3.0.0	3.0.0	Lately Settled
61	John McDonald	150	2.10.0		John McDonald	61		2.0.0	2.10.0	Richd. Christean
62	James Youmans	200	2.10.0	30.0.0	James Youmans	62		2.10.0	2.10.0	Lately Settled
63	Jon: & Bassil Bartow	300	4.0.0	48.0.0	Jon & Bassil Barton	63		4.0.0	4.0.0	J& Bas. Barton
64	Widow Bueys	150	3.0.0	15.0.0	Widow Buys	64		3.0.0	3.0.0	Widw. Buys
65	Philip Steanbaugh	150	3.0.0	23.16.0	Philip Steanbaugh	65			3.0.0	Phil Steanbaugh
66	Wm: Colegrove	100	3.0.0	10.0.0	Will: Colegrove	66			3.0.0	Lately Settled
67	Richd: Christean	100	2.0.0		Ricd. Christean	67			2.0.0	Do.
68	Cors: Tomkins	150	3.0.0	6.0.0	Cors. Tomkins	68			3.0.0	Do.
69	Richd: Denny	200	3.0.0	9.0.0	Richd Denny Jr.	69			3.0.0	Do.
70	John Winn	300	3.0.0	9.0.0	John Winn	70			3.0.0	Do.
71	John Still Purdy	150	3.0.0	40.0.0	John Still Purdy	71			3.0.0	Do.

Tenant List Lot Number 4 - 1768 and 1777 continued

72	Keirser & Sparling	150	3.0.0		6.0.0	Kierser & Spauling	72		3.0.0
73	John Langdon Junr:	150	2.0.0		4.0.0	John Langdon	73	2.0.0	2.0.0
74	Joseph Sherwood	15	2.0.0			Joseph Sherwood	74		2.0.0
		14659	£ 353.15		1285.6.7			304.9	353.15
	unsettled Lands	22341						£ 131.1	

Do.
Thos. Woodard
lately Settd.

Tenants in possession but not in rent books:

John Youmans	100	3.0.0
William White	50	1.10.0
Roger Tomkins	100	3.0.0
Saml. Jenkins	150	2.0.0
Will: Shaw	200	0.10.0
Abm. Birdsall	140	4.4.0
John Ager	100	3.0.0
Robt. Tomkins	150	2.0.0
David Hennion	50	1.10.0
Gabl. Kings	150	4.10.0
Lazarius Light	200	
David Haree	100	
John Brinkerhofe	300	6.0.0
Elwin Smith	100	3.0.0
John Simkin	150	3.0.0
Jediah Frost	100	3.0.0
Saml. Brewer	150	3.0.0
Jona. Pine	200	6.0.0
John Wood	100	3.0.0
Geo: Scot	150	3.10.0
	2740	

TENANT LIST LOT NUMBER 7 - 1768 and 1777
American Loyalist Claims - Public Record Office, London

Rent Roll of Colonel Beverley Robinsons Estate in the County of Dutchess in New York in North America

Number of farms on Lot (No 7)	Tenants Names on Lot (No 7) in Philips's Precinct	no. of Acres in Each farm by Estimation	Rent pr Annum	Amt of Rent due from Each Tenant to the 1st May 1777	Tenants Names	Lot No 7	Rents per Annum			Old Tenants before 1768
							in 1755 (from memory) £ s	1 May 1768 (from rent book)	1 May 1777	
1	sold to	20								
2	Duncan Campbell									
3	Isaac Haviland	119	6.0.0	12.7.0	Isaac Haviland	3	3.0.0	6.0.6	6.0.0	Edwd. Hall
4	Benjm: Chase 174 acs of 10h sold 4	170	20.0.0	54.8.0	Benjm. Chase	4	4.0.0	16.0.0	20.0.0	Tho Corbin
5	Benjm: Chase	229	10.0.0		Do.	5	3.0.0	10.0.	10.0.0	Henry Gray
6	Archd: Campbell	440	20.0.0	16.2.4	Archd. Campbell	6	10.0.0	20.0.0	20.0.0	Moses & Amos Northrup
7	(Bev: Robinson)	150				7	5.0.0			Chrisn. Dickinson
8	ditto	160			Alexander Grant	9	5.0.0	24.0.0	100.0.0	Benjm. Gifford
9	ditto	184				10	5.0.0			James Calkins
8	Dennis Wright	578	45.4.0	111.15.8	Dennis Wright	8	5.0.0	8.0.0	48.4.0	Malh. Hatch
	James Calkins		3.0.0	10.3.0	James Calkins Junr.					
11	David Akin	300	17.0.0	4.19.11	David Akin	11	3.0.0	10.0.0	17.0.0	Widow Porter
12	Barns Hatfield	203	10.0.0	20.0.0	Barnes Hatfield	12	3.0.0	10.0.0	10.0.0	Dd. Akins, lease out 1786
13	Wm: Calkins	195	8.0.0	47.18.8	Wm. Calkins	13	2.0.0	8.0.0	13.0.0	Jos. Barlow
	Josiah Akin		5.0.0	5.0.0	Joseph Akins					
14	Thos: Menzies	336	18.0.0		Thos. Menzies	14	2.10.0	18.0.0		Noah Smith
15	ditto	255	12.0.0	30.0.0	Do.	15	5.0.0	12.0.0	12.0.0	John Calkins
16	Alexd: McDonald	338	16.0.0	30.8.3	Alex. McDonald	16	5.0.0	16.0.0	16.0.0	Wm. Gray
17	Jedediah Willis	195	6.0.0	15.12.0	Jedediah Willis	17	2.0.0	6.0.0	6.0.0	Elijah Hungerford
18	John Robinson	177	10.0.0	58.18.0	John Robinson	18	2.0.0	12.0.0	10.0.0	Micael Newland
19	John McArther	262	20.0.0	14.1.11	John McArther	19	2.0.0	9.0.0	10.0.0	Benjm. Burch
20					ditto	20	2.0.0	4.10.0	10.0.0	Timothy Clawson

A.O.13 Series II, piece 116 Temp. Assistance, page 571-2

A.O.12 Series I, piece 021, New York, page 78-79 (stamped) page 155-7 (pen)

Tenant List Lot Number 7 - 1768 and 1777 continued

Lot	Name				Lot				Name
21	Timy: Hatch	200	4.16.0	4.16.0	21	2.0.0	4.16.0		Steps. Hull
22	Ephraim Jones	119	4.0.0	20.15.6	22	2.0.0	4.0.0		-- Ludington
23	Abm: Birdsall	94	5.0.0	5.0.0	23	1.10.0	5.0.0		Fras. Baker
	Ely Wood		14.0.0	14.0.0					
24	Joseph Teed	437	12.0.0	24.0.0	24	5.0.0	10.0.	34.0.0	Benjm. Perry
25	Robert Watts		8.0.0	7.14.6	25				
26	David Heacocks	118	10.0.0	30.0.0	26	2.10.0	10.0.0	10.0.0	
27	Roswell Willcox	161	8.8.0	16.16.0	27	3.0.0	6.8.0	8.8.0	Josiah Willcox
28	Jacob Philips	115	20.0.0	55.6.9	28	3.0.0	4.16.0	20.0.0	Saml Calkins
29	James Covey	85½	6.0.0	12.0.0	29	2.0.0	6.0.0	6.0.0	Jas. Covey Senr.
30	David Nash	128	8.0.0	24.0.0	30	2.0.0	7.15.0	8.0.0	John Clauson
31	Robert Moony	146	6.0.0	18.0.0	31	2.10.0	6.0.0	6.0.0	Saml Utter
32	William Brady	105	6.0.0		32	2.0.0	4.16.0	6.0.0	Reuben Close
33	ditto	115	18.0.0	66.14.0	33	2.10.0	4.16.0	18.0.0	Abm. Hodge
34	Jona: Burch the 4th	112	15.0.0	16.2.2	34	1.10.0	3.0.0	15.0.0	Jonan. Burch the Widw.
35	Simeon Purdy	74	3.0.0	24.0.0	35	1.10.0	3.0.0	3.0.0	Obed. Beardsley
36	David Close	159	3.12.0	7.4.0	36	1.10.0	2.16.0	3.12.0	John Haynes
37	Widow Prindle	81	6.0.0		37	2.0.0	6.0.0	6.0.0	Elisha Ludington
part 38	(intended for a Glebe)	90			38	1.10.0	5.0.0	16.0.0	John Bogardus
	Lamuel Wilmot		16.0.0						Benj. Hatch
									pt of farm No. 33&[38]
39	John Newbery	125	3.12.0	3.12.0	39	1.10.0	2.16.0	3.12.0	John Newbery
40	John Burch	119	4.0.0	8.0.0	40	2.0.0	4.0.0	4.0.0	John Burch Senr.
41	Peter Scot	131	3.18.0	11.14.0	41	3.0.0	3.0.0	3.18.0	Isaac Hodge
42	David Dibble	122	4.0.0	9.15.0	42	2.0.0	3.0.0	4.0.0	Willm. Day
43	David Burch	122	3.10.0	14.0.0	43	1.10.0	3.10.0	3.10.0	David Burch
44	Jona: Burch	109	4.0.0	4.0.0	44	2.0.0	4.0.0	4.0.0	Jonath. Burch
45/46	Daniel Chase	194	9.14.0	14.2.0	45/46	3.0.0	9.14.0	9.14.0	Lionel Udall
47	Daniel Chase Junr:	135	20.0.0	40.0.0	47	3.0.0	5.0.0	20.0.0	Elihu Wing
48	John Terrill	338	22.12.0	45.4.0	48	3.0.0	6.0.0	22.12.0	Gideon Prindle
49	Malcom Morison	130	40.0.0	31.5.0	49	4.0.0	4.0.0	40.0.0	Abm.Hodge
50	Alexd: Kidd	111	7.0.0	14.0.0	50	2.10.0	7.0.0	7.0.0	Thos. Maggatt

Tenant List Lot Number 7 - 1768 and 1777 continued

Number of farms on Lot (No 7)	Tenants Names on Lot (No 7) in Philips's Precinct	no. of Acres in Each farm by Estimation	Rent pr Annum	Amt of Rent due from Each Tenant to the 1st May 1777		Lot No 7	Tenants Names	Rents per Annum			Old Tenants before 1768
								in 1755 (from memory) £ s	1 May 1768 (from rent book)	1 May 1777	
51	Malcom Morison	113	20.0.0	40.0.		51	Malcom Morison	2.10.0	5.0.0	20.0.0	Chas. Beardsley
52	Mathew Patterson	155	40.0.0	58.1.2		52	Math. Patterson	3.0.0	5.12.0	40.0.0	Saml Towner Senr.
53	Daniel Babbit	87	4.12.0	4.12.0		53	Danl. Babbitt	2.0.0	3.12.0	4.12.0	Elijah Calkins
54/55	John Kent	293	10.0.0	17.13.0		54/55	John Kent	3.0.0	7.0.0	10.0.0	Jehiel Beardsley
56	Elijah Oakly	264	10.0.0	27.1.8		56	Elijah Oakley	3.0.0	5.16.0	10.0.0	Do.
57	Alexd: Menzies	340	12.0.0	55.8.9		57	Alex. Menzies	3.0.0	12.0.0	12.0.0	Saml. Goodspeed
58	Asa Haynes	271	20.0.0	5.7.2		58	Asa Haynes	2.0.0	20.0.0	20.0.0	Joseph Craw
59	William Palmer	189	10.0.0			59	Wm. Palmer	3.0.0	10.0.0	10.0.0	Will Palmer
60	Nathl: Corsby	208	8.0.0	18.12.0		60	Nathan Crosby	2.10.0	8.0.0	8.0.0	Ebenr. Craw
61	Saml: Towner	269	10.16.0	11.8.6		61	Sam: Towner Jnr.	3.0.0	8.8.0	10.16.0	Simon Dakin
62	(wood lot)	95									
63	(wood lot)	504									
		11054	£667.14	1211.19				161.0.0	404.15	767.14	

Note: Generally speaking, tenants of Lot 7 farm lots 1 through 7, 40 through 47, and half of 48 were in Beekman's Precinct (1768 and prior) or Pawlings Precinct (from 1769 on). These lots were located in the Beekman Gore. The rest of the Lot 7 farm lots were in the South Precinct through 1771, then in Fredricksburgh Precinct or Frederick's Town until 1795, then in Franklin, which later became Patterson.

Tenant List Lot Number 8 - 1768 and Prior
A List of Tenants on Lott no./8/ Belonging to Mrs. Margret Philipse

No.	no. of acres	Tenants in possession at the time the farms were surveyed and run out	Tenants in Possession the 1st May 1768	Remarks	Rent pr Annum £.S.D.
1	65	Wm Rableyea	James Hughson	the greatest part of this farm is on Lott N 6	2.0.0
2	70 ½	Ruben Rableyea	Joshua Conklin	in the same Situation may be Rented @	3.0.0
3	67	Elisha Baker	Benj Green	in the same Situation	3.0.0
4	272 ½	Elisha Kellick & Jacob Burgis	Thomas Lovelass & Josiah Benjamin	Indiffferent farm	2.10.0
5	318 ½	Abenezar Chase	Malcom Morison	but a poor farm	3.0.0
6	309 ½	Jos Baker & Ezrh Burgis	Morison Rice on Burgis part & Benj Titus on Bakers part	poor farm	3.10.0
7	304	Bethuel Baker	the same	but a poor farm	2.10.0
8	195	Nathl Astin	Bethuel Baker has 1/2 of this farm	good farm	4.10.0
9	231	David Astin	Abrm Maybe	a good farm	5.0.0
10	358	Joshua Hinkley	Thos: Hinkley	very rough farm	2.0.0
11	543	Lazarus Griffin	Josiah Baker	Midling good farm	3.10.0
12	178½	Jacob Ellis	Gillson Clap	good farm	3.0.0
13	100	Edward Rice	the Same	good farm	3.10.0
14	17	Edmond Baker	the Same	Greatest part of farm runs into Lott no. 6	
15	90	Josiah Baker	the Same	good farm	3.0.0
16	96	John Finch	Gillson Clap	Midling good	3.0.0
17	90	Danl: Townsend Junr:	John Bircham	poor Land. but has Grist, Saw & fulling Mills	3.0.0
18	113	Moses Fowler	the Same	Sold by Executs: P P.	
19	27	Peter Robinson	Parish	not very good	1.10.0
20	225	Caleb Fowler	the Same	very good farm	5.0.0
21	167 ½	John Kelley	the Same	good farm	4.10.0
22	168 ½	Simion Ellis	the Same	good farm	4.10.0
23	144 ½	Gidion Ellis	Malcom Morison	Midling good	3.0.0
24	267 ½	Ebener: King and Edmond Baker		Midling	3.0.0

Tenant List Lot Number 8 - 1768 and prior, continued

No.	no. of acres	Tenants in possession at the time the farms were surveyed and run out	Tenants in Possession the 1st May 1768	Remarks	Rent pr Annum £.S.D.
25	203	Jonathan Kelly	the Same	Rough farm	2.10.0
26	352	Elnathan Doan & Son		Rough farm	5.0.0
27	290	Charles Townsend	the Same	good farm	5.0.0
28	172	Saml. Bangs	Haws & Wm Judd	good farm	4.10.0
29	153	Abner Bangs	David Crossby & Elisha Bangs	good farm	5.0.0
30	153	Wm Penny	the Same	good farm	5.0.0
31	334 ½	Eleazar Cools	Jon: Garrison & Jos: Vickery	good farm	6.0.0
32	258	Ebenezar Jones	the Same	good farm	5.0.0
33	202	Jacob Phillips	the Same	good farm	4.0.0
34	231	Nehemiah Jones	the Same & Thophilas Jones	good farm	4.0.0
35	203	Joseph Craw	Joseph Philips	good farm	5.0.0
36	103	Nathan Taylor	Josiah Swift	good farm - these two farms were left to arbitration	4.0.0
37	136	Silvanus Cole	the Same		5.0.0
38	170 ½	Isaac Chapman	Sold to Capt: Fleming Colgan		
39	297	Elijah Tomkins	the Same	good farm	7.0.0
40	505	David & Joa: Crossby	the Same	good farm	8.0.0
41	97	Ruben Crossby	the Same	good farm	3.10.0
42	158	Israel Cole	the Same	this farm was Ejected & therefore the Tenant has no Claim for Improvement	5.0.0
43	483	Thos: Paddock & Jonathan	the Same	very good farm	7.0.0
44	486	Jos: Vickery & Co	Jona: Vickery & Moss Kent	Midling good	4.10.0
45	162	Joseph Taylors	the Same	Midling good	4.0.0
46	133	Jon: Godferry & Rich Gray	Ezekiel Burgis	good farm	4.0.0
47	118	Moss Kent	the Same	Lease for ever	
48	80	Oliver Gray	Zebulon Bass	good farm	4.0.0
49	55 ½	Elijah White	the Same	good Land	2.10.0
-		George Hepburn		has a very fine piece of Swamp not Surveyed	

MILITIA LISTS

New York militia lists from the provincial and revolutionary periods have been transcribed and published at various times and in various books. This section is intended to bring together certain published lists that have a preponderance of men from the area that is now Putnam County, New York. These are not original transcriptions of those records, but are lists taken from transcribed records (originals are at the NY State Archives). And as with many colonial period records, not all militia lists survived, so this is not a comprehensive collection of men who served. Also, there are other militia lists or troops that included men from this area that are not included.

Of the thirteen muster rolls of New York Provincial Troops indicated as from Dutchess County,[1] three appear to have primarily or many south Dutchess men and are included herein.

In the Revolutionary period, two regiments of militia were drawn from men in the southern precincts of Dutchess County (see page 241 for descriptions of included lists). Other Dutchess men appeared on militia rolls or served in the Continental Troops, but such militia and muster rolls are not included herein.

Provincial Troops[1]

Muster Roll of a Company of Provincials in the Pay of the Province of New York for Dutchess County Commanded by Joseph Crane, Esq. - 1758[2]

Captain
Joseph Crane
Lieutenants
Richard Ray
Philip Paddock

Non Commissioned Officers
Benjamin Higgins
John Cannon
Simon Calkins
Jonathan Vickry

	Privates		Age	Where born	Trade	When enlisted
	John	McCrery	18	Jersey	Farmer	April 21
	Cornielus	Fuller	19	N. England	do	19
	Ebenezer	Baker	18	Boston	do	19
	Joseph	Barlow	17	Dutchess	do	3
5	Stephen	Fenton	26	Boston	do	19
	Noah	Jelett	49	Connecticut	Smith	7
	Eliphalet	Wheeler	20	do	Carpenter	29
	Joseph	Hollester	20	Connecticut	Labourer	19
	John	Bennett	31	do	do	20
10	Joseph	Phillips	19	do	do	3
	Phineas	Woodward	23	do	do	6
	Amos	Allen	17	do	do	14
	John	Frankland	20	do	do	7
	Moses	Allen	17	Boston	do	7
15	Samuel	Cogswell	45	do	Smith	19

---

1. *Muster Rolls of New York Provincial Troops 1755-1764 : Collections of the New-York Historical Society for the Year 1891* (New York: New York Historical Society, 1892). pp. 503 and 513 describe bounties and provisions.
2. Ibid, Muster Rolls for 1758, 108-113. All spellings from the published work have been retained.

Muster Roll of Provincials Commanded by Capt. Joseph Crane 1758 continued

	Privates		Age	Where born	Trade	When enlisted
	Daniel	Allen	35	Connecticut	Labourer	April 19
	James	Pingry	19	do	do	5
	Jeddiah	Carley	44	Boston	do	20
	Thomas	Inckly	31	do	Carpenter	19
20	Samuel	Boyington	18	Connecticut	Farmer	12
	James	Lovelace	42	do	Cordwainer	19
	John	Aston	22	Westchester	Labourer	10
	Charles	Barsleys	19	N. England	do	3
	Daniel	Atwood	50	Cape Cod	do	17
25	Andrew	Cowley	22	Connecticut	Cordwainer	17
	Mathew	Fuller	60	Boston	Labourer	3
	Michal	Tenry	29	Westchester	do	19
	Ruben	Rapeljea	20	L. Island	do	19
	George	Clasen	19	R. Island	do	14
30	Bethual	Baker	22	Boston	do	19
	David	Hodges	23	N. Engld	do	18
	John	Gray	20	Cape Cod	do	18
	George	Dickenson	19	R. Island	Sadler	3
	William	Calkins	17	Dutchess	Farmer	18
35	Caleb	Hill	17	N.England	Weaver	3
	Stephen	March	19	Connecticut	Cooper	3
	Gilbert	Clap	20	Westchester	Labourer	3
	Ebenezer	Gage	23	Boston	Smith	3
	David	Vickey	19	do	Cordwainer	12
40	Enoch	Seers	17	do	Labourer	12
	Eneas	Nicholson	20	do	Weaver	3
	Rowland	Rosall	19	do	Smith	3
	Asa	Cummins	19	Connecticut	Cooper	3
	Azariah	Parish	18	do	Farmer	17
45	Joshua	Barnum	21	do	do	5
	Daniel	Cash	19	Boston	do	4
	Jacob	Ellis	21	do	do	4
	Abel	Sherwood	33	Connecticut	Carpenter	12
	Bennonia	Gray	20	Boston	Farmer	12
50	Thomas	Cole	18	do	do	3
	Daniel	Townsend	36	L. Island	do	12
	Jezadiah	Frost	23	Connecticut	Cordwainer	12
	David	Sturdyvant	22	Dutchess	Farmer	12
	John	Perry	25	Boston	Joyner	12
55	William	Allen	19	Westchester	Farmer	3
	John	Franklin	20	Connecticut	do	5
	William	Earl	19	Dutchess	do	5
	Jacob	Leonard	24	Connecticut	do	8

Muster Roll of Provincials Commanded by Capt. Joseph Crane 1758 continued

	Privates		Age	Where born	Trade	When enlisted
	Rossel	Frankland	18	do	do	April 8
60	Henry	Grey	32	do	do	4
	Mathew	Standish	17	Dutchess	do	5
	Thomas	Evans	18	do	do	5
	Abner	Edie	25	Boston	Cordwainer	8
	Benjamen	Herrington	22	R. Island	Labourer	10
65	Zechariah	Herrington	21	do	do	10
	Benjamen	Shaw	25	Connecticut	Cordwainer	11
	Edward	Popple	30	R. Island	Labourer	19
	Isaac	Harrington	17	Dutchess	do	17
	Stephen	Hull	20	R. Island	Soldier	19
70	John	Barber	18	Boston	Farmer	12
	John	Martin	34	Ireland	do	9
	John	De Pew	24	Westchester	do	4
	Samuel	Blackman	29	do	do	29
	Conrad	Steenbergh	22	Dutchess	Cordwainer	20
75	Simon	Scouten	28	Fishkills	Taylor	8
	Philip	Pear	23	Westchester	Cordwainer	1
	John Wm.	Loudenburgh	26	Germany	Farmer	1
	Andrew	Silvernail	27	Dutchess	do	1
	Samuel	Brewster	20	do	do	3
80	Reuben	Crosby	23	do	do	4

Muster Roll of the Men Raised in the County of Dutchess and Passed Muster for Capt. Richard Rea's Company May the 1: 1760[3]

<u>Captain</u>
Richard Rea (militia Capt. Humphries)
<u>Lieutenant</u>
John Cannon (militia Capt. Bogardus)
Samuel Terry (militia Capt. Js. Livingston)
Isaac Ter Bush (militia Capt. Eleazer D.Bois)

Men's Names		Day Inlisted		Age	Where born	Trade	Co. of Militia
Oliver	Fox	Apl.	14	19	Connecticut	Farmer	Capt. Bogardus
William	Day	do	12	17	New England	do	do
Jeremiah	Parmer	do	23	16	Connecticut	do	do
Tilton	Eastman	do	16	18	Connecticut	do	do
William	Eastman	do	16	20	do	do	Capt. P.D.Bois
James	Richards	do	19	18	Dutchess	do	do
Samuel	Dalie	do	15	21	do	do	Eleazer D.Bois
Joshua	Hill	do	12	19	Rhode Island	Weaver	do
Joseph	Beavans	do	3	17	Rhode Island		Capt. Lyster

---

3. *Muster Rolls of New York Provincial Troops 1755-1764*, 262-267.

Muster Roll of Provincials in Capt. Richard Rea's Company 1760 continued

Men's Names		Day Inlisted		Age	Where born	Trade	Co. of Militia
Jacob	Pepper	Apl.	3	20	Dutchess	do	do
James	Lovelace	do	15	18	R. Island	do	do
Abner	Goodspeed	do	2	17	Boston	do	do
Ephariam	James	do	23	20	N. Carolina	do	do
John	House	do	12	45	Rhode Island	Cordwainer	do
Isaac	Wilcocks	do	3	18	Westchester	Sadler	do
John	Bennet	do	18	16	N. England	Labourer	do
Caleb	Worden	do	20	19	do	do	do
Jacob	Burges	do	20	16	Boston	do	do
John	Sunderling	do	4	29	Connecticut	Blacksmith	do
Samuel	Fox	do	14	24	do	Farmer	do
Simeon	Covel	do	18	25	Boston	Cordwainer	do
Gideon	Hollester	do	14	17	Connecticut	Farmer	Capt. Livingston
Samuel	Spalding	do	21	20	do	Cordwainer	do
Zephaniah	Little	do	8	18	do	Farmer	Capt. Rhodes
Elamuel	Fuller	do	18	18	do	do	do
Jeradiah	Davis	do	26	22	Long Island	Marriner	do
John	Dean	do	26	19	Connecticut	Farmer	do
Jonathan	Lawrence	do	8	18	W. Chester	do	do
James	Shaw	do	8	23	Dutchess	do	do
John	Hiames	do	5	50	R. Island	Carpender	do
Elijah	Hamlen	do	18	35	Boston	Farmer	do
James	Ravelje	do	26	28	Dutchess	do	do
Stephen	Fenton	do	26	28	Boston	Cooper	do
Zazares	Ellis	do	18	16	do	Labourer	do
Nathl.	Hollester	do	21	45	Connecticut	do	Capt. Ross
Andrew	Atwood	do	28	30	Boston	do	Capt. Rhodes
Plagery	Sprague	do	8	50	N. England	do	Capt. Delamater
Samuel	Nelson	do	12	16	Dutchess	do	Capt. Mead
Maher	Daggett	do	5	31	N. England	Black Smith	do
John	Nelson	do	26	19	Dutchess	Labourer	Capt. Dubois
John	Barber, Jr.	May	3	20	do	do	Capt. Rhodes
Samuel	Dimmick	do	3	34	do	do	do
Ebenezer	Robertson	do	3	24	Westchester	Cooper	Capt. Dickerson
William	Roe	do	23	22	do		Capt. Rhodes

Muster Roll of the Men Raised in the County of Dutchess and Past [sic] Muster for Capt. Isaac Ter Bush's Company 1762[4]

Men's Names	Inlisted		Age	Where born	Trade	Officers who Inlisted them	Stature Ft	In
Manchester Hawley	May	1	30	Philadelphia	Labourer	Lieut Concklin	5	9
Joseph Palmerton	April	27	17	Rhode Island	do	Lt Woodard	5	2
John Conet	do	25	18	Dutchess Co	do	Capt Haight	5	8½
William Moore	May	25	41	Ireland	Taylor	Lt Concklin	5	1
Nehemiah Smith	Aprill	16	32	Long Island	Blacksmith	Capt Bush	5	6

---

4. *Muster Rolls of New York Provincial Troops 1755-1764*, 450-453.

Muster Roll of Provincials in Capt. Isaac Ter Bush's Company 1762 continued

Men's Names	Inlisted		Age	Where born	Trade	Inlisted By	Stature	
Joseph Calkins	June	8	18	Dutchess Co	Labourer	Lt Woodard	5	2
John Smith	April	10	54	New England	Carpenter	Lt Concklin	5	8
Richard Murch	do	29	19	do	Black Smith	do	5	10
John Bruster	do	29	16	Dutchess Co	Labourer	do	5	6
Able Merrick	do	29	16	do	Cooper	do	5	2
Thomas Burgis	do	29	17	New England	Labourer	do	5	6
David Cash	do	30	19	Dutchess Co	Cooper	do	5	9¼
William Murch	April	30	17	New England	Labourer	do	5	8½
Jeremiah Barly	do	10	19	Dutchess Co	do	do	5	6
Willm. Richardson	June	8	22	do	do	Lt Woodard	5	7
John Evans	April	15	18	do	do	do	5	6
Prince Haws	May	1	18	Cape Codd	do	Lt Concklin	5	6
Barny Seers	June	6	19	Boston	Weaver	Lt Woodard	5	10
Pelethia Bruster	do	8	21	Dutchess Co	Labourer	do	5	10
Joseph Hornet	April	30	32	do	do	Capt Bush	5	10½
George Hicks	do	30	23	North Castle	Turner	do	5	11
Moses Prindle	May	20	34	New England	Labourer	do	5	7
John Kane	do	19	52	Ireland	Weaver	Lt Concklin	5	5
Jon Penree	April	1	20	Wales	Labourer	do	5	1
Jacob Schouten	do	29	19	Dutchess Co	do	Capt Bush	5	6
Lewis Du Bois	do	17	18	do	Carpenter	do	5	7
Henry Lewis	do	18	16	do	Labourer	do	5	5
Joseph Worden	do	26	18	New England	do	Lt Woodard	5	7½
Jones Odle	do	16	20	Dutchess Co	do	do	5	8½
Jonathan Woodard	do	6	18	New England	do	do	5	6
James Birch	do	13	18	do	do	do	5	6½
Jonathan Hammond	do	18	17	do	do	do	5	4
Elisha Willcocks	do	20	20	do	do	do	5	11½
Amos Willcocks	do	19	23	do	do	do	5	11¾
John Finch	do	20	17	do	do	do	5	4
John Finton	June	13	32	do	Joyner	do	5	8½
Richard Hornet	May	29	50	Ireland	Labourer	Lt Concklin	5	3
Benjm. Vredinburgh	do	25	21	Dutchess Co	Cordwainer	do	5	10
Jacobus Ostrander	do	26	18	do	Labourer	do	5	3
Peter Palmatier Junr.	April	3	20	do	do	Capt Harris	5	9
Daniel Earnst	do	24	22	Germany	do	Capt Bush	5	3½
James Pickett	do	29	18	New England	do	do	5	6
Martin Smith	do	30	17	do	do	do	5	6
Stephen Finton	do	17	30	Dutchess Co	do	do	5	8
John Langley	May	25	18	do	Cordwainer	Lt Concklin	5	3½
John Austin	do	11	55	Ireland	Weaver	Capt Bush	4	10
Lodawick Miller	April	26	16	Dutchess Co	Labourer	do	5	8
Isaac Romane	do	26	17	do	do	do	5	6

Militia Regiments in South Dutchess County 1776–1781

Two regiments organized in May 1776 included primarily south Dutchess men: the Third Regiment under Col. John Field, and the Seventh Regiment under Col. Moses Dusenberry (soon succeeded by Henry Luddington). Col. Field's regiment covered Pawling and South East Precincts, and Philipse Lots 7 and 8 of Fredricksburgh Precinct. Col. Luddington's regiment included Philipse Precinct and the rest of Fredricksburgh Precinct (Philipse Lots 5, 6, and 9). Each was subdivided into companies under command of a captain. The previous Southern Regiment had encompassed all of Dutchess County and, with twelve companies, exceeded the ten company limit.[5]

The Provincial Congress of New York, in session at New York City on 22 August 1775 adopted requirements for the enlistment, organization, and equipment of the militia. It was ordered:

> That every man between the ages of 16 and 50 do with all convenient speed furnish himself with a good Musket or firelock & Bayonet Sword or Tomahawk, a Steel Ramrod, Worm, Priming Wire and Brush fitted thereto, a Cartouch Box to contain 23 rounds of cartridges, 12 flints and a knapsack agreeable to the directions of the Continental congress under forfeiture of five shillings for the want of a musket or firelock and of one shilling for want of a bayonet, sword or tomahawk, cartridge or bullet. That every man shall at his place of abode be also provided with one pound of powder and three pounds of bullets or proper size to his musket or firelock.[6]

The cost of serving in the militia took a toll on many South Dutchess men whose wealth paled in comparison with men to the north. Col. Henry Ludington complained in 1781: "I can affirm that ten farmers in Coll. Brinckerhoff's Regiment is able to purchase the whole of mine. In this uneaquil way, I have been obliged to turn out my men untill they are so much impoverish'd that they almost dispair."[7] In 1777 it was said that "the Drafts in Dutchess were few and would not serve [because] the People were wore out last year. Those in the Army lost the opportunity of seeding their ground and were now starving for Bread."[8]

LOYALIST OR REBEL?

In 1775, many Fredricksburgh and Philipse farmers followed the prodding of their Loyalist landlords (Robinson and Morris) in opposing Whig causes. According to one Whig leader, referring to southern Dutchess County: "British Agents ... have corrupted the minds of many of the ignorant and baser sort of men among us, maliciously telling them the whigs are in rebellion: the King would conquer them, and their estates be forfeited; and if they take up arms against them, the King for their services will give them the whigs' possessions."[9] Once the Revolution began, Tory agents offered tenants free land if they helped the King win the war. Whigs countered with a Land Bounty militia, giving soldiers payment in land grants.[10]

---

5. Berthold Fernow, *New York in the Revolution* (Baltimore: Clearfield, 1999), 102, reprint of *Documents Relating to the Colonial History of the State of New York*, v. 15 (Albany: 1887)

6. Willis F Johnson, *Colonel Henry Ludington: A Memoir* (New York: Ludington family, 1907), 60-61.

7. Staughton Lynd, "Who Should Rule at Home? Dutchess County, New York, in the American Revolution," *The William and Mary Quarterly*, v. 18. n.3 (Jul 1961), 339, citing Henry Ludinton to George Clinton, 1 May 1781, *Clinton Papers*, VI, 817.

8. Lynd, "Who Should Rule at Home?", 339, citing William Smith, *Historical Memoirs*, 119.

9. Ibid, 336. citing Samuel Dodge to the President of the New York Provincial Congress, 5 Dec 1775, *Journals of the Provincial Congress, Provincial Convention, Committee of Safety and Council of Safety of the State of New-York* (Albany, 1842), II, 106. For loyalist men transported to Exeter, NH see *Minutes of the Committee and of the First Commission for Detecting and Defeating Conspiracies in the State of New York : December 11, 1776–September 23, 1778 with Collateral Documents*, v. I (NY: NY Historical Society, 1924).

10. James A. Roberts, *New York in the Revolution as Colony and State*, Second Edition (Albany: 1898), 12.

Egbert Benson, addressing the New York Congress on utilizing the Dutchess militia in securing positions for the war, reported: "we have always obliged the tories to appear in the ranks and be subject to be drafted, because we knew that in most cases they would hire others to serve in their stead, (I mean when the drafts were intended to form a part of the army) and such as were not of sufficient ability for that purpose, have deserted and lurked in the woods, and were the occasion of the late insurrection."[11]

The following support the reported Tory leanings of southern Dutchess:

- Col. Beverly Robinson, testifying in 1785, boasted of raising a Loyalist regiment of 250 men primarily from his own tenants.
- In 1779, James Fallon of Quaker Hill (just north of South East Precinct) reported "only four whigs" there, with the rest being the "very essence and quintessence of Tories."
- The militia regiment of southern Dutchess County was reportedly nonfunctional since "greater part of them by farr Refuse to March," due to indifference or their Tory sympathies.[12]
- The chairman of the Dutchess County Committee of Safety expressed concern in 1776 that the county's militia as a whole was untrustworthy and should not be called out. He believed that perhaps one in four of the county's militiamen were disloyal.[13]

While Robinson and Morris were loyalists, the third proprietor, Philip Philipse, died in 1768 and his lots (2, 6, and 8) were partitioned among his non-Loyalist heirs. Presumably, Philipse and South East tenants were not pressured to be Tories like their counterparts on Robinson's and Morris's lands.

MILITIA LISTS

The following militia lists extracted from the Alphabetical Roster of the State Troops[14] include men issued certificates for payment (pursuant to a 1784 law) for serving in the Field or Luddington Regiments. Captains of companies within the regiments changed over time, and some men served in more than one company.

For additional information, consult other published lists grouping enrollments, muster rolls, pay book records, and bounty land claims by regiment. Men aged between 16 and 50 (raised to 60 in April 1778) were to be enrolled by the colonel. Able bodied men were to serve, but could provide a substitute. Enrolled but exempt Quakers, Moravians, and United Bretheren paid money in lieu of service. Also exempt were one miller for each grist mill, three powder makers for each powder mill, five men to each furnace, three journeymen in each printing office, and one ferryman for each public ferry.[15]

For information on Loyalist soldiers, see the Loyalist American Regiment (LAR) Muster Rolls at http://www.royalprovincial.com/military/musters/loyamregt/mrlarmain.htm. Also consult the UK, American Loyalist Claims at Ancestry.com. Note that many loyalists migrated to Canada after the war.

---

11. *Journals of the Provincial Congress, Provincial Convention, Committee of Safety and Council of Safety of the State of New-York 1775-1776-1777* (Albany: Thurlow, 1842), II, 309. Egbert Benson (at Red Hook) to the New York Provincial Convention, 15 July 1776.

12. Sung Bok Kim, "Impact of Class Relations and Warfare in the American Revolution: the New York Experience," *The Journal of American History*, v 69, no. 2 (Sep 1982), 341-42, and n41.

13. Lynd, "Who Should Rule at Home?", 338, citing Egbert Benson to the New York Provincial Convention, 15 July 1776, *Jour. Prov. Cong.*, II, 309.

14. Berthold Fernow, *Documents Relating to the Colonial History of the State of New York*, v. 15, State Archives, v.1 (Albany: Parsons, 1887), 311-524.

15. NY Office of State Comptroller, *New York in the Revolution as Colony and State*, v.1 (Albany: Lyon, 1904), 11.

Roster of Troops[16] 1775–1781
Field's Third Militia Regiment

Colonel	Other Regimental
Field, John, Colonel	Crane, Joseph Jr, Surgeon
Captains	Crane, Solomon, Adj't
Barnum, Aza, Capt	Crosby, Reuben, Qr Mr.
Dykeman, Jos., Capt	Paddock, Jon'n, 1st Major
Hecock, David, Capt	Paddock, Nath'n, Sgt Major

Name and Rank (if other than Private) are listed alphabetically by Company.
Combined companies list men who served in more than one company.
See Appendix B for location of Company "Beats"

Barnum/Hecock Cos.
- Birdsall, Thomas
- Cornwell, David

Barnum's Company
- Baldwin, David
- Barnum, Jonah, Cpl
- Barnum, Noah, Cpl
- Barnum, Stephen
- Burch, George
- Burch, Silas
- Cable, Platt
- Carley, John, Cpl
- Chapman, Enoch
- Clinton, Wm
- Closson, Wilber
- Cole, Benjamin
- Crane, Iza, drummer
- Crane, Will.
- Crocker, Tim'y
- Crosby, Jon'n
- Crosby, Joseph
- Dean, Elijah
- Elwell, Ezra
- Elwell, Jabez
- Elwell, John
- Field, Jesse
- Foster, Sam'l
- Gage, Alden, Cpl
- Gage, Anth'y, Sgt (Ens.)
- Gage, Mark
- Gilchrist, Sam'l
- Green, Nathan(Jr), Ens/Lt
- Hall, Morton
- Hall, Sam'l
- Haviland, John
- Hempstead, Nath'l, Sgt
- Hewman, Zach'h
- Higgins, Thomas
- Hinckley, Elkany
- Hinman, Zach'h
- Holmes, Joseph
- Honeywell, Matt's
- Hopkins, Berry, Sgt
- Jones, Thomas
- King, Caleb
- Marsh, John
- Morehouse, Stephen
- Morrell, Ab'm
- Mott, Jacob
- Mott, Tho's
- Mott, Will. Jr
- Murray, And'w
- Nickerson, Thos.
- Olmsted, Eben'r
- Osburn, Ezekiel
- Ragon, Thomas
- Rider, Christ'r
- Rider, David
- Rider, John
- Rider, Simeon
- Rider, Simeon Jr
- Roberts, Benj'n Jr
- Rockwell, Stephen
- Russell, Roland
- Sealy, Will
- Sears, Banj'n
- Sears, Peter
- Sears, Seth
- Sears, Seth Jr
- Sears, Stephen
- Smith, Alpheus, Cpl/Pvt
- Smith, Jon'n
- Spencer, Sam'l
- St. John, Thos.
- Thomas, Thomas
- Townsend, Isaac
- Townsend, John
- Townsend, Solomon
- Weed, John
- Wixon, Eben'r
- Wooster, Will.
- Wright, Edmond
- Young, Elkany
- Young, Shaw

Dykeman/Barnum Cos.
- Burlison, Joel
- Foster, Seth
- Hall, John
- Sears, Thomas, Lieut
- Sears/Seers, Enoch, Cpl
- Smith, Joseph, drummer

Dykeman's Company
- VanDuzen, Christ., Capt
- Bennit, Amacy
- Birch, Isaiah
- Bisbuit, Francis
- Brewster, Peltiah
- Brown, Moses
- Buckler, Jabez
- Campbell, Robison
- Cannon, Abr'm
- Carter, Jabez, Cpl
- Chapman, Tho's
- Chase, Seth
- Chase, Thomas, Cpl/Pvt
- Clossen, Wm., Sgt
- Cockshuer, Jonas
- Cole, Sylvanus
- Crandle, Jerem'h
- Crosby, Abner
- Crosby, David
- Crosby, Eleazer
- Crosby, Elemuel, Cpl
- Crosby, Eli
- Crosby, James
- Crosby, Joshua, 1st Lt
- Crosby, Josiah, Sgt

---

16. extracted from Fernow, *Documents Relating to the Colonial History of the State of New York*, 15: 311-524.

Field's Third Militia Regiment, continued

Dykeman's Company, cont.
- Crosby, Moses
- Davis, Paul
- Dean, Dan'l, Ensign
- Doan(n), Daniel, Lt/Ens
- Done, Elnathan
- Ellis, Thos, Cpl
- Elliss, Elijah
- Fermilar, Philip
- Ferres, Justus
- Fox, Oliver Jr
- Franklin, Nathan
- Gage, Justus
- Gage, Sylvanus
- Gay, Jason
- Goodspeed, Abner
- Green, Isaac
- Green, Jno.
- Hall, Jesse
- Hazard, Sam'l
- Hicox, Noah
- Hinkley, Elkanah, Cpl
- Hinkley, Josiah
- Hinkley, Reuben, Cpl
- Holliday, John
- Holliday, Simeon
- Hunt, Thomas
- Johnson, Joseph
- Jones, Eben'r
- Jones, Elias
- Jones, Isaac
- Jones, Joseph
- Jones, Levi
- Jones, Samuel
- Kelly, David
- Kelly, Jon'n
- Kelly, Reuben
- Kelly, Sylvanus
- Kent, Moses
- Ketcham, Dan'l
- King, Merrick, Fifer
- King, Nath'l
- Lockwood, Henry
- Lockwood, Solomon
- Mayerson, Thomas
- Mills, Benajah
- Nickerson, James
- Parish, Azariah, Sgt
- Parish, Uriah
- Penney, John
- Penny, Ed'd, 2nd Lt
- Perkins, Elijah
- Perry, Simeon
- Philips, Joseph
- Reed, Jacob
- Richardson, Isaac
- Runnalds, David
- Sabens, Billings
- Shaw, Ichabod, Sgt
- Shurman, Darius
- Slocum, Benj'n, Ensign
- Slocum, George
- Snow, Will.
- Stark, Henry
- Stark, John
- Stephens, Thomas, Cpl
- Thomson, Dan'l
- Thorrington, Thomas
- Tubbs, Benijah
- Vickry, Thos.
- Wairing, John
- Webb, Noah
- Weekson, Elijah
- Wilson, John
- Wixon, Elijah
- Wixon, Isaac

Dykeman/Hecock Cos.
- Ashbey, Ant'y
- Bouton, Noah
- Burling, Gillard/Gilead
- Lindsay/sey, David
- Morehouse, Isaac
- Moshier, Johiel
- Perry, Samuel

Hecock's Company
- Akins, David
- Atkins, Isaac
- Babbett, Daniel
- Banvert, Abr'm
- Barlow, Nathan
- Bennet, Increase
- Birdsall, Squire
- Bollard, Tracy
- Brewer, Garrey
- Brown, Elisha
- Bruster, John
- Bruster, Sam'l
- Burch, Benj'n
- Burch, Charles
- Burch, Danl.
- Burch, David
- Burch, Jerem'h
- Burch, John
- Burch, Jon'n
- Burling, Eben'r Sam'l
- Butler, Tim'y
- Button, Peter
- Calkin, James, Cpl
- Cameron, Dougle
- Cerley, Albert
- Cerley, John
- Cerley, Oliver
- Cerley, Peter
- Chandler, Jos., 1st Lt
- Clerk, John
- Clossen, Wilbert
- Closson, Jacob
- Colkin/Calkin, Simon
- Colkin/Calkin, Will.
- Colkins/Calkins, Eli
- Colkins/Calkins, Joshua
- Covey, Joseph
- Covey, Walter
- Cushman, Consider
- Dibble, Joel
- Douglass, John
- Ellis, Jerem'h
- Farris, Ezra
- Fisher, Nath'l
- Flemming, Thomas
- Freman, George
- Furman, Joseph
- Gilchrist, Will.
- Gorden, James
- Gray, John, fifer
- Gray, Jon'n
- Gray, Will.
- Grimes, James
- Hains, Asa, Lieut
- Hall, Ambrose
- Hartwell, James
- Hays, James
- Hays, John
- Hays, Nath'l
- Hecock, David Jr
- Hecock, John, Sgt
- Hecock, Joss
- Hecock, Noah
- Hill, David
- Hill, Elijah
- Howland, Obadiah
- Johnson, Sam'l
- Jones, Eph'm, Cpl
- Jones, Nathan Jr
- Kidd, Alex'r
- Lockwood, Daniel
- Ludington, Comfort
- Manvell, Adrian
- Measureall, Corn's

Field's Third Militia Regiment, continued

Hecock's Company, cont.
- Mills, Alex'r
- Mills, Brown
- Nash, David
- Newberry, Joseph
- Newbury, Joshua, Cpl
- Nickenson, Bassett
- Nickenson, Levi
- Nickerson, Uriah
- Nickinson, Aaron
- Ogden, Edmund
- Ogden, Humphrey
- Ogden, Joseph
- Ogden, Nathan
- Palmer, Will.
- Pell, David
- Philips, Amos, Cpl
- Phillips, Isaac
- Pineer, Ab'm
- Pineer, David
- Post, Ant'y
- Potter, David
- Rivers, Ant'y
- Robinson, John
- Robinson, Lewis
- Rowley, Dan'l
- Rowley, Elijah
- Scott, Abm
- Scott, Peter, Sgt
- Smith, Major
- St. John, Abr'm
- Stebens, Lewis
- Stebens, Neh'h
- Stephens, Russell
- Taylor, Joseph
- Townsend, Levi
- Turner, Dan'l
- Utter, Amos
- Utter, Eben'r
- Utter, John
- Utter, Samuel
- Ventress, Wm., drum'r
- Ward, Chas.
- Ward, James
- Warring, Ephraim
- Watts, John
- Watts, Robert
- Weed, Jehiel Jr
- Wilcock, Benj'n
- Wilcock, Rosal
- Willes, Jedediah
- Willes, Rich'd
- Willes, Thomas
- Willess, James
- Wilson, Samuel
- Yale, Stephen
- Yale, Uriah
- Yales, Enos
- Yarns, Reuben
- Young, Samuel

Van Duser's Company
- Hammond, John, Sgt
- Tuthill, John W, Lieut
- Wilkins, James

Luddington's Seventh Militia Regiment

Colonel
Luddington, Henry, Col.

Other Regimental
Baker, Eleazer, Qtr Mstr
Baker, Joshua, Qtr Mstr
Baker, Stephen, A Major
Ferris, Reuben, Lt.Col.
Robinson, Eben'r, [2d] Maj
Townsend, Elijah, Adjt

Captains
Baker, Edmund, Capt
Crane, John, Capt
Kidd, Alex'r, Capt
Knapp, Israel, Capt
Lane, George, Capt
Mead, Hezekiah (Jr), Capt
Mead, Joel, Capt
Scribner, Nath'l, Capt
Waterbury, David, Capt

Name and Rank (if other than Private) are listed alphabetically by Company.
Men who served in more than one company are listed first, with companies noted.
See Appendix B for location of Company "Beats"

Companies	**Soldier**	**Companies**	**Soldier**
Mead/Waterbury	Adams, Gilbert	Waterbury/Knapp	Conklin, Sam'l
Mead/Crane	Adams, John	Mead/Knapp	Drew, Isaac
Lane/Mead	Barret(t), John	Scribner/Waterbury	Everitt, George
Lane/Baker	Barrett, Isaac	Scribner/Knapp	Ferguson, Thomas
Waterbury/Crane/Knapp	Berry, Jabez, Sgt	Scribner/Waterbury	Finch, Reuben
Ludinton	Carrigan, Gilbert	Waterbury/Mead-H	Fuller, Elijah, Lieut
Mead/Baker	Chadwick, Comfort	Waterbury/Scribner	Ganong, Reuben
Robinson/Mead	Chase, Obadiah	Waterbury/Scribner	Gregory, Ezra, Pvt/Sgt
Lane/Knapp	Chase, Robert	Crane/Lane	Gregory, Joseph, Ensign
Lane/Knapp	Christian, John	Scribner/Waterbury	Gregory, Sam'l
Lane/Scribner	Colbroth, Thomas	Mead/Waterbury	Hadley, Moses

MILITIA LISTS

Luddington's Seventh Militia Regiment, continued

Companies	Soldier	Companies	Soldier
Baker/Knapp	Hall, John, Lt/Sgt	Waterbury/Mead	Platt, Rich'd
Mead/Knapp	Hawkins, Sam'l	Scribner/Waterbury /Knapp	Raymond, Thaddeus
Scribner/Waterbury	Hazen, Caleb, Ens/Lt		
Scribner/Waterbury	Hazen, Moses, Cpl	Waterbury/Mead /Scribner	Rice, Sam'l, Sgt/Pvt
Lane/Knapp	Hills, Thomas		
Mead/Lane	Hopkins, Isaiah, Pvt/Sgt	Waterbury/Lane	Richards, Ezra, Sgt/Pvt
Mead/Scribner	Hyatt, Alvan/Elvin	Scribner/Mead	Robinson, Eben'r
Scribner/Baker	Jenkins, Nath'l, Pvt/Cpl	Scribner/Mead	Robinson, Is(s)achar
Waterbury/Baker	King, Heman, Pvt/Sgt	Mead/Baker	Russell, James, Cpl/Pvt
Scribner/Lane	Kircum/kum, Solomon	Mead/Lane	Simkins, John
Scribner/Waterbury	Kniffen, Sam'l	Mead/Baker	Small, James
Scribner/Mead /Waterbury	Kniffen/in, Amos	Crane/Knapp	Smith, Elisha, Sgt/Pvt
		Mead/Lane	Smith, James
Mead/Waterbury	Knott, Nath'l	Crane/Lane	Smith, Solomon
Waterbury/Knapp	Maker, Solomon	Mead/Lane	Sprague/Sprage, John
Mead/Baker	Mead, Jacob, Sgt/Ens	Mead/Baker	Swift, Isaiah, Cpl
Waterbury/Scribner	Myrick/Marick, Isaac	Waterbury/Mead	Townsend, James, /Sgt
Waterbury/Baker	Nickerson, Isaachar	Mead/Knapp	Towns(h)end, Amos
Knapp/Kidd	Nickerson, Thos.	Paddock	Tryon, Simon
Hecock/Kidd	Oakley, Elijah, Pvt/Sgt	Scribner/Lane	Veal, John
Swartwout	Parrish, Silas	Mead/Waterbury	Waterbury, Enos
Mead/Waterbury	Pearce/Pearse, Isaac	Scribner/Mead	Wilson, Daniel

continued, by company

Baker's Company
- Bailey, Peleg
- Benjamin, Elijah T.
- Brown, Isaac
- Dan, Thaddeus
- Dean, Benjamin
- Dean, Caleb
- Dean, Ezelkiel
- Dean, John
- Fuller, Robt., Sgt
- Gregory, Tim'y
- Huson, Jerem'h
- Jenkins, Solomon
- Jones, Wm.
- King, Barley
- King, Stephen
- Lovelass, Wm
- Mabee, Peter
- Parish, Dan'l
- Robards, Peter
- Russell, Robt
- Russell, Thomas, Lt
- Sloot, Isaac
- Van Scoy, Jacob, Cpl

Crane's Company
- Austin, Jobe, Sgt
- Austin, Robert
- Austin, Smith
- Bisley, Oliver
- Bohker, Jacob
- Cayton, Isaac
- Crab, John
- Elsworth, John
- Hate, Sam'l
- Hedger, Joseph
- Hedger, Robert
- Hill, Wm
- Howe, Jesse
- Knapp, Daniel
- Nelson, Elijah
- Smith, David, Lieut
- Smith, Sam'l
- Sorine, Charles
- Sorine, Israel
- Wirson, Dan'l
- Wirson, John

Kidd's Company
- Bennet, Isaiah, Sgt
- Birdsall, John
- Browden, Eben'r
- Calkin, Will., Ensign
- Chase, Jebes
- Crosby, Theod's
- Cullen, Charles, Lt
- Elwell, Isaac
- Elwell, Jabus
- Gage, Eben'r
- Johns, Neh'h
- Nickerson, Uriah
- Sell, Uriah

Knapp's Company
- Barret, Samuel
- Boaly, Elias
- Burnell, Thomas
- Carey, John
- Champlin, Thomas
- Cooper, George
- Crosby, Lemuel
- Denny, Barber
- Doty, Joseph
- Downer, Israel
- Downin, Corn's
- Dusenbury, Will.
- Eldridge, Joseph
- Elliott, Dan'l
- Frost, Thomas
- Goodspeed, Israel
- Gray, Jon'n
- Hager, Thos
- Harrington, Reuben
- Kelley, John
- Lewis, Thomas, Qr Mr
- Marin, Charles
- McCredey, Charles

Luddington's Seventh Militia Regiment, continued

Knapp's Company, cont.
- Morrel, Ab'm, Sgt
- Mott, Zebulon, Sgt
- Nicholson, Basset
- Odle, Aaron
- Parker, Nath'l
- Penny, Joseph
- Perry, Sam'l
- Robinson, Esseker
- Rockwell, Silas
- Rogers, Richard
- Sampson, George
- Smally, James
- Smith, Alpheus
- Taylor, Gam'l
- Thompson, Dan'l
- Thompson, Thomas
- Townsend, Gilbert
- Vail, Israel, Lieut
- Ward, Moses
- Weight, Christ'r
- Witchson, Eben'r

Lane's Company
- Adams, Major
- Armstrong, J. Jr.
- Armstrong, John
- Arnul, Seymour
- Barger, Peter
- Barton, Elijah T.
- Barton, Gilbert
- Bartow, Andrew
- Bashford, James
- Begal, Stephen
- Beyes, Isaac
- Brewer, Hendk
- Brewer, Saml.
- Byington, Sam'l
- Christian, Charles
- Christian, George
- Christian, Rich'd
- Covert, Silvenus
- Drake, John
- Dusenberry, Chas
- Dusenberry, Jervis
- Dusenberry, Moses
- Dusenberry, Wm
- Dusenberry, Wm Jr
- Eakerly, Banj'n, Cpl
- Gager, Nath'l
- Green, John
- Holley, Daniel
- Knap, Gabriel
- Lane, Nathan, Sgt
- Lane, Nathan Jr, Sgt
- McCabee, Benj'n
- McTassel, Peter
- Oakley, Robt, Sgt
- Oakley, Tim'y
- Odell, Amos
- Odell, John
- Owens, Jesse
- Post, Henry, Sgt
- Read, Jacob
- Rhades, Rich'd
- Rhoades, Isaac
- Rhoades, John
- Rose, Will., Cpl
- Rush, John
- Sarrine, Isaac
- Simkins, John Jr
- Simkins, Robt
- Sloot, John
- Smawley, Zaccheus
- Smith, Abr'm, drum'r
- Smith, Gilbert
- Smith, John
- Smith, Rich'd
- Smith, Thomas
- Steward, Geo.
- Tomkins, Corn's Jr
- Tomkins, James, fifer
- Tomkins, Stephen
- Travis, George, Cpl
- Travis, James
- Travis, Titus
- Travis, Will.
- Wiksom, John, Cpl
- Williams, Thos.
- Willsey/tsie, Henry, Ens
- Wilsie, Daniel, Lieut

J&H Mead's Companies
- Abbett, Elijah T.
- Adams, John Jr.
- Adams, Thomas
- Akley, Jon'n
- Astin, John
- Baker, Joshua Jr.
- Baker, Josiah, Ens.
- Ballard, Caleb, Cpl
- Ballard, Peleg
- Barret, Isaac Jr.
- Barrett, Justus
- Barrett, Will.
- Bartine, Sam'l
- Bayley, Elias
- Benjamin, Darius
- Berry, Sam'l
- Brewster, John, Sgt
- Brooks, Will.
- Brown, Corns
- Bugbee, Ezekiel
- Burdick, Amos
- Burdick, Caleb
- Carl, Jonas
- Carver, Barnabus
- Carver, Tim'y
- Chase, John
- Chase, Judah
- Classon, Will.
- Cole, Reuben
- Colwell, James
- Colwell, Joseph
- Colwell, Wm.
- Crosby, Enoch
- Cushman, Consider
- Davis, John
- Daykins, Elisha
- Daykins, Johnson
- Demick, Shubab, Sgt
- Derley, John
- Dickson, James
- Dickson, Theodorus
- Disbrow, David, Sgt
- Disbrow, Nathan Jr, Cpl
- Dotton, Will.
- Drew, Gilbert, Sgt
- Drew, Sam'l
- Drew, Wm.
- Dyckman, Hezekiah
- Fisher, Nath'l, Sgt
- Frost, David
- Fuller, David
- Fuller, Isaac
- Furman, Joseph
- Giffords, Elisha
- Giffords, Sam'l
- Griffith, Joshua
- Griffith, Lazarus
- Hall, Elisha
- Hawkins, James
- Hazelton, David
- Hezelton, Daniel, Cpl
- Hopkins, Jerem'h
- Hopkins, Solomon, Lt
- Horton, Thomas
- Hyatt, Elias
- Hyatt, Minor
- Jewel, Jacob
- Jones, Annanias

Luddington's Seventh Militia Regiment, continued

J&H Mead's Companies, cont.
Kelley, Benj'n
Kelley, Zebedee, Ens.
Kerby, Albert
Knapp, Banj'n
Langdon, Benj'n
Light, Henry
Lockwood, Eben'r
Lockwood, Peter, Cpl
Ludinton, Comfort
Mane, Sebeus
Maze, Ab'm
Mead, Abner
Mead, Billey
Mead, Isaac
Mead, James
Mead, Moses
Morehouse, John
Moss, Will.
Paddock, Peter
Parse, Dan'l
Pinckney, Lewis
Pinkney, Israel
Porter, David, Lieut
Price, James
Raymond, Moses
Robinson, John, Lieut
Russell, John, Cpl
Scoffield, Ezra
Shaw, James Jr
Shaw, Joshua
Small, James Jr
Small, Zach'h
Smith, Benajah
Smith, Edward
Smith, Major
Smith, Philip
Smith, Seth
Sprague, Elijah
Sprague, Jerem'h
Taylor, Dan'l
Terry, Sam'l
Tidd, Nathan
Townsend, Chas., drum
Townsend, Eber
Townsend, Levy, Cpl
Townsend, Zeph'h
Turner, John
Turner, Stephen
Utter, Will.
Van Scoy, Abel
Waring, Theod's, Sgt

Whealey, James
Wood, Israel
Woodlin, John
Wright, Will

Scribner's Company
Baldwin, Elisha
Baldwin, Henry
Baldwin, James, Cpl
Ballard, Tracy
Bouton, Saml.
Brundage, John
Davis, Sam'l
Dean, Joseph
Everitt, Isaac, Sgt
Ferguson, John
Finch, Nath'l
Finch, Silvanus
Ganong, Isaac
Ganong, Jacob
Ganong, Marcus
Gregory, Dan'l
Gregory, Joshua
Gregory, Josiah, Sgt
Gregory, Russell, Cpl
Gregory, Thomas
Hall, Thomas
Hamblin, Benj'n
Hazen, Eleazer, Sgt
Hopkins, Eli
Hopkins, Jon'n
Hopkins, Joseph
Hopkins, Thomas
Hyatt, Stephen
Jenkins, Sam'l
Maline, Dan'l
McLean, John, Lieut
Merrick/Marick, David, Lt
Odell, Isaac
Parish, Silas
Raymond, Eben'r
Robinson, Peter
Simeons, John'n
Vermylea, Will.
Wilson, Thomas, Cpl
Wright, Zebulon

Waterbury's Company
Arnold, Pelick
Arnold, Semeur, Cpl
Bailey, Joseph
Bogington, Sam'l
Bogington, Solomon
Bouten, Saml

Buckley, Jabez
Bugby, Silvester
Covey, Walter
Cowen, David
Cowing, Isaac
Crosby, Solomon
Dan, Will.
Delavan, Timothy, Lt/Ens
Delivan, Abr'm
Disbrow, Andrew
Disbrow, Nathan, Cpl
Dixson, James
Gage, Moses
Ganong, John
Ganong, John Jr
Hadley, Will.
Howes, Job, Cpl/Pvt
Howes, John, Sgt
Howes, Moody
Hows, Daniel
Huson, Robert
Jean, John
Kelly, John
Kelly, Jude, Sgt
King, David
King, Obadiah
Martine, James
Martine, Samuel
Myrick, John
Nickerson, Aaron
Paddock, David
Paddock, Judah, Cpl
Paddock, Seth
Paddock, Stephen, Cpl
Petton, Philip
Pinkney, Fred'k
Platt, John
Rice, Edward
Richards, David
Richards, Moses
Rider, John
Smith, Asa
Smith, Jeremiah
Smith, Nath'l, Sgt
Townsend, Daniel, fifer
Townsend, Isaac, Lt/drum
Townsend, John
Vermilyea, John
Webb, Jonathan
Williams, Ichabod
Wood, John

FIRST CENSUS OF THE UNITED STATES, 1790
REPORTED THE THIRD DAY OF JANUARY 1791[1]

The first census of the United States began in 1790. Per the US Census Bureau:

> The law required that every household be visited, that completed census schedules be posted in "two of the most public places within [each jurisdiction], there to remain for the inspection of all concerned..."[2]

The seven data categories in 1790 are abbreviated as follows in the accompanying lists:

No.	Number of Families
Head	Names of Heads of Families
m≥16	Free white Males of 16 Years & upwards including Heads of Families
m<16	Free white Males under 16 Years
fem	Free white Females including Heads of Families
free	All other free Persons
slave	Slaves

Three census divisions existed in south Dutchess County in 1790:
    Township of Frederickstown, 914 families, 5932 people.
    Township of Phillipstown, 331 families, 2079 people.
    Township of Southeast, 141 families, 921 people.

Referencing the Philipse 1754 survey, Phillipstown comprised Philipse Lots 1–4; Frederickstown comprised the portion of Lots 5–9 that had been in the South Precinct; and Southeast comprised The Oblong east of Lots 7–9. By 1790, most of the farm lots in Philipse Lots 1, 3, 4, 5, 7, and 9 had been sold by the Committee of Forfeiture. Many farm lots in Philipse Lots 2, 6, and 8 and The Oblong had also been sold by the proprietors.[3]

The following schedules for south Dutchess were reported by Samuel Augustus Barker, Assistant to the Marshal of New York District. Indeed, he is the first person listed in the Township of Frederickstown.[4]

---

1. First Census of the United States, 1790, New York volume 2, NARA microfilm publication M637 roll 6; images from *FamilySearch.org* digital microfilm 004440870.
2. United States Census Bureau, *First Congress, Sess. II, Ch. 3, Sec. 7,* www.census.gov/history/pdf/1790_Census_Act.pdf.
3. see Henry S. Concklin, *Maps of eight lots of the Philipse upper patent : compiled and drafted from descriptions in records in Dutchess and Putnam counties and based in part on the field book of John Conklin's survey made in 1810* (1885-1887), and William T. Ruddock, *Confiscated Properties of Philipse Highland Patent, Putnam County, New York 1780-1785* (Westminster: Heritage, 2012) for maps and schedules and of properties sold. Northern portions of Lots 6 and 7 were in Pawling or Rombout.
4. He lived near Haviland's Tavern in the area of Frederickstown that became the Town of Patterson, according to Pelletreau, *History of Putnam County NY*, 641.

CHAPTER 5

Township of Frederickstown in the County of Dutchess 1790

pg	No	Head		m≥16	m<16	fem	free	slave
1		Samuel Augustus	Barker	4	1	6		5
		Caleb	Frisbie	2	3	3	1	2
		Medad	Palmer	1		4		
		Samuel	Huggins	3	2	4		
		David	Gilbert	1	2	2		
		Stiles	Peet	1	1	1		1
		Jacob	Burtch	1	1	1		
		Ephraim Beach	Hubbard	1	1	4		
		James	Phillips	2	2	5		
	10	John	Douglass	2		1		
		Alexander	Kidd	1		1		3
		Richard Samuel	Bryan	1	2	6		1
		Justus	Weed	2	2	6		
		William	Calkin	1	2	6		
		Benjamin	Platt	2	2	4		
		Samuel	Townsend	3	3	4		
		Enoch	Lewis	2	1	1		1
		Stephen	Hayt	3	2	3		
		Edmund	Ogden	2	1	1		
	20	Matthew	Patterson	6	1	4		3
		Mary	Sturgis	1	2	3		
		Losee	Ketcham	1	2	1		
		Nathaniel	Newman	1	1	3		
		David	Beebe Jnr:	1	2	2		
		John	Beebee	1	2	3		
		Samuel	Cornwall	3	2	3		1
		Anthony	Ashby	1	5	2		
		Moses	Williams	1	1	2		
		Stephen	Yale	2	5	5		
	30	William	Palmer			1		
			Total	54	51	92	1	17
2		Nathaniel	Palmer	1	1	5		
		Abel	Hodge	1	4	2		
		Ebenezer	Jones	1	4	1		
		Eli	Crosby	1	1	8		
		Aaron	Stocker	1	2	1		
		Sarah	Tomkins		1	2		
		Simeon	Perry	1	1	3		
		George	Murch	1	3	4		
		Lemuel	Crosby	1	1	3		

pg	No	Head		m≥16	m<16	fem	free	slave
	40	Reuben	Crosby	2	1	1		
		James	Crosby	1	1	1		
		Abiel	Crosby	1		2		
		Darius	Crosby	1		1		
		Ruth	Doane	2		1		
		Nathaniel	Foster	1	3	6		
		Thomas	Paddock	1		2		
		Thomas	Chapman	2	2	3		
		Jonathan	Paddock	6	2	7		
		Nathan	Paddock	1	3	5		
	50	William	Crane	1	1	2		
		Mary	Austin			1		
		Zeruiah	Disbrow		1	3		
		Theddorus	Crosby	3	3	4		
		Jeremiah	Burgess	2	3	6		
		Ebenezer	Arnold					2
		Ichabod	Lewis	1		3		
		Jonathan	Brown	1		1		
		Elias	Benjamin			1		
	60	Jacob	Weed	1	2	1		
		Edward	Rice	1	1	2		
		Eli	Gage	1	1	1		
		John	Rice Jnr:	1	1	1		
		Edward	Rice	1	2	3		
		William	Rice	1	2	3		
		Moody	Howes Jnr:	1	2	3		1
		Solomon	Meeker	1	1	1		
		David	Paddock	2	5	5		
		James	Paddock	1	2	5		
		Moody	Howes Sen:	5	1	4		
			Total	51	56	103	3	
3	70	Job	Howes	1		3		
		Ephraim	Marvin Jnr:	1	1	1		
		William	Brown	1	1	1		
		Uriah	Townsend	2	4	5		
		Nathan	Brundage	1	1	3		
		Reuben	Rider	1	3	2		
		Seth	Paddock	2	4	5		

Township of Frederickstown in the County of Dutchess 1790, continued

pg	No	Head		m≥16	m<16	fem	free	slave
		Elkanah	Hinckley	1	1	3		
		Stephen	Paddock	2	2	7		
		David	Baldwin	1	2	4		
	80	Jonathan	Crane	2	3	5		
		John	Place	1	1	5		
		Silas	Paddock	4		9		
		Isaac	Birdsall	2	2	3		
		Eunice	Smith		2	1		
		Jonathan	Waring	1		4		
		Jabez	Close	1	4	2		
		Moses	Gage	4		3		
		Joseph Coles	Fields	4	3	2		
		William	Bartlet	2	1	4		
	90	Bugby	Gage			1		
		Timothy	De La Van	5	2	4		
		John	Dan	1	2	3		
		William	Dan	1	1	1		
		Selleck	Dan	1	2	2		
		Isaac	Fields	1	1	6		
		Solomon	Fields	3	3	4		
		John	Platt	5	1	5		
		Moses	Richards	3	1	3		
		Stephen	Fields	2	1	7		
	100	Sylvanus	Palmer	1	3	3		
		James	Veal	2		2		
		James	Bland	1		1		
		John	Jeans	1	2	4		
		Samuel	Byington	1		4		
		Solomon	Byington	2	1	4		
		Daniel	King	1		2		
		Ezra	Richards	1	3	4		
		Nehemiah	Smith	2	3	8		
				69	61	140		
4		Jeremiah	Mead	1	2	3		
	110	Phillip	Mead	1	1	2		
		Nehemiah	Richards	2	1	4		
		Timothy	Lockwood	1	1	3		
		Daniel	Bull	2		4	1	6

pg	No	Head		m≥16	m<16	fem	free	slave
		Horace	Bull	1	1	2		
		Ichabod	Marvin	4	4	6		
		Solomon	Crosby	1	2	2	1	
		Priscilla	Cowen			1		
		Joseph	Lovelace	1	1	1		
		David	Cowen	2	3	4		
	120	Zachariah	Paddock	2	1	3		
		Isaac	Paddock	2	3	2		
		Frederick	Pinckney	2	2	5		
		Ephraim	Marvin	2		6		1
		Isaac	Townsend	2	3	8		
		Samuel	Fairbanks	1		1		
		Jesse	Fields	1		4		
		Anthony	Westcott				4	
		Jonathan	Minor	1	2	2		
		Daniel	Ketcham Jnr:	1	1	3		
	130	Asa	Cummins	1	1	4		
		Daniel	Ketcham	4	1	4		1
		David	Crosby Jnr:	3	1	6		
		Jeremiah	Lincoln	2	1	1		
		John	Waring	4	4	5		
		Peter	Crosby	2		4		
		Samuel	Lawrence	2	1	3		
		Elijah	White	1	1	4		
		John	Penny	2	2	7		
		George	Penny	2	4	5		
	140	Abijah	Benedict	1		2		
		Phillip	Brown	1	4	2		
		William	English	1	2	4		
		Ammiel	Penny	1	4	4		
		Stephen	Clements	2	2	2		
		John	Raymond	1	1	3		
			Total	60	57	126	6	8
5		William	Snow	1	2	3		
		James	Foster	2	2	5		
		Joshua	Crosby Jnr:	2		5		
		John	Howes	1	1	3		
	150	Sylvanus	Seely	2	4	2		

1790 US Federal Census

Township of Frederickstown in the County of Dutchess 1790, continued

pg	No		Head	m≥16	m<16	fem	free	slave
		Jacob	Reed	1		5		
		Phinehas	Baker	1	6	6		
		Beverly	Burch	2	2	3		
		Neil	McGlaughlin	1	4	2		
		Thaddeus	Waring	2	1	8		
		William	Burroughs	1	2	1		
		John	Crosby	2	4	4		
		Moses	Crosby	2	2	4		
		Joshua	Crosby			1		
	160	Amos	Jones	1		2		
		Thoeophilus	Jones	2		2		
		Abner	Crosby	2	4	3		
		Thomas	Crosby	2	1	2		
		Nathaniel	Jones	1		1		
		Nehemiah	Jones	3		4		
		Joseph	Phillips	2	2	2		
		Samuel	Crosby	2	2	7		
		William	Palmer Jnr:	1	2	3		
		Isaac	Crosby	2		4		
	170	Zebulon	Homan	3	3	2		
		Samuel	Towner	2	2	6	2	
		Gideon	Baxter	2	1	2		
		Francis	Gilding	1	1	1		
		Basset	Nickerson	1	2	1		
		John	Townsend the 1st	1	4	2		
		Elizabeth	Watts	2	2	7	2	
		David	Hill	3	2	3		
		Roswell	Willcox	3	1	4		1
		Samuel	Mills	3	2	2		2
	180	Job	Hicock	1	1	3		
		Abigail	Mills			4	1	1
		Eli	Calkins	1	2	2		
		Agnis	De La Van			4		1
		Total		61	65	125	5	5
6		Richard	Dixon	2		3	4	
		Abraham	Fancher	2	5	3		
		David	Beebe	2	1	4		
		John	Newbury	2	1	6		
		Joshua	Newbury	1	2	3		

pg	No		Head	m≥16	m<16	fem	free	slave
		Eady	Newbury	1	2	5		
		Abrose	Hall	1		1		
	190	Abigail	Dean		1	2		
		Joshua	Jeacocks	1	2	5		
		Edward	Hulford	1	4	3		
		Comfort	Ludinton	2	4	4		
		Stephen	Hurlbutt	1		2		
		Jachin	Hoyt	1	1			
		Timothy	De La Van Jnr:	1	1	2		
		Nathaniel	Fisher	2	3	5		
		John	Watts	1	3	3		
	200	James	Graham		3	2		
		Gilbert	Utter	1		1		
		Edward	Mooney	1	1	2		
		Silas	Dailey	2	1	3		
		John	Olmstead	1		2		1
		Joseph	Trusdell Jnr:	1	2	6		
		Bela	Alford	1	3	5		
		Ephraim	Waring	1	2	3		
		Abraham	St. John	1	2	5		
		Jonathan	Squire	1	1	2		
	210	Josiah	Miller	1		1		
		Joseph	Trusdell Sen:	1		1		
		George	Cleveland	1	2	2		
		Ebenezer	Bennet Jnr:	2		6		
		Ezekiel	Tharp	1	2	1		
		James	Hays	4	3	5		
		Eli	Northroup	1		4		
		Silas	Brown	1		2		
		Aaron	Calkins	1		2		
		David	Hicock	3	2	2		
		Total		47	53	105	4	1
7	220	Prince	George				5	
		James	Stenson	1	1	1		
		John	Allen	1	1	1		
		Issachar	Nickerson	2	3	6		
		Abraham	Mead	1	2	1		
		John	Terry	3	1	6		

Township of Frederickstown in the County of Dutchess 1790, continued

pg	No	Head		m≥16	m<16	fem	free	slave
		Ebenezer	Bennet Sen:	2	1	2		
		Abraham	Maybee	4	1	5		
		Nathaniel	Baker	1	3	4		
		Abraham	Hill	4	2	6		
230		Avery	Baker	1		1		
		John	Hinckley		4	5		
		Caleb	Spencer	1	5	2		
		Thomas	Hinckley	1	1	2		
		Abraham	De Puy	1	2	3		
		Elijah	Wixson	2		4		
		Jacob	Pyers	1	2	2		
		Michael	Bowen	1	2	2		
		Elisha	Gifford	3	1	4		
		Duncan	McGregor	2	4	4		
240		Joseph	Dyckman Jnr:	1	2	2		
		Benjamin	Dyckman	1	2	2		
		John	Ellis	1	2	4		
		Thomas	Ellis	1	4	3		
		David	Kelly	1	4	4		
		Shubael	Kelly	2	2	5		
		Simeon	Ellis	3	1	5		
		Jonathan	Kelly	1	1	2		
		Elizabeth	Doane	1	3	3		
		Abel	Merrick	1	2	4		
250		Elnathan	Doane	1	4	2		
		Caleb	Fowler Jnr:	1	4	4		
		Barzillai	King	4	2	4		
		Merrick	King	1	3	3		
		Nathaniel	King	1	2	4		
		John	King			1		
		John	Green	1	1	6		
		Caleb	Fowler Sen:	2		5		
			Total	58	76	124		5
8		Enoch	Ferris	1	1	3		
		Heman	King	2	2	3		
260		Heman	King Jnr:	1		2		
		Jeremiah	Bailey	1	4	6		
		Joseph	Hoskins	2	1	3		
		William	Lovelace	3	6	6		

pg	No	Head		m≥16	m<16	fem	free	slave
		Isaac	Townsend Jnr:	1	3	3		
		Daniel	Townsend	1		1		
		Enos	Tuttle	1		2		
		David	Rider	1	2	3		
		John	Gage	1		2		
		James	Egleston	1	2	3		
270		Aaron	Hull	3	4	4		
		Stephen	Rusco	3	1	2		
		Thaddeus	Dan	2	6	8		
		Hill	Sturgis	1		2		
		Solomon	Steenrod	1	1	1		
		Peleg	Bailey	2	3	5		
		Robert	Townsend	1	1	2		
		Elihu	Townsend	1		3		
		Elisha	Haines	1	6	3		
		Samuel	Bailey	1	2	6		
		Christopher	Townsend	2	3	3		
		William	Arnold	1	2	2		
		Samuel	Robbins	1	2	4		
		Edward & Seymour	Arnold	4	1	4		
		John	Ballard	1	6	9		
		John	Townsend the 2d	3	1	5		
		Nehemiah	Wood	3	2	5		
		John	Gilbert	1	1	3		
		Jabez	Trusdell	1	2	4		
		Philetus	Phillips	1	2	3		
		Ezekiel	Stewart	2		1		
		Edward	Haines	1	1	4		
		Peter	Brower	2	4	5		
		Aaron	Haines	1	2	3		
		John	Haines	1	2	3	3	
		Gideon	Townsend	1		1		
		Joseph	Requa	1		3		
		Johnson	Yumans	2	5	5		
			Total	61	83	140	3	
9		David	Birdsall	1	1	1		
		Noah	Robinson	1	4	3		
300		Abraham	Mott	1	1	1		
		John	Ambler Jnr:	1	2	4		

1790 US FEDERAL CENSUS

Township of Frederickstown in the County of Dutchess 1790, continued

pg	No		Head	m≥16	m<16	fem	free	slave
		Joseph	Langdon	2	2	2		
		Jacob	Mead	2	4	4		
		John	Byington	1		4		
		Abraham	De La Van	3		1		
		Jacob	Benedict	1		3		
		Caleb	Palmer	3	2	5		
		Zebediah	Brown	2		3		
		Mordecai	Dickens	1	4	3		1
	310	Deliverance	Purdee	1	3	2		
		Edward	Nickerson	2	4	6		
		Selah	Finch	1		1		
		Samuel	Ackerly	1	1	2		
		Jeremiah	Webb		4	1		
		Samuel	Kniffin Jnr:	2	1	3		
		Rachel	Genont	3	3	8		
		Isaac	Genont Sen:	1	3	5		
		John	Genont	2	2	4		
		Isaac	Pearce	2	2	4		
	320	Reuben	Genont	1	2	3		
		John	Genont Jnr:	1	4			
		Ebenezer	Genont	1		2		
		John	Mead	1	1			
		Merriby	Mott		3	1		
		Lucy	Cullen			3		
		Jotham	Smith	1	2	2		
		David	Garretson	3	4	2		
		John	Barber	5	3	5		
		Thomas	Wanser	1		2		
	330	Joshua	Gregory	1	3	3		
		William	Huson	1	3	3		
		Isaiah	Robinson	2		2		
		John	Tomkins	2		2		
		Isaac	Barns	1		2		
		Enoch	Crosby	2	2	4		2
		John	Mark	1	2	2		
		Joseph	Moss	1	3	5		
		William	Fowler	2	4	2		
		Samuel	Kniffin Sen:	2	2	3		
			Total	64	82	120		3

pg	No		Head	m≥16	m<16	fem	free	slave
10	340	Jeremiah	Kelly	1	2	2		
		Foster	Ellis	1	1	1		
		Jacob	Ellis	2	3	3		
		Nathan	Hawley	3	2	4		
		Stephen	Fowler	1	2	2		
		Matthew	Beal	3	2	2		
		George	Beal	1	1	1		
		Silas	Griffin	2	1	3		
		Zebulon	Phillips	4		3		
		David	Read	1	5	1		
	350	Gideon	Close	1		1		
		Isaac	Seely	2	3	3		
		John	Rider	1	1	1		
		Daniel	Gay	2	4	5		
		Thomas	Kelly	2	1	4		
		Josiah	Baker Jnr:	4	2	4		
		Zebulon	Washborn	3	3	3		
		Stephen	Mead	2		4		
		Absolom	Gifford	1	2	1		
		Amos	Rogers	1	2	3		
	360	Levi	Molineaux			2		
		John	Molineaux	1		2		
		Israel	Molineaux	2	2	3		
		Joseph	Blatchly	2	2	2		
		James	Mead Jnr:			1		
		Abijah	Townsend	2	1	3		1
		James	Caldwell	2	2	3		
		Gilbert	Merritt	1	2	6		
		Phillip	Pelton	3	3	4		
		Benjamin	Pelton	1	4	4		
	370	Nathan	Brooks	1	4	2		1
		Jane	Foster			2		
		Moses	Fowler	4	2	4		
		Israel	Hamlin	2	3	6		
		Benjamin	Griffin the 1st	1	1	2		
		James	Willson	2	3	2		3
		Daniel	Gregory	2	4	4		
		John	Neal	2	3	3		
		Elisha	Smith	2		1		
		Samuel	Bradly	1	1	1		

Township of Frederickstown in the County of Dutchess 1790, continued

pg	No	Head		m≥16	m<16	fem	free	slave
11	380	John	Frost	5	3	4		
		Total		76	76	109	1	4
		John	Langdon	1	1	1		
		John	Varnill	1	1	2		
		Nathaniel	Jenkins	1	4	3		
		Jacob	Genont	1	5	3		
		Reuben	Smith	1	1	3		
		Samuel	Trusdell	1	2	1		
		Ezra	Rundle	1		5		
		Daniel	Tillotson	3	1	3		
		Elizabeth	Genont	1	1	5		
	390	Lemuel	Mosier	1		1		
		Abraham	Bloomer		1	1		
		Henry	Neil	1		1		
		Ebenezer	Wright	1	1	3		
		Jacob	Bailey	1	1	6		
		Robert	Wright	4	2	5		
		Mary	Kniffin	1		6		
		Robert	Wright Jnr:	2		1		
		Devereux	Bailey	2	6	2		2
		Isaac	Genont Jnr:	1		3		
	400	John	Maybee	3	3	4		
		Isaac	Sloet	2	2	4		
		Isaac	Bashford	1	2	5		
		William	Kennicut	1	3	5		
		Luther	Gregory	1	4	2		
		Abijah	Drake	2	2	3		1
		John	Barker	1	2	5		
		Martha	Smith	4		3		
		Abel	Hull	1	1	6		
		Eliphalet	Hull	2	4	2		
		Hezekiah	Hitt	1	2	2		
	410	Jared	Early	1	2	4		
		Absolom	Kniffin	1	2	1		
		Jacob	Gray	1	5	2		
		John	Trowbridge	1	5	4		
		Bille	Chapman	2		5		
		Richard	Gregory	4	7	2		1
		Joseph	Burgess	1	1	2		
		Jonathan	Kniffin	1		4		
		John	Sloet the 1st	1		1		
	420	James	Cambey	1	1	1		
		Henry	Hitt	1		3		
		Nathaniel	Brundage			2		
			Total	61	73	127		4
12		William	Falconer	1		5		
		Benjamin	Crosby	3	5	4		
		John	Devereux	1		2		
		Joshua	Merrick		2	3		
		John	Beyea	2	2	4		
		Isaac	Stocum	1	3	2		
		James	Whitney		1	1		
	430	Isaac	Lounsbury	3	3	3		
		Thomas	Crosby	1	4	5		
		William	Webb	1	2	5		
		Peter	Scutt	1	3	3		
		James	Sovrine	3	1	2		
		Charles	Sovrine	2		1		
		Elizabeth	Minthorne	1		3		
		Major	Simpkins	1	2	3		
		Esther	Crane		2	4		
		Paul	Secoy	2		1		
	440	William	Derbyshire	1	2	5		
		John	Badeau	1	1	2		
		James	Crawford		2	2		
		Clarkson	Herroy	1	4	2		
		Benjamin	Golden	2		1		
		Elizabeth	Herroy		1	3		
		Peter	Herroy	2	4	3		1
		John	Doty	2	3	2		
		Jacob	Yumans	1	2	2		
		Harry	Garrison	3		3		2
	450	William M.	Smith	1	3	3		3
		James	Cock	1	1	5		
		William	Porter	3		3		
		Joseph	Angevine	1	3	3		
		Peter	Badeau	3	1	3		1
		Thomas	Kircum	4	1	6		

1790 US Federal Census

Township of Frederickstown in the County of Dutchess 1790, continued

pg	No	Head		m≥16	m<16	fem	free	slave
		Lydia	Kircum	1	2	4		
		John	Griffin	1	1	2		
		Jacob	Badeau	1	1	3		
		Charles	Sovrine Jnr:	1	1	2		
	460	Catharine	O'Brien	1		3		
		Isaac	Keating	2		4		
		Joshua	Ketcham	1	1	6		
	Total			60	65	123		7
13		William	Roe	1	1	3		
		Daniel	Knap	2	2	2		
		John	Curtiss	1	1	2		
		Benjamin	Knap	1	4	3		
		Solomon	Farrington	1		1		
		Charles	Herroy	1	2	3		
		Joseph	Ketcham	1		2		
	470	Jeremiah	Genont	1	1	3		
		John	Berry	2	1	2		
		Jacob	Bonker	3		5		
		John	Secoy	5	2	3		
		Isaac	Secoy	4	3	8		
		Daniel	Hawley	1	1	2		
		Peter	Badeau Jnr:	1	1	3		
		Isaac	Pioneer	2	3	2		
		David	Demarest	1	3	4		
		Abijah	Wright	1	2	1		
	480	Peter	Bonker	1		2		
		Jemima	Burch	2		1		
		Joseph Gidney	Haines	1	2	5		
		Isaac	Badeau	1	4	3		
		Peter	Maybee	3	1	5		
		Daniel	Maybee	2	2	6		
		John	Ferguson	1	3	3		
		Elias	Sloet	1	3	3		
		Michael	Sloet	4	3	5		
		John	Halket	1		1		
	490	John	Sloet the 2d	1	2	4		
		William	Vermillia	1	6	3		
		Joseph	Tidd	2		4		
		Benajah	Beardslee	2	4	4		
		Jonathan	Austin	2	1	6		1
		Josiah	Nichols	2	2	4		
		Ebenezer	Robinson	4	3	7		3
		Simeon	Sloet	1	1	2		
		John	Sloet the 3d	1	2	2		
		Edward	Genont	1		1		
	500	Hannah	Barker			1		
		Jacob	Ackerly	1	3	2		
		Samuel	Jenkins	3	4	7		
		Solomon	Jenkins	4	3	5		
		Henry	Ludenton Jnr:	1		1		
		David	Bouton	2	4	2		
	Total			74	81	138		4
14		Asa	Haines	2	2	6		4
		James	Calkins	1	4	5		
		Daniel	Haines	1	2	1		
		Enoch	Haines	1	1	1		
	510	William	McGilvray	1		3		
		Jonathan	Gray	1	3	2		
		Peter	McIntire	1		2		
		William	Gray	2	1	3		
		Abijah	Starr	2	4	4		
		Ebenezer	Palmer	1	1	3		
		Nathan	Sheldon	3	2	8		
		Darius	Stone	1	2	2		
		Elijah	Stone	1	2	5		
		John	McLean the 2d	3	1	4		
	520	Darius	Atkins	1		4		
		David	Lyndsay	1		1		
		Auley	McAuley	1		1		
		David	Birdsall	2	1	2		
		Benjamin	Cole	2	1	4		
		Nathan	Weed	1	2	4		
		Lucy	St John	1	2	5		
		Joseph	Weed	1		1		
		Gershom	Jones	1		1		
		Robert	Jones	1		2		
	530	William	Birdsall	2	2	6		
		Ephraim	Jones	2	2	5		

Township of Frederickstown in the County of Dutchess 1790, continued

pg	No	Head		m≥16	m<16	fem	free	slave
		Jehiel	Stevens	3		4		
		Jonathan	Parrish	2	2	4		
		David	Stone	1	1	2		
		Russell	Stevens	1		3		
		Joshua	Conklin	3		3		
		Eleazer	Baker Jnr:	1	2	4		
		Jachin	Lockwood	1	1	2		
		Edmund	Baker	2		3		
	540	Elijah	Abbot	1	4	4		
		Samuel	Terry	3	4	3		
		Henry	Lockwood	3	3	4		
		Joshua	Baker	1	1	2		
		Josiah	Baker	1	1	1		
		Elijah	Fuller	2	1	4		
		David	Egleston	1		5		
		Bethuel	Barnum	1		1		
			Total	64	55	133		4
15		Andrew	Disbrow	3	6	3		
		William	Jones	1	1	2		
	550	David	Fuller	2	3	7		
		Zepheniah	Townsend	1	3	3		
		Seth	Foster	1	2	2		
		Judah	Kelly	2	2	5		
		Benjamin	Isaacs	2				
		John	Wooden	2		2		
		Thomas	Sears	3	4	5		
		Desire	Stone			2		
		Enoch	Green	1	1	1		
		Jeremiah	Huson	3		3		
	560	Alpheus	Hayden	2	1	6		
		Thatcher	Hopkins	4	2	5	2	
		Isaac	Smith	1	2	2		
		William	Frost	2		1		
		William	Warren	1	3	1		
		Rebecca	Hopkins			4		
		Ira	Bouton	1	2	1		
		Reuben	Cole	1	2	3		
		Caleb	Veal	2	6	4		
		John	Veal	1	1	1		
	570	Jonas	Yumans	1	1	4		
		William	Drew	1		5		
		John	Golding	2	1	5		
		Joseph	Hopkins	2	2	8		
		Solomon	Reynolds	1	3	3		
		John	Ambler Sen:	2	2	3		
		Jonathan	Hopkins	1	1	2		
		Samuel	Conklin	2	3	3		
		Thomas	Hopkins	1	1	2		
		Mille	Handly			1		
	580	Abner	Mead	3	3	4		
		Jesse	Genont	3	2	1		
		Roger	Dickens	1	1	1		
		Thaddeus	Raymond	4	3	8		
		David	Robinson	2		4		
		Thomas	Ferguson	1	1	1		
		Thomas	Ferguson Jnr:	2	2	3		
		Abraham	Ferguson	1	3	3		
		Jane	Davis		1	5		
		Henry	Baldwin	1	2	3		
	590	Isaac	Fuller	1	1	3		
		Thomas	Fowler	1	1	3		
			Total	70	76	138	2	
16		Mary	Waters			1		
		Thomas	Kirk	1		3		
		John	Brewer	1		1		
		James	Baldwin		3	7		
		Caleb	Tomkins	1	1	2		
		John	McLean the 1st	1	1	7		
		Elisha	Baldwin	4	2	6		
		Solomon	Kireum	1	1	1		
	600	Benjamin	Griffin the 2d	1	2	2		
		David	Smith	1	2	3		
		Isaac	Ferguson	1	3	5		
		John	Adams	2	1	7		
		Tracy	Ballard	1	2	3		
		Matthew	Bump	1		1		
		Jesse	Smith	1	1	3		
		Elisha	Smith	1	3	4		

1790 US FEDERAL CENSUS

Township of Frederickstown in the County of Dutchess 1790, continued

pg	No		Head	m≥16	m<16	fem	free	slave
		Samuel	Smith	1	2	3		
		Edmond	Foster	1	1	2		
	610	Elizabeth	Hall	2		1		
		Absolom	Simmons	2	1	4		
		Caleb	Hazen	4	4	4		
		Solomon	Chase	1	1	1		
		Moses	Hazen	1	4	2		
		Eleazer	Hazen	3	2	4		
		Abel	Smith	1		2		
		Isaac	Everett	5	1	3		
		Isaac	Merrick	4	3	5		
		David	Merrick	1		2		
	620	George	Everett	3	3	3		
		John	Lounsbury	3	1	4		
		Thomas	Smith	3	5	6		
		Jacob	Cronk	1	3	3		
		Isaac	Barret	1	3	4		
		Joshua	Shaw	2	1	3		
		Phillip	Smith	1	5	5		
		James	Sacket	3		2		
		Frederick	Margetson	1	2	3		
		Edmond	Hopkins	1		3		
	630	Hezekiah	Rowland	2	3	3		
		John	Roberts	1		4		
		Isaac	Chase	1		2		
		Total		69	67	134		
17		John	Kelly	3	3	5		
		Benjamin	Ogden	1	4	4		
		Obadiah	Chase	2	2	4		
		Jonathan	Washbourn	2	2	1		
		Peter	Mead	1	2	3		
		Ezekiel	Deane	1		4		
		Isaiah	Swift	1	5	1		
	640	Caleb	Deane	1	2	2		
		Michael	Evans	3		4		
		Stephen	Welding				5	
		John	Deane	4	2	6		
		David	Hazleton	1	2	2		
		James	Russell	2	2	2		
		Robert	Freeman				5	

pg	No		Head	m≥16	m<16	fem	free	slave
		William	Calwell	2	1	2		1
		Joseph	Calwell	4	4	4		
		Joel	Mead	2	2	6		
	650	Nathan	Crosby	4	3	5		
		William	Wooden	4	4	4		
		Thomas	Hammond	1		4		
		John	Gifford	1	2	5		
		Joseph	Knap	1	4	4		
		Daniel	Sunderland	1	3	3		
		Jacob	Smith	1	2	2		
		Edward	Smith	3	3	5		
		John	Smith	2		6		
		Paul	Northroup	1		3		
	660	Elihu	Secoy	2	3	5		
		Reuben	Ferris	3	1	4		
		Jacob	Birdsall	1	4	3		
		Stephen	Northroup	1	1	4		
		Joseph	Dyckman	4	1	8		
		John	Robinson the 2d	1	4	3		
		Lewis	Robinson	1	3	2		
		John	Robinson the 1st	3	1	5		
		Walter	Covey	3	3	5		
		James	Hopkins	1		1		
	670	Michael	Nowland	3	3	4		
		Noah	Scovil	2		3		
		James	Lyon	1		2		
		David	Hicock Jnr:	1	2	1		
		Isaac	Lañterman	1	2	2		
		Total		77	82	141	10	1
18		Caleb	Burdeck	2		4		
		Elizabeth	Maine	1	3	2		
		Joseph	Covey			1		
		Elishama	Holcomb	3	4	3		
		Moses	Fowler Jnr:	1	1	1		
	680	Elisha	Brown	1		3		
		Isaac	Wixson	1	2	2		
		John	Price	1	2	2		
		Samuel	Ludenton Jnr:	1	3	3		
		Elijah	Wixson	1	1	3		

Township of Frederickstown in the County of Dutchess 1790, continued

pg	No		Head	m≥16	m<16	fem	free	slave
		Daniel	Burch	1	1	7		
		Jeremiah	Burch	2	2	3		
		John	Bartow	1	2	3		
		William	Daily	1	1	4		
		Zachariah	Burch	1	2	2		
	690	Henry	Ludenton	3	2	4		1
		James	McFarlin	2		2		
		Mary	Dimick		1	4		
		John	Wood	1	1	4		
		James	Mead Sen:	1	3	3		
		David	Mory	3	2	3		
		Robert	Booth	1	4	2		
		Isaac	Booth	1	4	2		
		Lemuel	Carl	1	3	2		
		David	Disbrow	1	1	6		
	700	Seth	Kelly	1	2	1		
		Zebediah	Kelly	1	1	2		
		Joseph	Northroup	3		6		
		William	Mead	2	5	1		
		John	Sprague Jnr:	1	1	1		
		Shubael	Dimick	1	2	2		
		Enoch	Robinson	1	1	3		
		Elijah	Sturdevant	1	1	2		
		Johnson	Dakins	2		3		
		Elisha	Dakins	1	3			
	710	Jacob	Scoit	1	1	2		
		John	Patrick	2	1	6		
		Abel	Scoit	1		2		
		William	Utter	1	5	4		
		Morris	Smith	1	4	3		
				53	72	114		1
19		John	Williams Jnr:	1	1	3		
		Joseph	Phillips Jnr:	1	1	2		
		Samuel	Hayt	1	1	3		
		Mary	Neilson	3		1		
		Joseph	Farrington	3	5	3		
	720	William	Foster	1		5		
		James	Shaw	1		3		
		Joseph	Lee	2		2		

pg	No		Head	m≥16	m<16	fem	free	slave
		David	Mead	1		6		
		Henry	Charlock	2	3	6		
		Nathaniel	Parker	1	1	1		
		Samuel	Parker	1		1		
		Joseph	Randall	1		6		
		Isaac	Cronk	1		2		
		Consider	Cushman	3	2	4		
	730	Richard	Cook	1	1	3		
		Reuben	Barrett	1	1	3		
		Thomas	Horton	4	1	5		
		Joseph	Huntly	1	1	4		
		Thomas	Horton Jnr:	1	2	1		
		Israel	Knap	1		2		
		Moses	Knap Jnr:	1	1	5		
		William	Knap	1		4		
		Benjamin	Knap the 2d	1	3	3		
		Thomas	Carl	3	4	4		
	740	John	Dingy	1	1	2		
		Ezra	Scovil	1		4		
		Joseph	Randal Jnr:	1	2	4		
		Ebenezer	Boyd Jnr:	1	1	1		
		Cornelius	Brown	1	3	6		
		Samuel	Scoit	1		2		
		Isaiah	Smalley	1	1	2		
		Richard	Ayres	1	1	3		
		Daniel	Wixson	1	2	4		
		John	Booth	3	1	5		
	750	John	Williams Sen:	1	4	2		
		Richard	Williams, the 1st	1		3		
		Abraham	Williams	1	1	2		
		Teunis	Cronk	3		6		
		Matthew	Williams	1	1	2		
		Lemuel	Munger	2	6	2		
		Richard	Williams, the 2d	1	1	2		
			Total	60	55	134		
20		Samuel	Jones	4	1	6		
		Joseph	Jones	1	1	2		
		Isaac	Drew	1	1	5		
	760	Samuel	Barret	1		2		

1790 US FEDERAL CENSUS

Township of Frederickstown in the County of Dutchess 1790, continued

pg	No		Head	m≥16	m<16	fem	free	slave
		John	Matross	1	3	2		
		Robert	Shaw	2	4	6		
		Jacob	Tomkins	1	2	4		
		Samuel	Hunt	2	2	5		
		Jesse	Howe	1	4	2		
		Thomas	Adams	3	3	5		
		John	Rhodes	1	1	3		
		Isaac	Horton	2	2	5		
		William	Hedden	3	2	6		
	770	John	Post	1	5	2		
		Thomas	Richards	3		5		
		Stephen	Lawrence	1	1	4		
		John	Barret Jnr:	1	1	1		
		John	Barret Sen:	2	3	4		
		Ebenezer	Boyd Sen:	2	2	5		1
		William	Cudney	2		2		
		James	Rhodes	1		2		
		Calvin	Whedon	1		1		
		James	Randall	1	1	1		
	780	Isabelle	Hawkins	1		2		
		Stephen	Scoit	1		1		
		James	Hawkins	1	1	5		
		Nathan	Sturdevant	1	6	3		
		Jesse	Barret	2	3	4		
		Elijah	Chase	1		2		
		Moses	Mead	2	1	3		
		David	Webb	2	2	4		
		Henry	Laight	2	3	6		
		John	Sprague	1	1	2		
	790	James	Carl	1		3		
		Abijah	Russell	1		2		
		Samuel	Hawkins	1	1	3		
		James	Russell Jnr:	2	2	6		
		Elijah	Sprague	2	2	6		
		Jeremiah	Sprague	3	3	2		
			Total	62	64	134		1
21		William	Ballard	1		1		
		Caleb	Ballard	1		2		
		Lewis	Mead	1	3	1		
		Peter	Robinson	2	2	2		

pg	No		Head	m≥16	m<16	fem	free	slave
	800	Jonathan	Close	2	3	5		
		Hezekiah	Dyckman	1	1	2		
		Ebenezer	Robinson	1		1		
		Peleg	Ballard Jnr:	1	2	1		
		John	Robinson, the 3d	2	2	5		
		Joseph	Northroup Jnr:	1	2	4		
		William	Moss	2	1	7		
		Isaiah	Hopkins	2		2		
		Thomas	Russell	2	2	5		
		Joseph	Parker	1		2		
	810	William	Barret	1	2	6		
		Aaron	Whitney	3		3		
		Ebenezer	Brown	4	2	4		
		Elijah	Townsend	1	4	4		
		James	Townsend	3	1	6		
		Gilbert	Drew	3	2	6		1
		Thomas	Chase	3	1	4		
		Comfort	Paddock	3		1		
		Thomas	Townsend	1	3	4		
		Benjamin	Higgins	1		4		
	820	Gilbert	Townsend	3	3	1		
		Amos	Towsend	1	3	2		
		David	Frost	5	3	3		
		Nathan	Cole	1	4	5		
		Joshua	Cole	1	1	2		
		Ephraim	Baldwin	2	3	5		
		Joseph	Fuller	1	1	2		
		Jeremiah	Hopkins	2	4	3		
		Solomon	Hopkins	3	1	3		
		Caleb	Hall	1	3	4		
	830	Jahoida	Whedon	1	2	1		
		James	Smalley	1		3		
		John	Wixson	1	2	3		
		Moses	Hedden	1	2	1		
		John	Morgan	1	2	2		
		Mary	Lockwood	2		6		
		Daniel	Cole	2	3	7		
		Isaac	Barret Jnr:	1	3	3		
			Total	71	75	138		1

Township of Frederickstown in the County of Dutchess 1790, continued

pg	No	Head		m≥16	m<16	fem	free	slave
22		James	Barret	2	1	7		
		James	Barret Jnr:	1	3	4		
	840	Zachariah	Smally	1		2		
		Daniel	Chaddock	1		1		
		Reuben	Hedden	1	1	1		
		John	Beyea	1	2	1		
		Peter	Lockwood	1	1	3		
		Gilbert	Adams	1	5	2		
		Justus	Adams	1	1	2		
		James	Williams	1	2	2		
		John	Adams Jnr:	1		4		
		John	Cole	2	2	2		
	850	Elisha	Cole	4	4	4		
		Isaac	Rhodes	2	1	2		
		Gilbert	Carrigan	1	2	3		
		Timothy	Carver	2	4	5		
		Jeremiah	Huson	1		1		
		James	Smalley Jnr:	1	3	2		
		William	Anderson	1		1		
		Barnabas	Carver	2	1	2		
		Peleg	Wixson	3	1	5		
		Shubael	Wixson	4	2	2		
	860	James	McGuire	1	1	2		
		Charles	Green	1	1	1		
		Joseph	Cole	2	4	4		
		Nehemiah	Brewer	1	3	2		
		Joseph	Crane Jnr:	1	2	4		1
		Peleg	Ballard	1	3	3		
		Jabez	Berry Jnr:	1	1	4		
		Samuel	Berry	1		3		
		Jabez	Berry	2	1	2		
		James	Sloane	1		1		
	870	Stephen	Evans	1	2	2		
		Caleb	Craft	4	2	3		
		John	Crane	3	1	5	1	
		George	Huson	1	1	2		
		Robert	Huson	2		6		
		Edward	Stevens	1		4		
		Sylvanus	Traverse	1	2	2		
		Nathan	Conklin	1	1	2	1	1
			Total	61	62	110	1	2
23		John	Sweeny	1	1	2		
		William	Hill	2	1	3		1
		Jonathan	Stocum	3	1	3		
		Noah	Hill	1	1	3		
		William	Hill Jnr:	1	2	2		
		Charles	Ager	3		2		
		Daniel	Pearce	1	5	4		
		Abraham	Williams	1	2	1		
		William	Osborn	1	1	3		
		Israel	Pinckney	2	2	2		
		William	Hitchcock	2	3	4		
		David	Hitchcock	2	2	3		
	890	Jehiel	Tyler	3	1	2		
		David	Longwall	2	3	4		
		Gilbert	Hayt	1	3	4		
		John	Crookston	1	3	2		
		John	Simkins	1	1	2		
		Peter	Anderson	2	2	3		
		Robert	Hedger	1		3		
		Job	Austin		1	3		
		Benjamin	Austin	1	1	2		
		Isaac	Austin	2	2	2		
	900	Moses	Knap Sen:	2		3		
		Robert	Austin		1	2		
		Smith	Austin	1	1	4		
		Elijah	Neilson	1	1	5		
		Josiah	Ingersoll	3	1	3		
		John	Ingersoll	1		3		
		Isaac	Ridgeway	1	1	3		
		Solomon	Smith	1	1	6		
		Henry	Handtrot	1	1	1		
		Henry	Brewer	1		3		
	910	Abigail	Yumans			1		
		Lebbens	Howe	1	4	2		
		Elijah	Wright	1	3	2		
		Samuel	Edy	2	1	4		
		Joseph	Conklin	1		2		

Township of Frederickstown in the County of Dutchess 1790, continued

pg	No	Head	m≥16	m<16	fem	free	slave
		Total	54	53	103		1
		Brot forward from Page No 1	54	51	92	1	17
		Do: Do: from Page No 2	51	56	103	3	
		Do: Do: from Page No 3	69	61	140		
		Total	228	221	438	4	18
24		Brot forward from Page No 4	60	57	126	6	8
		Do: Do: from Page No 5	61	65	125	5	5
		Do: Do: from Page No 6	47	53	105	4	1
		Do: Do: from Page No 7	58	76	124	5	
		Do: Do: from Page No 8	61	83	140	3	
		Do: Do: from Page No 9	64	82	120		3
		Do: Do: from Page No 10	76	76	109	1	4
		Do: Do: from Page No 11	61	73	127		4
		Do: Do: from Page No 12	60	65	123		7
		Do: Do: from Page No 13	74	81	138		4
		Do: Do: from Page No 14	64	55	133		4
		Do: Do: from Page No 15	70	76	138	2	
		Do: Do: from Page No 16	69	67	134		
		Do: Do: from Page No 17	77	82	141	10	1
		Do: Do: from Page No 18	53	72	114		1
		Do: Do: from Page No 19	60	55	134		
		Do: Do: from Page No 20	62	64	134		1
		Do: Do: from Page No 21	71	75	138		1
		Do: Do: from Page No 22	61	62	110	1	1
		Do: Do: from Page No 23	228	221	438	4	18
	914	Total of Frederickstown	1437	1540	2851	41	63

Township of Phillipstown in the County of Dutchess 1790

pg	No	Head		m≥16	m<16	fem	free	slave
24		Peter	Weeks	1		1		
		John	Brewer	2	4	2		
		Abraham	Losee	1		1		
		Isaac	Jones	1	1	2		
		John	Smith	1	6	4		
		Girardus	Cronk	1	4	5		
		James	Smith	1		1		
			Total	8	16	16		
25		Solomon	Smith	1	1	3		
		Levinus	Covert	1	1	3		
	10	Abraham	Smith	1	2	3		
		James	Covert	1		3		
		Joseph	Smith	2		3		
		John	Hyatt	3	1	2		
		Nathan	Lane	3	2	3		
		Isaac	Rhodes	2	1	1		
		George	Currie	1	1	1		
		Isaac	Beyea	2		4		
		Matthew	Covert	1	1	2		
		Isaac	Rhodes Jnr:	2		2		
	20	John	Every	1	1	2		
		John	Russell	1	3	3		
		John	Barret	2		2		
		Francis	Williams	5	1	2		
		Abraham	Post	3		2		
		Thomas	Obriant	1	1	2		
		Joshua	Tomkins	2	2	4		
		Joshua	Tomkins Jnr:	1	1	3		
		John	Tillotson	1		3		
		William	Pearce	1	4	1		
	30	Titus	Traverse	1	3	4		
		Abraham	Lockwood	1	2	6		
		Solomon	Avery	3	1	2		1
		Timothy	Rhodes	1	3	2		
		James	Tomkins	1	3	2		
		Cornelius	Tomkins	1	3	3		
		Amos	Odell	1	2	3		
		Nathaniel	Tomkins	3	4	4		

Township of Phillipstown in the County of Dutchess 1790, continued

pg	No.	Head		m≥16	m<16	fem	free	slave
		Charles	Currie	1	4	3		
		Stephen	Tomkins	1	3	2		
	40	John	Denny	1	2	3		
		John	Delany	2	1	2		
		Nathaniel	Gager	1	3	7		
		John	Berger	1	3	5		
		Cornelius	Berger		1	1		
		Amaziah	Dusenbury	1	1	1		1
		William	Dusenbury	4	2	7		
		Moses	Dusenbury	5	2	4		
26		**Total**		**68**	**67**	**115**		**2**
		Francis	Strang	4	2	4		
		John	Bashford	3	1	4		
	50	John Gold	Selleck	6	4	3		
		Andrew	Barton	2	2	3		
		Andrew	Barton Jnr:	1	1	3		
		Jesse	Owens	1	4	4		
		James	Sherwood	1	2	3		
		Jasper	Drake	1	1	3		
		John	Drake	2	5	6		
		Obadiah	Hunt	1	3	3		
		William	Drew	7	1	5		
		Ira	Gale	1		1		
	60	Joseph	Gale	2	2	2		
		Gilbert	Oakley Jnr:	1		3		
		Peter	Berger	1	5	6		
		Jeremy	Chapman	2	2	2		
		Peter	Terrel	1	1	8		
		Samuel	Cromwell	1		5		
		Paul	Berger	1	2	2		
		Jacob	Reed	2	3	2		
		George	Lane	2		4		1
		Timothey	Oakley	1	2	5		
	70	Mary	Conklin	3	1	2		
		Hannah	Knap	5	3	6		2
		Tobias	Waggoner	1	3	3		
		Richard	Rhodes	1	1	4		
		Jeremiah	Conklin	1	3	1		
		Gilbert	Traverse	1		2		

pg	No.	Head		m≥16	m<16	fem	free	slave
		Aaron	Odell	1	1	1		
		Oliver	Odell	3		4		
		John	McDonald	3		2		
		Reuben	Tomkins	1	4	2		
		James	Tomkins	1	1	3		
	80	Abraham	Holliday			2		
		Richard	Satterlee	2		1		
		Gilbert	Oakley Sen:	3	4	5		
		William	Dotton	1	4	2		
		William	Nichols		2	3		
		Isaac	Odell Jnr:	1	3	1		
		Total		**74**	**73**	**125**		**3**
		Barthene	Bailey		1	5		
		Mark	Dingy	1	1	2		
		Seth	Kircum	1	3	3		
	90	John	Nichols	2		5		
		Judah	Baker		3	1		
		William	Lane	1	3	2		
		Daniel	Amy	1	2	6		
		Joseph	Horton	5	2	3		
		Peter	Ryal	1	4	2		
		Woolsey	Laight	1	1	4		
		Jesse	Lane	1	2	1		
		John	Ryal	1		1		
		George	Tomkins	1	2	1		
	100	Thomas	Town	2	2	4		
		John	Goodman	1	4	1		
		Gilbert	Barton	1	1	5		
		Samuel	Phillips	2		3		
		John	Rush	2	2	4		
		Israel	Lockwood	1	2	7		
		James	Sovrine	1	2	5		
		Hannah	Mangle			3		
		Elizabeth	Doyl			2		
		Joseph	Hyatt	1	2	1		
	110	Stephen	Cale	1	3	1		
		Jane	Owens	2	3	4		
		James	Campbell	1	1	1		
		Thomas	Bashford	3	4	4		

1790 US Federal Census

Township of Phillipstown in the County of Dutchess 1790, continued

pg	No.	Head		m≥16	m<16	fem	free	slave
		Jonathan	Owens	1	2	1		
		Silas	Palmer	1		1		
		Phinemon	Smith	1	3	3		
		Sylvanus	Lockwood	1	3	5		
		John	VanTassell	2	1	2		
		Joshua	Horton	2	5	3		
	120	Ebenezer	Cole	2	4	2		
		Sibert	Cronk	1	1	6		
		Joseph	Chase	1	2	2		
		Jeremiah	White	1	2	2		
		Margaret	Traverse			3		
		John	Lickley	2	3	5		
		Henry	Ducher	1	3	3		
		Thomas	Hunt	1	5	2		
		David	Ducher	2		4		
		Henry	Post	2	4	4		
	130	Isaac	Odell	2		1		
		Total		58	88	130		
28		John	Odell	1	3	3		
		John	Horton	1	6	3		
		Peter	Bell	3	1	6		
		Samuel	Smith	2	3	5		
		Samuel	Smith Jnr:	1	2	2		
		Joseph	Bell	1		2		
		William	Colegrove	2	1	3		
		William	Colegrove Jnr:	1		1		
		John	Colegrove	1				
	140	Charles	Post	2	3	5		
		John	Elsworth	1	1	3		
		Phillip	Steenbanck	3	1			
		Nathan W.	Miner	1	2	2		
		Jacob	Armstrong	1	3	3		
		Matthew	Mc Abe	3	1	2		
		Stephen	Mc Abe	1	4	4		
		Benjamin	Mc Abe	1	2	2		
		George	Traverse	1	1	2		
		Francis	Tercotte	1	3	1		
	150	Jacob	Armstrong Jnr:	1	1	2		
		William	Christian	1	3	2		
		Gabriel	Armstrong	1	1	3		
		John	Conolly	1		1		
		John	Armstrong	3	3	4		
		Charles	Armstrong	1	3	5		
		James	Hall	1		2		
		Thaddeus	Tomkins		1			
		James	Perry	1	4	3		
		Richard	Christian	2		2		
	160	Richard	Christian Jnr:	2	4	1		
		George	Christian	1	2	2		
		Robert	Armstrong		3	3		
		Amos	Odell	1	1	1		
		James	Christian	2	1	1		
		Isaac	Sovrine	1	3	5		
		Thomas	Ryan	1		1		
		John	Jeacocks	2	2	2		
		James	Jeacocks	1	6	3		
		Ezekiel	Gee	2	1	2		
	170	Isaiah	Jeacocks	1	1	6		
		Henry	Kearse	3		1		
		Total		59	80	106		
29		Abraham	Craft	3	2	2		
		Elisha	Barton	2		1		
		John	Barton Jnr:	1	1	1		
		James	Ascough	1		1		
		William	Shaw Jnr:	1	4	3		
		Isaac	Springer	1		4		
		William	Springer	1	3	1		
		Ephraim	Storm	1	1	2		
	180	Eli	Shaw	1	1	2		
		Elisha	Pelham	1		1		
		Isaac	Washbourn	1	5	1		
		Isaac	Shaw	1	1	3		
		Solomon	Lane	2	1	1		
		Reuben	Shaw	1	3	2		
		Matthew	Boyce	1	4	1		
		John	McFarden	1		3		
		Charles	Wright	1	2	1		
		Joseph	Wright	1	2	2		

Township of Phillipstown in the County of Dutchess 1790, continued

pg	No.	Head		m≥16	m<16	fem	free	slave
	190	David	Hangen	1		4		
		John	Haight	3	7	4		2
		Thomas	Scovil	1		1		
		Mary	Knap	2	3	3		
		Eleazer	Heely	1		5		
		John	Heely	1	1	5		
		Squire	Baker	1		1		
		William	Hill	1		2		
		Robert	Matross	1	1	1		
		Cornelius	Matross	1		4		
	200	John	Knap	1	4	2		
		Jesse	Lawrence	1		1		
		John	Barton	4	2	3		
		Israel	Lawrence	1	1	2		
		John	Snook	1		1		
		James	Neilson	2	1	5		
		Ephraim	Scovil	1	1	3		
		Miles	Scovil		3	3		
		Sylvanus	Wood	1	1	3		
		William	Wright	2	2	2		
	210	Gilbert	Weeks	3	3	3		
		Elijah	Barton	1	1	2		
		Charity	Husted	2	2	5		
		Joseph	Husted	2	3	6		
		Robert	Husted			2		
		Total		56	68	105		2
30		Paul	Sparling	3	2	3		
		Benjamin	Bloomer	4	1	3		
		William	Smith	1		1		
		Elisha	Bloomer	1		1		
		John	Boyce	1	1	3		
	220	Joshua	Mead	2	3	5		
		Jonathan	Odell	3	2	6		
		Timothy	Wood	1	3	3		
		William	Bloomer	1		1		
		John	Van Ambrough	4	1	2		1
		John	Arkills	2		1		
		Thomas	Latimore	2	1	2		
		Andries	Scouten	1	1	2		
		Robert	Golden	1	3	4		
		Judith	Cromwell	3	2	5		
	230	Peter	Du Bois	4	3	3		9
		George	Bump Jnr:	1	1	2		
		Daniel	Bloomer	1	3	3		
		Gilbert	Bloomer	1	2	4		
		Peter	Weaver	1	1	1		
		William	Sprague	1		1		
		Mary	Davenport	1	3	2		
		Thomas	Pioneer	1	2	3		
		William	Davenport	4	2	3		
		William	Davenport Jnr:	2	2	6		
	240	Thomas	Davenport	4		2		4
		James	Snook	2		1		
		Daniel	Sheilds	1		1		
		Reuben	Bunn	2	1	2		1
		Nehemiah	Traverse	1	3	1		
		Moses	Swims	1	1	3		
		Uriah	McKeel	3		2		
		Matthew	Snook	2	1	3		
		Isaac	Dapenport [sic]	1	3	3		
		Beverly	Warren	1	1	2		
	250	Robert	Welsh	1	2	2		
		Peter	Budd	1	2	1		
		Elijah	Budd	2		1		1
		Sarah	Sawyer	2		3		
		Gilbert	Budd	2	3	2		
		William	Butler			1		
		Total		74	57	100		16
31		James	Yumans	1	2	2		
		John	Budd	2	3	2		
		Peter	Sine	1	1	4		
		Sarah	Sherwood	1	2	3		
	260	William	Sarls	1	2	1		
		John	Warren	3	4	4		
		Thomas	Sarls	1	3	4		
		Absolom	Early	1		2		
		Elijah	Early	1	1	1		
		Andrew	Denny	2	4	4		

1790 US Federal Census

Township of Phillipstown in the County of Dutchess 1790, continued

pg	No.	Head		m≥16	m<16	fem	free	slave
		Richard	Denny	6	4	3		
		Joseph	Hultz	1	3	2		
		John	Coonradt	1		1		
		John	Hancock	1	1	3		
	270	Thomas	Hill	4	4	4		
		Francis	Gee	1		2		
		Joseph	Beard	2	2	5		
		Teunis	Brewer	1		2		
		John	Christian	1	2	6		
		Richard	Rogers	1	3	7		
		David	Hill	1	1	1		
		Henry	Brewer	1	2	3		
		William	Manning	1	4	4		
		Benjamin	Rogers	2	3	4		
	280	Abraham	Garrison	1	2	4		
		Daniel	Ferris	2	2	1		
		Charles	Hill	1	2	1		
		Timothy	Scott	1	2	3		
		Peter	Snook	1	5	4		
		Richard	Hopper	4	1	4		
		Edward	Eldridge	1		2		
		Joseph	Hopper	2		5		
		Isaac	Mead	1	2	2		
		Stephen	Hayt	1		4		
	290	Abraham	Baker	1	4	2		
		Samuel	Jeffers	1	3	2		
		Ruth	Arkills	2	2	3		
		James	Finn	1	2	2		
		John	Johnson	1	1	2		
		John	Meeks	3	1	2		
		Total		61	80	117		
32		John	Meeks Jnr:	1	2	2		
		Thomas	Oakley	3	2	7		
		Joshua	Lancaster	1	3	3		
		William	Lancaster	1	6	3		
	300	Richard	Arundale	3		6		
		Ruth	More	1		2		
		John	Hopper	2	2	3		
		John	Gee	2	3	2		
		John	Dalton	1	1	4		
		Sylvanus	Hayt	1	2	7		1
		Joshua	Neilson	2	1	4		1
		Jacob	Neilson	2	4	3		
		Isaac	Garrison	3	1	3		
		Cornelius	Neilson	1	1	3		
	310	Caleb	Neilson	3		3		
		Peter	Matross	1	2			
		Samuel	Matross	1	2	6		
		Justus	Neilson	3	5	7		
		Jonathan	Austin	1	1	4		
		Daniel	Lane	1	2	2		
		Mark	Obryant	1		3		
		Phenas	Neilson	1	2	4		
		Tatlock	Rhinehart	1	2	4		
		Christopher	Fowler	1		1		
	320	Daniel	Hayt	1		4		
		William	Hayt	2	5	5		
		Thomas	Hinyon	5	3	2		
		William	Houston	2		3	2	
		Mikiah	Avery	3	1	4		
		Jacob	Ten Eyck	1	1	2		
		Robert	Ten Eyck	1		3		
		John	Neilson	2	4	8		
		Eli	Neilson	1		1		
		Richard	Meeks	1		4		
	330	Edward	Meeks	1	3	3		
		James	Craft	1	1	3		
		Total		59	64	128	2	2
		Brot forward from Page 24		8	16	16		
		Do from Page 25		68	67	115		2
		Do from Page 26		74	73	125		3
		Total		209	220	384	2	7
33		Brot forward from Page 27		58	88	130		
		Do. from Page 28		59	80	106		
		Do. from Page 29		56	68	105		2
		Do. from Page 30		74	57	100		16
		Do. from Page 31		61	80	117		
		Do. from Page 32		209	220	384	2	7
	331	Total of Phillipstown		517	593	942	2	25

Township of Southeast in the County of Dutchess 1790

pg	No.	Head		m≥16	m<16	fem	free	slave
33		Thomas	Baldwin	2	1	2		
		Edmund	Wright	1	3	1		
		Stephen	Keley	2	1	5		2
		Jacob	Brush	3		8		1
		Elijah	Dean	1	2	3		
		John	Feilds	4	1	6		
		Joseph	Bailey	1	3	4		
		William	Fields	3	3	5		
		Isaac	Townsend	2	1	2		
	10	Uriah	Townsend	1	2	3		
		Gilbert	Fields	2				
		Elijah	Benjamin	1	3	2		
		Shubael	Bouton	2	3	9		
		Phineahas	Weed	1	1	2		
		Rebecca	Wood			3		
		Isaac	Crane	2	3	3		
		Eleazer	Rider	3		3		
		Joshua	Hinckley	1	1	2		
		Jabez	Rockwell	2	2	2		
	20	Joseph	Crane	3		1		1
		Seth	Sears Jnr:	2	2	7		
		William	Wooster	2	5	4		
		Joseph	Crane Jnr:	2	1	3		
			Total	43	40	80		4
34		Benjamin	Sears Jnr:	4	1	5		
		James	Green	2		4		
		Morton	Hall	1	1	4		
		David	Hall	2		1		
		Elnathan	Field	1	2	4		
		John	Weed	1	3	4		
	30	Benjamin	Titus	3	3	3		
		Richard	Smith	2	1	3		6
		Ichabod	Doolittle	1		1		
		William	Young	1	3	3		
		Nathan	Green	2	1	3	1	
		Stephen	Sears	1		3		
		Stephen	Crane	2	2	5		

pg	No.	Head		m≥16	m<16	fem	free	slave
		Stephen	Frost	1		3		
		Samuel	Hall	3	3	4		
		Mary	Rider			2		
	40	William	Case	1		2		
		Abigail	Benedict			2		
		Zadoc	Rider	1	4	2		
		Shaw	Young	3	2	8		
		William	Penny	4		2		
		Ebenezer	Gage	2	2	2		
		Seth	Sears	2	1	3		
		Isaac	Crosby	3	2	6		
		Ezra	Elwell	1	4	4		
		Anthony	Gage	4	6	9		
	50	Lambert	De Forest	2	2	1		
		John	Starr	1	2	6		
		Elihu	Gage	2	2	2		
		Christopher	Rider	1	3	2		
		Thomas	Higgins	2	3	7		
		Maria	Briggs	4	1	4		
		Simeon	Rider	2	3	2		
		Elkanah	Young	1	2	5		
		Darius	Benjamin	1	2	3		
		Thankful	Bangs		1	1		2
	60	Nathaniel	Scrivener	4	3	8		
		Thomas	Russell	1				
		Caleb	Roberts	1	1	2		
			Total	71	67	136	1	8
35		Enos	Comstock	2	3	4		
		Noah	Bouton	1	3	2		
		Benjamin	Roberts	1		1		
		Phebe	Roberts		1	1		
		Rowland	Russell	2		1		
		Sylvanus	Cole	1	1	4		
		Elias	Jones	2	3	3		
	70	John Gray	Akins	1	3	2		
		Zaccheus	Raymond	1	1	1		
		Jonah	Barnum	1	2	6		

1790 US FEDERAL CENSUS

Township of Southeast in the County of Dutchess 1790, continued

pg	No.	Head		m≥16	m<16	fem	free	slave
		Joshua	Barnum	4	2	4		
		Azor	Barnum	3	2	6		
		Charity	Foster			2		
		Obadiah	Crosby	1	3	2		
		Peleg	Meeker	1	2	2		
		Peter	Olney	1	1	3		
		Isaac	Elwell	2	1	3		
	80	Ebenezer	Olmstead	2	3	3		
		Matthew	Honeywell	1	5	1		
		Berry	Hopkins	1	2	5		
		Phebe	Elwell	1	2	2		
		Jabez	Elwell	5	2	5		
		Jonathan	Carly	1	3	4		
		Jabez	Elwell Jnr:	1		5		
		Obadiah	Howland		1	2		
		Seth	Nickerson Jnr:	1	2	2		
		Jason	Gay	1	3	2		
	90	Mary	Nickerson		1	1		
		William	Utter			1		
		Nathan	Taylor	1	1	2		
		John	Hopkins	2	2	3		
		Joshua	Nickerson	1	1	2		
		Thomas	Haviland	2	3	2		
		William	Stow	2	5	3		
		Jesse	Lane	2	4	4		
		Seth	Nickerson	2	1	2		
		Moultroup	Nickerson	1	1	3		
	100	Abraham	Haviland	1	2	1		
		Daniel	Haviland Jnr:	1	2			
			Total	56	75	104		
36		Daniel	Haviland	3	2	6		
		Jonathan	Nickerson	1		2		
		Stephen	Hyatt		1	2		
		Roger	Haviland Jnr:	1	2	1		
		Nathaniel	Covill	1		2		
		Warren	Covill		4	4		
		John	June	1	1	1		
		Peter	June	1	1	3		
	110	Joshua	Hayt	1	1	2		1
		John	Bradshaw	1	2	4		
		Samuel	Brewster	1	1	3		
		Isaac	Squires	1	3	3		
		Isaiah	Hayt	1		3		
		Francis	Franklin				2	
		David	Haviland	2	1	3		
		Benjamin	Haviland Jnr:	2	2	3		
		Benjamin	Haviland Sen:	2	2	3		
		Violet	Morrison			3		
	120	James	Birdsall	4		2		
		Uriah	Sill	1	1	2		
		John	Tweedy	3	1	4		
		Gilbert	Birdsall	1	3	1		
		William	Birdsall	1	2	2		
		Anne	Hepburn	2		4		
		James	Hartwell	2	4	2		
		Peter	Ritton		3	1		
		Daniel	Burch	3	1	4		
		Amos	Leech	1		5		
	130	Amos	Leech Jnr:	1	1	2		
		Jonathan	Wright	1	2	4		
		Silas	Burch	2	1	2		
		James	Burton	3	1	4		
		Joseph	Burch	2	2	1		
		Zachariah	Hinman	1	2	3		
		Joseph	Arnold	2	3	6		
		James	Fairchild	3	1	6		
		George	Burch	1	1	1		
		Thomas	Birdsall	1	4	3		
	140	Jacob	Miller	3	1	2		
		John	Willcox	1	2	4		
37			Total	61	59	113	2	1
		Brot forward from Page 33		43	40	80		4
		Do. from Page 34		71	67	136	1	8
		Do. from Page 35		56	75	104		
		Do. from Page 36		61	59	113	2	1
	141	Total of Southeastown		231	241	433	3	13

APPENDIX A

BOOK OF TAXES 1729 to 1748, VOLUME C, DUTCHESS COUNTY CLERK FEBRUARY 1739/40 — FISHKILLS PRECINCT

The names were extracted for those also on the South Precinct tax list in February 1740/1 or those on the Fishkills list in 1739/40 but not 1740/1. The names are cross referenced to those on the 1740/1 tax list; parentheses indicate surnames in 1740/1 with a different given name. The names on page 205 likely lived along the Hudson River.

Page	Line	Name	Assessment	On Feb 1740/1 List	
Page 205	2	Abraham Otter	0.1	Otter	11
	3	Samul Taylor Jur	0.2	-	
	4	Ebbenezer Jons	0.3	Jones	12
	5	Samul Jons	0.3	Jones	13
	6	Joseph Erkils	0.1	Arkills	3
	7	Edward Willer	0.1	-	
	8	John Tamkins	0.1	Thompkins	14
	9	Obadya Tamkins	0.1	Thompkins	15
	10	Jurry Sprengstin	0	(Springsteen)	(4)
	11	Francis Nelson	1.6	Nellson	1
	12	Francis Drack	0.8	Drake	16
	13	James Walden	0.3	Willden	18
	14	Thomas Devenport	3.5	Davinport	2
	15	Albart Swiem	0.3	Swim	5
	16	Daved Hussted	0.9	Hustis	6
	17	William Lambe	0.2	Lamb	19
	18	Isack Fortin	0.3	Fontyn	20
	19	John Van Amburgh	0.9	Van Amburgh	21
	20	Isack Van Amburgh	0.2	Van Amburgh	22
	21	Hendrick Van Amburgh	0.7	Van Amburgh	23
	22	Piter Dubois Jur	1.1	Du Bois	24
Page 208	1	William Umpris	0	-	
	3	John Leneback	0.1	-	
	4	Hendrick Bell	0.1	-	
	5	Jacob Sprengstin	0.1	Springsteen	4
	6	Bangaman Jacobs	0.3	Jaycocks	25
	7	Henry Brower	0.4	Brewer	26
	30	Edward Hall	0	-	
	31	Nattan Broster	0.2	(Brooster)	(46)
	32	John Corken	1.5	Calkin	7
	33	Jeremia Corken	1.5	Calkin	8
Page 209	1	Abraham Oter	0.1	-	
	7	John Jons	0.1	(Jones)	
	10	Bangaman Roy	0.5	-	
	11	Jonatan Stordevelt	0.4	Sturdefunt	27
	12	Jonatan Stordevelt Jur	0.3	Sturdefunt	28
	23	Jacob Mandevil	0.5	Mandavil	29
	24	Jacobus Henion	0.5	Hennion	30
Page 210	1	Joseph Jacobs	0.2	(Jaycocks)	
	3	John Roggars	0.4	Rogers	9
	13	Ebenezer Jons Jur	0.2	(Jones)	(12)
	14	Joseph Barla	0.2	-	
	15	William Jarns	0.2	([Y]Earns)	(44)
	16	Joseph Corbin	0.2	-	
	17	John Tamkins	0.2	(Thompkins)	(17)
	19	Joseph Gregory	0.6	-	(47)
	21	Martin Ocken	0.2	-	
	22	Daved Gray	0.4	-	

APPENDIX B

DUTCHESS COUNTY MILITIA BEATS

Fredricksburgh and South East 1775–1776

Under date of 15 March 1776, the Dutchess general committee submitted the officers for six companies of militia to the Committee of Safety of New York, "pursuant to a resolve of the Provincial Congress of New-York, passed the 9th of August, 1775."[1] The committee members inspected and selected the officers, consisting of captain (cpt), first lieutenant (1st lt), second lieutenant (2d lt), and ensign (ens). The following chart places the beats in Fredricksburgh and South East precincts based upon known residences of one or more officers and a logical numbering system. North is up, but it is not drawn to scale.

Fredricksburgh				SouthEast
Long Lots 5 and 6		Short Lots 7-9		Oblong
Beat 5		**Beat 6**		
committee:	Wm Colwell, cpt	*committee:*	David Hecock, cpt	
Solomon Hopkins	Joel Mead, 1st lt	Isaac Chapman	Wm Calkin, 1st lt	
Joshua Myrick	Steph. Ludinton, 2d lt	Joshua Crosby	Moses Sage, ens	
	David Porter, ens			
Beat 4		**Beat 3**		
committee:	John Crane, cpt	*committee:*	Jonthn Paddack, cpt	
Solomon Hopkins	Elijah Townsend, 1st lt	Jonthn Paddack	Simeon Tryon	
David Myrick	David Smith, 2d lt	Simeon Tryon	Jeremiah Burges, 2d lt	
David Smith	John Berry, ens	David Crosby	Joseph Dykeman, ens	
Beat 1		**Beat 2**		
committee:	Ebenz Robinson, cpt	*committee:*	David Waterbury, cpt	
Joshua Myrick	Nathl Scribner, 1st lt	David Waterbury	Isaac Townsend, 1st lt	
Daniel Mertine	Hezek. Mead Jr, 2d lt	Moses Richards	Jonathan Webb, 2d lt	
David Myrick	Obadiah Chase, ens		Timothy Delavan, ens	

A notation indicates Simeon Tryon (Beat 3) was appointed lieutenant in the Continental Army. Also, for Beat 6, "Increas Bennet afterwards refused to serve as lieutenant."[2]

---

1. *Journals of the Provincial Congress, Provincial Convention, Committee of Safety and Council of Safety of the state of New-York : 1775-1776-1777* (Albany: Weed, 1842), 1:390.
2. Ibid.

APPENDIX B CONTINUED

Beats for Luddington's and Field's Regiments 1778

In May 1778, the Council of Appointment, meeting in Poughkeepsie, approved the officers for the beats of Colonel Henry Luddington's Regiment, and followed in June 1778 with the same for Colonel Field's Regiment.[3] These charts depict the geographical area of the ten beats specified in the minutes of the committee that fall within the precincts of Philipse, Fredricksburgh, and South East. The chart does not include those beats of Field's Regiment that lay in Pawling Precinct to the north.

Seventh Regiment - 1778			Third Regiment - 1778	
Henry Luddington, col		Eben. Robinson, 2nd maj	John Field, col	Jonathan Paddock, 2d maj
Reuben Ferris, lt col		Hosea Hamilton, Adj	Andr. Morehouse, lt col	Isaac J. Talman, 2d maj
Wm Gee, 1st maj.		Eleazer Baker, qtr master	Solomon Crane, adj	Reuben Crossby, qtr mstr
Lots 1-4	Long Lot 5	Long Lot 6	Short Lot 7	Oblong
George Lane, cpt Danl: Willsey, 1st lt Reuben Drake, vice John Drake, 2d lt Henry Willsey, ens	(was Elijah Townsend, commander) Joel Mead, cpt David Porter, 1st lt Steph. Luddington, 2d lt		David Heacock, cpt Joseph Chandler, 1st lt Peter Hatfield, 2d lt John Hatch, ens	Benjamin Higgins, cpt Azor Barnum, 1st lt Thomas Sears, 2d lt Nathan Green, ens
			Short Lot 8	*SE Pct Assoc Exempts:*
	John Crane, cpt David Smith, 1st lt John Berry, 2d lt Jos. Gregory, ens	Hezek. Mead Solomon Hopkins Elijah Fuller Josiah Baker	Jos. Dykeman, cpt Joshua Crosby Jr, 1st lt Edward Penny, 2d lt Daniel Doan, ens	Alexander Kidd, cpt Charles Cullen, 1st lt William Calkin, ens
John Haight, cpt Israel Knap, 1st lt Jos. Garrison, 2d lt John Nelson, ens	Nathl Scribner, cpt David Merrick, 1st lt William Martine, 2d lt Caleb Hazen, ensign		Short Lot 9	
			David Waterbury, cpt Isaac Townsend, 1st lt Tim^y: Delivan, 2d lt James Egleston, ens	

For the above, cpt=captain, 1st lt= first lieutenant, 2d lt=second lieutenant, ens=ensign.

The Seventh Regiment included Water Lots 1–3, Long Lots 4–6, and Short Lot 9. The Third Regiment included Pawling Precinct (not shown), Southeast Precinct (the Oblong), and Short Lots 7 and 8. Figure above is not drawn to scale.

---

3. *Minutes of the Committee and of the First Commission for Detecting and Defeating Conspiracies in the State of New York : December 11, 1776–September 23, 1778 with Collateral Documents* (New York: NYHS, 1925), 2:11-13, 32-33.

APPENDIX C

TENANT FARM LOT MAPS

The proprietors commissioned surveys of their lands in the 1760s to satisfy the laws regarding leasing to tenants. Few of the field books of survey and maps from this period survive. The following maps were re-created through use of tenant lists, one surviving survey field book, sales of loyalist lands in the 1780s, Concklin's maps of those sales, and other deeds and records. For Lots 4 and 7, the reader is cautioned to use these lot boundaries as guides, not absolutes, as only the map of Lot 6 was created from survey notes at the time. These maps provide relative positions of the tenants and allow for identification of neighbors. Please refer to the tenant lists for Lots 4, 7, and 8 included on pages 226–234. All maps were created by the author with invaluable assistance from a metes and bounds deed mapping software program and Concklin's maps (see bibliography of maps).

ROBINSON'S LONG LOT 4 – THE SOUTHERN PORTION

This map depicts only the southern portion of Lot 4. Settlement of the more mountainous northern portion occurred in the mid to late 1770s or 1780s. As noted in the tenant lists, farms 1–52 were surveyed and are included on the map with aproximate boundaries. However, for farms 53–74 the map provides a tentative location only for those numbered farms where the purchaser in the 1780s matches a tenant from Robinson's list; these farm numbers appear with dots (*e.g.,* •53•) to indicate the tentative nature of the location and size. Of farms 53–74, only farms 53–56, 61, 65–67, and 69 are included on the map; the other listed tenants either did not purchase a farm in the 1780s, or located a farm in the northern portion of the lot.

PHILIPSE'S LONG LOT 6

This map depicts the farm lot lines based upon the metes and bounds in Benjamin Morgan's 1762 field book of survey. One section of the lot (on the west side) was not surveyed. The field notes specify the locations of the houses and mills on the farm lots. The accompanying list includes tenants and occupants of each farm as identified in the field notes. Some farms along the east and west boundaries extended into the neighboring lots (Morris's lot 5 to the west and the three short lots 7, 8, and 9 to the east).

ROBINSON'S SHORT LOT 7

A significant portion of Lot 7 extended into Beekman/Pawling Precinct. The tenants in those precincts will not be found in the accompanying tax lists. As with lot 4, some of the boundaries of the farm lots shown may vary from the original survey. As noted earlier, squatters occupied much of this land prior to the initial 1754 patent survey and into the mid 1760s. Many of those early settlers do not appear on Robinson's tenant lists since they had left, or been tossed out, prior to 1768.

PHILIPSE'S SHORT LOT 8

The original surveys for Lot 8 are not extant. Most subsequent deeds and mortgages do not specify farm lot numbers, thereby complicating identification of the original lots on a map. Of the 49 lots included in the tenant list, 48 appear on the map, though many do not indicate boundaries. This map is a work in progress.

The Farms of the Southern Portion of Robinson's Long Lot 4

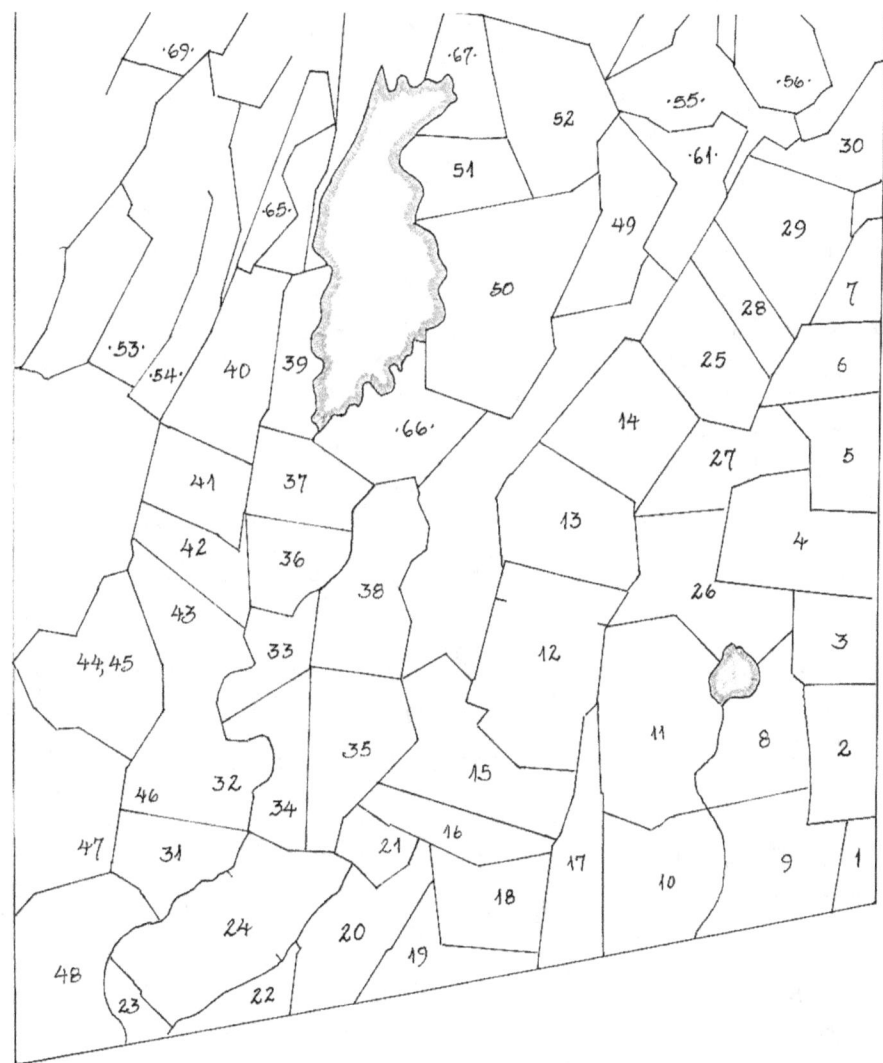

The map above sits about 10° off of true north (so as to fit better on the page). However, in the 1760s and early 1770s when the land was surveyed, the surveyors considered the bottom line of the lot to be due east – west ("as the compass now points" rather than using true north).

The large body of water is Conopus Pond, now called Oscawana Lake. The smaller one is Knapp's Pond. Peeks Kill creek enters the lot between farms 22 and 24 and courses up through the middle of farms between 21 and 30. Lake Peekskill is near the south west corner of the lot around farm 23.

Both farms 24 and 12 indicated two tenants in Robinson's lists. The small lines along the edges show the approximate location of dividing line between the two tenants.

The Farms of Robinson's Short Lot 7

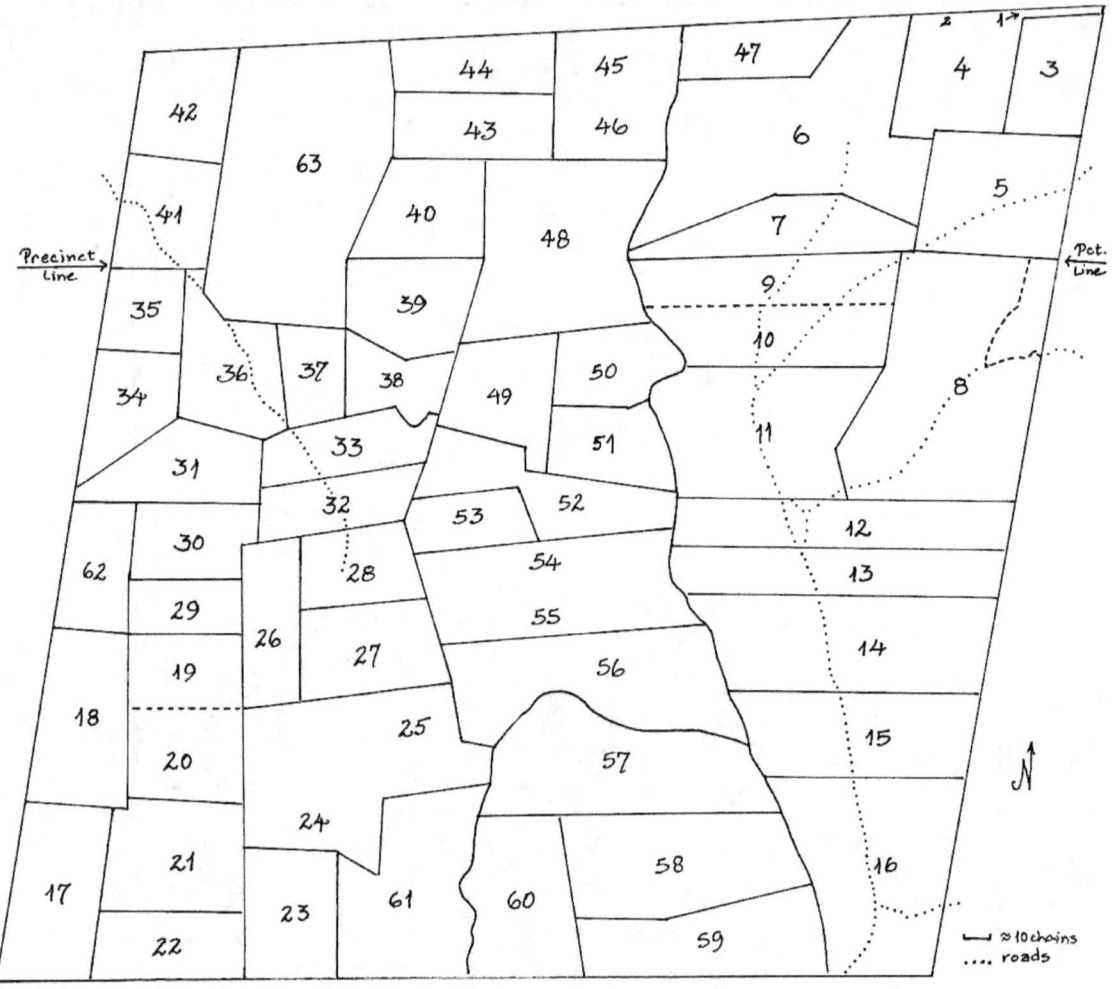

The above map is off kilter from true north. Surveys made in the 1750s and 1760s used measurements based upon uncorrected compass readings and considered the bottom line of this lot as due east – west. Current maps use modern surveying methods which adjust for magnetic declination.

The arrows indicating the precinct line show the *approximate* location of the dividing line between the South Precinct and Beekman (Pawling, beginning in 1769) Precinct. The lands above the line lie in Beekman/Pawling and remained in Dutchess County (for the most part) upon the creation of Putnam County.

The dividing lines between farms 19 and 20 and 9 and 10 represent approximate divisions between those farms. The section in the upper right corner of farm 8 represents the farm allocated by 1777 to James Calkins in Robinson's tenant list.

The northern part of Philip Philipse's Lot 6 is to the left and the Oblong is to the right. The westerly borders of farms 47, 6, 7, and 9 to 16 are along the Croton river.

The Farms of Philipse's Short Lot 8

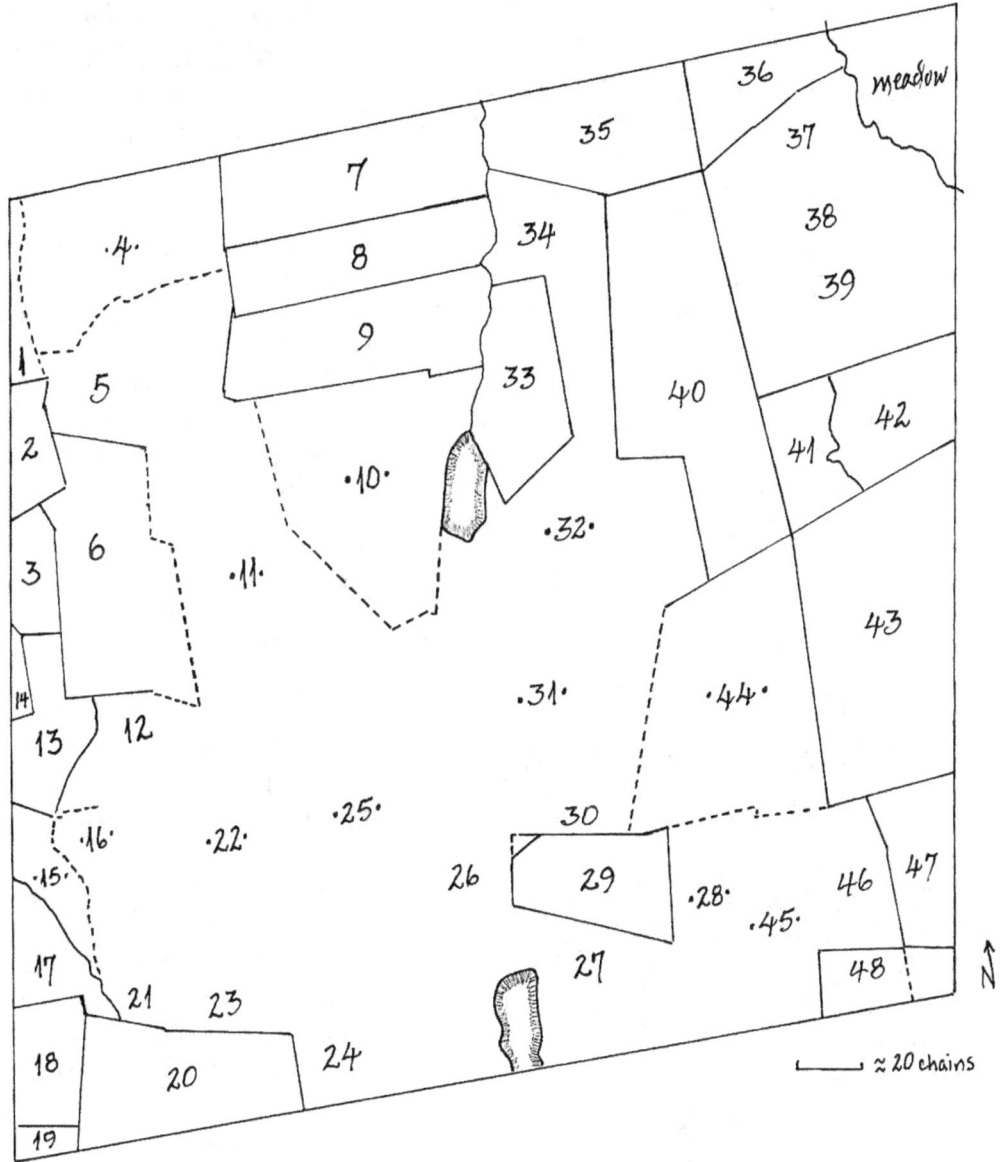

Due to incomplete available information, the map portrays approximate original surveyed farm lot lines and locations. Solid lines indicate boundaries identified in early deeds or mortgages. Dotted lines depict approximate farm lot lines, which may be inaccurate. Dots around farm lot numbers (*e.g.*, •4•) denote possible or likely locations not verified through deed or mortgage references. Farm numbers without dots are located based upon references in deeds or mortgages, even when the boundaries are not known. Farm lot 49 is not identified above.

Many of the farms along the western edge continued into adjacent Long Lot 6, also inherited by Philip Philipse. The Oblong is to the east.

Some lots were sold prior to the revolutionary war. 1770 to 1771 purchasers not on the tenant list included Peter Chapman, Uriah Raymond and Samuel Bangs in the southern part of farm 43; John Daniels a portion of farm 29; and John Tweedy a part of the meadow.

APPENDIX C CONTINUED

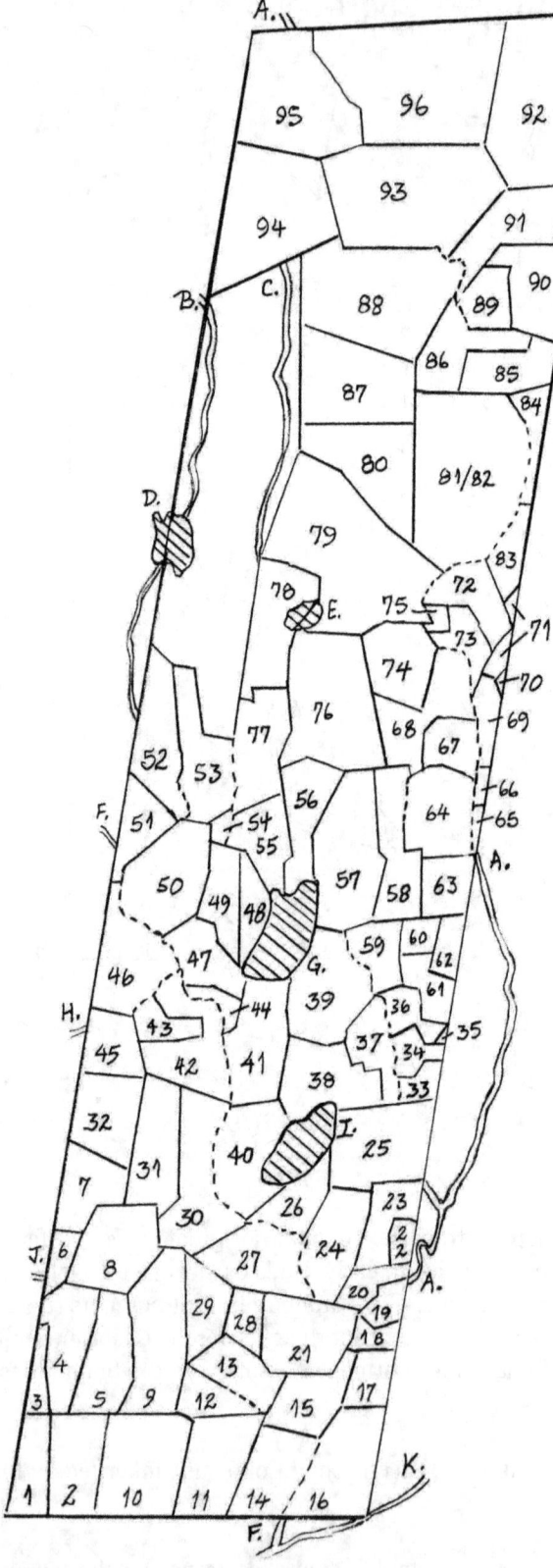

Map based upon Morgan's Survey of Long Lot 6, dated from 12 April to 10 May 1762[1]

Morgan's meets and bounds descriptions of the farm lots surveyed in 1762, and his comments regarding houses and mills on those lots serve as the basis for this map and tenant list. Dotted farm boundary lines indicate waterways, which are extended beyond the farm lots to assist with identification.

The named rivers, brooks, and ponds are:
A. Townsend Mill Brook,
B. Pine Pond Brook,
C. Phillips Mill River,
D. Pine Pond,
E. Meeds Pond,
F. West Branch Croten River,
G. Shaw's Pond,
H. Fish Brook,
I. Dean's Pond,
J. Broad Brook, and
K. East Branch Croten River.

Where the farm lot is along the east or west line, the farm may extend to adjacent lands in Long Lot 5 or Short Lots 7, 8, or 9.

1. Benjamin Morgan, *Feild* (sic) *Work & Book of Survey of Mr. Phillip Phillips Lot No. 6 of the High Land Patent*; Philipse-Gouverneur family property records 1762-1901, New York Historical Society, New York. Watercourses based on Benjamin Morgan, map of Lot 6 dated 15 February 1773; map #193, image provided by the Bureau of Land Management, Office of General Services of New York State.

Tenant List from Morgan's Survey of Lot 6, April and May 1762

Farm Lot	Acres	Tenant or Occupant
1	140½	Samuel Peters Esq:
2	221	Daniel Talor
3	41	Abraham Mabey
4	216	Isaac Loun(Lowne)sberey
5	227	Thomas Karles
		house:
		Thomas Baxter
6	47	Michael Slutt
7	176	John Craffs [Craft]
8	264	Daniel Phillips
9	352	Soloman Jenkens
10	370	Joseph Bates
11	262	Elisha Okley [Oakley]
12	96	Jonathen Hobbey (Hubbey)
13	144	Edward Ganong(ue)
14	220	Abenezar Robeson [Robinson]
15	186	Temothy Gregory
		houses and mills:
		Thomas Kelock [Kellick]
		— Woodsen
16	300	Helkiah Brown Esq:
		& Phillip Ruff
		other house:
		John Ruff
17	89	Isaac Perce
18	48	Hanah Finch
19	61	Nathaniel Robeson [Robinson]
20	72½	John Mabey
21	257	James Willson
22	40	John Hanes
23	127½	Uriah Larrance
24	231	William Stone
25	305	Abraham Hartwell
26	174	Calib Brund[a]ge
27	236	Rusel Gregory
28	89	Joseph Ganounge
29	147	John Ganoung
30	386	Francis Briar
31	239	Thomas Forgason
32	221	James Sears
		sawmill:
		James Rusel
33	60	John Tompkins
34	65	Betha Ballard
35	2.4	Josiah Peck
36	92	Wheten Robeson [Robinson]
37	126	Jeremiah Hughson (Huston)
		other house:
		Widow Kerkin [Kercomb?]
38	243	Rev.Mr. Elnathen Gregory
		other house:
		— Burbank[s]
39	292	Thomas Crosbey
40	226	Samuel Lukis
41	256	John Merrick
		houses:
		David Merrick
		Isaac Merrick
42	243	Calib Hasel [Hazen]
43	71	Samuel Gates
44	81	Samuel Gates 2nd lot
45	128	Eleazer Hamblin (Hambling)
46	253	Jesse Smith (Smyth)
47	161	Benjamin Barber
48	84	John Barber Jun:
49	140	John Barber Sen:
50	292	Thomas Phillips Esq:
51	122	Marey Hopkins
52	218	Robert Fullar
53	250	Jonathen Hopkins
54	34	Benj: Barber – meadow
55	141	Joseph Barber
56	197	Samuel Perce
		other house:
		David Perce
57	380	Silas Washborn
58	217	Seth Merrick
59	121	Matthew Bomp (Bump)
60	58	Abenezar Robeson [Robinson]
61	108	John Sprage (Sprague)
62	58	Moses Fowlar [Fowler]
63	132	Daniel Townsend
		& William Merrit
64	256	Amos Fullar & Company
		other houses:
		Peter Robeson [Robinson]
		Cornelius Fullar Jnr:
65	9	John Farris
66	14	Edward Rise [Rice]
67	122	Eleazer Baker
		& Edea (Edey) Baker
68	217	Abegal Terrey
69	71	Edmond Baker
70	10	Elisha Baker
71	36	Benj: Weed
72	134	Isaac Smith
73	106	William Rabley(e)a Jnr:
74	196	John Pordey (Purdy)

APPENDIX C - TENANT FARM LOT MAPS

Tenant List of Lot 6, April and May 1762 continued

Farm Lot	Acres	Tenant or Occupant	Farm Lot	Acres	Tenant or Occupant
75	20	Wm: Rableyea - meadow	88	583	Moses Northorp
76	477	Wm: Dean	89	98	Steven Ozbon & Samuel Daley
77	204½	John Paddock			
78	285	Hezekiah Meed	90	273½	Elisha Colkins [Calkins] & Aaron Colkins
79	802	James Colwell & Widdow Colwell	91	252	Edward Dolph & Jacob Phillips
80	346	Amos Northorp			
81/82	737	Hope Covey	92	754	Joshua Bordox [Burdick]
83	123	William Rableyea Sen:	93	688	Samuel Cartor [Carter] & Son
84	98	Isaiah Bennet			
85	168	Nechemiah Barlow *farm lots:* — Brown — Bonday [Bundy]	94	627	Joshua Burdick ~~William Bordon~~ *originally for:* Jonathen Tuttle
86	211	Wm: Daley	95	492	Jonathen Gray
87	395	Joseph Northorp	96	818	Jonathen Hill

The spelling used by Benjamin Morgan has been retained. Parentheses enclose alternative spellings from the text. Where spelling deviations are not obvious, a more common spelling appears in brackets. A trailing "s" may or may not be a part of the surname.

A portion of the northern farm lots of Long Lot 6 lay outside of the South Precinct, in either Rombout or Beekman Precincts.

May 1765 Agreement Over Disputed Lands

On 25 May 1765, two opposing groups agreed to settle their legal disputes over certain farms and tenements west of the Oblong. Philip Philipse, Beverly Robinson, and Roger Morris claimed these properties by virtue of the original Adolph Philipse patent and their patent granted in 1761 by the Province of New York. Six other men also claimed these farms and tenements under a 1707 grant from the Colony of Connecticut to Captain Nathaniel Gold. The parties agreed to allow a panel of arbitrators and trustees determine ownership and award the lands and tenements within one year's time.

Philipse, Robinson, and Morris held lands possessed by Thomas Maggot, Nathaniel Porter, William Palmer, and Nathan Taylor. The Connecticut claimants held lands possessed by William Gray, Isaac Chapman, Silvanus Cole, Josiah Bobbit, Samuel Munroe, Noah Smith, David Akins, and Christopher Dickinson. On 12 March 1766, the panel settled the dispute and awarded the lands and tenements to Philipse, Robinson, and Morris.[2]

The following map depicts the boundaries of the 1761 New York patent and the relationship of that patent to the farms included in the 1765 settlement.

---

2. Deed of Trust from Philip Philipse et al to William Earl of Sterling et al dated 25 May 1765, *Philipse-Gouverneur family papers, [ca 1653]-1874*, Pocket II, Rare Book and Manuscript Library Columbia University.

Farms Included in the May 1765 Agreement

Descriptions of the parcels with farm numbers:

In Short Lot 7, possessed by (see also p. 274):
- 7-Christopher Dickinson, formerly held by Malatiah Hatch: 150 acres, south east corner meets Phineas Pecke farm formerly possessed by Christopher Dickinson.
- 11-Nathaniel Porter: 300 acres, north by Samuel Calkins (10), east by Nathaniel Hatch (8), south by David Akins (12).
- 12-David Akins "formerly Fuller's": 203 acres, north by Nathaniel Porter (11) and Nathaniel Hatch (8), south by Barlow's lot (13). Part thereof possessed by "Akins father of the said David [,] Josiah Akins & ___ Hatch"
- 14-Noah Smith, formerly held by his father John Smith: 336 acres, north by Barlow's lot (13), south by John Calkin's (15).
- 16-William Gray: 338 acres, bounded on the north by John Calkin (15).
- 50-Thomas Maggot, formerly held by Abraham Hodges: 111 acres, north by Gideon Prindle (48) and west by Benjamin Hatch (49).
- 59-Josiah Swift and William Palmer: 300 acres, north by Ebenezer Craw (58).

In Short Lot 8, possessed by (see also p. 275):
- 36-Nathan Taylor: 103 acres, south by Silvanus Cole (37), west by Joseph Craw (35), north by Robinson's short lot line.
- 37-Silvanus Cole: 136 acres, south by Isaac Chapman (38), west by David Crossby (40) and Joseph Craw (35), north by Nathan Taylor (36).
- 38-Isaac Chapman: 170½ acres, bounded south by Elijah Tomkins (39), west by David Crossby (40) and north by Silvanus Cole (37).

South Precinct (not specified) - Josiah Bobbit on farm "lately possessed by Philip Cannon."

Beekman Precinct, Samuel Munroe: east by Benjamin Gifford Jr., west by Jedediah Wing, north by Oliver Shed, north east by John Solomon.

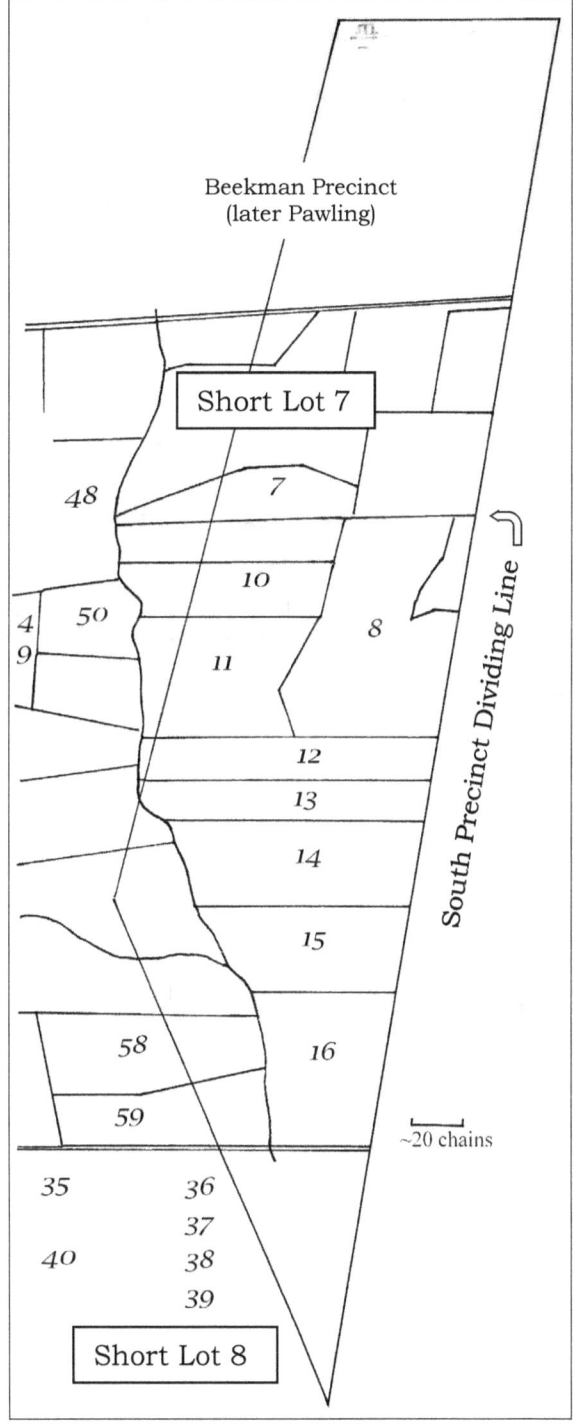

Tenants of Short Lots 7 and 8 mentioned in 1765 Agreement, lying in Beekman and South Precincts

APPENDIX C - TENANT FARM LOT MAPS

Dutchess County

BIBLIOGRAPHY

DUTCHESS COUNTY TAX LISTS:

Dutchess County, New York. *Book of Taxes 1729 to 1748 Dutchess County Clerks Office* v. C and *Supervisor's Record 1753 to 1757, Dutchess County Clerks Office* v. E. *FHL microfilm 925054.*

Dutchess County, New York. *Supervisor's Record 1757 to 1761 Dutchess County Clerks Office v. F and Supervisor's Record 1761 to 1764 Dutchess County Clerks Office v. G. FHL microfilm 925902.*

Dutchess County, New York. *Supervisor's Record 1764 to 1770 Dutchess County Clerks Office v. H and Supervisor's Record 1771 to 1779 Dutchess County Clerks Office v. I. FHL microfilm 925055.*

the above microfilms have been digitized and can be viewed at the Family History Library, Family History Centers, and allied libraries.

BOOKS:

American Annual Register, for the Years 1827-8-9, or the Fifty-Second and Fifty-Third Years of American Independence. Second Part. Volume 4, ed. Joseph Blunt. New York: Blunt, 1830. [pp. 45-56, for New York case Jackson et al vs. James Carver] (books.google.com)

Benton, R.C. *The Vermont Settlers and the New York Land Speculators.* Minneapolis: Housekeeper, 1894. (HathiTrust.org)

Blake, William J. *History of Putnam County, N.Y.; with an Enumeration of its Towns, Villages, Rivers, Creeks, Lakes, Ponds, Mountains, Hills, and Geological Features; Local Traditions; and Short Biographical Sketches of Early Settlers, Etc.* New York: Baker & Scribner, 1849. (Archive.org)

Broadhead, John Romeyn. *Documents Relative to the Colonial History of the State of New York: procured in Holland, England and France,* VII. Albany: Weed Parsons, 1856. (HathiTrust.org)

Commissioners of Statutory Revision State of New York. *The Colonial Laws of New York from the Year 1664 to the Revolution, including the Charters to the Duke of York, the Commissions and Instructions to Colonial Governors, the Duke's Laws, the Laws of the Dongan and Leisler Assemblies, the Charters of Albany and New York and the Acts of the Colonial Legislatures from 1691 to 1775 inclusive.* Albany: Lyon, state printer, 1894. Volume 1-4. (books.google.com)

Doherty, Frank J. *The Settlers of the Beekman Patent, Dutchess County, New York: An Historical and Genealogical Study of all the 18th Century Settlers in the Patent.* Pleasant Valley, NY: author, 1990. (FHL digital image)

Fernow, Berthold, ed. *Documents Relating to the Colonial History of the State of New York, Vol. XV: State Archives Vol. I.* Albany: New York State Archives, 1887. (HathiTrust.org). Also published as Fernow, Berthold. *New York in the Revolution.* Reprint, Baltimore: Clearfield, 1999. (Ancestry.com)

From English Colony to Sovereign State: Essays on the American Revolution in Dutchess County, Province of New York, ed. Richard B. Morris, Jonathan C. Clark, and Charlotte Cunningham Finkel. Millbrook, NY: Dutchess County American Revolution Bicentennial Commission, 1983.

Haacker, Frederick C. *Early Settlers of Putnam County, New York.* Typescript: author, 1946. FHL microfilm 529189, item 4.

Haacker, Frederick C. *Early Settlers of Putnam County and Cortlandt Manor, New York*. Typescript: author, 1954. FHL microfilm 529189, item 5.

Hasbrouck, Frank. *The History of Dutchess County New York*. Poughkeepsie: S.A. Matthieu, 1909. (Archive.org)

Historical and Genealogical Record Dutchess and Putnam Counties New York. Poughkeepsie: A.V. Haight, 1912. (Archive.org)

Johnson, Willis Fletcher. *Colonel Henry Ludington: A Memoir*. New York: Ludington Grandchildren, 1907. (Archive.org)

Journals of the Provincial Congress, Provincial Convention, Committee of Safety and Council of Safety of the State of New-York 1775-1776-1777, Vol. I and II. Albany: Thurlow Weed, 1842. (Archive.org)

Kim, Sung Bok. *Landlord and Tenant in Colonial New York: Manorial Society 1664-1775*. Chapel Hill: Institute of Early American History and Culture, 1978.

Lynd, Staughton. *Anti-Federalism in Dutchess County, New York: A Study of Democracy and Class Conflict in the Revolutionary Era*. Chicago: Loyola University, 1962.

Mark, Irving. *Agrarian Conflicts in Colonial New York 1711-1775*. New York: Columbia U, 1940.

Minutes of the Committee and of the First Commission for Detecting and Defeating Conspiracies in the State of New York : December 11, 1776–September 23, 1778 with Collateral Documents : to which is added Minutes of the Council of Appointment State of New York April 2, 1778–May 3, 1779. Vol. I and II. New York: New York Historical Society, 1924. (Archive.org)

Minutes of the Council of Appointment April 4, 1778-May 3, 1779 (included in above volume II). New York: New York Historical Society, 1924. (Archive.org)

Muster Rolls of New York Provincial Troops. 1755-1764 : Collections of the New-York Historical Society for the Year 1891. New York: New York Historical Society, 1892. (Archive.org)

O'Callaghan, E.B. *The Documentary History of the State of New York*; Arranged under Direction of the Hon. Christopher Morgan, Secretary of State. Albany: Van Benthuysen, 1851. (Archive.org) [see pp 205-208 for Dutchess freeholders 1740]

New York Office of State Comptroller. *New York in the Revolution as Colony and State: A Compilation of Documents and Records*, v. 1. Albany: J.B. Lyon, printers, 1904. (Archive.org). Prev. pub. as Roberts, James A., Comptroller. *New York in the Revolution as Colony and State*, 2nd Ed. Albany: Brandow, 1898.

Pelletreau, William S. *History of Putnam County, New York, with Biographical Sketches of its Prominent Men*. Philadelphia: W.W. Preston, 1886. (Archive.org)

Roebling, Emily Warren. *The Journal of the Reverend Silas Constant: Pastor of the Presbyterian Church at Yorktown, New York*. Philadelphia: Lippincott, 1903 (books.google.com)

Ruddock, William T. *Confiscated Properties of Philipse Highland Patent, Putnam County, New York, 1780-1785*. Westminster, Md.: Heritage Books, 2012. [revised edition will correct the placement of Lot 7 to be farther north on the modern map]

BIBLIOGRAPHY

Smith, James H., Hume H. Cale, William E. Roscoe. *History of Duchess* [sic] *County, New York: with Illustrations and Biographical Sketches of Some of its Prominent Men and Pioneers*. Syracuse: D. Mason, 1882. (Archive.org)

Smith, Philip H. *General History of Duchess* [sic] *County from 1609 to 1876, Inclusive: Illustrated with Numerous Wood-Cuts, Maps, and Full-Page Engravings*. Pawling, NY: author, 1877. (Archive.org)

Transformations of an American County: Dutchess County, New York, 1683-1983, edited by committee. Poughkeepsie: Dutchess County Historical Society, 1986.

ARTICLES:

Edson, Obed. "Pioneers of Chautauqua Lake : William Prendergast" *The Chautauquan* vol. 59 no. 2 (July 1910): 203-209. (books.google.com)

Handlin, Oscar. "The Eastern Frontier of New York." *New York History* 18, 1 (January 1937): 50-75. (JSTOR.org)

Handlin, Oscar and Irving Mark. "Chief Daniel Nimham v. Roger Morris, Beverly Robinson, and Philip Philipse – An Indian Land Case in Colonial New York, 1765-1767." *Ethnohistory* vol. 11, no. 3 (Summer 1964): 193-246. (JSTOR.org)

Humphrey, Thomas J. "5 Crowd and Court : Rough Music and Popular Justice in Colonial New York." *Riot and Revelry in Early America*. edited. University Park, PA: The Pennsylvania State University, 2002: 107-124. (books.google.com)

Humphrey, Thomas J. "'Extravagant Claims' and 'Hard Labour': Perceptions of Property in the Hudson Valley, 1751-1801." *Explorations in Early American Culture Pennsylvania History* vol. 65 Special Supplemental Issue (1998):141-166. (journals.psu.edu/phj/issue/view/1604)

Kim, Sung Bok. "Impact of Class Relations and Warfare in the American Revolution: The New York Experience." *The Journal of American History*, v. 69, no. 2 (Sept 1982): 326-346. (JSTOR.org)

Lynd, Staughton. "Who Should Rule at Home? Dutchess County, New York, in the American Revolution." *The William and Mary Quarterly*, v. 18, no. 4 (July 1961): 330-359. (JSTOR.org)

McDermott, William P. "Colonial Land Grants in Dutchess County, N.Y.: A Case Study in Settlement," *The Hudson Valley Regional Review*. Poughkeepsie, NY: Hudson River Valley Institute, 1986.

Mark, Irving and Oscar Handlin. "Land Cases in Colonial New York, 1765-1767: The King vs. William Prendergast." *New York University Law Review* XIX (Jan. 1942): 165-194. (HeinOnline)

Tryon, Winthrop P. "Whig Strategy on Dutchess County Border: Work of Fredericksburgh Precinct Committee and New York Provincial Committee in Checking Tory Activities (1776-1777)." *The New-York Historical Society Quarterly Bulletin* v. VI no. 4 (Jan. 1923): 111-129. (books.google.com)

—— "The Loyal American Regiment 1777-1783." www.loyalamericanregiment.org/reghist.htm (2010). and see http://www.loyalamericanregiment.org/docs/LAR-Muster_Rolls.pdf.

THE SOUTH PRECINCT OF DUTCHESS COUNTY NY 1740-1790

MANUSCRIPT COLLECTIONS:

Beverly Robinson (1722-1792) collection, 1756-1774. New York Historical Society Mss Collection. AHMC – Robinson, Beverly (1722-1792) Non-circulating.

Henry Livingston Collection 1751-1833 (bulk 1787-1811) SC 19687. New York State Library.

John Tabor Kempe Papers 1678-1782. New York Historical Society Mss Collection MS#344.

[Oblong or Equivalent Land papers], [17--]. New York Historical Society Mss Collection. BV New York State – Boundaries, Oblong Tract.

Philipse – Gouverneur family papers, [ca. 1653]-1874. Rare Book and Manuscript Library, Columbia University Library (New York City). MS#0994.

Philipse – Gouverneur family property records, 1762-1901. New York Historical Society Mss Collection. BV Philipse-Gouverneur. [incl 1762 and 1771 field books of survey of Lot 6]

Philipse patent agreement 1771 Jan. 26. NY Hist. Soc. Mss Collection. AHMC – Philipse patent.

MAPS:

Colden, Cadwallader. Map in "The Answer of the Proprietors of the Equivalent Lands to the Attorney Generals Bill in Chancery Before Governor Cosby." ca 1732. *[Oblong or Equivalent Land Papers]*. New York Historical Society Mss Collection.

Colden, Cadwallader and Alex^r Colden. *[?ant] of Survey Decr 30th 1760 for Phillip Phillipse Beverly Robinson & Roger Morris Contiguay to the Patent of Adolph Phillips in Dutchess County.* State Archives Record Series A0272, New York State Department of State Applications for Land Grants 16:24. image provided by New York State Archives Reference Services (A0272_16_24.pdf).

Concklin, Henry S. *Maps of eight lots of the Philipse upper patent : compiled and drafted from descriptions in records in Dutchess and Putnam counties and based in part on the field book of John Conklin's survey made in 1810.* 1885-1887. New York Public Library. Map Div. (photostatic copies)

Erskine, Robert. *Map No. 35 Draught of the Roads from Fishkill to Danbury, &c &c.* 1778. at New York Historical Society #4601.

Erskine, Robert. *Map No. 131 : [Map of Roads in the Area Bounded by Peekskill and Fishkill (NY), Quaker Hill and Ridgeberry (Conn.)].* Between 1778-1780. New York Historical Society #4616.

Erskine, Robert. *Map No. J-1, J-2 & J-3 : Surveys in New York & Connecticut States for His Excellency General Washington.* 1778. New York Historical Society #4641.

Hampton, Jona. *Draft of the lands disputed by Philipse Patent against Beekmans & Rambaults.* 1753. Peter Force map collection, 163. Library of Congress.

Holland, Samuel, and Robert Sayer and John Bennett, *The provinces of New York, and New Jersey; with part of Pensilvania, and the province of Quebec* (London: Printed for Robt. Sayer & John Bennett, 1775), map, https://www.loc.gov/item/74694272/.

Morgan, Benjamin. Map of Lot 6 dated 15 February 1773. Map #193 digital image provided by the Bureau of Land Management, Office of General Services of New York State.

INDEX

SURNAMES: Alternative spellings from the records appear in parentheses. Surnames are combined only if (1) they are very near in the alphabet, (2) the differences are not significant, and (3) the alternate spellings appear to have been used for the same family (though other families may have also used them). Some surnames have so many alternative spellings, it was not feasible to combine them all. No cross referencing is provided. The actual spelling is on the applicable page.

GIVEN NAMES: Given names with spelling variations appear herein by the most common spelling. The spelling in a record may vary from this either by an abbreviation or by vowel or consonant changes. Ambiguous spellings or abbreviations are not standardized. Scribes also made mistakes, so check alternatives.

BRACKETS: Names in brackets indicate corrections to the record primarily for scribe errors or possible errors (denoted "?").

Abbett/Abbot - Elijah 257; Elijah T. 247
Ackerly - Jacob 256; Samuel 254
Adams - Gilbert 245, 261; John 113, 118, 123, 128, 133, 138, 144, 149, 154, 160, 165, 172, 180, 187, 195, 245, 257; John Jnr: 247, 261; Justus 261; Major 247; Thomas 103, 108, 113, 118, 123, 128, 133, 139, 144, 149, 154, 160, 165, 172, 180, 187, 196, 205, 214, 247, 260
Agar/Ager - Charles 169, 174, 182, 189, 197, 206, 215, 261; John 192, 194, 221, 229
Agard - John 210
Agors - John 178
Aikins - Isaac 29
Airs - Richard 173, 180, 187, 196, 205, 214
Akelson - James 157, 162
Akens - David 172
Akesley - Annanias 209, 218
Akin(s) - Daniel 47, 51; David 55, 58, 62, 66, 70, 75, 79, 84, 89, 142, 179, 187, 195, 204, 213, 230, 244, 278, 279; David Jnr: 95, 100, 105, 110, 116, 120, 126, 131, 147, 153, 158, 164; David's farm 81, 86, 91, 96, 102, 107, 112, 117, 122, 127, 132, 136, 138, 208, 217; John Gray 267; Josiah 76, 81, 86, 91, 96, 101, 106, 111, 116, 121, 127, 132, 137, 230, 279; Josiah's farm 175, 182, 189, 197, 207, 215
Akley - Jon'n 247
Aldridge - Henry 156, 161, 167, 176, 177
Alford - Bela 252
Allen - Amos 235; Ben: 24, 26; Benjamin 22; Daniel 236, 238; John 252; Moses 235; William 236
Ambler - John Jnr: 253; John Sen: 257
Amy - Daniel 263
Anderson - James 71, 76, 80, 85, 90, 95, 101; Nathaniel 178, 192, 194, 210, 212; Peter 81, 86, 91, 96, 113, 118, 123, 128, 133, 138, 144, 149, 154, 183, 190, 198, 207, 216, 261; William 261
Andrews - Benjamin 20, 22, 24
Angerine - Peter 31, 38, 42, 45, 49, 53, 57, 61
Angevine (Anguwine) - Joseph 255; Lewis 168; Peter 65, 69, 135, 141, 146, 152, 157, 163, 171, 179, 186, 195; Peter's estate 213
Angwine - Peter 73, 83, 88, 93, 98, 104, 109, 114, 119, 125, 130
Anjerijn (-rine) (-ryn) - Peter 24, 26, 29, 35
Anthony - Joseph 209, 217
Archer - Gabriel 193, 212, 227
Arcles/Arclas (Arcler)(Arcly) - Joseph 19, 20, 21, 23, 25; Joshua 19, 20, 21, 23
Arcy - John 24, 26, 28
Arison [Garrison] - Richard 140
Arkills (Arkles) - John 225, 265; Joseph 15, 16; Ruth 266; Widow 176, 178, 192, 194, 210, 211, 212, 225
Arkills (Erkils) - 269
Armstrong - Gabriel 264; J. Jnr: 247; Jacob 169, 176, 178, 192, 194, 210, 221, 221, 264; Jacob Jnr: 264; John 113, 118, 123, 128, 133, 138, 144, 149, 154, 160, 165, 176, 177, 192, 193, 210, 211, 220, 228, 247, 264; John Jnr: 113, 118, 123, 128; Jos. 228; Robert 264
Arnold (Arnul) - Benjamin 20, 22, 23, 28, 30, 34, 38, 41, 45, 49, 52, 56, 60, 64; Benjn 26; Ebenezer 151, 156, 161, 167, 250; Edward 175, 182, 189, 197, 206, 215, 253; Joseph 171, 184, 186, 201, 202, 203, 219, 268; Nathaniel 81, 86, 91, 96, 102, 107, 117, 122, 127, 132, 138, 143, 148, 171; Pelick 248; Richard 140, 145, 150, 155, 160, 166, 176, 177, 192, 193, 210, 212, 220, 225; Seymour 247, 248, 253; William 253
Arrawah (Arrewah) - Charles 134, 139, 144, 149, 155, 160
Arsher - Gabriel 194, 210
Arundal(l)(e) - Richard 59, 63, 71, 75, 79, 85, 90, 266
Arundel - Richard 55, 67
Arwah (Arwa) (Arway) - Charles 166, 172, 180, 187, 196, 205, 214, 215; Charles Jnr: 168, 174, 181, 189, 197, 206; Peter 208, 217; Peter Jnr: 200
Ary - John 31, 34, 38, 42, 45, 49
Ascough - James 264
Ashb(e)y - Anthony 244, 250
Ashcraft - Joseph 238
Askel - James 221
Astin - David 17, 18, 20, 21, 23, 25, 27, 30, 34, 37, 233; John 247; Jonathan 32, 35, 39, 42; Nathl 233; place 33
Aston - John 236
Atkins - Darius 256; Isaac 244
Attwood (Atwood) - Andrew 134, 139, 144, 149, 155, 160, 190, 239; Daniel 236
Augwine - Peter 78
Austin (Austen) - Benjamin 261; Charity 150, 156, 161, 167, 173, 181, 188, 196, 205, 214; David 41, 45, 48, 52, 56, 60, 64, 68, 72, 77, 82, 87, 93, 98; Isaac 145, 150, 156, 161, 167, 173, 181, 188, 196, 205, 214, 261; Job 261; Jobe 246; John 240; Jonathan 46, 50, 53, 57, 61, 65, 69, 73, 78, 83, 182, 197, 213, 256, 266, 88, 94, 99, 104, 110, 115, 120, 125, 130, 136, 169, 174, 189, 211; Jonathen's farm 141; Mary 250; Nathaniel 134, 140; Robert 246, 261; Silas 183, 190, 198; Smith 246, 261
Avery - Ezekiel 220; Hezekiah 150, 156, 161, 167, 225; John 134,

285

THE SOUTH PRECINCT OF DUTCHESS COUNTY NY 1740-1790

140, 162, 168, 176, 178, 192, 193, 210, 212, 220, 225, 226; John's farm 144; Micajah 176, 177, 192, 193, 210, 212; Mikiah 266; Solomon 262

Ayres - Richard 259

Babbit(ett) - Daniel 232, 244

Backer - Ede (Edey) (Edy) 103, 108, 113, 118, 123, 128, 154, 172, 180; Eleazer 172; John 48, 51; Josiah 28; Silas 24, 26

Baddock [Paddock] - Jonathan 171; Silas 171

Badeau (Baddeau) - Isaac 208, 217, 256; Jacob 256; John 255; Peter 186, 195, 204, 213, 255; Peter Jnr: 256

Bailey (Baily) - Barthene 263; Devereux 255; Hugh 71, 76, 80, 85, 90, 95, 101, 106, 111, 116, 121, 126; Jacob 255; Jeremiah 29, 33, 36, 40, 43, 47, 50, 54, 58, 62, 66, 70, 74, 79, 84, 89, 94, 175, 182, 189, 197, 206, 215, 253; Joseph 248, 267; Nathan 183; Nathaniel 33, 36, 39, 191, 199, 208, 216; Nehemiah 124, 129, 134, 139, 144, 149, 154, 160, 166, 180, 187; Oliver 169, 175, 182, 189, 197, 209, 218; Peleg 174, 182, 189, 197, 206, 215, 246, 253; Samuel 253; Widow 100, 105, 110, 115, 120, 125, 131, 136, 142, 147, 152, 158, 164; Widow's farm 183, 190

Bailiff (Bailif) (Bailyff) - Nathan 78, 84; Nathaniel 43, 47, 50, 54, 58, 62, 66, 70, 74, 94, 99, 105, 110, 115, 120, 125, 131, 136, 142, 147, 152, 158, 164; Nathen 89

Baker - Abraham 220, 266; Avery 253; Bethuel 233, 236; Ebenezer 187, 235; Ede (Edey) (Edy) 133, 138, 143, 148, 159, 165, 277; Edmund 35, 39, 179, 233, 277, 245, 32, 42, 46, 50, 53, 57, 61, 65, 69, 74, 78, 83, 88, 94, 99, 104, 130, 136, 141, 147, 152, 158, 164, 171, 186, 195, 204, 213, 257; Edward [Edmund] 110, 115, 120, 125; Eisha 49; Eleazer 124, 129, 134, 139, 144, 149, 154, 160, 166, 180, 198, 207, 216, 245, 271, 277; Eleazer Jnr: 257; Elisha 29, 31, 35, 38, 42, 46, 53, 134, 140, 233, 277; Francis 32, 36, 39, 43, 46, 50, 54, 57, 61, 65, 69, 74, 78, 83, 88, 94, 99, 105, 110, 115, 120, 125; Francis's farm 140; Fras. 231; John 55, 59, 63, 67, 70, 75, 79, 84, 140, 145; Jos 233; Joseph 32, 35, 39, 43, 46, 50, 54, 72, 92, 97, 102, 107, 112, 117, 122, 127, 133, 138, 143; Joshua 245, 257; Joshua Jnr: 247; Josiah 31, 34, 38, 42, 45, 49, 53, 57, 61, 65, 68, 73, 77, 83, 88, 93, 98, 104, 109, 114, 119, 125, 130, 135, 141, 146, 152, 157, 163, 171, 179, 186, 195, 204, 213, 233, 247, 257, 271; Josiah Jnr: 168, 174, 181, 189, 197, 206, 215, 254; Judah 263; Mathuel 149; Matuel 134, 140, 145; Nathaniel 253; Phinias 157, 162, 168, 174, 181, 188, 196, 206, 215, 252; Squire 221, 265; Stephen 175, 182, 189, 198, 207, 215, 245

Baker [Brown?] - Jessel 157, 162, 168

Baker [Kelly] - Thomas 204, 213

Baldwin - David 243, 251; Elisha 191, 199, 208, 216, 248, 257; Ephraim 260; Henry 191, 199, 208, 216, 248, 257; James 139, 144, 149, 155, 160, 166, 172, 180, 187, 196, 205, 214, 248, 257; Thomas 138, 143, 148, 154, 159, 165, 170, 185, 200, 202, 203, 218, 267

Baldwyn - Thomas 138, 143, 148, 154, 159, 165, 170, 185, 200, 202, 203, 218, 267, 184

Bales - Oliver 182

Baley - Peleg 169

Balie - Ebenezer 238

Baliff - Nathaniel 171

Ball - Allen 22, 204, 219; Dan 86, 204, 219; Daniel 81, 91, 96, 101, 106, 112, 117, 122, 127, 132, 137, 143, 148, 153, 159, 165; Daniel's farm 170; Dan's farm 184, 185; Elifelet 22, 24, 26, 28; Wait (Weight) 201, 204, 219

Ballard - Betha 277; Caleb 247, 260; John 253; Peleg 32, 36, 39, 43, 46, 50, 54, 58, 62, 66, 69, 74, 78, 84, 89, 247, 261; Peleg Jnr: 32, 36, 39, 43, 46, 50, 54, 58, 62, 66, 69, 74, 78, 84, 89, 260; Tracy 248, 257; Widow 103; William 17, 18, 20, 22, 32, 36, 39, 43, 46, 50, 54, 58, 62, 66, 69, 74, 78, 84, 89, 94, 99, 105, 110, 115, 120, 125, 260

Ballid - John 169

Bancker - Peter 187, 195, 213

Bangs (Bang) - 36; Abner 33, 36, 40, 43, 47, 50, 54, 58, 62, 66, 70, 74, 79, 84, 89, 94, 100, 105, 110, 115, 120, 125, 234; Abner's estate 131, 136; Elisha 32, 36, 65, 69, 74, 78, 105, 110, 115, 120, 125, 131, 136, 141, 147, 152, 158, 234; Joseph 40, 43, 47, 51; Samuel 104, 109, 114, 119, 125, 130, 135, 141, 146, 152, 157, 163, 170, 183, 185, 200, 202, 203, 218, 234, 275; Samuel's farm 175, 182, 189, 198, 207, 215; Thankful 267

Banker - Peter 102, 179

Banks - Elisha 39, 43, 46, 50, 54, 58, 61, 83, 88, 94, 99; Samuel 31, 35, 38, 42, 69, 73, 78, 83, 88, 93, 99, 29, 45, 49, 53, 57, 61, 65

Banvert - Abr'm 244

Barber - Benj:'s meadow 277; Benjamin 122, 127, 277; Benjamin's farm 132, 137; John 20, 22, 24, 26, 28, 31, 34, 38, 41, 45, 49, 52, 56, 60, 64, 68, 73, 77, 82, 87, 93, 98, 104, 109, 114, 119, 124, 237, 254; John Jnr: 123, 129, 239, 277; John Sen: 277; Jonathan 20, 22, 24, 26; Joseph 92, 97, 102, 107, 209, 218, 277

Barcrum - Eliakim 171, 184

Bard - Joseph 176, 178, 194, 211, 212, 221, 228

Bardsley - Andrew 180; Jehiel 180; Obediah 179

Barger - Andrew Jnr: 103, 108, 110, 176, 227; Andrew Sen: 227; John 227; Peter 178, 247

Barker - Hannah 256; Martha 255; Richard 191, 199, 208, 217; Samuel Augustus 249, 250

Barker [Baker] - Edmund 179, 186

Barla - Joseph 269

Barleu - Benjamin 91, 96, 107

Barley - Joseph 17, 18

Barlow - Benjamin 101, 112, 117; farm lot 279; Jos. 230; Joseph 235; Nathan 244; Nechemiah 278; Nehemiah 81, 86, 91, 96, 101, 107, 112, 117, 122

Barly - Jeremiah 240; Jo: 43, 46, 50, 54, 58, 61, 65, 69, 74, 78; Joseph 16, 20, 21, 32, 36, 39

Barnam - Bethual 62, 66, 74, 79; Bethuel 33, 36, 40, 43, 47, 50, 54, 58, 62, 66, 70, 74, 79; Joshua 71, 75, 79

Barnod - Samuel 148, 154

Barns - Isaac 254; Joshua 140, 145; Joshua's farm 150

Barnum - Asa 169, 170; Aza 243; Azor 184, 201, 203, 219, 268, 271; Bethuel 84, 89, 94, 99, 105,

INDEX

110, 257; Eliakum 201, 203, 219; Jonah 243, 267; Joshua 55, 59, 63, 67, 85, 90, 95, 100, 106, 111, 116, 121, 126, 131, 137, 142, 147, 153, 158, 164, 170, 184, 185, 200, 202, 236, 268; Joshua Jnr: 82, 86, 91, 96, 102, 107, 112, 117, 122, 127, 132, 138, 143, 148, 153, 159, 165, 170, 184, 185, 200, 202, 203, 218; Joshua's farm 156, 161, 167; Noah 243; Stephen 243

Barret(t) - 92, 97, 118; Isaac 128, 133, 154, 160, 165, 173, 180, 188, 196, 205, 245, 258; Isaac Jnr: 247, 260; James 144, 149, 155, 160, 166, 172, 180, 205, 214, 261; James Jnr: 200, 261; Jesse 260; John 189, 197, 215, 245, 262; John Jnr: 191, 199, 217, 260; John Sen: 260; Justus 191, 199, 208, 217, 247; Reuben 259; Samuel 246, 259; Will. 247; William 200, 208, 260

Barrick - John 174

Barrit(t) - Isaac 123, 139, 144, 149, 214; James 134, 139, 187; John 182, 206, 221; John Jnr: 208; William 217

Barsleys [Baseley?] - Charles 236

Bartine - Sam'l 247

Bartlet - William 251

Bartley - Ephraim 108

Barto - John 92, 97; John's farm 102, 107, 112, 117, 138, 143, 148, 154, 159, 165; Philip 29; Thomas's farm 122, 127, 133

Barton - Andrew 220, 263; Andrew Jnr: 263; Bassil 228; Elijah 265; Elijah T. 247; Elisha 221, 264; Gilbert 247, 263; Isaac 33, 36, 39, 43, 47, 50, 54, 58, 62, 66, 70, 74, 78, 84, 89, 94, 99, 105; John 176, 178, 192, 194, 210, 212, 221, 265; John Jnr: 264; Jon: 228; place 113, 118

Bartow - Andrew 247; Bassil 228; John 259; Jon: 228

Baseley(ly) - Augustin 71, 76, 80, 85, 90, 95, 101, 106, 111, 116, 121, 126, 132, 137, 142; Charles 92, 97, 102, 107, 112, 117, 122, 127, 132, 138; Jehiel 71, 103, 108, 113, 118, 123, 128, 133, 138, 143, 148, 154; Obediah 71, 75, 80, 85, 90, 95, 101, 106, 111, 116, 121, 126, 131, 137, 142, 147, 153, 158, 164

Baseter - Thomas 134, 140

Bashford - Byal 134, 144, 149, 155, 160, 166; Byally 176, 177; James 194, 211, 212; John 263; Ryal 139; Thomas 178, 192, 194, 210, 212, 221, 263; William 191, 255

Bass - Zebulon 140, 145, 150, 155, 161, 166, 173, 180, 234; Zebulon's widow 205, 214

Bassford - Bryaly 227

Bates - Isaac 183, 190, 198, 207, 216; John 81, 86, 91, 96, 101, 145, 150, 155, 161, 166, 173, 180, 187, 196; John's estate 205, 214; Joseph 118, 129, 162, 168, 277; Oliver 175, 189, 198, 207, 215; Samuel 150, 156

Bauldin - 87

Baulding - 92; Thomas 97, 102, 107, 112, 117, 122, 127, 132

Bawlding - James 134

Baxter (Baxtert) - Gideon 252; Lockart 20, 22; Marcus 20, 22, 23, 26, 28, 30, 34, 38; Thomas 72, 145, 149, 155, 160, 166, 180, 188, 196, 277; Thomas's estate 205, 214; William 15, 16

Bayly (ey) - Elias 247; Nehemiah 172; Susana 171

Bayly [Baliff] - Nathaniel 171

Bazely - 32, 36, 39, 43

Bea - John 198, 207

Beadle - Elisha 124, 129, 134, 139

Beagle - Daniel 145

Beal - George 254; Matthew 254

Beamus - Benjamin 238

Beard - Joseph 266

Beardslee - Benajah 256

Beardsley(ly) - Andrew 145, 150, 155, 161, 166, 173, 188, 196; Chas. 232; Doctor 145, 150; Jehiel 159, 165, 172, 232; Obadiah 172, 187; Obed. 231

Beavans - Joseph 237

Beckus - Daniel 16, 17, 18

Bedunah - Ebenezer (hatter) 200

Bee - John 216

Beebe(e) - David 252; David Jnr: 250; John 250

Beekman - Henry 6

Begal - Stephen 247

Belden - William 157, 162, 168

Bell - Hendrick 269; James 102, 108, 113; Joseph 264; Peter 178, 192, 221, 227, 264

Benedict(ck) - Abigail 267; Abijah 251; Ebenezer 132, 137, 143, 148, 153, 159, 165, 170, 184, 185, 200, 202, 203, 218; Jacob 254; Mathew 63, 67, 71, 80, 90, 95, 100; Mathias's farm 185, 200; Matthew's farm 75, 85, 106, 111, 116, 121, 126, 131, 137, 142, 147, 153, 158, 164, 170, 184, 202, 203, 218; Samuel 71, 76, 90, 95, 101, 106, 111, 116, 121, 126, 132, 137, 142, 148, 153, 159, 164, 170, 184, 185, 200, 202, 203, 218

Benit - Peter Jnr: 16

Benjamin(s) (-men) - Darius 247, 267; Elias 198, 204, 219, 250; Elijah 267; Elijah T. 246; Joseiah 123; Josiah 72, 128, 145, 150, 155, 161, 166, 173, 180, 233

Bennedict - Samuel 80, 85

Bennet(t) (-ent) - Amacy 243; Benjamin 25, 27, 29, 238; Ebenezer 71, 76, 132, 137, 142, 147, 153, 158, 164, 172, 179, 187, 195, 204, 213; Ebenezer Jnr: 252; Ebenezer Sen: 253; Eleazer 80, 85, 90, 95, 101, 106, 111, 116, 121, 126; Increase 183, 190, 198, 207, 216, 244, 270; Isaiah 140, 145, 150, 155, 208, 217, 246, 278; John 235, 239; Jonathen 180, 140, 145, 150, 155, 161, 166, 173; Old 71, 76; Peter 19, 20, 21, 23; Peter Jnr: 17, 18, 20, 21, 23, 25; Thomas 80, 85, 90, 95, 101

Benson - Egbert 242

Berger - Andrew Jnr: 44, 116, 120, 126, 131, 136, 142, 147, 153, 158, 164, 177, 192; Andrew Jnr: the 2nd 113; Andw. Sen: 227; Cornelius 263; Francis 140, 145, 150, 155, 160, 166, 176; Francis's widow 192, 193; Frans 177; John 140, 145, 150, 155, 160, 166, 176, 210, 212, 220, 263; Paul 263; Peter 140, 145, 150, 155, 160, 166, 193, 194, 210, 221, 263

Bergis - Andrew Jnr: 95, 100, 105

Bernard - Samuel Jnr: 113

Bernod - Samuel 103, 108, 113, 118, 123, 128, 133, 138, 144, 159

Berrit(t) - James 196; John 169; John Jnr: 169

Berry - Asahel 209, 217; Jabez 171, 179, 186, 195, 204, 213, 245, 261; Jabez Jnr: 261; Jaby 29, 31, 35, 38, 42, 45, 49, 53, 57, 61, 65, 69, 73, 78, 83, 88, 93, 99, 104, 109, 114, 119, 125, 130, 135, 141, 146, 152, 157, 163; John 183, 190, 198, 207, 216, 270, 271, 256; Samuel 247, 261

Bessee (Bessie) - Joseph 92, 97, 102, 107

Bexster - Thomas 173

Beyea - Isaac 262; John 255, 261

Beyes - Isaac 247

Bill - Peter 194, 210, 212

287

THE SOUTH PRECINCT OF DUTCHESS COUNTY NY 1740-1790

Birch [Burch?] - Isaiah 243; James 240
Bircham - John 233
Birdsall (-sell) (-sill) - Abm: 229, 231; Abraham 183, 190, 198, 207, 216; Benjamin 145, 150, 156, 162, 167, 173, 180, 188, 196, 205, 214; Benjamin (south) 155, 161, 167; David 253, 256; Elemuel 171, 184; Gilbert 268; Isaac 183, 190, 198, 207, 216, 251; Jacob 191, 199, 208, 217, 258; Jacob Jnr: 198; James 125, 131, 136, 142, 147, 152, 158, 164, 170, 175, 182, 184, 185, 189, 198, 200, 202, 203, 207, 215, 218, 268; John 37, 40, 44, 47, 51, 54, 58, 62, 66, 70, 74, 79, 84, 89, 94, 100, 105, 110, 115, 120, 126, 131, 136, 145, 150, 155, 161, 166, 173, 180, 187, 196, 246; John's estate 205, 214; John's farm 142; Jonathan [Nathan] 62, 66; Nathan 33, 36, 40, 43, 47, 50, 54, 58, 70, 74, 79, 84, 89, 94, 99, 102, 105, 107, 110, 112, 115, 120, 138, 143, 148, 154, 159, 165, 170, 184, 185, 200, 202, 203, 218; Nathen Jnr: 117, 122, 127, 132; Squire 244; Thomas 171, 184, 186, 201, 202, 203, 219, 268; William 199, 207, 216, 256, 268
Bisbuit - Francis 243
Bisley - Oliver 246
Blackman - Samuel 237
Blake - (William) 10
Bland - James 251
Blatchly - Joseph 254
Bloomer - Abraham 255; Benjamin 140, 145, 150, 155, 161, 166, 176, 177, 192, 193, 210, 212, 220, 265; Daniel 265; Elisha 265; Gilbert 169, 176, 178, 192, 193, 210, 212, 220, 265; John 71, 72, 76, 76, 80, 80, 85, 85, 90, 90, 95, 96, 101, 101, 106, 106, 111, 111, 116, 116, 121, 121, 126, 127, 132, 132, 137, 142, 147, 153; John (nr river) 137, 142, 148, 153, 159, 165; John's farm 162, 168; Reubin 123, 129; Robert 72, 76, 80, 80, 85, 85; William 20, 22, 24, 26, 28, 265
Blosum - John 103
Boaly - Elias 246
Bobbet/Bobbit - Christopher 32, 36, 39, 43, 46, 50, 54, 58, 62, 66, 69, 74, 78, 83, 89, 94, 99, 105; Christopher's farm 110, 115; Daniel 162, 168, 174, 181, 188, 197, 206, 215; Isaiah 138, 143; Josiah 103, 108, 113, 118, 123, 128, 133, 278, 279; Old 32, 35, 39, 43, 46, 50, 54, 57, 61; Old's farm 65, 69, 74
Bogardus - Capt 237, 238; John 67, 71, 75, 80, 85, 90, 95, 100, 106, 111, 116, 121, 126, 131, 231
Bogington - Sam'l 248; Solomon 248
Bohker - Jacob 246
Boice - Henry 59; John 193, 194, 210, 212
Bollard - Tracy 244
Boncker/Bonker - Adolphus 211; Jacob 256; Peter 87, 91, 97, 107, 112, 117, 122, 127, 132, 138, 143, 148, 154, 159, 165, 256
Bond - Reubin 134, 140, 144
Bonday - farm 278
Booth(e) - Isaac 259; John 259; Robert 259; Stephen 151, 156, 200
Bordon - William 278
Bordox - Joshua 278
Borland - Joel 208, 217
Borlew - Benjamin 81, 86
Boss - Zebulon 187, 196
Bottom - Hickin 31, 35, 38, 42, 46, 49, 53, 57, 61, 69; Jickin 29
Bouton (-ten) - David 256; Ira 257; Noah 244, 267; Saml 248; Shubael 267
Bowen - Michael 253
Boyce - Henry 63, 67, 71, 75, 80, 85, 90, 95; John 178, 265; Matthew 264
Boyd - Ebenezer Jnr: 259; Ebenezer Sen: 260
Boyington - Samuel 236
Brade(y) (Braide) - John 81, 86, 91, 96, 101, 107
Bradly(ley) - Daniel 22, 24, 26, 28, 31, 34, 38, 41, 45, 49, 53, 56, 60, 64, 68, 73, 77, 83, 88, 93, 98, 104; Samuel 16, 17, 18, 254
Bradshaw - John 268
Braidy (Brady) - William 162, 168, 174, 181, 188, 197, 206, 215, 231
Brewer - Garrey 244; Hendrick (Hend:k) 16, 18, 19, 21, 23, 27, 247; Hendrick Sen: 17; Henry 15, 33, 43, 261, 266; Jacobus 92, 97, 102, 107, 112, 117, 122, 128; Johannis 47; John 55, 162, 168, 174, 181, 188, 197, 257, 262; Nehemiah 261; Peter 215; Samuel 20, 22, 24, 26, 28, 55, 59, 63, 67, 71, 177, 229, 247; son of Hendrick 18, 19, 21, 23; Teunis 44, 47, 51, 55, 58, 62, 66, 70, 74, 79, 84, 89, 266, 95, 100, 105, 110, 115, 120, 126, 131
Brewer (Brower) - 269
Brewster - Ebenezer 29; Edward [William] 21; John 201, 247; Nathan 19; Peltiah 243; Samuel 237, 268; William 16, 20, 23, 25, 28
Briar/Brier - Francis 180, 277
Bridges [Burgis] - Thomas 140
Briggs (Brigs) - Jacob 92, 97; Maria 267; Zebedee 102, 107, 112, 117, 122, 127, 132, 138, 143, 148, 154, 159, 165, 170, 184, 185, 200, 202, 203, 219; Zebulon 92, 97
Brinckerhoff - Coll:'s farm 192, 210, 176, 178, 194, 212
Brinkerhoff (-ofe) - Col. 241; farm 221; John 229
Broadwick - Joseph 221
Brock (Brok) - Even 15, 16
Brooks - Joseph 48, 51, 55, 59, 62, 66, 70, 75, 79; Nathan 254; Will. 247
Brooster - William 15
Broster - Nattan 269
Brouer - Jacobus 87
Browden - Eben'r 246
Brower - Hend:k 25; Henry 36, 40, 269; Jacobus 91, 97, 102, 107; Peter 253; son of Hend:k 25
Brown - Capt. 118, 123, 128, 133, 139, 144, 149, 154, 160, 166, 172, 180, 187, 196, 205, 214; Capt.'s place 118, 123, 128, 133, 138, 144; Charles 175, 182, 189, 198; Cornelius 209, 218, 259; Corns 247; Eben (nr Capt.) 138, 144; Ebenezer 81, 86, 91, 96, 102, 107, 112, 117, 122, 127, 132, 138, 143, 148, 153, 159, 165, 172, 179, 187, 195, 205, 213, 260; Elias 145; Elisha 244, 258; farm 278; Helkiah Esq: 277; Isaac 246; Israel 209, 218; James 134, 140; Jesse 183, 190; John 81, 86, 91, 96, 101, 107, 112, 117, 122, 127, 140, 169, 208, 217; Jonathan 250; Mordicai 211, 212; Moses 243; Phillip 251; Silas 252; William 250; Zebediah 254
Brown [Wilson] - James 187
Brown? [Baker?] - Jessel 162, 168, 157
Brownell - William 92, 97, 102, 107, 112, 117, 122, 127
Bruister - David 103, 108
Brundage (-didge) (-dige) - Bartlet 20, 22, 23, 26, 28, 36, 40, 43, 47,

INDEX

51, 54; Ben: Jnr: 43, 47, 50, 54, 58, 62, 66, 70; Benjamin 23, 26, 28, 30, 34, 38, 41, 45, 49, 52, 56, 60, 64, 68, 73, 77, 82, 87, 93; Benjamin Jnr: 33, 36, 40; Benjamin's farm 98; Caleb 17, 18, 20, 21, 23, 25, 27, 30, 34, 37, 41, 45, 48, 52, 56, 60, 64, 68, 72, 77, 82, 87, 93, 98, 103, 109, 114, 119, 124, 130, 135, 141, 146, 151, 157, 163, 171, 179, 208, 217; Calib 277; Daniel 72, 76, 81, 86, 90, 96, 101, 106, 111, 116, 121, 127, 132, 137, 143, 148, 153, 159, 165, 172, 179, 187, 195, 205, 213; John 248; Jona: 228; Jonathan 169, 176, 178; Joseph 44, 47, 51, 55, 151, 156, 162, 167, 173, 181; Josiah 200, 208, 217; Marcus 191, 199; Moses 52, 55, 59, 63, 67, 71, 75, 79, 84, 89, 95, 100, 105; Nathan 250; Nathaniel 81, 86, 255; Silvenus 156, 162, 167; Solomon 33, 36, 40, 72, 76, 81, 86, 91; Solomon's farm 96
Brush - Jacob 267
Bruyster/Bruster - David 113, 118; John 171, 240, 244; Pelethia 240; Samuel 175, 182, 189, 197, 206, 215, 244
Bryan - Richard Samuel 250
Bryant - Jonathan 37, 40, 44, 47, 51, 54, 58, 62, 66, 70, 74, 79, 84, 89, 94, 100, 105, 110, 115, 120, 126, 131, 136, 142, 147, 152, 158, 164, 172, 179, 186, 195, 204, 213; Richard 190, 199, 207, 216; Samuel (Doctor) 190, 199, 207, 216; Thomas 140, 145, 150, 155, 160, 166, 176, 177, 192, 193, 210, 212, 227
Bryer (-or) - Francis 113, 118, 123, 128, 133, 138, 144, 148, 154, 159, 165, 173; Francis's farm 188; Jane 198
Buckley - Moses 190, 199, 208, 216
Buckley (-er) - Jabez 243, 248
Budd - Elijah 122, 127, 133, 138, 143, 148, 154, 159, 165, 178, 193, 194, 210, 212, 220, 265; Elisha 92, 97, 102, 107, 112, 117; Gilbert 151, 156, 161, 167, 176, 177, 192, 193, 210, 212, 220, 265; John 265; John Sen: 221; Peter 265
Bueys/Buys - Widow 228
Bugbee (Buggbee) (Bugby) - Daniel 193, 194, 210, 212, 221, 227; Ezekiel 200, 208, 217, 247;

Silvester 248
Buis - Abraham 19, 20; Abram 21, 23, 25; Hannis 20, 21, 23, 25, 28; Johannis 19
Bull - Daniel 67, 71, 75, 80, 85, 90, 95, 100, 106, 111, 116, 121, 126, 131, 137, 142, 147, 153, 158, 164, 172, 179, 187, 195, 204, 213, 251; Horace 251
Bump - 29; George Jnr: 265; Mathew 31, 35, 38, 42, 46, 49, 53, 57, 61, 65, 69, 73, 78, 83, 88, 93, 99, 104, 109, 114, 119, 125, 130, 136, 169, 175, 182, 189, 197, 206, 215, 257, 277
Bundy - farm 278; George 238; James 151; Simeon 97, 102, 108, 113, 118, 145, 150; Simeon Jnr: 140; Simeon's farm 155
Bundy [Moss] - Benjamin 122
Bunker - Peter 172, 205
Bunn - Reuben 149, 155, 160, 166, 176, 177, 192, 193, 210, 211, 265
Burbanks(cks) - 277; Noah 32, 35, 39, 42, 46, 50, 53, 57, 61, 65, 69, 74, 78, 102, 108, 113, 118, 122, 128, 133, 138, 143, 148, 154, 159, 165, 209, 217
Burch - Benjamin 81, 86, 91, 96, 101, 107, 230, 244; Beverly 252; Charles 244; Daniel 244, 259, 268; David 231, 244; George 243, 268; Jemima 256; Jeremiah 244, 259; John 244; John Jnr: 231; John Sen: 231; Jona: the 4th 231; Jona: the widow 231; Jonath: 231; Jon'n 244; Joseph 268; Silas 243, 268; Zachariah 259
Burchad - David 71, 76, 80, 85, 90
Burchard - Isaiah 29; Samuel 123, 129, 134, 139, 144, 149; Samuel's farm 154, 160, 166
Burdeck/Burdick/Burdock - Amos 247; Caleb 247, 258; Joshua 151, 156, 161, 167, 181, 188, 196, 206, 214, 278; Tobias [Joshua] 173
Burger - John 177, 192, 193; Peter 212
Burges(s) - Archibald 255; Jacob 239; Jeremiah 250; Matthias 184
Burgis(s) - 37, 40, 43; Andrew Jnr: 47, 51, 55, 58, 62, 66, 70, 75, 79, 84, 89; Ezekiel 32, 36, 39, 43, 46, 50, 54, 57, 61, 65, 69, 74, 78, 83, 88, 94, 99, 105, 110, 115, 120, 125, 130, 136, 141, 147, 152, 158, 164, 171, 179, 234; Ezrh 233; Jacob 92, 97, 102, 107, 112, 117, 122, 127, 133, 138, 233;

Jeremiah 134, 140, 145, 149, 155, 160, 166, 173, 180, 187, 196, 205, 214; Jeremiah's farm 186, 201, 202, 203, 219; Mathias 47, 51, 54, 58, 62, 66, 70, 74, 79, 84, 89, 94, 100, 105, 110, 115, 120, 126, 131, 136, 142, 147, 152, 158, 164, 170, 185, 200, 202; Mathias's wife 203, 218; Thomas 140, 145, 150, 155, 161, 166, 170, 184, 185, 201, 202, 203, 240
Burlesson - Ebenezer 182
Burling - Eben'r Sam'l 244; Gillard/Gilead 244
Burlingson - Job 169
Burlinson - Joel 183
Burlison (-isson) (-osson) - Amos 190, 198; Ebenezer 175, 201; Ebenezer's widow 204, 219; Job 174, 190, 198, 207, 216; Joel 190, 243
Burnell - Thomas 246
Burnum - Azer 185, 202
Burroughs - William 252
Burtch - Daniel 201, 204, 219; George 186, 201, 202, 203, 219; Jacob 250; Jeremiah 198, 207, 216; Jonathen 198, 207, 216; Joseph 201, 204, 219; Silas 201, 204, 219
Burton - James 268
Bush [Ter Bush] - Capt 239, 240
Butler - Daniel 81, 86, 91; Daniel's farm 96; Jeremiah 86, 91, 97, 102, 107; Tim'y 244; William 265
Buttom - Hickin 65
Button - John 169, 175, 182; Peter 244
Byington (Byngton) - John 254; Nathaniel 24, 26, 28, 31, 34, 38, 42, 45, 49, 53, 57, 60, 65, 68, 102, 123, 129, 133; Samuel 247, 251; Solomon 102, 108, 113, 118, 122, 128, 133, 138, 175, 182, 189, 198, 207, 215, 251
Cable - Platt 243
Caby - Eliza 135
Caldwell - James 254
Cale - Stephen 263
Calkin (Corken) - 269
Calkin(s) - Aaron 32, 35, 39, 42, 46, 50, 53, 57, 61, 78, 83, 88, 94, 99, 104, 110, 115, 120, 125, 130, 136, 252, 278; Abram [Aaron] 65, 69, 73; David 82, 86, 91, 96, 102, 107, 112, 117, 122, 127, 132, 138, 159, 165; David Jnr: 143, 148, 153; Eli 244, 252; Elijah 32, 35, 39, 42, 46, 50, 72,

289

76, 81, 85, 90, 96, 101, 106, 111, 116, 121, 127, 132, 137, 143, 148, 153, 159, 165, 172, 232; Elisha 54, 57, 61, 65, 69, 74, 78, 83, 88, 94, 99, 123, 128, 133, 139, 144, 149, 154, 160, 166, 278; James 145, 150, 155, 161, 167, 173, 180, 188, 196, 205, 214, 230, 244, 256, 274; James Jnr: 230; Jeremiah 15, 16, 17, 18, 19, 21, 23, 25, 27, 82, 86, 91, 97; Jeremiah Jnr: 72, 76, 81, 85, 90, 96, 101; John 19, 37, 41, 44, 48, 52, 56, 60, 64, 68, 72, 77, 82, 87, 92, 98, 103, 108, 114, 119, 124, 129, 135, 230, 279; John (Doctr:) 140; John (Justice) 26, 28, 30, 33; John 3rd: 22, 24, 71, 76, 80; John 3rd:'s estate 85; John Jnr: 15, 16, 17, 18, 21, 23, 25, 27, 30, 33, 37, 41, 44, 48, 52, 56, 60, 64, 68, 72, 77, 82, 87, 92, 98, 103; John's farm 140; Joseph 240; Joshua 198, 207, 216, 244; Nathaniel 140, 145, 150, 155, 161, 166, 173; Samuel 17, 18, 20, 21, 23, 25, 28, 30, 34, 37, 41, 45, 48, 52, 56, 60, 64, 68, 72, 77, 82, 87, 93, 98, 103, 109, 114, 119, 124, 130, 135, 231, 279; Samuel Jnr: 32, 35, 39, 42, 46, 50, 54, 57, 61, 65, 81, 86, 91, 96, 101, 107, 112, 117, 122, 127, 132, 137, 143, 148, 153; Simon 82, 92, 97, 134, 140, 235, 244; Will. 244, 246; William 102, 108, 113, 118, 122, 128, 133, 138, 163, 168, 174, 181, 188, 197, 206, 215, 230, 236, 250, 270, 271

Calwell - Joseph 258; William 258

Calwill - Thomas 50

Cambey - James 255

Cameron (Camaron) - Allen 190, 199; Dougle 244

Campbell (Cambell) (Campell) - Archd: 230; Duncan 230; James 263; John 16, 17, 18, 19, 21; Robison 243

Cannon (Canon) - Abraham 204, 219; Abr'm 243; John 118, 123, 128, 235, 237; Philip 24, 27, 29, 31, 34, 38, 42, 45, 49, 53, 56, 60, 64, 68, 73, 77, 83, 88, 93, 98, 104, 109, 114, 279

Carey - John 246

Carl(e) (Carll) - Adonijah 199; James 134, 140, 145, 149, 155, 160, 166, 173, 180, 187, 196, 214, 260; Jonas 247; Lemuel 259; Samuel 33, 36, 39, 43, 47, 50, 63, 67, 71, 75, 80, 134, 140, 145, 149, 155, 160, 166, 173, 180, 187, 196, 214; Thomas 157, 174, 181, 259; Thomas Jnr: 191, 199; Thomas Jnr:'s estate 217; Thomas's estate 206; Thomas's widow 215; William 191, 199, 208

Carley (-ly) - Jeddiah 236; John 92, 97, 102, 107, 112, 117, 122, 127, 132, 138, 143, 148, 154, 159, 165, 170, 184, 185, 200, 202, 203, 219, 243; John Jnr: 151, 156, 161, 167, 170, 184, 185; Jonathan 185, 186, 201, 202, 203, 219, 268

Carpenter - Abiel 29; Ephraham 168, 182; Ephram 174, 189, 197; Gabriel 145, 150, 155, 161, 167, 173, 180, 200; John 162, 168, 174, 181, 188, 197, 206, 215; Joseph 183, 190; Richard 134, 139; Stephen 27; Thomas 29; William 169, 174, 182, 189, 197

Carrigan - Gilbert 245, 261

Carter - Hezekiah 82, 86, 91, 97, 102, 107, 112, 117, 122, 127, 132, 138; Jabez 243; Jared 118, 123, 128, 133, 139, 162, 168; Lucas 103, 108, 113, 118, 123, 128; Samuel 72, 76, 81, 86, 90, 96, 101, 106, 111, 116, 121, 127; Samuel & son 278

Cartwright (Cartryt) - Christopher 48, 51; Nicolas 25, 27, 29, 31, 35, 38, 42, 45, 49

Carver - Barnabas 247, 261; Timothy 209, 218, 247, 261

Cary - George 60, 64, 68, 73, 77, 83, 88, 93, 98, 104, 109, 114, 119

Casby - Joshua 83

Case - 20; William 22, 267

Cash - Daniel 236; David 238, 240

Casten (Casston) - Samuel 33, 52, 55

Cayton - Isaac 246

Cercome (-omb) - Thomas 18, 20, 21, 23, 25

Cerley - Albert 244; John 244; Oliver 244; Peter 244

Chace - Isaac 81; Obadiah 238

Chaddock - Daniel 261

Chadwick - Comfort 245, 182

Chaise - place 118, 123, 128

Champlin - Thomas 246

Chandler - Jos. 244; Joseph 175, 182, 189, 198, 207, 215, 271

Chapman - 221; Enoch 243; Isaac 24, 26, 28, 31, 34, 38, 41, 45, 49, 52, 56, 61, 65, 69, 73, 78, 83, 88, 93, 98, 104, 109, 115, 120, 125, 130, 136, 141, 146, 152, 158, 164, 171, 179, 186, 195, 204, 213, 234, 270, 278, 279; Jeremy 263; Peter 169, 170, 184, 275; Peter's estate 208, 217; Richard 151, 156, 162, 167, 173, 181, 200, 208, 217, 255; Thomas 243, 250

Charlock - Henry 191, 208, 217, 259

Chase - Abenezar 233; Benjn: 230; Berry 209, 218; Caleb 32, 35, 39, 42, 46, 50, 53, 57, 61, 65, 69, 74, 78, 83, 88, 94, 99, 104, 110, 115, 120, 125; Caleb Jnr: 32, 35; Daniel 231; Daniel Jnr: 231; Ebenezer 32, 35, 39, 42, 46, 50, 53, 57, 61, 65, 69, 74, 78, 83, 88, 94, 99, 104, 110, 115, 120, 125; Ebenezer's farm 131, 136; Elijah 260; Isaac 32, 36, 39, 43, 46, 50, 54, 200, 208, 217, 258; Jabish 191, 199, 208, 217; Jebes 246; Jeremiah 142, 147, 152, 158, 164, 171, 179; John 190, 199, 207, 216, 247; Joseph 264; Judah 247; Obadiah 169, 174, 182, 189, 197, 206, 215, 245, 258, 270; place 133; Reuben 123, 129, 134, 139, 144, 149, 154, 160, 166, 172, 180, 187, 196; Reuben's estate 205, 214; Robert 245; Seth 243; Solomon 258; Thomas 243, 260

Chatterdon/Chetterton - Joseph 29, 76, 81, 86, 91, 96, 101, 106, 111, 117, 121, 127, 132; Will 47, 55, 58, 62; William 44, 66, 95, 100, 105, 110, 116, 120, 126, 151, 156, 162, 167, 173, 181, 193, 194, 210, 212

Cheeseman (Chesman) - Benjamin 190, 199, 208, 216; Thomas 204, 219

Chittenton (-don)/Chitterton - Jo: 57, 46, 50, 54; Jos 39, 43; Joseph 32, 36; Will 51; William 70, 75, 79, 84, 89, 131

Christian (Christean) - Charles 221, 247, 264; George 247, 264; James 264; John 221, 245, 266; Richard 44, 169, 176, 178, 221, 221, 228, 228, 247, 264; Richard Jnr: 264; William 221, 264

Chugal/Chugel - John 44, 47, 51, 55

Church - Josiah 33, 36, 39

Clap - Gilbert 124, 129, 134, 144, 149, 155, 160, 166, 172, 236; Gilbert's farm 139; Gilson 67, 71, 75, 80, 233

Clarke (Clark) - Capt's farm 145,

INDEX

150; John 47, 51, 55, 59, 62, 66, 70, 75, 79, 84, 89, 95, 100, 105, 110, 116, 121, 126, 131, 136, 142, 147, 153, 168, 174, 182, 189, 197, 206, 215; John Jnr: 123, 129; William 16, 17, 217
Clasen - George 236
Classon - Will. 247
Clauson/Clawson (-sen) - Caleb 16, 17, 18, 20, 21; John 71, 76, 80, 85, 121, 126, 132, 137, 142, 147, 153, 158, 164, 231; John's estate 90, 95, 101, 106, 111, 116; Timothy 29, 31, 35, 38, 42, 46, 49, 53, 57, 61, 65, 69, 73, 78, 83, 88, 93, 99, 104, 109, 114, 119, 125, 130, 136, 141, 146, 152, 158, 163, 230
Clemens/Clements - Peter 168; Stephen 251; Thomas 47, 51, 55, 58, 62, 66, 70, 74, 79, 84, 94, 100, 105, 110, 115, 120, 126, 131, 136, 142, 147, 201, 89; Thomas's farm 152
Clemmons/Clemons - Peter 163
Clemons - Thomas 44
Clerk - John 244
Cleveland - George 252
Clinton - Joseph 20, 22; Philip 155, 160; William 140, 145, 149, 171, 184, 185, 201, 202, 203, 219, 243
Close (Cloos) - David 231; Gideon 254; Jabez 251; Jonathan 260; Mr David 190, 199, 207; Reuben 76, 81, 86, 91, 96, 101, 106, 111, 116, 121, 127, 132, 137, 143, 148, 153, 159, 165, 172, 231; Reubin Jnr: 151, 156, 161, 167
Closs - farm 183
Clossen/Closson - farm 171, 179; Jacob 244; place 186; Wilber(t) 243, 244; Wm. 243
Cobert - Abraham 199
Cock(e) - 134; James 151, 156, 162, 255; Joseph 144; Jurdin 134
Cocker - 184, 186
Cockshuer - Jonas 243
Coevert - Abraham 140; Luke 141
Cogswell - Samuel 235
Colbroth - Thomas 245
Colden - Cadwallader 4, 5, 8
Cole - 17, 18, 20, 21, 37, 40, 43; Benjamin 243, 256; Daniel 183, 260; Ebenezer 264; Eleazer 23, 25, 28, 30, 34, 37, 41, 45, 48, 52, 56, 60, 64, 68, 72, 77, 82, 87, 93; Elisha 32, 35, 39, 42, 46, 50, 53, 57, 61, 65, 69, 74, 78, 83, 158, 261; Elisha Jnr: 172; Israel 40, 44, 47, 51, 55, 58, 62, 66, 70, 74, 79, 84, 89, 234; John 261; Joseph 161, 173, 181, 261; Joshua 260; Nathan 161, 173, 181, 260; Reuben 247, 257; Silvanus Jnr: 161, 173; Solomon 238; Sylvanus 86, 91, 159, 234, 243, 267, 278, 279; Thomas 236
Colegrove - John 264; William 169, 176, 178, 192, 194, 210, 212, 220, 228, 264; William Jnr: 264
Coles - Rufus 47, 51, 54, 58, 62
Colgan - Fleming (Capt:) 234
Colkin(s) [Calkin(s)] - Aaron 278; Eli 244; Elisha 278; James 173, 180; Joshua 244; Nathaniel 173; Simon 244; Will. 244; William 181
Coller - James 92, 97, 102, 107
Collins - 156; Joseph 81, 86, 91, 122; Joseph Jnr: 96, 101, 107, 112, 117
Collvill - Joseph 205
Collwell - 22; Joseph 172; William 174, 181
Colvel - James's farm 116
Colvil(l) (Colville) - James 95, 100; James's farm 106, 111, 121, 126; Joseph 123, 128, 133, 139, 144, 149, 154, 160, 166, 214; Thomas 89, 94, 99, 105, 110, 115, 120, 125, 131, 136, 152; William 215
Colwell/Colwill - James 247, 32, 36, 39, 43, 46, 50, 55, 59, 63, 67, 71, 75, 80, 85, 90, 278; Joseph 180, 187, 196, 247; Thomas 32, 36, 39, 43, 46, 54, 58, 62, 66, 69, 74, 78, 84, 147; Widdow 278; William 162, 168, 188, 196, 206; Wm. 270, 247
Comstock - Enos 267
Comwell - John 193
Concklin (Conklin) - Gilbert 44, 47, 51, 55, 58, 62, 66, 70, 75, 79; Jeremiah 221, 263; Jo: 42, 46, 49, 53, 57, 61, 65, 69, 73, 78, 83, 88, 93, 99, 104, 109, 115, 120; John 33, 36, 40, 43; Joseph 29, 31, 35, 38, 125, 130, 136, 141, 146, 152, 158, 163, 261; Joshua 145, 150, 155, 161, 167, 173, 180, 188, 196, 205, 214, 233, 257; Lieut 239, 240; Mary 220, 263; Nathan 261; Richard 169; Samuel 191, 199, 208, 216, 245, 257; Stephen 87, 91, 97, 102, 107, 123, 128, 133, 138, 144, 149, 154, 176, 178, 192, 194, 210, 212, 226; Timothy 25, 27, 30, 33, 37, 41, 44, 48, 52, 56, 60, 64, 68, 72, 77, 82, 87, 92, 98, 103, 109, 114, 119, 124, 129, 135, 141, 146, 151, 157, 163, 175, 191, 193, 226; Timothy's estate 209, 211
Conet - John 239
Conkling - Timothy 177
Conolly - John 264
Cooee - James 238
Cook - James 167; Richard 259
Cooke - 139; Jorden 140
Cool(e) - Daniel 190, 198; David 216; Ebenezer 217; Eleazer 98, 103, 109, 114, 119; Elijah [Elisha] 179; Elisha 88, 94, 99, 105, 110, 115, 120, 125, 130, 136, 141, 147, 152, 164, 171, 186, 195, 204, 213; Elisha Jnr: 134, 139, 144, 149, 155, 160, 166, 180, 187, 196, 205, 214; Israel 94, 100; Joseph 150, 156, 167, 188, 196, 205, 214; Nathan 150, 156, 167, 188, 196, 205, 214; Silvenus 81, 96, 101, 107, 112, 117, 122, 127, 132, 137, 143, 148, 153, 165; Silvenus Jnr: 151, 156, 167, 181, 190
Cools - Eleazar 234
Coonradt - John 266
Cooper - Cornelis 71, 75, 80; George 246, 63, 67, 71, 75, 80, 92, 97
Corben (-ban) (-bin) - Joseph 17, 18, 19, 21, 269; Tho 230
Corby [Carly] - John 92; John Jnr: 185
Corken - Jeremia 269; John 269
Corkum - Hezekiah 24, 26
Cornell - Daniel 31, 35, 38; David [Daniel] 29; John 194; John's farm 210, 212; Richard 173, 180; Samuel 176, 178
Cornwall - 184; John 225, 225; Samuel 250
Cornwell - Danll 27; David 243; Richard 145, 150, 156, 161, 167; Solomon 220
Corum [Cowen] - David 151
Cosby - Daniel 31; David 29, 35, 38, 42, 45, 49, 53, 57, 61, 65, 69, 73, 88, 93, 99, 104, 109, 114, 119, 125, 130, 135, 141, 146; Joshua 31, 35, 38, 42, 45, 49, 53, 57, 61, 65, 69, 73, 78, 88, 93, 99, 104, 109, 115, 120, 125, 130, 136, 141, 146
Cotton - Thomas 22
Covan - James 204, 213
Covell (Covel) - 27; Seth 29, 31, 35, 38, 42, 45, 49, 53, 57; Simeon 239; Zeth 238
Coven - James 171, 179, 186, 195
Covert - Abraham 102, 108, 113, 208, 217; James 262; Levinus

262; Luke 18, 20, 21, 23, 25, 28, 30, 34, 37, 41, 45, 48, 52, 56, 60, 64, 68, 72, 77, 82, 87, 93, 98, 103, 109, 114, 119, 124, 130, 135, 146, 151, 157, 163; Matthew 262; Sylvanus 221, 247

Covey (Covy) - Hope 29, 38, 42, 45, 49, 53, 57, 61, 65, 69, 73, 78, 83, 88, 93, 99, 104, 109, 114, 119, 125, 130, 135, 278; Hope Jnr: 29, 31, 35; James 103, 108, 113, 118, 122, 128, 133, 138, 143, 172, 180, 187, 195, 205, 214; James Jnr: 148, 154, 159, 165, 231; Jas. Sen: 231; John 29, 31, 35, 38, 42, 45, 49, 53, 57, 61, 65, 69, 73, 78, 83, 88, 93, 99, 104, 109; Joseph 29, 244, 258; Walter 209, 218, 244, 248, 258

Covil(l) - Nathaniel 268; Simon 72, 76, 81, 85, 90; Thomas 141; Warren 268

Cowban - Joseph 16

Cowen - David 151, 156, 162, 167, 173, 181, 188, 196, 206, 214, 248, 251; James 32, 35, 39, 43, 46, 50, 54, 57, 61, 65, 69, 74, 78, 83, 88, 94, 99, 105, 110, 115, 120, 125, 130, 136, 141, 147, 152, 158, 164, 238; Priscilla 251

Cowing - Isaac 248

Cowley - Andrew 236

Cox - James 206, 215

Coxwell - Samuel 238

Crab(b) - John 199, 208, 217, 246

Craft - 97, 102, 108; Abraham 124, 129, 134, 139, 144, 149, 155, 160, 166, 172, 192, 194, 210, 212, 221, 264; Caleb 261; Henry 191, 199; James 220, 266; John 277; John Thauny 113, 117, 122, 128, 133, 138, 143, 148, 154, 159, 165, 172, 180, 187, 195, 205, 214; William 190, 199

Cragg/Craig - Robert's estate 209, 217

Craine - Joseph 16

Cräkhyt - Jacobus 21; Sibet 21

Cranckheit/Cranckhyt - Siber 15, 16, 17

Crandle - Jerem'h 243

Crane - Esther 255; Isaac 267; Iza 243; John 162, 168, 174, 181, 188, 197, 206, 215, 245, 261, 270, 271; Jonathan 170, 184, 185, 201, 202, 203, 219, 251; Joseph 17, 18, 19, 21, 23, 25, 27, 30, 34, 37, 41, 44, 48, 52, 56, 60, 64, 68, 72, 77, 82, 87, 92, 98, 103, 109, 114, 119, 124, 170, 183, 185, 200, 202, 203, 218, 267; Joseph (Capt) 235; Joseph Jnr: 22, 24, 26, 28, 30, 34, 37, 41, 44, 48, 52, 56, 60, 64, 68, 72, 77, 82, 87, 93, 98, 103, 109, 114, 119, 124, 130, 135, 141, 146, 151, 157, 163, 243, 261, 267; Solomon 201, 203, 219, 243, 271; Stephen 81, 86, 91, 96, 102, 107, 112, 117, 122, 127, 132, 138, 267; Will. 243; William 250

Crank - Isaac 209, 218

Crankhirt - Jasper 51

Crankhite/Crankhyt - Caus [Hans] 81; Cobus 41, 45, 52, 56, 60, 64; Cobus Jnr: 41, 45, 52, 56, 60, 64; Hark's: 19, 20, 21; Henry 71; Jacobus 17, 18, 20, 23, 25, 27, 227; Jacobus Jnr: 17, 18, 20, 21, 23, 25, 27; John 67, 71, 75, 80; Sib. A 227; Sibert Jnr: 227; Sibet 18, 19, 23; Teunis 23, 43, 47, 50, 54

Crankright/Crankwright - Teunis 18, 21

Craw - Ebenezer 22, 24, 26, 50, 54, 58, 61, 65, 69, 92, 97, 102, 107, 112, 232, 279; Jacob 16, 17, 18, 19, 21, 23, 25, 27; Joseph 16, 17, 18, 19, 21, 23, 25, 27, 50, 54, 58, 61, 65, 69, 74, 78, 83, 88, 94, 99, 105, 110, 115, 120, 125, 232, 234, 279; Joseph's farm 131, 136

Crawfoot - 33

Crawford - 33, 36; Daniel 40, 43, 47, 50, 54, 58, 62, 66, 70, 87, 91, 97, 102, 107, 112, 117, 122, 127, 132, 138, 143, 148, 153, 159, 165, 172, 200; Daniel's estate 208, 217; James 191, 199, 208, 217, 255

Crinnell (Crimell) - Thomas 32, 36, 39, 43

Crocker - Tim'y 243

Crofoot - Gedion 111, 121, 127, 132

Croft - Abraham 178

Crommel(l) - Joseph 89, 94, 100, 105, 110, 115, 120, 126, 131, 136, 142, 147, 152, 158, 164; Joseph's estate 175, 177, 191, 193, 209, 211; Judah 220; Samuel 192, 194, 210; Thomas 90, 96, 101, 106, 111, 116, 121, 127, 132, 137, 143, 148, 159, 165, 176, 177

Cromton - Jer. 227

Cromwell - Joseph 66, 70, 74, 79, 84; Judith 265; Samuel 212, 226, 263; Thomas 72, 76, 80, 85, 226

Cronckhite - John 63

Cronk - Girardus 262; Isaac 259; Jacob 258; Sibert 264; Teunis 259

Croofoot - Gedion 116

Crookston - John 261

Crosbie - Theodoras 238

Crosbury/Crosbary - Thomas 63, 67, 75, 80, 85, 90, 95, 100, 106, 111, 116, 121, 126, 131, 137

Crosby (-bee) (-bey) - 36, 40, 43; Abiel 250; Abner 140, 145, 150, 155, 161, 166, 173, 180, 187, 196, 205, 214, 243, 252; Benjamin 255; Darius 250; David 78, 82, 83, 86, 91, 96, 102, 107, 112, 117, 122, 127, 132, 152, 157, 163, 171, 179, 186, 195, 204, 213, 243, 270; David Jnr: 138, 143, 148, 153, 159, 165, 172, 179, 187, 195, 205, 213, 251; Eleazer 243; Elemuel 243; Eli 183, 190, 198, 207, 216, 243, 250; Enoch 247, 254; Isaac 24, 28, 31, 34, 38, 42, 45, 49, 53, 57, 61, 65, 69, 73, 77, 83, 88, 93, 98, 104, 109, 114, 119, 125, 130, 135, 141, 146, 152, 157, 163, 170, 183, 185, 200, 202, 203, 218, 252, 267; Isaac Jnr: 170, 184, 190, 199; James 243, 250; John 183, 190, 201, 219, 252; John Jnr: 203; Jon'n 243; Joseph 243; Joshua 29, 152, 155, 158, 161, 164, 171, 179, 186, 195, 204, 213, 243, 252, 270; Joshua Jnr: 140, 145, 150, 151, 156, 161, 166, 167, 173, 180, 187, 196, 205, 214, 251, 271; Josiah 183, 190, 198, 207, 216, 243; Lemuel 246, 250; Moses 200, 208, 217, 244, 252; Nathan 71, 76, 80, 85, 90, 95, 101, 106, 111, 116, 121, 127, 132, 137, 142, 148, 153, 159, 164, 172, 179, 187, 195, 204, 213, 232, 258; Obadiah 268; Peter 251; Reuben 81, 86, 91, 96, 102, 107, 112, 117, 122, 127, 132, 138, 143, 148, 153, 159, 165, 172, 179, 187, 195, 205, 213, 237, 243, 250; Samuel 169, 174, 182, 189, 197, 252; Solomon 190, 199, 207, 216, 248, 251; Theodorus 123, 129, 134, 139, 144, 149, 154, 160, 166, 172, 180, 187, 196, 205, 214, 250; Theod's 246; Thomas 252, 255, 277

Crossbary - Thomas 71

Crossby - David 234, 234, 279; Isaac 26; Joa: 234; Reuben 234, 271

Crow - Ebenezer 32, 36, 39, 43, 46;

INDEX

Isaac 238; Joseph 32, 36, 39, 43, 46
Crowfoot - Gedion 72, 76, 81, 86, 90, 96, 101, 106, 137, 143, 148, 153
Crummel - Thomas 153
Crummill - Samuel 178
Crumpton - John 176, 178
Crumstock - Thomas 203, 219, 170
Cudney - William 260
Cullen (-on) - Charles 162, 168, 170, 184, 185, 201, 202, 203, 219, 246, 271; Lucy 254
Cummins (Cummings) - Asa 236, 238, 251
Cumstock - Thomas 184, 185, 201, 202
Currie - Charles 263; George 262
Curry - George 22, 24, 26, 28, 31, 33, 34, 38, 42, 45, 49, 53, 56, 125, 130, 135, 141, 146, 152; George Jnr: 191, 199; George's farm 157, 163, 171, 179; place 33, 36; Richard 20, 22, 24, 26, 28, 226; Thomas 17, 18, 20, 21, 23, 25, 33, 36, 39, 43
Curtis(s) - John 55, 59, 256
Cushman - Consider 209, 217, 244, 247, 259
Dacon(s) - Johnson 167, 181; Simon 153, 158, 164
Daggett - Maher 239
Daily (Dailey) - Edward 19, 20, 92, 97; Samuel 140; Silas 252; Will:'s farm 35, 38, 46, 49; William 19, 20, 21, 23, 29, 92, 97, 102, 107, 112, 117, 122, 259; William Jnr: 81, 91, 92, 96; Will's farm 42, 53, 57, 61; Wm's farm 31
Dakin(s) (-ons) - Elisha 259; Johnson 145, 150, 156, 161, 173, 205, 214, 259; Simon 172, 179, 232; Thomas 198
Daley (Dalie) (Daly) - Samuel 237, 278; William Jnr: 86; Wm 278
Dalton - John 266
Dan(n) - Elnathen 145; John 174, 181, 188, 196, 206, 215, 251; John Jnr: 169, 175, 182, 189, 197, 206, 215; Selleck 251; Thaddeus 246, 253; Will. 248; William 251
Daniels - Doctor 145, 150, 155, 161, 167, 173, 180; John 275
Dapenport [sic] - Isaac 265
Darbey (Darby) - George 81, 86, 91, 96, 101, 107, 112, 117, 122, 127, 132, 137, 143, 148, 153, 159, 165, 172, 179, 187; George Jnr: 175, 182, 189; James 198,

207, 216; Joseph 134, 140, 144, 149, 155, 160, 166, 227
Darling - Ephraim 238
Davinport (Devenport) - 269
Davinport/Davenport - Isaac 220; Mary 265; Mary Jnr: 220; Stephen 192, 194; Thomas 15, 16, 18, 19, 21, 23, 25, 27, 30, 33, 37, 41, 44, 48, 52, 56, 60, 64, 68, 72, 77, 177, 191, 193, 194, 209, 211, 220, 265; Thomas (Capt.) 17; Thomas Jnr: 18, 20, 21, 23, 25, 27, 30, 33, 37, 41, 44, 48, 52, 56, 60, 64, 68, 72, 77; William 21, 23, 25, 27, 177, 191, 193, 209, 211, 220, 220, 265; William Jnr: 265
Davis - Jane 257; Jedediah 124, 129, 134, 139, 191, 199; Jerediah 239; John 247, 209, 218; Paul 244; Sam'l 248
Dawn - John 157, 162, 168
Day - William 237; Willm. 231
Daykins - Elisha 247; Johnson 247
Dayton - Thomas 48, 51, 55
Deacon - Johnson 188, 196; Joshua 135, 140; Simon 63, 67, 71, 75, 80, 85, 90, 95, 100, 106, 111, 116, 121, 126, 131, 137, 142, 147
Dean - 31, 35, 38; Abigail 252; Benjamin 191, 199, 246; Caleb 157, 162, 167, 174, 181, 188, 196, 206, 215, 246; Dan'l 244; Elijah 32, 243, 267; Ezekiel 174, 181, 189, 197, 206, 215, 246; John 157, 162, 167, 173, 181, 188, 196, 206, 215, 239, 246; Joseph 175, 248; Richard Jnr: 169; Seth 17, 18, 20, 21, 23, 25, 28, 30; Seth Jnr: 22, 24, 26, 28; William 48, 51, 52, 55, 59, 59, 63, 67, 70, 75, 80, 85, 90, 95, 100, 106, 111, 116, 121, 126, 131, 137, 142, 278; William Jnr: 55; William's farm 147
Deane - Caleb 258; Ezekiel 258; John 258
Deason - Simon 59
DeForest - Lambert 267
Delamater - Capt 239
Delany - John 263
DeLavan (Delivan) - Abraham 205, 214, 254; Abr'm 248; Agnis 252; Daniel's farm 220; Timothy 118, 123, 128, 133, 139, 144, 149, 154, 160, 165, 172, 180, 187, 196, 205, 214, 248, 251, 270, 271; Timothy Jnr: 252
Demarest - David 256
Demick - Shubab 247
Dennen - William 220

Dennick - Widow 220
Dennis - Richard Jnr: 178, 192, 193
Dennis & Fowler - 59, 63, 67, 71, 75, 80, 85, 90, 95, 100
Denny - Andrew 265; Barber 246; John 263; Richard 212, 220, 266; Richard Jnr: 176, 228
DePew - John 237
Depie - John 33
DePuy - Abraham 253
Derbyshire - William 255
Dergey - Henry 221
Derley - John 247
DeVel - Sander 98, 114
Devenport (Devinport) - Stephen 169, 176, 178; Thomas 82, 108, 114, 119, 124, 129, 135, 140, 146, 151, 157, 163, 175, 269; Thomas Jnr: 82, 87, 92, 98, 103; Thomas's estate 87, 92; Thomas's farm 98, 103; William 108, 108, 112, 114, 119, 124, 129, 135, 140, 146, 151, 157, 163, 175
Devereux - John 255
DeVil - Sander 109
Dewell (-wel) (-wall) - Alexander 28, 31, 34, 38; Sander 42, 45, 49, 53, 56, 60, 65, 68, 73, 77, 83, 88
Dewey - John 80, 85, 90; Joseph 95, 101, 106, 111, 116, 121, 126; Joseph Jnr: 81
Dewil - Peter 27; Sander 104
Dibble - David 231; Joel 244
Dickens - James Jnr: 131, 136, 142; Mordecai 254; Roger 257
Dickenson & Wallis & Co - 171, 179
Dickenson (Dickinson) - Amos 20, 22, 24, 28, 30, 34, 37, 41, 45, 48, 52, 60, 64, 68, 73, 77, 82, 87, 104, 109, 114, 119, 124, 130, 135, 141, 146, 152, 157, 163; Amos Jnr: 66, 70, 75, 79, 84, 89; Amos's estate 93, 98; Chrisn. 230; Christopher 67, 71, 75, 80, 85, 90, 151, 156, 278, 279; Christopher's farm 62; farm 208, 217; George 236; James 19, 20, 22, 23, 28, 30, 34, 37, 41, 45, 48, 52, 60, 64, 68, 73, 77, 82, 87, 93, 98, 104, 109, 114, 119, 124, 130, 135, 141, 146, 151, 157, 163, 171, 179, 186, 195; James Jnr: 147, 152, 158, 164, 199, 208; James's farm 190; John 20, 22, 24, 28, 30, 34, 37, 41, 45, 48, 52, 60, 64, 68, 73, 77, 82, 87, 93, 98, 104, 109, 114, 119, 124, 130, 135, 141, 146, 152, 157, 163, 171, 179, 186, 195, 204, 213; Samuel 133, 139, 144, 149, 154,

293

THE SOUTH PRECINCT OF DUTCHESS COUNTY NY 1740-1790

160, 165, 172, 180, 187, 196, 205; Samuel's farm 214; Tertullis's mill 155; Tertullus 129, 134, 139, 144, 149, 169, 174, 182, 189, 197; Tertullus's estate 206, 215; Widow's farm 32, 36, 39, 46, 50, 54, 58

Dickenson [Dickson] - Gilbert 118, 123, 128, 172, 180, 187

Dickenson/Dickerson - Capt 238, 239

Dickerson - Widow's farm 43

Dickeson - Amos 26; James 26; John 26

Dicketson - Amos 56; James 56; John 56

Dickinson [Dickson] - Gilbert 165, 195

Dicks - William 44, 47

Dickson - Gilbert 118, 123, 128, 133, 139, 144, 149, 154, 160, 165, 172, 180, 187, 195, 205; Gilbert's estate 214; James 247; Theodorus 247

Dike - John 134

Dikeman - Joseph 169

Dillevan - Timothy 113

Dimmock/Dimick (Dimmick) - Mary 259; Samuel 239; Shubael 200, 217, 259, 208

Dinge(e) (Dinger) - Elijah 178, 192, 194, 226

Dingy - John 259; Mark 263

Dinnis - Richard 210

Disbrow - Andrew 248, 257; David 247, 259; Nathan 162, 168, 174, 181, 188, 197, 206, 215, 248; Nathan Jnr: 247; Zeruiah 250

Disbury - Jacob 199; Nathan Jnr: 200, 208, 217

Dixon/Dixson - James 248; Richard 252

Doan(e) - Daniel 198, 244, 271; Elizabeth 253; Elnathan 198, 253; Elnathan & son 234; Ruth 250

Dolf(f) (Dolph) - Edward 106, 111, 116, 121, 126, 132, 137, 142, 147, 153, 169, 278; Simon's farm 31, 34, 38, 41, 45, 49

Dolph (Dolf) or Wolf - Edward 71, 76, 80, 85, 90, 95, 101

Donaldson - Thomas 200

Done (Doone) - Andrew 194, 211, 213; Daniel 173, 180, 207, 216; Elithan 40; Elnathan 44, 47, 51, 173, 180, 207, 216, 244

Doolittle - Ichabod 267

Dortlandt - 6, 7

Dotton - William 221, 263, 247

Doty (Doughty) - Abner 184, 186, 209, 218, 238; Elijah 201, 203, 219; Jacob 20, 22, 24, 26, 55, 123, 129; John 255; Joseph 246

Douglass - John 244, 250

Dowel(l) - Alex: 24, 26; farm 129, 134, 139, 144

Downer - Israel 246

Downin - Corn's 246

Doyl - Elizabeth 263

Drack - Francis 269

Drake - farm 220, 221, 221; Francis dec'd 15; Jasper 263; Jere.'s farm 32; John 16, 17, 18, 19, 21, 23, 25, 27, 30, 34, 37, 41, 44, 48, 52, 56, 60, 64, 68, 72, 77, 82, 87, 92, 98, 103, 109, 114, 119, 124, 129, 135, 141, 146, 151, 157, 169, 176, 178, 192, 194, 210, 212, 220, 227, 247, 255, 263, 271; John Jnr: 163; Joseph 204, 219; Peter 108, 112, 117, 122, 128, 133, 138, 143, 148, 227; Peter's farm 154, 159, 165, 176, 177, 192, 193, 210, 211; Reuben 140, 145, 149, 155, 160, 166, 176, 177, 192, 193, 210, 227, 271; Reuben's farm 211; Saml. Sen: 226, 227; Samuel 59, 63, 67, 71, 75, 80, 85, 90, 95, 100, 106, 111, 116, 121, 126, 131, 137, 142, 147, 153, 158; Samuel Jnr: 164, 176, 177, 192, 193, 210, 211, 227; Uriah 59, 63, 67, 71, 75, 80, 85, 90, 95, 100, 106, 111, 116, 121, 126, 131, 137, 142, 147, 153, 158, 164, 176, 177, 192, 226; Uriah's farm 193, 210, 211; William 22, 24, 26, 27, 30, 34, 37, 41, 44, 48, 52, 56, 60, 64, 68, 72, 77, 82, 87, 92, 98, 103, 109, 114, 119, 124, 129, 135, 141, 146, 151, 157, 227

Drees - Gilbert 178

Drew - Gilbert 169, 176, 191, 199, 208, 216, 226, 247, 260; Isaac 209, 218, 245, 259; Sam'l 247; William 209, 218, 257, 263; Wm. 247

Drew & Gals - 220

DuBois (DuBoys) (Duboise) - Abraham 48, 51, 55, 59, 63, 67; Capt. Peter 98; John's 19; Lewis 240; Mathew 20, 21; Mathew Jnr: 48, 51; Mathias 18; Peter 15, 16, 17, 18, 19, 21, 23, 25, 27, 30, 33, 37, 41, 44, 48, 52, 56, 60, 64, 68, 72, 77, 82, 87, 92, 103, 108, 114, 119, 124, 220, 265; Peter (Capt) 129, 135, 140, 146, 151, 157, 163, 175, 177, 191, 193, 209, 211; Peter Jnr: 220; Piter Jnr: 269

DuBois/D.Bois - Eleazer (Capt) 237, 239; P. (Capt) 237, 239

Ducher - David 264; Henry 264

Dunn (Dun) - Daniel 140, 145, 150, 155, 161, 166, 187; Elnathen 140, 150, 155, 161, 166, 187

During - John 16, 17, 18, 19, 21, 23, 25

Dusenbury (-Berry) - 33, 36; Amaziah 263; Chas 247; Jacob 190; Jarvis 211, 212; Jervis 247; Moses 40, 43, 47, 50, 54, 58, 62, 66, 70, 74, 79, 84, 89, 94, 99, 105, 110, 115, 120, 126, 131, 146, 150, 156, 161, 167, 176, 177, 192, 193, 210, 212, 220, 226, 247, 263; Moses (Col) 241; Moses Jnr: 194, 211, 213, 221; William 40, 44, 47, 51, 54, 58, 62, 66, 70, 74, 79, 84, 89, 94, 100, 105, 110, 115, 120, 126, 131, 136, 142, 147, 152, 158, 164, 176, 177, 191, 193, 210, 211, 220, 226, 246, 247, 263; William Jnr: 221; William Jnr: (Moses's son) 221; Wm Jnr: 247

Dutcher - Barent 211; Hendrick 220

Dutton - William 191, 199, 208, 217

Duvel - Sanders 93

Duwey - John 76; Joseph 71; Joseph Jnr: 86

Dyck - John 139; John's farm 144; Samuel 200

Dyckman - Benjamin 253; Hezekiah 247, 260; Joseph 174, 182, 189, 197, 206, 215, 258; Joseph Jnr: 253

Dykeman - Jos. 243, 271

Eagar(-er) - farm 151, 156, 162, 167; John 87, 91, 97, 102, 107, 112, 117, 122, 127, 132, 138, 143

Eagleston - John 16

Eakerly - Banj'n 247

Earl - Capt 238; Nathl. 238; William 236

Early - Absolom 255, 265; Elijah 265

Earnell/Earnoll - Benjamin 17, 18, 19, 21, 23

Earns - Benjamin 15, 16

Earnst - Daniel 240

Eastman - Tilton 237; William 237

Edderton - 33, 36, 40, 43, 47, 50, 54, 58

Edie - Abner 237

Edy - Samuel 261

Egeleston/Egilston - James 182, 215

294

INDEX

Egleston/Egelston (Egg-) - David 257; James 169, 174, 189, 197, 206, 253, 271; John 17, 18, 19, 21, 23

Eldridge - Edward 221, 266; Henry 150, 210, 212; Henry's widow 192, 193; Joseph 246

Elliott - Dan'l 246

Ellis (Ellice) - Christopher 48, 51, 55, 59, 63, 66, 70, 75, 79, 84, 89, 95, 100, 105, 111, 116, 121, 126, 131, 136, 142; Foster 254; Gideon 32, 36, 39, 43, 46, 50, 54, 58, 62, 66, 124, 129, 134, 139, 144, 233; Jacob 22, 24, 26, 28, 31, 34, 38, 41, 45, 49, 53, 56, 60, 64, 68, 73, 77, 83, 88, 103, 108, 113, 118, 123, 128, 133, 138, 143, 148, 154, 159, 165, 172, 180, 187, 195, 205, 214, 233, 236, 254; Jerem'h 244; John 253; Simeon Jnr: 175, 182, 189, 198; Simon 33, 36, 39, 43, 46, 50, 54, 58, 62, 66, 69, 74, 78, 84, 89, 94, 99, 105, 110, 115, 120, 125, 131, 136, 141, 147, 152, 158, 164, 171, 179, 186, 195, 204, 213, 233, 253; Thomas 191, 199, 208, 217, 244, 253; Zazares 239

Ellis? (Wood?) - Christopher 147, 153, 158

Elliss - Elijah 244

Elsworth - John 246, 264

Elwell (Ellwell) - Ezra 243, 267; farm 185; Isaac 71, 75, 80, 85, 90, 95, 101, 106, 111, 116, 121, 126, 131, 137, 142, 147, 153, 158, 164, 170, 184, 185, 200, 202, 203, 218, 246, 268; Jabez 71, 76, 80, 85, 90, 95, 101, 106, 111, 116, 121, 127, 132, 243, 268; Jabez Jnr: 268; Jabish 137, 142, 148, 153, 159, 164, 170, 184, 185, 200, 202, 203, 218; Jabus 246; John 171, 184, 186, 201, 202, 203, 219, 243; Phebe 268; Samuel 29, 31, 35, 38, 42, 45, 49, 53, 57, 61, 65; Samuel 69, 73, 78, 83, 88, 93, 99, 104, 109, 114, 119, 125, 130, 135, 141, 146, 152, 157, 163, 170, 183, 185, 200, 202; Samuel Jnr: 71, 75, 80, 85, 90, 95, 101, 106, 111, 116, 121, 126, 131, 137, 142, 147, 153, 158, 164, 170, 184

Emmery - Robert 18, 20, 21, 23

English - William 251

Erkils - Joseph 269

Ernold - Nathaniel 112

Esmon - Peter 81

Evans - John 240; Michael 81, 86, 91, 258; Stephen 261; Thomas 237

Everitt (Everett) - Abraham 175; George 182, 189, 198, 207, 215, 245, 258; Isaac 175, 182, 189, 198, 207, 215, 248, 258; Isaac Jnr: 175, 182, 189, 198

Every - John 262

Fairbanks - Samuel 251

Fairchild - James 268; Jesse 238

Falconer - William 255

Falkanier/Falkenier (-ennar) - Josiah 181, 188, 197

Fallon - James 242

Fancher - Abraham 252

Farrington - Joseph 259; Robert 28; Robert's widow 31, 34, 38, 42, 49, 53, 56, 60, 65, 68, 73, 77, 83, 88, 93, 98, 104; Solomon 33, 36, 40, 105, 111, 116, 131, 137, 256; Stephen 44, 47, 51, 55, 58, 62, 66, 70, 75, 79, 126, 131; Thomas 31, 34, 38; Tom 28

Farrinton - Robert 24, 26; Tim: 24; Tom 26

Farris - Ezra 244; John 277

Feilds - John 277, 267

Fenton - Stephen 102, 108, 113, 118, 122, 128, 133, 138, 143, 148, 154, 235, 239; William 97, 102, 108, 113

Ferguson (-geson) - Abraham 257; Ephraim 17, 18; Isaac 257; John 199, 217, 248, 256; Lewis 190, 198, 207, 216; Thomas 123, 128, 133, 139, 144, 149, 154, 160, 166, 187, 196, 205, 214, 245, 257; Thomas Jnr: 257; William 23

Fermilar - Philip 244

Ferres - Justus 244

Ferrington - Robert's widow 45; Solomon 52, 55, 59, 63, 67, 71, 75, 79, 85, 89, 95, 100, 121, 126; Stephen 84, 89, 95, 100, 105, 110, 116, 120, 136, 142

Ferris - Daniel 266; Enoch 253; John 51, 55, 59, 63, 67, 70, 75, 79, 84, 89, 95, 100, 105, 111, 116, 121, 126; John's farm 131, 137; Reuben 198, 207, 216, 220, 245, 258, 271

Field(s) - Anthony 113, 118, 123, 128, 133, 176, 178, 192, 194, 210, 212, 228; Daniell 18, 20, 21, 23, 25; Elnathan 267; George 63, 67, 71, 75, 80; Gilbert 267; Isaac 251; Jesse 243, 251; John 33, 36, 40, 43, 47, 50, 54, 58, 62, 66, 70, 74, 78, 84, 89, 94, 99, 105, 110, 115, 120, 125, 131, 136, 142, 147, 152, 158, 164, 170, 184, 185, 200, 202, 203, 207, 215, 218, 243; John (Col) 241; John's farm 175, 182, 189, 198; Joseph 20, 22, 24, 26, 28, 30, 34, 37, 41, 45, 48, 52, 56, 60, 64, 68, 73, 77, 82, 87, 93, 98, 104, 109, 114, 119, 124, 130, 135, 141, 146, 151, 157, 163, 170, 183, 185, 200, 202, 203, 218; Joseph Coles 251; Joseph Jnr: 184, 186, 201, 202, 203, 219; Nathan 27, 29; Peter 201, 204, 219; Salomon 172; Samuel 19, 20, 22, 23, 25, 28, 30, 34, 37, 41, 45, 48, 52, 56, 60, 64, 68, 73, 77, 82, 87, 93, 98, 104, 109, 114, 119, 124, 130, 135, 141, 146, 151, 157, 163, 170, 183, 185, 200, 202, 203, 218; Solomon 81, 86, 91, 96, 102, 107, 112, 117, 122, 127, 132, 137, 143, 148, 153, 159, 165, 179, 187, 195, 205, 213, 251; Stephen 33, 36, 40, 43, 47, 50, 54, 58, 62, 66, 70, 74, 79, 84, 89, 94, 99, 105, 110, 115, 120, 125, 131, 136, 142, 147, 152, 158, 164, 170, 173, 180, 184, 185, 187, 196, 205, 214, 251; William 24, 26, 28, 201, 202, 203, 219, 267

Finch - Hanah 277; Isaac's widow 95, 100, 106, 111, 116, 121, 126, 131, 137, 142; Jacob 24, 26, 28, 31, 34, 38, 42, 45, 49, 53, 57, 60, 65, 68, 73, 77, 83, 88, 93, 98, 104, 109; Jacob Jnr: 103, 108, 113, 118, 123, 128; John 233, 240; Nathaniel 103, 134, 140, 145, 175, 182, 189, 197, 206, 215, 248; Reuben 245; Selah 254; Silvanus 248; Widow's farm 150, 156, 161, 167

Finckle [Hinkle] - Joshua 84, 89, 94

Finkle [Hinkle] - Joshua 100

Finn - James 266

Finton [Fenton] - John 240; Stephen 240

Firguson - John 208; Thomas 180

Fisher - Nathaniel 244, 247, 252

Fitch - Isaac 63, 67, 71, 75, 80, 85, 90

Flee - Joseph 238

Flemming - Thomas 244

Folcomer (Folcorner) - William 191, 199

Folkenier (Folkinar) - Josiah 168, 174

Fontyn - Isaac 15, 16

Fontyn (Fortin) - 269

295

THE SOUTH PRECINCT OF DUTCHESS COUNTY NY 1740-1790

Forgerson - Lewis 183
Forgeson (-gas-) (-gus-) - Ephraim 15, 16, 19, 21; Isaac 15, 16; Thomas 31, 35, 172, 277; Tom 25, 27, 29; William 17, 18, 20, 21
Forster - James 124, 129, 134, 134, 139, 140, 144, 149, 154, 160, 166, 173, 188, 196, 205, 214, 92, 97, 102, 107; John 96, 171, 186, 201, 202; John Wheeler 201, 203, 219; Joseph 92, 96, 97, 102, 107, 124, 129, 134, 139, 144, 149, 154, 160, 166, 170; Marmaduke 209, 218; Nathaniel 38, 42, 45, 49, 53, 57, 61, 65, 69, 73, 78, 83, 88, 93, 99, 104, 109, 114, 119, 125, 130, 135, 141, 146, 152, 157, 163, 170, 185, 200, 202, 203, 203, 218, 219; Nathaniel Jnr: 201; Thomas 130, 136, 141, 146, 152, 158, 163, 170, 183, 185, 200, 202, 203, 218; Thomas's farm 201; Tom 73, 78, 83, 88, 93, 99, 104, 109, 115, 120, 125
Fortin - Isack 269
Foster - Charity 268; Edmond 258; James 180, 251; Jane 254; John 81, 86, 91, 184; Joseph 81, 86, 91; Nathaniel 29, 31, 35, 183, 250; Sam'l 243; Seth 243, 257; Thomas 29, 31, 35; Thomas's farm 186; Tom: 38, 42, 46, 49, 53, 57, 61, 65, 69; William 259
Fowler - 24, 26; Caleb 106, 111, 116, 121, 126, 131, 137, 142, 147, 153, 158, 164, 172, 179, 187, 195, 204, 213, 233; Caleb Jnr: 253; Caleb Sen: 253; Christ. 225; Christopher 29, 31, 35, 38, 42, 45, 49, 53, 57, 61, 65, 69, 73, 78, 83, 88, 93, 98, 104, 109, 114, 119, 125, 130, 135, 141, 146, 152, 157, 163, 175, 177, 191, 220, 266; Christr. 225; Cristopher 193, 209, 211; David 183, 190, 198, 207, 216; John 27, 29; Jonathan 27, 29, 40, 44; Moses 118, 123, 128, 133, 139, 144, 149, 154, 160, 165, 172, 180, 187, 195, 205, 214, 233, 254, 277; Moses Jnr: 258; place 36; Stephen 254; Thomas 72, 76, 80, 85, 90, 96, 101, 106, 111, 116, 121, 127, 132, 137, 142, 148, 153, 159, 165, 172, 179, 187, 195, 257; Thomas's widow 205, 213; William 254
Fowler & Dennis - 59, 63, 67, 71, 75, 80, 85, 90, 95; Caleb 100
Fox - Isaac 92, 97, 102; Lemuel 92; Oliver 191, 199, 208, 217, 237; Oliver Jnr: 244; Samuel 239
Fräklin - Benjamin 22
Franch - Ebenezer 85, 90
Frankland - John 235; Rossel 237
Franklin (-len) - Benjamin 19, 20, 23, 26, 28, 238; Francis 268; John 236; Nathan 244
Freeman/Freman - George 244; Robert 258
French - David 72, 76; Ebenezer 81, 96, 101, 106, 111, 116, 121, 127, 132, 137, 143, 148
French man - The 97, 102, 108
Frisbie - Caleb 250
Frost - David 168, 174, 181, 189, 197, 206, 215, 247, 260; Jedediah 103, 108, 113, 118, 123, 192, 194, 210; Jediah 229; Jedidiah 212; Jerediah 176, 178; Jezadiah 236; John 17, 18, 20, 175, 182, 189, 197, 206, 215, 238, 255; Stephen 267; Thomas 17, 18, 20, 21, 23, 25, 28, 30, 34, 37, 41, 45, 48, 52, 56, 60, 64, 68, 72, 77, 82, 87, 93, 98, 103, 109, 114, 119, 124, 130, 135, 246; William 257
Frost [Green] - Nathaniel 123
Fullar - Cornelius Jnr: 277; Robert 277
Fullar & Company - Amos 277
Fuller - Amos 32, 36, 39, 43, 46, 50, 54, 58, 62, 66, 69, 74, 78, 84, 89, 94, 99, 105, 110, 115, 120, 125, 131, 136, 141, 147, 152, 158, 164, 171, 198; Cornelius 17, 18, 20, 21, 23, 25, 28, 30, 34, 37, 41, 45, 48, 52, 56, 60, 64, 68, 72, 77, 82, 87, 93, 98, 103, 109, 114, 119, 124, 130, 134, 135, 140, 141, 146, 151, 157, 163, 171, 179, 186, 195, 204, 213, 235; David 168, 174, 181, 189, 197, 206, 215, 247, 257; Elemuel 175, 182, 189, 197, 206, 215, 239; Elijah 145, 150, 156, 161, 167, 173, 181, 188, 196, 205, 214, 245, 257, 271; farm lot 279; Isaac 209, 217, 247, 257; John 168, 174, 181, 189, 197; Joseph 260; Mathew 236; Northrup 208, 217; Robert 48, 51, 55, 59, 62, 66, 70, 75, 79, 84, 89, 95, 100, 105, 110, 116, 121, 126, 175, 182, 189, 198, 207, 215, 246; Robert's farm 131, 136; Samuel 33, 36, 39, 43, 47, 50, 54, 58, 62, 66
Fuller [Tompkins?] - Cornelius 141
Furman - Joseph 244, 247
Gage - Alden 243; Anthony 71, 76, 80, 85, 90, 95, 101, 106, 111, 116, 121, 126, 132, 137, 142, 147, 153, 159, 164, 170, 184, 185, 200, 202, 203, 218, 243, 267; Bugby 251; Ebenezer 81, 86, 91, 96, 102, 107, 112, 117, 122, 127, 132, 138, 143, 148, 153, 159, 165, 170, 184, 185, 200, 202, 203, 218, 246, 267, 236; Eli 250; Elihu 71, 76, 80, 85, 90, 95, 101, 106, 111, 116, 121, 126, 132, 137, 142, 147, 153, 158, 164, 170, 200, 202, 203, 218, 267; Elisha [Elihu] 184, 185; John 253; Justus 244; Mark 171, 184, 185, 201, 202, 203, 219, 243; Moses 71, 76, 80, 85, 90, 95, 101, 106, 111, 116, 121, 126, 132, 137, 186, 201, 202, 203, 219, 248, 251; Silvanus 201, 203, 219, 244; Thomas 32, 35, 39, 42, 46, 50, 54, 57, 61, 65, 69, 74, 78, 83, 88, 94, 99, 104, 110, 115, 120, 125, 130, 136, 141, 147, 152, 158, 164, 170, 184, 185, 200; Thomas's farm 202
Gager - Nathaniel 220, 247, 263
Gale - Ira 263; Joseph 263
Gals & Drew - 220
Ganung (-nnung)/Gano(u)ng - Edward 22, 33, 36, 40, 43, 47, 50, 54, 58, 62, 66, 70, 74, 79, 84, 89, 94, 99, 105, 110, 115, 120, 125, 131, 136, 142, 147, 152, 158, 164, 171, 186, 195, 277; Gilbert 169, 175, 182, 189, 197; Gilbert's estate 206, 215; Isaac 150, 156, 161, 167, 173, 181, 198, 207, 209, 216, 218, 218, 248; Isaac Jnr: 209; Jacob 175, 182, 189, 197, 206, 215, 248; John 103, 108, 113, 118, 123, 128, 133, 138, 175, 182, 189, 197, 207, 215, 248, 277; John Jnr: 200, 248; Joseph 103, 108, 113, 118, 123, 128, 133, 138, 143, 148, 154, 159, 165, 172, 180, 187, 195, 205, 214, 277; Marcus 248; Reuben 245
Gardner - James 151, 156, 162, 167, 173, 181, 188; John 162, 190
Garlick (-leck) - Henry 134, 139, 144, 149, 155
Garlinghousen - John 19; John George 16, 17, 18
Garner - John 183
Garrason/Garretson - David 254; Isaac 177
Garrison - Abraham 266; David 190, 198, 207, 216; Harry 255;

INDEX

Isaac 29, 59, 134, 139, 144, 149, 155, 160, 166, 176, 210, 211, 225, 266; John 71, 76, 80, 85, 90, 95, 101, 106, 111, 116, 121, 127, 132, 137, 142, 148, 153, 159, 164, 172, 179, 187, 192, 193, 195, 204, 213; John (nr Wekepe) 72, 76, 81, 86, 90; Jon: 234; Jos. 271; Joseph 211, 212; Richard 140, 145

Garson - David 183

Gates - Samuel 20, 22, 24, 26, 28, 30, 34, 38, 41, 45, 49, 52, 56, 60, 64, 68, 73, 77, 82, 87, 93, 98, 104, 109, 114, 119, 124, 277; Samuel's 2nd lot 277; Samuel's farm 130, 135

Gay - Daniel 201, 204, 219, 254; Jason 244, 268; John 27; William 27

Gea - Cornelis 63; Fredrick 51, 55, 59, 63, 67, 70, 75, 79; Joshua 59, 63, 67

Gean - John 72, 76

Gee - Cors. 228; Ezekiel 32, 59, 63, 67, 71, 86, 91, 97, 176, 178, 192, 194, 210, 212, 220, 264; Francis 266; John 30, 34, 37, 41, 45, 48, 52, 56, 60, 64, 68, 72, 77, 82, 87, 93, 98, 103, 109, 114, 119, 124, 129, 135, 225, 266; Joseph 81, 86, 91, 96, 101, 106, 112, 117, 121, 127, 132, 137, 143; Joshua 71, 75, 80, 85, 90, 95, 100, 106, 111, 116, 121, 126, 131; Rossell 113, 118, 123; Roswell 128; William 30, 34, 37, 41, 45, 48, 52, 56, 60, 64, 68, 72, 77, 82, 87, 93, 98, 103, 109, 113, 114, 118, 119, 123, 124, 128, 130, 133, 135, 139, 141, 144, 149, 154, 160, 165, 176, 177, 192, 193, 210, 211, 271; Willm. Sen: 227; Wm: Jnr: 227

Geen - John 79, 84, 89, 94, 100, 105, 110, 115, 120, 126, 131, 136, 142, 147, 152, 158, 164

Genont - Ebenezer 254; Edward 256; Elizabeth 255; Isaac Jnr: 255; Isaac Sen: 254; Jacob 255; Jeremiah 256; Jesse 257; John 254; John Jnr: 254; Rachel 254; Reuben 254

George - Prince 252

Gerretsen - Cornelis 19; Elijah 19

Gifford(s) - Absolom 254; Benjamin 67, 71, 75, 80, 85, 90, 95, 100, 106, 111, 116, 121, 126, 131, 137, 142, 147, 153, 158, 164, 172, 179, 187, 230; Benjamin Jnr: 183, 279; Elisha 199, 207, 216, 247, 253; Jeremiah 48, 51, 55, 59, 62, 66, 70, 75, 79, 84, 89, 95; John 258; Samuel 191, 199, 208, 217, 247

Gilbert - David 250; John 253

Gilchrist - Sam'l 243; Will. 244

Gilding - Francis 252

Goarman - Ichabud's farm 202, 203, 219

Godferry - Jon: 234

Gold - Nathaniel 278

Golden - Benjamin 255; Benjamin's estate 208, 217; Robert 265

Golding - John 257

Goldsilluk - John 221

Good - Francis 169, 175, 182, 189, 197

Goodman - John 263

Goodspeed - Abner 239, 244; Israel 246; Samuel 32, 35, 39, 43, 46, 50, 54, 57, 61, 65, 69, 74, 78, 83, 88, 94, 99, 104, 110, 115, 120, 125, 130, 136, 232

Gorden - James 244

Gorum - Ichabud 186; Ichabud's farm 201

Gould - John 103, 108

Graham - James 252

Grant - Alexander 145, 150, 155, 161, 166, 173, 180, 187, 196, 224, 230; James 162, 168, 174, 181; James's farm 188

Gray - 17, 18, 20; Benoni 124, 129, 134, 139, 144, 149, 154, 160, 166, 173, 180, 188, 196, 236; Daniel 22; Daved 269; Edward 21, 23, 25, 28, 29, 30, 34, 37, 41, 45, 48, 52, 56, 60, 64, 68, 72, 77, 82, 87, 93, 98, 103, 109, 114, 119, 124, 130, 135, 141, 146, 151; Edward Jnr: 31, 35, 38, 42, 45, 49, 53, 57, 61, 65, 69, 73, 78, 83, 93, 99, 104, 109, 114, 119, 125, 130, 135, 141, 146, 152, 157; Edward Jnr:'s farm 163; Edward's farm 170, 183; Eldest son of Wm 33, 36; Henry 230; John 48, 51, 55, 169, 176, 178, 192, 194, 210, 212, 236, 244, 255; Jonathan 256, 278; Jon'n 244, 246; Oliver 29, 31, 35, 38, 42, 45, 49, 53, 57, 61, 65, 69, 73, 78, 83, 88, 93, 99, 104, 109, 234; Rich 234; Richard 124, 129, 134, 139, 144, 149, 154, 160, 170, 184; Richard Jnr: 166; Silas 82, 86, 91, 96, 102, 107, 112, 117, 122, 127, 132, 138; son of Edward 88; son of Will: 40, 43, 47, 50, 62; Thomas 36, 40; Will. 244; William 30, 33, 37, 41, 44, 48, 52, 54, 56, 58, 60, 62, 64, 66, 68, 70, 72, 74, 77, 79, 82, 84, 87, 89, 92, 94, 98, 100, 103, 105, 108, 110, 114, 115, 119, 120, 124, 126, 129, 131, 135, 136, 230, 256, 278, 279

Green - Benjamin 145, 150, 155, 161, 166, 173, 180, 188, 233; Charles 261; Edmund 151, 156, 161, 167; Enoch 257; Isaac 244; James 169, 170, 184, 185, 199, 204, 219, 267; James's farm 207, 216; Jno. 244; John 29, 40, 44, 47, 51, 55, 58, 62, 66, 70, 74, 81, 199, 207, 216, 247, 253; Jonathen Jnr: 86, 91; Nathan 29, 31, 35, 38, 42, 46, 49, 53, 57, 61, 65, 69, 73, 78, 83, 88, 93, 99, 104, 109, 114, 119, 125, 130, 135, 141, 146, 152, 157, 163, 170, 173, 183, 185, 185, 200, 202, 267, 271; Nathan Jnr: 81, 124, 129, 134, 139, 144, 149, 154, 160, 166, 170, 184, 200, 202, 203, 219, 243; Nathaniel 81, 86, 91, 103, 108, 113, 118, 123, 128, 133, 138, 143, 148, 154, 159, 165, 170, 183, 190, 238; William 175, 182, 189

Green [Geen] - John 79, 84, 89, 94

Gregory - Abijah 255; Dan 102; Daniel 33, 36, 108, 113, 118, 122, 128, 133, 138, 191, 199, 208, 217, 248, 254; Elnathan 209, 217; Ezra 209, 217, 245; Isaiah [Josiah] 189; Jos. 271; Joseph 30, 34, 37, 41, 44, 48, 52, 56, 60, 64, 68, 72, 75, 77, 79, 82, 84, 190, 198, 207, 216, 245, 255, 269; Joseph Jnr: 77; Joshua 209, 217, 248, 254; Josiah 16, 17, 18, 19, 21, 23, 25, 27, 143, 175, 197, 206, 215, 248; Josiah's farm 122, 128, 133, 138; Moses 32, 36, 39, 43, 46, 50, 54, 57, 61, 65, 69, 74, 78, 83; Moses's estate 88, 94, 99; Mr. 129, 134, 139, 144, 149, 155, 160, 166, 172, 187; Rev. Mr. Elnathen 277; Russel 22, 24, 26, 28, 31, 34, 38, 41, 45, 49, 53, 56, 60, 64, 68, 73, 77, 83, 88, 93, 98, 104, 109, 114, 119, 125, 130, 135, 208, 217, 248, 277; Samuel 183, 190, 198, 245; Sebel 108; Sebel's farm 112; Sias 30, 34, 37, 41, 44, 48, 52, 56, 60, 64, 68, 72, 77, 82, 87; Sias's estate 92; Silas's farm 117; Temothy 277; Thomas 209, 217, 248; Tim'y 246

Grey - Henry 237

297

THE SOUTH PRECINCT OF DUTCHESS COUNTY NY 1740-1790

Griffen (Griffin) - Benjamin the 1st 254; Benjamin the 2d 257; Doane 198; Edward 31, 35, 39; John 256; Lazarus 33, 36, 40, 43, 47, 50, 54, 58, 62, 66, 70, 74, 79, 84, 89, 94, 99, 105, 110, 115, 120, 125, 131, 136, 142, 147, 151, 152, 158, 161, 164, 171, 214, 233; Lazarus Jnr: 156, 167, 173, 181, 188, 196, 205; Richard 59, 63, 67, 67, 71, 75, 80, 85, 90, 95, 100, 106, 111, 116, 121, 126; Silas 254; Stephen 175; Thomas 182, 189, 198; William 183, 190, 198

Griffen [Burtch] - Jonathen 198

Griffis - Thomas 175

Griffith - Joshua 247; Lazarus 247; Stephen 208, 217; William 207, 216

Grigory/Grigery - Isaiah [Josiah] 182; Joseph 183; Mr. 180

Grimes - James 244

Guage - George 238

Gunning - Edward 24, 26, 28

Habond - Peter 92, 97

Haborn - George 81, 86, 91, 96

Haddon/Hadden - Alpheus 209, 218; William 199, 208, 217

Haddy - John 55, 58, 62, 66, 70, 75, 79, 84, 89, 95, 100, 105

Hadge - Abram 20, 21

Hadley - Moses 245; Will. 248

Hagelston - Murte 178

Hager /Hagur/Hagar - Charles 140, 145; John 82, 86, 91, 97, 102, 107; Thos 246

Haight – Abraham 157, 162, 168; Capt 239; Daniel 194, 211, 212, 220; Eburir 174; Eburn 162, 168, 181, 188; James 191, 199, 208, 217; John 176, 178, 192, 194, 210, 212, 220, 265, 271; Joseph 155, 160, 162, 167, 176, 177, 192, 193; Joseph (Highlands) 156; Samuel 156, 162, 167, 200, 208, 217; Silvanus 176, 178, 192, 194, 220, 225; Stephen 220

Hains (Haines) - Aaron 253; Asa 162, 167, 173, 181, 188, 196, 206, 214, 244, 256; Daniel 256; Edward 253; Elisha 253; Enoch 256; John 18, 20, 28, 30, 34, 37, 41, 45, 48, 52, 56, 60, 64, 68, 72, 77, 82, 87, 93, 98, 103, 109, 114, 119, 124, 130, 135, 141, 146, 151, 157, 163, 171, 206, 215, 253; John (reed maker) 183, 190, 198; John Jnr: 175, 182, 189, 197; Joseph Gidney 256; Mary, widow 217; Samuel 175, 182, 189, 197, 206; Solomon 190, 198

Hains [Hairs] - Richard 140

Hairs - Richard 140, 145, 149

Hale - Caleb 20, 22, 24, 26, 28; Josiah 238

Halket - John 256

Hall - Abraham 177; Abrose 252; Ambrose 244; Caleb 260; David 267; Edward 32, 36, 39, 43, 46, 50, 54, 57, 57, 61, 230, 269; Elisha 247; Elizabeth 258; Henry 92, 97, 102, 107, 112, 117; Isaac 178, 192, 194; James 264; Jesse 244; John 49, 53, 61, 65, 69, 74, 78, 83, 88, 94, 99, 105, 178, 192, 226, 243, 246; John 's farm 211, 212; Josiah 81, 86; Morton 157, 162, 168, 170, 184, 185, 201, 202, 203, 219, 243, 267; Nathaniel 151, 156, 161, 167; Peter 32, 35, 39, 42, 46, 50, 54, 57, 61, 65, 69, 74, 78, 83, 88, 94, 99, 104, 110, 115, 120, 125, 130, 136, 141, 147, 152, 158, 164, 170, 183, 185, 200, 202, 203, 218; Samuel 123, 129, 133, 139, 144, 149, 154, 160, 166, 170, 184, 185, 200, 202, 203, 219, 243, 267; Stephen 238; Thomas 168, 174, 181, 189, 197, 206, 215, 248; Widow 134, 139, 144, 149, 155, 160, 166

Hallock - Thomas 82, 87, 92, 98, 103, 108, 114

Halloway - John 207, 216

Hallowday - John 178, 193, 199

Hallsted/Halstead - David 27, 29

Hambleton - Doctor 200, 208, 217

Hamblin (Hamlin) (Hamlen) - 32; Barnabas 20, 22, 24, 26, 28, 30, 34, 38, 41, 45; Benj'n 248; David 87, 91, 97, 102, 107, 112, 117, 122, 127, 132, 138, 143, 173, 181; David (Joshua's son) 145, 150, 156, 161, 167; Deacon 20, 22, 24, 26, 28, 31, 34, 38, 41, 45, 49, 53, 56, 60, 64, 68, 73, 77, 82, 87, 93, 98, 104, 109, 114, 119, 124, 130, 135, 141; Ebenezer 35, 39, 42, 46, 49, 53, 57, 61, 65, 69, 73, 78, 187; Eleazer 92, 97, 102, 107, 112, 117, 122, 127, 132, 138, 143, 148, 154, 159, 165, 172, 179, 198, 207, 216, 277; Elijah 239; Israel 254; Joshua 32, 35, 39, 42, 46, 50, 53, 57, 61, 65, 69, 73, 78, 83, 88, 94, 99, 104, 110, 115, 120, 125, 130, 136, 141, 146, 152, 158, 164, 171; Reubin /Ruben 47, 51, 55, 59, 62, 66, 70, 75, 79, 84, 87, 89, 91, 95, 97, 102, 107, 112, 117, 122, 127, 132, 138, 143; Silvanus 175, 182, 189

Hamen - Thomas 211

Hamerday - Samuel 191

Hamilton - Hosea 271

Hammond - John 245; Jonathan 240; Thomas 212, 258

Hampson/Hamson/Hanson - Caleb 178, 192, 194, 210, 212, 227

Hampstead - Nathaniel 170

Hanan - Thomas 194

Hancock - John 266

Handly - Mille 257

Handtrot - Henry 261

Hanen - David 194

Hanes - Henry 55, 58, 62, 66; John 277; Mary, widow 209; Samuel 215

Hangen - David 265

Hannis - Elisha 191, 199, 208, 216

Hannon - David 211, 212

Haree - David 229

Hares - Richard 155, 160, 166

Harps - Conrad 200

Harrick - John 24, 26

Harrick? - John 28

Harrington - Isaac 237; Reuben 246

Harris - Capt 240

Hartwell - Abraham 119, 124, 130, 277; Abraham's place 135; Abrm. 238; farm 141, 146, 152, 157; James 244, 268; Peter 20, 22, 24, 26, 28, 31, 34, 38, 41, 45, 49, 52, 56, 60, 64, 68, 73, 77, 82, 87, 93; Peter's farm 98, 104, 109, 114

Hasel - Calib 277

Hason - Eleazer 208

Hass - Isaac 65, 99

Hatch - 19; Abiel 22; Benjamin 81, 86, 91, 96, 101, 107, 112, 117, 122, 127, 132, 137, 143, 148, 153, 159, 165, 172, 179, 187, 195, 231, 279; Isaac 32, 36, 39, 43, 46, 50; John 271; Malatiah 279; Malh: 230; Mallethiah 97, 102, 107; Malthia 32, 36, 43, 46, 50, 54, 58, 62, 66, 69, 74, 78, 84, 89, 94, 132, 138; Melthia 39, 92, 112, 117, 122, 127; Melthia's farm 143; Nathaniel 23, 25, 28, 30, 34, 37, 41, 45, 48, 56, 60, 64, 68, 72, 77, 279; Nathaniel Jnr: 72, 76, 80, 85; Richard 20, 21; Timothy 103, 134, 140, 145, 149, 155, 160, 166, 173, 180, 187, 196, 205, 214, 231

Hate - Sam'l 246

Hater - Alpheaw 190

Hatfield (Hatsfield) - Barnes 230; Barus 201, 202; Joshua 145, 150,

INDEX

204, 219; Joshua's farm 155, 161, 166, 170, 184, 185; Peter 190, 199, 207, 216, 271
Hath - Nathaniel 52
Haukins - David 103
Hause - Isaac 69, 73, 78, 83, 104, 109, 114, 119, 125, 130
Haviland (-val-) (-vel-) (-vyl) - Abraham 268; Benjamin 81, 86, 91, 96, 117, 122, 127, 132, 137, 143, 148, 153, 159, 165, 170, 184, 185, 200, 202, 203, 218; Benjamin Jnr: 268; Benjamin Sen: 268; Benjamin's farm 101, 107, 112; Daniel 151, 156, 162, 167, 170, 184, 185, 201, 202, 203, 219, 268; Daniel Jnr: 268; David 268; Ebenzer 27, 29; farm 186; Isaac 202, 203, 219, 230; James 184, 186, 201, 202; Jane 201; John 243, 92, 124, 129, 134, 139, 144, 149, 155, 160, 166, 170, 184, 185, 201, 202, 203, 219; Roger 123, 128, 133, 139, 144, 149, 154, 160, 166; Roger Jnr: 268; Roger's farm 170, 184, 185, 200, 202, 203, 219; Solomon's farm 201, 202; Thomas 27, 29, 44, 47, 51, 55, 59, 204, 219, 268; Thomas Jnr: 204, 219; William 81, 86, 91; William's farm 96
Haw - John 84, 89, 94
Hawborn - George 101, 107, 112, 117, 122, 127, 132, 137, 143; Widow 150, 156, 161, 167
Hawkins - David 108, 113, 118, 123, 128, 133, 138, 143, 148, 154, 159, 165, 172, 180, 187, 195; David Jnr: 205, 214; Isabelle 260; James 247, 260; Samuel 246, 260
Hawley - Daniel 256; Manchester 239; Nathan 254
Haws - 27; Edmund 44, 47, 51, 55; Edward 40; Isaac 29, 31, 35, 38, 42, 45, 49, 53, 57; Prince 240
Haws & Judd - 234
Hayden - Alpheus 257
Haydon - Tom's farm 30, 33, 37, 41, 44, 48, 52, 56
Haynes (Hayns) - Asa 156, 232; Henry 44, 47, 51; John 17, 21, 23, 25, 231; John's farm 156
Hays - James 244, 252; John 244; Nathaniel 103, 108, 113, 118, 244
Hayser - Caleb 52, 56, 60, 64, 68, 73, 77, 82, 87, 93, 98, 104, 109, 114, 119, 124
Hayson - Caleb 130

Hayt - Daniel 266; Gilbert 175, 261; Isaiah 268; Joshua 268; Samuel 259; Stephen 250, 266; Sylvanus 266; William 266
Haywood - Thomas 169, 176, 178
Hazard - Sam'l 244
Hazel(l)/Hazer - Caleb 30, 34, 38, 41, 45, 49, 135, 141, 146, 152, 157, 163, 171, 179, 186, 195
Hazelton (Hazleton) - Daniel 209, 218; David 247, 258; Martin 192, 194
Hazen (-zon) (-zor) - Caleb 207, 215, 246, 258, 271, 277; Caleb Jnr: 175, 182, 189, 198; Eleazer 217, 248, 258; Moses 246, 258
Heacock/Hecock - David 145, 150, 155, 161, 167, 173, 180, 188, 196, 205, 214, 231, 243, 270, 271; David Jnr: 244; John 209; Joss 244; Noah 244
Headon (Headen) - Thomas 15, 16, 17, 18, 19, 21, 23, 25, 27
Heady (Headdy) - John 25, 27, 29, 51
Hearns - Thomas 81, 86, 91, 96, 101, 107, 112, 117, 122, 127, 132, 137
Hebburn - Widow 170
Hedden - Moses 260; Reuben 261; William 191, 260
Heddy - 150, 156, 161, 167; John 44, 47
Hedger - Henry 27; Joseph 246; Robert 246, 261; William 32, 36, 183
Heeley (Heely) - Eleazer 265, 221; John 265
Height - Abraham 118, 123, 128, 133, 138, 144; James 145, 150; Joseph 139, 144, 149; Joseph (in Highland) 151; Samuel 151
Heirs - Richard 134
Heley - John 211, 212, 221
Hellick - Thomas 64, 68, 72, 77
Hempstead/Hemsted - Nathaniel 184, 243
Henderson - John 190, 199, 207, 216; William 151, 175, 189, 197
Hennion (Henion) - David 229; Jacobus 15, 17, 18, 19, 269, 16
Henry - James 137
Hepburn - Anne 268; George 234
Herriton/Herrington - Benjamen 237; Ebbert 55, 59, 63, 67, 71, 75, 79, 85, 89, 95; Zechariah 237
Herroy - Charles 256; Clarkson 255; Elizabeth 255; Peter 255
Hewman - Zach'h 243
Heycock - John 218
Hezelton - Daniel 247

Hiames - John 239
Hibburn - Widow 184
Hicks - George 240
Hicock - David 252; David Jnr: 258; Job 252
Hicox - Noah 244
Hide - Jabish 22, 24, 26; James 22, 24, 26, 28; Joseph 32, 35, 39
Higbee (-by) Higgbee (-by) - Stephen 140; Stephen's farm 145, 150, 155; William 163, 168, 208, 217
Higgins (Higgens) - Benjamin 156, 162, 167, 170, 184, 185, 201, 202, 203, 219, 235, 238, 260, 271; Benjamin Jnr: 151; Thomas 40, 44, 47, 51, 55, 58, 62, 66, 70, 74, 79, 84, 89, 94, 100, 105, 110, 115, 120, 126, 131, 136, 142, 147, 152, 158, 164, 170, 243, 267; Thomas Jnr: 140, 145, 150, 155, 161, 166, 170, 184, 185, 201, 202, 203, 219
Highet - Abraham 113
Hill – Abraham 198, 207, 216, 253; Andrew 44, 47, 51, 55, 58, 62, 66, 70, 75, 79, 84, 89, 95; Anthony 15, 16, 17, 18, 19, 21, 23, 25, 27, 72, 76, 81, 86, 90, 96, 191, 199; Caleb 236; Charles 266; Daniel 190; David 81, 86, 91, 96, 101, 107, 112, 117, 122, 127, 132, 137, 183, 198, 207, 216, 244, 266, 252; Elijah 244; John 29, 31, 35, 38, 42, 45; John Jnr: 72, 76, 81, 85, 90, 96; Jonathan 32, 36, 39, 43, 46, 50, 54, 58, 61, 65, 69, 74, 78, 83, 88, 94, 99, 278; Joshua 237; Noah 209, 217, 261; Thomas 266; Uriah 22, 24, 26, 28, 33, 36, 40, 43, 51, 55, 59, 63, 67, 71, 75, 79; Widow 100, 105, 110, 116, 121, 126, 131, 136, 142, 147, 153, 158, 164, 179, 187, 195, 204, 213; Widow's farm 172; William 32, 35, 39, 42, 46, 49, 53, 57, 61, 65, 69, 73, 78, 83, 88, 93, 99, 104, 109, 115, 120, 125, 130, 136, 141, 146, 152, 158, 164, 171, 179, 186, 195, 204, 213, 261, 265; William Jnr: 261; Wm 246
Hills - Cornelius 221; Joes 19, 20; Thomas 177, 178, 192, 194, 210, 212, 221, 228, 246
Hinckley - Elkanah 251; Elkany 243; John 169, 174, 182, 189, 197, 209, 253; Joshua 105, 110, 115, 120, 126, 131, 142, 147, 152, 158, 164, 172, 267; Nathan

299

THE SOUTH PRECINCT OF DUTCHESS COUNTY NY 1740-1790

190; Reuben 183, 190, 198, 207, 216; Thomas 169, 174, 182, 189, 197, 206, 215, 253
Hinderson - William 182
Hinkle - 37, 40, 43, 47, 51; Joshua 54, 58, 62, 66, 70, 74, 79, 84, 89, 94, 100
Hinkley (Hinkly) - Elkanah 244; Elkeny 71, 76, 80; John 218; Joshua 136, 233; Josiah 40, 44, 47, 51, 55, 58, 62, 66, 70, 74, 79, 244; Reuben 244; Thomas 40, 44, 47, 51, 55, 58, 62, 66, 70, 74, 79, 84, 89, 94, 100, 105, 110, 115, 120, 126, 233
Hinman - 201; Zachariah 204, 219, 268; Zach'h 243
Hinyon - David 221; Thomas 266
Hitchcock - David 261; Joseph 162, 168, 174, 181, 188, 197, 208, 217; Joseph (at stores) 191, 199; Joseph Jnr: 200; Samuel 198; William 191, 199, 208, 217, 261
Hitt - Henry 255; Jared 255
Hoag(g) - David Jnr: 184, 186; Jonathan 81
Hobey (Hobbey) - Jonathen 81, 86, 91, 96, 101, 107, 112, 117, 122, 127, 132, 137, 143, 277
Hodges - Abel 250; Able's farm 170, 184, 185; Abm. 231; Abraham 19, 93, 99, 104, 109, 115, 120, 125, 130, 136, 279; Abram 16, 17, 18, 19, 21, 23, 25, 27, 35, 39, 42, 46, 49, 53, 57, 61, 65, 69, 73, 78, 83, 88; Abram Jnr: 32; David 236; Isaac 231; Thomas's farm 71, 76, 80, 85, 90, 95, 101, 106, 111, 116, 121, 127, 132, 137, 142, 148, 153, 159, 164
Hoeg - Jonathan 86
Hoems - Seth 81, 86, 91, 96
Hogg - Job 32, 35, 39, 42, 46, 50, 54
Hokum (Hokam) - Elijah 175, 182, 189, 198
Holaday - John 190
Holcomb - Elishama 258
Hollester - Gideon 239; Joseph 235; Nathl. 239
Holley - Daniel 247
Holliday - Abraham 263; John 210, 244; John's farm 212; Simeon 244
Hollowday - John 194
Holmes (Holms) - Joseph 243; Seth 92, 101, 106, 112, 117, 121, 127, 132, 137, 143, 148, 153, 159, 165, 170
Homan - Zebulon 252
Honeywell (Honywell) - David 31,
35, 38, 42, 46, 49, 53, 57, 61, 65, 69, 73, 78, 83, 88, 93, 99, 104, 109, 114, 119; Israel 44, 47, 51, 55, 59, 62, 66, 70, 75, 79, 84, 89, 95, 100; Israel Jnr: 29; Israel Jnr:'s farm 31; Matthew 268; Matt's 243; Richard 186, 201, 202
Hopkins - Benjamen 238; Berry 157, 162, 168, 170, 184, 185, 201, 202, 203, 219, 268, 243; Edmond 258; Eli 248; Freeman 190, 199, 208, 216; Isaiah 123, 129, 133, 139, 168, 181, 189, 197, 206, 215, 246, 260; James 258; Jeremiah 247, 260; John 46, 50, 53, 57, 171, 184, 186, 201, 202, 203, 219, 268; Jonathen 48, 51, 55, 59, 62, 66, 70, 75, 79, 84, 89, 95, 100, 105, 110, 116, 121, 126, 131, 136, 142, 147, 153, 158, 164, 172, 179, 187, 195, 204, 213, 257, 277; Jon'n 248; Joseph 40, 44, 47, 51, 55, 58, 62, 66, 70, 74, 79, 84, 89, 94, 100, 105, 157, 162, 168, 191, 199, 208, 216, 257, 248; Joseph's widow 110, 115, 120, 126, 131; Josiah [Isaiah] 174; Marey 277; Prince 92, 97, 102, 107, 112, 117, 122, 127, 132, 138, 143, 148, 154, 159, 165, 170, 184; Rebecca 257; Salomon 172; Samuel 238; Silvenus 92, 97, 102, 107, 112, 117, 122, 127, 133, 138; Silvenus's farm 143, 148, 154, 159; Solomon 123, 129, 133, 139, 144, 149, 154, 160, 166, 180, 187, 196, 205, 214, 247, 260, 270, 271; Stephen 81, 86, 91, 92, 96, 97, 101, 106, 134, 140; Stephen's farm 145, 149, 155, 160, 166; Thatcher 204, 219, 257; Thomas 248, 257
Hopkins [Kelley] - Reuben 213
Hopkins [Tompkins] - Elijah 171
Hopkins? - John 32, 35, 39, 42; Joseph 32
Hoppe - Richard 55, 59, 63, 67, 71, 75, 79, 85, 90, 95, 100, 106
Hopper - John 194, 211, 212, 266; Joseph 266; Richard 111, 116, 121, 126, 131, 137, 142, 147, 153, 158, 164, 169, 176, 177, 192, 193, 210, 211, 220, 225, 266
Horner [Horton] - Isaac 29
Hornet - Joseph 240; Richard 240
Horsemore - 33
Horskins - Joseph 145, 150, 156, 161, 167, 173, 181, 188, 196, 205, 214
Horten [Hall] - Morten 170
Horton (-ten) (-tin) - David 37, 40, 44, 47, 51, 54; Dennis 181, 189, 197; Elijah 155, 160, 166, 176, 227; Elisha 134, 139, 144, 149; Isaac 29, 31, 35, 38, 42, 46, 49, 53, 57, 61, 65, 69, 73, 78, 83, 88, 93, 99, 104, 109, 115, 119, 125, 130, 136, 140, 151, 156, 162, 167, 176, 177, 192, 227, 260; Isaac Jnr: 169, 176, 178, 227; John 220, 264; Joseph 221, 263; Joshua 221, 264; Nehemiah 32, 36, 39, 43, 46, 50, 113, 118, 123, 128; Obediah 124, 129, 134, 139, 227; Samuel 145, 150, 156, 161, 167, 173, 181, 188, 196; Samuel's estate 205, 214; Thomas 191, 199, 208, 217, 247, 259; Thomas Jnr: 259; William 178
Hose - Nathaniel's farm 74, 78
Hoskins - Joseph 253
Hoss - Isaac 61
Hoton - Isaac 193
House - Isaac 88, 93, 135, 141, 146; Isaac's farm 152; John 239; Moody 35, 39, 43, 46, 50, 54, 57, 61, 65, 69, 74, 78, 83, 88, 94, 99, 105, 110, 115, 120, 125, 130, 136, 141, 147, 152, 158, 164, 171, 179, 186, 195, 204, 213; Moody Jnr: 199, 207, 216; Nathanel's farm 69; Nathaniel 32, 35, 39, 42, 46, 50; Nathaniel's farm 54, 57, 61, 65, 83, 88
Houston - William 266
How - Charles 134, 139; John 37, 40, 43, 47, 51, 54, 58, 62, 66, 70, 74, 79, 100, 105, 110, 115, 126, 131, 136, 142, 147, 152, 158, 164, 176, 177, 226
Howard - John 120
Howe - Jesse 246, 260; Lebbens 261
Howes (Hows) - Daniel 248; Job 248, 250; John 248, 251; Modak [Moody] Jnr: 190; Moody 32, 248; Moody Jnr: 250; Moody Sen: 250
Howland - Benjamin 48, 51, 55; Obadiah 244, 268; Samuel 185
Hoyt - Jachin 252; Joseph 134; Waterbury 163, 168, 174, 181
Hubbard - Ephraim Beach 250
Hueson - Jeremiah 48, 51; Walter 59, 63, 67, 70, 75, 79
Huested (Huestead) - 183, 190, 198, 207, 216; Caleb 76, 81, 86, 91, 96, 101, 106, 111, 116, 121, 127, 132, 137, 143, 148, 153, 159, 165, 176, 177, 192, 193,

INDEX

211, 212; Charity 220; Joseph 76, 81, 86, 91, 96, 101, 106, 111, 116, 121, 127, 132, 137, 143, 148, 153, 159, 165, 176, 177, 192, 193, 210, 211, 220; Moses 94

Huestin (Huesten) - George 87; Jeremiah 95, 100, 105, 110, 116, 120, 126, 136, 142, 147, 153, 158, 164

Huestis - Moses 66, 70, 74, 79, 84, 89

Hueston - George 15, 16, 17, 18, 19, 21, 23, 25, 27, 30, 34, 37, 41, 44, 48, 52, 56, 60, 64, 68, 72, 77, 82; Jeremiah 44, 47, 51, 55, 59, 62, 66, 70, 75, 79, 84

Huggins - Samuel 250

Hughson (Huston) - Jeremiah 277

Hughson (-stin) (-sen) - George 92, 98, 103, 109, 114, 119, 124, 129, 135, 141, 146, 151; James 134, 140, 140, 145, 149, 155, 160, 166, 233; Jeremiah 172, 179, 187, 195, 204, 213; Nathaniel 118, 123; Robert 108, 112, 117, 122, 128, 133, 138, 143, 148, 154, 159, 165, 172, 187, 195, 205, 214; Susannah 162, 168; Thomas 145, 150, 156, 161, 167, 173, 180, 188, 196; Walter 84, 89, 95, 100, 105, 111, 116, 121, 126; William 200, 208, 217

Huiston - Jeremiah 89

Hulford - Edward 252

Hull - 157, 162; Aaron 253; Eliphalet 255; Hezekiah 255; Joseph 168, 170, 184, 185, 201, 202, 203, 219; Oliver 162, 168, 170, 184; Stephen 237; Steps. 231

Hulse (Hultes) - Richard 19, 20, 22, 29

Hultz - Joseph 266

Humphries - Capt 237

Humstead (Humsted) - Ebenezer 107, 112, 117, 122, 127, 132, 138, 143, 148, 154, 159, 165, 171, 184, 186, 201, 202; Ichabud 201; John 134, 140; Nathaniel 185, 201, 202, 203, 219

Hungerford (-gar-) - Elijah 140, 145, 150, 155, 161, 166, 230; Jonathan 81, 86, 91, 96, 101, 107

Hunlock - Jonathen 71, 75, 80, 85, 90, 95, 101, 106, 111, 116

Hunt - Edward 151, 156, 162, 167; Elijah 191, 199, 208, 216; farm 40, 183, 190, 198, 207, 216; John 76, 81, 162, 168; Joseph 24, 26, 28, 31, 34; Joseph's widow 38, 42, 45, 49, 53; Obadiah 263; Samuel 145, 150, 155, 161, 167, 260; Theophilus 151; Thomas 244, 264; Wil:'s farm 37; William 15, 16, 17, 18, 19, 21, 23, 25, 27, 30

Huntly - Joseph 259

Hunywell - David 29

Hurlbutt - Stephen 252

Hurt - Edward's estate 173

Huson - George 261; Jeremiah 246, 257, 261; Robert 248, 179, 261; Walter 51, 55; William 254

Hussted - Daved 269

Husted - Charity 265; Joseph 265; Mossis 15; Robert 265

Hustin - Jeremiah 131

Hustis - David 15, 16, 17, 18, 19, 21, 23, 25, 27, 30, 33, 37, 41, 44, 48, 52, 56, 60, 64, 68; Moses 16, 17, 18, 19, 37, 40, 44, 47, 51, 54, 58, 62

Hustis (Hussted) - 269

Hutchens (Hutchins) - Benjamin 108, 113, 118, 123

Hyat(t) - Abraham 149, 154, 174; Alvan/Elvin 246; Caleb 37, 40, 43, 47, 51; Elias 247; Gilbert 182, 190, 198, 207, 216; John 262; Joseph 263; Minor 247; Stephen 248, 200, 208, 217, 268

Inckinbottom (-ken-) - Richard 113, 103, 108

Inckly - Thomas 236

Ingersol(l) - John 261; Josiah 162, 168, 261

Ingerson - Josiah 59, 63, 67, 71, 75, 80, 85, 90, 95, 100, 106, 111, 116, 121, 126; Josiah's farm 131

Isaacs - Benjamin 257

Isinghart - Christopher 27, 29

Ismond (Ismon) - Peter 86, 91, 96, 101

Jacobs - Bangaman 269; Joseph 269

Jacocks - Isaiah 221; James 178, 212, 221

Jagger (Jager) - Nathaniel 140, 145, 150, 155, 160, 176, 177, 192, 193, 210, 212, 226

James - Ephariam 239

Jarns - William 269

Jaycocks - Benjamin 15, 16, 17, 18, 19, 21, 23, 25, 27, 30, 33, 37, 41, 44, 48, 52, 56, 60, 64, 68, 72, 77, 82, 87, 92, 98, 103, 109, 114, 119, 124; Isaiah 37, 40, 44, 47, 54, 58, 62, 66, 70; James 192, 194, 210; Joseph 16, 17, 18, 19, 21, 23, 25, 27, 30, 34; Josiah 74, 79; Josiah [Isaiah] 51

Jaycocks (Jacobs) - 269

Jeacocks - Isaiah 264; James 264; John 264; Joshua 252

Jean(s) - John 172, 179, 186, 195, 204, 213, 248, 251

Jeffers - Samuel 266

Jelett - Noah 235

Jenkins (Jinkins) - John [Solomon] 137, 143; Nathaniel 208, 217, 246, 255; Samuel 20, 22, 24, 26, 28, 175, 176, 178, 182, 189, 192, 194, 197, 206, 210, 212, 215, 229, 248, 256; Solomon 72, 76, 81, 86, 90, 96, 101, 106, 111, 116, 121, 127, 132, 148, 153, 159, 165, 172, 179, 187, 195, 205, 213, 246, 256, 277

Jennings - Joseph 171

Jewel - Jacob 247, 209, 218

Jey - John 17, 18, 20, 21, 23, 25; William 17, 18, 20, 21, 23, 25

Johns - Neh'h 246

Johnson - Jeremiah 177; John 266; Joseph 244; Sam'l 244

Joice - James 171

Jones - 118, 133, 138, 162, 168; Amos 252; Annanias 247; Benjamin 144, 149, 154; Benjamin Jnr: 169, 175, 182, 189, 197; Daniel 102, 108, 113, 118; Ebenezer 15, 16, 17, 18, 19, 21, 22, 23, 24, 25, 27, 30, 33, 37, 41, 44, 48, 52, 56, 60, 64, 68, 72, 77, 82, 87, 92, 98, 103, 109, 114, 119, 124, 129, 135, 140, 146, 151, 157, 158, 163, 171, 179, 186, 225, 234, 250; Ebenezer (Peeks Mill hollow) 164; Ebenezer Jnr: 32, 35, 39, 42, 46, 50, 53, 57, 61, 65, 69, 73, 78, 83, 88, 94, 99, 104, 110, 115, 120, 125, 130, 136, 141, 146, 152; Ebenezer's widow 195, 204, 213; Eben'r 244; Elias 190, 201, 203, 219, 267, 244; Eph'm 244; Ephraham (upper) 181; Ephraim 113, 118, 123, 128, 133, 138, 144, 148, 151, 154, 159, 165, 208, 217, 231, 256; Ephraim (upper) 156, 161, 167, 173; farm 183, 190; Gershom 256; Henry 113, 134, 139, 144, 149, 155, 160, 166, 227; Isaac 244, 262; Jeremiah 24, 26, 28, 31, 34, 38; John 51, 55, 59, 63, 67, 70, 75, 79, 84, 89, 95, 100, 105, 106, 111, 116, 121, 126, 131, 137, 142, 147, 153, 158, 164, 176, 177, 227; Jonathan 63, 67, 71, 75, 80, 85, 90, 95, 100; Joseph 244, 259; Josiah 169, 174, 182, 189,

301

197, 206, 215; Levi 244; Lewis 77, 82, 87, 87, 91, 93, 97, 102, 107, 112, 117, 122, 127, 132, 138, 143, 148, 153, 159, 165, 176, 177, 192, 193, 227; Luwis Jnr: 134; Nathan Jnr: 244; Nathaniel 252; Nathen 168; Nehemiah 81, 86, 91, 96, 102, 107, 112, 117, 122, 127, 132, 138, 143, 148, 153, 159, 165, 172, 179, 187, 195, 205, 213, 234, 252; Robert 19, 20, 21, 256; Samuel 15, 16, 17, 18, 19, 21, 23, 25, 27, 30, 34, 37, 41, 45, 48, 52, 56, 60, 64, 68, 72, 77, 82, 87, 87, 91, 93, 97, 98, 102, 103, 107, 169, 174, 182, 189, 197, 206, 207, 215, 216, 244, 259; Samuel Jnr: 190, 198; Theophilus 32, 35, 39, 42, 46, 50, 53, 57, 61, 65, 69, 73, 78, 83, 88, 94, 99, 104, 110, 115, 120, 125, 130, 136, 141, 146, 152, 158, 164, 171, 179, 186, 195, 204, 213, 234, 252; Thomas 243; Widow 29; William 175, 182, 189, 197, 206, 215, 257; Wm. 246

Jons [Jones] - Ebbenezer 269; Ebenezer Jnr: 269; John 269; Samul 269

Judd - William 123, 129, 134, 139, 144, 234

June - John 81, 86, 91, 96, 101, 107, 112, 117, 122, 127, 132, 137, 143, 148, 153, 159, 165, 170, 184, 185, 200, 202, 203, 218, 268; Peter 268

Kane - John 240

Kangs - Israel 220

Karl(e) - James 205; Jonas 209, 218; Samuel 205; Thomas 162, 168, 188, 196, 277; Thomas Jnr:'s estate 208

Kearse - Henry 264

Keating - Isaac 256

Keeler - James 86, 91, 96

Keirser & Spauling - 229

Kelek (Kelik) - Thomas 16, 17, 18, 19, 27

Keler - James 81

Keley - Stephen 267

Kelk - Edmund 94; Elemuel 32, 35, 39, 42, 46, 50, 53, 57, 61, 65, 69, 73, 78, 83, 88, 99; Elisha 32, 35, 40, 44, 47, 51, 54, 58, 62, 66, 70, 74, 79, 84, 89, 94, 105, 110, 115, 120, 126, 131, 136, 142, 147; Thomas 21, 23, 25, 30

Kelley (Kelly) - Benj'n 248; David 28, 32, 169, 182, 189, 197, 206, 215, 244, 253; Ebenezer 71, 76,

80, 85, 90, 96, 101, 106, 111, 116, 121, 127, 132, 137, 142, 148, 153, 159, 165; Jeremiah 254; John 19, 20, 21, 23, 25, 32, 35, 39, 42, 46, 50, 53, 57, 61, 65, 69, 73, 78, 83, 88, 94, 150, 156, 161, 167, 173, 181, 188, 196, 205, 214, 233, 246, 248, 258; Jonathen 32, 36, 39, 43, 46, 50, 54, 57, 61, 65, 69, 74, 78, 83, 88, 94, 99, 105, 110, 115, 120, 125, 130, 136, 141, 147, 152, 158, 164, 171, 179, 186, 195, 204, 213, 234, 253; Jon'n 244; Judah 257; Jude 248; Reuben 32, 36, 39, 43, 46, 51, 55, 59, 63, 67, 70, 75, 79, 84, 89, 95, 105, 111, 116, 121, 126, 131, 137, 142, 147, 153, 158, 164, 172, 179, 187, 195, 204, 213, 244; Seth 259; Shubael 253; Silvanus 169, 182, 189, 197, 206, 215, 244; Thomas 32, 32, 35, 36, 39, 42, 46, 50, 53, 57, 61, 65, 69, 73, 78, 83, 88, 94, 99, 104, 110, 115, 120, 125, 130, 136, 141, 147, 152, 158, 164, 171, 186, 195, 204, 213, 254; Zebedee 169, 182, 189, 197, 206, 215, 248; Zebediah 259

Kellick - Elisha 100, 233; Thomas 33, 37, 41, 44, 48, 52, 56, 60

Kellick (Kelock) - Thomas 277

Kempe - William 5

Kennicut - Luther 255

Kent - Elisha Jnr: 124, 129, 134, 139, 144, 149, 154, 160, 166; John 190, 199, 207, 232; Jonathan 55, 59, 63; Moses 244; Moss 83, 92, 97, 102, 107, 112, 117, 122, 127, 132, 138, 143, 148, 154, 159, 165, 170, 172, 179, 184, 205, 213, 234, 234; Moss's farm 185, 187, 195, 200, 202, 203; Mr: 32, 35, 39, 42, 46, 50, 53, 57, 61, 65, 69, 73, 78, 83, 88, 94, 99, 104, 110, 115, 120, 125, 130, 136, 170, 183, 185, 200; Revd: Mr 141, 147, 152, 158, 164

Kerby - Albert 248

Kercomb/Kercome - Elijah 32; Hezekiah 29, 31, 34, 38, 42, 45, 49, 53, 57, 61, 65; Thomas 17, 27

Kerk - Thomas 36, 39, 43, 46, 50, 54

Kerkin [Kercomb?] - Widow 277

Ketcham (-em) (-um) - 150, 156, 161; Daniel 162, 168, 174, 181, 188, 197, 206, 215, 251; Daniel Jnr: 251; Dan'l 244; Joseph 256; Joshua 256; Losee 250; Richard

191; Zephas/Zophas 191, 199

Ketterfield - 118, 128

Kidd (Kid) - Alexander 175, 182, 189, 197, 206, 215, 231, 250, 271; Alex'r 244, 245; Capt. 169; Joseph 198, 207, 216

Killey - David 174; Silvanus 174; Thomas 179; Zebedee 174

Killog(g) - Thomas 171, 184

Killy - Reubin 100

King - Barley 246; Barzilla 172, 179, 187, 195, 205, 214, 253; Baseley 92, 97, 102, 107, 112, 117, 122, 128, 133, 138, 143, 148, 154, 159, 165; Caleb 243; Daniel 251; David 206, 215, 248; Ebenezer 24, 26, 28, 31, 34, 38, 42, 45, 49, 53, 57, 61, 65, 68, 73, 77, 83, 88, 93, 98, 104, 109, 114, 119, 125, 130, 135, 141, 146, 152, 157, 233; Haman 95, 100, 105, 110, 116, 121, 126, 131, 136, 142, 147, 153, 158, 164, 172, 179, 187, 195, 204, 213; Heman 48, 51, 55, 59, 62, 66, 70, 75, 79, 84, 89, 246, 253; Heman Jnr: 253; James 103, 108, 113, 118, 123, 128, 133, 138, 143, 148, 154, 159, 165, 172, 180; John 253; Merrick 244, 253; Nathaniel 244, 253; Obadiah 248; Stephen 246

Kings - Gabl. 229

Kingsley - 102, 107, 112, 117, 122, 127; John 92, 97

Kinkle [Hinkle] - 51; Joshua 79

Kinkly [Hinkly] - Thomas 70

Kirk - Thomas 32, 257

Kirkham (Kirkhum) - Solomon 208; Thomas 163, 188, 197, 206; Zebulon 163, 181, 188, 197; Zopher 200

Kirkum/Kircum (-kem) - Ezekiel 199; Hezekiah 87; Lydia 256; Seth 209, 217, 263; Solomon 191, 199, 216, 246, 257; Thomas 168, 174, 215, 255; Zebulon 168, 174, 206, 215

Kitterfield - 123

Knap(p) - Banj'n 248; Benjamin 191, 199, 208, 217, 256; Benjamin the 2d 259; Daniel 151, 156, 162, 167, 173, 181, 188, 196, 206, 214, 246, 256; Gabriel 35, 39, 42, 46, 61, 65, 69, 73, 78, 83, 88, 94, 99, 221, 226, 247; Gabriel's estate 104, 110, 115, 120, 125, 130; Hannah 136, 141, 146, 152, 158, 164, 175, 177, 191, 193, 209, 211, 220, 226, 263; Israel 169, 176, 191, 192,

INDEX

194, 199, 208, 210, 212, 217, 245, 259, 271; James 124, 129, 134; John 211, 212, 265; Jonathen 44, 47, 124, 129, 134, 139; Joseph 176, 178, 192, 194, 210, 212, 258; Mary 265; Moses 157, 162, 168, 183, 188, 190, 196, 205, 214; Moses Jnr: 157, 162, 168, 198, 259; Moses Jnr:'s estate 207, 216; Moses Sen: 261; William 259

Kniffen (Kniffin) - Amos 246; J.'s place 174; Jacob 168, 174, 182, 189, 197, 206, 215, 255; Jacob's place 188; Jonathan 255; Mary 255; Samuel 173, 181, 188, 196, 205, 214, 217, 246; Samuel Jnr: 209, 254; Samuel Sen: 254

Knilsen [Kniffen] - Jacob 174, 182; Jacob's place 181

Knop - Israel 178

Knott - Nathaniel 204, 219, 246

Kool - Daniel 207; Ebenezer 208

Krackheit - John 173

Krain - Jonathen 169

Kranck [Harrick?] - John 28

Kranckheyt (-hyt) - Hark:S 28; John 188; Sibert 176

Kranheyt/Kranhite - Cobus Jnr: 68; Sibert 193

Krankheyt/Krankhite (-hyt) - Abraham 89, 95, 100, 105; Abram 44, 47, 51, 55, 58, 62, 66, 70, 74, 79, 84; Cobus 48, 68; Cobus Jnr: 48, 72, 77; Hans 86, 91, 96, 101, 106; Hark s: 23, 25; Henry 67, 75, 80, 85, 90, 95, 100, 106, 111, 116, 121, 126, 131, 137, 142, 147, 153, 158, 164; Jacobus 30, 34, 225; Jacobus Jnr: 30, 34; John 151, 156, 162, 167; Kobus 37; Kobus Jnr: 37; Sibert 44, 47, 51, 55, 58, 62, 66, 70, 74, 79, 84, 89, 94, 100, 105, 110, 115, 120, 126, 131, 136, 140, 142, 145, 147, 153, 158, 164, 177, 192, 210, 212, 220; Sibert Jnr: 150, 155, 160, 166, 176, 177; Teunis 33, 36, 39, 89; Teunis' Jonse/Johnse 55, 58, 62, 66, 70, 79; Teunis Sen: 44, 47, 51

Krankhites/Krankhight - John 181; Teunis 84

Krankite/Krankright - Teunis 20; Tunis' Johnse 74

Kuatson [Kniffen] - Samuel 181

Kurkham - Thomas 181

Laight - Henry 174, 182, 189, 197, 206, 215, 260; Lazarus 176, 178; Woolsey 263

Lain - David 169

Lamb(e) - William 15, 16, 17, 269

Lamesie - John 67, 71, 75, 79, 84

Lamonaux - James 176; Joshua 176, 177

Lamoreaux (-iaux) - Elisha 194, 211, 213, 227; Isaac 176; Jas. 228; John 207, 216; Joshua 192, 193, 210, 211, 228

Lamorie/Lamory - John 89, 95, 100, 105, 111, 116, 121, 126, 131, 137, 142, 147, 153, 158

Lancaster - David 15, 225; Joshua 266; William 194, 210, 212, 220, 266

Lancastor - Aaron 171

Lane - 129, 134; Daniel 266; David 176, 178, 192; David's farm 194; G 227; George 129, 135, 139, 141, 144, 146, 151, 157, 163, 175, 177, 191, 193, 209, 211, 220, 226, 245, 263, 271; Gilbert 134, 139; Jesse 170, 184, 185, 200, 202, 203, 219, 263, 268; John 27, 40, 44, 47, 51, 55, 58, 62, 66, 70, 74, 79, 84, 89, 94, 100, 105, 110, 115, 120, 126; Jonathan 29, 31, 35, 38, 42, 46, 49, 53, 57, 61, 65, 69, 73, 78, 83, 88, 93, 99, 104, 109, 115, 119, 125; Jonathan Jnr: 63, 67, 67, 71, 71, 75, 75, 80, 80, 85, 90, 95, 100, 106, 111, 116, 121, 126, 131; Jos: 226; Joseph 17, 18, 20, 21, 23, 25, 27, 30, 34, 37, 41, 45, 48, 52, 56, 60, 64, 68, 72, 77, 82, 87, 92, 98, 103, 109, 114, 119, 124, 129, 135, 141, 146, 151, 157, 163, 175, 177, 191, 193; Justice 52; Nathan 15, 16, 17, 18, 19, 21, 23, 25, 27, 30, 33, 37, 41, 44, 48, 52, 56, 60, 64, 68, 72, 77, 82, 87, 92, 98, 103, 109, 114, 119, 124, 145, 150, 155, 161, 167, 173, 180, 188, 194, 196, 211, 213, 226, 226, 247, 262; Nathan Jnr: 213, 221, 247, 211; Nathan Sen: 221; Nathan's farm 214, 205; Solomon 134, 139, 144, 149, 155, 160, 264; Solomon's farm 162, 168; William 37, 40, 44, 47, 51, 54, 58, 62, 66, 70, 74, 79, 84, 89, 94, 100, 105, 110, 115, 120, 126, 131, 136, 142, 147, 152, 158, 164, 176, 177, 221, 227, 263

Lang - Robert 145

Langdon - Benj'n 248; farm 145, 150, 156, 162, 168; Isaac 59, 63, 67, 71, 75, 80; Jno: (Isaac's bro) 67, 75, 80, 85; John 16, 17, 32, 35, 39, 59, 63, 67, 71, 75, 80, 85, 90, 95, 100, 106, 111, 116, 121, 126, 131, 137, 140, 142, 145, 147, 150, 153, 155, 200, 208, 217, 255; John (Isaac's bro) 59, 63, 71, 90, 95, 100, 106, 111; John Jnr: 160, 166, 173, 180, 229; Joseph 211, 212, 254

Langley - John 240

Lankeston - William 178, 193

Lańterman - Isaac 258

Larkwood - Ebenezer 180

Larrance - Uriah 277

Latham - 22, 24; Samuel 26, 28, 31

Lathen - Widow 122; Widow's place 97, 102, 108, 113, 117

Latimore - Thomas 265

Lawrence (-ance) - 81, 86, 91; farm 147; Israel 265; Jesse 265; John 40, 44, 47, 51, 55, 58, 62, 66, 70, 74, 79, 84, 89, 94, 100, 105, 110, 115, 120, 151, 156, 162, 167, 173, 181; John's farm 188; Jonathan 239; Samuel 251; Stephen 178, 192, 194, 210, 212, 260; Uriah 32, 36, 39, 43, 46, 50, 54, 57, 61, 65, 69, 74, 78, 83, 88, 94, 99, 105, 110, 115, 120, 125, 130; Uriah's farm 136; William 209, 217

Lea - John 20

LeClair (Leclear) - John 162, 168, 174, 181, 188, 197, 206, 215

Lee - John 22; Joseph 97, 102, 259; Noah 81, 86, 91, 96, 101, 107, 112

Leech - Amos 268; Amos Jnr: 268

Legget (Leggit) - 135; Gabriel 141, 146, 152, 157, 163, 171, 179

Leneback - John 269

Leonard - Jacob 236

Lester - John 190, 199, 207, 216

Levet - Nehemiah 20

Lewis - Enoch 250; Henry 191, 199, 208, 216, 240; Ichabod 250; Joshua 92, 97; Thomas 246

Lickely/Likely (Likeley) - John 177, 178, 192, 194, 210, 212, 221, 227, 264

Light - Doctor 163, 168; Henry 169, 248; Lazarus 211, 229

Light? - Suzanne 212

Linch - 162

Linchlon - Jeremiah 175; Samuel 175, 182

Linckhorn(e) - Jeremiah 89, 94, 105, 110, 115, 120, 125, 131, 142

Lincoln - Jeremiah 251

Lindsay/sey - David 244

Linkhorn(e) - Jeremiah 33, 36, 40, 43, 47, 50, 54, 58, 62, 66, 70, 74, 79, 84, 99, 136, 147, 152, 158,

303

THE SOUTH PRECINCT OF DUTCHESS COUNTY NY 1740-1790

164, 171
Little - Zephaniah 239
Livingston - Henry 11, 12; James (Capt) 237, 238, 239
Lockwood - Abraham 221, 262; Caleb 102, 113, 118, 123, 128, 133, 139, 144, 149, 154; Daniel 244; Eben 92, 97, 102, 107, 112, 117, 122, 127, 133, 138, 143, 148, 154, 159, 165; Ebenezer 172, 187, 195, 205, 214, 248; Ephraim 162; Gilbert 221; Henry 190, 199, 208, 216, 244, 257; Israel 221, 263; Jachin 257; John 70, 74, 79, 84; Jonathen 37, 40, 43, 47, 51, 54, 58, 62, 66, 94, 100, 105, 110, 115, 120, 126, 131, 136; Joseph 20, 22, 24, 26, 28; Mary 260; Peter 248, 261; Solomon 169, 190, 198, 207, 216, 244; Sylvanus 221, 264; Timothy 251
Lomree - Elisha 183; John 183
Long - Robert 150, 156, 161
Longwall - David 261
Lookwood - Jonathen 89
Lord - Benjamin 36, 40, 81, 86, 91, 96, 113, 134, 145, 150, 156; Benjamin's place 118
Losee - Abraham 262
Loudenburgh - John Wm. 237
Loudinton - Asa 238; Cumfort 238
Lounsburg - Michael 67
Lounsbury (-burry) (-berey) - Isaac 255, 277; John 172, 258
Louwnsbury - Michael 191
Lovelace (-lass) (-less) (-lis) - James 22, 29, 31, 35, 38, 42, 46, 49, 53, 57, 61, 65, 69, 236, 239; Joseph 251; Joshua 238; Thomas 92, 97, 102, 107, 112, 117, 122, 127, 132, 138, 143, 148, 154, 159, 165, 172, 179, 233; William 183, 190, 198, 207, 216, 246, 253
Lownsburg - Michael 63
Lownsbury (-berry) - Isaac 102, 108, 113, 118, 122, 128, 133, 138, 143, 148, 154, 159, 165, 172, 179, 187, 195, 205, 214; John 103, 108, 113, 118, 123, 128, 133, 138, 143, 148, 154, 159, 165, 180, 187, 195, 205, 214; Michael 59; Thomas 103, 108, 113, 118, 123, 128, 133, 138, 143, 148, 154, 159, 165, 172, 180
Lucas - Israel 191; Samuel 102, 108, 113, 118, 122, 128, 133, 138, 143, 148, 154, 159, 165, 172, 180, 187
Luddington/Ludington - -- 231; Comfort 123, 128, 133, 139, 157, 162, 244; Elisha 231; Henry 145, 150, 155, 161, 167, 245; Henry (Col) 241; Steph. 271
Ludenton/Ludinton - Comfort 271, 168, 174, 188, 196, 206, 215, 248, 252, 181; Henry 173, 180, 188, 196, 205, 214, 259; Henry Jnr: 256; Samuel Jnr: 258; Steph. 270; Timothy 209, 218
Lukis - Samuel 277
Lumery (-erey) (-arey) - Elisha 190; Isaac 113, 118, 123, 128, 133, 138, 144, 149, 154; James 113, 118, 123, 128, 133, 138, 144, 149, 154, 160, 165; John 76, 81, 86, 91, 190, 198; Joshua 134, 139, 144, 149, 155, 160, 166
Luttington - Elisha 16, 17, 18, 20, 21, 29, 31, 35, 38, 42, 46, 49, 53, 57, 61, 65, 69, 73, 78, 83, 88, 93, 99, 104, 109, 114, 119
Lynch - 168; Thomas 174, 181, 188, 197; Thomas's estate 206, 215
Lyndsay - David 256
Lyon - James 258
Lyster - Capt 237
Mabee/Maybey - Abraham 277; Abram 63, 67, 71, 75, 80, 85; Abram Jnr: 63, 67, 71, 75, 80, 85; John 277; Peter 246
Mack - Orlander 32, 36, 39, 43, 46
Mackel [McKeel] - Uriah 178
Macklean - 199
Maggot (Maggatt) - farm 169; Thomas 131, 137, 142, 147, 153, 158, 231, 278, 279
Mahew - John 32, 35, 39, 43, 46, 50, 54, 57, 61, 65, 69, 74, 78, 83, 88; John Jnr: 32, 35, 39, 43, 46, 50
Main - Joshua 198, 207, 216
Maine - Elizabeth 258
Maker - Peleg 190; Solomon 170, 184, 190, 246
Maline - Dan'l 248
Mandavill/Mandevil(l)(e) - Jacob 15, 16, 17, 19, 21, 23, 25, 27, 30, 33, 37, 41, 44, 48, 52, 56, 60, 64, 68, 72, 77, 82, 87, 92, 98, 103, 108, 114, 119, 124, 129, 135, 140, 146, 151, 157, 163, 175, 177, 191, 193, 209, 211, 225, 269
Mane - Sebeus 248
Mangle - Hannah 263
Manley/Manly - John 33, 36, 40, 43, 47, 50, 54, 58, 62, 66, 70, 74, 79, 84, 89, 94, 99, 105, 110, 115, 120, 125, 131, 136, 139, 142, 144, 147, 152, 158; John Jnr: 124, 129, 134
Manning - William 266
Mansell - Ebenezer 133, 139
Manuel - Jacob 191
Manvell - Adrian 244
March - Richard 238; Stephen 236
Margetson - Frederick 258
Marin - Charles 246
Mariner - William 220
Mark - John 254
Marks - Levi /Levy 82, 86, 91
Marsh - Elnathan 201, 203, 219; John 243; Simeon 155, 161; William 59, 70, 163, 168, 174, 186
Martin - Daniel 188; John 237; William 190
Martine (-tyne) (Matine) - Daniel 162, 168, 174, 181, 196; James 248; John 130, 136, 141, 147, 152, 206, 214; Samuel 248; William 271
Marvin - Ephraim 251; Ephraim Jnr: 250; Ichabod 251
Mash - Simeon 145, 150; William 55, 62, 66, 75, 79, 84
Mast - William 55, 62, 66, 75, 79, 84, 44, 47
Masters - William 22
Matross - Cornelius 265; John 260; Peter 266; Robert 265; Samuel 266
Matthews - James 194; Joseph 191, 199
Maurade - James 24
Maurode - James 26, 28
Maxfield - William 92, 97, 102, 107, 112, 117
Maxvell - William 156
Maybee - 118; Abraham 90, 95, 100, 106, 111, 116, 121, 126, 131, 131, 137, 142, 147, 153, 158, 164, 253; Abraham (tailor) 137; Abraham Jnr: 90, 95, 100, 106, 111, 116, 121, 126, 131, 137, 142, 147, 153, 158, 164, 172, 179, 187, 195, 204, 213; Abrm 233; Daniel 256; Jacob 146, 150, 156, 161, 167, 173, 181, 188, 196; Jacob's estate 205, 214; John 123, 128, 133, 139, 162, 168, 174, 181, 188, 197, 206, 215, 255; John's estate 144; Peter 103, 108, 113, 118, 123, 128, 133, 138, 143, 148, 154, 159, 165, 172, 180, 187, 195, 205, 214, 256; Widow's farm 150; Widow's place 156, 161
Mayerson - Thomas 244
Mayhew - John 99, 105, 110, 115; John's estate 120, 125, 130, 136

INDEX

Maze - Ab'm 248
McAbe/McCabe - Benjamin 264; Matthew 220, 228, 264; Stephen 264
McArthur - John 230
McAuley - Auley 256
McCabee - Benj'n 247
McCaby - Matthew 81, 86, 143, 148, 153, 159, 91, 96, 101, 106, 112, 117, 121, 127, 132, 137, 165, 176, 177, 192, 193, 210, 211
McCrady - Charles 172, 179
McCredey - Charles 246
McCreedy - William 63, 67
McCrery - John 235
McCudney/McCudny - Jeremiah 176, 178, 227
McCurdy [McCudny] - Jeremiah 227
McDaniel - John 220
McDonal - Capt.'s farm 207
McDonald (-old) - Alexd: 230; Capt.'s farm 190, 199; John 176, 178, 192, 194, 210, 212, 228, 263; Lauchlan 173; Laughlin 187, 196; Locklan(d) 145, 150, 155, 161, 166; Loughlin 180
McDonnel - John 169
McDougall - Capt.'s farm 216
McFarden - John 264
McFarlin - James 208, 217, 259
McFarthing - James 200; John 40, 44, 47, 51, 55, 58, 62, 66, 70
McGilvray - William 256
McGlaughlin - Neil 252
McGregor - Duncan 253
McGregory - Duncan 175, 182, 189, 198, 207, 215; Joseph 15, 16, 17, 18, 19, 21, 23, 25, 27
McGuire - James 261
McIntire - Peter 256
McKee - John 169, 174, 182
McKeel - Uriah 178, 193, 194, 220, 265, 210, 212
McKinney - Rodrick's estate 202, 203, 219
McKinsey - Rodrick 170, 184, 185, 201; Rodrick's estate 202, 203
McKudney - Jeremiah 192, 194, 210, 212
McLane/McLean - John 162, 168, 174, 181, 188, 196, 206, 207, 215, 216, 248; John the 1st 257; John the 2d 256; Mr 190
McNeal/McNiel - James 238; Neal 162, 168
McNichols - John 170, 184
McNill - 156
McReady - Charles 81, 86, 91, 96, 101, 106, 112, 117, 121, 127, 132, 137, 148, 153, 159, 165; John 116; William 75, 85, 90, 95, 100, 106, 111
McReedy (McReed) - Charles 143; James 31, 34, 38, 42, 45, 49, 53; James's farm 56, 60, 65, 68, 73, 77; William 59, 71, 80
McTassel - Peter 247
Mead(e)/Meed - Abner 162, 168, 174, 181, 188, 197, 206, 215, 248, 257; Abraham 252; Azariah 71, 76, 80, 85, 90, 96, 101, 106, 111, 116; Billey 248; Capt 239; David 259; Elisha 44, 47, 51, 55, 58, 62, 66, 70, 75, 79, 84, 89, 95, 100, 105; Ezekiel 31, 35, 39, 42, 46, 48, 49, 51, 53, 55, 57, 59, 61, 62, 65, 66, 69, 70, 73, 78, 83, 88, 93, 99, 104, 109, 115, 120, 125, 130, 136, 141, 146, 152, 226; Hezek Jnr: 270; Hezek. 271; Hezekiah 55, 59, 63, 67, 92, 97, 121, 127, 132, 137, 142, 148, 153, 159, 165, 172, 179, 187, 195, 278; Hezekiah Jnr: 102, 107, 112, 117, 122, 127, 133, 138, 143, 148, 154, 159, 165, 172, 179, 187, 195, 204, 213, 245; Isaac 211, 213, 220, 248, 266; Jacob 198, 207, 216, 246, 254; James 209, 218, 248; James Jnr: 254; James Sen: 259; Jeremiah 175, 182, 189, 197, 206, 215, 251; Joel 191, 199, 208, 216, 245, 258, 270, 271; John 254; Joseph 17, 18, 20, 21, 23, 25, 27, 30, 34, 37, 41, 45, 48, 52, 56, 60, 64, 68, 72, 77, 82, 87, 92, 98, 103, 109, 114, 119, 124, 129, 135, 162, 168, 174, 181, 188, 226; Joseph's farm 141; Joshua 194, 211, 213, 220, 265; Lewis 260; Moses 134, 139, 144, 149, 155, 160, 166, 172, 180, 187, 196, 205, 214, 248, 260; Peter 258; Phillip 251; place 134, 139, 144, 149, 155, 160, 166; Stephen 124, 129, 134, 139, 254; William 168, 174, 181, 189, 197, 206, 215, 259
Measureall - Corn's 244
Meeker - Peleg 268; Solomon 250
Meeks (Meckes) - Edward 220, 266; John 33, 36, 39, 43, 47, 50, 54, 58, 62, 66, 69, 74, 78, 84, 89, 113, 118, 123, 128, 133, 139, 144, 149, 154, 160, 165, 176, 177, 192, 193, 210, 211, 220, 225, 225, 266; John Jnr: 266; Richard 266
Menger - Benjamin 191; Lemuel 191
Menzies (Mensus) (Menzus) - Alexander 145, 150, 155, 161, 166, 173, 187, 196, 232; Alexander's estate 205, 214; Thomas 145, 150, 155, 161, 167, 173, 180, 188, 196, 205, 214, 230
Mercy - Jesse 182, 189, 197
Merrick (Merick) - Abel 240, 253; Benjamin 22, 24; David 154, 159, 205, 214, 248, 258, 271, 277; Isaac 139, 149, 154, 160, 166, 172, 180, 196, 205, 214, 258, 277; John 32, 35, 39, 43, 46, 50, 54, 57, 61, 65, 69, 74, 78, 83, 88, 94, 105, 110, 115, 152, 158, 186, 277; John Jnr: 108; Joshua 183, 190, 207, 216, 255; Seth 32, 36, 39, 43, 46, 50, 54, 58, 62, 66, 69, 74, 78, 84, 89, 94, 105, 110, 115, 277; Thomas 238; Widow 150, 156, 161, 167, 181
Merrit [Mirrick] - David 172
Merrit(s)/Merritt(s) - Cornbury 198; Ebenezer 52, 55; Gilbert 183, 190, 198, 207, 216, 254; Hachaliah 162, 168, 174, 181, 188, 197; Hachaliah's widow 206, 215; John 200, 208, 217; Joseph 27, 29, 79, 84, 89, 95, 100, 105, 111, 116, 121, 126, 131, 137, 142, 147, 153; Joseph's farm 51, 55, 59, 63, 67, 70, 75; Josiah's farm 48; Silvanus 191; William 72, 76, 80, 103, 108, 113, 118, 123, 128, 133, 138, 143, 148, 154, 159, 165, 180, 187, 195, 205, 214, 277
Mertain - William 183
Mertains - 183
Mertine - Daniel 270
Meruce - David 59, 63
Meyhew - John 94
Millard - Jacob 201, 202, 203, 219
Miller - Eleazer 72, 76, 81, 85, 90, 96, 101, 106, 111; Jacob 268; Jonathan 211, 213; Josiah 252; Lodawick 240
Mills - Abigail 252; Alex'r 245; Benajah 244; Brown 245; Samuel 252
Minck [Mirrck?] - John 195, 204, 213
Miner - Nathan W. 264
Minor - Jonathan 251
Minthorn(e) - Benjamin 175, 182, 189; Elizabeth 255; Philip 16, 17, 18, 19, 21, 134, 140, 145, 149, 155, 160, 166, 173; Philip Jnr: 134, 140, 145, 149, 155, 160
Minzies - Alexander 180
Mirck - Dirck 187; John 120, 125,

305

THE SOUTH PRECINCT OF DUTCHESS COUNTY NY 1740-1790

130; John Jnr: 113, 118, 123
Mirrck? - John 195, 204, 213
Mirrick (-eck) - David 143, 148, 165, 172, 195; David Jnr: 133, 138; Isaac 123, 129, 133, 144, 187; John 99, 136, 141, 147, 164, 171, 179; John Jnr: 103, 128; Joshua 198; Seth 99, 120, 125, 131, 136; Seth's estate 141; Widow 173
Mitchel - Thomas 209, 218
Mitchel [McKeel] - Uriah 193, 194
Mock [Moe] - Peter 133, 139
Moe - Abraham 175, 182, 189, 197, 206, 215; Peter 113, 118, 123, 133, 139, 144, 149, 154, 160, 165, 172, 180, 187, 191, 199
Molineaux - Israel 254; John 254; Levi 254
Mondavill - Jacob 18
Money - Robert 146, 157, 163
Monhouse - Stephen 184, 186, 201
Montros(s) - Peter 193, 194
Mooney (Moony) - Edward 252; Robert 130, 135, 141, 152, 171, 179, 186, 195, 204, 213, 231
Moore - Samuel 38, 69, 225; William 239
Mora - Samuel 63
Morce - Samuel 49
Morcy - Jesse 169, 175
More - Ruth 266; Samuel 29, 31, 35, 42, 46, 53, 57, 61, 65, 73, 78, 83, 88, 93, 99, 104; Thomas 134, 139
Morehouse (-ause) (-ous) - Andr. 271; Elisha 71, 76, 80, 85, 90, 96, 101, 171; Isaac 244; John 248; Stephen 171, 202, 243
Morgan - Benjamin 272, 276, 278; John 260
Morrel(l) - Ab'm 243, 247
Morres - Peter 178
Morris - Iabah 29; Roger 2, 9, 11, 169, 174, 182, 189, 197, 241, 242, 278
Morrison (Morison) - Malcom 124, 129, 134, 139, 144, 149, 155, 160, 166, 172, 180, 187, 196, 205, 231, 233, 233; Malcom's farm 214; store 198; Violet 268
Mors - Abraham 87, 91, 97, 102, 107, 112, 117, 122; Joseph Jnr: 218; William 218
Morse - Joseph Jnr: 209; William 209
Mory - David 259
Moshier - Johiel 244
Mosier - Lemuel 255
Moss - Abraham 127; Abram 63, 67, 71; Benjamin 97, 102, 108, 113, 118, 122, 128; John Jnr: 134, 139, 144, 149, 155, 160, 166; Joseph 191, 199, 208, 217, 254; Joshua 33, 36, 40, 43, 47, 50, 54, 58, 62, 66, 70, 74, 79, 84, 89, 94; Will. 248; William 260
Most - William 51
Mott - Abraham 253; Jacob 243; Merriby 254; Tho's 243; Will. Jnr: 243; William 186, 201, 202, 203, 219; Zebulon 247
Mowe - Peter 128
Mullinaus (-eaux) - Israel 209, 218
Munger - Elemuel's farm 208, 217; James 199; Lemuel 199, 259
Munroe - Samuel 278, 279
Munrowe - John 200; Justus 218
Munsell - 118; Ebenezer 123, 128
Munson - Ebenezer Jnr: 124, 129, 134, 139, 144, 149, 154
Murch - George 250; Richard 240; Stephen 124, 129; William 184, 202, 203, 240
Murik - William 184, 202, 203, 240, 219
Murowe - Justus 209
Murray - And'w 243
Murrit - William 172
Mursh - William 201
Mustoon (Muston) - Gershom 32, 35, 39, 42
Myrick (Myrck) - David 180, 270; Isaac 246; John 248; Joshua 270
Nail [Vail] - Caleb 181, 188
Names - Isaac 15
Nap - Gabriel 32, 50, 53, 57
Nash - David 231, 245
Nath - David 208, 217
Nauthrop (Nauthorp) - Benjamin 92, 97; Joseph 92, 97, 102, 103, 107, 112, 117, 122, 127, 132, 138, 143, 148, 154, 159, 165; Moses 20, 22, 24, 26, 28, 33, 36, 40, 43, 47, 50, 54, 58, 62, 66, 70, 74, 79, 84, 89, 94, 99, 105, 110, 115, 120
Neal - John 254
Neil - Henry 255
Neilson - Caleb 266; Cornelius 266; Eli 266; Elijah 261; Jacob 266; James 265; John 266; Joshua 266; Justus 266; Mary 259; Phenas 266
Nellson/Nelson - Absolom 211, 212; Alexander 29; Caleb 107, 112, 117, 122, 128, 133, 138, 143, 148, 154, 159, 165, 176, 177, 192, 193, 210, 211, 220; Eli 163, 175, 177, 191; Elie 18, 20, 21, 23, 25, 28, 30, 34, 37, 41, 45, 48, 52, 56, 60, 64, 68, 72, 77, 82, 87, 93, 98, 103, 109, 114, 119, 124, 130, 135, 141, 146, 151, 157; Elijah 246; Ely 225; Francis 15, 16, 17, 18, 19, 21, 23, 25, 27, 30, 33, 37, 41, 44, 48, 52, 56, 60, 64, 68, 72, 77, 269; Francis's estate 82, 87, 92; Francis's farm 98; Jacob 220; James 211, 213, 221; Jeremiah 133, 138; John 21, 23, 25, 33, 36, 40, 43, 47, 50, 54, 58, 62, 66, 70, 74, 79, 84, 89, 94, 99, 105, 110, 115, 120, 125, 131, 136, 142, 147, 152, 158, 164, 175, 177, 191, 193, 209, 211, 220, 239, 271; Joshua 108, 113, 118, 123, 128, 133, 138, 144, 148, 154, 159, 165, 176, 177, 192, 193, 210, 211, 220; Justice 107, 113, 117, 122, 128, 133, 138, 143, 148, 154, 159, 165, 177, 192, 193; Justus 176, 210, 211, 220; Machor 216; Mahar 182, 190, 198, 207; Samuel 239; William 37, 40, 44, 47, 51, 54, 58, 62, 66, 70, 74, 79, 84, 89, 94, 100, 105, 110, 115, 120, 126, 131, 136, 142, 147, 152, 158, 164, 172, 179, 186
Newberry (-bery) (-bury) - Eady 252; John 22, 24, 26, 28, 31, 34, 38, 41, 45, 49, 53, 56, 60, 64, 68, 73, 77, 83, 88, 93, 98, 104, 109, 114, 119, 125, 130, 135, 141, 146, 152, 157, 163, 171, 179, 186, 195, 204, 213, 231, 231, 252; Joseph 245; Joshua 245, 252
Newland - Michael 173, 230
Newman - Nathaniel 250
Nicholls - 19, 19, 20, 20; Ephraim 22
Nichols - John 263; Josiah 256; William 263
Nicholson - Basset 247; Eneas 236
Nickenson - Bassett 245; Levi 245
Nickerson - Aaron 248; Basset 252; Comfort 198; Edward 169, 254; Elipet A. 128; Eliphel(et) 113, 118, 123; Eliphet A.'s farm 133, 138; Ephraim 175, 182, 189, 198, 207, 215; Irane 174; Iranen 169; Issachar 246, 252; Izaker 108, 113, 118, 123, 128; James 24, 26, 244; Jonathan 268; Joseph 72, 76, 80; Joshua 204, 219, 268; Mary 268; Moultroup 268; Nathaniel 108, 113, 118, 123, 128, 133, 138, 205, 214; Nathaniel's estate 144; Nathaniel's widow 181; Nathaniel's widow 150, 156, 161, 167, 188, 196; Seth 29, 31, 35, 38, 42, 46, 49, 53, 57, 61, 65, 69,

INDEX

73, 78, 83, 88, 93, 99, 104, 109, 114, 119, 125, 130, 135, 141, 146, 152, 157, 163, 170, 183, 185, 200, 202, 203, 218, 219, 268; Seth Jnr: 151, 156, 162, 167, 170, 184, 185, 201, 202, 203, 268; Thomas 72, 76, 80, 108, 113, 118, 123, 128, 169, 174, 182, 189, 197, 204, 206, 215, 219, 243, 246; Thomas's farm 133; Uriah 245, 246; Widow 118, 123, 128, 133, 139, 144, 149, 154, 173; William 160, 165
Nickinson - Aaron 245
Nickrey [Vickrey] - Jonathan 182
Nickry [Vickry] - David 182
Nnipfin [Kniffen] - Jacob 168
Northroup (-rop) (-rup) (-orp) - Amos 230, 278; Eli 252; Joseph 172, 179, 187, 195, 205, 213, 259, 278; Joseph Jnr: 260; Moses 230, 278; Paul 258; Stephen 258
Norton - place 220
Nowland - Michael 145, 150, 155, 161, 167, 180, 188, 196, 205, 214, 258
Oakley (-ly) - 118; Elijah 146, 182, 190, 198, 207, 216, 232, 246; Elijah's farm 150, 156; Elisha 81, 86, 91, 96, 101, 106, 111, 117, 121, 127, 132, 137, 143, 148, 153, 159, 165, 176, 228, 277; farm 161; Gilbert 176, 178, 192, 194, 210, 212, 220, 228; Gilbert Jnr: 263; Gilbert Sen: 263; Robert 123, 128, 133, 139, 144, 149, 154, 160, 165, 176, 177, 192, 193, 210, 211, 228, 247; Thomas 44, 47, 51, 55, 59, 220, 266; Timothy 193, 194, 210, 212, 221, 247, 263; William 226
Oar - John 163, 168
Obrian(t) - Thomas 220, 262
O'Brien - Catharine 256
Obryant - Mark 266
Ocken - Martin 269
Odell & Post - 227
Odell (Odel) (Odle) - Aaron 247, 263; Amos 221, 247, 262, 264; Benjamin 63, 67, 71, 75, 80, 85, 90, 95, 100, 106, 111, 116, 121, 126, 131, 137, 142, 147, 153, 158, 164, 176, 177, 192, 193, 210, 211, 226; Daniel 178; Isaac 178, 192, 194, 210, 212, 221, 248, 264; Isaac Jnr: 263; John 247, 264; Jonathen 113, 169, 176, 178, 192, 194, 210, 212, 220, 265; Jones 240; Joseph 25, 27, 238; Old 25, 27; Oliver 51, 55, 59, 63, 67, 70, 75, 79, 169, 176, 178, 192, 194, 210, 212, 220, 228, 263

Ogden - Benjamin 258; Edmund 245, 250; Humphrey 245; Joseph 245; Nathan 245
O'Hara - Daniel 201
Olmstead (Olmsted) - Ebenezer 203, 219, 243, 268; Ichabud 204, 219; John 252; Seth 123, 129
Olney - Peter 268
Osborn (Osburn) - Daniel 151, 156, 161, 167; Ezekiel 204, 219, 243; Stephen 103, 108, 113, 151, 156, 161, 167, 170; William 261
Ostrander - Jacobus 240
Otter (Other) (Oter) - Abraham 269, 269; Abram 15, 16, 17, 18, 19, 21, 23, 25, 27, 30, 33, 37, 41, 44, 48, 52, 56, 60, 64, 68, 72, 77, 82; Isaac 32, 35, 39, 42, 46, 50, 53, 57, 61, 65, 69, 73, 78, 83, 88, 94, 104; Jabish 128; Samuel 31, 34, 38, 41, 45, 49, 53, 56, 60, 64, 68, 73, 77, 83; Samuel's estate 88, 93, 98, 104, 109
Owens/Owen - Jane 220, 263; Jedediah 169, 176, 227; Jesse 220, 247, 263; Jona. 225; Jonan: 227; Jonathan 211, 212, 220, 264
Owins - Benjamin 20, 22, 24; Jonathen 194
Ozbon - Steven 278
Paddock - Comfort 260; David 16, 17, 18, 19, 21, 23, 25, 27, 30, 34, 37, 41, 44, 48, 52, 56, 60, 64, 68, 72, 77, 82, 87, 92, 98, 103, 109, 114, 119, 124, 129, 132, 135, 137, 141, 142, 146, 151, 157, 163, 171, 195, 204, 213, 248, 250; David Jnr: 71, 76, 80, 85, 90, 95, 101, 106, 111, 116, 121, 126, 147, 153, 159, 164, 179, 186; farm 87, 92; Isaac 184, 251; James 16, 17, 18, 19, 21, 23, 25, 27, 72, 76, 80, 85, 90, 96, 101, 106, 250; John 29, 31, 35, 39, 42, 46, 49, 53, 57, 61, 65, 69, 73, 78, 83, 88, 93, 99, 104, 109, 115, 120, 125, 130, 136, 141, 146, 152, 158, 163, 171, 179, 186, 195, 278; John's widow 204, 213; Jonathan 29, 31, 35, 38, 42, 45, 49, 53, 57, 61, 65, 69, 73, 78, 83, 88, 93, 99, 104, 109, 114, 119, 125, 130, 135, 141, 146, 152, 157, 163, 171, 179, 186, 195, 204, 213, 234, 250, 270, 271; Jonathan's farm 171, 201, 204, 219; Jonathan's land 184; Jon'n 243; Judah 248; Nathan 169, 170, 184, 190, 201, 206, 215, 250;

Nathaniel 190, 199, 207, 216; Nath'n 243; Peter 22, 24, 26, 28, 31, 34, 38, 41, 45, 49, 53, 56, 60, 64, 68, 73, 77, 83, 88, 248; Peter's estate 93, 98, 104; Philip 33, 36, 40, 43, 47, 50, 54, 58, 62, 66, 70, 74, 78, 235; Seth 32, 35, 39, 42, 46, 50, 53, 57, 61, 65, 69, 73, 78, 83, 88, 94, 99, 104, 110, 115, 120, 125, 130, 136, 141, 146, 152, 158, 164, 173, 180, 187, 196, 205, 207, 214, 216, 248, 250; Seth Jnr: 183, 190, 198; Silas 33, 36, 39, 43, 47, 50, 54, 58, 62, 66, 70, 74, 79, 84, 89, 94, 99, 105, 110, 115, 120, 125, 131, 136, 142, 147, 152, 158, 164, 171, 179, 186, 195, 204, 213, 251; Stephen 190, 199, 207, 216, 248, 251; Thomas 22, 24, 26, 28, 31, 34, 38, 41, 45, 49, 53, 56, 60, 64, 68, 73, 77, 83, 88, 93, 98, 104, 109, 114, 119, 125, 130, 135, 141, 146, 152, 157, 163, 171, 179, 186, 195, 204, 213, 234, 250; Zachariah 33, 173, 181, 188, 196, 205, 251; Zachariah Jnr: 33; Zachariah's place 157; Zachary 36, 40, 43, 47, 50, 54, 58, 62, 66, 70, 74, 79, 84, 89, 94, 100, 105, 110, 115, 120, 125, 131, 136, 145, 150, 156, 158, 161, 167, 214; Zachary Jnr: 36, 40, 43, 47, 50, 54, 58, 62, 66, 70, 74, 79, 84, 89, 94, 99, 105, 110, 115, 120, 125, 131, 136, 142, 147, 152; Zachary's place 162, 168
Palmatier - Peter Jnr: 240
Palmer - 92, 97, 102, 107, 112, 117, 122, 127; Caleb 124, 129, 134, 139, 144, 149, 154, 160, 166, 172, 180, 187, 196, 205, 214, 254; Ebenezer 256; Jonathan 33, 36, 39; Medad 250; Nathan 183, 190, 198, 207, 216; Nathaniel 250; Silas 264; Sylvanus 251; Thomas 150, 156; Will. 245; William 22, 24, 26, 28, 31, 34, 38, 41, 45, 49, 53, 56, 60, 64, 68, 73, 77, 83, 88, 93, 98, 104, 109, 114, 119, 125, 130, 135, 141, 146, 152, 157, 163, 171, 179, 186, 195, 204, 213, 232, 250, 278, 279; William Jnr: 183, 190, 198, 207, 216, 252
Palmerton - Joseph 239
Pardy - Ebenezer 81, 86, 91, 96, 101, 106, 112, 117, 122, 127; James 81, 86, 91, 96, 101, 106, 112, 117, 122, 127, 132, 137,

THE SOUTH PRECINCT OF DUTCHESS COUNTY NY 1740-1790

143, 148, 153, 159, 165; Stephen 81, 86, 91, 96, 101, 106, 112, 117, 122, 127, 132, 137, 143, 148, 153, 159, 165
Parish - Azariah 236, 244; Benjamin 49, 29, 31, 35, 38, 42, 46, 53, 57, 61, 65, 69, 73, 78, 83, 88, 93, 99, 104, 109, 114, 119, 125; Benjamin's farm 130, 136; Daniel 22, 29, 31, 35, 38, 42, 46, 49, 53, 57, 61, 65, 69, 92, 97, 102, 108, 112, 117, 122, 128, 133, 138, 209, 218, 246; farm 233; Jonathan 182, 189, 197, 206, 215; Joseph 97, 102, 108, 112; Silas 169, 175, 248; Uriah 244
Parker - Joseph 260; Joshua 103, 108, 113, 118, 123, 128; Nathaniel 259; Nath'l 247; Samuel 259
Parks - Dan'el 238
Parmer - Jeremiah 237
Parmiter - Ichabud 238
Parre - Solomon 81, 86
Parrish - Jonathan 169, 174, 257; Silas 246
Parse - Dan'l 248
Patrick - John 259
Patterson (Pater-) (Patti-) - Anthony 22, 24, 26, 28; David 22, 24, 26, 28, 183, 190, 198; Matthew 162, 168, 174, 181, 188, 196, 206, 215, 232, 250; Nathaniel 28
Pear - Philip 237
Pearce - Daniel 151, 161, 167, 196, 205, 214, 261; David 123; Ephraim 76, 81; Isaac 158, 164, 195, 204, 213, 246, 254; Samuel 160; Silas 36; William 262
Pearish - Joseph 92
Peck - 105; Eliphalet 110, 115, 120; Josiah 277; Mr (minister) 131, 136
Pecke - Phineas 279
Peers/Pears - Alexander 191, 199; Alexander's estate 217; Caleb 191, 199; Samuel 124, 129, 199; Samuel's estate 208, 217
Peet - Stiles 250
Peirce - Isaac 32, 35, 39, 42, 46, 50, 53, 57, 61, 65, 69, 74; Silas 32, 40, 43
Pelham - Elisha 264
Pell - 31, 35, 38; Caleb 29; Caleb's farm 31, 33, 36, 40, 43, 75, 79, 84, 89, 95, 100, 105, 111, 116, 121, 126, 131, 137, 142, 147, 153, 158, 164, 176, 177, 192, 193, 210, 211; David 245; Joseph 29

Pelletreau - (William) 12
Pelton - Benjamin 254; Capt. 209, 218; Daniel 209, 218; Philip 207, 209, 216, 218, 254; Philip's farm 221
Pembleton - 46, 50, 54
Penny (Penney) - Ammiel 170, 191, 199, 208, 217, 251; Ed'd 244; Edward 183, 190, 198, 204, 219, 271; George 151, 156, 161, 167, 173, 181, 188, 196, 206, 214, 251; John 29, 31, 35, 38, 42, 46, 49, 53, 57, 244, 251; Joseph 247; Mial 151, 156, 161, 167; William 29, 31, 35, 38, 42, 46, 49, 53, 57, 61, 65, 69, 73, 78, 83, 88, 93, 99, 104, 109, 115, 120, 125, 130, 136, 141, 146, 152, 158, 163, 170, 171, 179, 184, 186, 195, 204, 213, 234, 267; William Jnr: 169, 185, 201, 202, 203, 219; William's farm 171, 184, 186, 201, 202
Penoyer - Isaac 220
Penree - Jon 240
Pepper - Jacob 239
Perce - David 277; Isaac 277; Samuel 277
Perece [Pierce] - Samuel 166
Perkins - 19, 20; Elijah 244; Valentine 22, 23, 25, 28, 30, 34, 37, 41, 45, 48, 52, 56, 60, 64, 68, 73, 77, 82, 87, 93, 98; Valentine's farm 103, 109, 114, 119, 124
Perre - Elisha 81, 86, 91, 96; James 81, 86, 91, 96; Solomon 96
Perry - 17, 18; Benjamin 29, 33, 36, 40, 43, 47, 50, 54, 58, 62, 66, 70, 74, 78, 84, 89, 126, 131, 137, 142, 147, 153, 158, 164, 231; Benjamin Jnr: 59, 63, 67, 71, 75, 80, 85, 90, 95, 100, 106, 111, 116, 121; Benjamin's estate 94; David 171, 184, 201, 202; David's farm 185; Ebenezer 81, 86, 91, 96, 101, 107; Elisha 102, 107, 112, 117; Isaac 37, 40, 43, 47, 51, 54, 58, 62, 66, 70, 74, 79, 84, 89, 94, 100, 105, 110, 115, 120, 126, 140; James 102, 107, 112, 117, 122, 127, 132, 138, 143, 177, 178, 221, 264; John 170, 201, 236; Rowland 33, 36, 40, 43, 47, 51, 54, 58, 62, 66, 70, 74, 79, 84, 89, 94, 100, 105, 110, 115, 120, 126, 131, 136, 142, 147, 152, 158, 164, 172, 179; Rowland's farm 186; Samuel 123, 128, 133, 139, 157, 162, 168, 244, 247; Seth 135, 140; Simeon 244, 250; Solomon 91, 102, 107,

112, 117, 122, 127, 132, 138, 143, 148, 153, 159, 165; Solomon's farm 170, 184, 185, 200
Peters (Peter) - Capt.'s place 162, 168; Richard 134, 139, 144, 149, 155, 160, 166, 172, 180, 187; Samuel 33, 36, 40, 43, 47, 50, 54, 58, 62, 66, 70, 74, 79, 99, 105, 110, 115, 120, 125, 131, 136, 142, 147, 152, 158, 164, 171, 179, 186, 195, 204, 213, 277; Samuel's farm 84, 89, 94; Thomas 162, 168, 174, 181, 188, 197; Thomas's estate 206, 215; William 198
Petton - Philip 248
Pew - Thomas 72, 76, 81, 86, 90, 96, 101, 106, 111, 116, 121, 127, 132, 137, 143, 148, 153
Peyn - Stephen 112, 117
Philip - Daniel 15, 47, 50, 54, 58, 62, 66, 70, 74, 79, 99, 105, 110, 115; David 84, 89, 94; Jacob 34, 38, 41, 45, 49, 53, 56, 60, 64, 68, 73, 77, 82, 87, 93, 98, 104, 109, 114, 119, 124, 130, 135, 141, 146, 152, 157, 163; Jacob Jnr: 80, 158, 164; Joseph 45, 47, 49, 50, 53, 54, 57, 58, 62, 66, 70, 74, 79, 84, 89, 156; Thomas 31, 38, 42, 45, 49, 53, 57, 61, 65, 68, 73, 77, 83, 88, 93, 98, 104, 109, 114, 119, 125, 130
Philips - Amos 245; Daniel 16, 17, 33, 36, 40, 43; Jacob 22, 24, 26, 28, 31, 132, 137, 142, 231; Jacob Jnr: 71, 75, 111, 116, 121, 147, 153, 187, 195, 204, 213; James 22, 24, 26, 32; John 190, 198, 207; John's farm 216; Joseph 27, 31, 33, 35, 36, 38, 40, 42, 43, 94, 100, 105, 110, 115, 145, 150, 161, 167, 173, 188, 196, 205, 214, 234, 244; Joshua 189, 197, 206, 215; Philip 22, 29, 31, 63, 67, 71, 75, 80, 95, 106, 111, 116, 121, 126; Thomas 24, 26, 28, 34; Thomas's estate 135, 141; Widow 156
Philipse - Adolph 1, 2, 6, 7; Frederick 2; Isaac 175; Jacob 126; Jacob Jnr: 85, 90, 95, 101, 106; Joshua 175; Philip 85, 90, 100, 119, 2, 9, 242, 275, 278; Philip (Major) 92, 98, 103, 108, 114, 124; Widow 150
Philipse Morris - Mary 2, 11
Phillips - Daniel 277; Isaac 245; Jacob 234, 278; Jacob Jnr: 172, 179; James 250; John 183;

INDEX

Joseph 29, 180, 235, 252; Joseph Jnr: 259; Joshua 169, 174, 182; Philetus 253; Samuel 263; Thomas Esq: 277; Zebulon 254
Pick - Eliphalet 125
Pickett - James 240
Pierce - Daniel 156, 173, 181; David 129, 133, 139; Ephraim 86, 91, 92, 96, 97, 101, 102, 106, 111, 116, 121, 127, 132, 137, 143; Isaac 83, 88, 94, 99, 104, 110, 115, 120, 125, 130, 136, 141, 147, 152, 171, 186; Samuel 134, 139, 144, 149, 155, 166, 172; Thimoty (sic) 238
Piere - Isaac 78
Piers - Alexander's estate 208
Pinckney - Frederick 251; Fredrick 175, 189, 197, 206, 215; Israel 209, 218, 261; Lewis 248
Pine - Amos 71, 76, 80; Daniel 188; Jona. 229; Jonathen 124, 129, 134, 139, 157, 162, 168, 176; Jonathen Jnr: 192, 193, 178; Samuel 180, 187; Stephen 87, 108, 122, 128, 133, 138, 143
Pine [Pierce] - Isaac 179, 186
Pineer - Ab'm 245; David 245
Pingry - James 236
Pinkerton - William 200
Pinkney - Fred'k 248; Fredrick 182; Israel 248
Pioneer - Isaac 256; Thomas 265
Place - John 251
Platt - 162, 168; Benjamin 250; John 174, 181, 188, 197, 206, 215, 248, 251; Judge's farm 220; Rich'd 246
Plumstead (-sted) (-steed) - Nathaniel 72, 76, 127, 132, 137, 143, 148, 153, 159, 165; Nathen 80, 85, 90, 96, 101, 106, 111, 116, 121
Popple - Edward 237
Porter - David 140, 145, 150, 155, 161, 166, 173, 180, 188, 248, 270, 271; John 26, 28, 81, 86, 91, 96, 175; John's farm 101, 107; Joseph 17, 18, 20, 21, 23, 25, 27; Joshua 55, 59, 63, 67, 71, 75, 80, 85, 90, 95, 123, 129, 134, 139, 144, 149, 154, 160, 166; Nathaniel 16, 17, 18, 20, 21, 23, 32, 36, 39, 43, 46, 50, 54, 57, 61, 65, 69, 74, 78, 83, 88, 94, 99, 105, 110, 115, 120, 125, 131, 136, 278, 279; Nathaniel's estate 141; place 27, 30, 34, 37, 41, 44; Robert 102, 108, 211, 212; Widow 150, 230; William 92, 97, 102, 107, 112, 117, 122, 127, 132, 138, 143, 255; William's farm 148, 154, 159, 165
Porter or Smith - Nath-ll 25
Post - Abm: 227; Abraham 169, 176, 178, 192, 194, 210, 212, 220, 262; Anthony 209, 218; Ant'y 245; Charles 211, 212, 220, 264; Henry 178, 192, 194, 210, 212, 221, 247, 264; John 260; Martin 218; Nathaniel 209, 218
Post & Odell - 227
Potter - David 245; John 22, 24; Rob: 227
Potter [Porter] - David 155, 161
Powers - Laurence 193, 194; place 32, 36, 39, 43
Powers & Sherwood - 227
Pray - John 44, 47, 51
Price - Elemuel 92, 97, 102, 107, 112, 117, 122; James 248; John 55, 59, 191, 199, 258; Richard 191, 199, 208, 216; Simon 19
Price [Prince?] - Samuel 81
Pricket(t) - William 19, 20
Prince - Samuel 86, 91, 96
Prindle - Gedion's estate 145; Gideon 134, 140, 231, 279; Joseph 145; Moses 240; Widow 231
Purdee - Deliverance 254
Purdy - Francis 24, 26, 28, 31; James's farm 170, 184; John 277; John Still 177, 178, 192, 194, 210, 212, 228; Peter 48, 51, 55, 59; Simeon 162, 168, 231; Stephen's farm 170
Purlsend [Burlison] - Job 190
Purtesend [Burlison] - Amos 190
Pyers - Jacob 253
Quimby/Quinby - James 33, 36, 40, 43, 47, 50, 54, 58, 62, 66, 70, 74, 79, 84, 89, 94
Rableyea - Ruben 233; William Jnr: 277; William Sen: 278; Wm 233; Wm:'s meadow 278
Ragon - Thomas 243
Raly [Baily] - Jeremiah 33, 36
Ramond - Jno's farm 184; John 184; Uriah 181
Randal(l)/Randel(l) - James 260; Joseph 191, 199, 208, 217, 259; Joseph Jnr: 259; Night 209, 218; Peter 22, 24, 26
Randolph - David 51, 55
Rapalyea/Rapelyea (-je) (-jea) - Andrew 20, 22, 32, 36, 39, 43, 46, 50, 54; Ruben 236; William 20, 22, 24, 26, 28, 30, 34, 38, 41, 45, 49, 52, 56, 60, 64, 68, 73, 77, 82, 87, 104, 109, 119; William Jnr: 71, 76, 80, 85, 90, 121
Rappelyea (-jea) - William 93, 98, 114, 124, 132, 135, 137, 142; William Jnr: 95, 101, 106, 111, 116, 126; William's farm 130
Rathburn (-born) - Edmund 151, 156, 161, 167
Ravelje - James 239
Ray - Richard 235
Raymond - Eben'r 248; Jno's farm 186; John 151, 156, 161, 167, 186, 198, 207, 216, 251; Moses 248; Thaddeus 209, 218, 246, 257; Uriah 151, 156, 161, 167, 173, 188, 196, 206, 214, 275; Zaccheus 267
Rea - Richard (Capt) 237
Read - David 254; Jacob 247
Recke - Peter 178
Reed/Reade - Archer 211; Archer's farm 212; Isaac 151, 156, 161, 167; Jacob 190, 199, 207, 211, 212, 216, 221, 244, 252, 263
Requa - Joseph 253
Reyders - John 24, 27; Simon 24, 26
Reynolds - Moses 209, 218; Solomon 257
Reynolds [Runnels] - Daniel 100
Rhades - Rich'd 247
Rhinehart - Tatlock 266
Rhodes (Rhoades) - Isaac 17, 18, 68, 72, 77, 82, 87, 183, 226, 226, 247, 261, 262; Isaac Jnr: 262; James 260; John 75, 80, 85, 247, 260; Richard 263; Timothy 262
Rice - Edward 71, 76, 80, 85, 90, 96, 101, 106, 111, 116, 121, 127, 132, 137, 142, 148, 153, 159, 165, 172, 179, 186, 187, 195, 205, 213, 233, 248, 250, 277; Edward Jnr: 250; Edward's farm 201, 202, 203, 219; John 250; Morison 233; Sam'l 246; William 32, 36, 39, 43, 46, 50, 54, 61, 65, 69, 74, 78, 83, 250; William's estate 88, 94, 99
Richards - 183, 190, 198; David 248; Edward 24, 26; Ezra 207, 216, 246, 251; James 237; Moses 183, 190, 198, 207, 216, 248, 251, 270; Nehemiah 251; Thomas 260
Richardson - Isaac 244; Thomas 20, 21, 23; Thomas Sen: 19; Tom. 31, 35; Willm. 240
Rickerson - Thomas 29
Ricks (Ricky) - Peter 193, 194, 227
Rider - Christopher 267; Christ'r 243; David 243, 253; Eleazer 267; John 243, 248, 254; Mary 219, 267; Reuben 250; Simeon

309

183, 243, 267; Simeon Jnr: 243; Zadoc 267
Ridgeway - Isaac 261
Right - David 24, 26; Robert 168
Rise [Rice] - Edward 277; William 57
Ritton - Peter 268
Rivers - Ant'y 245
Roades/Roads - Capt 239; Isaac 92, 98, 103, 109, 114, 119, 124, 135, 141, 146, 151, 157, 163, 175, 177, 191, 193, 209, 211, 220, 221; Isaac Jnr: 169, 174; James 113, 118, 123, 128, 133, 138, 144, 149, 154, 160, 165, 172, 180, 187, 195, 205, 214; John 95, 100, 106, 111, 116, 121, 126, 131, 137, 142, 147, 153, 158, 164, 172, 179, 187, 195, 204, 213; John [Isaac] 129; Richard 29, 31, 35, 38, 42, 46, 49, 53, 57, 61, 65, 73, 78; William 44, 47, 51
Robards - Peter 246
Robbins - Samuel 253
Robenson - Giles 24, 26
Roberts - Benjamin 29, 31, 35, 38, 42, 46, 49, 53, 57, 61, 65, 69, 73, 78, 83, 88, 93, 99, 104, 109, 114, 119, 125, 130, 160, 166, 184, 267; Benjamin Jnr: 71, 76, 80, 85, 90, 123, 129, 134, 139, 144, 149, 154, 243; Caleb 184, 186, 267; John 123, 129, 134, 139, 144, 149, 154, 160, 166, 170, 184, 185, 200, 238, 258; Peter 198, 207, 216; Phebe 267
Robertson [Robinson] - Beaverly (Capt.)'s farm 102; Ebenezer 100, 106, 111, 116, 121, 239; N.'s place 100; Nathal:'s place 95; Peter 99, 104; Wheton 101
Robeson [Robinson] - Abenezar 277, 277; Nathaniel 277; Peter 277; Wheten 81, 277
Robins - Joseph 72, 76, 81, 85, 90, 123, 129, 134, 139, 144, 149, 154, 160, 166, 238
Robinson - Abenezar 277; Abenezar (nr Brown) 277; Beverly 2, 5, 7, 8, 9, 176, 177, 192, 193, 230, 241, 242, 277, 278; Beverly (Capt) 132, 138, 143, 148, 153, 159, 165; Beverly (Capt.)'s farm 82, 86, 91, 97, 107, 112, 117, 122, 127; Beverly Jnr:'s farm 208, 217; Beverly's farm 210, 211; David 257; Eben 108, 113, 271; Eben (nr Capt Brown) 118, 123, 128, 133; Ebenezer 59, 63, 67, 71, 75, 80, 85, 90, 95, 126, 131, 137, 142, 147, 151, 153, 156, 158, 162, 164, 172, 179, 187, 195, 204, 213, 256, 260; Ebenezer Jnr: 167, 173, 181, 188, 196; Eben'r 245, 246; Ebenz 270; Enoch 259; Esseker 247; Giles 16, 22, 28; Isaiah 96, 101, 107, 112, 117, 122, 127, 254; Issachar 246; John 175, 182, 189, 197, 207, 230, 245, 248; John (nr store) 198, 216; John the 1st 258; John the 2d 258; John the 3d 260; Josiah 86, 91; Lewis 245, 258; N.'s farm 118; Nathaniel 17, 18, 20, 21, 23, 25, 27, 30, 34, 37, 41, 45, 277; Nathaniel Jnr: 32, 36, 59, 63, 67, 71, 75, 80, 102, 108, 113, 118, 122, 128; Nathaniel Jnr:'s farm 133, 138, 143; Nathaniel's farm 59, 63, 67; Nathaniel's place 71, 75, 80, 85, 90; Noah 253; Peter 32, 35, 39, 42, 46, 49, 53, 57, 61, 65, 69, 73, 78, 83, 88, 93, 109, 115, 120, 125, 233, 248, 260, 277; store 207, 216; Susanna 2; Wheaton 86, 91, 96, 107, 112, 117, 122, 127, 132, 137, 143, 148, 153, 159, 165, 277; Wheaton's place 134, 139
Robison - Josiah 81
Rockwell - Jabez 267; Joseph 113, 118, 123, 128, 133; Silas 247; Stephen 71, 76, 80, 85, 90, 96, 101, 106, 111, 116, 121, 127, 132, 137, 142, 148, 153, 159, 164, 170, 184, 185, 200, 202, 203, 218, 243
Rodes - Isaac 16, 19, 21, 23, 25, 27, 30, 34, 37, 41, 44, 48, 52, 56, 60, 64; John 63, 67, 71, 90; Richard 69
Roe - Mathew 22, 28; William 239, 256
Rogers (Rodgers) - Amos 254; Benjamin 194, 209, 211, 220, 266; John 15, 16, 17, 18, 19, 21, 23, 27, 30, 33, 37, 41, 44, 48, 52, 56, 60, 64, 68, 72, 77, 82, 87, 92, 98, 103, 108, 114, 119, 124, 129, 135, 140, 146, 151, 157, 163, 175, 177, 191, 193; John Jnr: 177; Richard 266, 266
Roggars/Roggers - John 25, 269
Romane - Isaac 240
Rosall - Rowland 236
Rose - Iccabud 67, 71, 75, 80; Will. 247
Ross - Capt 238, 239
Row - Mathew 24, 26
Rowland - Hezekiah 258
Rowley - Dan'l 245; Elijah 245
Rowly - Mathew 22, 24, 26, 28, 33, 36, 40, 43, 47, 51, 54, 58, 62; Shubal 22, 24, 26, 28, 31, 34, 35, 38, 39, 41, 43, 45, 46, 49, 50, 53, 54, 56, 57, 60, 61; Shubal Jnr: 32
Roy - Bangaman 269
Royal - Peter 221
Rubbelyea (-yeer) - Andrew 103, 108
Rubelyeer (-year) (-jear) (-ye) - Andrew 113, 118, 123, 128, 133, 138, 143, 148, 154, 159, 165; John 124, 129
Rubly (-ey)/Rublee (-eey) - Andrew 172, 180, 187, 195, 205, 214; Nathaniel 183, 190, 198, 207, 216; Reubin 92, 97, 102, 107, 112, 117, 122, 127, 132, 138
Ruff - Humfrey 48, 51, 55, 59, 63, 67, 70, 75, 79, 84, 89, 95, 100, 105, 111; John 277; Philip 48, 51, 55, 59, 63, 67, 70, 75, 79, 84, 89, 95, 100, 105, 111, 116, 121, 126, 131, 137, 142, 277
Rundle - Ezra 255
Runnalds/Runalds - Daniel 37; David 244
Runnells (-nels) - Daniel 40, 44, 47, 51, 54, 58, 62, 66, 74, 79, 84, 89, 94, 100, 105; David 70; Joel 169; Jonathan 32, 36, 39, 43
Ruscky - Isaac 134, 140, 145, 149, 155, 160, 166
Rusco - Stephen 253
Rush - John 211, 213, 247, 263
Rusky (-key) - Isaac 173, 180, 187, 196, 205, 214
Russel(l) (Rusel) - Abijah 260; James 40, 44, 47, 51, 55, 58, 62, 66, 70, 74, 79, 84, 89, 94, 100, 105, 110, 115, 120, 126, 246, 258; James Jnr: 260; James's sawmill 277; John 209, 217, 221, 248, 262; Robert 199, 208, 217, 246; Roland 243; Rowland 201, 203, 219, 267; Rowlin 134, 140, 145; Thomas 191, 199, 208, 216, 246, 260, 267
Ryal - John 263; Peter 29, 44, 47, 51, 55, 58, 62, 66, 70, 75, 79, 84, 89, 92, 95, 97, 102, 108, 112, 117, 122, 128, 263
Ryan - Thomas 264
Rycks - Peter 210, 212
Ryder(s) - David 201; Ebenezer 151, 156, 161, 167, 170, 184, 185, 201; Ebenezer's estate 202; John 29, 31, 40, 44, 47, 51, 54, 58, 62, 66, 70, 74, 79, 84, 89, 94, 100, 105, 110, 115, 120, 126, 131, 136, 142, 147, 152, 158,

INDEX

164, 170, 184; John's farm 185; Jonathan 33, 36, 40, 43, 47; Mary, widow 201, 203; Reuben 201, 203, 219; Robert 33, 36, 39, 43, 47, 50, 54, 58, 62, 66, 70, 74, 78, 84, 89, 94, 99; Robert's farm 110; Simeon/Simon 29, 31, 35, 38, 42, 45, 49, 53, 57, 61, 65, 69, 73, 78, 83, 88, 93, 98, 104, 109, 114, 119, 125, 130, 135, 141, 146, 152, 157, 163, 170, 185, 200, 202, 203, 218; Zadoc 201, 203, 219
Sabens - Billings 244
Sacket - James 258; Nathaniel 163
Sacor - Isaac 196; John 189
Sage - Moses 198, 270
Salomons - Albert 174
Sampson - George 247
Sarls - Joseph 191, 199; Thomas 92, 97, 102, 107, 112, 117, 122, 128, 133, 138, 143, 148, 154, 159, 165, 192, 193, 210, 211, 220, 265; Thomas Jnr: 194; William 220, 265
Sarrine - Isaac 247
Saterly (-lee) - Richard 221, 228, 263
Saunders - Eliphalet 151, 156, 162, 167
Sauthier - Claude Joseph 11
Sawyer - Daniel 191, 199; Peter 191, 199; Sarah 265
Sayca [?] - Jacob 200
Sayers - Mr. James's estate 208, 217
Schoolfield - Ephraim 220; Miles 220
Schot(t) - Timothy 211, 212
Schouten/Scouten - Andries 265; Jacob 240; Simeon/Simon 134, 237
Scoffield - Ezra 248
Scoit - Abel 259; Jacob 259; Samuel 259; Stephen 260
Scot(t) - Abm. 245; farm 92, 97; Geo: 229; John 67, 71, 75, 79, 84; Peter 231, 245; Timothy 266
Scovil - Ephraim 265; Ezra 259; Miles 265; Noah 258; Thomas 265
Scribner - 22; Abell 22, 24, 26, 28; Enoch 175, 182, 189, 197; John 32, 36, 39, 43, 46, 50, 54, 58, 61; Nathaniel 175, 182, 189, 197, 206, 215, 245, 270, 271; Zadock 32, 92, 97, 102, 107, 112, 117
Scrivener - Nathaniel 267
Scutt - Peter 255
Seabrandt - 6, 7
Seacord - John 140, 145
Seails [Searls] - James 174
Sealy - Will 243
Seamons - Absolom 217; Rachel 217
Searls - James 168, 174; Thomas 176, 177
Sears - Banj'n 243; Ben: 24, 26; Benjamin 28, 31, 34, 38, 42, 45, 49, 53, 57, 61, 65, 69, 73, 78, 83, 88, 93, 98, 104, 109, 114, 119, 125, 130, 135, 141, 146, 152, 157, 163, 170, 183, 185, 200, 202, 203, 218; Benjamin Jnr: 124, 129, 134, 139, 144, 149, 154, 160, 166, 170, 184, 185, 200, 202, 203, 219, 267; David 86, 91, 97, 102, 107, 112, 117, 122, 127, 132, 138, 143, 148, 153, 159, 165, 172; Enoch 243; James 20, 22, 24, 26, 32, 35, 39, 42, 46, 50, 53, 57, 61, 65, 69, 74, 78, 83, 88, 94, 99, 104, 110, 115, 120, 125, 130, 136, 141, 147, 152, 158, 164, 170, 183, 184, 277; James Jnr: 157, 162, 168; Peter 243; Seth 102, 108, 113, 118, 122, 128, 133, 138, 143, 148, 154, 159, 165, 170, 184, 185, 200, 202, 203, 219, 243, 267; Seth Jnr: 184, 186, 201, 202, 203, 219, 243, 267; Silas 22, 24, 26, 28, 31, 34, 38, 41, 45, 49, 53, 103, 108; Stephen 243, 267; Thomas 169, 170, 184, 185, 201, 202, 203, 219, 243, 257, 271
Secord/Secor/Secar - 113, 118; Daniel 103, 108, 113, 118, 140, 145, 150, 155, 161, 166, 173, 180; Elihu 209, 218; Isaac 140, 145, 150, 155, 161, 166, 173, 180, 187, 205, 214; James 123, 128, 133, 138; James's farm 144; John 123, 128, 150, 155, 161, 169, 175, 182, 197, 206, 215; Paul 183, 190
Secoy - Elihu 258; Isaac 256; John 256; Paul 255
Seelass (-lis) - Daniel 167, 173, 181, 206, 214
Seely - Isaac 254; Sylvanus 251
Seers - Barny 240; David 82; Enoch 236
Seless (-lass) - Daniel 151, 156, 162, 188, 196
Sell - Uriah 246
Selleck - John Gold 263
Sely - 33
Sention/Senition - Thomas 201, 204, 219
Serring - Benjamin 72, 76, 81, 86, 90, 96; Benjamin's farm 101, 106, 111
Serrings - Amos 162, 168, 174, 181, 188
Shad - Michael 34, 38
Shadwick - Comfort 190, 198, 207, 216
Shafer/Shaifer - Jeremiah 157, 162, 167, 181
Sharlock - Henry 199
Shaw - Benjamen 237; Eli 264; Enoch 200, 208, 217; farm 81, 86, 91; Gilbert 209, 217; Ichabod 244; Isaac 264; James 239, 259; James Jnr: 248; John 191, 199; Joshua 248, 258; Michael 20, 22, 24, 26, 28, 30, 41, 45, 49, 52, 56, 60, 64, 68, 73, 77, 82, 87, 93, 98; Michael Jnr: 58, 62, 66, 70, 75, 79, 84, 89, 95, 100, 105, 110, 116, 120, 126, 131, 136, 142, 147, 153, 158, 164, 172, 179, 186, 195, 204, 213; Migell Jnr: 47, 51, 55; Reuben 221, 264; Robert 104, 109, 114, 119, 124, 130, 135, 141, 146, 152, 157, 163, 171, 179, 186, 195, 204, 213, 260; Robert's place 102, 97, 108; Tim:'s farm 31; Timothy 20, 22, 24, 26, 28, 150, 156, 161, 167, 173, 181, 188, 196; Will: 229; William 47, 48, 51, 55, 58, 62, 66, 70, 75, 79, 84, 89, 95, 100, 105, 110, 115, 120, 126, 176, 178, 192, 194, 210, 212; William Jnr: 44, 264
Shead - Ephraim 76, 81
Shearman - Benjamin's farm 204, 219
Shearwood/Sheerwood - 108; David 112, 117, 122, 128, 133, 138; Jeremiah 210; Joseph 81, 86, 91, 96, 101, 107, 112, 117, 122, 127, 132, 143
Shed - Oliver 279
Sheifer - Jeremiah 174
Sheilds - Daniel 265
Sheldon - Nathan 256
Sheperdson (-ardson) (-erson) - Nathaniel 22, 24, 26, 87, 91, 92, 97, 102; Steph. 228
Sherwood & Powers - 227
Sherwood & Smith - 227
Sherwood/Shurwood - Abel 236; David 143; James 220, 263; Jeremiah 193, 194, 212; John 193, 194, 210, 212, 227; Joseph 137, 151, 156, 162, 167, 176, 177, 192, 212, 227, 229; Joseph's farm 210, 210; Sarah 265
Shurman - Darius 244
Sill - Uriah 268

THE SOUTH PRECINCT OF DUTCHESS COUNTY NY 1740-1790

Silvernail - Andrew 237
Simeons - John'n 248
Simkins/Simpkins - John 44, 47, 51, 55, 58, 62, 66, 70, 229, 246, 261; John Jnr: 247; Major 191, 199, 208, 217, 255; Robt 247
Simmons - Absolom 208, 258; Rachel 200, 208
Sine - Peter 265
Single - John [?] 37
Sirrine - James 178
Skolfield - Arnold 176, 178, 192
Slaigh - Benajah 157, 162, 168
Slaterly - Richd: 228
Slatt - Benjamin 177, 178; Michael 179
Sloakum/Slocum - Benj'n 244; George 244; William 168
Sloane - James 261
Sloet - Elias 256; Isaac 255; John the 1st 255; John the 2d 256; John the 3d 256; Michael 256; Simeon 256
Slott (Slut(t)) (Sloot) - Abraham 35; Abram 32, 33, 36, 39, 40; Hendrick 200, 208, 217; Isaac 134, 139, 144, 209, 217, 246; John 33, 36, 40, 43, 51, 55, 59, 63, 183, 190, 198, 247; John's estate 207, 216; Michael 29, 31, 35, 38, 42, 46, 49, 53, 57, 61, 65, 69, 73, 78, 83, 88, 93, 99, 104, 109, 115, 120, 125, 130, 136, 141, 146, 152, 158, 163, 171, 186, 195, 204, 213, 277
Smalley (-lly) (-wley) (Small) - Isaiah 259; James 246, 247, 260; James Jnr: 248, 261; Zaccheus 247; Zachariah 261; Zach'h 248
Smith - 27, 30, 34, 37, 41, 44, 145, 150, 156; Abel 255, 258; Abm. 226; Abraham 18, 87, 93, 98, 103, 109, 114, 119, 124, 221, 262; Abraham's estate 130, 135, 141; Abram 20, 21, 23, 25, 28, 30, 34, 37, 41, 45, 48, 52, 56, 60, 64, 68, 72, 77, 82; Abr'm 247; Alpheus 243, 247; Asa 248; Benajah 248; Charles (Isaac's brother) 54, 58; David 33, 36, 40, 42, 46, 50, 53, 57, 61, 65, 69, 74, 78, 83, 88, 94, 99, 104, 110, 115, 120, 125, 130, 136, 141, 183, 190, 198, 207, 216, 246, 257, 270, 270, 271; Edward 209, 218, 248, 258; Elijah 87, 91, 97, 102, 107, 176, 178, 192, 194, 210, 212; Elisha 191, 199, 208, 216, 246, 254, 257; Elwin 229; Ephraham's farm 184; Ephraim 71, 76, 80, 85, 90, 96, 101, 106, 111, 116, 121, 127, 132, 137, 142, 148, 153, 159; Ephraim's farm 186; Eunice 251; farm 36, 40; Gilbert 247; Isaac 29, 31, 35, 38, 42, 45, 49, 53, 57, 61, 65, 69, 73, 78, 83, 88, 93, 99, 104, 109, 114, 119, 125, 130, 135, 141, 199, 257, 277; Isaac's brother 37, 40, 43, 47, 51; Jabish 208, 217; Jacob 258; James 221, 246, 262; Jeremiah 183, 190, 248; Jesse 20, 22, 23, 26, 28, 30, 34, 38, 41, 45, 49, 52, 56, 60, 64, 68, 73, 77, 82, 87, 93, 98, 104, 109, 114, 119, 124, 130, 133, 135, 157, 162, 168, 174, 181, 257, 277; Jesse Jnr: 113, 118, 123, 128, 139; John 27, 29, 31, 35, 38, 42, 45, 48, 49, 52, 56, 60, 64, 68, 72, 77, 102, 108, 113, 118, 145, 150, 156, 161, 168, 174, 181, 189, 197, 206, 211, 212, 215, 221, 240, 247, 258, 262, 279; John (Highlands) 169; John Jnr: 174, 182, 189, 197; Jonathen 169; Jon'n 243; Joseph 162, 168, 176, 178, 192, 193, 210, 212, 226, 243, 262; Jotham 254; Judge 10; Major 245, 248; Margaret 150; Margit 156; Martin 32, 36, 240; Maurice 220; Morris 259; Nath'l 248; Nehemiah 183, 190, 198, 207, 216, 239, 251; Noah 36, 40, 43, 47, 51, 54, 58, 62, 66, 70, 74, 79, 84, 89, 94, 100, 105, 110, 115, 120, 126, 131, 136, 142, 147, 152, 158, 164, 170, 184, 185, 200, 202, 203, 218, 230, 278, 279; Philip 200, 208, 217, 248, 258; Phinemon 221, 264; Reuben 255; Richard 247, 267; Samuel 221, 246, 258, 264; Samuel Jnr: 264; Seth 248; Solomon 248, 137, 142, 147, 153, 158, 164, 176, 177, 192, 193, 210, 211, 212, 220, 226, 246, 261, 262; Solomon Jnr: 211; Thomas 27, 29, 31, 35, 38, 42, 45, 49, 53, 57, 61, 65, 69, 73, 78, 83, 88, 93, 99, 104, 109, 114, 119, 125, 130, 135, 141, 146, 152, 157, 163, 171, 179, 186, 195, 204, 211, 212, 213, 247, 258; William 20, 22, 24, 26, 28, 31, 34, 38, 265; William M. 255
Smith & Sherwood - farm 227
Smith or Porter - 25
Sniffen - 150, 156, 161, 167
Snook (Snouk)(Snock)(Snoke) - James 265; John 221, 265; Matthew 211, 213, 220, 265; Peter 211, 213, 225, 225, 266
Snow - Will. 244; William 169, 175, 182, 189, 201, 208, 217, 251
Soames - farm 198
Solomon - John 279
Solomons - Albert 182; Elbert 169
Songworth - John 42
Sorine - Charles 246; Israel 246
Southerland (-lyn) (-hill) - Daniel 30, 33, 37, 100, 116, 121, 126, 140, 145, 150, 155, 161, 166, 187; Daniel Jnr: 134, 139, 144, 149, 155, 160, 166; Joseph 134, 139, 198
Sovrine - Charles 255; Charles Jnr: 256; Isaac 264; James 255, 263
Spalding - Samuel 239
Sparling - Paul 220, 265
Sparling/Spauling & Keirser - 229
Spencer - Caleb 201, 202, 203, 219, 253; Samuel 201, 202, 243; Theophilus 151, 156, 162, 167
Sprague/Spragg(e)/Sprag(e) - Eleazer 32, 36, 39, 43, 46, 50, 54, 57, 61, 65, 69, 74, 94, 99, 105, 110; Elijah 248, 260; Ezekiel [Eleazer] 78, 83, 88; farm 36; Jeremiah 248, 260; John 17, 18, 20, 21, 23, 25, 27, 30, 34, 37, 41, 45, 48, 52, 56, 60, 64, 68, 72, 77, 82, 87, 93, 98, 103, 246, 260, 277; John Jnr: 81, 86, 91, 96, 101, 107, 112, 117, 259; Plagery [John?] 239; William 265
Sprengstin - Jacob 269; Jurry 269
Springer - Isaac 177, 178, 192, 194, 264; William 198, 264
Springsteen - Jacob 15, 16, 17, 18; Jeremiah 63, 67, 71, 75, 80, 85, 90, 95
Springsteen (Sprengstin) - 269
Squire(s) - Isaac 268; Jonathan 252
St John - Abraham 252; Abr'm 245; Lucy 256; Thos. 243
Stacker - Joseph 95, 100
Standish - Mathew 237
Standly (-ley) - James 51, 55, 59, 63, 67, 70, 75, 79
Stanley - Henry 225
Stare - John 186
Stark - Henry 244; John 244
Starr (Star) - Abijah 256; John 201, 202, 203, 219, 267
Stebens - Lewis 245; Neh'h 245
Stedwell (Steadwell) - Gilbert 201, 202, 203, 219; James 201, 202; James's farm 203, 219; John 149, 160, 166, 173, 180, 188, 205, 214; Jonathen 134, 139, 144; Joseph 171, 184; Joseph's farm 186

INDEX

Steenbanck/Steebonck - Phillip 140, 264
Steenbaugh - Philip 176, 177, 192, 193, 210, 212, 220, 228
Steenbergh - Conrad 237
Steenbuck (-bock) - Philip 145, 150, 155, 160, 166
Steenrod - Solomon 253
Stenson - James 252
Stephans - John 80, 85; Timothy 80, 85
Stephens (Stephen) (Stevens) - 19, 20; Edward 261; Jehiel 103, 108, 113, 118, 123, 128, 133, 138, 151, 169, 174, 182, 189, 197, 206, 215, 257; John 72, 76, 90, 96, 101, 106, 111, 116, 121, 168, 174, 181, 188; John Jnr: 169, 174; Mathew 151, 156, 161, 167, 170, 184; Nathaniel 22, 23; Russell 245, 257; Thomas 244; Timothy 55, 59, 63, 67, 71, 75, 90, 171; Timothy's farm 95, 100, 106; William 31, 35, 39, 238
Stephenson(s) - Nathaniel 171, 184, 186
Steward - Geo. 247
Stewart - Ezekiel 253
Stickney (-ny) - Amos 27; Thomas 17, 18, 20, 21, 23, 25
Stidwell/Stidwill - John 155, 196
Stoakum - William 162
Stock - Anthony 145, 150, 156, 161
Stocker - Aaron 250; Joseph 71, 75, 80, 85, 90, 106, 111, 116, 121, 126
Stockham - Jonathen 139, 144, 149, 155, 160, 166, 187, 214
Stocum/Stockum (-em) - Isaac 255; Jonathen 134, 196, 205, 261; William 174, 181, 188, 197
Stone - Abner 157; Abraham 162; Darius 256; David 257; Desire 257; Ebenezer 151; Elijah 256; Nathaniel 81, 86, 91, 96, 101, 107, 112, 117, 122, 127, 132, 137, 143, 148, 153, 159, 165, 173, 196; Nehemiah [Nathaniel] 180, 188; William 32, 35, 39, 42, 46, 50, 53, 57, 61, 65, 69, 74, 78, 83, 88, 94, 99, 104, 110, 115, 120, 125, 140, 145, 150, 155, 161, 184, 185, 201, 202, 203, 219, 277
Stordevelt - Jonatan 269; Jonatan Jnr: 269
Storm - David 168, 174, 182, 189, 197; Ephraim 264
Stosckum/Stoukum - Jonathan 172, 180
Stow - William 151, 156, 161, 167, 170, 268
Strang/Strong - Francis 220, 263
Stringham (-gum) - Sam. 40, 44, 37; Samuel 157, 162, 168
Stuart - John 190, 199, 207, 216
Sturdefunt - David 29, 32, 35, 39, 42, 46, 49, 53, 57, 61, 65, 69, 73, 78, 83, 88, 93, 99, 104, 109, 114, 119, 125, 130, 136; Jonathan 49, 15, 16, 17, 17, 18, 19, 21, 29, 31, 35, 38, 42, 46, 53, 57, 61, 65, 69, 73, 78, 83, 88, 93, 99, 104; Jonathan Jnr: 15, 16, 18, 19, 21, 29, 31, 35, 38; Nathen 190, 199, 207, 216; Richard 199, 200, 208, 217; William 16, 17, 18, 29, 31, 35, 38, 42, 46, 49, 53, 57, 61, 65, 69, 73, 78, 83, 88, 93, 99, 104, 109, 114, 119, 125, 130, 136, 141, 146, 152, 158, 163
Sturdefunt (Stordevelt) - 269
Sturdevant - Elijah 259; Nathan 260
Sturdewand - William 173
Sturdyvant - David 236
Sturgis - Hill 253; Mary 250
Sunderhill - Daniel 63, 67, 71, 75, 80, 85, 90, 95, 106, 111
Sunderland (-lin) - Daniel 173, 180, 258; Daniel Jnr: 173, 180; Daniell 27; Jacob 169, 174, 182, 189, 197; Joseph 183, 190, 207, 216
Sunderling - John 239
Surine (-ene) (-rrine) - Charles 168, 174, 181, 189, 197, 206, 215; James 191, 192, 199, 208, 217; William 168, 174
Sutton - Thomas 176, 178, 192, 194, 210, 212, 220
Swartwout - farm 221
Sweeny - John 261
Sweet - Caleb 22, 24, 26, 28, 31, 34, 38, 41, 45, 49, 53, 56, 60, 64, 68, 73, 77, 83, 88, 93, 98, 104, 109, 114, 119, 125, 130, 135, 141, 146, 152, 157, 163, 170, 183, 185; Caleb's place 108, 112; Eliah 171; Joseph 19, 20, 22; Timothy 71, 76, 80; William 19, 20, 22, 23, 25, 28, 30, 34; William's farm 37
Swiem - Albart 269
Swift - Isaiah 209, 218, 246, 258; Josiah 72, 76, 81, 85, 90, 96, 195, 205, 213, 234, 279; Josiah Jnr: 72, 76, 81, 85, 90, 96, 101, 106, 111, 116, 121, 127, 132, 137, 143, 148, 153, 159, 165, 172, 179, 187
Swim (Swiem) - 269
Swim(s) - Albert 15, 177, 178, 192, 194, 210, 212, 225; Cornelius 150, 156, 161, 167, 176; Moses 265
Tallor - Isaac 178
Talman - Isaac J. 271
Talor - Daniel 277
Tamkins - John 269, 269; Obadya 269
Tanner - Cornelius 169; Samuel 103
Tarbell - John 63, 67
Tarhill - Isaac 42
Tarwell - John 71, 75, 80, 85, 90, 95, 100, 106
Tayler - William 29
Taylor - 136; Daniel 17, 44, 47, 51, 55, 58, 62, 66, 70, 74, 79, 84, 89, 95, 100, 105, 110, 115, 120, 126, 131, 147, 153, 158, 164; Daniel's estate 136, 142; Dan'l 248; Gam'l 247; Isaac 169, 174; Israel 31, 35, 39, 42, 46, 49, 53, 57, 61, 65, 69, 73, 78, 83, 88, 93, 99, 104, 109, 115, 120, 125, 130, 136, 141, 146, 152, 158, 163, 175, 177, 191, 228; John 141, 147, 157, 162, 168, 174, 181, 188; Joseph 29, 31, 35, 38, 42, 45, 49, 53, 57, 61, 65, 69, 73, 78, 83, 88, 93, 99, 104, 109, 114, 119, 125, 130, 135, 141, 146, 234, 245; Joseph's farm 152; Lieut: 24, 26, 28, 31, 34, 38, 42, 45, 49, 53, 57, 61, 65, 68, 73, 77, 83, 88, 93, 98, 104, 109, 114, 119, 125, 130, 135; Nathan 234, 268, 278, 279; Nathan Jnr: 22, 24, 26, 28, 48, 51, 55, 59, 63, 67, 70, 75, 79, 84, 89, 95, 100, 105, 111, 116, 121, 126, 131, 137; Nathaniel Jnr: 31, 34, 38, 42; Samuel Jnr: 269; William 29, 31, 34, 38, 42, 45, 49
Taylor [Teller] - William 29, 31, 34, 38, 42, 45, 49, 18
Teed - Benjamin 113, 118, 123, 128; Joseph 231; Joseph Jnr: 209, 218; Nathen 191, 199, 208, 217
Teller - Isaac 107, 112, 117, 122, 128; Jeremiah 107, 112, 117, 122, 128; Wellem 24, 26; William 18, 20, 21, 23, 25, 28, 30, 34, 37, 41, 45, 48, 52, 56, 60, 64, 68, 72, 77; William's estate 82, 87, 93, 98; William's son 55, 59, 63, 67
Ten Eyck - Jacob 266; Robert 266
Tenry - Michal 236
Terbos(s) (-bus) - Henry Jnr: 55, 59, 63; Simeon 113, 118, 123
TerBush - Isaac 237; Isaac (Capt)

313

THE SOUTH PRECINCT OF DUTCHESS COUNTY NY 1740-1790

239
Tercotte - Francis 264
Terey - John 189
TerHill - Isaac 24, 26, 28, 31, 34, 38, 45, 49, 53, 56; Isaac's widow 60, 64, 68, 73, 77; Peter 44; Peter's farm 52; Widow 225
Terril(l)/Terrel - John 151, 156, 161, 167, 173, 181, 188, 196, 214, 231; Peter 194, 212, 263
Terry (Terrey) (Terre) - Abegal 277; John 168, 174, 181, 197, 206, 215, 252; Peter 81, 81, 86, 91; Samuel 168, 174, 181, 189, 197, 206, 215, 237, 248, 257; Widow 168
Tharp - Ezekiel 252
Theal(e) - Charles 169, 175, 182, 189, 197, 206, 215
Thomas - Thomas 243
Thompkins (Thomkins) - 269; Cournelius 177; Elijah 16, 17, 18, 19, 87; John 15, 16, 17, 18, 19, 80; Joseph 15, 16, 17; Joshua 100; Nathaniel 77; Obediah 15, 16, 17, 18, 19; Silvenis 102; Thomas 180
Thompson (Tomson) - Dan'l 244, 247; Thomas 247
Thorrington - Thomas 244
Tidd - David 15, 16, 17, 18, 19, 21, 23, 25; John 22, 24; Joseph 256; Nathan 248
Tidd [Kidd] - Joseph 198
Tillotson - Daniel 255; John 262
Tirrill - John 262, 205; Peter 211
Titus - Benjamin 150, 156, 233, 267
Tomkins [Hopkins?] - John 39
Tompkins (Tomkins) - Caleb 257; Cornelius 32, 36, 39, 43, 46, 50, 54, 58, 62, 66, 69, 74, 78, 84, 89, 94, 99, 105, 110, 115, 120, 125, 131, 136, 146, 150, 156, 161, 167, 176, 192, 193, 210, 212, 220, 262; Cornelius Jnr: 221, 247; Cors: 226, 228; Elijah 21, 23, 25, 27, 30, 33, 37, 41, 44, 48, 52, 56, 60, 64, 68, 72, 77, 82, 92, 98, 103, 108, 114, 119, 124, 129, 135, 140, 146, 151, 157, 163, 171, 179, 186, 195, 234, 279; Elijah's widow 204, 213; George 263; Jacob 211, 212, 260; James 211, 212, 247, 262, 263; John 21, 23, 25, 71, 76, 132, 137, 142, 147, 153, 159, 164, 173, 180, 188, 196, 205, 214, 254, 277; John Jnr: 85, 90, 95, 101, 106, 111, 116, 121, 126; Joshua 59, 63, 67, 71, 75, 80, 85, 90, 95, 106, 111, 116, 121, 126, 131, 137, 142, 147, 153, 158, 164, 176, 177, 192, 193, 210, 211, 220, 227, 262; Joshua Jnr: 262; Nathaniel 27, 30, 34, 37, 41, 45, 48, 52, 56, 60, 64, 68, 72, 82, 87, 93, 98, 103, 109, 114, 119, 124, 130, 135, 141, 146, 151, 157, 163, 175, 177, 191, 193, 209, 211, 220, 226, 262; Obediah 225; Reuben 194, 211, 212, 221, 228, 263; Robt. 229; Roger 229; Sarah 250; Silvanus 108, 113, 118, 177, 178, 192, 194, 210, 212, 221; Stephen 124, 129, 134, 139, 144, 149, 154, 160, 166, 176, 227, 247, 263; Thaddeus 264; Thomas 140, 145, 150, 155, 160, 166, 173
Tompkins [Hopkins?] - John 32, 35, 42; Joseph 32
Tompkins? - Cornelius 141
Totters - farm 37, 40
Toweur - Samuel 171
Town - Thomas 263
Towner - Ethiel 145, 150; Phineas 81, 86, 91, 96, 101, 107, 112, 117, 122; Saml Sen: 232; Saml: Jnr: 232; Samuel 98, 103, 109, 114, 119, 124, 129, 135, 141, 145, 146, 150, 151, 155, 161, 167, 183, 190, 198, 207, 216, 252
Townsend (Townsen) - 19; Abijah 254; Amos 209, 217, 246; Benjamin 30, 34, 38, 41, 45, 49, 52, 56, 60, 64, 68, 73, 77, 82, 87, 93, 98, 104, 109, 114, 119, 124, 130, 135, 141, 146, 152, 157, 162, 163, 170, 171, 179, 183, 185, 186, 195, 200, 202, 203, 204, 213, 218; Benjamin Jnr: 168; Caleb 209, 218; Charles 29, 30, 34, 37, 41, 45, 49, 52, 56, 60, 64, 68, 73, 77, 82, 87, 93, 98, 104, 109, 114, 119, 124, 130, 135, 141, 146, 152, 157, 163, 171, 179, 186, 195, 204, 213, 234, 248; Christopher 71, 76, 80, 85, 90, 95, 101, 106, 111, 116, 121, 126, 132, 137, 142, 147, 153, 159, 164, 173, 180, 188, 196, 205, 214, 253; Daniel 16, 17, 19, 21, 23, 25, 27, 30, 34, 37, 41, 45, 48, 52, 56, 60, 64, 68, 73, 77, 82, 87, 93, 98, 104, 109, 114, 119, 124, 130, 135, 141, 146, 152, 157, 163, 171, 179, 186, 186, 195, 204, 213, 236, 248, 253, 277; Daniel (Leuts son) 30, 34; Daniel D. 38, 41, 45, 49, 52, 56, 60, 64, 68, 73, 77, 141, 146, 152, 157, 163; Daniel Jnr: 30, 34, 38, 41, 45, 49, 52, 56, 60, 64, 68, 73, 82, 87, 93, 98, 104, 109, 114, 119, 124, 130, 171, 179, 195, 233; Daniel Sen: 135; Eber 248; Elihu 22, 24, 26, 28, 30, 34, 37, 41, 45, 49, 52, 56, 60, 64, 68, 73, 77, 82, 87, 93, 98, 104, 109, 114, 119, 124, 253; Elijah 175, 182, 189, 198, 207, 215, 245, 260, 270, 271; Gideon 253; Gilbert 247, 260; Isaac 198, 207, 216, 243, 248, 251, 267, 270, 271; Isaac Jnr: 209, 218, 253; James 123, 128, 133, 139, 144, 149, 154, 160, 166, 173, 180, 188, 196, 205, 214, 246, 260; John 151, 156, 162, 167, 173, 181, 188, 196, 201, 206, 214, 243, 248; John the 1st 252; John the 2d 253; Joseph 186; Levi 245; Levy 168, 174, 182, 189, 197, 206, 215, 248; Robert 20, 22, 23, 26, 28, 30, 30, 34, 34, 37, 41, 45, 48, 52, 56, 60, 64, 68, 73, 77, 82, 87, 93, 98, 104, 134, 140, 141, 145, 146, 149, 152, 155, 157, 160, 163, 166, 170, 171, 179, 183, 185, 186, 195, 200, 202, 203, 204, 213, 218, 253; Robert Jnr: 30, 34; Robert R. 38, 41, 45, 49, 52, 56, 60, 64, 68, 73, 77, 82, 87, 93, 98, 104, 109, 114, 119, 124, 130, 135; Robert U. 38, 41, 45, 49, 52, 56, 60, 64, 68, 73, 77, 82, 87, 93, 98, 104, 109; Samuel 250; Solomon 243; Thomas 20, 22, 24, 26, 28, 30, 34, 37, 41, 45, 48, 52, 56, 60, 64, 68, 73, 77, 82, 87, 93, 98, 104, 109, 114, 119, 124, 173, 180, 260; Thomas Jnr: 37, 38, 41, 71, 76, 80, 85, 90, 95, 101, 106, 111, 116, 121, 126, 132, 137, 142, 147, 153, 159, 164; Uriah 22, 24, 26, 28, 82, 86, 91, 96, 102, 107, 130, 135, 141, 146, 152, 157, 163, 170, 183, 185, 200, 200, 208, 217, 250, 267; Uriah's farm 202, 203, 218; Zebulon 30, 34, 37, 41, 45, 49, 52, 56, 60, 64, 169, 191, 199, 208, 217; Zepheniah 257; Zeph'h 248
Townsend [Robinson] - Ebenezer Jnr: 196
Towsend/Towsen - Amos 260; Daniel Jnr: 77; Daniell 18
Trahill [TerHill] - Widow 225
Traverse - George 264; Gilbert 263; Margaret 264; Nehemiah 265; Sylvanus 261; Titus 262
Travis (-ers) (Trevers) - Amos 145,

INDEX

150, 155, 161, 167; Gabriel 178; George 247; Gilbert 81, 86, 91, 96, 102, 107, 112, 117, 122, 177; James 247; Shuerman 103, 108, 113, 118, 123, 128, 133, 138, 143, 148, 154; Silvanus 208, 217; Titus 145, 150, 155, 161, 167, 221, 227, 247; Will. 247

Treadwell - Samuel 29

Trobridge (-brig) (Trowbridge) - Bille 255; Thomas 81, 86, 91, 96, 101, 107, 112, 117, 122, 127, 132, 137, 143, 148, 153, 159, 165, 170, 184

Trusdell/Truesdell - Jabez 253; Joseph Jnr: 252; Joseph Sen: 252; Richard 151, 156, 162, 167, 173, 181, 188, 196, 206, 214; Samuel 255

Tryon - Simeon 175, 182, 189, 197, 270; Simon 246

Tubbs - Benajah 201, 203, 219, 244

Tucker - Joseph 102, 108

Turner - Dan'l 245; Edw. 228; John 248; Stephen 248

Tuthill - John W 245

Tuttle - David 76, 81, 86, 91, 96, 101, 124, 129, 134, 139; Enos 253; Jabes 106, 111; Jabish 102, 108, 113, 116, 118, 121, 122, 127, 132, 137; Jonathen 128, 133, 138, 278

Tweedy (Twedy) - John 169, 170, 184, 185, 201, 202, 203, 219, 268, 275; John Jnr: 171, 184, 186, 201, 202; John's farm 175, 182, 190, 198, 207, 216; Samuel 171, 184; Samuel Jnr: 171

Tyler - Berzelel 81, 86, 91, 96, 101, 107; Jehiel 261

Udall - Lionel 231

Ulsbron - Clark 178

Umpris - William 269

Umpstead (Umstead) - Stephen 198, 207, 216

Underhill - Abraham 89, 105, 110, 115, 120, 126, 131, 136, 142; Abram 40, 44, 47, 51, 55, 58, 62, 66, 70, 74, 79, 84, 94, 100; Augustin 123, 129, 134, 144, 149, 154, 160, 166, 172; Benjamin 59, 63, 67, 71, 75, 80, 85, 90, 95, 100, 106; Cap: 27; Thomas 52, 55, 59, 63, 67; William 20, 22, 24, 26, 28, 123, 129, 134, 139, 144, 149, 154, 160, 166, 172, 180, 187, 196; William Jnr: 163, 168, 174, 181, 188

Underwood - Joseph 44, 47, 51, 55, 58, 62, 66, 70, 74, 79

Unisted - Ebenezer 92, 97, 102

Utter - Amos 209, 218, 245; Benjamin 22; Eben'r 245; Gilbert 252; Isaac 99, 110, 115, 120, 125; Jabish 103, 108, 113, 118, 123; John 22, 200, 208, 217, 245; Samuel 22, 24, 26, 28, 156, 162, 167, 173, 181, 231, 245; Samuel's estate 114, 119, 125; Will. 248; William 209, 218, 259, 268

Vail - Caleb 181, 188, 196, 206, 214; Israel 247

Van Ambrough - John 265

Van Ambur (Amber) - Isaac 178; John 220

Van Amburgh - Hendrick 269; Henry 15, 16, 17, 18, 19, 21, 23, 27, 30, 33, 37, 41, 44, 48, 52, 56; Henry's widw: 60; Isaac 15, 16, 17, 18, 193, 269; John 15, 16, 17, 18, 19, 21, 23, 27, 30, 33, 37, 41, 44, 48, 52, 56, 60, 64, 269; John's estate 68, 72, 77, 82, 87, 92, 98, 103, 108, 114, 119, 124, 129, 135, 140, 146, 151, 157, 163, 175, 177, 191, 193, 209, 211

Van Amburgt - Henry 25; John 25

Van Courtlandt - Col. 1

Van Duzen - Christ. 243

Van Heyning - Henry 91

Van Scoy (Scey) - Abel 209, 218, 248; Jacob 246

Van Tessel(l)/Van Tassel(l) - John 24, 26, 32, 35, 39, 42, 46, 50, 53, 57, 61, 65, 69, 73, 78, 83, 88, 94, 99, 104, 110, 115, 120, 125, 130, 136, 141, 146, 152, 158, 164, 211, 212, 227, 264; William 113, 118, 123, 128, 133, 138, 144, 149, 154, 160, 165, 176, 177, 192, 193, 210, 211, 227

Vanheyning - Henry 87

VanVore - John 33

Varney - Nathaniel 201

Varnill - John 255

Veal(l) - Caleb 151, 156, 162, 167, 173, 257; James 251; John 246, 257

Ventress - Wm. 245

Verkilyer/Verkylyer - John 191, 199, 208, 217; William 200, 208, 217

Vermillia (-yea) - John 248; Will. 248; William 256

Verney - Nathaniel 186

Viccary - Iccabud 16, 17, 18, 19, 21, 23, 25, 27; Iccabud's estate 41, 44; Iccabud's widow 34, 37, 30

Viccorie (-ry) Vickorie - Benjamin 51; Joseph 51, 55, 59, 63, 67, 70;

Timothy 51

Vickery & Co - Jos: 234

Vickry (-ery) (-rey) - Benjamin 82, 86, 91, 97, 102, 107, 112, 117, 122, 127; David 169, 174, 182, 189, 197, 236, 238; Jona: 234; Jonathen 102, 107, 112, 117, 122, 127, 132, 138, 175, 182, 235; Jos: 234; Joseph 92, 97, 102, 107, 112, 117, 122, 127, 133, 138, 143, 148, 154, 159, 165, 172, 179, 187, 195, 205, 214; Thomas 175, 183, 190, 244

Viere(e) - Jonathan 81, 86, 91, 96

Vredinburgh - Benjm. 240

Waggoner - Tobias 263

Wairing - John 244

Wakeman - David 171, 184; Squire 221

Walden - James 269

Wallis & Dickenson & Co - 171, 179

Wallis (Wallace) - John 169; John's farm 190

Wanser - Jacob 103, 108; Thomas 254

Wantsell - John 20, 22, 24

Ward - Chas. 245; Ebenezer 82, 86, 91, 209, 218; Israel 151, 156, 161, 167, 173, 181, 188, 196; Israel's estate 206, 214; James 245; Moses 247

Waring - Ephraim 252; John 174, 251; Jonathan 251; Thaddeus 252; Theod's 248

Warren - Beverly 265; Daniel 134, 139, 144, 149, 155, 160, 166; John 169, 220, 265; Peter 168, 176, 178, 192, 193, 210, 212, 225; Samuel 169, 176, 178, 192; Samuel's farm 194; Tanier 220; William 257

Warring - Ephraim 245; Peter 163; Richard 170, 184

Wasebun - Silus 16

Washburn (-bourn) (-born) (-bun) - Ebenezer 175, 182, 189, 198; Isaac 193, 194, 210, 212, 264; Jonathan 258; Jonathen 123, 129, 133, 139; Samuel 134, 139, 144, 149, 155, 160, 166, 172, 180, 187, 196, 205, 214; Silas 17, 33, 55, 59, 63, 67, 71, 75, 79, 85, 89, 95, 100, 105, 111, 116, 121, 126, 131, 137, 277; Widow 144, 149, 154, 160; Zebulon 183, 190, 198, 207, 216, 254

Waterbury - David 163, 168, 174, 181, 188, 197, 206, 215, 245, 270, 271; Enos 246

Waters - Joseph 59, 63, 67, 71, 75,

THE SOUTH PRECINCT OF DUTCHESS COUNTY NY 1740-1790

80; Mary 257

Watts (Wats) - Elizabeth 252; John 245, 252; Robert 145, 150, 155, 161, 167, 173, 180, 188, 196, 205, 214, 231, 245

Wealer - Justice 51

Wearing - John 182, 189, 197, 206, 215; Richard 71, 76, 80, 85, 90, 95, 101, 106, 111, 116, 121, 126, 132, 137, 142, 147, 153, 159, 164, 185; Thaddeus 190, 199, 207, 216

Weaver - Peter 29, 265

Webb - David 175, 182, 190, 198, 207, 216, 260; Jeremiah 254; Jonathan 169, 175, 182, 189, 197, 248, 270; Noah 209, 218, 244; William 255

Weed - 183, 190; Benjamin 118, 123, 128, 133, 139, 277; Jacob 250; Jehiel Jnr: 245; John 243, 267; Joseph 256; Justus 250; Nathan 256; Phineahas 267

Weeks - Gilbert 220, 265; John 94, 99, 105; Peter 262

Weekson - Ebenezer 72, 76, 85, 90, 96, 116, 121; Ebenezer's estate 127; Elijah 62, 66, 70, 74, 79, 84, 89, 94, 100, 105, 110, 115, 120, 126, 131, 136, 142, 147, 152, 158, 164, 180, 187, 196, 205, 214, 244; Peleg 105, 110, 115, 120, 126, 131, 136, 142, 147, 152, 158, 164, 179, 186, 195, 204, 213; Peleg (Robert's son) 54, 58, 62, 66, 70, 74, 79, 84, 89, 94, 100; Robert 32, 35, 39, 42, 46, 50, 53, 57, 61, 65, 69, 73, 78, 83, 88, 94, 99, 104, 110, 115, 120, 125, 130, 136, 141, 146, 152, 158, 164, 171, 179; Robert's eldest son 33, 36; Robert's son 40, 43, 47, 51; Shubell 174, 182, 189, 197, 206, 215

Weight - Christ'r 247

Welch - John 183, 190

Welding - Stephen 258

Wellden - James 15

Welsh - Robert 265

West - Thomas 76, 81

West Gate - by the store 183

Westcott - Anthony 251

Wever - Peter 24, 27

Whealer/Wheeler - Eliphalet 235; Justice 55, 59, 63

Whealey - James 248

Whebney/Whibley - Jeremiah 179, 187

Whedon - Calvin 260; Jahoida 260

White - Elijah 76, 80, 85, 90, 96, 101, 106, 111, 116, 121, 127, 132, 137, 142, 148, 153, 159, 164, 172, 179, 234, 251; Elisha [Elijah] 71; Jeremiah 194, 211, 213, 264; John 22, 24, 26, 28, 31, 34, 38, 41, 45, 49, 53, 56, 60, 64, 68, 73, 77, 83, 88, 93, 98, 104, 109, 114, 119, 125, 130, 135, 169, 174, 182, 189, 197, 206, 215; Jonathan 22, 24, 26, 28; Joseph 190, 199, 207, 216; William 178, 192, 194, 210, 212, 221, 229

Whitney - Aaron 260; Elijah 171, 205, 214; James 255; Jeremiah 195, 205, 213; Uriah 123, 129, 134, 139

Wickham - Shugel 168

Wickson - Ebenezer 80, 106, 111; Elijah 173; Peleg 172

Wieder - 185

Wiksom - John 247

Wilcocks/Willcox/Willcocks - Amos 240; Benj'n 245; Elisha 240; Isaac 239; James 245; Jeremiah 186, 201; John 201, 268; Josiah 118, 123, 128, 133, 139, 231; Rosal 245; Roswell 145, 150, 155, 161, 167, 173, 180, 188, 196, 205, 214, 231, 252; Stephen 140; Thomas 238; Widow 32, 36, 39, 43

Willden (Walden) - 269

Willer - Edward 269

Willes - Hezekiah 190; Jedediah 245; Rich'd 245; Thomas 245

Willess - James 245

Willet - Coll: 27, 29; Collo:'s farm 48, 51, 55, 59; Isaac 29

Williams - 27; Abraham 259, 261; Francis 262; Ichabod 248; James 261; John 29, 31, 63, 67, 71, 75, 80, 85, 90, 95, 100, 182, 190, 198; John Jnr: 259; John Sen: 259; John's estate 207, 216; Matthew 259; Moses 103, 108, 250; Richard 162, 168, 174, 181, 188, 197, 206, 215; Richard the 1st 259; Richard the 2d 259; Samuel 145, 150; Thomas 210, 212, 247

Williamson - Thomas 150, 156, 161, 167, 176, 177, 192, 193, 225

Willis - 171, 179, 186; Hezekiah 183, 195; Jedediah 161, 167, 206, 214, 230; Jerediah 173, 181, 188, 196

Willmot(t)/Wilmot - Lemuel 156, 162, 167, 173, 181, 188, 196, 231

Wilsie (Willsey) - Daniel 192, 194, 210, 212, 226, 247, 271; Henry 193, 194, 210, 212, 227, 247, 271

Wilson/Willson - 150, 156; Daniel 163, 168, 174, 181, 188, 206, 215, 246; James 118, 123, 128, 133, 139, 144, 149, 154, 160, 166, 172, 180, 187, 200, 208, 217, 254, 277; James Jnr: 163, 168, 174, 181, 188; John 162, 168, 174, 181, 188, 197, 206, 215, 244; Robert 161; Samuel 209, 217, 245; Thomas 248

Wiltse - Daniel 178; Henry 178

Win/Winn - John 134, 139, 144, 166, 176, 177, 192, 193, 210, 211, 228; Peter 183, 190, 198, 207, 216

Wing - Elihu 231; Jedediah 279

Winter - Benjamin 32, 35, 39, 42; Lewis 33, 218; Lewis Jnr: 209; Mathew 20, 22, 23, 26, 28, 30; Moses 191, 199, 208, 217; Moses Jnr: 209, 218

Wirson - Dan'l 246; John 246

Witchson - Eben'r 247

Witnah (Witerah) - Jeremiah 76, 81, 86, 91, 96, 101, 106, 111, 116, 121, 127, 132, 137, 143, 148, 153, 159, 165, 172

Wixson (Wixon) - Daniel 259; Ebenezer 101, 243; Elijah 54, 58, 244, 253, 258; Isaac 244, 258; John 260; Peleg 261; Shubael 261; Shubal 54, 58

Wolf [Dolf?] - Simon 22, 24, 26, 28

Wood - Ely 231; Israel 248; John 140, 145, 229, 248, 259; Nehemiah 48, 51, 55, 59, 62, 66, 70, 75, 79, 84, 89, 95, 100, 105, 111, 116, 121, 126, 131, 136, 142, 147, 153, 158, 164, 173, 180, 187, 196, 205, 214, 253; Obediah 134, 140; Rebecca 267; Solomon 191, 199; Sylvanus 220, 265; Timothy 265; Titus 20, 22, 24, 26, 28

Wood [Ellis?] - Christopher 147, 158

Wood? [Ellis?] - Christopher 153

Woodard - Jonathan 240; Lieut 239, 240; Phineas 238; Thomas 97, 102, 107, 112, 117, 122, 128, 133, 138, 143, 148, 154, 159, 165, 176, 177, 192; Thomas's farm 193, 211

Wooden - Henry 129, 134, 139, 144, 149, 155, 160, 166, 172, 180, 187, 196, 205, 214; John 257; William 162, 168, 174, 181, 188, 197, 206, 215, 258

Woodlin - John 248

Woodsen - 277

INDEX

Woodward - Phineas 235; Thomas 92; Thomas's farm 210
Wooster - Will. 243; William 267
Worden - Caleb 239; Joseph 240
Worten/Wortman - Dennis 168, 174
Wright - Abijah 256; Augustin 124, 129, 134, 139, 144, 149, 154, 160; Austin 238; Charles 264; David 29; Dennis 156, 162, 167, 173, 181, 188, 196, 206, 214, 230; Ebenezer 255; Edmund 243, 267; Elijah 261; Hezekiah 16, 17, 18, 19, 21, 23; Isaac 162, 168, 174, 181, 188, 197; John 24, 26, 29, 55, 59, 63, 67, 71, 75, 79, 85, 89, 95, 100, 105, 111, 116, 121, 126, 131, 137, 142, 147, 153, 158, 162, 164, 168, 174, 176, 178, 181, 188, 197, 206, 215; John Jnr: 140, 145, 149, 155, 160, 166; Jonathen 193, 194, 210, 212, 268; Joseph 264; Robert 151, 156, 162, 167, 173, 181, 188, 196, 206, 214, 255; Robert Jnr: 255; Samuel 24, 26, 140, 145; Uriah 183, 190, 198; Will 248; William 151, 156, 162, 167, 176, 177, 192, 193, 209, 210, 212, 218, 220, 265; Zebulon 200, 208, 217, 248
Wright [Light?] - Suzanne 212
Wyllis - Jedediah 151, 156
Wynn - John 149, 155, 160
Yaeres/Yarus - Benajah 175, 182
Yager - Nathaniel 166
Yale(s) - Enos 245; Stephen 245, 250; Uriah 245
Yarns - Reuben 245
Yearns - Benajah 189, 198; Nathan 183; William 23, 25
Yearns (Jarns) - 269
Yerns - William 16, 18, 20, 21, 27, 30; William's farm 77; William's widow 34, 37, 41, 44, 48, 52, 56, 60, 64, 68, 72, 92; William's widow's farm 82, 87
Yoemans/Yeomans - Abraham 103; Absalom 169, 174, 182, 189, 197; Anthony 48, 103, 108, 113, 118, 123, 140, 145, 150, 155, 161, 166, 176, 177, 192, 193, 210, 212; Eleazer 91, 96, 101, 106, 112, 117; James 220; John 99, 105, 110, 115, 120, 144, 149, 154, 160, 165, 172, 180, 187, 195, 205, 214; John Jnr: 125, 131, 133, 136, 139, 142, 147, 152, 158, 164, 171, 179, 186, 195; John Sen: 118, 123, 128; John's estate 204, 213; Johnson 208, 217; Samuel 48, 63, 67, 71, 75, 80, 85, 108, 113, 118, 123, 128, 133, 138, 144, 148, 154, 159, 165, 176, 177, 192, 193, 210, 212; William 129, 134, 139, 144, 149, 155, 160, 166, 172, 180, 187, 196, 205, 214
Youmans - Anth: 227; Eleazer 81, 86; James 228; John 229; Johnson 199; Saml: 228
Young [Ganung] - Edward 179, 186
Young(s) - Alkanah 219; Eleany 183; Elkanah 267; Elkany 243; Elkney 186, 201, 202, 203; Samuel 245; Shaw 140, 145, 149, 155, 160, 166, 170, 184, 185, 201, 202, 203, 219, 243, 267; William 175, 185, 186, 201, 202, 203, 219, 267
Yumans - Abigail 261; Jacob 255; James 265; Johnson 253; Jonas 257
Yurns - William 17

LIST OF MAPS

Figure 1: The Philipse Patent Survey 1754 2
Figure 2: The Gore Lands Resolved in 1758 and 1771 3
Figure 3: Sketch of the 20-Mile Lands 4
Figure 4: Rendition of 1760 Patent Survey and Map 5
Figure 5: The 1761 20-Mile Tracts 6
Figure 6: Rendition of the Native Indians' Plan 7
Figure 7: Precincts in 1772 9
Figure 8: Topography of Putnam County, NY 11

Map: The Farms of the Southern Portion of Robinson's Long Lot 4 273
Map: The Farms of Robinson's Short Lot 7 274
Map: The Farms of Philipse's Short Lot 8 275
Map: Map Based upon Morgan's Survey of Long Lot 6 276
Map: Farms Included in the May 1765 Agreement 279

www.ingramcontent.com/pod-product-compliance
Lightning Source LLC
Chambersburg PA
CBHW051400070526
44584CB00023B/3233